Sustainable Finance

Series Editors

Karen Wendt
CEO. Eccos Impact GmbH, President of SwissFinTechLadies
Cham, Zug, Switzerland

Margarethe Rammerstorfer
Professor for Energy Finance and Investments
Institute for Finance, Banking and Insurance WU Vienna
Vienna, Austria

Sustainable Finance is a concise and authoritative reference series linking research and practice. It provides reliable concepts and research findings in the ever growing field of sustainable investing and finance, SDG economics and Leadership with the declared commitment to present the theories, methods, tools and investment approaches that can fulfil the United Nations Sustainable Development Goals and the Paris Agreement COP 21/22 alongside with de-risking assets and creating triple purpose solutions that ensure the parity of profit, people and planet through choice architecture passion and performance. The series addresses market failure, systemic risk and reinvents portfolio theory, portfolio engineering as well as behavioural finance, financial mediation, product innovation, shared values, community building, business strategy and innovation, exponential tech and creation of social capital. Sustainable Finance and SDG Economics series helps to understand keynotes on international guidelines, guiding accounting and accountability principles, prototyping new developments in triple bottom line investing, cost benefit analysis, integrated financial first plus impact first concepts and impact measurement. Going beyond adjacent fields (like accounting, marketing, strategy, risk management) it integrates the concept of psychology, innovation, exponential tech, choice architecture, alternative economics, blue economy shared values, professions of the future, leadership, human and community development, team culture, impact, quantitative and qualitative measurement, Harvard Negotiation, mediation and complementary currency design using exponential tech and ledger technology. Books in the series contain latest findings from research, concepts for implementation, as well as best practices and case studies for the finance industry.

More information about this series at http://www.springer.com/series/15807

Karen Wendt
Editor

Theories of Change

Change Leadership Tools, Models and Applications for Investing in Sustainable Development

Springer

Editor
Karen Wendt
ECCOS Impact GmbH
Cham, Switzerland

ISSN 2522-8285 ISSN 2522-8293 (electronic)
Sustainable Finance
ISBN 978-3-030-52274-2 ISBN 978-3-030-52275-9 (eBook)
https://doi.org/10.1007/978-3-030-52275-9

This Springer imprint is published by the registered company Springer Nature Switzerland AG.
The registered company address is: Gewerbestrasse 11, 6330 Cham, Switzerland

Foreword

Why Research and Use Cases About Theories of Change?

The sheer volume of articles on "sustainable finance" accompanied by conferences and business events on the topic is an excellent indication that the tipping point in the world of finance and investment may be reached: sustainable finance has the credentials to become the new paradigm in the investment world! A number of spin doctors have been working on this movement for at least two decades, including a broad variety of players from diverse backgrounds: The Global Alliance for Banking on Values has been showing that impact investing is feasible and NGOs have been chasing banks and wealth managers, like Unfriend Coal, who convinced a number of insurance companies to divest coal. Think tanks like the World Resources Institute and the Carbon Tracker have been creating awareness about the stranded costs of carbon and carbon value at risk, the insurance industry has been starting to divest coal, investors like the 100% divest invest movement, pension funds like the Norwegian Pension Fund, multilateral banks, and development finance institutions have been changing their investment and finance strategies and policies, multilaterals like the OECD with its responsible business conduct approach hold OECD country players liable for their business conduct, politicians managed to find a new societal contract, with the Paris Agreement, scientists provided input and models for a revised portfolio engineering, the Rockefeller Foundation coined the term impact investing, and most recently, also Blackrock spoke about introducing.

The question has evolved from "why would we care" and "what are we talking about" to an impressive granularity of perspectives and approaches in redefining investment and finance. Paul Polman has repeatedly pointed to the finance and investment industry as the biggest lever of change to realize the Sustainable Development Goals (in short SDGs). Recently, the EU has published the first parts of the EU Action Plan for sustainable growth including the taxonomy, development of two low carbon benchmarks, increased reporting requirements, and its envisaged green bond scheme. A lot has happened and more is underway.

So do we need to talk about theories of change or are we all in the middle of the change in an effective and efficient manner already? Looking at the EU Action Plan, it becomes clear that investors need green assets to invest in and that these assets have to be created by asset owners. Low carbon benchmarks and investors' awareness are still to be created. The UN has estimated the funding gap as large as 3–5 trillion USD annually for infrastructure alone (including power, transport, buildings and industrial, communication, agriculture, forestry, and water). The focus has been for too long on investors only, leaving out sustainability-linked finance and asset owners. ESG has been used a lot as a differentiation tool from other players, but achieving too little on the ground.

Also, the EU is looking at both sides now: to the investors and to the asset owners in order to accelerate the green to brown ratio.

At the moment it appears that all efforts bundled together will not take us to achievement of the goals fast and consistent enough. As an example we look at recent statements by members of the Club of Rome. "Despite all good efforts from Sustainable Finance experts, so far, the underlying global challenges have not yet been sufficiently resolved and approaches have not been able to steer the world to a more sustainable development path", says Olivier Jaeggi, Founder and CEO of ECOFACT. Early September 2015, investors met with the Club of Rome and Prof. Jørgen Randers, co-author of *Limits to Growth* and author of *2052: A Global Forecast for the Next Forty Years*, in Berlin to engage in a dialogue about the "next forty years". He was shockingly pessimistic. In his view, no relevant progress had been made over the past 36–43 years. One reason may be that the efforts have been too idiosyncratic and too scattered and measures and measurements not consistent. Another reason may be that thinking is still in old models, rather than in ecosystem approaches and circular economy thinking. Perhaps we are still working with wrong models, which are not fit for providing us clear guidance on the impacts of our decisions? A holistic approach appears to be still missing. Are our approaches really fully assessment based or do we trust some easy KPIs? Do we really consider all the relevant variables and do we have quantitative models able to show us the impacts of various decision practices and paths correctly. Is sustainability at the core of the activities or just an add-on filter at the end of our "systemic" assessment? Can we sketch out pathways on how transformation works and how it fails?

With its 17 Sustainable Development Goals, the UN has abandoned to accumulate more problem knowledge and has turned the page to describe the solutions. With its 17 Sustainable Goals (SDGs) the United Nations (short UN) has defined the "what" of the global sustainability agenda but not the "how". The societal transition trajectories and transformation knowledge need additional study, in particular the creation of transformation knowledge—on how to achieve the goals—the creation of transformation knowledge is still in its nascent stages. This publication contributes to the discussion in various ways. First it breaks the challenge down in various areas. New pathways need new collaboration, new networks, and ecosystems. A quantification and clear description of the impacts of any decisions made contributes to transparency in decision-making. As we are already using resources beyond planetary boundaries, growth (often seen as the key in abating poverty) needs to happen without additional resource usage. Hence a decoupling approach, decoupling growth from resource usage, is a relevant topic. We need intelligent technologies, a transparent circular economy (potentially based on block chain), ease of access to funds for entrepreneurs, and sound management procedures, but also clear investment guidance from the ESG companies leading the field.

The Paris Agreement foresees a breakdown of the 1.5 degree target in nationally determined contributions (NDCs). The EU is at the forefront to lead the way with the creation of a framework it seeks to share and apply with others.

A lot needs to be done in the sphere of sustainability risk integration in financial decision-making, and on the need for a change in banks and insurers' prudential treatment of assets with a favourable environmental and social impact. Likewise asset owners need to know about how a sustainable asset looks like and what it entails. Internal management systems and change management procedures are relevant in order to allow asset owners, multinational companies, and smaller players to increase their green to brown ratio quickly. The field for creation of transformation knowledge is large. A clear integration of outside-in risk to complement inside-out risks is required in order to deal with topics like climate adaptation risk.

The EU has created its International Platform on Sustainable Finance for Public Authorities (exchange, compare initiatives, institutional learning, best practice). This seems to be the first useful step to create more consistency and coherence in the field of sustainable finance. Another benefit is that this approach makes sustainable finance accessible to a corporate audience.

In this volume, we have diligently assembled the best practice use cases and emerging topics in the field of sustainability that work under the umbrella of a theory of change and we raise and discuss inconsistencies and offer top-notch solutions on sustainability measurement, decision-making quantification, alternative assets, alternative finance, change management, and the role of creating an ecosystem and offer food for thought for new business strategies. Is the volume exhaustive? It cannot be, as the topics are emergent and solutions in the making. However, this compendium offers a wide range of best practice models and solutions to pave the way in the creating process of theories of change.

Cham, Switzerland Karen Wendt

Preface

Synthesis of Rational and Emotional Decision-Making

The following three articles focus on rational theories of change—rational both in the sense of the word "calculable" and in the sense of using the reason which of course is related. Not only in the age of computing, our rational minds use numbers to explain the world around us, to weigh the consequences of the options at our disposal, and to support our decisions with evidence. Rational decision-making is a common thread in our history, traceable back to the Romans and beyond.

However, the critique of reducing humans to their reason and to numbers is equally old and permeates all eras. Not only does modern neurology place great emphasis on the irrationality of our decision-making, ironically supported by statistical studies of decisions in lab settings. Also, philosophies emphasizing rational thinking, from Plato to Kant to name just two eminent rational minds, have always been challenged by more mystery or empirically oriented philosophers.

Is there a place at all for a theory of change based on rational decision-making given all the rational evidence showing that our decisions are steered by emotions to a large extent? However, do we really need to choose *between* a quantitative and a qualitative approach, *between* thinking and feeling, and *between* numbers and storytelling? Are not fundamental large-scale transitions supported by both mind and emotion?

We will pick three large-scale changes that required the cooperation of many decision-makers against their own short-term vested interests: the peaceful end of apartheid in South Africa, the pre- and postwar introduction of Western social security systems, and the fast and decisive worldwide substitution of fluorocarbons (CFC) to halt the depletion of the ozone layer. In all three cases, the moral pressure was forcefully complemented by a strong element of fear shared by many actors and decision-makers: loss of reputation and investments, the communist alternative, and the imminent threat of skin cancer at an unprecedented scale. However, in all three cases, data and calculations ensured that the changes could be achieved at an affordable price, opening new opportunities, and most importantly, that the option of business as usual was not the safest and most economical option.

Good and sustainable change requires both reason and emotion, numbers and narratives, qualitative and quantitative. The more connected, the more sustainable the change is. After all, we work best when our parts of the brain work together, not against each other.

A Theory of Change Underlying Rational Approaches

The theory of change underlying "Sustainable Impact through Simulation and Action Leverage" (SISAL, first article in the series) generally applies to rational approaches with explicit links to the qualitative world. It is based on three postulates:

1. Individual and collective *commitment arises from transparency* about the effects of actions.

From the perspective of an involved community, better transparency of interconnectivities enables us to have a better understanding of the effects of decisions. This leads to broader commitment for sustainable solutions. Perceived dilemmas between individual profit and societal benefit are often a consequence of the way complex questions are cast, considering only one perspective or channel of transmission. Transparency will help overcome such perceived trade-offs.

Example: Since centuries, the interdependencies between alp farming activities, mechanisms in nature (soil, weather, plants), and economic developments have been well known. Respecting these interconnections has assured traditional alp farming to provide a basis for living throughout centuries without destroying the fragile alpine pastures.

2. We need *level playing fields* that do not put the persons acting sustainably at an undue disadvantage. A political and societal debate sets the goals and leaves the pathways open to reach them. Transparent analysis provides the technical answers on feasibility and execution.

Regulators and lawmakers play an important role by creating a level playing field with rules that do not put the person or entity deciding and acting sustainably at a disadvantage, for example via the attribution of externalities caused. These rules need to consider desired and potentially undesired effects as well as limited resources. In political and societal debates, we often lack an open and transparent agreement on the desirable outcomes. Instead, assertions on the feasibility of assumedly common goals inhibit the required progress. However, as soon as an agreement on the intended outcomes has been reached, data analytics and computer simulation help all involved actors to find the best means to reach these outcomes by producing reproducible and consistent analysis results.

Examples of already established policies: Financial accounting standards have been established to make sure business results are comparable. Social contract including protection of property helps prevent recurring and losing battles over resources. Taxation systems enable public entities to run essential infrastructures and provide essential services to all. Financial stability rules establish the trust the financial system is based on.

Examples of debate on desirable outcomes: The Sustainable Development Goals have been agreed on as a framework of goals to be reached, leaving the execution up to the individual signing countries. Employing the similar principles, the preceding Millennium Development Goals have largely been reached.

3. *Transparency and comparability of complex* problems can be established through data integration and computer simulation.

A comprehensive and consistent understanding of *all* relevant implications of decisions will enable conscious decisions for a holistically more sustainable solution. Complex questions that are phrased considering only one aspect or time horizon are prone to being answered in an oversimplified way. Integrated simulation of those questions will allow qualitative and quantitative comparisons and consequently will eliminate statement against statement.

Example: Phaseout of fossil fuels and nuclear energy—How to assure a sufficient energy supply, with which economic opportunities, and at what cost?

Example: Underwriting decisions in the insurance industry ensuring future claims payout without putting the business at risk.

Example: Ensuring monetary stability while providing the necessary financial liquidity to economies: Computer simulation has successfully been established in central banking.

Article Series on Data Analysis and Computer Simulation

The following three articles focus on leveraging analytics and simulation to support the transition to holistically sustainable investments at scales that matter. Transparent connections between investment strategies and their impact are the common thread in this article series. The series consists of three contributions:

The first article introduces the SISAL model for the first time, a comprehensive simulation metamodel for transition planning and decision analysis. It provides insight on the effects of a proposed agenda ahead of time and supports an optimization of resources available to decision-makers to reach their goals across different time horizons and considering different quantities of relevance.

The second article introduces a new materiality-enhanced environmental, social, and governance (ESG) scoring methodology including unbiased factor scores, an unbiasing model with connections to various key performance indicators.

The third article highlights a key role insurance and more generally finance can play in combating climate change and its impacts by attaching a price tag on risk. This core expertise puts insurance at the nexus of capital markets and society, paving the way for a sustainable future.

Adliswil, Switzerland Salomon Billeter
Riehen, Switzerland
April 27, 2021

Contents

Contributors

Mihai Alisie AKASHA Foundation, Zug, Switzerland

Stefanie Auge-Dickhut Business Engineering Institute, St. Gallen, Switzerland

Christian Betz Business Engineering Institute, St. Gallen, Switzerland

Salomon Billeter scaling4good, Riehen, Switzerland

Marc Burkhalter Institute of Information Management, University of St. Gallen, St. Gallen, Switzerland

Sandeep Chandur Adapt Ready, New York, NY, USA

Daniel Fasnacht Department of Banking and Finance, University of Zurich, Zurich, Switzerland

Ruben Feldman ESG Strategy & Business Development Department, Swisscanto, Zürich, Switzerland

Katherine A. Foster Green Digital Finance Alliance (GDFA), Geneva, Switzerland

Daniel Gächter Swiss Impact Finance Network, Zug, Switzerland

Paul Garte Munich, Germany

Ulrike Glatz Global Impact Alliance, Berlin, Germany

Peter W. Heller Canopus Foundation, Freiburg, Germany

Maximilian Horster ISS Climate Solutions, ISS ESG, Kronberg, Germany

Marc Johnson Bunker Trace, Westminster, London, UK

Reinhard Jung Institute of Information Management, University of St. Gallen, St. Gallen, Switzerland

Swee-Sum Lam Asia Centre for Social Entrepreneurship and Philanthropy, NUS Business School, National University of Singapore, Singapore, Singapore
Finance Department, NUS Business School, National University of Singapore, Singapore, Singapore
Asian Pastoral Institute, Singapore, Singapore

Laubie Li SKEMA Business School, Suzhou, China

Deanna MacDonald BLOC, Copenhagen, Denmark

Will Mackay UniSA Business, University of South Australia, Adelaide, SA, Australia

Marcel Malmendier Qualitates GmbH, Darmstadt, Germany
Investmentkontor RheinRuhr GmbH, Bochum, Germany

Greg Meredith APA Group, Sydney, NSW, Australia

Katharina Miller 3C Compliance, Madrid, Spain

Michal Natora Emerald Technology Ventures AG, Zürich, Switzerland

Tobias Peylo University of Applied Sciences, Kempten, Germany

Efi Pylarinou Efi Pylarinou Advisory, Fribourg, Switzerland

Shruthi Rao Adapt Ready, New York, NY, USA

Jakob Roth Center for Innovative Finance, Basel, Switzerland

Kuno Roth Greenpeace International, Zurich, Switzerland

Fabian Schär Center for Innovative Finance, Basel, Switzerland

Aljoscha Schöpfer Center for Innovative Finance, Basel, Switzerland

Siddhartha Sharma CredFIC Inc, Jaipur, Rajasthan, India

Michael Sonntag Y.1–Seminar for Evolutionary Leadership and Economy, Bern, Switzerland

Erwin Stahl Munich, Germany

Martin Suhr Swiss Impact Investing Network, Zug, Switzerland

Xiang Ru Amy Tan Asia Centre for Social Entrepreneurship and Philanthropy, NUS Business School, National University of Singapore, Singapore, Singapore
Centre for Ageing Research and Education, Duke-NUS Medical School, Singapore, Singapore

Bernhard Villhauer Weltethos-Institut (World Ethos Institute), University of Tübingen, Tübingen, Germany

Georgette Vun University of Queensland, Brisbane, QLD, Australia
University of St. Gallen, St. Gallen, Switzerland

Karen Wendt Sustainable Finance Association, Cham, Switzerland

Katya Wisniewski Greenpeace, Zürich, Switzerland

Lei Xu UniSA Business, University of South Australia, Adelaide, SA, Australia

Xin Xu SKEMA Business School, Suzhou, China

Markus Zeilinger fair-finance, Vienna, Austria

Part I
Theories of Change: Defining the Research Agenda, Leadership and Change

Theory of Change: Defining the Research Agenda

Karen Wendt

> *You cannot create the future using the old strategy tools. . . .*
> *The big challenge in creating the future is not predicting the future; instead the goal is to try to imagine a future that is plausible, that you can create.*
> *Charles Handy*

Abstract Theories of change revisited. In the context of the Sustainable Development Goals (SDGs) and the challenges ahead, actors must think beyond an innovation strategy above and foremost about the impact they want to achieve. They need to realise that impact does not stem from innovation but from the scaling of innovation results. Thus the outcomes of their theory of change in terms of what their innovation should achieve becomes of key importance. There needs to be a paradigm shift: Today we move from problem solving concepts like environmental and social governance to creating a future based on the SDGs, which provide target knowledge. How does economy 3.0 look like in 2030, 2400 or 2050?

Keywords Theory of change · Theories of change · Programme theory · Target knowledge · Transformation knowledge · SDGs · Transition · SDG pathways · ESG · Impact assessment · Impact · Risk · Value at risk (Transition, Rational decision-making, Synthesis, Paradigm, Change management) · Systems theory · VUCA · Leverage point analysis · Impact investing · Positive impact investing · Impact assessments

---

K. Wendt (✉)
Sustainable Finance Association, Cham, Switzerland
e-mail: karen@sustainable-finance.io

K. Wendt (ed.), *Theories of Change*, Sustainable Finance,
https://doi.org/10.1007/978-3-030-52275-9_1

1 Relevance of Topic: Why a Research Agenda for Theories of Change in the Investment Context Is Necessary

The United Nations (UN) Sustainable Development Goals (SDGs or Global Goals) provide a global framework for addressing the most urgent social and environmental challenges. Investors and the financial industry are seen as important levers to implement the SDGs. The EU processes the EU action plan for financing sustainable growth.

Unfortunately, most discussions around economic changes, environmental degradation, societal well-being and individual thriving look at environmental and social domains in a very compartmentalized and incomplete manner. A holistic approach is missing. With the SDG a societal contract has been established and at the same time society is moving away from just understanding the problem (problem knowledge) and looking for solution creation. It is the beginning of the search for new models, methodologies and frameworks to create a greener and more sustainable economy. However, the pathways to solutions is new ground, with a lot of Volatility, uncertainty, complexity and ambiguity (VUCA) and the creation of transformation knowledge is in its nascent stages. Therefore we need to define the research agenda for the transformation. Each framework currently developed and tested contributes to transformation knowledge, however the approaches differ and apply different programme theories. A Program theory has been described by evaluATOD as underlying rationales for programs, describing how and why a program should lead to the intended outcomes. A logic model connects activities of a program with the expected outcomes of a program in a clear, logical fashion. In short, the outcomes need to be explicit, observable and correlated to the programme theory and attributable to the elements of the theory in a logical manner. Creating and evaluating transformation knowledge therefore requires the evaluation of programme theories, the impact of the programmes, the impact of decisions made in the programme and a benchmark to compare it to other programmes. Finally it should take companies to a greener business model with new strategies, products and increased green/brown ratio and lower emissions. Programme theory, a construct and tool originated in the field of program evaluation, is also referred to as theory of change. The change must be a logical derivation from the theory. Such theory of change can, and should be a core element in the evaluation of impact investing.

The **term 'theory of change' originates in the field of program evaluation. Sometimes also called 'program theory', it refers to the construction of a model that specifies (usually visually) the underlying logic, assumptions, influences, causal linkages and expected outcomes of a development program or project. Through the collection and analysis of performance data, this model can be tested against the actual process experienced, and results attained, by the intervention (Funnell and Rogers** 2011; **Morra-Imas and Rist** 2009; **Rogers** 2008**).**

How can impact investing be defined? How can it be evaluated? In a metrics-rich and increasingly data-driven industry, it could be argued that all stakeholders in the emerging field of impact investing are concerned with these questions. The most reknown definition for impact investing is that of the Rockefeller Foundation: Impact investments are investments made into companies, organizations, and funds with the intention to generate social and environmental impact alongside a financial return. This definition leaves the black box intact. The why, and how, the programme, the logical connection between the programme elements, their execution, the calculation of the impacts and outcomes of various decisions prior to making the decisions remain all in the dark. The definition argues in the comfortable confines of an Input Output or stimulus reaction (SR) model, commonly used in the financial industry, while for estimating the impacts of a programme theory we clearly need a stimulus, organism, reaction (SOR) model. Only when the logical link between the stimulus and the processes within the organism can be explained and a causal link to the reactions can be established we can understand the effects of the programme theory.

Impact investments are made in both emerging and developed markets, and across asset classes, including bonds, listed shares, and private equity. With the original definition of the Rockefeller Foundation impact investing is no different from Triple Bottom Line Investing, a term coined by John Ellington in 1994. In recent years the definition therefore has evolved and the elements of additionality, profitability as a prerequisite (to distinguish it from philanthropy) and key performance indicators for measuring the impact (KPIs) have been added. However, an important element is often underdeveloped in the discourse and practice on performance assessment in the sector. That element is theory of change.

Fortunately, theory of change is already a part of the practice of the impact investing industry at a number of levels. Nevertheless, there are two problems. First, in some areas of the field's practice, in particular in the large equity asset classes like listed stocks theory of change is still invisible, not explicit or missing altogether. And second, there has not yet been an assessment of the overall state of play of this pivotal element in the field as a whole and how it can be applied to the maximum effect. This contribution will argue that making the theory of change explicit, making the programme theory traceable and the individual impact of each factor measurable enables all stakeholders and investors, intermediaries and investees to better understand and strengthen the processes of change, help to calculate in advance the impact of managerial decisions, allow for alignment of decision making to the programme theory and therefore evaluate the effects of the implementation of existing theories of change. Therefore effectiveness of (ToC) results can be maximized and the extent to which results and processes actually align with the expected profitability can be tested. Successful establishment of the impacts of the various elements of a programme theory then finally can be used in the portfolio engineering approach and intervention planning or even the creation of a systematic intervention theory.

So thus far there has not been a clear answers on why does theory of change matter to the evaluation of impact investing? Why should actors in the impact investing industry who are not using it now consider adopting this approach? What is its value added? Why should mainstream investors adopt this approach and what are the missing links to show the value added to a ToC to an investment or portfolio strategy. The following benefits have been mentioned in the literature on the value add of ToC inclusion into investment decision making.

2 Addressing the Research Gaps

The ecosystem for impact investing is growing since the impact G8 and so is the academic interest in the field. The main organizing instrument of the industry is the Global Impact Investing Network (GIIN), which serves a membership of 50 institutions, firms and funds on its Investors' Council. Till date, most of the major players in this field have been based in the United States or Europe, but there is also evidence of a growing number of networks and actors based in Asia, Africa and the Americas (Jackson and Harji 2012; Harji and Jackson 2012). There is an on-going (and healthy) debate on what, in fact, constitutes an 'impact investment'. However, leading proponents of the industry generally would agree that they are mobilizing capital for 'investments intended to create positive social impact beyond financial return'. Two key components of this definition are, first, the intent of the investor to achieve such impacts, and, second, tangible evidence of the impacts themselves and most recently an exploration about whether or not a "Theory of change exists". This third component in the definition of an impact investment theory of change allows for a structured and longterm approach to investing and finance and should answer the following question. What is the theory of change of the investors? What that of the investee? Is there pattern matching? What outcomes and impacts do they expect? For investor—will the investment be catalyzed by the capital they are channeling to enterprises or projects on the ground? Why and how do impact investors apply and implement their theory of change. Why do mainstream investors do not have, expect or implement a theory of change?

It is unclear at the current point in time what the connecting logical model that ties the actions of the programme to the outcomes is unclear and so is the question how the elements of impact measurement and theory of change could fit into any portfolio theory unsolved. It needs to be clarified how a theory of change can be implemented in passive investing strategies, other than by the regulator that rules out certain business models. However in active portfolio management, ToC would be considered portfolio engineering and asset selection process, should theories be able to establish the link between the programme theory and the outcome in all respects (financial, societal, environmental). In the current environment many mainstream players have advocated for a passive portfolio management approach which means nothing else than buying the market index or reconstructing it—which leads to finally buying the dip and the assets that have the biggest weighting in an index, neglecting impact and theories of change as well as intent. Using the logics of portfolio engineering—the contribution of the ToC could install an early warning system for emerging trends. For ToC to be fit for entering into a portfolio engineering concept and portfolio theory, therefore the core factors that determine the success of a programme theory in achieving impact have to be identified and analyzed.

While building sector-wide measurement systems for the impact investing industry is underway, there has also been a flourishing of customized or decentralized metrics and tools at the level of individual institutions or organizations. How the centralized and decentralized measurement systems can interact productively with each other is a key question for industry leaders. Moreover a magnitude of over 1000 different impact measurement criteria is hard to introduce into portfolio industry with its variance based systemic risk. As pointed out "Until recently, it could accurately be said that impact investing was metrics-rich but data poor."

On-going reporting of funds dedicated to impact investing (notably, Acumen Fund, IGNIA, Root Capital and others)—have begun to mobilise and analyse larger and more granular data sets from microfinance institutions and small and growing businesses, in particular, to better understand the scope, nature and performance of impact investments in aggregate and by industry sector and investment type (among others, see Bouri et al. 2011; Saltuk et al. 2011).

3 Process Elements of Theories of Change are missing

Nevertheless, the current data collection and metrics driven impact measurement approaches, which are—recognizably first attempts follow the input–output scheme and forget about the process element. In other word they do not look into impact investing as an input—process—output model or stimulus organism reaction model. Therefore it is difficult to provide the connecting logical model that ties the actions of the programme to the outcomes. This is exactly where theory of change is kicking in. As Jackcon (2013) argues, "current practice in the evaluation of impact investing still tends to focus on counting inputs and outputs, and telling stories." Impact investing therefore may have to draw from the wisdom and the successfully implemented concepts from development banks, multilaterals and program evaluation in development aid. At the same time a theory of change wants to influence other market actors, which will be called external intervention. The impact investors organized via GIIN have stated in their report that they aim to influence intermediaries, other investors and market players as well as investees through the use of a ToC in their investment philosophy.

4 Benefits of Applying a Theory of Change

This exercise involves the interrogation of the theory of change: Is the program theory valid, appropriate, relevant and accurate? Does change actually occur in the ways the intervention proponents have expected? Are there other change dynamics or pathways at work? Are there unforeseen actors and factors who promote or constrain change? Are there obstacles that stymie or render ineffective the theory of change? How can those obstacles be minimized or eliminated altogether? These are just some of the questions that evaluators ask as they examine an intervention's theory of change. And the answers to these questions can usefully inform program managers and funders as to how they can modify the design of the intervention under review to improve outcomes, or whether the intervention should be terminated altogether. A quantitative approach to answer these questions is provided in this anthology in the quantitative analysis section.

Applying the theory of change approach is not as expensive as some other options for evaluating impact investing, such as large-scale experimental studies. Theory of change is a generally cost-effective way to frame and inform an evaluation that is suited to help de-risk assets as the author posits. Theory of change can, and should be interrogated at all levels: the field as a whole, multi-firm platforms, individual organizations, specific investments and the beneficiary level of communities, households and individuals in order to distil the elements that are effective in de-risking assets in a way that it can be modeled into mainstream investment models like portfolio theory, quality assurance, ISO Standards, and process assurance in the auditing industries. Network analysis can be a helpful tool in achieving these outcomes. Theories of Change—well prepared—provide the forward-looking potential to inform the asset selection process of an active investor.

The GIIRS platform is one of the first networks that uses an approach informed by a logic model that requires each impact investment manager it rates to make explicit the firm's own theory of change relating to social impact. In other words, the company's theory of change is embedded in each ratings report (GIIRS 2012a). The GIIRS platform provides access by investors to a pool of companies with different theories of change. Investors can thus choose the investees that most closely match their own intent, theories and strategies (see the GIIRS website for more detail; GIIRS 2012b). There are other examples around like Root Capital or the NEXI, a social stock exchange based in South Africa with however minimal trading volumes. 'An articulated theory of change illustrating the link between intention, action and outcome becomes the centre-piece of impact due diligence', says Nexii (2012, 1). Prospective investors can test the logic of the firm's theory as a whole as well as interrogate its individual parts. Nexii argues that applying such due diligence processes can improve investor confidence and increase the impact of investments, as well as enabling the investor to hold its investees to account.

At the level of individual investments, Rockefeller Philanthropy Advisors has published a widely distributed handbook on how to design, implement and evaluate impact investments. Using a logic model that details the 'impact value chain' for a given investment, this guide distinguishes clearly between outputs (defined as the 'activity results', such as the number of people served by a project), on the one hand, and outcomes (defined as the collection 'of all results, intended and/or unintended'. However there is thus far no tool available that makes ToC application compatible to mainstream investment measurement and due diligence efforts, portfolios or investment theories or quality assurance procedures. Therefore the Rockefeller

Philanthropy Advisors responsible for the handbook suggest as ideal systemic solution, building and refining impact metrics that are standardized across the impact investing industry. They clearly support the efforts of IRIS, GIIRS and other actors working towards this goal (Godeke and Pomares 2009).

The following elements provide helpful:

1. Theory of Change is a cost-effective way of mapping complex and complicated processes of cause and effect in impact investing using network analysis and ecision making analysis quantitative models for calculating the effects of interventions serving the imperative of establishing a systematic, disciplined and continuous analysis that can be translated into an explicit (even quantifiable) contribution for an investor using the ISO Plan Do Check Act (PDCA) philosophy. Over time the permanent improvement of the programme theory and its outcomes will be the rewardand competitive edge.
2. Constructing and refining the theory of change helps investors to purposefully and clearly understand the change they are trying to create and to learn and adjust their strategies and instruments as they proceed forward.
3. The act of investors publicly communicating their theory of change serves to engage other key stakeholders (partner investors, social enterprises, local organizations) in the implementation and learning process.
4. An explicit theory of change can be used by governments, NGOs, employees and citizens at large to hold the asset owner accountable for the results. In a generally unregulated and emerging industry, checks and balances matter.
5. And finally theory of change can be productively blended with other evaluation methods and applied at various levels to generate even more useful findings and insights.

5 Defining the Research Agenda

Currently ToC is currently more of a framework than a tool and not sufficient to understand the multiple levels and dimensions of the emergent field of impact investing and the success factors of interventions and therefore do not provide the necessary **leadership guidance in decision making**.

In order to find out, what leaders really need Open-ended qualitative interviews with leaders, as well as closed-ended surveys can be deployed.

Programme theories can be analysed and ranked to the extend to which they builds on organizational assessment tools like PESTO analysis, Porters Five Forces, the Strengths weakness, opportunities and threat model (SWOT), to what extend they consider physical risks, transition risks and stranded assets that can be applied on individual, policy and universal level are important.

Sets of tools able to build an overall integral assessment of organizational performance on the basis of three pillars (1) first the external environment (legal and administrative, political, cultural and economic) (2) second, of its organizational 'motivation' (history, mission, rewards and incentives); and (3) third, of its organizational capacity (strategic leadership, human resources, program management, financial management, inter-organizational linkages may provide a good starting point for developing qualitative research when combining these three analyses to generate an overall assessment of the organization's effectiveness, efficiency and financial viability (Canadian International Development Agency 2006; IDRC and Universalia n.d.).

This approach can be applied to organizations operating at any level across the industry's spectrum. However in order to get to this point and potentially find variables that represents organizational capacity or any other integral variable that can serve as a dummy for ToC, the concepts of theories of change why they exist, how they are crafted, why they are used or not used by market participant with what intention has to be clarified first.

Whereas the approach of organizational assessment can be used in case study analysis to create a body of knowledge for impact investors and academia and serve for comparative analysis of organizational performance and change segmented either by industries, roles (investor, investee, intermediary) or intention. And therefore could also be useful for organisations to construct self-assessment tools. Currently, in its uneven and fragmented state, and with most impact investments still in their early stages, qualitative methods, such as 'most significant change' stories, could be very useful (see Davies and Dart 2005). Moreover, qualitative tools for understanding cause and effect relationships in a given investment, like contribution analysis (Mayne 2008), are also appropriate.

Another general approach to assess micro-level impacts that is often qualitative in nature but can also involve quantitative methods is that of participatory evaluation. This approach aims to expand the breadth and depth of stakeholder participation, which could be integrated in a first step using secondary data. Within individual investments, there are methods from social accounting and cost–benefit analysis that can also be mobilized. Social return on investment (Harji 2008a; SROI Network 2012) and the expanded value-added statement (Harji 2008b; Mook 2013) as well as the shared values approach from Porter and Kramer are methods for monetizing the otherwise invisible and unaccounted for, social value created by an investment. However these methods are too fragmented and too little standardized, as to be expanded into a ToC that can be applied universally in Portfolio and Investment Theory and in mainstream portfolio engineering. Moreover they disregard they disregard the effect on other market players, whereas a ToC should also be able to make statements about the proliferation effect of the theory to an industry or a group of players.

Randomized controlled trials (RCTs) and other experimental or quasi-experimental methods could also have a role in the evaluation of impact investing There is no doubt that RCTs can be applied to measuring the social impacts of impact investments. However, it is also true that RCTs are generally expensive to implement. In addition, they can sometimes involve serious political challenges in interacting with control groups that have not received the same interventions as the experimental groups.

The author can draw from a variety of relevant Research Questions ranging from Why does theory of change matter to the evaluation of impact investing to what are the obstacles of ToC?

Why should actors in the impact investing industry who are not using it now consider adopting this approach?

What is the role of a theory of change in solving dilemmas and leadership problems? This exercise involves the interrogation of the theory of change itself—for those who already apply it: Is the program theory valid, appropriate, relevant and accurate? Does change actually occur in the ways the intervention proponents have expected? Are there other change dynamics or pathways at work? Are there unforeseen actors and factors that promote or constrain change? Are there obstacles that stymie or render ineffective the theory of change? What are investors motives.

In what areas do or don't they apply ToC. This could include a network analysis, or comparative analysis as there is no stochastically sample, but networks and distinct industry players applying a ToC.

A simpler alternative way would be to review existing case studies, identify Success Factors. However the research would be restricted by the existence of a very narrow database only.

References

Bouri, A., Fonzi, C. J., Gelfand, S., Gromis, A., Lankester, K., Leung, G., McCarthy, K., et al. (2011). *Data driven: A performance analysis for the impact investing industry*. New York: Impact Reporting and Investment Standards (IRIS), Global Impact Investing Network.

Canadian International Development Agency. (2006). *Guide to organizational assessment*. Gatineau: Canadian International Development Agency.

Davies, R., & Dart, J. (2005). *The 'most significant change' technique: A guide to its use*. Cambridge: Care International.

Funnell, S. C., & Rogers, P. J. (2011). *Purposeful program theory: Effective use of theories of change and logic models*. San Francisco: Jossey-Bass.

Global Impact Investing Rating System (GIIRS). (2012a). *GIIRS quarterly analytics report: Q1 2012*. Global Impact Investing Rating System.

Global Impact Investing Rating System (GIIRS). (2012b). *Appendix III: TIIRS and theory of change logic model*. Retrieved from http://www.giirs.org/about-giirs/how-giirs-works/173

Godeke, S., & Pomares, R. (2009). *Solutions for impact investors: From strategy to implementation*. New York: Rockefeller Philanthropy Advisors.

Harji, K. (2008a). *Social return on investment*. Ottawa: Carleton Centre for Community Innovation, Carleton University.

Harji, K. (2008b). *Expanded value added statement*. Ottawa: Carleton Centre for Community Innovation, Carleton University.

Harji, K., & Jackson, E. T. (2012). *Accelerating impact: Achievements, challenges and what's next in the impact investing industry*. New York: The Rockefeller Foundation.

International Development Research Centre (IDRC) and Universalia Management Group. (n.d.). *Organizational assessment framework*. Ottawa. Retrieved from https://books.google.de/books?id=iNffAgAAQBAJ&printsec=copyright&hl=de&source=gbs_pub_info_r#v=onepage&q&f=false

Jackson, E. T., & Harji, K. (2012). *Unlocking capital, activating a movement: Final report of the strategic assessment of the Rockefeller Foundation's impact investing initiative*. New York: The Rockefeller Foundation.
Mayne, J. (2008). *Contribution analysis: An approach to exploring cause and effect*. ILAC Brief 16.
Mook, L. (Ed.). (2013). *Accounting for social value*. Toronto: University of TorontoPress.
Morra-Imas, L., & Rist, C. (2009). *The road to results: Designing and conducting effective development evaluations*. Washington, DC: World Bank.
Nexii. (2012). *Due diligence in impact investing*. Retrieved June 30, 2017, from http://www.nexii.com/blog/due-diligence-in-impact-investing/
Rogers, P. J. (2008). Using programme theory to evaluate complicated and complex programmes. *Evaluation, 14*(1), 29–48. Root Capital. 2012. [online] Various. Retrieved from http://www.rootcapital.org
Saltuk, Y., Bouri, A., & Leung, G. (2011). *Insight into the impact investment market*. New York: J.P. Morgan and Global Impact Investing Network. e-book.
SROI Network. (2012). *Social return on investment guide*. London: SROI.

Karen Wendt is editor of the Sustainable Finance Series with Springer Science Publishing. She merges 20 years investment banking with social and green economy finance, leadership 4.0, design thinking and ideation. She implements Portfolio engineering, assessment and value based decision making, choice architecture and theories of change and advises on Sustainable Development Goals Economics (SDG Economics) in her programme scaling4impact. Karen co-created the Equator Principles, the First Global Sustainability Standard in investment banking—based on impact assessments, creating mitigation strategies and impact action plans. She won the Financial Times Sustainability Award together with peers for this pioneering and created Responsible Investment Banking.

About Bridges and Goals: On the Art of Change Management as a Bridge to the Goals for a Sustainable World and a World of Sustainable Investing

Marcel Malmendier

Abstract This essay outlines a comprehensive perspective on how a transitional path to sustainable living can be fostered. To date, most decision-makers see this process predominantly as a management task, focusing on instruments like policy-making, management of technology-development, economic incentives, and strategic goal-setting. Within a change management perspective, the view is broader: In addition to management instruments processes of meaning construction and understanding, especially various practices of discourse, are considered to be essential. As such practices do not aim at specific predefined impacts they are often ignored as being fundamental for the success of change processes.

The essay outlines this guiding distinction between management and change approaches together with other fundamental insights of the social sciences and practitioners into the functioning of change processes. Aspects that are relevant from a change perspective in order to shape and promote a transition from investment banking to sustainability are highlighted. Comparisons are also being made between this sector and the transition to renewable energies.

The author proposes that the integration of change management know-how with knowledge about the management of political and economic developments as well as with technological knowledge is essential for leading this global change project to success.

Keywords Change management · Multi-level change · Sustainable investment · Sustainable finance · Transition to sustainability · Practice theory · Instrumental change · Goal-setting · Discourse

---

M. Malmendier (✉)
Qualitates GmbH, Darmstadt, Germany

Investmentkontor RheinRuhr GmbH, Bochum, Germany
e-mail: m.malmendier@qualitates.de; marcel.malmendier@ikrr.de

K. Wendt (ed.), *Theories of Change*, Sustainable Finance,
https://doi.org/10.1007/978-3-030-52275-9_2

1 Introduction

The journey toward sustainability is on its way. Cornerstones of the process become visible. This process is an open experiment of mankind.

This essay takes a closer look at what we know about how change processes should be designed and fostered to be successful, illustrating these insights with aspects of the transition to renewable energy and sustainable investment.

The process of bringing more sustainability into our ways of living, producing and consuming makes necessary both,

- a search of what we can learn from existing knowledge and which new knowledge resources are lacking and
- a continuous reflection of the process itself, in its parts and as a whole.

To accomplish this, multiple efforts are required. We need extensive scientific research, thinking beyond the status quo in every faculty and a huge entrepreneurial drive with a lot of trial and error experiments to find feasible solutions for many challenges, large and small. Natural sciences are on their way, in particular taking the part of convincing the public of a man-made climate change. Economic and political thinkers have introduced concepts on how to encourage change and how to organise our living in sustainable ways. Engineering and information technology have contributed by developing new technologies e.g. for the production of energy and communication devices to reduce traffic. And a lot of practitioners in many fields, for instance, politicians, NGOs, engineers, enterprises, communities, consumers, farmers, etc. are already contributing to the process.

I would wish that the humanities would be far more aggressive to contribute to these reflections from their point of view. This would shed more light on the procedural and cultural aspects of the change process to sustainability. These aspects tend to be underestimated, thus running high risk of inefficiency and even failure.

It's not only the goals that matter, it is also the bridges to reach these goals. To use a comparison from the world of organisations: Every company knows that producing good results requires good inputs as well as good processes. Both product and process go hand in hand. The same is true for the transition to sustainability, in particular to sustainable investment. If we just try to put into practice ideas of smart people, that are fascinating and convincing, practice will teach us, that we have forgotten about designing, fostering and continuously re-reflecting the process of becoming more and more sustainable. Many leaders have experienced this pitfall in their own change projects. Shall we make all these mistakes again? Or can we do better, saving time and resources?

2 Requirements for Complex Change Processes: Post-modern Organising as Catalyser for the Transition to Sustainability (Thesis One)

Sustainability is probably the greatest change project that humanity has seen in modern times. The transition to sustainability is playing on so many different levels: individuals, small groups such as households, communities, cities, regions, companies and other organisations, states, state unions up to the United Nations. And it involves such wide-spread subject areas like technology, politics, economy, science, ethics, legislation, local cultures and even religions.

Considering such complexities and the necessity for change, sustainability is both a fascinating and thrilling challenge. The core of this challenge lies in the fact that very different sets of knowledge have to be brought together and a large number of activities have to be coordinated across regional, cultural and political borders.

From a change management perspective, the overarching question is, whether we as mankind have experiences and developed practices in order to clear a path through such a jungle of challenges as a forward-looking process and not as an adaptation to crises and disasters.

Here at least I see possible solutions. Today we know from organisational practice and science that heterogenous groups are able to master particularly great challenges, insofar as they manage to combine different abilities productively. However, we also know that finding or developing such abilities within teams, organisations and society is not an easy task, but it is also not the real difficult one. The real challenge lies in bringing those different abilities together productively.

Let's think of the transition to sustainability as a huge and manifold change project. And let's imagine that those striving to manage this change are linked by some kind of organisation. This may be a locally and culturally dispersed team or a decentralised organisation scattered over cultures and time zones or a swarm of different organisations that do not know each other directly or entities that are loosely coupled by shared activities, by the idea of sustainability or by personal contact.

Whatever form of organisation we imagine, all these forms are basically capable of bringing together at least some different faculties in order to pursue a specific organisational purpose. According to the purpose this may be such heterogenous faculties as politics, technology, economy, ethics, legislation, local cultures and others. While such areas in modern societies are functionally separated, many organisations make use of several different subject areas. Thus, organisations can be understood as a purposeful process of amalgamation of different faculties and their different know-how and knowledge resources.[1] It goes without saying that

[1] The question of the connection between functional differentiation and the described ability of organisations to integrate very different bodies of knowledge and perspectives is discussed, for example, by Schimank (2001) and Bode and Brose (2001).

organisations differ considerably in regard to this capability of amalgamation. Especially this depends on the extent to which post-modern and flexible forms of organising and open-minded cultures are actually realised or not.

The idea of organisations as processes based on different practices and views is not new. For example, it has been developed partly in organisational theory and practice (Weick 1979; Mintzberg 1979; Mintzberg and Westley 1992; Volberda 1999; Oestereich and Schröder 2017) and partly in the debate on organisational culture describing various bodies of knowledge within organisational parts and how they work together (Smircich 1983; Schein 2010; Czarniawska-Joerges 2000). The notion of diversity management also takes up the topic of heterogeneity, here as a characteristic of the workforce. In recent decades, change managers and organisational developers have established a huge variety of tools to bring together different views and convictions.

Considering this wide-spread capability of organisations to integrate various bodies of knowledge and considering the concreteness of the Sustainable Development Goals (SDGs), which outline the purpose of the global sustainability project, I see a good chance to master the challenge using post-modern organisational and change abilities to moderate diverse subject areas and cultures.

However, we should avoid projecting our hopes solely on some of the leading faculties as we tend to do today, in particular on technological innovations and political institutions. Instead for this change project we should cultivate a post-modern approach by appreciating and seriously checking every idea, every subject area for solutions and every imaginable change practice for benefits and possible pitfalls. This open-minded thinking lies at the heart of holistic change management approaches, which provide important know-how on how further processes of change can be initiated and steered. These approaches in particular make it possible to put the change process on a much broader and more solid footing than is possible with the paradigm of change in the field of sustainability that is prevalent today, and which focuses primarily on technology development, political measures (e.g. Cato 2008) and sociotechnical transformation processes (Geels 2010; Dolata 2011). By scrutinising today's procedures from a perspective informed by change management and social science know-how, a number of problems of inefficiency and at least partial ineffectiveness with possible dramatic consequences are revealed. As fascinating as it is, what has already been achieved today with the SDGs, the regular international consultation mechanisms, as well as in the field of technologies and the development of some regulatory instruments, it is also clear that the present state of knowledge on the requirements of change projects is not taken into account.

Illustration Here I will focus on illustrating how different professions are involved in change processes. Whereas other challenges of postmodern change management, in particular the practical questions of how to generate different ideas and how to bring different perspectives into a fruitful discourse, are not the subject of this illustration. Some aspects of these questions are taken up in the following theses.

Renewable Energy In some respects, the process of introducing the renewables to the market is a shining example of change expertise. By integrating many different subject areas, this process shows a pragmatic and post-modern open-minded approach. As a result, different renewable energy acts in many countries have motivated investments in various segments.

In the common discourse, government incentives and state guarantees over the investment cycle are seen as key factors. Another central point is witnessed in the fact that these incentives have been created for both small and large electricity producers. The success is obvious: the demand has grown a market for different actors such as suppliers of components, producers of power plants, large energy suppliers, manufacturers of tools and materials for network infrastructure, craftsmen and households. In addition, various areas like science and technology, different economic segments as well as political, legislative and regulatory processes on different levels have been involved.

From the perspective of change management, the mere inclusion of several professional perspectives is important but not sufficient. Getting ideas and inspirations from various professions is only half the way. In order to ensure the success of a concrete change project, it is particularly important that different perspectives are integrated in one framework in such a way that both, their solution-oriented inputs and their critical potential are taken into account. In the transition to renewables this has been done for many though not all relevant areas. I will revisit this point in thesis four.

Sustainable Investment In the area of sustainable investment, there is no change approach today that would be nearly as comprehensive as the approaches in the area of renewable energies. However, in recent years we have seen an increasing number of activities in the investment segment. These are no longer solely initiated by smaller and firmly convinced actors. Increasingly, even powerful players in the financial market are seeing an advantage in taking at least the first steps into the direction of sustainability. One such lighthouse project is, for example, the sale of coal investments from the Norwegian State Fund.

But in recent years it is not only the number of activities that is increasing, initiatives are also getting more wide-spread including different faculties. For example, the relationship of sustainable investment and risk-reward-relations has been scrutinised by scientists and practitioners. The topic of sustainable finance has become a field for journalism. New entrepreneurs are entering the scene like fund-managers and advisors integrating ESG-criteria into their financial analyses. Such criteria are applied to parts of some of the very large investment portfolios today, sometimes as free initiative, sometime as a regulatory requirement. There are discussions on more regulations for the investment sector where the clearest step in the last years has been the introduction of CSR-reporting standards as a requirement for larger listed companies, thus making information available for investors.

This spreading of the topic over faculties can be used as a fertile ground for decision-makers in the political arena to prepare steps that have the quality of a comprehensive change framework. Until today all activities represent individual initiatives. This is so, although it has been shown for more than 20 years that successful sustainable investments are feasible on the basis of the description and control of sustainable investment criteria. States have long been impressing by non-action. Big companies tend to be mainstream oriented since they run widespread activities and are not just specialising in niches. A structural conservatism emerging from such business models explains non-action in the past as there was no broad sustainable finance trend that one could miss. This also explains first steps that we see at present as today's widening of activities in this area may be interpreted as the starting point of an accelerating development.

3 Change Management in Social Contexts Means Addressing Practices: Insights in the Structure of Practice as a Fundament for Change Management (Thesis Two)

What does change mean when talking about change in social contexts? Whenever we talk about change as a social phenomenon we refer to a shift in what we do and the way we are acting. If bundles of action and ways of acting typically differ from those before, we talk of a change in a social sense. Following a tradition in social philosophy and sociology for bundles of action and ways of acting I will use the notions of meaningful activity and practice (Schutz 1967; Bourdieu 1972; Giddens 1984; Turner 1994; Schatzki 1996; Schatzki et al. 2001; Malmendier 2003; Honer and Hitzler 2015).[2] Practices/activities (in the following I only use the notion 'practice') are neither single actions, nor structures, strategies, artefacts or other entities, that influence the course of action. Practice encompasses intentional procedures, habitual routines and non-intentional processes as can be observed for example in practices of energy production and supply, practices of investment decisions or practices of analysing sustainability impacts. Consequently, change in social contexts means changing practices, not single actions nor just entities, that might influence practice. And thus, using this notion of practice, change management means addressing practices.

To provide a deeper understanding of what change means in social contexts, I will make three remarks. The first and fundamental one is important to clarify the idea that change management in social contexts means addressing practices, while most authors are talking about change as a change of structures, rules, procedures, technologies, goals, strategies, etc. Using a modern, empirically based notion of practices I will clarify why all these elements should be understood as means of

[2]The terms 'action' in the tradition of phenomenological theory of action, 'practice' in the more recent discussion of the so-called practice theory, as well as the theoretically more neutral word 'activity' are all used to emphasize that what we do does not depend so much on individual decision making or will, but to a large extent on patterns of meaning and processes of meaning creation. This includes the use and creation of subconscious or implicit knowledge. An interdisciplinary empirical research underpins this point of view, mainly from micro-sociology (Garfinkel 1967; Goffman 1974), cultural anthropology (Geertz 1973), cognitive science and cognitive psychology (Varela 1990; Goldstein 2011).

change and not as change itself. The second remark is on the role of stability in change processes, a point that is clear for any change management practitioner. The third remark very shortly states the role of artefacts, which is in particular important in the transition to the renewables as this process is very much driven by technology and infrastructure.

(a) How practices can be seen adequately in the light of modern empirical research? Traditionally in everyday life as well as in science there is an understanding that action and cognition are two separate phenomena, that are linked at certain points. However, empirical research deems this traditional view as misleading. The traditional view that is still vital had sequential and hierarchical views on this linkage of action and cognition.

    For example, in this traditional view, rational action is often understood as action following plans; often a good organisational practice is seen in the postulate that structure and process should follow strategy; and hierarchical and sequential organisation of projects for a long time have been the leading paradigm. Today many innovative researchers have shown that rationalisations and action are interwoven processes. It is acknowledged that flexible and post-modern organisations with lots of trial and error activities and communication structures beyond hierarchies are more adaptive to environmental requirements and thus are sometimes able to create even better strategies than the thinking of leaders could imagine. And situational project management approaches often called agile project management like scrum and others, first introduced in complex software projects, are on the forefront because of higher innovativeness and higher efficiency.

    The decisive outcome of the underlying empirical research is that, what we do can be understood in a better way when we see action and sensemaking not as two linked processes but as simultaneous aspects of the same process. According to this research, cognitive processes run in parallel with activities. In this view planning and replanning, understanding, accounting for and explaining are intrinsic constituents of practice. Acting and meaning patterns are two sides of the same coin. And the normality of practices within a cultural context can now be understood as the fact that people are able to recognise certain patterns of meaning within the course of action, using explicit and implicit cultural knowledge (Garfinkel 1967; Goffman 1974).

    Consequently, change should be understood not only as change of acting, but also as a change of patterns of meaning. And so, if I talk about designing structures, setting strategies, etc. as means of change I, want to point out that changing structures, strategies, etc. does not change per se the patterns of meaning within practice nor the course of action.

(b) What is the role of stability in change processes? When discussing change, we refer to the change of certain practices. No change process changes everything. Most of the existing practices are not even affected.

    Whenever we initiate change we are forced to deal with this tension between change and preservation. While a change is occurring or deliberately infused into social systems, most of the existing practices remain as they have been before. If existing practices are not specifically addressed in change processes they are secured against change by their normality. What is normal does change, if ever, in small portions and in rather slow processes. Stability is therefore inherent and part of a change process.

(c) Why artefacts matter in change processes? We have to keep in mind that artefacts like technologies, organisations, infrastructures, etc. are lasting results of former actions, shaping today's practices. Thus, saying that addressing the ways we act is key for any change management project typically includes the production of new artefacts as well as the change of existing ones.

What is the outcome of these remarks for change management? When talking about change management we refer to a deliberate change that aims at diminishing effects identified as negative (e.g. pollution, hunger, global warming, infringements) and introducing or promoting new practices that shall have positive effects (e.g. renewable energy, sustainable investment). For change management it is vital to address both the course of action through certain means of change such as goals, rules, technologies, infrastructures, strategies, etc. and the patterns of meaning through various practices of discourse. In a rough and sketchy argument, one could say: With goals, rules, structural changes, etc. we change what we should or must do. By questioning the meaning patterns, we address what is normal and thus accepted or even appreciated.

For change management it is also crucial to keep in mind the stability of social practices. Usually this is done by concepts of resistance (e.g. action against change) and persistence (e.g. ignoring change action) (Argyris 1990). As far as I see, this idea is essential for authors and practitioners who do care about people, their habits and cultures. Caring about these tangible and palpable social facts arouses an understanding of the rigorous sanctioning reality and the trust-generating preservative characteristics of normality (Malmendier 1995). Other authors and practitioners arguing and acting along classical management approaches often lack this understanding and are therefore pursuing ways that may initiate quick change movements, but can't reach the deeper levels of meaning patterns and thus lack the capability to bring change processes to sustainable ends (e.g. Kotter 2012).

Finally, investing in changing artefacts is vital when old practices with clearly identified negative outcomes such as fossil energy or certain distribution practices are based on such artefacts as technologies, infrastructures and organisations.

Illustration In this illustration I will describe *to what extent* we have succeeded in driving new activities forward effectively. Some aspects of the question of *how* we can address practices in change projects is dealt with in the following theses.

Renewable Energy Concrete practices have changed in this field in the last years. State activities have been able to encourage wide-spread activities and subsequently boost a market. After basic technological possibilities had been established to invite existing and new actors into that market we could observe that the initiation of regulatory frameworks led to unleashed investments. The capacities of renewable energy generation are on a path of exponential growth.

Old energy suppliers are searching for new investment opportunities such as large onshore and offshore wind parks, photovoltaic, solar-thermal or hydroelectric power stations, investments into the electricity grid, and into the distribution of smart home technologies. At the same time the market of energy production is about to change from a clearly centralised system to a more decentralised structure. This has infused a variety of activities in the area of engineering, craftsmanship, foundation of new actors like local cooperatives of energy production and tech companies, etc. New entrepreneurial chances arise like the networking of the production of renewable energies and traffic from local to industry level.

Sustainable Investment In the area of sustainable investment the number and size of activities is increasing. However, they are still scattered. We find various initiatives from private to institutional levels to invest assets according to sustainability criteria. This ranges from the use of single negative or positive criteria to coherent concepts and clearly defined impact approaches that pursue concrete social or ecological goals. Some major investors have announced strategies to transfer their assets according to certain sustainability criteria. International initiatives of stakeholders and legislators for corporate sustainability reporting (CSR reporting) have forced at least a group of large and listed companies to provide information on economic, ecological, social and governance performance. Engagement activities in the segment of large companies have become commonplace. Studies show that sustainable investments have become possible in many areas and generate competitive returns. Some further regulations in the area of sustainable finance are discussed at the professional and political level, e. g. for public investments and sustainability standards for financial products (e.g. EU HLEG 2017; EU EP 2018).

4 Actors Differ: A Categorisation by Micro-, Meso- and Macro-Level Helps to Identify and Address Carriers and Drivers of Change (Thesis Three)

Practices are not only based on patterns of acting and meaning, but as well on actors as carriers and drivers of action. In some of the older social philosophies, cultivating an emphatic concept of individuals and subjects as primary actors, this remark sounds superfluous and trivial. Within modern views as stated in thesis two, starting with an understanding of the dynamics of meaning and acting, actors are not just subjects, but part of and suspended in these dynamics.

For change management, one of the important questions for addressing practice is how to find ways of addressing actors. Good change managers know that the basis for successful change action is about getting into contact with and establishing a relation of resonance (Rosa 2016) to actors. This is a precondition to address actors in a way that they are inclined to change their practice which means changing their acting and re-examining their guiding patterns of meaning.

Actors can be individuals, but a lot of influential actors that are relevant for the transition to sustainability are not single individuals. They are organisations like companies, administrations, associations on local, national and international levels. They are more or less clearly organised groups based on ideas or personal acquaintance. They are actors in discourses like journalists, experts or thought leaders very often embedded in professional contexts. They are states, alliances of states and formally organized state unions. And a group of actors that has become increasingly relevant especially in investment, belonging to the realm of artefacts, are software programs and robots.

I will use the scheme of micro-, meso- and macro-levels to sort actors by size and level of aggregation. This scheme also serves for the methodological questions on how to typically understand actors on different levels. Here I apply this scheme as an easy to use heuristic. It is clear that a concrete change project needs more work at this point.

We find individuals and groups with personal relations (micro-level). When dealing with companies or other organisations (meso-level), multi-national corporations (meso- up to macro-level) we usually have contact to various persons or interfaces. Addressing robots and software-programs (might be relevant on micro-, meso- and sometimes macro-level) needs contact to responsible experts. States, governments, multi-national institutions and confederations (mostly macro-level) have established their own paths for consultations.

This broad perspective on different actors promotes a holistic view of change processes. It helps to avoid two misunderstandings of change management, namely that change is just about addressing minds (psychological pitfall) or just about addressing the logic of societies and their social functional sub-systems (social theory pitfall).

Illustration In the following remarks I will point out the fact that in the transitions to the renewables and sustainable investment change is driven by small units serving as incubators of change. Typically, only after such incubation periods change activities are taken up by larger units.

Renewable Energy Decades ago, renewable energy technologies were developed and such diverse actors as households and space experts haven proven their usability. On this ground, today's renewable energy acts typically integrate all levels from micro to macro. Local actors on the micro-level were invited into the market. On the meso-level the old players running large power plants and energy grids are still present developing their activities increasingly into the direction of renewable energy supply. Professional associations have emerged. States as actors on the meso- and macro-level have set up the existing frameworks through laws, regulations and budget decision, in particular on subsidies for energy producers and research.

Sustainable Investment As in the case of renewable energies, the first movers were also located mostly on the micro-level and some on the meso-level. Decades ago, private individuals started to look for sustainable ways to save their money. Individual investment managers and smaller specialised banks were offering the first sustainable investment opportunities. Churches, foundations and some philanthropic small to medium-sized institutional investors began to more and more reflect on the possible social or environmental impacts of investments and set up approaches to use assets as a lever bound by ethical criteria. Today, rating-agencies and some scientists provide further insight into whether companies act in accordance to certain sustainability criteria and into impacts of certain economic activities and technologies. Associations promoting the ideas of sustainable finance are initiated in some countries.

On the meso- and macro level, larger investment companies and insurances (some of them multi-national corporations,) are entering the scene by offering some products for sustainable investors, by announcing strategies to grow the share of sustainable assets or by generally applying some criteria e.g. no investments in coal or controversial weaponry. Whether these activities are typically value driven or instead motivated by marketing rationales and the fear to miss a new trend is an open question today.

However, all these activities only account for a small share of the market. But we can assume, that the pioneering period of sustainable finance is over. Today actors on the macro level, especially states, state unions and the international community, find a foundation to base their legal and regulatory activities on. In the illustration of thesis two I gave some hints that activities on this level have started in recent years.

5 Systems of Meaning and World Views: On the Stability of Self-absorbed Perspectives as Challenge for Change (Thesis Four)

Whenever we perceive, reflect, judge or take decisions, we are selective. We don't see everything, and we cannot use every option, even if we would grasp them. When we speak of a perspective we exactly point out this selectivity.

For the successful implementation of change projects, it is important to understand that such ways of perceiving, reflecting, judging and decision-taking, often become a stable part of practices and identities, related to certain roles or social groups. Change managers should keep in mind that as a normal process in every social entity certain relevance structures (Schutz 1970) are emerging, which lead to certain types of perception, understanding, judgement or decision-making, and to certain self-conceptions. One should always be aware of the fact, that by defining what is relevant and what is not, all social entities draw distinctions between themselves and their environment. In other words, social entities become social entities on the one hand through developing ways of acting and self-images and on the other hand through distinguishing themselves from other social entities by establishing boundaries. Sometimes one aspect is in the foreground, sometimes the other.

By using the notion of systems of meaning in this essay I want to refer to these two characteristics of all social entities: The emergence of meaning through various processes of sensemaking and the establishment of boundaries.

We should not ignore the empirical hustle and bustle of various social contexts and their specific cultures. However, in this essay I suggest to take a brief look at some of the systems of meaning that are relevant in many contexts. Because the transition to sustainability is a broad process encompassing many facets of society, I consider such meaning systems to be particularly important in that transition. Here we can build on various authors who broadly discussed the following topics (e.g. Habermas 1981; Luhmann 1984; Rammert 2016).

Technological meaning systems are centered around questions of functioning. Science is oriented toward processes of finding and testing hypotheses. Politics deals with power and influence. Economy is focused on costs, profits and the availability of goods. Legal systems provide procedures to establish rules and apply them to cases. Ethics is about finding criteria to identify the appropriateness of action. Local and organisational cultures are centered around processes of community, belonging, and lived group identities.

Understanding that such meaning systems are providing specific and intrinsically coherent and logical meanings suggests that not dealing with one of the dominant meaning systems in change processes probably will lead to misunderstandings, feelings of personal or professional negligence and resistance. Here Clifford Geertz gave us a nice metaphor, talking of man as an "animal suspended in webs of significance he himself has spun" (Geertz 1973, p. 5). If this is an appropriate view on social reality negligence of such engrossing and absorbing webs of significance is likely to lead to trouble.

Finally, I want to point to the empirical observable fact that meaning systems tend to develop self-referential and self-absorbed perspectives and as such develop far reaching claims to offer viable world views. By providing convincing and coherent meaning, integrating contradictions, drawing and maintaining boundaries and controlling what is relevant, a strong tendency arises to believe that one's own perspective is superior. Meaning systems show a tendency to marginalise or even ignore alternative views. This always creates a breeding ground for frictions.

Coming back to thesis one on the requirements of complex change projects it is now becoming clear that even though using and integrating various knowledge and different perspectives in the project of change toward sustainability is a convincing idea but difficult to put into practice. A lot of negotiation and mediation work has to be an essential part of the process.

Illustration Here, I take a closer look at the aspect mentioned in the illustration under thesis one, namely that a strong framework that integrates different perspectives is probably one of the central success factors in change management. In the following brief illustrations, I will outline the quality of the prevailing change regimes in this respect. I will not dwell on the manifold stories of adversary discussions, interest conflicts, and ethical aporia that emerge in the light of various meaning systems in the fields of the renewables and sustainable investment.

Renewable Energy In retrospect the start into the age of renewable energy production at the beginning of the millennium looks simple and logical. However, as usual with success stories, it was far from clear over many years that this story would develop so favourably. From the point of view of change management a key point has already been outlined in thesis one: Various expert views were brought together. In combination with the points made in this thesis four, we can now see very clearly how important it was that professional expertise from different areas has been integrated into one project and for one purpose in such a way that technical, scientific, political, legal, and economic perspectives could not develop their antagonistic potentialities. As I see it, this became possible because in many countries, politics has set up a strong legal and regulatory framework with monetary incentives, thus bridging economic gaps in the calculations of a large number of investors and setting the ground for further investments in photovoltaics, wind turbines, or infrastructural measures for net stability.

As a result, the observable lack of political continuity in some countries has been able to slow down, but not stop, the transition to renewable energy (e.g. decrease in the rate of expansion of renewables and reduction or cancelation of the feed-in tariffs in some countries after the financial crises). Even though political will is an unsteady factor over the years, this multi-professional framework still drives and defends this development against strong adversary interests, e.g. cost arguments, loss of labour force in the old economy or loss of power of large companies running conventional plants.

From a change management perspective that is interested in mid- to long-term change success it is to be assumed that the prevailing exclusion of local cultures (not single local actors) from this transition to the renewables will likely be unfavourable. Further, as a cautious change manager one should assume that this will be as unfavourable as the exclusion of any other meaning system that today is integrated into the change framework, since with existing know-how we are not able to identify criteria to prefer one meaning system over another in change processes. As energy installations and infrastructures are immovable property, they are important at local levels. Here they are noticed. Here people talk and complain about them. And here the nutshells of resistance will most likely find their water and wind for sailing, with all kinds of resonance in the political systems. I am not saying that the inclusion of local cultures into the change frameworks to renewable energy would have been an easy task. We could have done more in this direction, I will therefore come back to this in the following theses.

Sustainable Investment In the field of investment, today we are not discussing about a comparable framework combining different professions, although this would be much easier regarding technology: Classical and sustainable investments use the same technological platforms. In the last 10 years, politics used its regulatory energy for measures for the stabilisation of the capital market. Incentives are still oriented towards pension schemes while ESG-criteria are rarely relevant. Professionally, a change framework encompassing ethical, legal, and regulatory as well as economic aspects could be set up today. But this is a professional view without taking political processes into account. Majorities in the political system are not yet organised which is not an easy task against strong adversary interests. In a comparative view to the renewables, there is a great challenge to catch up. An essential element of a comparable change framework will be discussed in the next thesis.

6 Goal-Setting and Sensemaking: The Two Sides of Change (Thesis Five)

In thesis two I introduced an empirically based notion of activity and practice, pointing out that acting and construction of meaning are two aspects of the same process and not two separate processes that are linked. While one side of practice is to interfere in and to try to influence aspects of the world, therefore using the action itself as instrument, meaning construction is about ongoing processes of cognition and recognition. These cognitive processes are embedded in the course of action or they are more elaborate procedures of reflection and understanding.

In the field of change management there is a group of practitioners and authors that uses such a concept of practice. With their interventions into social systems these change managers try to address instrumental action and processes of meaning construction on an equal base (Doppler and Lauterburg 2014; Oestereich and Schröder 2017). Other authors focus more on the instrumental side (Kotter 2012; Doppelt 2010).

Within this discourse on change management as well as within organisational science the discussion on organisational design is important because it highlights the consequences of differentiating activity and meaning. Here, first we have to mention the criticism of organisation models based on metaphors of machines. At least since the 60s it was clear that such organisational designs led to inefficient results even in industrial mass production. Machine-oriented organisation designs are an extreme form of differentiation between activities and meaning, separating these aspects of practice across roles of management and roles of mere execution.

Today however, goal-oriented approaches to management and change-management dominate. Here some authors use scientific concepts of organism and evolutionary processes as metaphors. These approaches are still trying to optimise the instrumental activity side of practice to improve performance alongside certain measurable parameters. What was new in comparison to machine-oriented designs was that the importance of sensemaking abilities has partly been reintroduced by searching for resources to self-optimise work practices of individuals and teams (e.g. practices of continuous optimisation cycles, kaizen, total quality management) as well as to streamline business processes (e.g. reengineering practices).

A full reception of the outlined notion of practice leads to address both instrumentality and meaning construction processes on an equal footing. In this light, it is not surprising that today we see many experiments of holistic forms of organisation that explicitly create space for processes of self-organisation. In contrast, working with such reduced and fictitious notions of the actor as a rationally calculating maximiser of utility (as many economists still do) seems astonishing and non-empirical.

What can we learn from an empirically based notion of practice for change management? To put it briefly for the context of this essay we have to address both sides of the coin. A hierarchy between instrumental and discursive elements should be avoided. Both basic perspectives, instrumental and discursive, should be brought into a dialogue. Understanding this interconnection of instrumentality and discursive elements within practice gives an idea, that the so-called "colonization" of discourses by instrumental imperatives (Habermas 1981) is one of the greatest dangers in change processes in the modern age.

Rapid progress in change processes at instrumental level should not be overestimated. Resistance can still strike back years and decades later. Equating change with achieving change goals sounds very convincing, but unfortunately it is shortened and therefore simply wrong, inefficient and in the worst case completely ineffective. With a balanced approach, the instrumental aspect of practice is typically addressed through goals, goal achievement criteria and resource specifications for projects, while the aspect of significance is addressed through various forms of discourse. This means to always address both sides of the following pairs of notions: norms and normality, instrumental leadership and thought leadership, criteria of measurement and understanding, KPIs as tools and discourse as a process. For reasons of brevity I will not further develop these ideas here.

Illustration In the following illustrations I will give a brief sketch of examples how patterns of meaning have been addressed. I will not focus on practices of goal setting and similar methodologies, as decision-makers today seem to have a preference for this specific side of practice. Those that have to pursue and display specific results in time and in budget are naturally more at ease with methods that sell themselves as being clearly calculable. The writer Max Frisch (1957) called this side of man the side of Homo Faber. Economists often talk about the homo economicus in their context.

From the point of view of a holistic change management approach, the risks within the process design of the transition to sustainability lie above all on the side of sensemaking and meaning. I'm not saying that the side of instrumental action is no longer an exciting challenge. But we can see that these instrumental aspects of change are in the focus of decision-makers and are more or less common sense today. On the other hand, many do not understand the often completely different dynamics of the cultural space. So, this side is more urgent to be discussed. We need examples of good practice to address the meaning side and we need ideas how to set up structures so that discourses on various levels can grow.

Renewable Energy Over the last 10–15 years we have established a new professional structure of production, supply, consultancy, and service for renewable energies. This development only became possible by setting up a new field of activities with new rules.

The development of the renewables is a good example that this can be achieved by creating new structures and dealing with the resistance of old regimes (Geels 2014). In the case of the renewable energies, a break of power structures was achieved by subsidies and an equal access to the electric grid for small and big as well as new and old investors. Today, we find a lively discourse on renewables accessible to any investor, any household and any interested person. This discourse can be observed within the professional structure and beyond in the public and in education.

Important drivers on the path to a new structure were among others: Giving proof of the feasibility of new practices, convincing powerful actors in the political system as counter-power against large corporations, initiating and fostering new structures.

Sustainable Investment In the field of investment, the situation is different. As traditional structure we find corporations like banks and investment companies that initiate investment products as well as its supply in the market. The major difference to the field of the renewables is that to date we do not see any concept seriously supported on national and international levels to set up a new structure beside the old one. The addressees of the current ideas on sustainability primarily are the leaders of large corporations. The main argument is that they sit in front of the levers with the possibility to move large amounts of capital into investments with ESG-criteria. Obviously, this argument is true. But as obvious as this, this is not the whole story. There are plausible ideas in the market that would require a new structure. I will outline three of them.

(a) One such idea is to set up investment advice as a new profession with requirements for each single professional on the level of doctors and lawyers. Standards to inform on ESG-criteria could be established. This path will not be a quick fix. One charming point about this idea is that today in the finance industry only few investment consultants are sufficiently educated to give advice on the level of actual know-how in science and practice and thus to bring a high-quality discourse to investors. This means that setting up a profession would require huge educational efforts. As in every industry good examples can be found as a starting point. A growing number of persons in large corporations, small investment companies and advisories, rating agencies and specialised associations, science and journalism promote and organise a professional discourse in workshops and fairs to show possibilities and developments in the field of sustainable, impact and mission investing.
(b) Another idea is to fully separate product development/market making and investment advice. This idea should not be mixed up with the idea of a separate banking system initiated to secure bank deposits against investment risks (see for example within the debate on sustainability von Weizsäcker and Wijkman 2018). The separation of product development and advice might have some

quicker effects than education and would open a gap where discourse can get back into a system where today a concentration of interests and power form structural barriers. An illustrative comparison clarifies this point: When today you wish to get access to know-how in the field of the renewables, it will take some hours to find a couple of relevant doors. When you try the same in the field of investment and you cannot enter the scene as a major investor you will have a hard time. Here, large corporations have an egoistic advantage to enclose their know-how in internal discourses and display their abilities through marketing measures. Positive examples to resolve conflicts of interest and to reduce the concentration of power through fully legal and structural separations of business areas can be found in the energy market (separation of power grids and power generation) or in consulting (separation of consulting and auditing).

In other words, this idea leads to an opening of gaps to infuse possibilities of discourse that have been squeezed out of the system by concentration of power and interests. However, without professional consultants with know-how on the described level, such a structural measure will get as far as a limping man crossing a rugged mountain range. Taking into account social science and change management know-how it is clear, although unpopular for the mainstream of the industry, that structural changes have to take place, if sustainability is a serious goal that shall be pursued in the finance industry. Consequently, to spread the idea of ESG-related investments, fostering discourse and know-how processes will be required to develop a fertile ground on which the idea of sustainable investment can grow in every place.

(c) A short remark should be added on ideas mentioned by some high-level politicians to shutting down the broad retail markets together with parts of the market on which smaller institutional investors get their advice, by organising state run funds and defining strict regulatory rules that allow only a small range of possible products. It is common knowledge that excluding practically the whole discourse on a broad level out of the market will not lead to more quality. Even more seriously this will hinder change towards sustainability as it should have become clear in this thesis.

7 Interests and Change: On Interests Linked to Roles and Positions as Primary Targets for Change Management (Thesis Six)

As we know from psychology and sociology, interests are strong motivators for action. Ideas themselves do not have this quality of action drivers. Often, the way from an idea to action is a long one and some good ideas get lost on their journey to practice. Therefore, if we want to change the way we are doing business and our habits of consuming we should focus on asking what the main interests of people are and how we can address them. We should intentionally dwell less on the side of appeals, ethics and beautiful stories, what would be possible if we were better people. As human beings we are doing that anyway. We are continuously more or less active originators of thoughts. But exploring and addressing interests is the difficult work on reality after having left the platonic heavens of pure and ideal ideas.[3]

When talking about interests, many various facets are mentioned. For example, in concepts of stakeholder analyses we find expectations, possible demands and claims, general attitudes, or the willingness to use power. But what is the core of the concept of interest?

Some understand an interest as the fact, or rather the underlying structure producing the fact, that our awareness is drawn to something. If we look at sustainability in this way, we can see that it is a fascinating success story. Today, so many people around the globe are thinking about sustainable issues. In the beginning, only a few people initiated this idea, in particular the members of the Club of Rome. Today, many are interested in and concerned about sustainable issues.

Others understand interests as motivational structures. Here, interests are not a question of attention, focus, or relevance, but rather a relatively stable inclination to do something or to avoid certain actions. This is not about being interested, but about having an interest. In other words, having an interest means having a stable predisposition to act or to avoid to act.

While some interests are deeply rooted in habits and identities, other interests are part of social positions and roles. Changing habits or cultures and the interests embedded therein is a medium- to long-term process, that can't be clearly directed in a particular pathway. By contrast, interests associated with positions or roles can usually be addressed more specifically, which makes them an excellent target for goal-oriented change measures.

On this side of role- and position-linked interests we especially find some topics I have been already talking about in the part of meaning systems. Let's have a short look on these topics again, here not under the aspect of sensemaking, but under that of interest as a driver of action. Economic interests are about getting goods, paying little and achieving profits. Interests in technology are achieving intended results. Interests in politics aim at reaching certain decisions. Legal interests aim at the correct application of rules, whereby law is often used as a means of political enforcement. And ethical interests are oriented towards justice.

Illustration What can we get into focus from a perspective on interests having a closer look on our examples?

While interests seem to be rather easy to understand when viewed from afar, on closer inspection they appear to be fluid and granular. This effect is well known by social scientists, change managers and other practitioners when proceeding from a sketchy stakeholder analysis to an exploration of interests. Due to the observable

---

[3]For an instructive discussion on the dynamics between ideas and interests and the vagueness of this conceptual distinction by Max Weber see Münnich (2011).

complexity of interests, it is not possible to provide a more or less encompassing overview in the following remarks. I will instead confine myself to just casting a spotlight on the scene.

Renewable Energy In the illustrations above I was talking about integrating different professions and meaning systems into the process of the transition to renewable energies. This means to bundle together the typical interests embedded in such professions and meaning systems.

In thesis four I pointed out that there is an overall lack of awareness towards the importance of local cultures. Reading thesis five on the distinction and interrelations of instrumental and discursive practices could lead to the guess, that to address cultures merely means to initiate various discourses. This may lead to the familiar bad practice of telling hollow stories, which at best remain without resonance but in the worst-case lead to mistrust of the audience because of a deep feeling of not being understood.

The important and feasible step is to explore typical interests related to roles and positions. While it is in the interest of mankind and countries to grow the capacities of renewable energy, unfortunately social tensions may be encouraged on local levels through the prevailing regimes of the renewable energy acts. Here the economic fact that everybody has to pay for state funding that support those who are already able and willing to invest can become a cultural experience in neighbourhoods. In addition, on the local level it happens that what some see as the art of engineering e.g. for large wind turbines and other immovable properties to produce renewable energy affect aesthetic sensibilities and is experienced as too large, too noisy, too smelly, etc.

To understand such experiences not only as personal attitudes but as interests related to positions and roles gives new opportunities. For example, we could seriously think about a third opportunity for investments between private and communal investments by shaping the possibility to run local energy suppliers collectively. Why not foster structures that make citizens participate in the investments into renewable energies in their municipality to better align local interests with overarching goals? This idea of collective or partly collective investments and profits is not new. In the light of interests on a local level it gets interesting again.

Sustainable Investment As illustrated in the preceding theses there is no comparable framework of action in the field of investment. So, we are confronted with a classical market with large, medium-sized and small actors. This market is primarily centered around the interests of making profits and avoiding risks: On the one side, issuers, product developers, and investment advisors are selling certain reward-risk-combinations. On the other side, clients and investors are buying these.

On the level of economic interests, sustainable investments have been working on getting a neutral situation in comparison to conventional investments, i.e. equal risk-reward-relations. This is important since in almost every investment decision economic interests are most relevant or at least highly important. The degree to which other interests such as political, technological, environmental, ethical, or religious interests get crucial depends on the predispositions of the investor and the discourse in the consulting he is confronted with.

Nonetheless, even equal risk-reward-relations with ethical advantages for many actors are still a weak argument for change as far as economic interests are crucial. Public effort should focus on regimes to change this. This is the same situation as with the renewables before cost parity will be reached. As long as we are talking about equal economic outcomes the benefit lies at the ethical level. For advisors and product developers who are not intrinsically driven by ethical and sustainable concerns, the balance sheet for sustainable investments is still negative because change needs an investment, e.g. for education of the consultants and for the development of new products.

8 Structures and Strategies: On Means for Change and on Avoiding a Cockpit-Effect (Thesis Seven)

In the discourse on change, structures, infrastructures, and strategies are prominent concepts. They are powerful means to initiate change. In particular, decisions on (infra-)structures and strategies are important for top-down approaches that are promoted by high-level decision-makers in the public and private sector, as is the case with changes at the level of states, state alliances and large organisations. Instruments are required here that can drive changes in widths.

There is a broad discourse on the possible effects of structural and strategic decisions. From this discourse it is clear, that with change measures targeting structures and strategies we primarily address realities on meso- and macro-levels such as infrastructural facilities, high-level decision-structures, general rules, or procedures of resource allocation. Surprisingly little is discussed in science and practice about how transmission belts can be designed between the upper meso- and macro-levels and the basic micro-level. Likewise, we find little on how an interaction between top-down- and bottom-up-transmissions can be fostered beyond the usual tendency of the top-down-infusing of desired actions and the bottom-up-complaining about an assumed irrational use of power by decision-makers. But as many change experts see it, the transfer in both directions is essential for sustainable change.

From an empirically based notion of practice it is clear, that relevant change has to reach not only the doing, but also the patterns of meaning embedded in practice. As I see it, there is still a huge lack of awareness that changes at the level of (infra-)structures and strategies are not relevant in the first place. Such changes only become relevant when they reach practice. As long as we read about decisions and change projects in discussion papers, colourful presentations, image campaigns, and even in results measured at short notice, we can assume that changes have not yet arrived in practice. Adaptation in practice must be verifiable over a longer period of time. Here, decision-makers are all too often subject to a kind of cockpit phenomenon and succumb to the illusion that they could control things like pilots control their aircrafts via switches.

So, what can be done? For large change projects like the transition to sustainability we need means with possible broad impact. This is the strength of structural and strategic change measures. At the same time, we should keep asking the question of how structural and strategic decisions can have a lasting effect on people's practices. This question is not only about the development paths from technological innovations to their wide-spread use in "sociotechnical regimes" (Geels and Schot 2007; Geels 2010) or about the interrelationships between state regulation and social practice. We also need to consider how to transform certain social contexts in order to promote sustainability issues.

For this we will need intelligent discourses to enable transmission in both directions from micro to meso and macro and from macro and meso to micro. There are already tried and tested tools in the area of change management, such as local and digital open space forums and many others.

Similarly, the understanding of the concepts of (infra)structure and strategy should be clearly oriented towards practice, which is hardly the case at present. In a view in which practice is the central focus, (infra)structures and strategies are means and as already stated above only relevant insofar as they induce real consequences in everyday live.

Illustration Intuitively it is clear that change without a strategy is merely a directionless movement. Than the interaction between structure and strategy, one of the famous topics of the early organisation sciences in the last century, should be kept in mind. We are talking here above all about top-down approaches. In particular, activities from the political system, the main actor on the macro level, are coming into focus.

Renewable Energy Here, many countries have formulated strategies for the transition, with the focus of mobilising private capital on a broad basis. The predominant structural element of the time before the start of this transition was the fossil- and nuclear-based energy production in large central plants. On the structural level we in particular find legal regulations (e.g. separation of energy production and electricity grids), economic measures (e.g. subsidies) and technological and scientific measures (e.g. financing of research).

Sustainable Investment Transitional strategies are emerging in the area of investment. Today, we see some clearly instrumental regulatory elements but hardly any interventions aiming at initiating discourse and reflection. Also, no relevant structural measures can be identified today.

The interesting thing about this perspective of strategic and structural measures is that previous and projected measures, such as CSR reporting, standards for investment criteria, divestment requirements from e.g. coal investments, interventions into rating practices by forcing to take ESG-criteria into account, or the request to talk about ESG-issues with clients correspond to today's structures of the investment industry. A fundamental change in strategy for integrating ESG criteria, processes of reflection on ESG issues, and related discourses at all levels of organisations into procedures for financial analysis as well as into distribution and training of investment advisors is not being pushed with the seriousness it necessitates. It is hard to believe that such a defensive attitude of the political system will go far. Single instrumental measures of the political system can and by many actors will be responded to instrumentally, in particular through buying or generating of data and displaying of ESG-indicators in the assets.

The overall effect is likely to be that we will see measurable, presumably and hopefully significant effects in the first few years. I suspect that many people will interpret changed actions as changed practices and therefore will forget about the importance of disputes and professional reflections underestimating the driving force of discourses. I have already mentioned general reasons as well as industry specific aspects in the previous theses. In particular, I have outlined a structural conservatism in the investment sector which, as far as we are talking about big banks and investment companies, is unlikely to lead to a pioneering role, despite the fact that a considerable and growing proportion of assets were invested in absolute figures according to ESG criteria. However, this development should not blind us.

9 Conclusion

Is there a conclusion? Certainly, there should not be one in the sense of a simple result like some checklists or a master framework. As change is an open process so is change management. The art of change management is to design, and whenever necessary, redesign change frameworks, to use tools in a situational and highly selective way, to manage in a targeted manner and simultaneously to look for opportunities for stepping back in order to leave developments and discussions to themselves. The aim always is to promote developments and to prevent obstacles.

With regard to the description of target states, a holistic change management approach takes an offensively ambivalent stance: Notified target states are welcomed in terms of their strategic function in the here and now, while the insight into the empirical structure of practices as a unit of instrumental and discursive aspects of activity necessarily leads to acknowledge the variability and blurriness of such targeted states.

The prevailing paradigm of instrumentally oriented change succumbs to the fiction of feasibility. And, in the short term, the effectiveness of instrumental change approaches also creates the collective illusion that set goals are reachable. Luckily, we have discursively oriented actors, especially in the education system, in journalism and to some extent in science, politics and investment practice, who remind us that change management is not akin to a composition of a musical work, which then only has to be orchestrated by instrumentalists. Change processes are more like improvisations on a composed melody than playing a prefabricated composition.

Discursive elements in change processes serve both, creativity on the one hand and construction or (re-)actualisation of meaning patterns on the other hand. As can be derived from an empirically based understanding of practice, instrumental and discursively oriented acts of change principally have to be placed on an equal footing. Sometimes within the course of a change process one pole, sometimes the other pole may come to the fore. Hopefully it will become increasingly clear to all responsible decision-makers that change can never be carried out in a strictly targeted and sustainable manner at the same time. If we overemphasise instrumental aspects, processes of meaning will be marginalised which will lead to resistance and obstacles. Conversely, of course, without any strategically targeted framework change will happen, but it may lead anywhere.

What does this mean for the transition to sustainable investment in general? As we have not yet defined a clear framework for change in the area of sustainable investment we live on individual initiatives and individual political interventions. In my view, a comparatively comprehensive approach such as in the field of renewable energies is also conceivable and feasible for sustainable investments in the near future.

There are many indications that the economy needs external impulses to really act for a change. This point should be seen in the light of the intrinsic mainstream-orientation of large enterprises in any industry sector. Large enterprises tend to focus on a direct and already visible and predictable future so that visionary and aggressive change is to be expected less. Why should that be different when it comes to sustainable finance? It is likely that strategically targeted frameworks of change have to be infused into current logics of action. These are the bridges an industry has to pass, bridges that the industry itself is only partly able to build.

How can we propose a practical heuristic for change projects encompassing not only one organisation but many actors on micro- to macro-levels?

To the current state of our knowledge, this is possible partly as an art, and partly as secured professional knowledge. For example, we know that instrumentally oriented change approaches always reach their limits, but that it is basically not possible to describe the point where exactly these limits lie due to the described double-sided structure of practice as instrumental acting and (re-)construction of meaning. To highlight another example, we know that integrative approaches have advantages over non-integrative change designs. Integrative approaches intrinsically deal with resistance from individual areas through developing a more discursive culture since integrative work means going through processes of discourse.

The following heuristic takes up some of the pivotal points of the preceding theses:

(a) For each aggregation level, it should be asked which practices within the change project are instrumental and which are discursive. Both sides should always be addressed (Table 1).
(b) Efforts should be made to find measures that generate the densest possible network of effective relationships between different fields, between different levels, between discursive and instrumental modes of action and between fields that are diagonal to each other.

Table 1 Heuristic for multi-level change projects

Level of aggregation of involved actors	Instrumental practices	Discursive practices
Macro	E.g. state regulations, development of technologies to market maturity	E.g. journalism, general educational measures
Meso	E.g. structural separation of commercial and investment banks	E.g. opening up of discourse between consulting and product development
Micro	E.g. formal investigation of strategic ESG-goals and ethics used by investors	E.g. concrete professional education on ESG-issues

(c) It is recommended to ask different meaning systems for their possible input and resistances.
(d) And a framework should be sought in which these meaning systems can interact productively.

Such a heuristic inevitably leads to questions. Here, I will outline some of these as examples and without any claim to completeness.

How soon will the political system as an actor on the macro-level recognise available insights into the limits of single regulatory interventions as instrumental policy tools? Will there be political majorities to set the field for a comprehensive framework of change as was designed for the transition to the renewable energies aiming at micro- to macro-levels and encouraging action on both sides of the above table, instrumental and discursive?

Will the possibilities of instrumental regulations be effectively used to infuse productive discursive elements into the market beyond expert panels and research which means bringing sustainability issues into the discourse with any investor? Here one concrete point is: Will rules that oblige advisors to talk about ESG issues with investors effectively encourage discourse or will this become another formal element in the interaction like aspects as costs and risks?

Will the structural barriers—on the meso- and macro-level—against discourses be tackled, barriers arising from the conglomeration of interests within banks and investment companies as they act at the same time as advisors and as initiators or market makers? If measures are taken along the lines of other industries, how clear will they be?

Will governments—as in the area of renewable energies—act as a catalyst of change by using existing subsidies for pension schemes (macro level) to promote ESG-related investment? Will the opportunity be seized that such subsidies already exist while in the field of the renewables they had to be introduced as new measures producing new costs and requiring new political legitimation?

What different perspectives can contribute to the transition to a sustainable financial system? What role can ethics, social sciences and philosophy play? How can technological developments enable or jeopardise sustainable finance? What role can other views and meaning systems play?

How do we find ways to include ESG studies by rating agencies and scientists in investment decisions? Will we put into practice the well thought-out concept of ESG integration, which aims to integrate financial analysis and ESG issues? And will this happen above all at the level of instrumental procedures through data analysis or in addition at the level of reflection, debate and engagement as a targeted discourse with companies?

How can discursive elements in investment management, which are micro-level and difficult to identify by external investors, be promoted as a central quality aspect? Is it possible to share this information with customers in general? And is it possible to establish high national and international quality standards in investment advice as a macro-level measure based on the model of other professional groups?

Acknowledgement I thank Marcel Caspar for his review of the manuscript and I thank him and Ulrich Markowiak for the fruitful discussions over many years. Both are change experts and organizational developers (koelnteam). And I thank my partners at Qualitates for many insights into the market of sustainable investments.

References

Argyris, C. (1990). *Overcoming organizational defenses: Facilitating organizational learning*. Upper Saddle River: Prentice-Hall.

Bode, I., & Brose, H.-G. (2001). Zwischen den Grenzen. Intersystemische Organisationen im Spannungsfeld funktionaler Differenzierung. In V. Tacke (Ed.), *Organisation und gesellschaftliche Differenzierung* (pp. 112–139). Wiesbaden: Westdeutscher Verlag.

Bourdieu, P. (1972). *Esquisse d'une théorie de la pratique. Précédé de trois études d'ethnologie kabyle*. Genf: Librairie Droz.

Cato, M. S. (2008). *Green economics: An introduction to theory, policy and practice*. London: Earthscan.

Czarniawska-Joerges, B. (2000). Symbolism and organization studies. In G. Ortmann, J. Sydow, & K. Türk (Eds.), *Theorien der Organisation. Die Rückkehr der Gesellschaft* (pp. 360–384). Wiesbaden: Westdeutscher Verlag.

Dolata, U. (2011). *Wandel durch Technik. Eine Theorie soziotechnischer Transformation*. Frankfurt: Campus.

Doppelt, B. (2010). *Leading change toward sustainability: A change-management guide for business, government and civil society* (2nd ed.). Sheffield: Greenleaf.

Doppler, K., & Lauterburg, C. (2014). *Change Management. Den Unternehmenswandel gestalten* (13th ed.). Frankfurt: Campus.

EU EP (European Parliament). (2018). *Draft report on sustainable finance (2018/2007(INI))*. Committee on Economic and Monetary Affairs. Rapporteur Molly Scott Cato. Retrieved February 10, 2018, from http://www.europarl.europa.eu/committees/en/search-in-documents.html

EU HLEG (High-Level Expert Group on Sustainable Finance). (2017). *Interim report, July 2017*. Financing a Sustainable Economy. Retrieved from https://ec.europa.eu/info/sites/info/files/170713-sustainable-finance-report_en.pdf

Frisch, M. (1957). *Homo faber*. Frankfurt: Suhrkamp.

Garfinkel, H. (1967). *Studies in ethnomethodology*. Englewood Cliffs: Prentice-Hall.

Geels, F. W. (2010). Ontologies, socio-technical transitions (to sustainability), and the multi-level perspective. *Research Policy, 39*, 495–510. https://doi.org/10.1016/j.respol.2010.01.022.
Geels, F. W. (2014). Regime resistance against low-carbon transitions: Introducing politics and power into the multi-level perspective. *Theory, Culture & Society, 31*(5), 21–40. https://doi.org/10.1177/0263276414531627.
Geels, F. W., & Schot, J. (2007). Typology of sociotechnical transitions pathways. *Research Policy, 36*, 399–417. https://doi.org/10.1016/j.respol.2007.01.003.
Geertz, C. (1973). Thick description: Toward an interpretive theory of culture. In C. Geertz (Ed.), *The interpretation of cultures: Selected essays* (pp. 3–30). New York: Basic Books.
Giddens, A. (1984). *The constitution of society: Outline of the theory of structuration*. Cambridge: Polity Press.
Goffman, E. (1974). *Frame analysis: An essay on the organization of experience*. New York: Harper and Row.
Goldstein, E. B. (2011). *Cognitive psychology: Connecting mind, research, and everyday experience* (3rd ed.). Wadsworth: Cengage Learning.
Habermas, J. (1981). *Theorie des kommunikativen Handelns (Vol. 1: Handlungsrationalität und gesellschaftliche Rationalisierung, Vol. 2: Zur Kritik der funktionalistischen Vernunft)*. Frankfurt: Suhrkamp.
Honer, A., & Hitzler, R. (2015). Life-world-analytical ethnography. A phenomenology-based research approach. *Journal of Contemporary Ethnography, 44*(5), 544–562. https://doi.org/10.1177/0891241615588589.
Kotter, J. P. (2012). *Leading change: Edition with a new preface by the author*. Boston, MA: Harvard Business Review Press.
Luhmann, N. (1984). *Soziale Systeme. Grundriß einer allgemeinen Theorie*. Frankfurt: Suhrkamp.
Malmendier, M. (1995). *Selbstverständlich, adäquat, normal. Überlegungen zur Soziologie der Normalität*. Master thesis, University Bielefeld.
Malmendier, M. (2003). *Kommunikations- und Verhaltenstraining in Organisationen. Zur Interventionspraxis in der Personalentwicklung*. Frankfurt: Campus.
Mintzberg, H. (1979). *The structuring of organizations: A synthesis of the research*. Englewood Cliffs: Prentice-Hall.
Mintzberg, H., & Westley, F. (1992). Cycles of organizational change. *Strategic Management Journal, 13*, 39–59.
Münnich, S. (2011). Interest-seeking as sense-making. Ideas and business interests in the new deal. *European Journal of Sociology, 52*(11), 277–311. https://doi.org/10.1017/S0003975611000117.
Oestereich, B., & Schröder, C. (2017). *Das kollegial geführte Unternehmen. Ideen und Praktiken für die agile Organisation von morgen*. München: Vahlen.
Rammert, W. (2016). *Technik – Handeln – Wissen. Zu einer pragmatistischen Technik- und Sozialtheorie*. Wiesbaden: Springer VS.
Rosa, H. (2016). *Resonanz – Eine Soziologie der Weltbeziehung*. Frankfurt: Suhrkamp.
Schatzki, T. R. (1996). *Social practices: A Wittgensteinian approach to human activity and the social*. Cambridge: CUP.
Schatzki, T. R., Knorr-Cetina, K., & von Savigny, E. (2001). *The practice turn in contemporary theory*. London: Routledge.
Schein, E. H. (2010). *Organizational culture and leadership* (4th ed.). San Francisco: Jossey-Bass.
Schimank, U. (2001). Funktionale Differenzierung, Durchorganisierung und Integration der modernen Gesellscchaft. In V. Tacke (Ed.), *Organisation und gesellschaftliche Differenzierung* (pp. 19–38). Wiesbaden: Westdeutscher Verlag.
Schutz, A. (1967). *The phenomenology of the social world*. Evanston, IL: Northwestern University Press.
Schutz, A. (1970). *Reflections on the problem of relevance*. New Haven: Yale Univ. Press.
Smircich, L. (1983). Concepts of culture and organizational analysis. *Administrative Science Quarterly, 28*, 339–358.

Turner, S. P. (1994). The social theory of practices. In *Tradition, tacit knowledge and presuppositions*. Chicago: Polity.
Varela, F. J. (1990). *Kognitionswissenschaft, Kognitionstechnik. Eine Skizze aktueller Perspektiven*. Frankfurt: Suhrkamp.
Volberda, H. W. (1999). *Building the flexible firm. How to remain competitive*. Oxford: Oxford University Press.
von Weizsäcker, E. U., & Wijkman, A. (2018). *Come on! Capitalism, short-termism, population and the destruction of the planet*. A Report to the Club of Rome. New York: Springer.
Weick, K. E. (1979). *The social psychology of organizing* (2nd ed.). New York: Random House.

Marcel Malmendier is an Asset-advisor and insurance broker, founder and director of two companies in the field of sustainable investment: Qualitates GmbH and Investmentkontor RheinRuhr GmbH.

Areas of Expertise: Sustainable and ethical investments, mission related investment-banking, risk management, change management and organizational design, personnel development.

After eight years of experience in change management as a scientist (Universities of Bielefeld and Dortmund: empirical research project on interventions in organizations), as internal advisor (Opel (GM)), as external consultant (Accenture) and after co-founding the koelnteam, a network of change management experts based in Germany, Marcel Malmendier moved to asset-advisory and investment-banking.

After three years as an asset-advisor at a leading German banking and financial service provider he launched his own bank-independent company for asset advice and investment-banking in 2007, the Investmentkontor RheinRuhr. Here he assists private investors and institutions with advice on asset allocation, asset selection and sustainability. In 2010 he initiated the first sustainable liability umbrella in Germany, the Qualitates GmbH. Together with seven partners he founded this company. Since then he has become one of the directors, responsible for organization, risk management and legal affairs. The Qualitates initiated the "Marktplatz für Nachhaltiges Investment", a fair for asset-advisors in the field of sustainable investment, impact investment and mission investing.

Regular lectures on financial markets and entrepreneurial risk management are held by Marcel Malmendier since 2008 at the Ruhr-University in Bochum and since 2014 at the Hochschule Bochum.

Since 2020 board member of ökofinanz-21 e.V., the leading German network of financial advisors in the field of sustainable investments and insurance.

My Network: Qualitates GmbH, ökofinanz-21 e.V, FNG, CRIC e.V., koelnteam, sponsor of the German Sector of Junior Chamber International, international network with asset managers ranging from smaller companies to multinational corporations.

Hobbies and Social Engagement: Encourages asset-advisors and asset-managers to endorse sustainability; helps young people to become entrepreneurs; likes philosophical, sociological and ethical thinking; writes blogs on financial questions.

Analysing the Credibility of Theories of Change

Georgette Vun

Abstract Simply put, and most unfortunately, current interpretations and applications of the Theory of Change concept have drifted so far from their origins as to render them useless. As inflammatory a statement as that may appear to be, it is also the single biggest and most annoying elephant in the development world's room. And as the development world continues to shift focus from solely philanthropic and development finance funding to self-funded social enterprises and the very trendy impact investing, this elephant has grown well beyond the confines of that room.

Keywords Stakeholder · Feedback · Consultation · Listening · Sustainable improvement · Financial returns · Mythbusting

1 Theory of Change: Does It Do What It Says on the Box?

Simply put, and most unfortunately, current interpretations and applications of the Theory of Change concept have drifted so far from their origins as to render them useless. As inflammatory a statement as that may appear to be, it is also the single biggest and most annoying elephant in the development world's room. And as the development world continues to shift focus from solely philanthropic and development finance funding to self-funded social enterprises and the very trendy impact investing, this elephant has grown well beyond the confines of that room.

What was originally a perfectly viable academic concept and school of thought debated and developed by respectable and intelligent academics, has become a trendy, over-used and illogical methodology that has as much value as a postage stamp: it may get a message from A to B, but by design it is not useful or valid beyond that short-term one-off use.

G. Vun (✉)
University of Queensland, Brisbane, QLD, Australia

University of St. Gallen, St. Gallen, Switzerland

K. Wendt (ed.), *Theories of Change*, Sustainable Finance,
https://doi.org/10.1007/978-3-030-52275-9_3

In 1997, Carol Weiss, one of the originating academics on the topic published *How Can Theory-Based Evaluation Make Greater Headway*[1] which explored the problems with the evaluation that follows the attempted implementation of a theory of change. Therein she readily acknowledged that much had been written and debated in the literature about the value of a Theory Based approach, i.e. the evaluation based on the Theory of Change. And in doing so, she also posed, "*Yet, given all the interest and the praise, little evidence has surfaced that evaluators are adopting the approach widely. Why?*" She then helpfully and logically set out 12 reasons and or explanations as to why the theory is not yet ready for widespread adoption.

Ten years later, Patricia Rogers publishes *Theory Based Evaluation—Reflections Ten Years On.*[2] In that, she notes that practitioners seem to have forgotten, or rendered less relevant, the issues and challenges raised by Weiss. Given that funders now routinely require the projects theory of change and evaluation methodology, projects are having to comply with this requirement or miss out on funding altogether.

What results is a situation where funders thereby become imperialists of the development project universe. Projects are expected to, and will in fact, align their theories of change and implementation thereof, for the purpose of securing funding. This in turn results in an adaptation of the original objective of the project, converting it to a colonial project of the funder.

Evaluation poses the same relative problems for projects, and as Weiss also points out, there is a significant risk of evaluations being done to verify process as opposed to understand the causal elements of the desired (or not desired) change.[3]

2 Old-School Development Theory

Arguably Development Theory has been, and still is, the least helpful when looking for a solid, reliable reference point to build up and implement a program of change. What has perhaps not been so obvious is that the reality of development, or more accurately put, the lack thereof, is a social construction.[4] Without the genuine and authentic intention to achieve meaningful development, such theory will forever be limited in its application.

---

[1]Weiss, C.H., 1997 *How can Theory-Based Evaluation Make Greater Headway* Evaluation Review: A Journal of Applied Research Vol 21 (4): 24 – Aug 1 pp. 501–524.

[2]Rogers, P.J., 2007 *Theory Based Evaluations: Reflections Ten Years On,* New Directions for Evaluation, no 114 Summer, Wiley Periodicals Inc DOI: 10.1002/ev.225

[3]Weiss, C.H., 1997 *How can Theory-Based Evaluation Make Greater Headway* Evaluation Review: A Journal of Applied Research Vol 21 (4): 24 – Aug 1, pp. 501–524.

[4]Nederveen Pieterse, J., 2010 *Development Theory: Deconstructions/Reconstructions* Chapter 1: *Trends in Development Theory* pp. 2–3. DOI: http://dx.doi.org/10.4135/9781446279083.n1

This means looking at two key elements of development theory: (1) That it originated from the West and from colonialist heritage and (2) That it grew, and was perpetuated, in sync with neo-classical economics. One perhaps the fan, the other the fire—or, even interchangeable, they are both.

The adoption of neoclassical economics as the most powerful and dominant, yet not positive, element of modern development is frequently acknowledged in academic and popular literature.[5] As the close sibling of neoclassical economics, neo-colonialism has covertly and silently accompanied his brother, jinxing and haunting many a failed development project.

Implementation of a development project is never simple, the challenges should not be underestimated. It cannot be implied that there is a simple and always predictable leap from a viable theory to practical implementation. What appears, inter alia, to be lacking, however, is the inherent recognition within the theory itself that there is a very real risk of failure. Yet if we look at the organic link that exists between neoclassical economics and neo-colonialism, we would easily see that not only is the risk very real, but its manifestation can easily, and through no act of bad faith, become a reality. When put in the context of a complex development project, where human players are abundant and human decision-making is for Western minds, we create over and over again imperial framework, often the very framework that the development project is seeking to dismantle and replace.

The most prevalent example of this is the covertly forced financial systems of the West that are imposed upon the South. If development means adoption of Western standards of policy and systems of financial accounting to align economies and financial regimes,[6] then it truly has become a breeding system for inefficiency, with means to retard innovation and keep the targets of development projects in their colonized, undeveloped, unprogressive state. Sometimes labelled as modernization and also, popularly, as globalization, the policies underpinning development theory are not necessarily incorporating the lessons learned from failed policies of the past, but rather shuffled, somewhat re-organised and updated for the latest political trends, yet remain otherwise unevolved.[7]

---

[5]Goodland, R., Ledec, G., *Neoclassical economics and principles of sustainable development*, Environmental and Scientific Affairs, Projects Policy Department, The World Bank, Washington, DC 20433, U.S.A. DOI: doi.org/10.1016/0304-3800(87)90043-3

[6]Nederveen Pieterse, J., 2010 *Development Theory: Deconstructions/Reconstructions* Chapter 1: *Trends in Development Theory* p. 5. DOI: http://dx.doi.org/10.4135/9781446279083.n1

[7]Kothari, U., & Minogue, M. (2002). *Development Theory and Practice: Critical Perspectives*. Basingstoke: Macmillan Publishers Ltd. ISBN: 0333800710

3 How Do We Go Forward: Learning from Models That Bring About Effective, Long-Lasting and Sustainable Change

Its high time to look beyond the above theories, which were intended from their inception to bring about effective, long-lasting and sustainable change but due to faulty design, were unsuccessful. We now grant ourselves the explicit permission to look to one of more other theories. And these are theories that, in practice, have proven that change, improvement, development, evolution, growth and advancement can be achieved. What these theories each have in common is the insistence to implement, as a minimum, the following basic principles:

- Involving the target beneficiaries, and their families and the relevant parts of their communities.
- Empower all related humans, be they beneficiaries or other stakeholders—they are all customers.
- Build a relationship with and between the customers.
- Permit and regularly obtain, digest and integrate customer feedback.
- Do not punish mistakes made in project implementation, instead provide pathways for learnings to be disseminated.
- Give them space, or create that space, to innovate and learn and develop.
- Acknowledge that without a customer's own intrinsic motivation, the project will fail—do not disturb the triggers for this motivation.

In a word, its about allowing for *engagement* of stakeholders. Emotional commitment to the project? No, its emotional commitment to the other humans in the project. Recognition that it is a team effort, without one or another team member equally committed the project will fail. So let us look at a few examples to verify how, practically, such engagement has allowed successful change.

Organisational Transformation, Leadership and Employee Engagement
Organisational Transformation (or "change" as it was once known!) is an interesting topic for corporate entities looking to improve their entire organization and its operations. It explicitly acknowledges the involvement and relevant of the employee human beings as a fundamental resource also in the context of the transformation. What distinguishes successful transformations from failed can be attributed to the approach and attitude of the organisation's leader.

McKinsey's 2007 article summarized: *The CEO helps a transformation succeed by communicating its significance, modeling the desired changes, building a strong top team, and getting personally involved.*[8]

[8]Aiken, C.B., Keller, S.P. 2007 *The CEOs Role in Leading Transformation* website: McKinsey February 2007 available at: https://www.mckinsey.com/business-functions/organization/our-insights/the-ceos-role-in-leading-transformation

Apparently, it is possible to distill four key functions of a CEO that support a successful transformation:

1. Making the transformation meaningful. People will go to extraordinary lengths for causes they believe in, and a powerful transformation story will create and reinforce their commitment. The ultimate impact of the story depends on the CEO's willingness to make the transformation personal, to engage others openly, and to spotlight successes as they emerge.
2. Role-modeling desired mind-sets and behavior. Successful CEOs typically embark on their own personal transformation journey. Their actions encourage employees to support and practice the new types of behavior.
3. Building a strong and committed top team. To harness the transformative power of the top team, CEOs must make tough decisions about who has the ability and motivation to make the journey.
4. Relentlessly pursuing impact. There is no substitute for CEOs rolling up their sleeves and getting personally involved when significant financial and symbolic value is at stake.

In each of these four functions, the CEO ought to be creating, nurturing and making further space for the engagement of employees. What is perhaps implicit but unfortunately not mentioned explicitly by McKinsey is the effectiveness of these functions in the absence of fear and the possibility of failure.

The Harvard perspective although expressed somewhat more technically, mentions this albeit mildly. Theory O, in contrast to Theory E, is "*geared toward building up the corporate culture: employee behaviors, attitudes, capabilities, and commitment. The organization's ability to learn from its experiences is a legitimate yardstick of corporate success.*" Theory E, on the other hand is easily recognised as a neo-colonial and neoclassical economic model, whereby, the leader's "*strategies usually involve heavy use of economic incentives, drastic layoffs, downsizing, and restructuring. Shareholder value is the only legitimate measure of corporate success*".[9]

Jason Saltzman points out more directly and arguably quite helpfully that successful leaders should start "with shedding the fear that looms in every room and rejecting failure as a setback rather than accepting it as a teacher".[10] Acknowledging the crippling affect that fear and (the fear of) failure within an organisation is fundamental to understanding why changes fail, and furthermore, why engagement lies at the heart of successful change.

[9]Nohria, N., Beer, M., 2000 *Cracking the Code of Change,* Harvard Business Review May-June 2000 Issue available at: https://hbr.org/2000/05/cracking-the-code-of-change

[10]Saltzman, J. 2018 *How CEOs can inspire social change within their organizations* Forbes Councils August 29 available at: https://www.forbes.com/sites/forbesnycouncil/2018/08/29/how-ceos-can-inspire-social-change-within-their-organizations/#256636116052

Then what of the employee engagement? Where there is little or no employee engagement managing that as a change within the transformation might initially appear complex. Joseph Folkman would suggest trust and integrity are two key features of a competent leader, in addition to their technical or intellectual competencies. Those of us that that reflect upon our emotional states might also describe this as the emotional intelligence of the leader. In addition, positivity in the work environment should be fostered together with giving a clear strategy and direction. It would quite naturally follow that the ability to change is a mindset originated from the leader and adopted by employees as their relationship with each other and with the management or leadership teams evolve to include trust.[11]

Going further, various studies have shown that there is a direct correlation to an employee's feeling of well-being and their level of engagement.[12] Since the feeling of well-being is entirely subjective and internally generated by that human and for that human, looking for an external means of creating well-being is likely to be disproportionately onerous. The better approach has been to simply give the human support in self-generating the feeling of well-being. And it is this support that Saltzman, Folkman, Harvard and McKinsey argue opens the door for successful and sustainable change.

Effecting Changes in an Institution: Education

Much like the challenges of changing an organisation, institutional change is thwart with challenges. Two key reasons for this is the long-standing history of education and its heavily institutionalised delivery and the number of stakeholders involved. To follow the logic argued above, each stakeholders' opinions, mindsets and levels of well-being needs to be taken into consideration. By sheer volume of stakeholder numbers, this may indeed first seem an onerous and extremely resource intensive task. But is it?

Paolo Friere offered up these observations in 1970[13]: "*Those who authentically commit themselves to the people must re-examine themselves constantly. .they almost always bring with them the marks of their origin, their prejudices and their deformations, which include a lack of confidence in the people's ability to think, to want and to know.*" If one will learn, and thereby evolve, ones means of learning ought similary to evolve. Unfortunately, the evidence shows clearly that traditional educational systems and frameworks have not evolved. There was never a mechanism within the framework to consider the opinions and well-being of the stakeholders, which would have lead to continuous evolution.

[11]Folkman, J., 2018 *Measuring Engagement Does Not Improve It,* Forbes March 13 2018 available at: https://www.forbes.com/sites/joefolkman/2018/03/13/measuring-engagement-does-not-improve-it/#73436273775f

[12]Brunetto, Y., Teo, S.T.T., Shacklock, K., Farr-Wharton, R., 2012 *Emotional intelligence, job satisfaction, well-being and engagement: explaining organisational commitment and turnover intentions in policing in* Human Resource Management Journal 22(4) November 2012 DOI: 10.1111/j.1748-8583.2012.00198.x

[13]Friere, P., (2000) *Pedagogy of the Oppressed* (30th anniversary ed.) New York: Continuum.

"Those who engage in true dialogue with the people have a faith in their abilities that prevents their work from falling into a pattern of 'paternalistic manipulation'".

So little progress seems to have been made, that one cannot help wondering if it is even possible to apply the critical viewpoints of Friere to bring about the changes that so many institutions in the educational sector publicly espouse. Otherwise it would have been done already, no?

Well, perhaps it has been done albeit in isolated instances.

Take the example of the Building Assets, Reducing Risks Model (BARR Model), developed by Angela Jerabek, a US high-school counsellor frustrated by the persistently high failure-rates of her students. The eight pillars of the Model focus explicitly on the stakeholders: students, teachers, school administrators (principals), students' families. Additionally, the specific pre-requisites of those stakeholders to have a feeling of well-being. Lastly, but certainly not least, it includes the making tailor-made programmes for student most at risk. At each stage of the programm, the Model has ensured practical and realistic engagement of the stakeholder in what is an efficient and effect interaction and collaboration.[14]

The BARR website provides key and quite frankly impressive impact data which not only supports the programm and Model itself, but the elements of its design.

Let's zoom in for a moment on one of the crucial pillars: "I-time" a lesson during which teachers and students learn and can practice communication, goal-setting, and in doing so build their relationship in a emotionally connected and authentic way. A positive environment to tackle even more difficult topics such as grief and loss and substance use.

What do you think? Are there any parallels with this approach and Theory O? Is there space and time for fear and failure to spawn and or proliferate? Has this Model drawn together the principals resulting from McKinsey studies and embodied them in a programm that elicits the very positive type of change a CEO might wish for his organisation and employees?

What might this mean for a universally applicable Theory of Change? What would a program or project need to include to benefit from these approaches, theories and models? It is clear that the focus of the project must be the beneficiaries as well as the stakeholders. More precisely, the projects design will need to focus on the engagement of the stakeholder, or in other words their well-being.

Proper research and interaction with the stakeholder is necessary before the design can be finalized and ultimately implemented. Projects designed before this will only be partially successful, if at all.

[14]The Barr Center, *The Barr Model* available at: https://barrcenter.org/strategies

4 Proposing a Viable, Efficient Alterative to the Classic Theories of Change and Their Inefficient Evaluations

Based on the above discussion, it would make sense to devise an alternative framework which should guide projects to success. Such framework must be simple, and where possible ought to be universally relevant and applicable.

The two stages of creating and implementing a project are of course dealt with separately. The creation of a project, its initial design could only be produced after proper research was done on all the stakeholders of the project. The beneficiaries, their families, their immediate community, the different service-providers and or dependents of the beneficiaries, and usually those controlling the infrastructure of the beneficiaries are the key stakeholders. Project staff will also be stakeholders and will therefore also need to be included.

The research would enable the project to have mapped out a kind of stakeholder ecosystem, and have the project lead understand the relationships between stakeholders but also between the stakeholder and the desired or intended change.

A checklist of sorts to support the creation of the project would include the following:

The Project design

(i) was based upon feedback from Stakeholder 1, 2, 3, 4 etc.
(ii) incorporates one or more collaborative forums for the stakeholders to communicate and build their relationships
(iii) contains a clear pathway for stakeholders to communicate feedback and where constructive, additional pathway for a focus group to address this feedback
(iv) provides sufficient space and time for stakeholder to feel engaged without imposing pushy incentives
(v) has a timeline realistically reflecting the resources and abilities of stakeholders as perceived by the stakeholders

Project implementation would be according to the project design. Measuring and monitoring of milestone achievements and other changes can be tailored to the projects budget and of course be project specific. Failures that lead to lessons learned, without punishment or reprimand, must also be included in the monitoring. Measurement and monitoring in this sense becomes a complementary task to project implementation. It cannot be seen as the sole reflection of the project's success or lack of success.

Then what about evaluation of the project? What about collecting reliable data to prove to funders and other stakeholders that the project has affected the intended positive impact? Its clear that stakeholders may require such reporting, however, this is for their purposes and not for the purposes of the project per se. It therefore would be sensible and certainly fair that any such reporting is undertaken by that stakeholder and at that stakeholders expense.

The above discussion boldly argues that the success of any project depends entirely on the stakeholders engagement, the stakeholders feeling of well-being. Separately, there can be technical reviews of achievements, quality assurance checks and other evaluations that are industry specific and or based on industry standards for the appropriate stage of a projects lifetime. However, as evidenced by the countless number of failed projects which included these evaluations, they are of little value when trying to implement a successful project.

5 Conclusion

As soon as the development world has the courage to reflect upon its current practices and move from those current misguided practices to adopt a 3-dimensional project design consisting of emotional, intelligent and practical fundamentals and based genuinely on stakeholder engagement, it would find that projects success will increase dramatically. Simultaneously, better use will be made of available resources for the project as opposed to the project monitoring, reporting and evaluation. Evaluations are done when they are indeed necessary to be done and not just because the methodology requires it.

Georgette Vun Is a qualified Australian lawyer and has been working in the banking and finance industry for over 18 years. She is from a mixed racial background, one of five siblings and has a passion for problem-solving and human nature. She specialises in alternative investment structures, as well as the ongoing study of sustainable practices for renewable energy and human resilience. She has worked within investment banks, asset management firms, consulted family offices and nextgen investors. Challenging the norms is, she believes, the best catalyst to meaningful change. She intends to pilot simple yet resilient finance models based on the research conducted for this chapter.

Failed Theories of Change: Misperceptions About ESG Investment and Investment Efforts to Combat Climate Change

Maximilian Horster

Abstract Sustainable Investing is joining the mainstream. This development is due to transformations in the financial system and regulatory landscape. This article explores the effectiveness and failure of new investor approaches to address sustainable investing.

Keywords Theory of change · Theories of change · 1.5 Degree · Climate · Climate benchmarks · Climate change · Climate finance · Climate impact · Climate risk · Climate strategy · Climate stress test · Climate voting · Engagement · ESG · EU action plan · EU regulation · Green bonds · Green financing · Investments · Investors · Maximilian Horster · Net zero · Paris-aligned · Physical risk · Proxy voting · Risk disclosure · Scenario analysis · Score cards · Shareholder proposals · Taxonomy · TCFD · Theory of change · Transition risk · Voting · Sustainable development goals · SDGs

One basic theory of change behind ESG (Environmental, Social, and Governance) investing is that the financial industry can impact the real economy for positive environmental and social outcomes. In the area of climate change, for example, many see investors as the key lever to decarbonize the economy. If that is the case, we should be on a good path to preventing the most catastrophic consequences of climate change.

As of the end of 2018, an estimate of approximately USD 31 Trillion are invested sustainably. This represents astonishing average of more than 30% growth rates over the past 2 years in Europe (11%), the U.S. (38%), Canada (42%) and Australia and New Zealand (46%). Japan joined the club with growth in ESG assets of 306%, which brings the figure of ESG assets as a percentage of all managed assets in this country to almost 20%. This figure is still low in comparison to the other geographies, where ESG assets are now being seen to make up to over 50% of overall managed assets.[1] These trends come at a time when the European Union set out to

[1]Global Sustainable Investment Alliance (GSIA), 2018 Global Sustainable Investment Review.

M. Horster (✉)
ISS Climate Solutions, ISS ESG, Kronberg, Germany
e-mail: maximilian.horster@iss-esg.com; https://www.iss-esg.com

K. Wendt (ed.), *Theories of Change*, Sustainable Finance,
https://doi.org/10.1007/978-3-030-52275-9_4

"green" the financial markets, Green Bonds are reaching record volumes, and hundreds of investment houses globally join collective climate engagement initiatives such as "Climate Action 100+".[2]

Considering these trends, one may conclude that the financial industry is doing its part in changing the world into a more sustainable place. Unfortunately, that is not the case. Unimpressed by these investor initiatives, global greenhouse gas emissions keep increasing to unprecedented levels, reaching a new annual all-time high in 2018, the very same year when low-carbon investments peaked as well.[3]

One wonders why we do not see a reversal in emissions despite global efforts on the investment front. Is the financial system too slow to counter the accelerated emission of greenhouse gases? Or is there a fundamental flaw in the theory of change that a lot of ESG investing is based on? This essay argues the latter. While investors can play a key role in changing the real economy, current approaches are often not sophisticated enough to achieve the intended results. Many regulators have not fully embraced how financial markets can impact the economy and, despite enormous regulatory efforts, are unlikely to efficiently achieve their goals. Effective impact-focused ESG investing requires a deep understanding of the respective asset class and its dynamics and institutionalized and implicit levers of influence, including geographic specificities and a surgical precision in the choice of means.

1 Understand the Investor Intention

USD 31 Trillion of ESG-guided assets is indeed an enormous amount of money to help create a more sustainable world. It is, however, important to note that not all this invested money has the intention to create positive impact. Increasingly, ESG analysis is seen to address and measure material risks that matter to any investor. The exposure to companies that emit large amounts of Greenhouse Gas Emissions, a typical factor measured by ESG analysis, should be of concern for any investor who expects politics to introduce a price on carbon as that might negatively impact financial returns. ESG analysis is, hence, seen to recognize and address investment risks that are routed in environmental, social, or governance circumstances. If ESG approaches are used in this way, they enhance existing risk measurement frameworks which may result in re-allocation of capital and can help generate alpha.

Such ESG-based reallocation of capital, however, does not automatically impact the underlying sources of ESG risk. Take the logic of divestment, exclusion, and negative screenings in equity investing, for example—to date still the dominant ESG investment approach (Fig. 1).

In 2018, the exclusionary screening approach executed on almost USD 20 trillion assets under management (AuM), can be found in active strategies or indexes that systematically exclude stocks with certain ESG risks. Such an approach results in

[2]Climate Action 100+ combines over 300 investors with over USD 30 trillion of assets under management to engage with the 160 largest greenhouse gas emitting companies to change course.

[3]Global Carbon Budget 2018, Earth Syst. Sci. Data, 10, 2141–2194, https://doi.org/10.5194/essd-10-2141-2018, 2018.

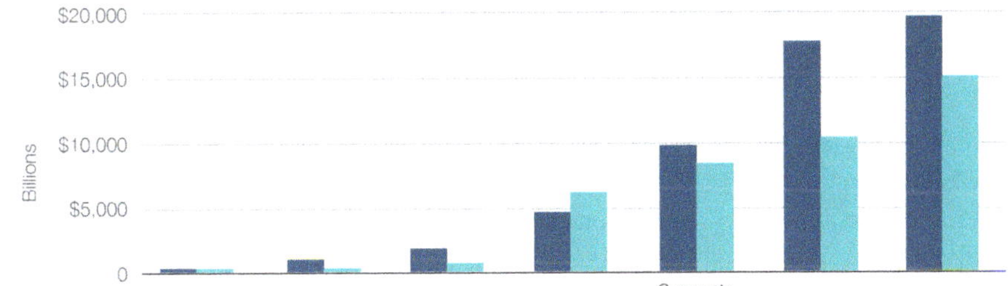

	Impact/ community investing	Sustainability themed investing	Positive/ best-in-class- screening	Norms-based screening	Corporate engagement and shareholder action	ESG integration	Negative/ exclusionary screening
2018	$444.26	$1,017.66	$1,841.87	$4,679.44	$9,834.59	$17,543.81	$19,770.96
2016	$248.47	$276.16	$818.01	$6,195.40	$8,385.17	$10,353.20	$15,063.57
Growth 2016–18	79%	269%	125%	-24%	17%	69%	31%
CAGR	33.7%	92.0%	50.1%	-13.1%	8.3%	30.2%	14.6%

Note: Asset values are expressed in billions.

Fig. 1 Global growth of sustainable investing strategies 2016–2018, 2018 Global Sustainable Investment Review, ISS ESG

investors reducing their exposure to these risks. However, given that stock markets are secondary markets, such a de-risking does not result in an impact on the real economy—the sources of ESG risks will most likely continue to exist.

One of the most common exclusion topics exists around weapons. However, by not investing in stocks of weapon companies, investors are not reducing the amount of weapons in the world and weapon companies do not go out of business. The same is true for climate change. By divesting from fossil-fuel companies or high carbon emitters, those companies do not go out of business. On the contrary, a divestment is only possible if another investor buys the stocks from the divesting investor. However, many divesting investors repeatedly claim to contribute to fighting climate change, and some regulators and civil society see divestment as key to combat climate change via financial markets.

A further iteration of this theory of change is that, if enough investors divest, a company will change course, as the share price drops to levels that will impact the business. This theory is based on a false understanding of financial markets. Even if the share price drops due to a global divestment, a company will not cease its business activities. The company may be undervalued, and management might simply buy back shares or even take the company private.

Overall, not investing into a company on the secondary markets of equities and bonds has very little impact on the real economy, but it does reduce an investor's exposure to that asset. Divesting or reducing exposure to a certain company is therefore an appropriate risk management approach. However, divestment is not effective way to create a real impact. In other words, divesting is a good way to decarbonize a portfolio, but divestment does not decarbonize the economy.

The USD 20 trillion AuM using a negative screening did change little to nothing for the climate challenge and can certainly not be counted towards unlocking the USD 2 trillion annually that are needed to stay within 1.5 °C of average global warming.[4]

[4]Unlocking the trillions to finance the 1.5 °C Limit, World Future Council 2017, https://www.worldfuturecouncil.org/unlocking-the-trillions/

2 EU Regulation: Good Intention, Lots of Action—But Missing the Point?

In late 2017, the European Union set out to use its regulatory power in financial markets to close address climate change. The aim was nothing less than ensuring that the EU financial industry would contribute its part to help the EU achieve its climate goals. This constitutes an enormous paradigm shift: In the past, regulators would have regulated the real economy for the greater good of society and the money would follow. With this approach, money—the blood in the economic system—would be regulated and therefore enable or disable the intended outcome in the real economy.

At the time of writing this essay in Summer 2019, the results of the regulatory efforts are out, albeit in the details note quite final yet. It must be concluded that the regulation, although enormous in effort, will not help achieve the regulatory goal of combating climate change through financial markets. The reason is that the wrong theories of change lead to an outcome with probably large impact on the financial industry itself but very little impact on the climate.

The regulatory effort comes in five different proposals. To increase transparency, the EU suggests to (1) mandate climate risk disclosure in the investment process as well as (2) towards retail investors at the point of sale, (3) devise a taxonomy of what type of companies are sustainable or green, (4) introduce standards for Green bonds and a label for green funds, and (5) develop a series of climate benchmarks that only sustainable of green companies can join. The logic of the regulation is that an increase in transparency towards stakeholders and internally will help finance climate-friendly companies and withdraw financing from companies harming the climate. While the first part—creating transparency—will be helpful and effective to de-risk portfolios vis-à-vis climate change implications, it will—at large—not help funnel money from climate-harming to climate-friendly economic activities.

Regulation focuses predominantly on equities and so-called Green Bonds. Both asset classes do not have a direct and efficient impact on the real economy. Equities and bonds are traded in secondary markets, so the money that investor A pays for a stock or bond goes to investor B who sells that security, and not directly to the company for its operations. In addition, Green Bonds are instruments to get exposure to green activities of a firm, but they cannot claim to enable such activities: Green Bonds, in their current form, are not a solution to climate change.[5] So by better understanding a company's sustainability profile and (not) investing in it due to this in secondary markets, that company will neither disappear nor receive a boost. The regulatory efforts, not able to differentiate between cause and effects in public markets, fail to achieve their goal: Climate change will not be impacted by these approaches.

---

[5]Shooting for the moon in a hot air balloon, 2° Investing Initiative, https://ec.europa.eu/info/law/better-regulation/feedback/14080/attachment/090166e5bd23089a_en

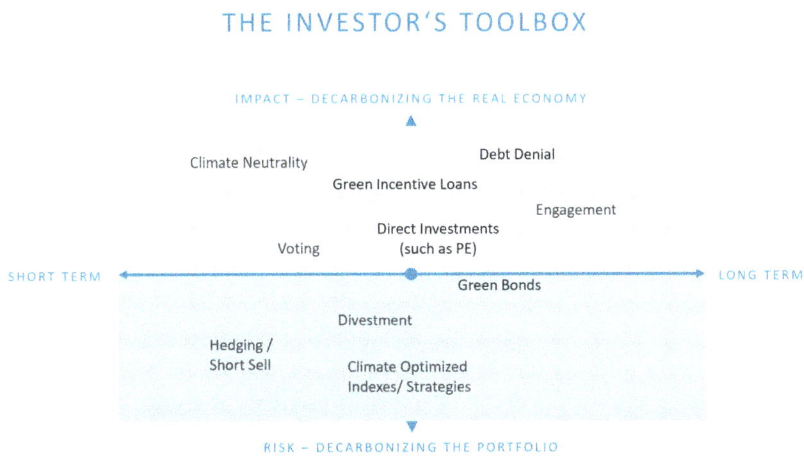

Fig. 2 The Investor's Toolbox, ISS ESG

3 How Can Financial Market Participants Combat Climate Change?

At this point, one might conclude that equity and fixed income investors are not able to impact the real economy, because they are operating in secondary markets. The opposite is true: Financial market participants can efficiently change the course of companies and so can equity investors. What is needed, though, is a more nuanced, asset-class specific approach that understands the respective dynamics as well as the available instruments in the "Investor's Toolbox".

Some of the tools at hand are geared towards decarbonizing a portfolio (lower part of Fig. 2), while others aim to decarbonize the real economy (upper part of Fig. 2). For equities, approaches such as divestment and climate-optimized equity strategies can help from a risk management angle. However, engagement and proxy voting can change the course of companies. On the debt side, not participating in the issuance of bonds or not lending to certain companies due to their ESG performance is an effective means to impacting economic activity and providing cheaper capital to companies that achieve certain ESG targets (positive incentive loans).

To delve deeper into this analysis, we should first make a distinction between investment and financing. Unlike an investor, a financier (a bank, loan giver, participant in debt issuance) can impact the real economy by not financing specific activities. For example, a bank may opt to not finance a coal exploration or to finance the development of an environmentally-friendly automotive engine. The theory of change is that not lending money to climate-harming activities will drive up the cost of capital and might result in aborting the activity all together. Conversely, a competition of money to finance a climate transformation should bring down the cost of capital and foster such activities. There are now plenty of examples of how lending instruments aim to foster more sustainable development, such as so-called "positive incentive loans" that offer cheaper loans for companies that can prove a positive transformation.[6]

For investors, from an impact perspective, it is further important to differentiate between taking ownership through direct investments into primary markets and taking ownership through investments in secondary markets. In short, there is very little data available for primary markets although there is a lot of impact potential, while there is a lot of data for secondary markets that results in—so far—very little impact.

Primary market investments include taking stakes through direct private equity or real asset investments as well as participation in Initial Public Offerings (IPOs). Here, investors have the option to withstand investing into certain assets, which can make it ultimately difficult for these assets to access capital or negatively impact valuations. Same goes for Venture Capital Investments that can help enable to jumpstart a new technology or service that positively impacts the real economy. There is now an increasing amount of real asset and direct investments in the primary market that takes climate change considerations into account. A challenge is, however, that ESG data and service providers typically do not have "off-the-shelf" information on these assets: They are typically "one-off" small investments into projects and companies that often do not publish any information on their positive or negative impact, ESG governance, strategy, risks, or metrics. One increasingly popular approach is that of "scorecards" that are being used by investors during the due diligence process: Climate change and other sustainability key performance indicators (KPIs) are being collected systematically by investors themselves and automatically taken into account for different types of technologies and industries. The investment will then only be deployed if the project or company achieves a specific threshold of points in the weighted KPIs. That way, an investor ensures to invest in climate-supporting technologies or at least avoids investing into climate-harming ones (Fig. 3).

Secondary market investments (typically listed equity and listed fixed income), on the other hand, offer the most sophisticated data and approaches, and tools exist to identify climate-helping and climate-harming assets. Such data can help avoid climate risks by not investing into climate-harming companies and it can support seizing opportunities by investing into companies that develop climate solutions. As shown, though, this only helps decarbonize the portfolio, not the real economy.

There are, however, ways for secondary market investors to also create an impact on the real economy: By making use of informal as well as institutionalized approaches to make the investor's voice heard in a company's boardroom and enable companies to change its climate course. The most effective approaches are those of climate engagement and—as an extension—making use of shareholder votes ("proxy voting"). By engaging with executives of companies that are not in line

[6]The green and sustainability loan market: ready for take-off, Environmental Finance, https://www.environmental-finance.com/content/analysis/the-green-and-sustainability-loan-market-ready-for-take-off.html

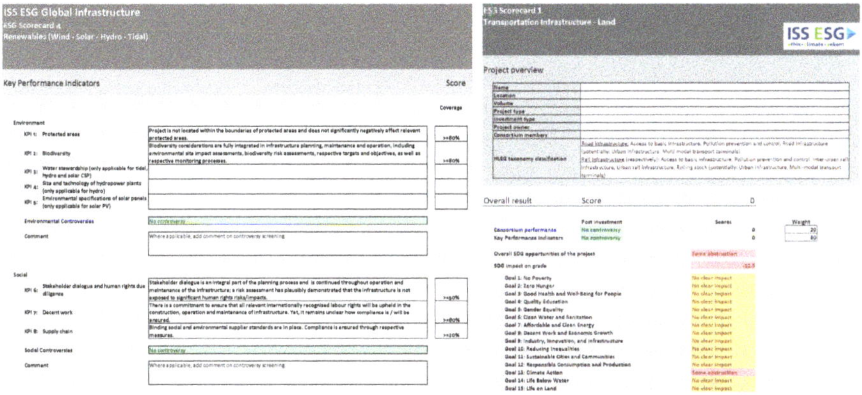

Fig. 3 Examples of ESG score cards for direct real asset investments, ISS ESG

with investors' climate change expectations, the executives might be prompted to adopt a climate change strategy. This carrot can be complemented with the stick of proxy voting: If the engagement endeavor fails in adequate results, an investor can vote against the company management or its remuneration plans in the annual general meeting.

4 Engagements and Voting for Creating Impact in Secondary Markets

Typically, an investor interested in understanding climate impact and climate risks of a portfolio starts with a climate impact assessment. In listed equity and fixed income markets, such assessments can now be automatically performed via online tools and can be as holistic as including a carbon analysis, transition risk analysis, physical risk analysis and scenario analysis—ideally balancing qualitative and quantitative analyst driven elements to be forward-looking.

An example of such analysis is shown below. It helps to understand if the greenhouse gas emissions of a portfolio are aligned with the carbon budget necessary to stay within 2° of average global warming (Fig. 4).

In the example in Fig. 4, the grey shade shows the "2 degree decarbonization pathway", i.e., how global greenhouse gas emissions have to decrease until 2050 to limit global warming to below 2 °C versus pre-industrial levels. The dotted line is an example portfolio of European equities that is not 2 °C aligned: By assuming that the portfolio companies continue their current business practice and grow in line with overall growth expectations, the portfolio companies' greenhouse gas emissions will outgrow their greenhouse gas budget at around the year 2035.

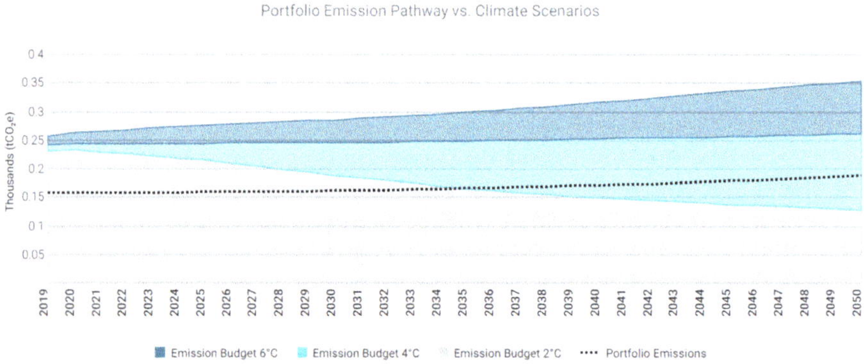

Fig. 4 A portfolio level scenario analysis, standard climate impact report ISS ESG

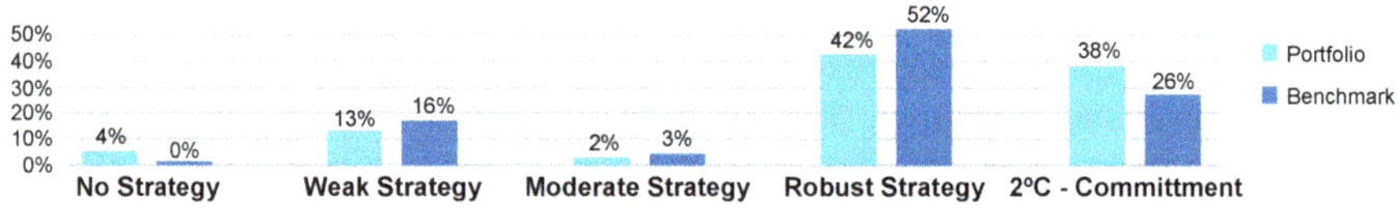

Fig. 5 Climate Strategy Assessment (%Portfolio Weight), ISS ESG

Listed equity and fixed income investors now have two options: To either just de-risk the portfolio from a climate perspective, or to also decarbonize the real economy.

To do so, a climate impact assessment can complement the aforementioned scenario analysis with qualitative information on the individual companies, such as on companies that have no or a weak climate strategy, versus those having adopted a 2 °C target and committed to transition in line with greenhouse gas budget requirements.

In Fig. 5, the sample portfolio of European equities can be seen on a scale from not having a climate strategy (left) to having set a 2° target (far right).

For de-risking the portfolio vis-à-vis an economy that transitions towards a below 2 °C world, the investor needs to simply sell all companies that drive the future portfolio emissions above the 2 °C budget thresholds, i.e., those further to the left of the graph. To also impact the real economy, on the other hand, the investor can opt to encourage companies further to the left to start transitioning in a way that they are not exceeding their specific future greenhouse gas budget—i.e., to move further over to the right of the graph. If successful, the portfolio is not only less risky, the climate impact of the real economy should have also decreased.

The equity investor's influence on the transitioning of companies for a more climate-friendly economy can be achieved by the means of engagement and by using voting rights.

Engagement describes an interaction in which investors communicate to companies their expectations on how they should address certain topics. Engagement is hence seen as an investor's instrument to execute on environmental, social and governance, targets but it is not always clear to what extent engagement truly affects companies.[7] Climate change has been a topic of engagement since quite some time and seen so-called "collective engagement" approaches. The idea is that different shareholders pool their shares to have a louder voice in a company's boardroom and can increase the urgency of the matter. At time of writing this essay, the largest climate change focused engagement initiative is the "Climate Action 100+": More than 300 investors globally with more than USD 30 trillion of assets under management put their weight into the interaction with the world's "100 plus" (currently about 160) largest greenhouse gas emitters to adopt a meaningful climate strategy. If successful, such an investor initiative should, indeed, change the real economy. Despite operating for over 2 years,[8] and with impressive investor weight behind it, however, the initiative has yielded remarkably low success announcements. Obviously, engagement on transition of a company's business practice is a longer process but there is a certain danger that such exchange might not yield meaningful results or drag of for too long, given the urgency of the challenge.[9]

Therefore, aside from the "carrot" of having a collaborative exchange with companies, shareholders also have the "stick" of framing their opinion through votes at a company's annual general meeting (AGM). Typically, the topic of climate change comes on the agenda via shareholder proposal, i.e. agenda items at AGMs that shareholders put up for voting. In 2018 in the US alone, an all-time high of 90 shareholder proposals was counted that addressed climate change in one form or another (Figs. 6 and 7).

Investors use shareholder proposals to encourage companies to adopt a climate strategy. It is important to note that such proposals are now increasingly coming from large asset owners rather than advocacy groups. Also, these mainstream asset owners are increasingly voting in favor of shareholder resolutions addressing climate change.

In many jurisdictions, however, shareholder resolutions are not as common. What can investors do, however, if a company is not addressing climate change but the topic of climate change does not come to vote at the AGM? For such cases, investors have the option to make use of their regular voting rights.

If there is no agenda item to vote on climate change at the AGM of a company that does not address the topic adequately, investors can opt to simply use their regular vote against one or more directors, against a remuneration plan, or whatever agenda item seems appropriate to express dissent with climate change management. To do so, investors must understand a company's climate profile, namely climate disclosure practices and the company's performance on embracing the risks and

[7]How ESG engagement creates value for investors and companies, PRI, https://www.unpri.org/download?ac=4637

[8]Launched 2017, success stories so far: Royal Dutch Shell, Glencore, Equinor, Maersk and BP.

[9]ClimateAction100+: Engagement 2.0? Responsible-investor.com, https://www.responsible-investor.com/home/article/climateaction100_engagement_20/P0/

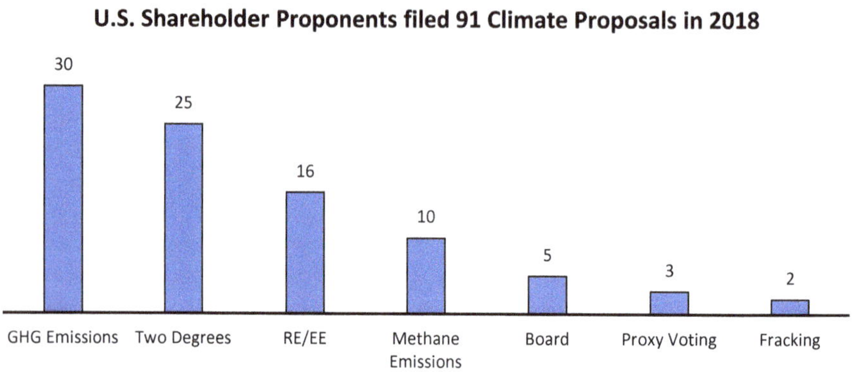

Source: ISS Analytics

Fig. 6 91 Climate Proposals (US 2018). *Out of these proposals, four received majority shareholder backing when turned into resolutions*

Company	Shareholder Resolution	Support
Sturm Ruger & Company, Inc.	Report on Gun Safety	68.8%
Depomed Inc.	Governance Measures Related to Opioids	62.3%
Kinder Morgan	Report on Sustainability	60.4%
Kinder Morgan	Climate Risk - Two Degree Scenario	59.7%
Middleby Corporation	Report on Sustainability	57.2%
Genesee & Wyoming	Adopt GHG Emissions Reduction Goals	57.2%
Ameren Corporation	Report on Coal Ash Risks	53.2%
Anadarko Petroleum	Climate Risk - Two Degree Scenario	53.0%
Range Resources Corp.	Report on Methane Emissions Reduction	50.3%

Fig. 7 Successful E&S shareholder resolutions in the US in 2018. Underlined: Climate change focused resolutions, ISS Analytics

opportunities of climate change. One way to assess a company's climate risk profile is to consult "climate awareness scorecards" that flag where companies lag in climate disclosure and performance and highlight the overall climate risks of the respective sector as well as any potential climate norm violations, such as oil spills (Fig. 8).

Elior Group SA (ELIOR) Meeting Date: 30 August 2019
POLICY: Catholic Meeting ID: 1350373

Climate Awareness Scorecard

Climate Risk Exposure

INDUSTRY CLIMATE RISK EXPOSURE

Industry Level Risk	High

Different industries have different exposure to climate change. The ISS industry climate risk exposure differentiates between industries with low, medium and high climate risk exposure. A company is assigned a sector risk level based on its specific industry and business activities.

INCIDENT-BASED RISK EXPOSURE

Norms Violation	-

The Paris Agreement and other universally accepted climate norms set "do no harm" standards for a corporate climate practice. Certain companies, however, might be violating such norms. ISS Norm-Based Research differentiates between the level of failure to respect norms.

Climate Performance

CURRENT CLIMATE PERFORMANCE

Greenhouse Gas Emissions	Total
Total Emissions (Scope 1&2)	543,737 tCO_2e
Total Emissions (Scope 3)	3,036,970 tCO_2e
Emission Intensity (Scope 1&2 /m$ revenue)	77 tCO_2e
Average Peer Emission Intensity (Scope 1&2 /m$ revenue)	82.1 tCO_2e

FORWARD-LOOKING CLIMATE PERFORMANCE

Carbon Risk Rating	Total
Category	Climate Laggard
Rating (0-100)	12

To meet climate targets and avoid climate risks, the current and future performance on climate challenges matters. Current direct and indirect greenhouse gas emissions, normalized by revenue, provide an indicator for the climate efficiency of a company in comparison with average emissions of its peers. This can be contrasted to the average emission intensity of industry peers with a similar emission profile. The Carbon Risk Rating provides a future-oriented analysis of CO2-related risks through an assessment of not only industry-specific challenges and risk profiles, but also companies' positive impact. It differentiates between leaders, performers, underperformers and laggards on a scale from 0 (worst) to 100 (best).

Climate Disclosure

CLIMATE RISK DISCLOSURE

Climate Disclosure Pillars	Disclosure Alignment
Governance	STANDARD UNMET
Strategy	STANDARD UNMET
Risk Management	STANDARD UNMET
Metrics & Targets	PARTIAL ALIGNMENT

A key indicator of a robust strategy to address the risks and opportunities of climate change is a company's disclosure of its activities. The Climate Disclosure assessment follows the nomenclature of the Task Force on Climate-related Financial Disclosure (TCFD) to score a company on disclosure regarding climate governance, strategy, risk management, and metrics and targets with the classifications: Standard Unmet, Partial Alignment, Meets standard, and Exemplifies standard.

ISS' Climate Awareness Scorecard reflects publicly disclosed data and reporting on the company's climate change-related disclosures and performance. The Scorecard uses a range of climate-related factors to indicate a company's disclosure practices and performance record including its industry risk group. Companies are evaluated on overall disclosure (Governance, Strategy, Risk Management, Metrics & Targets) and performance factors (Norms, GHG Emissions, Performance Ratings). For more information or questions regarding ISS' Climate Awareness Scorecard, please contact: esghelpdesk@iss-esg.com.

Fig. 8 Example of a "Climate Awareness Scorecard", ISS ESG

By combining engagement and voting, investors address climate risks of existing portfolio companies, and they potentially change the course of companies and therefore the real economy.

5 Theories of Change: Good Intention, Poor Execution

In assessing the status quo of the regulatory and investor landscape in Summer 2019, it becomes clear: There are very good intentions for the financial industry to contribute in solving the climate change challenge. When looking into approaches and execution, however, poor understanding of financial market mechanics may result in a lot of action without real impact. Only by making use of the entire investor's toolbox of means to address climate change and by systematically and clearly evaluating the effects of each approach, investors and regulators alike can execute on their respective theories of risk or change.

Maximilian Horster Head of ISS ESG Climate Solutions. Dr. Maximilian Horster is Managing Director and Head of ISS ESG Climate Solutions, a unit of Institutional Shareholder Services that enables investors, agencies and governments to understand, measure, and act upon the implications of climate change on investments. In 2010 and while with Zurich-based South Pole Group, Max developed the leading methodology to gauge and assess climate impacts on investment portfolios. Under his stewardship, the group established the world's largest database of company-level climate change data and pioneered the development of leading, standardized investment carbon screening tools, resulting in the screening for climate change implications of more than US$ 2 trillion of assets under management. Max currently leads two EU funded investment-related greenhouse gas accounting projects, is working in several industry organizations dealing with financial greenhouse gas accounting, and advises governments on the matter. Prior to joining the South Pole Group, Max worked in equity and fixed income research capacities as well as in business development with Capital Group Companies in Los Angeles, Toronto, Tokyo, Geneva and London. Prior to that, Max was an academic researcher and worked with a Member of the European Parliament. He holds a PhD in History from the University of Cambridge.

Y.1: The Biological Code for Evolutionary Transformation and Strategic Investment Decisions

Including the Svensca Handelsbanken Transformation Case

Michael Sonntag

Abstract How does transformation occur in living systems? How do they manage to transform themselves in a direct, fast, safe and extremely energy efficient manner? What principles do they follow? And what can we learn about governing transformation as investors?

Coming from a rather medical standpoint, I strongly emphasize the ultimate need to have a clear understanding of healthy, living systems. Only then will we have the ability to govern the necessary radical transformations in economy, society and politics instead of only managing symptoms. It is not news that our traditional, reductionist, closed-system assumptions have led us into the muddle-headedness we experience today. Unfortunately, the same is true for our concepts of change and transformation. Learning from living systems, we learn how desperately wrong our current transformation models are: nature is able to undergo radical transformations, erasing its previous identity completely and rebuilding a new identity directly. Without dying. Without changing its genes. The cell has the information needed to actively transform itself into a radical new "Y.1" prototype.

The difficult point is that in nature there are no hybrid or dual solutions—it is either-or. You must DECIDE. If we truly seek to transform our world into a sustainable, evolutionary system through our investment strategy, we must be prepared to make brutal decisions. This article shall provide the Y.1 information code necessary for governing this transformation directly, fast, safe and efficiently. It also offers a new and comprehensive framework for positive impact investors, (real) green growth and sustainable finance.

By doing so, the gap between people, planet and profit is vanished. Our soul will be able to return and inspire our actions, endowing a feeling of grace and pleasure, while building a truly evolutionary and meaningful economy.

Keywords Theory of change · Theories of change · Evolutionary transformation · System change · Paradigm change · Change management · Transdifferentiation ·

M. Sonntag (✉)
Y.1–Seminar for Evolutionary Leadership and Economy, Bern, Switzerland
e-mail: m.sonntag@yd1.ch

K. Wendt (ed.), *Theories of Change*, Sustainable Finance,
https://doi.org/10.1007/978-3-030-52275-9_5

Field of meaning · Active information · Evolutionary information · Operating system change · Evolutionary investment · Positive impact investing · Impact investing · Evolutionary leadership · Governing transformation · Evolutionary transformation · Transdisciplinarity · Transleadership · Sustainability leadership · Systems leadership · Svenska handelbanken · Swedish handelbanken · Jan wallander · Evolutionary economy · Evolutionary purpose · Meaningful economy · Conscious capitalism · Strategic decision-making · Evolutionary cooperation · Generic principles · Living systems · 1st law of living systems · 1st law of evolutionary systems · Complexity · Mimic life · Biomimicry · System thinking · Self-organisation · Connectivity · Emergence · Creativity · Co-location · Network · Furure of creativity · Postnormal times · Post-covid transformation · Academy for system change · Sustainable future · World pulse · World evolutionary forum · SDGs · Sustainable development goals

1 Theory of Change: From Evolutionary Purpose to Evolutionary Investment

In my previous publications I have focused on how living systems function in our existing natural reality (Unpredictability, Openness, Limited Resources, Emergence, Dynamical Disequilibrium). Coming from biology, quantum physics and neuroscience I have defined the 1st Law of an Evolutionary Economy as the capacity to co-create a maximum of shared value for all involved stakeholders by organizing all functional activities towards this end in the most energy efficient way, while expanding the economy's potential to transform itself and its environment, reaching optimal evolvability through continuously generating diversity, novelty and complexity (Sonntag 2018). The ultimate evolutionary purpose is to enhance the energy in the system through expanding evolutionary cooperation capacity. I then described which generic principles living systems follow to achieve this purpose in the energetically most efficient way (Self-organization, Connectivity, Co-location, Co-creativity, Coherence—see Sonntag 2018). I am strongly convinced that the change needed in our world to achieve the UN SDGs and to globally create a sustainable and even meaningful economy (Drewell and Larsson 2017) lies in our investment decisions. As "information gives form to energy" (Bohm and Peat 2000) the generic information patterns underlying our strategic and investment assessments must be absolutely clear to really have a strong positive impact on our social, economic, leadership and political decisions. In practice this means that our strategic decision-making must be strictly coherent with the described five generic principles and the evolutionary purpose (for further details see Sonntag 2017, 2018; Sonntag et al. 2020 including cases, a framework for strategic investment decision-making and a detailed bibliography).

Our aim is to take this a step further. Our positive impact investment strategies will obviously miss the global challenge of saving our world from a looming ecologic, social and economic breakdown, as long we do not have a clear, integral concept of transformation.

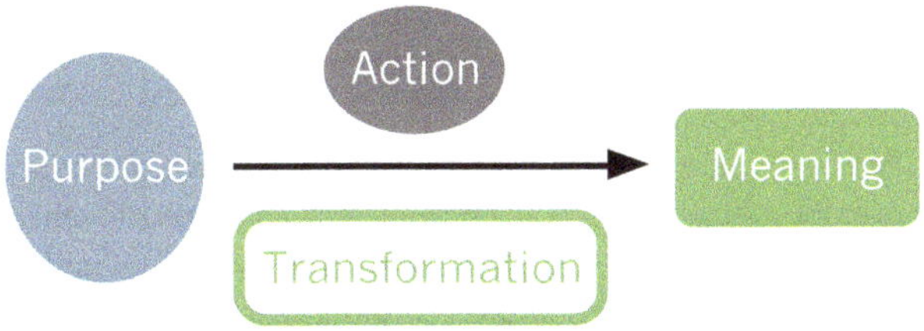

Fig. 1 Transformation: From purpose to meaning

Only by including a concept of transformation ("Theory of Change", ToC) that enables our existing, traditional paradigm of economics and society to transform in a direct, fast, safe and very energy efficient way, will we be able to generate a truly sustainable, purposeful and meaningful economy within the very limited time we are given (Fig. 1).

In this sense I would define "meaning" as that special tone or feeling within ourselves, in our companies and in our society which occurs when we know that the energy and time we have are invested in the most energy efficient way to sustainably co-create a maximum of shared value for all stakeholders (children, family, society, environment, economy, political system) ensuring that we are able to actively maintain our and all involved stakeholders integrity.

Meaning thus has to do with the ability to actively influence and change or even transform our environment. This article addresses the topics of learning from living systems just how transformation happens in the most energy efficient way, and how meaning is generated.

2 Towards a New Paradigm of Transformation

The problem with our existing ToC models is that—largely unconsciously—they are still based on the same absolutely obsolete assumptions as our traditional scientific, economic and social theories.

These are based on assumptions made in virtually closed systems, completely denying—as we intuitively all know—the given natural reality. The corresponding human nature concepts are those of a Type X (McGregor 1960) behavior. In a more updated version, I personally like to call them "homo algorithmicus" human nature assumptions. Within the closed system conventions, we behave as if things are stable, predictable, measurable, controllable and can be planned for. We define strategic goals and fixed targets and then roll out our plans, projects and strategic decisions with predefined milestones, building a tremendous bureaucracy and internal control system, and micro-managing employees' behavior and performance through extrinsic incentives. Big data then provides us with the illusion of omnipotent control and the ability to even predict and manipulate our future and our destiny. For instructive examples of how these assumptions still drive our management decisions see Robert E. Quinn and Anjan V. Thakor (HBR 2018).

In management and especially in software development, we have widely recognized this difficulty and have started to establish more agile, dynamic and adaptable models (for good examples see: Agile Manifesto n.d.; the Beyond Budgeting Round Table BBRT 2020; Denning 2018; Hope and Fraser 2003; Laloux 2014; Morlidge and Player 2012; Ramaswamy and

Gouillart 2010). And we have recognized that the Type X human nature concept in management has killed intrinsic motivation and has therefore made companies (and society) unable to innovate and evolve (Gulati 2010; Hamel and Zanetti 2019; Hamel and Zanetti 2020).

Traditional biology is also still trapped in a paradigm in which phenomena are only described that can be reduced to a collection of particles, the movement of which is governed by linear dynamics rules, driving the overall system toward a deterministic, predictable fate. Molecular biology is also continuously trying to explain biological processes within this single-molecule-to-specific-target-dogma. Under the aegis of genetic determinism, they consider change solely as a consequence of a linear translation of the DNA code. This has deeply influenced our scientific and popular conception of transformation: cell differentiation and organism development are traditionally described as a genetic, centrally controlled and provoked, clockwork-like, predesigned, programmed, hierarchical, unidirectional and stepwise process. Within this limited mindset change can only occur through genetic changes, which, in turn, only happens through spontaneous and random mutations. The new cells then need to undergo natural selection, allowing only the fittest to survive.

Even though critics of this traditional reductionist viewpoint have increased in number, the ultimate breakthrough occurred only recently when Jarriault et al. (2008) showed in real time with live animals how a fully differentiated cell was able to transform itself into an entirely altered differentiated cell: the cell was able to completely convert its identity in a single, direct, transformational process! This is groundbreaking. It shows how deeply incorrect our previous assumptions where and how unbelievably dynamic, plastic and decisive living biological systems are (Jarriault et al. 2008; Richard et al. 2011; Zuryn et al. 2014).

3 Switching the Operating System: Transdifferentiation as a Model for Paradigm Change

Following their observations on intestinal cells, which transformed into motoneuron cells, Jarriault et al. described a model for "Y-to-PDA transdifferentiation". It depicts how an intestinal cell "Y" of the nematode *Caenorhabditis elegans* in vivo undergoes a process which begins with a complete erasure of its initial identity (Fig. 2). It then goes through a stage that lacks both the initial and the final identity (Y.0). From there it begins rebuilding its new identity from scratch; first, only early neural identity is acquired (Y.1) before the cell develops into an entirely differentiated "PDA" motoneuron cell. The cell does not die; it remains alive through this

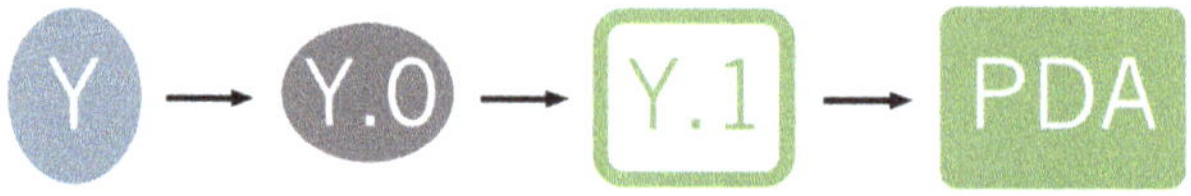

Fig. 2 Transdifferentiation: A model for direct transformation (simplified from Richard et al. 2011)

process. It is not influenced by any outside environmental or biomechanical interventions, and the genes are no way altered—they remain the same.

This offers an entirely new perspective on the capacity for transformation in healthy living systems.

Today we know that this kind of direct physiological transformation often occurs in nature, suggesting that cells have an inherent flexibility. Photoreceptor conversion during metamorphosis in a fly or the formation of coronary arteries from venous cells are prime examples.

In nature, this method of transformation is:

- **The most direct** and least wasteful. It need not randomly innovate and experiment with wide ranging mutations of possible new creatures, which then would subsequently undergo an uneconomical natural selection process;
- **The fastest**. It does not need to wait several generations to see which random mutation will prove to be the fittest;
- **The safest**. It does not go through a stage of mixed identities, in which the risk of creating dysfunctional or cancerous variants could arise.
- **The highest energy efficient**. It bypasses the complex process of dedifferentiating into stem cell mode, then having to rebuild the entire system.

Transdifferentiation is not incremental: previous functional principles are completely erased. And it is decisive: with high invariant precision the cell converts directly into the cell it however decided to be.

From a biological perspective, this kind of transformation is not governed by mutations in the genes, but by changes in the genes' control functions—the epigenetic code. Transdifferentiation goes far beyond reorganizing or fixing a few dysfunctional symptoms or readjusting some organizational culture issues—it is about completely transforming the operating system.

We are accustomed to thinking that shifts like these require several years or even several generations. Nature shows us that this is not true. Switches in the epigenetic code can happen in seconds.

This is a complete paradigm shift regarding our understanding of transformation. It forces us to radically rethink our previously held traditional concepts of change and transformation. However, we will not have to manipulate our genes to do so. We will remain the same, but the purpose of and the way in which we work—the assumptions and principles our new operating will follow—will change radically.

Learning from the biological process of transdifferentiation, we see that nature follows very strict principles. There is no hazard or unintentional 'innovation', but instead a very clear, decisive, highly precise, biological process. It is the logical conclusion and application of the 1st Law of Evolutionary Systems to transformation: to create as much shared value (new identity serving the whole system) in the most efficient way, executing the generic principles (Self-organization, Connectivity, Co-location, Co-creativity, Coherence) throughout the transformation process.

There seems to be absolutely no randomness and minimal risk taking in this process.

(For more detailed information see my article "Evolutionary investment and leadership as agents for rapid transformation", 2020)

4 Y.1: The Code for Evolutionary Transformation

As we have seen, closed systems strive for simplicity, homogeneity and equilibrium, while energy is consumed and dissipates. These are the opposite features of living, evolutionary systems, which generate diversity, novelty and complexity (Sabelli 2008; Sabelli and Kauffman 2014), while energy is liberated and enhanced (Grandpierre et al. 2014; Kafatos et al. 2015).

Looking at transformation from the perspective of quantum theory, after having erased the previous identity (stage Y.0), a new code or matrix of active information is implemented or activated. This code includes all information necessary to enable the cell to actively develop its new identity and function. This information creates—according to Bohm—a "field of meaning".

In quantum theory, towards the end of 1980s, David Bohm introduced the notion of "Active Information" into his ontological interpretation of quantum theory. There seemed to be a "Hidden Variable" that influenced quantum processes so that a single physical outcome emerged out of a multiplicity of possibilities. The quantum potential seemed to contain information to actively influence the outcome. This information has the potential to 'in-form' raw 'un-formed' energy: information gives 'form' to energy. These "morphogenetic fields" (Goodwin 1982; Sheldrake 1987), following David Bohm, create a "field of meaning". Bohm understood the principle of active information as a new general principle alongside matter and energy (Bohm and Peat 2000).

In analogy to the discoveries of Jarriault et al. I termed this new code "Y.1". It contains a matrix of active information allowing the self-organizing proliferation of a large number of viable, creative systems. You can understand "Y.1" as the new evolutionary information prototype, directing the energetic flow toward evolutionary cooperation while continuously applying the generic principles of evolutionary systems (Self-organization, Connectivity, Co-location, Co-creativity and Coherence). This gives 'meaning' to transformation. As Laszlo has put it very clearly: This "biological and physical survival imperative permits no alternatives" (Laszlo 1992).

Applying this evolutionary transformation process to change the paradigms of traditional economics and investment, we must realize that:

I. Direct, fast, safe and energy efficient transformation requires a complete erosion of the preexisting, traditional, closed system economic operating principles (state Y.0)
II. The liberated energy must be formed by the Y.1 information code to be enhanced and directed towards evolutionary cooperation, applying the generic principles from the very beginning.
III. To massively scale the Y.1 prototypes into sustainable, vibrant, productive and creative, co-local economies, the surrounding organizational culture, as well as the political and governance conditions must follow the 1st Law and be based on the generic principles (see also M. Sonntag on organizational culture in Sonntag 2018)

Now we might recognize why it is so important to have a clear and coherent understanding of the described concepts and principles. In order to undergo such a transformation and paradigm change we must deeply understand where we want to go. We must profoundly know how healthy, living systems function. Otherwise, we will not be able to break the symmetry when it comes to critical disturbances in our ongoing system, in a way that will lead to a new, healthy, coherent, evolutionary mode.

The purpose (1st Law) and the generic principles are the same on any level—impact investing, economy, social, scientific, pedagogic and political. If the outcome is not to be random (or even 'cancerous'), it takes a very decisive, brutal strategic decision to implement this new code as the transformational principle.

5 DECIDE: Governing Evolutionary Transformation

As we have seen, healthy, living systems:

- are radically self-organizing with decentralized, autonomous decision-making;
- have completely open information systems;
- organize themselves in pluripotent, co-local networks;
- actively enter into new interactions and co-dependent partnerships, co-creating emergent solutions and opportunities;
- are searching for dynamical disequilibrium, keeping themselves as far away from thermodynamic equivalence as possible, while actively and coherently directing the energy toward the purpose of evolutionary cooperation.

Coming from management concepts operating within the traditional closed, linear, reductionist, hierarchical control and micro-managing system, and wanting to transform into a healthy, evolutionary system, we often mistakenly think that it would be possible to transform the traditional system incrementally, bit-by-bit, trying to implement some hybrid or dual solutions or agile clusters, while keeping the old control systems going. From many experiences we know that this approach is extremely difficult, consumes a great deal of time, human and financial resources, and in nearly all cases has failed and has ceased into plenty of disappointment, frustration and pain. Meanwhile I personally refuse to support such transformation attempts. To implement a new system following the principles of the evolutionary paradigm we must first make very basic and radical decisions.

In all successful cases we know (Equinor/former Statoil, GAAIB Bern, Group Health Seattle, Iroquois Valley Farmland REIT, Morning Star, Novo Nordisk, Semco Partners, Swedish Handelsbanken, Tesla' household rooftop solar and battery storage program in South Australia, Valve Software, W. L. Gore & Associates, and others) the owners of the company decided to radically transform the entire operating, governance and leadership system. In most cases the starting point was purely economic:

> they realized that the traditional management and economic model was highly inefficient, demanding excessive costs from internal control systems while inhibiting the company from being flexible, adaptive and innovative, prohibiting them from having direct customer-centered interaction and was hindering them in the implementation of their purpose in an economically efficient way. They did not start with a few limited change or innovation

projects, but began to implement small, independent, self-organizing, in themselves coherently functioning, Y.1 prototypes and enabling them to spontaneously grow and spread, connecting with their own co-local networks and to start interacting and cooperating with similar-minded partners. Management's task was to eliminate all centralized controlling and HR structures and to actively support autonomous teams self-organizing around the locus of value creation.

Decisively building on Type Y (McGregor 1960) or Type I (Pink 2010)—I prefer to call them Y2Y—human nature concepts (Sonntag 2018), the transformation was carried out by autonomous intra- and entrepreneurs, all following the same purpose, while continuously applying and replicating the same coherent operational principles.

This is how living systems grow.

We must face the fact that there is no hybrid or dual solution, maintaining some of the traditional micro-management and control paradigm. It is either-or: either you work with the principles of living systems, or you work against them. In neurobiological terms, it is an on-off principle: either the brain is in a meaning-creating, pleasurable mode or it is in a blocked, fearful and painful mode. You must decide!

To let the "Y.1—prototype" emerge and grow in a self-organizing manner, you must first have the insight, knowledge and courage to erase the old operating system and allow a short Y.0—phase to happen. In traditional change conceptions this will create plenty of fear and resistance and you will have to manage and manipulate the employees involved top-down through heroic, authentic and hopefully more or less wise "penguins" (Kotter and Rathgeber 2017). However, having decided to govern an evolutionary transformation and by having your transformation code clear, upending the old control structures will release energy, hope and passion. The Y.1 information matrix will enable rapid scaling of this process with radically decentralized control and with a minimum energy investment.

The most educational and coherent transformation case is the Swedish Handelsbanken Transformation. My detailed case study ***Governing Evolutionary Transformation - The Blueprint for a New Paradigm of Change. The Svenska Handelsbanken Transformation Case*** can be sourced at the author or downloaded at the authors LinkedIn profile.

As the transformations needed so deeply impact the values, management beliefs, the organizational culture and operation of a company or society, the decisions must be made by the owners. On a company level, in the most cases, this is the investors' duty! On a societal level, it is the duty of the sovereign, the parliaments, government representatives and the political parties.

In analogy to the "Framework for Strategic Decision-Making" (Sonntag 2018) we now can outline how to govern Evolutionary Transformation.

6 Governing Evolutionary Transformation

The overall purpose is to enhance the energy and to govern the energy towards evolutionary cooperation.

First the two governing principles must be met:

Strategy

Have we decided to direct all free energy to increasing the capacity of evolutionary cooperation while sustainably co-creating shared value for all stakeholders?

Leadership

Are we willing and able to proactively, co-responsibly and continuously build the right conditions within which the co-creation of shared value is enabled and enhanced?

The generic principles must then be applied:

A. **Self-organization**

- *A1 Are we radically decentralizing decision-making?*
- *A2 Are we building through diverse, small, agile and autonomous teams?*
- *A3 Are these teams connecting with the stakeholders actively, dynamically and intensively?*

B. **Connectivity**

- *B1 Do our processes enable the perceiving and active sharing of complex information?*
- *B2 Are we providing information systems that are open, informal, dynamic and adaptable to a given situation?*
- *B3 Are we providing direct physical contact with the stakeholders, allowing resonance to occur spontaneously?*

C. **Co-location**

- *C1 Are we thoroughly building a decentralized network organizational structure with co-locally and autonomously acting operational units and engagement platforms?*
- *C2 Are we using and actively co-creating co-local, easily scalable synergies?*
- *C3 Do we anticipate a growth in diversity, novelty and complexity?*

D. **Co-creativity**

- *D1 Are we willing to admit our interactions on mutual interdependency?*
- *D2 Are we willing to let everyone become strongly engaged and develop long-term relationships built on empathy and concern?*
- *D3 Are we conscious and willing to accept that any co-creative process can involve transformational dynamics in which both interacting parts, including ourselves, can undergo transitions?*

E. **Coherence**

- *E1 Do we base all our decisions and actions on an Y2Y human nature concept?*

- *E2 Are we willing to build our decisions on a stakeholder engagement model (only win-win decisions are accepted)?*
- *E3 Are we willing to maintain the integrity of all stakeholders—also during a crisis?*

7 Evolutionary Investment: Giving Back the Soul and Closing the Socio-economic Gap

Considering the transformation our world needs, the essential change is in fact a healing process, leaving the track we embarked upon with Newton, Descartes, the industrialization, Taylor's principles of scientific management, globalization, centralization of decision-making and power and short-term shareholder profit maximization while exploiting nature and society. Within this traditional closed system, entropic mind-set any interaction was basically negative, because it would cost energy and finally lead to heat-death.

A virtual split between social welfare and ecologic sustainability on one side and economic prosperity on the other was created and is still growing (Fig. 3): In this logic the energy in the system (E) is caught and gets vandalized, not able to create any shared value (SV) or real "green growth" (Taherzadeh and Probst 2019).

On this track our economic and social system, and our very existence, has lost its purpose, meaning and soul.

With the evolutionary paradigm, the virtual socio-economic gap between value creation and profit is vanquished and the energy in the system is enhanced:

Applying the principles of living systems, economic profit and social welfare dynamically enhance each other, increasing the energy within the overall system: People, Planet and Profit merge.

Understanding how transformation into a sustainable economy must proceed so that it is direct, fast, safe and highly efficient enables us to launch a healing process, leading our energies and activities toward a truly vital, self-sustaining and self-enhancing, creative and self-healing business, economic, investment and social system.

I see this as the purpose of evolutionary investment: to be highly efficient and productive, while at the same time effectively co-creating a maximum of shared value for all stakeholders—and having the understanding and tools to govern self-

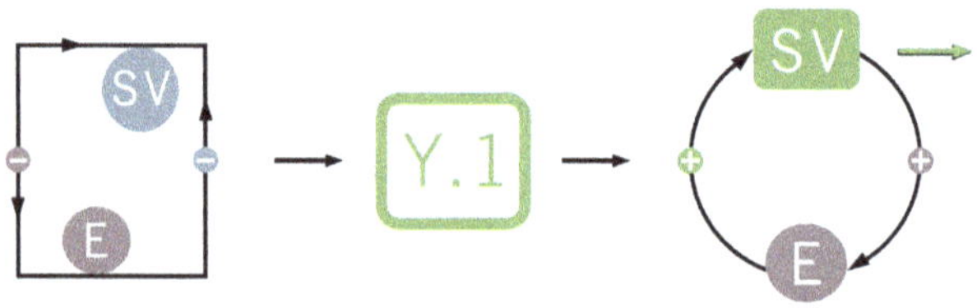

Fig. 3 Evolutionary Investment: Giving back the Soul

healing transformation. Living systems show us how to achieve this goal and enable us making our strategic investment decisions correctly.

Evolutionary investment, building on the principles of living systems (evolutionary paradigm) and actively inducing evolutionary transformation then becomes the catalyzer for a self-healing and self-enhancing evolutionary economy. It also provides a new framework for positive impact investors, (real) green growth and sustainable finance.

This allows our soul to return and inspire our actions, leading the evolutionary purpose to a deeper feeling of meaning, grace and pleasure, while building a truly evolutionary and meaningful economy.

Although I see the Y.1 transformation process in its core as a process giving us back our soul, for me it is not primarily about spirituality or consciousness. The feeling I get is more like working in the emergency room of our hospital: it is about having a clear mind, unbiased analysis, good understanding and especially about rational decision-making.

And it is about giving up our fight against nature and our natural human existence and learning how to work with nature and ourselves positively and co-creatively.

References

Agile Manifesto. (n.d.). Retrieved from https://agilemanifesto.org

Beyond Budgeting Round Table BBRT. (2020). Retrieved from https://bbrt.org

Bohm, D., & Peat, F. D. (2000). *Science, order and creativity* (2nd ed.). New York: Routledge.

Denning, S. (2018, May). HBR embraces agile at scale: Rethinking how we live and work. *Forbes*. Retrieved from https://www.forbes.com/sites/stevedenning/2016/04/21/hbrs-embrace-of-agile/

Drewell, M., & Larsson, B. (2017). *The rise of the new meaningful economy: A megatrend where meaning is a new currency*. Amazon Distribution. See also: *Meaning is the new currency*. Retrieved from https://medium.com/meaning-conference/meaning-is-a-new-currency-6324e0ae6d1b

Goodwin, B. C. (1982). Development and evolution. *Journal of Theoretical Biology, 97*, 43–55.

Grandpierre, A., Chopra, D., & Kafatos, M. C. (2014). The universal principle of biology: Determinism, quantum physics and spontaneity. *NeuroQuantology, 12*(3), 364–373.

Gulati, R. (2010). *Reorganize for resilience: Putting customers at the center of your business*. Boston, MA: Harvard Business Press.

Hamel, G., & Zanetti, M. (2019). *Blog post "the human movement"*. Retrieved from http://www.garyhamel.com/blog/human-movement

Hamel, G., & Zanetti, M. (2020). Humanocracy: Creating organizations as amazing as the people inside them. *Harvard Business Review*.

Hope, J., & Fraser, R. (2003). *Beyond budgeting*. Boston, MA: Harvard Business School Press.

Jarriault, S., Schwab, Y., & Greenwald, I. (2008). A Caenorhabditis elegans model for epithelial-neuronal transdifferentiation. *Proceedings of the National Academy of Sciences of the United States of America, 105*, 3790–3795.

Kafatos, M. C., et al. (2015). Biofield science: Current physics perspectives. *Global Advances in Health and Medicine, 4*(Suppl), 25–34.

Kotter, H., & Rathgeber, H. (2017). *Our iceberg is melting*. New York: Portfolio/Penguin.

Laloux, F. (2014). *Reinventing organizations*. Millis, MA: Nelson Parker.

Laszlo, E. (1992). *The age of bifurcation: Understanding the changing world*. New York: Gordon & Breach.
McGregor, D. (1960). *The human side of enterprise* (1st ed.). New York: McGraw-Hill.
Morlidge, S., & Player, S. (2012). *Future ready: How to master business forecasting*. West Sussex: Wiley.
Pink, D. H. (2010). *Drive: The surprising truth about what motivates us*. Edinburgh: Canongate.
Quinn, R. E., & Thakor, A. V. (2018, July–August). Creating a purpose-driven organization. *Harvard Business Review*, 78–85.
Ramaswamy, V., & Gouillart, F. (2010). Building the co-creative enterprise. *Harvard Business Review, 88*(10), 100–109.
Richard, J. P., et al. (2011). Direct in vivo cellular reprogramming involves transition through discrete, non-pluripotent steps. *Development, 138*, 1483–1492.
Sabelli, H. (2008). Bios theory of innovation. *The Innovation Journal, 13*(3), 12.
Sabelli, H., & Kauffman, L. H. (2014). The biotic logic of quantum processes and quantum computation. In *Nanotechnology: Concepts, methodologies, tools, and applications*. Hershey, PA: IGI Global.
Sheldrake, R. (1987). Mind, memory and archetype Morphic resonance and the collective unconscious. *Psychological Perspectives, 18*(1), 9–25.
Sonntag, M. (2017). Flow with purpose. The foundation and principles of a new evolutionary paradigm. Including the GAAIB case: Prototyping towards a new paradigm in health care. *COS Journal, 6*(2), 1182–1197. Retrieved from https://www.cos-collective.com/cos-journal/2017-volume-6-issue-2/
Sonntag, M. (2018). The biological Foundation of an Evolutionary Economy and its implications for organizational culture and leadership: A new framework for strategic decision making. In *Positive impact investing and organizational culture*. Springer International Scientific Publishing. Retrieved from https://link.springer.com/chapter/10.1007%2F978-3-319-10118-7_12
Sonntag, M., Mesesan, C., & Lau, A. (2020). Evolutionary investment and leadership as agents for rapid transformation. Including the Iroquois Valley Farmland REIT, PBCCase. In *Green and Social Economy Finance*. Taylor & Francis Group. In print.
Taherzadeh, O., & Probst, B. (2019, May 20). Five reasons 'green growth' won't save the planet. *The Conversation*. Retrieved from https://theconversation.com/five-reasons-green-growth-wont-save-the-planet-116037
Zuryn, S., et al. (2014). Sequential histone-modifying activities determine the robustness of transdifferentiation. *Science, 345*, 826–829.

Michael Sonntag is a medical doctor, psychiatrist, body-orientated psychotherapist (Bioenergetic Analysis) and management consultant. He strongly believes, that deep transformation is only possible, when we have a profound and coherent understanding of the operational and governing principles of healthy, living systems. This is true on an individual as well as on an organizational and economic level. He is teaching on these topics (Seminar for Evolutionary Leadership and Economy) and has been publishing in several journals. For more information see https://www.linkedin.com/in/dr-michael-sonntag/ or feel free to contact.

Part II
Creating Global Frameworks

Towards a Unifying Framework of Impact Assessment in Impact Investing

Swee-Sum Lam and Xiang Ru Amy Tan

Abstract This chapter highlights key challenges of impact assessment and argues for a unifying framework of impact assessment in impact investing. Given the current absence of a common language for *what* impact is, and the diversity in methodological approaches and methods for *how* impact may be assessed, a unifying framework would facilitate comparisons of performance of impact investment funds. Philanthropic organisations, foundations, investors and fund managers could benefit from such a unifying framework to assess, compare and aggregate impact across all investee firms, portfolios, and firm types in a spectrum of Social Purpose Organisations (SPOs) and over time. Furthermore, a unifying framework could provide contemporaneous assessment of a SPO's double or multiple bottom lines, as well as evaluate and manage intended and unintended outcomes of an intervention. These are essential for managerial decision making, business model pivoting or impact scaling. We advocate *social impact* as that which derives from an impact value chain where we distinguish outputs from outcomes and impacts. We further propose that the Global Impact Investing Network (GIIN)'s characterisation of impact investing can provide a unifying framework for impact assessment along this impact value chain.

S.-S. Lam (✉)
Asia Centre for Social Entrepreneurship and Philanthropy, NUS Business School, National University of Singapore, Singapore, Singapore

Finance Department, NUS Business School, National University of Singapore, Singapore, Singapore

Asian Pastoral Institute, Singapore, Singapore
e-mail: sweesum.lam@api.edu.sg

X. R. A. Tan
Asia Centre for Social Entrepreneurship and Philanthropy, NUS Business School, National University of Singapore, Singapore, Singapore

Centre for Ageing Research and Education, Duke-NUS Medical School, Singapore, Singapore
e-mail: amy.tan@duke-nus.edu.sg

K. Wendt (ed.), *Theories of Change*, Sustainable Finance,
https://doi.org/10.1007/978-3-030-52275-9_6

Keywords Impact investing · Social impact · Social impact assessment · Impact evaluation · Performance measurement · Unifying framework · UN sustainable development goals · Accountability · Social impact reporting

1 Pushing for Impact Assessment in Impact Investing

Funders—including development finance institutions, governments and quasi-government agencies, philanthropists, family offices and philanthropic organisations, venture philanthropists, impact investors, pension funds and insurance companies, financial institutions and corporations—are increasingly challenged to allocate resources more effectively and efficiently to unmet social needs whether for internal or external accounting and reporting. One of the challenges in accounting and reporting lies in assessing and aggregating social impact across projects, programs, social purpose organisations (SPOs), sectors, countries, regions and even time (Mudaliar et al. 2017a; Spiess-Knafl and Scheck 2017; Taskforce 2014).[1]

There is another challenge: There is also a diversity of causes or needs being addressed. These diverse needs arise endogenously from each country's socio-economic, political, historical and cultural contexts. In this conversation, the United Nations (UN) seeks to help all member countries better address the diversity of unmet social and environmental needs in their contemporary world by classifying these needs as goals and proposing possible indicators for how these goals may be managed. At the UN Sustainable Development Summit held in New York on 25–27 September 2015, the UN proposed and adopted the UN Sustainable Development Goals (SDGs) with their targets.[2] These 17 social and environmental goals is a call to action by all countries—rich, poor or middle-income—to have these targets met by 2030.

It should be noted that the Millennium Development Goals (MDGs) predate the SDGs. At the UN Millennium Summit in 2000, 189 countries signed the historic millennium declaration to eradicate extreme poverty in developing countries by

[1]In this study, we define a SPO as an organisation that seeks to generate a measurable and positive social impact, whether this be a charity (that embraces social impact as its sole mission), or a hybrid organisation, like a co-operative or a social enterprise (that seeks to generate social or environmental impact beside a financial return), or a for-profit firm (that embraces a CSR strategy that designs for and integrates social impact in its business model). For sustainability of these for-profit firms, social impact and financial return would tend to correlate positively so that its social impact tends to grow as it scales its financial performance. Therefore, a SPO is not defined by its legal constitution; it can take on different organisational forms. Moreover, what makes an organisation a SPO is dynamically determined by its nature as this innovates over time. For example, a co-operative can effectively cease to be a SPO if it drifts from its social mission to become more like a finance-first organisation. On the other hand, what was a social enterprise can also cease to be a SPO when it successfully attains its social goals and exits its social mission.

[2]United Nations Sustainable Development, Knowledge Platform, https://www.un.org/sustainabledevelopment/development-agenda/

2015. There are eight MDGs, ranging from universal primary education provision to child and maternal mortality prevention (Nations 2019). The SDGs can be considered as the sequel to the MDGs, but a key difference is that MDGs were targeted at the needs of the world's poorest and most vulnerable, while the SDGs set global targets that apply to both developing and developed countries. Nonetheless, both may function as frameworks to facilitate measurement, management and evaluation of the goals.

The Rockefeller Foundation is one of the key advocates of impact investing as the strategy to achieve these UN SDGs by means of a people-private-public partnership.[3] The Global Impact Investing Network (GIIN), a Rockefeller Foundation funded program, characterises impact investing in four tenets—intentionality, use of evidence and impact data in investment design, manage impact performance, and contribute to the growth of the industry (Network 2019b).

On the first characterisation—intentionality of creating social and/or environmental impact while generating financial returns—impact investors ought to articulate this as their mission or strategy in all their communications, if indeed they intend to create impact alongside generating financial returns. Some impact investors go further beyond self-reporting to evidence this intent by adopting a blended finance funding structure in a people-private-public partnership.[4] This funding structure would predispose impact fund managers to design, manage and sustain their social and/or environmental impact in all investing activities.

Secondly, impact investing is characterised as a practice whereby impact investors apply an evidence-based approach in designing impact through their investing to

[3]The Rockefeller Foundation conceived the term "impact investing" at Bellagio in 2007. Impact investing is defined as "investments made into companies, organisations, and funds with the intention to generate measurable and beneficial social and environmental impact alongside a financial return (Network 2019f).

[4]For example, general partners of an impact investment company could co-invest with international development agencies, government or quasi-government agencies as well as philanthropic organisations in a blended finance funding partnership. In this context, blended finance is the term given to the use of public or philanthropic capital to leverage private sector investment in SPOs. This funding structure would necessitate the impact fund to account for the generation of both social and/or environmental impact as well as financial returns. What is significant, however, is that the blended finance partnership structure allows for differentiated financial pay-offs. For example, individuals, foundations or multilateral agencies and governments may provide grants that have −100% return expectation. Mission-related investments of foundations and family offices, non-profit funds and individuals could join as venture philanthropic investors that have below-market return expectation. On the other hand, private equity funds are commercial impact investors that require market or near market returns. By leveraging private sector resources in this way, blended finance provides a stable funding mechanism that underpins impact investing to be a feasible strategy to attain the UN SDGs. What remains as a key challenge is the accounting and reporting of the social and/or environmental impact that may be attributable to such impact investing. Impact investors—especially philanthropic individuals, family offices, foundations, multilateral agencies and governments—need an evidence-based justification for why they are making grants or forgoing market rate returns when private equity funds are enjoying market or near market returns on the same investment.

address specified unmet social or environmental needs. This means the impact design and measurement, with learning from impact data, are integral to both the pre-investment and post-investment processes—in deal flow generation, deal filtering, due diligence, deal structuring, value creation, performance reporting and evaluation and deal exiting.

Thirdly, impact investing is characterised by impact management and performance—the measuring, monitoring and evaluating of impact that is attributable to the investing.

Lastly, GIIN characterises impact investing to generate an impact at the sector-level. That is, the practice of impact investing, including its impact structuring, origination, measurement, management and reporting, grows sector capacity and capability. Impact investors contribute to the growth of the sector through sharing their best practices and learning.

GIIN estimates USD 502 billion in impact investment assets currently (Mudaliar and Dithrich 2019). This growing market and interest in co-creating socio-environmental impact (henceforth "social impact") and financial returns through capital investments has placed social impact under much scrutiny regarding its accountability (Gray 2010; Molecke and Pinkse 2017; Nicholls 2018). Stakeholders are all eager to find out how much impact this 502 billion has achieved before scaling investments.

While conventional investments typically only adopt financial performance measurements to determine economic impact and efficiency, impact investing requires an integrated measurement system to account for economic and social impacts (Maas and Liket 2011). But such a holistic measurement system that can capture all dimensions of social, environmental and economic impacts is yet to be developed.

This chapter focuses on addressing some of the challenges of impact assessment in impact investing. Though the impact investing sector has grown significantly over the last 10 years, one key challenge remains. That is, social impact—those outcomes that ultimately address the targeted social and environmental goals that are attributable to the intervention programs or projects—cannot be readily compared nor aggregated across goals, projects, programs, sectors, countries and regions.

At a more fundamental level, the absence of a singular definition of "social impact" and how to measure it has generated immense confusion. For instance, in the impact investing community, output and operational performance metrics (not outcomes) are frequently used as claims for "impact". There are also different jargons and theoretical frameworks employed by the various disciplines that critically examine impact assessment as a subject matter. This is largely due to the writers imposing the languages and perspectives of their respective fields on impact assessment practices in impact investing.

There is another set of challenges with the use of quantitative indicators in performance measurement and assessment. Funders in social policies and development finance that often have in place performance measurement and reporting as funding requirements sometimes find unintended outcomes with undue use of quantitative indicators and performance measures.[5] In this study, we ask how far we should push for the use of quantitative indicators in performance measurement and assessment. What then is the appropriate mix of quantitative-qualitative data in performance measurement and assessment?

All these challenges—on what is impact, how and how much to measure, how to compare and aggregate impact—are likely to affect the flow and sustainability of impact investing, and ultimately the development of the sector and the fulfilment of the UN SDGs. Therefore, there is a need for a common language and a unifying framework for impact assessment.

2 Dealing with Varied Definitions of Impact and Assessment

We first outline the varied, and sometimes inconsistent, definitions of *impact* and approaches to measure *impact* across the impact investing community, international development organisations, and academic works. We then state our position on social impact—what it is, how and how much to measure and how to compare and aggregate.

In surveying the secondary literature, a ghastly realisation ensues. Practitioners, advocates, researchers, critics, consultants, public organisations and academics—each of these groups tends to use their own impact assessment jargons and methodologies, that which is familiar to them in their respective fields. As a result, there is often little attempt at addressing the critical differences in definitions (of what to measure) and methods for measurement (how to measure). This somewhat counter-productive diversity in impact assessment approaches and practices has been pointed out by other researchers in the field (Bull 2007; Ebrahim et al. 2014; Paton 2003).

Within the last two decades, social impact assessment discourses have drawn interests from a wide range of disciplines—including social accounting (Gibbon and Dey 2011; Luke et al. 2013; Morgan 2013), social finance (Chiappini 2017; Nicholls et al. 2015), voluntary and non-profit (Arvidson and Lyon 2014; Mook et al. 2015; Owen et al. 2015), business and management (Dufour 2019; Molecke and Pinkse 2017), organisational development (Ebrahim et al. 2014), social entrepreneurship (Haski-Leventhal and Mehra 2016; Ormiston and Seymour 2011), evaluation (Hatry 2013; Hoffman and Olazabal 2018; Ruff and Olsen 2018), economics and econometrics (Darby and Jenkins 2006).

[5]Quantitative indicators (vis-à-vis qualitative constructs) tend to be more objectively measured, easier to manipulate and communicate, and cost less. While measurement is essential for management and control in an organisation, an undue focus on quantitative indicators to proxy for the desired outcomes can be counter-productive. For example, Campbell's Law states, "The more any quantitative social indicator is used for social decision-making, the more subject it will be to corruption pressures and the more apt it will be to distort and corrupt the social processes it is intended to monitor." And, Goodhart's Law says, "When a measure becomes a target, it ceases to be a good measure" (Hoskin 1996).

Table 1 Definitions of social impact and its related terms (adapted from Maas and Liket 2011, p. 175)

Term	Author	Definition	Study field
Social impact	Latané (1981)	By social impact, we mean any of the great variety of changes in physiological states and subjective feelings, motives and emotions, cognitions and beliefs, values and behavior that occur in an individual, human, or animal, as a result of the real, implied, or imagined presence or actions of other individuals.	Psychology
Social impact	Freudenburg (1986)	Social impact refers to impacts (or effects, or consequences) that are likely to be experienced by an equally broad range of social groups as a result of some course of action.	Sociology
Social impact	Burdge and Vanclay (1996)	By social impacts we mean the consequences to human populations of any public or private actions that alter the ways in which people live, work, play, relate to one another, organise to meet their needs and generally act as a member of society.	Sociology
Social impact	Gentile (2000)	Social impacts are the wider societal concerns that reflect and respect the complex interdependency between business practice and society.	Business
Social value	Emerson et al. (2000)	Social value is created when resources, inputs, processes, or policies are combined to generate improvements in the lives of individuals or society as a whole.	Business/ practitioner
Impact	Clark et al. (2004)	By impact we mean the portion of the total outcome that happened as a result of the activity of the venture, above and beyond what would have happened anyway.	Business/ practitioner
Social impact	IAIA[a]	Social impacts are intended and unintended social consequences, both positive and negative, of planned interventions (policies, programs, plans, projects) and any social change processes invoked by those interventions.	Multi-discipline

[a]International Association for Impact Assessment, https://www.iaia.org/about.php

Arising from the discussions in these fields are various nomenclatures, including: social performance management, performance measurement, social impact accounting, social impact measurement, impact evaluation, and program evaluation (Ebrahim and Rangan 2014; Lall 2019; Nicholls 2018).

Spiess-Knafl and Scheck (2017) identify this lack of common language and terminology as one of the most critical challenges of social impact assessment in impact investing. Indeed, many of the aforementioned disciplines hold different perceptions of what impact assessment should entail because they conceptualise *social impact* differently. And ironically, what many scholars can actually agree on is the lack of agreement in existing literature on what *social impact* is (Chiappini 2017; Ebrahim and Rangan 2010; Grieco 2015).

A list of definitions is compiled by Maas and Liket (2011) to reflect the varied understandings of *social impact* and its related terms (Table 1).

It should be noted that *social impact* tends to be used interchangeably with other overlapping concepts such as "social value creation" (Emerson et al. 2000) and "social return" (Clark et al. 2004).

Consistent with Clark et al. (2004), we understand *social impact* as that which derives from an "impact value chain" where we distinguish outputs from outcomes and impacts (see Appendix).[6] Firstly, the definition accounts for the counterfactual by addressing "what would have happened anyway", that is, changes that would have taken place if the intervention had not taken place. This is important because valid measurements of social impact should aim to infer causality between the social outcomes observed and the activities/intervention introduced, by way of examining the counterfactual using adequate control groups. Ideally, samples should be randomly drawn to eliminate selection biases but realistically, randomised control trials are not commonly conducted due to ethical, operational and/or funding concerns. Secondly, this definition of impact as *what* is engendered from the impact value chain best resonates with GIIN's characterisation of *how* impact investing can help attain the UN SDGs in its theory of change.

To be sure, social impact is *not* unique to third sector organisations even though social impact typically refers to the value that non-governmental organisations (NGOs), social enterprises, social ventures, and social programs create (Costa and Pesci 2016). SPOs include those that span the third sector and the private sector. All kinds of organisations generate social impact—organisations with single, double or triple bottom lines. In the same vein, social impact is an inherently neutral concept. Activities and interventions can produce both negative and positive social impact, whether intended or unintended. In this discourse, we focus on organisations that that seek to generate a measurable and positive social impact.[7]

Beyond the issue of definitions, there is an attempt in extant literature to deconstruct the aspects of impact in impact investing. For instance, Brest and Born (2013) propose distinct dimensions of "enterprise impact", "investment impact" and "nonmonetary impact". Enterprise impact can be further deconstructed into "product impact" and "operational impact". The former refers to the impact of goods and services produced by enterprise; the latter refers to the impact of the enterprise's "management practices on its employees' health and economic security, its effect on jobs or other aspects of the well-being of the community in which it operates, or the environmental effects of its supply chain and operations". These are often understood as environmental, social, and governance (ESG) variables. Brest and Born maintain that each of these dimensions of impact will require its own assessment in

---

[6]While Clark et al. (2004) advance the notion of "social return" as *what* impact is, we note this does not imply necessarily a quantitative measure of impact in $ or % as is often associated with *how* financial return, a common referent, is being measured.

[7]Sometimes, the market may be confused by for-profit firms that are excluded by way of the negative screening in socially responsible investing—those in the alcohol, tobacco or gaming, also referred to as 'sin stocks', as well as weapons manufacturers, nuclear power producers or companies that use child labor—when these also have effective CSR programs generating positive social impact. We call these socially ambiguous grey stocks. See Lam et al. (2015).

order to comprehensively inform impact investors of the contributions their investments will actually make vis-à-vis the intended social/investment objectives.

The need for a consistent understanding of impact and social impact is pressing. This is more so when we learn from the findings in Rawhouser et al. (2019) that 10 out of the 71 relevant business journal papers they sampled provided no definition for social impact. A clear scoping of social impact will also allow practitioners in the sector and academics advancing the field of impact evaluation to discuss and evaluate impact in the same way.

3 Clarifying Approaches and Methods of Social Impact Assessment

The lack of consilience among differing approaches of social impact assessment also makes it challenging to establish standard measurements for aggregation and comparisons. Hubers (2017) suggests that some approaches place more emphasis on *what* to measure while others emphasise *how* to measure. The fundamental difference in motivation behind these approaches or methods results in diverse methodologies that confuse more than clarify. But in truth, both motivations need to be accounted for in a robust impact assessment. In this section, we seek to clarify what some of the key approaches or methods are or do in impact assessment.

Addressing *what* to measure typically undertakes periodic monitoring of social objectives using specific metrics; this type of approach tends to equate social impact measurement with social accounting or social performance management. It is primarily concerned with what indicators can be used to signal performance and what data can be used to keep track of these impacts regularly (Hubers 2017).

In contrast, addressing *how* to measure considers assessment as post- or mid project evaluation of the causal effects of the intervention on society. The focus in this field of study is less on what and more on how to measure social effects, in particular to estimate the casual link between the outputs of a given intervention and the social outcomes observed (Hubers 2017).

In a methods catalogue, Clark et al. (2004) classify a list of social impact measurement tools according to their functions. The purposive classification helps to clarify whether measurements are done at the output level or at the outcome and impact level. It also helps practitioners figure out which method(s) are more suitable for what they are trying to measure. Adapting their functional categorisation of the measurement tools, we find that methods can have different foci:

1. Process or operations focused methodologies tend to employ tools that track and monitor the efficacy of outputs, variables or indicators of ongoing operations. Output data alone cannot show if desired outcomes are achieved, but they can in turn be evaluated to gauge correlations with or causality of intended social outcomes.
2. Outcome or impact focused methodologies tend to employ tools that relate outputs and outcomes, and attempt to prove incremental outcomes relative to the

next best alternative. As outcomes are changes *resulting from* outputs, they are typically not within the direct control of ongoing operations. With this distinction, it becomes clear that generally, separate indicators would be needed and relevant data would have to be collected to test for intended outcomes and (longer term) impacts.

3. Monetising focused methodologies tend to employ tools that monetise outcomes or impact by ascribing a dollar value to them.

By surveying secondary sources (Clark et al. 2004; Maas and Liket 2011), we identify the following measurement tools as methods that evaluate at the outcome/impact level:

- Balanced Scorecard (BSc)
- Bottom of the Pyramid (BoP) Impact Assessment Framework
- Measuring Impact Framework (MIF)
- Millennium Development Goal Scan (MDG-scan)
- Ongoing Assessment of Social Impacts (OASIS)
- Participatory Impact Assessment
- Poverty and Social Impact Analysis (PSIA)
- Robin Hood Foundation Benefit–Cost Ratio
- Social Costs–Benefit Analysis (SCBA)
- Social e-Valuator
- Social Impact Assessment (SIA)
- Social Return on Investment (SROI)

There appears to be increasing efforts to develop new and more comprehensive tools of evaluation. While catalogues and summaries of measurement tools are helpful for practitioners looking for an appropriate way of conducting assessment, the problem remains that each method employs its own metrics and indicators. This would cause difficulty in making effectual cross references between results generated by different methods. Maas and Grieco (2017) point out that the absence of standardised methods and comparable data also causes measurements to take place only in terms of "business impact and financial results even when social goals or environmental goals are the primary drivers for operational choices" (Clark et al. 2004; Liket et al. 2014; Salazar et al. 2012; Schaltegger and Burritt 2018). This continues to be a hindrance for comparing performance of impact funds and portfolios.

In the next section, we review some frameworks of impact assessment and reporting.

4 Reviewing Existing Frameworks of Impact Assessment

SPOs may be located along a spectrum that maps the relative significance of their goals—social (and environmental) impact vis-à-vis financial returns—ranging from charities, foundations, social enterprises, impact investors and for-profits that engage in sustainable, socially responsible and ESG investing. To appreciate the challenges in comparing and aggregating social impact across SPOs, we review the major databases of SPOs and provide, where possible, direct comparisons among these databases. The existing databases include B Impact Assessment by B Corp, Calvert Social Index, Charity Navigator, DJSI, Foundation Transparency Index, FSTE4Good, GiveWell, GRI, MSCI ESG, and UN Global Impact.

B Corp The B impact assessment from B Corp has a total point of 200. Minimum qualifying point is 80. The rating is categorised under five categories such as governance, workers, community, environment, and impact business model. This is a qualifying assessment, not a ranking system. The companies are not ranked against one another.

Calvert Social Index The index measures seven categories such as environment, community relations, governance and ethics, human rights, indigenous peoples' rights, product safety and impact, and workplace. If the companies meet the criteria, they will be included in the index.

Charity Navigator The score and star rating system focuses more on the input and the process. It mainly focuses on charities. It does not provide developmental information on how to improve. It does not include environment factor. It focuses on (1) financial health and (2) accountability and transparency. It weights the two components.

DJSI DJSI uses the corporate sustainability assessment to score and rank firms according to their sustainability. It covers economic, environmental and social dimensions. The scores are cross-checked by public data disclosure and questionnaires. Their assessments are not catered for social enterprises but rather the normal for-profit firms.

Foundation Transparency Index The index measures the indicators on financial information, project information and donor information. It provides ranking for more than 2700 Chinese foundations against 47 "transparency indicators". This index is constructed based on public-released information. It does not cross-validate the collected information by other industry peers.

FSTE4Good It measures a company's ESG practices such as environmental, social and governance. It provides the risk (from zero to three) and score (from zero to five). It does not integrate the financial performance.

GiveWell It aims to find outstanding charities and provide details on them for donors to decide who to give. The top charities are supposed to be proven, cost-effective and scalable. They care about "$X per life saved" or "$Y per person enabled to get a job paying 20% more than they could gotten otherwise". It is not applicable to other types of organisations.

GRI GRI is not a ranking or scoring system. It is a framework that intends to guide firms on sustainability reporting. The specific standard disclosures include management approach and indicators on economic, environmental and social impacts.

MSCI ESG It measures a firm's ESG practices such as environmental, social and governance. It does not integrate with financial performance. Moreover, it does not apply to social enterprises whereby the key stakeholders are beneficiaries rather than customers.

UN Global Compact It aims to encourage global business to align their business strategies with ten universally accepted principles in human rights, labor, environment, and anti-corruption. It encourages the adoption of the standards and sharing of the best practices. It does not provide ranking among firms. It does not integrate the financial performance of the firms.

To give a sense of the extent to which these databases may allow for comparative and aggregative analyses, we check off whether each database allows for ranking across its constituents. At the same time, we also tabulate the extent to which a database covers the various dimensions—environmental-social-governance-financial (ESGF) and whether it allows for a qualifying assessment or validation of the organisation/firm's social impact (Table 2).

The DJSI distinguishes itself as having the broadest cover of the ESGF dimensions; it also allows for ranking across its constituents. However DJSI uses corporate sustainability scoring which may account for operational impact (in the sense of environment or governance in the ESG framework) but not necessarily the product impact in the sense of Brest and Born (2013). Such product impact may be assessed with reference to beneficiaries who may participate in the 'production' process as producers, workers or customers. The DJSI also does not cater for all types of firms that would include charities and social enterprises beside the regular for-profit firms.

B Corp, on the other hand, covers all firm types, but it does not allow for comparability or aggregation across firm, firm types and over time. Moreover, there are databases, like Calvert, FSTE4Good, MSCI ESG and UN Global, which assess the ESG dimensions but exclude financial performance.

This review of the diverse frameworks in impact assessment corroborate on the above-mentioned challenges—the various databases reflect the absence of a common language and understanding for *what* impact is and so what is to be assessed. It is not clear that these frameworks are assessing impact in the sense that we adopt here as *what* impact is—any measurable and positive change in societal outcomes that may be attributed to any intervention of a SPO. These diverse frameworks also reflect the related challenges of *how* impact may be assessed when an impact investor is confronted with diverse methodological approaches and methods.

A unifying framework for impact assessment could allow for a contemporaneous assessment of a SPO's double or multiple bottom lines to better understand, evaluate and therefore manage any trade-off or complementarity of the intended and unintended outcomes of a SPO's intervention. Such a contemporaneous assessment framework is essential for managerial decision making for business model pivoting or impact scaling. As well, this unifying framework could allow philanthropic organisations and foundations, investors and fund managers to assess, compare and aggregate impact across all investee firms, portfolios, and firm types in a spectrum of SPOs and over time.

Table 2 Review of existing databases

Name of databases	Environment	Social performance	Governance	Financial performance	Qualifying assessment	Ranking	Firm type
B Corp	X	X	X	X	X		All
Calvert	X	X	X		X		For-profit
Charity navigator			X	X	X	X	Charities
DJSI	X	X	X	X	X	X	For-profit
Foundation transparency index		X	X	X		X	Public
FSTE4Good	X	X	X		X		All
GiveWell		X	X	X	X		Charities
GRI	X	X		X	X		All
MSCI ESG	X	X	X		X	X	Not-for-profit
UN global	X	X	X		X		All

5 Assessing Impact Investing Practices

In this section, we seek to assess the state of impact investing practice, globally and in Asia, with reference to the four characterisations of impact investing—intentionality, use of evidence and impact data in investment design, manage impact performance, and contribute to the growth of the industry (Network 2019b).

In Sect. 5.1, we examine secondary literature from both industry and academic sources. This includes findings from key advocates, practitioners, and scholarly research. By looking at their reports and analyses, we try to find out if impact investors around the world are evidencing intentionality to create impact, using evidence-based impact data in investment design, measuring, managing and reporting on their impacts (whether to internal or external stakeholders) and contributing to the growth of the industry through sharing and learning in impact assessment. We also highlight information gaps and challenges in impact assessment as expressed by industry players, stakeholders and researchers. In Sect. 5.2, we present empirical data to demonstrate the state of play of impact assessment practices by impact investors in Asia.

5.1 Reviewing Secondary Data

We look into GIIN and its partners to get a sense of current practices in impact assessment and reporting. The GIIN network was officially launched in 2009 and it identifies itself as the "global champion of impact investing" with the core mission of "increasing its scale and effectiveness around the world" (Network 2019a). In its efforts to build the industry and promote best practices, the GIIN conducts surveys and publishes research findings on global impact investing activities. It also collates resources produced by partner organisations under its Impact Toolkit—an open resource designed to help investors navigate the landscape of impact measurement and management (IMM) tools. The Impact Toolkit allows for investors to tailor a list of fit-for-purpose resources; it professes to be the most comprehensive database of impact-focused systems, methods, indicators, and data in the world.

Notably, GIIN initiated the first version of Impact Reporting and Investment Standards (IRIS) around 2009 with the intention of providing a universal language for social, environmental, and financial performance reporting. IRIS has since evolved into a catalog of performance metrics managed by GIIN. It is supposed to facilitate aggregation of performance data across diverse portfolios and improve investment comparability and performance benchmarking. The latest version, launched as IRIS+ in 2019, exhibits efforts to increase user customisation and provides more defined concepts and structure for measuring impact according to the five dimensions they lay out. These are—identifying the outcomes to deliver, understanding baseline characteristics of stakeholders, understanding the degree of social changes, comparing performance with market benchmarks or control groups and lastly, understanding impact risks (Network 2019c, d).

We searched the GIIN online research portal (Network 2019e) for works produced or co-produced by the network from 2009 to date. Results show 48 reports, most of which provide overviews of the impact investing sector such as the size and reach of market, analyses of industry trends and (mainly financial) performance by organisation type, region and sector. There are also reports on impact investing benchmarking guidelines and sharing of best practices.

Of interest to us is their Annual Impact Investor Survey; reports are available for the period 2016–2019 (Mudaliar et al. 2016, 2017b, 2018, 2019). An increasing number of impact investors are participating in GIIN's annual survey. In 2016, 158 impact investors responded, while respondents grew to 266 in 2019. These respond on behalf of their organisations; they are not individual investors. In terms of sampling, the survey allows respondents to assess their own eligibility based on stipulated criteria, such as, respondents must have invested at least USD ten million in impact investments since their inception or have made at least five impact investments, or both (Mudaliar et al. 2019).

On the third characterisation of managing impact performance, the 2019 GIIN survey reports that 98% of the impact investors surveyed measure and manage their impact. Measurement can be in the form of qualitative information, proprietary metrics, IRIS metrics or other established frameworks. Results also indicate that more than 60% of investors specifically track their investment performance to the UN SDGs, reportedly motivated by the prospects of a convergent global development framework.

While the results seem optimistic, we are unable to ascertain if these impact investors are measuring at the outcome/impact level or at the output and operations level. As stated in Sect. 2 and more so in Sect. 3, social outcomes and impacts are distinct from outputs and activities generated by organisations. That's because social outcomes are changes that occur *as a result of* outputs, hence, different indicators would be needed and relevant data would have to be collected to test for intended outcomes and (longer term) impacts.

On the fourth characterisation of contributing to the growth of the industry, a separate report by GIIN highlights issues with the state of impact measurement and management practice (Mudaliar et al. 2017a). Firstly, impact is multifaceted and investments can generate both positive and negative impact concurrently. It calls for a more holistic understanding of impact so that negative externalities can be identified and addressed. Secondly, target setting is paramount for robust measurement. Without objectives and goals, there cannot be methodical deduction of the key impact indicators needed and what data to collect. Thirdly, more transparency, sharing of best practices and access to impact data build industry confidence and advance the field of practice. Fourthly, there should be greater coordination and standardisation of impact measurement practice.

5.2 *Reviewing State of Play of Impact Investors in Asia*

Based on publicly available information, we identify impact investors who are either based in or invest in Asia and their impact assessment practices. This review can give insights into the practice of impact investment fund managers, particularly in terms of social impact accounting and reporting. In addition to assessing information that is accessible online, we also abstract secondary sources in academic studies that may give a more critical analysis.

As stated in Sect. 2, we define social impact as "the portion of the total outcome that happened as a result of the activity of an organisation, above and beyond what would have happened anyway" (Clark et al. 2004). In terms of levels of measurement and reporting, we make distinctions between:

1. Impact evaluation (which makes causal inferences on the results of an intervention through adequate control groups or baseline survey data)
2. Outcome evaluation (which offer valid indicators to tests for change in social behavior or improved conditions)
3. Output reporting (which is akin to performance tracking of planned activities)

In our review, we look at investment funds that use financing instruments such as equity and/or loans to catalyze or develop businesses with specific social and/or environmental purposes.

On the first characterisation of intentionality, some specifically disclose that they manage their investments to the UNSDGs. Many generally self-identify as angel investors, seed impact funds or impact ventures; these generally provide financial backing for social enterprises up to certain milestones. Having a clearly stated vision and mission or identifying targets demonstrates the first characteristic of intentionality on the part of the impact investors (Hubers 2017; Lall 2017). It is also critical to prevent mission drifting (Ebrahim et al. 2014). The International Finance Corporation (IFC)'s subject paper lists "defining strategic impact objectives consistent with the investment strategy" as the very first principle of impact management (Corporation 2019).

Subject to the limits of self-reporting, our list of impact investors is collated from the Asian Venture Philanthropy Network (AVPN) member list on its website, AVPN's featured impact investors at their 2019 annual conference, and impact investors sourced from online searches. We reviewed a total of 44 impact investors or funds; this is not an exhaustive list.

On the second characterisation of impact investing, it is unclear if these impact investors or funds use evidence-based impact data in designing their investments. The IFC indicates that assessing the expected impact of each investment, based on a systematic approach is one of the principles of impact management; it is also vital for informing the investment design (Corporation 2019). However, such information is often not disclosed. The fund managers reviewed mostly claim to focus on creating social (and environmental) impact at scale, scalable impact or socially inclusive economic growth; some also mention their ESG goals and conscientiousness for responsible investments. All 44 publicly express their aim to achieve financial returns and social return on investment (Bugg-Levine and Emerson 2011).

The third characterisation of impact measurement and management may be induced from an impact investor or funder's self-reporting of output, outcome or impact of its investees or its investing. By reviewing information from their websites and annual reports (where available), we examine five key areas to make sense of what is publicly accessible:

1. Are UN SDGs used to represent their social and/or environmental goals?
2. Is any form of reporting publicly available? This may be primarily financial records, qualitative case studies or quantitative indicators.
3. Reporting of output measurement
4. Reporting of outcome measurement
5. Reporting of impact measurement (Table 3)

We find that about 36% of funders (16 out of 44) use relevant SDGs to represent their social or environmental goals. The majority does not reference the SDGs at all, instead they design the parameters of their targets themselves. 47% of the reviewed impact investors (20 out of 43, excluding one from the total sample of 44, as it is not in operation yet) avail some form of reporting to the public. For the rest, it is unclear whether such performance data do exist even though they may not be made public, or whether impact assessments are not being conducted.

The available information pertaining to the fund's performance ranges from snapshots of output or outreach tracking (such as the number of farmers supported, the number of products sold or the number of patients served etc.) to written annual reports with some detail on outcome evaluation. We differentiate the level at which the assessment is done and observe that 42% of the sample showed figures pertaining to performance tracking—which is data at the output level, and does not demonstrate outcome nor impact.[8]

24% of the sample (or 10 out of 42 investors) reported on outcomes, or conducted assessment beyond outputs at the process level. For instance, Bamboo Capital hired local third-party consultants in 2017 to survey the effects of the services provided by an investee healthcare service provider on their clients in India. Collecting data on the effects of the healthcare service would constitute assessment at the outcome level because the data could reflect positive, negative or nil social changes as experienced by the targeted beneficiaries. Omidyar Network commissioned a client feedback survey in 2018 to score the effectiveness of its investee companies. While client feedback on the effectiveness of, for instance, service delivery by investees does not measure social outcomes, it is an assessment that goes beyond output tracking to consider its reception.

[8]This is drawn from 18 out of 42 impact investors or funders—we exclude 2 from the total sample of 44, as one is not in operation yet and the other provides its annual report in a foreign language, and we were not able to review it.

Table 3 Review of impact investors' reporting

Impact investors & fund managers	UN SDG aligned	Public reporting	Output	Outcome	Impact
1. ADB Ventures Investment Fund	–	Not yet operational			
2. Ajooni Impact Investment	X	–	–	–	–
3. ANGIN	–	–	–	–	–
4. Ankur Capital	–	–	–	–	–
5. Anthem Asia Limited	–	–	–	–	–
6. B Current Impact Investment Inc.	X	–	–	–	–
7. Bamboo Capital Partners	–	X	X	X	–
8. Bharat Inclusion Initiative	–	–	–	–	–
9. Blue Orchard	X	X	X	X	–
10. Brightlight Investment Management	–	–	–	–	–
11. Capital4 Development Partners	–	X	X	X	–
12. Capria	X	X[a]	–	–	–
13. Circulate Capital	–	–	–	–	–
14. Conservation International	–	–	–	–	–
15. Cycle Group	X	–	–	–	–
16. D3 Jubilee Partners	–	–	–	–	–
17. Damson Capital	X	–	–	–	–
18. Ehong Capital	–	–	–	–	–
19. Evergreen Labs	–	X	X	–	–
20. Global Innovation Fund	–	–	–	–	–
21. IIX Growth Fund	X	X	X	–	–
22. Insitor Fund SCA	–	–	–	–	–
23. Japan SIIF	–	X	X	–	–
24. Kaizen Private Equity	–	–	–	–	–
25. Leapfrog Financial Inclusion Funds	–	X	X	–	–
26. Leping Social Entrepreneur Foundation	–	X	Non-English annual report		
27. Lok Capital	X	X	X	X	X
28. New Forests	X	X	X	X	–
29. Oikocredit International	X	X	X	X	–
30. Omidyar Network	X	X	X	X	–
31. One To Watch	X	X	X	X	–
32. Patamar Capital	–	–	–	–	–
33. Phitrust Asia	X	X	X	–	–
34. Quadria Capital Investment	–	X	X	–	–
35. responsAbility Investments	X	X	X	X	–
36. RS Group	–	X	X	X	–

(continued)

Table 3 (continued)

Impact investors & fund managers	UN SDG aligned	Public reporting	Output	Outcome	Impact
37. SEAF	X	–	–	–	–
38. Social Ventures Hong Kong	–	X	X	–	–
39. SOW (Asia) Foundation Limited	–	–	–	–	–
40. Unitus Capital	–	–	–	–	–
41. UnLtd India	X	X	X	–	–
42. UnLtd Indonesia	–	–	–	–	–
43. UOB Venture Management	–	–	–	–	–
44. YellowDog	–	–	–	–	–

Key: "X" = Yes; "–" = Not found
[a]Link to impact measurement report available online but requires login

We find only one case where the impact investor reported on impact evaluation using randomised control trials. It was a case of a microfinance institution's impact on serviced areas compared with non-serviced areas. Random assignment ensures that biases do not skew the sample. The setting up of a valid control group in the non-serviced areas allows the social changes observed in the serviced areas to be directly attributed to intervention provided. This practice coheres with our definition of social impact evaluation.

6 Discussion and Recommendations

This review is limited as the small sample and the short period of review only allows for a snap shot of the state of play of impact investing in Asia. Based on this limited review, it appears that transparency and disclosure are still at a nascent stage in the impact investing sector. Notwithstanding, we observe self-reporting of intentionality to create impact; 36% reference the UN SDGs. Even though it is unknown if impact investors or funders use evidence and impact data in investment design, there is a distribution of how impact assessment is being done. More than 40% report at the output level; about 25% report at outcome level, and an insignificant number report at impact level. There are also early indications of knowledge sharing and skills training by some impact funds, intermediaries like impact investing networks and research centres that contribute to the growth of the industry.

Our observations are consistent with those from other studies. In Hubers' assessment of the methods and criteria used by impact investors and philanthropists in Asia, he finds that "transparency among social investors is not optimal" and "social reporting happens mainly on the output level" (Hubers 2017). Additionally, Maas and Grieco who study social enterprises that measure their impact suggest that "the size of the organisation has a significant impact on impact measurement"(Maas and Grieco 2017). This size effect may be explained by legitimacy concerns; large organisations tend to have higher visibility and greater accountability needs (Meyer and Rowan 1977). We observe a similar phenomenon among impact investors that we sampled—the larger asset managers, particularly those who are members of the GIIN Investors' Council, tend to be the ones who report at the outcome level, and/or display more transparency in reporting. Perhaps these are better motivated to lead by example in contributing to the growth of the impact investing sector.

We offer possible explanations for why impact investors choose not to disclose the impact of their investing, or not to conduct impact assessment. First, impact evaluation that calls for an attribution of outcomes to the investment is difficult and costly. Second, the impact value chain takes time to take shape as different interventions are needed at different stages of business development to engender changes in social outcomes—early stage investing may not yet yield intermediate outcomes, much less impact which comes from inherently long term outcomes. Therefore, it is expected for investors/funders targeting early stage investments to measure (and report) outputs; those targeting growth stage investments to scale impact would measure (and report) outcomes, and possibly impact. Third, impact funds that do assess impact may also choose not to disclose till these have confirmed their strategic positioning, funding structure, investment instrument mix and therefore the target stakeholders to whom they account performance. Fourth, by self-selection, the poorer performing investors/funders may choose not to assess or disclose their assessment. Worst, non-disclosure may just point to impact washing.[9] While impact measurement is vital to inform internal learning and decision making (Lall 2019), there is still a lot in impact assessment that either remains to be done or disclosed.

To move this discourse forward, we recommend a unifying framework of impact assessment in impact investing:

1. That adopts the UN SDGs as the goals of impact investing, and defines impact to take the sense of what is being created along an impact value chain. That is, impact refers to the portion of the total outcome that happened as a result of the activity of the venture, above and beyond what would have happened anyway.
2. For all self-reporting impact investors/funders—these can opt in to participate in an annual survey as part of an independent and parsimonious validation of impact and its characterisations along the investor's impact value chain (see paragraph 3 below). Consistent with the economics of the size effect, validation fees can be structured on a sliding scale to incentivise the smaller impact investing funds to participate. The larger impact investors/funders may lead in conducting a fuller impact evaluation and reporting on impact of their investing for shared learning.

[9] In his cover letter for the 2018 *Annual Impact Investor Survey*, Global Impact Investing Network (GIIN) research director Abhilash Mudaliar included "industry integrity" as one of the noteworthy topics illuminated by the survey's findings: Specifically, 80% of respondents said that more transparency around impact investing strategies and results would help reduce the risks of impact washing or "industry mission drift." 41% pointed to "third-party certification of what qualifies as an impact investment," while others said that "shared principles" or a "code of conduct" could help address potential impact washing issues.

3. That measures the impact of an impact investor/funder in its four characterisations along the investor's impact value chain—intentionality, impact origination and design (along the pre-investing processes), impact measurement and management (along the post-investing processes including exit), sharing capability, capacity and learning to grow the impact investing sector.

A philanthropic organisation of good repute may want to fund an intermediary that serves as an independent validation agency of the sector. This agency builds and manages this unifying framework in impact assessment in impact investing. The instrument should be parsimonious and allow for aggregation of impact across goals, projects, organisations, firms, funds, countries, regions, and time. To avoid any conflict of interest that is often found with public auditing firms and rating agencies, fee-paying impact investors may not pay the validation agency directly. Independent validation of all self-reporting impact investors/funds could guard against impact washing as well as unintended negative impacts on beneficiary groups and build legitimacy of the sector. Notwithstanding, we acknowledge that too much focus on impact washing can be counter-productive.[10]

7 Conclusion

Impact investing, as advanced by the Rockefeller Foundation, is a strategy that can make operational the achievement of the UN SDGs through the leveraging of private sector resources. Five years into the launch of the UN SDGs, various surveys and studies point to a growing momentum to impact investing and a reference of its employ to attain the UN SDGs. However, the emerging sector needs to address various challenges, including that of evolving a common language on *what* impact is and *how* impact in impact investing may be assessed before it can scale.

In this study, we advocate *social impact* as that which derives from an impact value chain where we distinguish outputs from outcomes and impacts. We further propose that the GIIN's characterisation of impact investing can provide a unifying framework for impact assessment along this impact value chain. This unifying framework can give impetus to the attainment of the UN SDGs by 2030.

[10]The recent scandal surrounding funds misuse accusations leading to the eventual collapse of the Abraaj Group—which invests in private equity, private credit, real estate as well as impact investing in healthcare and clean energy—reminds us that adequate financial and social accounting is important and needs to be enforced, to go beyond warm glow. So that the intended socio-environmental impact can materialise and the targeted groups can live sustainable improved lives (Louch et al. 2018; Primack 2018).

Appendix

Impact Value Chain—adapted from Clark et al. (2004) and Maas and Liket (2011).

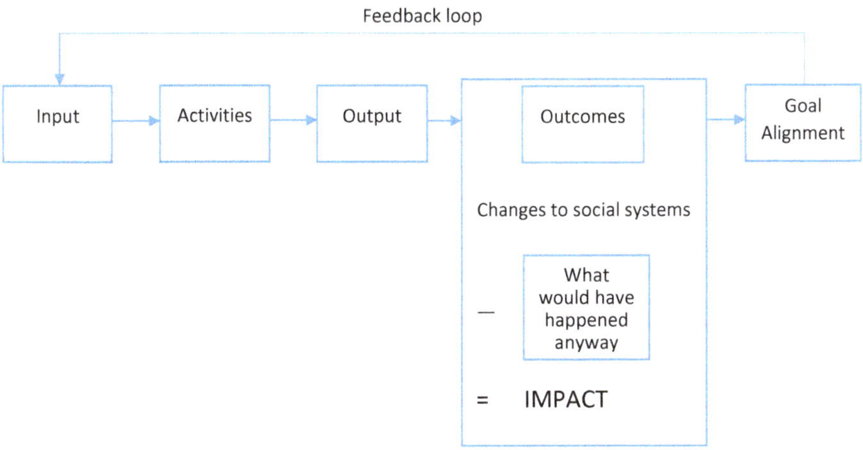

References

Arvidson, M., & Lyon, F. (2014). Social impact measurement and non-profit organisations: Compliance, resistance, and promotion. *Voluntas: International Journal of Voluntary and Nonprofit Organizations, 25*(4), 869–886. https://doi.org/10.1007/s11266-013-9373-6.

Brest, P., & Born, K. (2013). When can impact investing create real impact? *Stanford Social Innovation Review, 11*(4), 22–31

Bugg-Levine, A., & Emerson, J. (2011). *Impact investing: Transforming how we make money while making a difference* (1st ed.). San Francisco: Jossey-Bass.

Bull, M. (2007). "Balance": The development of a social enterprise business performance analysis tool. *Social Enterprise Journal, 3*(1), 49–66. https://doi.org/10.1108/17508610780000721.

Burdge, R. J., & Vanclay, F. (1996). Social impact assessment: A contribution to the state of the art series. *Impact Assessment, 14*(1), 59–86. https://doi.org/10.1080/07349165.1996.9725886.

Chiappini, H. (2017). *Social impact funds: Definition, assessment and performance*. Cham: Springer International Publishing.

Clark, C., Rosenzweig, W., Long, D., & Olsen, S. (2004). *Double bottom line project report: Assessing social impact in double bottom line ventures: Methods catalog*. Retrieved from https://escholarship.org/uc/item/80n4f1mf

Corporation, I. F. (2019). *Investing for impact: Operating principles for impact management*. Retrieved from https://www.ifc.org/wps/wcm/connect/Topics_Ext_Content/IFC_External_Corporate_Site/Impact-investing/Principles/

Costa, E., & Pesci, C. (2016). Social impact measurement: Why do stakeholders matter? *Sustainability Accounting, Management and Policy Journal, 7*(1), 99–124. https://doi.org/10.1108/SAMPJ-12-2014-0092.

Darby, L., & Jenkins, H. (2006). Applying sustainability indicators to the social enterprise business model: The development and application of an indicator set for Newport Wastesavers, Wales.

International Journal of Social Economics, 33(5/6), 411–431. https://doi.org/10.1108/03068290610660689.
Dufour, B. (2019). Social impact measurement: What can impact investment practices and the policy evaluation paradigm learn from each other? *Research in International Business and Finance, 47*, 18–30. https://doi.org/10.1016/j.ribaf.2018.02.003.
Ebrahim, A., & Rangan, V. K. (2010). Putting the brakes on impact: A contingency framework for measuring social performance. *Academy of Management Proceedings, 2010*(1), 1–6. https://doi.org/10.5465/ambpp.2010.54500944.
Ebrahim, A., & Rangan, V. K. (2014). What impact? *California Management Review, 56*(3), 118–141. https://doi.org/10.1525/cmr.2014.56.3.118.
Ebrahim, A., Battilana, J., & Mair, J. (2014). The governance of social enterprises: Mission drift and accountability challenges in hybrid organizations. *Research in Organizational Behavior, 34*, 81–100. https://doi.org/10.1016/j.riob.2014.09.001.
Emerson, J., Wachowicz, J., & Chun, S. (2000). Social return on investment: Exploring aspects of value creation in the nonprofit sector. In *The box set: Social purpose enterprises venture philanthropy in the new millennium* (Vol. 2, pp. 130–173). San Francisco, CA: The Roberts Foundation.
Freudenburg, W. R. (1986). Social impact assessment. *Annual Review of Sociology, 12*, 451–478.
Gentile, M. (2000). *Social impact management: A definition*. The Aspen Institute Business and Society Program Discussion Paper II. Retrieved from https://assets.aspeninstitute.org/content/uploads/files/content/docs/bsp/SOCIALIMPACTMANAGEMENT.PDF
Gibbon, J., & Dey, C. (2011). Developments in social impact measurement in the third sector: Scaling up or dumbing down? *Social and Environmental Accountability Journal, 31*(1), 63–72. https://doi.org/10.1080/0969160X.2011.556399.
Gray, R. (2010). Is accounting for sustainability actually accounting for sustainability…and how would we know? An exploration of narratives of organisations and the planet. *Accounting, Organizations and Society, 35*(1), 47–62. https://doi.org/10.1016/j.aos.2009.04.006.
Grieco, C. (2015). *Assessing social impact of social enterprises: Does one size really fit all?* Cham: Springer International Publishing.
Haski-Leventhal, D., & Mehra, A. (2016). Impact measurement in social enterprises: Australia and India. *Social Enterprise Journal, 12*(1), 78–103. https://doi.org/10.1108/SEJ-05-2015-0012.
Hatry, H. P. (2013). Sorting the relationships among performance measurement, program evaluation, and performance management. *New Directions for Evaluation, 2013*(137), 19–32. https://doi.org/10.1002/ev.20043.
Hoffman, S. A., & Olazabal, V. M. (2018). The next frontier for measurement and evaluation: Social impact measurement for impact investing and market solutions. *African Evaluation Journal, 6*(2), e1–e3. https://doi.org/10.4102/aej.v6i2.342.
Hoskin, K. (1996). The "awful idea of accountability": Inscribing people into the measurement of objects. In R. Munro & J. Mouritsen (Eds.), *Accountability: Power, ethos and the technologies of managing*. London: International Thomson Business Press.
Hubers, F. (2017). Assessing the impact of social enterprises: An exploration of the methods and criteria used by impact investors and philanthropists in Asia (ACSEP: Social Entrepreneurship in Asia Working Paper No. 6). Retrieved from https://bschool.nus.edu.sg/acsep/wp-content/uploads/sites/19/2018/10/SWP6.pdf
Lall, S. A. (2017). Measuring to improve versus measuring to prove: Understanding the adoption of social performance measurement practices in nascent social enterprises. *Voluntas: International Journal of Voluntary and Nonprofit Organizations, 28*(6), 2633–2657. https://doi.org/10.1007/s11266-017-9898-1.
Lall, S. A. (2019). From legitimacy to learning: How impact measurement perceptions and practices evolve in social Enterprise—Social finance organization relationships. *Voluntas: International Journal of Voluntary and Nonprofit Organizations*, 1–16. https://doi.org/10.1007/s11266-018-00081-5.

Lam, S.-S., Zhang, W., & Jacob, G. H. (2015). The mispricing of socially ambiguous grey stocks. *Finance Research Letters, 13*, 81–89. https://doi.org/10.1016/j.frl.2015.02.010.
Latané, B. (1981). The psychology of social impact. *American Psychologist, 36*(4), 343–356. https://doi.org/10.1037/0003-066X.36.4.343.
Liket, K. C., Rey-Garcia, M., & Maas, K. E. H. (2014). Why aren't evaluations working and what to do about it: A framework for negotiating meaningful evaluation in nonprofits. *American Journal of Evaluation, 35*(2), 171–188. https://doi.org/10.1177/1098214013517736.
Louch, W., Ballard, E., & Clark, S. (2018, February 2). Abraaj investors hire auditor to trace money. *The Wall Street Journal*. Retrieved from https://www.wsj.com/articles/abraaj-investors-hire-auditor-to-trace-money-1517598630
Luke, B., Barraket, J., & Eversole, R. (2013). Measurement as legitimacy versus legitimacy of measures: Performance evaluation of social enterprise. *Qualitative Research in Accounting & Management, 10*(3/4), 234–258. https://doi.org/10.1108/QRAM-08-2012-0034.
Maas, K., & Grieco, C. (2017). Distinguishing game changers from boastful charlatans: Which social enterprises measure their impact? *Journal of Social Entrepreneurship, 8*(1), 110–128. https://doi.org/10.1080/19420676.2017.1304435.
Maas, K., & Liket, K. (2011). Social impact measurement: Classification of methods. In *Environmental management accounting and supply chain management* (pp. 171–202). Cham: Springer.
Meyer, J. W., & Rowan, B. (1977). Institutionalized organizations: Formal structure as myth and ceremony. *American Journal of Sociology, 83*(2), 340–363.
Molecke, G., & Pinkse, J. (2017). Accountability for social impact: A bricolage perspective on impact measurement in social enterprises. *Journal of Business Venturing, 32*(5), 550–568. https://doi.org/10.1016/j.jbusvent.2017.05.003.
Mook, L., Maiorano, J., Ryan, S., Armstrong, A., & Quarter, J. (2015). Turning social return on investment on its head. *Nonprofit Management and Leadership, 26*(2), 229–246. https://doi.org/10.1002/nml.21184.
Morgan, G. G. (2013). Purposes, activities and beneficiaries: Assessing the use of accounting narratives as indicators of third sector performance. *Qualitative Research in Accounting & Management, 10*(3/4), 295–315. https://doi.org/10.1108/QRAM-04-2013-0016.
Mudaliar, A., & Dithrich, H. (2019). *Sizing the impact investing market*. Retrieved from https://thegiin.org/assets/Sizing%20the%20Impact%20Investing%20Market_webfile.pdf
Mudaliar, A., Schiff, H., & Bass, R. (2016). *Annual impact investor survey*. Retrieved from https://thegiin.org/knowledge/publication/annualsurvey2016
Mudaliar, A., Pineiro, A., Bass, R., & Dithrich, H. (2017a). *The state of impact measurement and management practice*. Retrieved from https://thegiin.org/research/publication/imm-survey
Mudaliar, A., Schiff, H., Bass, R., & Dithrich, H. (2017b). *Annual Impact Investor Survey*. Retrieved from https://thegiin.org/research/publication/annualsurvey2017
Mudaliar, A., Bass, R., & Dithrich, H. (2018). *Annual impact investor survey*. Retrieved from https://thegiin.org/research/publication/annualsurvey2018
Mudaliar, A., Bass, R., Dithrich, H., & Nova, N. (2019). *Annual impact investor survey*. Global Impact Investing Network (GIIN). Retrieved from https://thegiin.org/assets/GIIN_2019%20Annual%20Impact%20Investor%20Survey_webfile.pdf
Nations, U. (2019). *We can end poverty: Millennium development goals and beyond 2015*. Retrieved from https://www.un.org/millenniumgoals/
Network, G. I. I. (2019a). *About the GIIN*. Retrieved from https://thegiin.org/about/
Network, G. I. I. (2019b). *Core characteristics of impact investing*. Retrieved from https://thegiin.org/characteristics
Network, G. I. I. (2019c). *IRIS+*. Retrieved from https://iris.thegiin.org/
Network, G. I. I. (2019d). *IRIS+ and the five dimensions of impact*. Retrieved from https://iris.thegiin.org/document/iris-and-the-five-dimensions/
Network, G. I. I. (2019e). *Research*. Retrieved from https://thegiin.org/research
Network, G. I. I. (2019f). *What is impact investing?* Retrieved from https://thegiin.org/impact-investing/need-to-know/#what-is-impact-investing

Nicholls, A. (2018). A general theory of social impact accounting: Materiality, uncertainty and empowerment. *Journal of Social Entrepreneurship, 9*(2), 132–153. https://doi.org/10.1080/19420676.2018.1452785.

Nicholls, A., Paton, R., & Emerson, J. (2015). *Social finance* (1st Edition ed.). Oxford: Oxford University Press.

Ormiston, J., & Seymour, R. (2011). Understanding value creation in social entrepreneurship: The importance of aligning Mission, strategy and impact measurement. *Journal of Social Entrepreneurship, 2*(2), 125–150. https://doi.org/10.1080/19420676.2011.606331.

Owen, F., Li, J., Whittingham, L., Hope, J., Bishop, C., Readhead, A., & Mook, L. (2015). Social return on investment of an innovative employment option for persons with developmental disabilities. *Nonprofit Management and Leadership, 26*(2), 209–228. https://doi.org/10.1002/nml.21187.

Paton, R. (2003). *Managing and measuring social enterprises*. London: Sage.

Primack, D. (2018). *Private equity firm Abraaj Capital is in turmoil*. Retrieved from https://www.axios.com/the-1522167159-8ebfe0cb-7dcd-4385-8a00-27cf68cd39f2.html

Rawhouser, H., Cummings, M., & Newbert, S. L. (2019). Social impact measurement: Current approaches and future directions for social entrepreneurship research. *Entrepreneurship Theory and Practice, 43*(1), 82–115. https://doi.org/10.1177/1042258717727718.

Ruff, K., & Olsen, S. (2018). The need for analysts in social impact measurement: How evaluators can help. *American Journal of Evaluation, 39*(3), 402–407. https://doi.org/10.1177/1098214018778809.

Salazar, J., Husted, B. W., & Biehl, M. (2012). Thoughts on the evaluation of corporate social performance through projects. *Journal of Business Ethics, 105*(2), 175–186. https://doi.org/10.1007/s10551-011-0957-z.

Schaltegger, S., & Burritt, R. (2018). Business cases and corporate engagement with sustainability: Differentiating ethical motivations. *Journal of Business Ethics, 147*(2), 241–259. https://doi.org/10.1007/s10551-015-2938-0.

Spiess-Knafl, W., & Scheck, B. (2017). *Impact investing: Instruments, mechanisms and actors*. Cham: Springer International Publishing.

Taskforce, S. I. I. (2014). *Measuring impact: Subject paper of the impact measurement working group*. Retrieved from https://gsgii.org/reports/measuring-impact/

Swee-Sum Lam

Education 2016–2018: PhD (Theology), Durham University, St. John's College, UK; 1984–1988: Phd (Finance), University of Washington, USA; 1974–1977: B.Accountancy (Honors), Singapore University, Singapore.

Professional Qualifications 2004: Fellow CPA, Institute of Certified Public Accountants of Singapore, ICPA; 1995: CFA, Chartered Financial Analyst Institute, USA.

Professional Appointments 2019–present: Member, Scientific Committee, Geneva Centre for Philanthropy, University of Geneva; 2019:—Chairperson, Academic Committee, ISTR 2019 Asia Pacific Regional Conference, Bangkok, Thailand; 2015-present: Director, Asian Pastoral Institute; 2014–2020: Member, Income Tax Board of Review, Singapore; 2011–2020: Director, Asia Centre for Social Entrepreneurship and Philanthropy (ACSEP), NUS Business School, National University of Singapore; 1983–2020: Associate Professor of Finance, National University of Singapore; 2002:—Visiting scholar with Anderson School of Management, UCLA; 2001: Visiting scholar with Johnson School of Management, Cornell University; 1999–2001:

Vice-Dean (Academic Affairs, Finance & Administration), Faculty of Business Administration, National University of Singapore; 1998: Visiting scholar with the Swiss Institute of Banking and Finance, University of St. Gallen, Switzerland.

Xiang Ru Amy Tan

Education: Master of Social Sciences (Sociology), Faculty of Arts and Social Sciences, National University of Singapore.

Professional Experience: Research Associate, Centre for Ageing Research and Education (CARE), Duke-NUS Medical School, 2019—present. Research Associate, Asia Centre for Social Entrepreneurship & Philanthropy (ACSEP), NUS Business School, National University of Singapore, 2018–2019.

Selected Publications: Lam, S. S. & Tan, Xiang Ru Amy. (2020). Understanding social impact and how to measure it, in Gandhi, Oktoviano and Srinivasan, Dipti (Ed.), *Sustainable Energy Solutions for Remote Areas in the Tropics*. Green Energy and Technology series, Springer Nature. Tan, Xiang Ru Amy. (2016). Bloggers, Critics and Photographers in the Mediation of Food Consumption, in Lily Kong and Vineeta Sinha (Ed.), *Food, Foodways and Foodscapes: Culture, Community and Consumption in Post-Colonial Singapore* Singapore: World Scientific Publishing.

Social Reporting Standard (SRS): Making Social Impact Visible

Barbara Scheck

Abstract Social purpose organizations regularly assess and document the results of their work for a variety of stakeholders, such as funders or partners. However, so far, no standardized, generally accepted set of metrics or frameworks exists on how to derive a meaningful statement about the realized societal change. Consequently, social impact assessment remains a major obstacle and roadblock for the development of the social finance field. There is no consensus on what impact is, how it should be measured, or even the process by which metrics that matter could be developed. The Social Reporting Standard (SRS) has been developed roughly 10 years ago in Germany as one way and a first step to collect and account for information on social impact in a structured way and constitutes a standardized reporting tool with multiple possibilities for application.

Keywords Theory of change · Theories of change · Social reporting standard (SRS) · Making social impact visible · SRS · Impact reporting · Impact investing · Sustainable development goals · SDGs

1 Introduction

Social purpose organizations regularly assess and document the results of their work for a variety of stakeholders, such as funders or partners. However, so far, no standardized, generally accepted set of metrics or frameworks exists on how to derive a meaningful statement about the realized societal change. Consequently, social impact assessment remains a major obstacle and roadblock for the development of the social finance field. There is no consensus on what impact is, how it should be measured, or even the process by which metrics that matter could be developed. The Social Reporting Standard (SRS) has been developed roughly 10 years ago in Germany as one way and a first step to collect and account for information on social impact in a structured way and constitutes a standardized reporting tool with multiple possibilities for application.

B. Scheck (✉)
European Center for Social Finance, Munich Business School, Munich, Germany
e-mail: Barbara.Scheck@munich-business-school.de

K. Wendt (ed.), *Theories of Change*, Sustainable Finance,
https://doi.org/10.1007/978-3-030-52275-9_7

2 The Importance of Impact Reporting

Reporting is an instrument of information for external resource providers of a firm, mostly for investors regarding their financial resources. This information is economic information in the sense that it relates to the status and flow of scarce resources. This so-called decision-usefulness paradigm assumes that resource allocation will be more efficient when rational economic decisions are made possible (Jensen and Meckling 1976; Fama and Jensen 1983). In order to reduce potential conflicts due to different levels and types of information (e.g., between an investors and a social venture), reporting is used to standardize the communication between the parties and demonstrate accountability of management. Without standard and verifiable information that investors can trust, many social purpose organizations will to continue to struggle with the professional documentation of their work. A generally applied reporting could thus contribute to a more transparent investment universe, increase the quality as well as the quantity of investments in the social sector and ultimately lead to a more efficient capital allocation (GIIN 2016; Kramer 2005; Nicholls 2005).

Having said this, it is important to consider that the primary objective and defining characteristic of social purpose organizations is social impact. Traditional measurement and reporting systems used by commercially driven businesses that focus on operating performance and financial return are therefore not applicable to depict this different purpose. Consequently, a new tool needed to be developed reflecting the organizations' objectives. Like traditional reporting standards, the SRS does not value or rate the reported information, but aims to establish a common language and information structure as well as provide an easy-to-use framework for social purpose organizations to adopt impact management.

3 What Is Impact?

Any type of business has a social impact. The most prominent feature of social businesses is, however, the focus on intended positive social change. Unfortunately, a standard definition of impact does not exist yet. The way SRS thinks about impact can be depicted along the so-called impact value chain (synonymously also called I-O-O-I model, an abbreviation of the first letter of each step in the process; see also glossary (Table 1) at the end of this chapter; OECD/DAC (2000)):

- Inputs are all types of resources the organization uses, esp. financial resources, but also in-kind contribution or voluntary support.
- Outputs are the immediate consequences or results of the inputs, easily measurable or quantifiable.
- Outcomes are short- and medium-term changes in the lives of the target group. Outcomes coincide with the project goal or objective, and can still be causally and quantitatively attributed to the project.
- Impacts are long-term changes that occur during the lifetime of one project and/or after the project. Impacts go beyond the target group and therefore can be viewed as a change in society as a whole.

Table 1 Overview terminology (own depiction based on Wörrlein/Scheck (2016); GECES Sub-group on Impact Measurement 2014; Social Impact Investment Task Force 2014)

Activities	Actions, programs or projects the organization carries out.
Additionality	Referring to the extent to which an investment has made a difference and has resulted in change.
Attribution	Deducting the effect achieved by the contribution and activity of others.
Base case	Identifies what would have happened without the intervention and serves as a starting point for determining the additionality of an intervention.
Counterfactual	Measures what would have happened to beneficiaries in the absence of the intervention, often by means of a control group.
Deadweight	Changes that would have happened anyway, regardless of the intervention.
Displacement	Assessment of how much of the outcome has displaced other outcomes
Drop-off	Allowing for the decreasing effect of an intervention over time.
Impact	Long-term effects of interventions that go beyond the primary beneficiaries and reach additional target groups such as communities and families or that lead to changes on an institutional level.
Impact value chain	Illustration and logical link between inputs, activities, output, outcome and impact.
Input	Resources used in delivery of the intervention, these can be time, money or in-kind.
Materiality	Data that is of such relevance and importance that it could substantively influence the assessments of providers of financial capital with regard to the organization's ability to create value over the short-, medium, and long term.
Outcome	Social effect (change), both long-term and short-term achieved for the target beneficiaries as a result of the intervention undertaken.
Output	The tangible results from the intervention, effectively the points at which the services delivered enter the lives of those affected by them, expressed e.g., in terms of people reached, products or services.
Theory of change	The means (or causal chain) by which activities achieve outputs and outcomes, and use resources (inputs) in doing that.

If an organization would also report on measures of effectiveness, it can set outputs, outcomes and impacts in relation to input or in relation to pre-set goals.

SRS requires organizations to detail the link between the invested resources and the achieved societal change (the so-called causality and attribution). Whereas some organizations seek to explain this link through a narrative, it can also be reported by any existing impact measurement method. The essential requirement is, however, that the organization has to report on impact and cannot leave this chapter blank.

4 The Structure of the Social Reporting Standard

SRS is divided into sections A, B and C. Section A gives an overview by presenting the organization's vision and offering for its target groups. In section B, the detailed presentation of the offer forms the core of the impact reporting. By "offer" SRS means what an organization does to solve a social or environmental problem—such

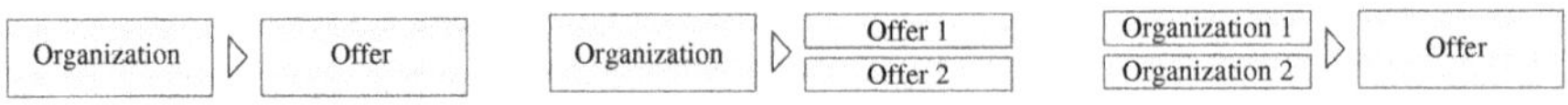

Fig. 1 Application possibilities for the Social Reporting Standard. Source: SRI e.v. (2019)

as distinct programs, projects or services. Organizational information, such as team, structure or finances is given in section C.

The framework allows to report on single or several offers, the entire organization or joint offerings by multiple organizations (Fig. 1):

Single activity reports should complete all parts (A to C) once, multiple activity reports should complete sections A and C once, and section B repeatedly for each individual activity. Joint reports by several organizations should complete section B once, and sections A and C repeatedly for each organization.

In each section, detailed instructions specify the information required to meet the standard, and examples guide users on how to collate and report the information. Sections that don't require annual updates, such as organizational structure, are highlighted to improve efficiency for repeat users.

Organizations are free to use whatever media or format (e.g., tables, diagrams, illustrations or organizational charts) suits their reporting purpose. Those seeking additional guidance can download templates and examples at www.social-reporting-standard.de/en. In addition, videos and other material is available for free for additional learning.

5 Limitations

While providing a common language and a standardized structure to inform about impact, SRS does not require a quantitative assessment of societal change in its guidelines. The purpose of it is to enable as many organizations as possible to use the framework, and is the result of the lack of an agreed-upon common measurement framework. Although this impedes absolute comparability between projects and organizations, SRS suggests a standardized reporting as a first step towards improved comparability.

In addition, the consortium promoting the standard (Universität Hamburg, TU Munich, Ashoka, Auridis, Vodafone Stiftung, Phineo, BonVenture, PricewaterhouseCoopers) has experienced that a useful application requires a certain degree of knowledge and interpretation on part of the report reader. Moreover, reporting can only be one part of impact management—other activities, such as planning and monitoring, are also necessary to put organizations on the path towards holistic impact management (EVPA 2013).

6 Conclusion and Outlook

In the roughly 10 years SRS has been applied in Germany, but also many other countries (the framework is currently available in German, English, Spanish, Polish, Turkish, French and Hungarian), the following insights have been generated.

By following a standardized and transparent process of logical steps to systematically report about achieved changes, SRS guides social purpose organizations through the assessment process and provides a basis for more structured discussions along the impact value chain. Consequently, many organizations had increasing success in fundraising along with a better visibility of their contributions to society. Equally if not even more important, organizations have used the framework and its results for quality improvement of their services and, lastly, as a tool for organizational development.

SRS has engaged many parties across the social finance field; this diversity of thought has proven to be invaluable in delivering meaningful results. The standard is provided to the public as an open-source framework. It might not be the silver bullet that will eliminate all issues related to impact management. However, we are confident that it can provide first steps in reporting in a systematic way about the social performance of social purpose organizations. It will take additional work to overcome the challenges linked to impact management to further strengthen the social finance system.

References

EVPA. (2013). *A practical guide to measuring and managing impact*. European Venture Philanthropy Association.

Fama, E. F., & Jensen, M. C. (1983). Separation of ownership and control. *Journal of Law & Economics, 26*(2), 301–326.

GECES Sub-group on Impact Measurement. (2014). *Proposed approaches to social impact measurement in European Commission legislation and in practice relating to EuSEFs and the EaSI*.

Global Impact Investing Network (GIIN). (2016). *The business value of impact measurement*. New York: Global Impact Investing Network.

Jensen, M. C., & Meckling, W. H. (1976). Theory of the firm: Managerial behavior, agency costs and ownership structure. *Journal of Financial Economics, 3*(4), 305–360.

Kramer, M. (2005). *Measuring innovation: Evaluation in the field of social entrepreneurship*. Boston: Foundation Strategy Group.

Nicholls, A. (2005). Measuring impact in social entrepreneurship: New accountability to stakeholders and investors? In *ESRC Research Seminar, April 2005*. London: Local Government Research Unit.

Organisation for Economic Cooperation and Development/The Development Assistance Committee [OECD/DAC]. (2000). *Results based management in the development co-operation agencies: a review of experience*. Retrieved from http://www.oecd.org/dac/evaluation/dcdndep/31950681.pdf

Social Impact Investment Task Force. (2014). *Measuring impact. Subject paper of the impact measurement working group*. Social Impact Investment Taskforce. Established under the UK's presidency of the G8.
Social Reporting Initiative (SRI) e.V. (2019). *Social reporting standard* (Version 2014).
Wörrlein, L., & Scheck, B. (2016). Performance management in the third sector: A literature-based analysis of terms and definitions. *Public Administration Quarterly, 40*(2), 220–255.

Barbara Scheck is the Professor for Entrepreneurship at Munich Business School. Her research focuses on the financing of social enterprises, impact and mission-related investing and impact assessment. Prior to joining MBS, Barbara was assistant professor for social investment at Hamburg University. During her Ph.D. she has developed the Social Reporting Standard, guidelines for impact-oriented reporting. Other significant experiences include consulting for a social venture capital fund and projects for development cooperation agencies on social entrepreneurship. She was a Visiting Fellow at the Asia Centre for Social Entrepreneurship & Philanthropy at NUS National University of Singapore and is a co-founder of the digital mentoring platform Volunteer Vision. Barbara was a member of the EU's GECES subgroup on impact measurement in social enterprise and the Impact Measurement Working Group of the Social Impact Investment Task Force established by the G8. She serves on the board of Hylea Foods and is member of the investment committee at GLS Treuhand.

Barbara Scheck holds a Diplôme de Grande Ecole and MSc from the European School of Management where she studied International Business Administration in Paris, Oxford and Berlin and a PhD from Technical University Munich.

Clustering of Negative Criteria: A Pragmatic Approach for the Implementation of SRI

Tobias Peylo and Bernhard Villhauer

Abstract In the Status Quo, Socially Responsible Investment (SRI) is still a niche strategy. While many investors are drawn to the concept, there are hurdles that prevent them from actually applying it. In the literature, both the fear of an underperformance and the lack of easily accessible standards have been addressed at large. From consulting experience, we highlight another problem: Especially with negative screening, some criteria are apt to result in fruitless and fundamental discussions that have led to the abortion of many SRI implementation processes especially in smaller organizations. This results from the fact that negative or exclusion criteria are drawn from different contexts and origins and may not be applicable to all investors. We thus propose a simple but differentiated system of criteria that is linked to the Sustainable Development Goals and can be used without the requirement of SRI professionals, giving small institutional investors a pragmatic and easy access to SRI implementation.

Keywords Socially responsible investment (SRI) · SRI-implementation · SRI criteria · SRI management · Exclusion criteria · Sustainable investment · Sustainable investing · Clustering · Theory of change · Theories of change · SDGs · Sustainable development goals

1 Introduction

In the last decades, SRI has been established as an investment style of its own. It comprises a set of methodologies to select and manage financial investments in the capital markets from a more comprehensive perspective. The idea behind SRI is to

T. Peylo (✉)
University of Applied Sciences, Kempten, Germany
e-mail: tobias.peylo@hs-kempten.de

B. Villhauer
Weltethos-Institut (World Ethos Institute), University of Tübingen, Tübingen, Germany
e-mail: villhauer@weltethos-institut.org

K. Wendt (ed.), *Theories of Change*, Sustainable Finance,
https://doi.org/10.1007/978-3-030-52275-9_8

enhance the investment process with information about the corporate sustainability of the financed companies, reflecting the impact of their strategies, products and production processes on the social and environmental spheres (Statman 2007). With mostly regional or notional differences, it is also known as Sustainable Investment, Triple Bottom Line Investment, ESG-investment (referring to the terminology of Environmental, Social and Governance criteria which are often used as a synonym for sustainability) or Ethical Investment (for a comprehensive terminology see Eccles and Viviers 2011).

The consideration of corporate sustainability in the investment process can prove beneficial from a material point of view—especially given the fact that corporate sustainability has become a noteworthy factor of influence in real economy with consequences on many corporate functions (Beckmann and Schaltegger 2014) including especially but not exclusively production processes and supply chains (Seuring and Müller 2008; Burritt and Schaltegger 2014). As a driver for innovation and aspect of corporate reputation (Peylo and Schaltegger 2010), corporate sustainability forms an integral part of the complex system of opportunities and risks companies are facing (Gramlich 2013).

Enhancing or even replacing material considerations, the integration of corporate sustainability in the investment process is often motivated by internal motives, based on ethics, moral, responsibility and ideals (Beal et al. 2005). While in the origin of SRI this perspective did have a strong link to religion and ethics (Sparkes 2006), nowadays the conceptual idea of sustainable development as defined by the Brundtland Commission (Hauff 1987) and more recently by the concept of the 17 Sustainable Development Goals (SDG) formulated by the United Nations (2018) and the Paris climate accord (COP21) often prevails as driver for the objective of the implementation of SRI in the investment process.

Presently, the initiative of the European Union (2018) to foster SRI—in this context termed Sustainable Investment—is apt to change the concept in several ways. Most importantly, its character as an unsolicited process driven by either material or ethical motives and hence personal persuasion is likely to be transformed into a matter of regulation and compliance. Despite the fact that this transformation bears complications of its own, it could deem SRI as a feasible instrument of effectively steering funds into a sustainable development. While this channeling of funds was at the central core of SRI all along, the new regulation could now provide a monetary volume that was only believed to be achievable by the most optimistic of advocates.

To substantiate the scope of optimism required until now, a mere glance at market shares will suffice. Despite its many benefits and the huge, yet largely untapped potential to contribute to a sustainable development, the status quo of SRI is largely disappointing. It is true that SRI has become an important element of finance market discussion all over the world for quite some time now, but the outcome in terms of investment effects and products is still that of a niche strategy. Especially in Germany which in other ways is certainly no stranger to the concept of sustainability, a lot of investors are yet to be convinced about SRI. This is not only true in hindsight to quantitative indicators like its diminutive market share—which according to Forum Nachhaltige Geldanlagen in Germany is only 2.8% of assets invested (FNG 2017). It is also true from a practitioner's perspective, where due to the enduring lack of standards and accepted recommendations each and every SRI-implementation project equals the repeated re-invention of the wheel.

As it is often the case in times of change, a crystal ball with the ability to look into the future would be most appreciated. Lacking this handy instrument, there always is the option to patiently wait for the regulation to crawl its way into practice and to hope that everything will turn to the best on its own. In this short chapter, however, we like to look at a third option, which is to define central problems at its core and to propose pragmatic ways to overcome them—independent but compatible to a regulation yet to come.

The major problem that we address is the lack of acceptance and impetus of SRI in Germany in the status quo. In order to identify the obstacles causing it, we are going to focus on project experience at investors that normally would be considered born advocates of SRI: public sector institutions and regional banks in Germany. As both are native agents of the idea of public welfare and hence sustainability, to scrutinize why many of them do not adhere to SRI in their investments processes is apt to reveal those problems of the concept that prevent even the willing from implementation. True to this idea, we have identified a significant stumbling block that have caused many initiatives in this field to fail.

2 Defining the Problem

There is no standard approach to implement SRI. Instead, methodology is divers and applies screens, filters and specially developed SRI rating systems. In a simplified distinction, both the underlying motivation of the investors and the methodology available can be separated into two pillars: "Avoiding the bad" and "fostering the good".

Thereby the "bad" refers to aspects of stock- and bond-emitting companies that are not compatible with the concept of sustainability, it is identified by the application of negative screens (e.g. Dillenburg et al. 2003; Lee et al. 2010).

The "good" comprises the investment in companies that are positive examples with regard to their implementation of sustainability-related objectives in their strategies, products or production processes (here, especially the focus on the start-up scene becomes more and more relevant). To implement this second pillar, there are several different approaches: Positive screening can be based on individual research, ESG-Ratings, the inclusion of securities into SRI-indices or the selection of categories of financial products like e.g. green bonds (e.g. Sullivan and Mackenzie 2006; Hill et al. 2007).

As an alternative, best-in-class or best-of-class approaches substitute the absolute decision of screens by a comparative assessment: Here SRI ratings are used to evaluate the position of a company or industry relative to its peers in order to channel the investment into "best practice approaches" within their respective frame conditions and boundaries (Schueth 2003; Benson et al. 2006; Statman 2007). Meanwhile the range of rating products has immensely increased and

cases, publically available lists of negative criteria are used instead as a starting point.

These lists are retrieved from the internet or from relevant books or journals. And they are, despite all good intentions, likely to cause serious problems. Indeed, different studies show that investors are confused about the value and significance of negative criteria as well as their impact in terms of sustainability (Bos 2014; Foltin et al. 2015). Especially problematic is the fact, that the lists constitute an amalgamation of criteria originating from a multitude of sources and thus very different contexts. All are associated with either social or ecological problems, but depending on the personal viewpoints they may not all be applicable to the context of the respective investor.

This is especially true for criteria with a religious context, that can be traced back to the origins of SRI as an ethical investment with calivinstic background (Sparkes 2006; Diefenbacher et al. 2008). Indeed, many lists of negative criteria for the exclusion of 'bad investments' that are publically available and thus often used in SRI implementation projects have been set up and discussed, for example in the field of church banks or religious institutions. Here, Bassler and Wulsdorf (2016) give an synoptic overview about the positions in Catholicism and Protestantism which make it easy for the investor to identify a "Christian investment".

While there are considerable overlaps between Christian ethic and sustainability, this is not true for all criteria involved. In the contemporary society, religious beliefs tend to be perceived as less important as in the past. But most importantly, in a pluralist world, the concept of sustainability is not shaped by a particular belief but refers to a wider understanding of social or ecological responsibility as it is reflected in the SDG's or climate goals.

A prominent example to highlight the resulting conflict is the exclusion of alcohol. While its banishment and exclusion is firmly embedded in the calvinistic view of the world, this criterion has led to serious, often fundamental debates in many SRI implementation processes. Without question the perils of alcohol-induced violence or alcoholism as an important health hazard are important social considerations. However, many forms of alcohol are part of the fabric of western European society. Considering both winemakers and breweries, one can find very positive examples and even pioneers of the sustainable economy. To give an example, the family-owned brewery Härle in Leutkirch has even been awarded the "Deutscher Nachhaltigkeitspreis" (German Sustainability Prize) in recognition of their exemplary ecological commitment (Brauerei Härle 2018). So how can companies like this—should they be listed—be defined as unsustainable and excluded from all investment considerations? It is easy to understand that such debates are likely to cause a great divide in the board meetings preceding the introduction of negative screening.

Another example, though not religiously motivated, is the exclusion of nuclear power plants. Here, the discussion whether their climate-friendly aspects or the risks involved are more dominant is often pursued in a rather radical manner, with both sides having highly principled advocates.

To give a third and final example, the exclusion of banned/controversial weapon systems is an accepted negative criterion that is very seldom debated. However it is a very different case with the exclusion of armaments in general. In SRI-implementation projects in a communal context, it often is feared that this exclusion could shed bad light on e.g. the local hunting-arms industry. With SRI projects in regional banks it could mean the loss of a long lasting customer relationship.

To sum it up, criteria like these are likely to cause strong emotions and enflame the advisory board-members in every implementation project, and they are not likely to find an easy consensus.

Interestingly, in situations like these it is an exception rather than the rule that only those criteria are implemented that find an easy consensus. More often a crisis evolves in the project. This is helped by the fact that prefabricated lists of negative criteria often give the impression that they have to be taken or disregarded as a whole. Consequently, in many cases the alienation caused by the debates leads towards a situation where the complete process is stopped or indefinitely postponed.

Thus a combination of awkwardness, emotional involvement and dissent regarding only a few criteria from a large, intermixed selection can be identified as one of the main hurdles to overcome when implementing SRI in small or medium sized companies or organizations. It is, however, a problem easily solved with a pragmatic solution.

3 Clustering Criteria: Because One Size Does Not Fit All

As we have argued above, many projects of SRI-integration are stalled and eventually abandoned in the wake of long and fruitless discussions concerning but a very few points—while about many other criteria there would have been a widespread agreement from the beginning. Thus it is not only the lack of standardization (as it is argued by EU 2018), but also the lack of the structuring of SRI criteria that causes many SRI-implementation projects to fail.

In the status quo, most sets of negative criteria do not recognize or highlight different levels of importance or impact—despite the fact that there is an obvious difference between criteria resulting from human rights or the UN on the one hand and criteria, that are based on individual ethics and beliefs on the other. There are approaches to differentiate between value-based and norm-based exclusions (FNG 2018), which are a helpful first step with hindsight to differentiation. We argue however, that this distinction is not sufficient, because between the value-based criteria a high degree of amalgamation still remains. There should be a distinction, for example, between the exclusion of gambling and the exploitation of child labor. Without further distinction the phenomenon of a processual stalemate due to different opinions concerning the value and impact of the criteria will still remain.

We thus propose a simple but effective building block-oriented approach that is strongly focused on the practitioners use. Drawing on an aggregation of publically available sets of negative criteria, we cluster them into three distinctive sets of

- MUST-Criteria,
- SHOULD-Criteria and
- CAN-Criteria.

Here, MUST-Criteria should only include legally binding or highly intercultural and interreligious accepted criteria. SHOULD-Criteria can be considered disputable from a legal perspective, but are intercultural und interreligious mostly accepted as having a strong (negative) connection to the goal of a sustainable development. CAN-Criteria, lastly, are not legally regulated but do cause affronts or disputes within specific cultural or religious contexts.

This distinction, of course, needs a guideline to what constitutes intercultural and interreligious accepted standards. While, sadly, the SDG's in their present formulation do not have many references to investments—which is quite astonishing because their success depends on the availability of ESG-motivated financing—they do represent a differentiated, common guideline to what should be achieved within the context of sustainability. Therefore we propose to use the SDG's as an orientation and guideline for the attribution of negative-criteria to the three clusters.

Here, as presented in Fig. 1, the MUST-Criteria should have the highest overlap with the SDG's with each following clusters allowing for a less tight fit.

With this three-level approach towards the use of negative criteria, institutions can start their SRI implementation process with a minimum of discussions, implementing only the first level at the beginning. Other criteria-clusters can later be added if sufficient agreement can be reached—if not, at the very least a low-level implementation of SRI has been reached successfully and the project has had at least a small impact.

Fig. 1 Overlap between negative criteria and SDG's

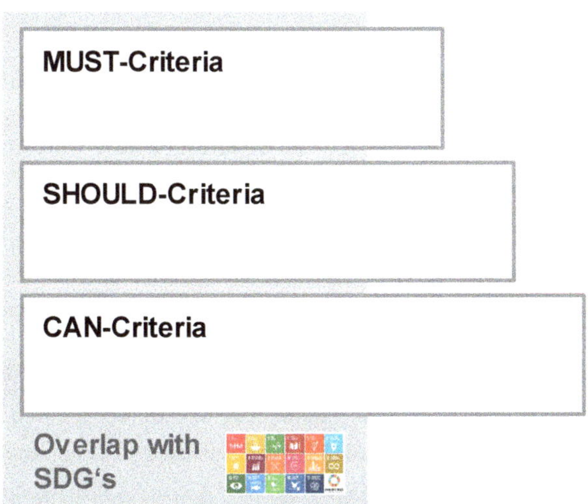

This approach is likely to help especially those institutions that strive to implement SRI on their own without professional guidance or access to professional information tools. The basic idea is to strive for the lowest common denominator in order to prevent fundamental discussions from destroying the process at an early stage.

In order to produce a first draft of this proposed clustering, we have summarized publically available criteria that are commonly used in the literature (e.g. Foltin 2014), prefabricated exclusion lists (e.g. from clerical organizations), ESG indexes, ESG rating systems and investments funds associated with SRI. While this list of criteria is not complete, it presents a good example of criteria available in standard SRI implementation processes where organizations have neither the time, desire nor knowledge to sort out and decide what might be useful or adequate for their respective investment strategy.

As an important notice, we have made no distinction between criteria that are used as exclusions (meaning they are not allowed into the portfolio at all) or as a negative criteria (meaning they are only allowed up to a predefined share of the portfolio) in the respective SRI instruments. However this distinction naturally is considered by the attribution of criteria towards the three clusters must, should or can.

When dividing the criteria into the three clusters, we have also considered the frequency with which the criteria occur in state-of-the-art SRI instruments, emitting criteria that are very seldom used (e.g. the production of water bottles).

In order to further highlight the motivation behind the attribution of the criteria, in Table 1 we do not only list the criteria within the three clusters but also add the reason why it should be considered a major concern, with the number and importance of concerns also guiding the attribution to the respective clusters. Here it should be noted that the term "legal" does not only refer to country-specific laws, but also to valid international norms and agreements (e.g. ILO norms and of course the human rights). This wide definition is, like all other aspects of the concept, open to discussion. We simply strife to reduce complexity in order to produce a user-friendly tool.

If there are criteria that are unequivocally handled within the same origin of concerns (like the rights of women in different religions) or dependent on thresholds (like the differentiation concerning Embryonic Research), this is indicated with an "x" in parentheses instead of a plain "x". Criteria that only apply to investments in Government Bonds are market have the enhancement "countries" in parentheses.

In line with the normal use of negative criteria in the SRI screening process, Table 1 gives an overview over the three clusters of criteria to be used when deciding about investments in companies and organizations.

With these clusters, the implementation process in organizations and companies can focus on the three following, easily applicable steps:

- Agree that no investments concerning MUST-Criteria should be added to the portfolios. With existing investments, an exit-strategy should be formulated with respect to other relevant factors.

Table 1 Clusters of negative criteria for companies and countries

	Negative/exclusion criteria	Origin of concern				Related SDG
		Legal	Social/ cultural	Environmental	Ethical/ religious	
Must-criteria	Banned/controversial Weapons	x	x		x	16
	Breaches of ILO conventions Exploitation of child labor	x	x		x	8.7, 16.2
	Breaches of Geneva Convention (countries)	x	x		x	–
	Discrimination of women	x	x		(x)	5.1
	Corruption	x	x		x	16.5
	Human rights violations	x	x		x	16.3
	Land grabbing (countries)	x	x		x	1.4
	Protection of species CITES violations	x		x	x	15.5
	Violation of environmental Laws and standards	x		x	x	15
Should-criteria	Abortion	(x)	x		x	–
	Biocides and pesticides		x	x		12.4
	Chlorine based chemicals And agrochemicals		x	x		12.4
	Death penalty (countries)		x		x	2
	Embryonic research	(x)	x		x	–
	Food speculation		x		x	2
	Fossile energy			x		13
	Genetic engineering		x	x		2.5
	Nuclear power		x	x		7.2
	Tobacco		x	x	x	–
Can-criteria	Adult entertainment		x		x	–
	Animal testing			x	x	–
	Alcohol		(x)		x	3.5
	Armaments				x	16.1
	Controversial environmental Behavior			x		15.5
	Fossile energy based Traffic and transportation			x		13

(continued)

Table 1 (continued)

Negative/exclusion criteria	Origin of concern				Related SDG
	Legal	Social/ cultural	Environmental	Ethical/ religious	
Gambling		x		x	–
Lack of consumer protection	(x)	x		x	–
Lobbying against Environmental standards			x		15
Non-ratification of Kyoto Protocol (countries)			x		13
Not certified forestry			x		15.2
Not certified fishery			x		14.4
Palmoil			x		–
Production in totalitarian Dictatorial countries		x	x		1.4
PVC			x		–
Totalitarian regimes (countries)		x		x	1.4

- Discuss whether and to which extent SHOULD-Criteria should be considered and used. These criteria can also be used to define strict limits, up to which share assets with reference to these criteria can be added to the portfolio. This step can also be postponed and be implemented after some experience with the previous step has been gained.
- Discuss whether and to which extent CAN-Criteria should be considered and used. These criteria can also be used to define less strict limits, up to which share assets with reference to these criteria can be added to the portfolio. This step can also be postponed and be implemented after some experience with the previous two steps has been gained.

Following these three steps, the first pillar of SRI ("avoiding the bad") has been implemented to a reasonable degree.

The adherence to this process is apt to enable more SRI implementations that are both manageable und impact-focused. However, the handling of criteria to "avoid the bad" should not be keep from "doing the good". This is why afterwards a differentiated discussion about the desired positive focus would be recommendable. It is, however, not within the scope of this chapter.

4 Conclusion and Perspectives

In this chapter, we have focused on the handling of negative criteria because we have found this aspect of the SRI implementation process as both difficult and hazardous especially for small or medium sized organizations.

Therefore, we have proposed a pragmatic, easy-to-use tool that tries to untangle the amalgamation of the negative criteria available. It allows a simple step by step process starting with the implementation of criteria that are beyond discussion with the option (but not the necessity) to enlarge this scope in the future. We argue that for many organizations and companies to start the implementation process with a high degree of consensus will make it much easier to achieve results and keep the process going and alive.

Despite all due considerations, the attribution of criteria to the three clusters and thus their valuation remains arbitrary. Thus our concept should be considered to be an impulse and not a final recommendation. With it, we hope to contribute to the ongoing discussions concerning the taxonomy and standardization of SRI and Sustainable Investment. The concept is open for discussion on all levels, as it focusses on pragmatic first steps—always following the persuasion that small steps achieved are better than large steps postponed.

We are sure that the concept will profit from the discussion with expert groups and are planning to evaluate and enhance it accordingly—with the aim to finalize it into an accepted, easy to use instrument that could prove most helpful to guide SRI implementation processes. It could then as well be used within the pragmatic conceptualization of SRI-products for the target groups concerned.

References

Bassler, K., & Wulsdorf, H. (2016). *Ethisch-nachhaltige Geldanlage. Die Positionen der evangelischen und katholischen Kirche. Eine Synopse*. Dortmund: ECOreporter.

Beal, D. J., Goyen, M., & Phillips, P. (2005). Why do we invest ethically? *The Journal of Investing, 14*(3), 66–77.

Beckmann, M., & Schaltegger, S. (2014). Unternehmerische Nachhaltigkeit (Corporate sustainability). In H. Heinrichs & G. Michelsen (Eds.), *Nachhaltigkeitswissenschaften (Sciences of sustainability)* (pp. 321–367). Berlin: Springer Spektrum.

Benson, K. L., Brailsford, T. J., & Humphrey, J. E. (2006). Do socially responsible fund managers really invest differently? *Journal of Business Ethics, 63*(2), 131–148.

Bos, J. (2014). Integrating ESG factors in the investment process. *CFA Institute Magazine, 25*(1), 15–16.

Brauerei Härle. (2018). *Umweltengagement*. Retrieved March 10, 2018, from https://www.haerle.de/5.html

Burritt, R., & Schaltegger, S. (Eds.). (2014). Accounting for sustainability in production and supply chains. *The British Accounting Review, 46*(4), 323–326. Elsevier, Amsterdam.

Diefenbacher, H., Foltin, O., & Teichert, V. (2008). Ethisches Investment und die Rolle der Kirchen – eine Einführung in den Sachstand und erste Empfehlungen. In: Th Begrich (ed.), *Stand und Perspektiven ethischen Investments in der evangelischen Kirche*, epd-Dokumentation (37), pp. 10–24.

Dillenburg, S., Greene, T., & Erekson, O. H. (2003). Approaching socially responsible investment with a comprehensive rating scheme: Total social impact. *Journal of Business Ethics, 43*(3), 167–177.

Eccles, N. S., & Viviers, S. (2011). The origins and meanings of names describing investment practices that integrate a consideration of ESG issues in the academic literature. *Journal of Business Ethics, 104*(3), 389–402.

European Union. (2018). *Sustainable finance: Commission's Action Plan for a greener and cleaner economy*. Retrieved March 15, 2018, from https://ec.europa.eu/clima/news/sustainable-finance-commissions-action-plan-greener-and-cleaner-economy_en

Foltin, O. (2014). *Methoden der Bewertung und Messung der Nachhaltigkeit von ethischen, sozialen und ökologischen Kapitalanlagen. Am Beispiel des Anlageverhaltens der Kirchen in Deutschland*. Marburg: Metropolis.

Foltin, O., Gunkel, T., Jüttner, D., & Nußbaumer, L. (2015). *Studie zur Bewertung von nachhaltigen Kapitalanlagen*. Heidelberg: FEST.

Forum Nachhaltige Geldanlagen (FNG). (2017). *Marktbericht Nachhaltige Geldanlagen 2016*. Berlin: Deutschland, Österreich und die Schweiz. FNG.

Forum Nachhaltige Geldanlagen (FNG). (2018). *Sustainable investments*. Retrieved March 10, 2018, from https://www.forum-ng.org/en/sustainableinvestments/sustainable-investments.html

Friede, G., Busch, T., & Bassen, A. (2015). ESG and financial performance: Aggregated evidence from more than 2000 empirical studies. *Journal of Sustainable Finance & Investment, 5*(4), 210–233.

Gramlich, D. (2013). Nachhaltigkeit und Risiko – ein Bezugsrahmen aus Sicht der Kreditinstitute. In H. Schäfer & K. Krummrich (Eds.), *Handbuch Nachhaltigkeit* (pp. 227–243). Stuttgart: DSV.

Hauff, V. (Ed.) (1987). *Unsere gemeinsame Zukunft. Weltkommission für Umwelt und Entwicklung* [Our common future. World commission on environment and development]. Greven: Eggenkamp.

Hill, R. P., Ainscough, J. E., Shank, T., & Manullang, D. (2007). Corporate social responsibility and socially responsible investing: A global perspective. *Journal of Business Ethics, 70*(2), 165–174.

Lee, D. D., Humphrey, J. E., Benson, K. L., & Ahn, J. Y. K. (2010). Socially responsible investment fund performance: The impact of screening intensity. *Accounting & Finance, 50* (2), 351–370.

oekom. (2017). *Methodology*. Retrieved December 30, 2017, from http://www.oekom-research.com/index_en.php?content=me-thodic

Orlitzky, M., Schmidt, F. L., & Rynes, S. L. (2003). Corporate social and financial performance. A meta-analysis. *Organization Studies, 24*(3), 403–441.

Peylo, B. T., & Schaltegger, S. (2010). Stakeholder-orientiert Reputationsrisiken managen. Nachhaltigkeitskonzept als solides Fundament. *Betriebswirtschaftliche Blätter, 59*(11), 641–649.

Renneboog, L., Jenke, T. H., & Chedi, Z. (2008). Socially responsible investments: Institutional aspects, performance, and investor behavior. *Journal of Banking and Finance, 32*, 1723–1742.

Schueth, S. (2003). Socially responsible investing in the United States. *Journal of Business Ethics, 43*(3), 189–194.

Seuring, S., & Müller, M. (2008). Core issues in sustainable supply chain management—A Delphi study. *Business Strategy and the Environment, 17*(8), 455–466.

Sparkes, R. (2006). A historical perspective on the growth of socially responsible investment. In R. Sullivan & C. Mackenzie (Eds.), *Responsible investment* (pp. 39–54). Leeds: Greenleaf Publishing.

Statman, M. (2007). Socially responsible investments. *Journal of Investment Consulting, 8*(2), 17–37.

Sullivan, R., & Mackenzie, C. (2006). The practice of responsible investment. In R. Sullivan & C. Mackenzie (Eds.), *Responsible investment* (pp. 332–346). Leeds: Greenleaf Publishing.

United Nations. (2018). *Sustainable development goals—17 goals to transform our world.* Retrieved March 14, 2018, from http://www.un.org/sustainabledevelopment/sustainable-development-goals/

Weber, O., Mansfeld, M., & Schirrmann, E. (2012). The financial performance of RI funds after 2000. In W. Vandekerckhove, J. Leys, K. Alm, B. Scholtens, S. Signori, & H. Schäfers (Eds.), *Responsible investment in times of turmoil.* Heidelberg: Springer.

Prof. Dr. Tobias Peylo is professor for economics and finance at the University of Applied Sciences, Kempten. His main areas of research are portfolio management, green finance and business development in East Africa.

Prior to his professorship, Dr. Peylo was working for several banks and management consultancies. As a consultant at savings bank association Baden-Württemberg, for the last ten years he has been developing strategies and instruments for the implementation of sustainability in regional banks. In this capacity and now as a professor, he has consulted more than 150 regional banks in Germany.

Dr. Peylo has authored several papers and studies concerning SRI and is lecturer for sustainable finance at Leuphana University, Lüneburg.

Bernhard Villhauer is the Managing Director of the Global Ethic Institute (WEIT) at the University of Tübingen since January 2015. After completing an apprenticeship as an industrial clerk, he studied philosophy, classical studies and history of art at the Universities of Freiburg i.Brsg., Jena and Hull (UK). After his PhD thesis on a cultural-philosophical topic (Aby Warburg and Ernst Cassirer) he worked for various companies in the publishing and media sector, most recently as editorial director of the publishing group Narr Francke Attempto. Before that he held positions in the middle management at the publishing houses Mohr Siebeck and Wissenschaftliche Buchgesellschaft (WBG). At the same time, he taught as a lecturer at the universities of Karlsruhe, Jena, Darmstadt and Tübingen. His lectures focused on cultural and media science issues as well as theoretical and practical philosophy and economics. He is co-founder of the Institute for Philosophy of Practice e.V. in Darmstadt. Since the summer 2013 he offers a seminar "Money and Ethics" at the Global Ethic Institute. He is also the initiator of the series "Klüger wirtschaften". His current work focuses on monetary theory, financial ethics and investment, topics he bloggs about in his "Finanz und Eleganz" Blog. Bernd Villhauer is Director of the Good Governance Lab at the European School of Governance (EUSG) and head of the research group "Finanzen und Wirtschaft" at the Weltethos-Institut. He is currently writing a book "Finanzmarkt und Ethik. Eine Einführung".

Part III
Impact Investing

Improving Early Childhood Development in Namibia with Result Based Financing

Daniel Gächter and Martin Suhr

Abstract High quality early childhood education programmes have been proven to create life-long positive learning outcomes among children—especially for those living in low income communities. In Namibia, many children from low-income families have limited access to high quality early education. To address this problem, we are exploring in this article the feasibility to support the launch of a Results Based Project financed through a Social Impact Bond that would provide high impact and quality education to preschool-aged children from low-income communities.

Keywords Impact investing · Result based finance · Social impact bond · Early childhood development · Impact philanthropy · SDG 4 · SDG 5 · Inclusive and equitable education · Learning opportunities for all · Education · Achieve gender equality · Empower all girls · Independent verifier · Theory of change · Theories of change · Sustainable development goals

List of Acronyms

CAFO	Church Alliance for Orphans
ECD	Early Childhood Development
EDF	European Development Fund
EU	European Union
GDP	Gross Domestic Product
IECD	Integrated Early Childhood Development
MoGECW	Ministry of Gender and Child Welfare
MoEAC	Ministry of Education, Arts and Culture
MoF	Ministry of Finance
MoHSS	Ministry of Health and Social Services
NAD/N$	Namibian Dollars
NDP	National Development Plan

D. Gächter (✉) · M. Suhr
Swiss Impact Investing Network, Zug, Switzerland

K. Wendt (ed.), *Theories of Change*, Sustainable Finance,
https://doi.org/10.1007/978-3-030-52275-9_9

NGO	Non-Governmental Organization
NICEF	United Nations Children's Fund
NIECD	National Integrated Early Childhood Development
PP	Pre-Primary
RBF	Result Based Financing
SIB	Social Impact Bond

1 Introduction

High quality early childhood education programmes have been proven to create positive learning outcomes among children—especially those living in low income communities. In Namibia, many children from low-income families have limited access to high quality early education. To address this problem, Fondation Botnar is exploring the feasibility to support the setting up and launch of a Social Impact Bond that would provide high impact and quality education to preschool-aged children from low-income communities. These services are intended to increase school readiness and academic performance and thereby reduce the very high repetition/dropout rates in later years at primary school level. In addition, the Directorates of Education, and other government entities would realize large cost savings due to the reduction in remedial services and related opportunity costs. In the medium term, private business and tertiary institutions would experience an intake of significantly better qualified apprentices and students graduating from secondary school level into apprenticeship or further studies. In order to create common ground the following framework (depicted in Table 1) was developed to align the interests of the partners involved. The framework defined motivations, objectives, the scope of the project regarding geography, target groups and outcome based payment fund.

To explore a result based financing project, an international working group was made up with representatives from the private and public sector, NGOs, foundations and aid organizations. Research and field engagement was led by Instiglio and was supported by various project partners. Interteam provided support for the local engagement. Swiss Impact Finance provided project management and coordination support. There were many other organizations involved in the project like the

Table 1 Framework for result based financing in early childhood development in Namibia

Motivation for Project	Children from low-income families have limited access to high quality early childhood education
Project objectives	• Increase school readiness and academic performance • Maximize and unlock human potential at a critical early stage • Reduce the high repetition rates (around 20%) of first grade students
Geography	Namibia
Issue area	Early childhood education
Outcome payer	Government of Namibia, outcome payer fund

European Union, Lifeline/Childline, the Roger Federer Foundation, UNICEF and many representatives from the different Ministries of Government of Namibia. Last but not least, the Namibian people, who welcomed us warmly and openly.

1.1 ECD Service Landscape and Involved Organization

Implementation of ECD services in Namibia is highly fragmented between 3 line ministries and hence guided by the IECD framework and the NDP5. The objective of the IECD framework is to ensure that all ECD services are comprehensively delivered in a manner that covers all the aspects which affect child development, namely health, education and social security. Oversight and coordination for the implementation of the IECD Framework is provided by the National High Level IECD Coordination Group. The IECD's main role is to ensure better coordination management and development of ECD services in Namibia and to allocate roles and responsibilities to the key ministries involved in the development of children.

The MoGECW leads initiatives aimed at children aged 0–4 years.[1] MoEAC is responsible for services to children aged 5–8 years which is the age of pre-primary and primary education and hence responsible for pre-primary education, and the training and curriculum development for pre-primary. All other aspects related to health and nutrition, among children in ECD facilities and home-based care settings are under purview of the MoHSS. Ministry of Home Affairs has also to be mentioned at this point, as birth registration constitutes the right to access all following relevant public services for a citizen of Namibia. All the above shows a highly fragmented approach to ECD within GRN. Figure 1 is outlining this policy framework influencing the ECD environment in Namibia. It highlights the leading role of the ministries involved, developing the strategic plans based on Namibian legislation.

The bilateral and multilateral partners mentioned below are emphasizing to close the ranks between the different GRN entities through active networking and facilitation of the National IECD forum. UNICEF is a major multilateral partner to GRN, in particular to MGECW and MOEAC in supporting from policy formulation up to implementation of frameworks and crucial infrastructure. EU dovetails' the above mentioned services by financing GRN through the 11th EDF, especially for ECD and PP development in Namibia. This support in particular is outstanding since Namibia is classified as an "upper middle income" country. The funding from EU is mainly channeled through the MoF on results-based conditions but some technical funding is implemented via UNICEF or other semi-public players in the sector. Civil society is much engaged since most ECD Centers are privately or community based with just a few that are owned by municipalities. Their relation and support is

[1]However, there are current discussions to transfer the responsibility of ECD from MoGECW to MoEAC in order to better integrate ECD with other aspects of education.

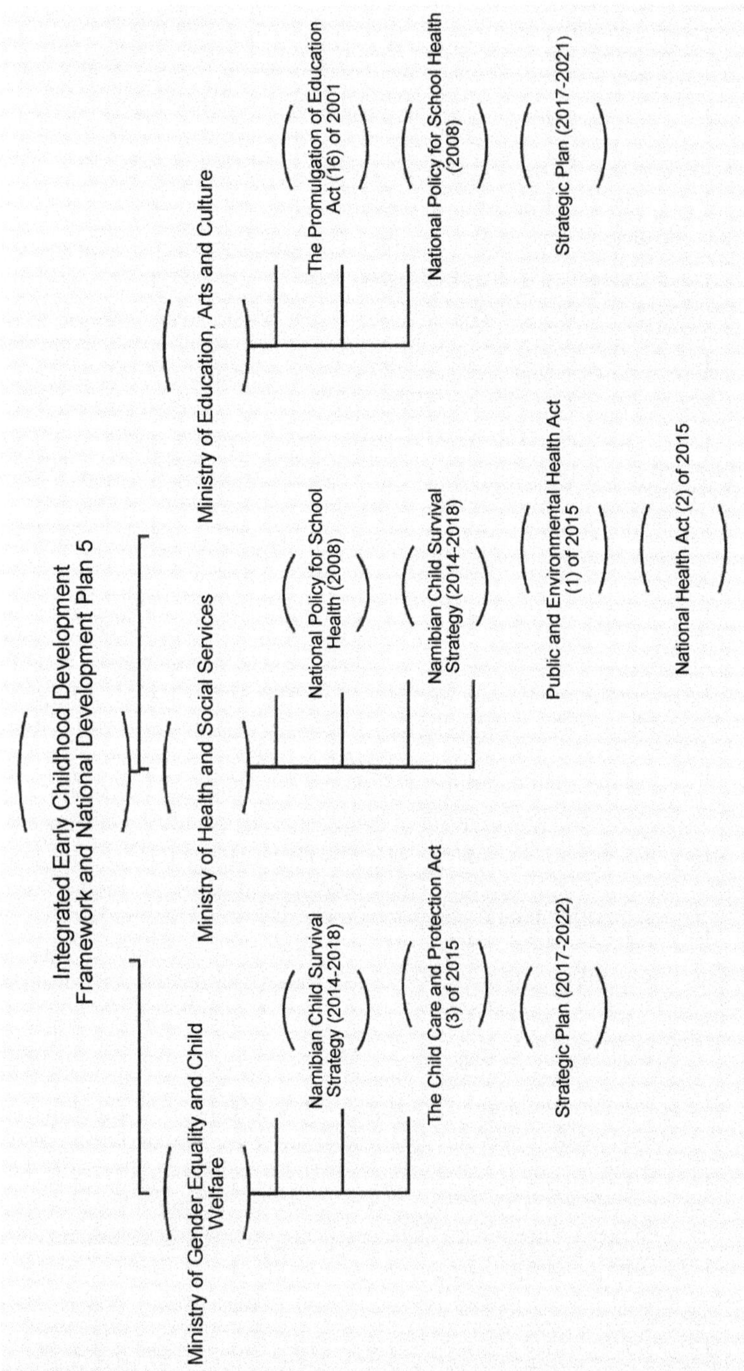

Fig. 1 Schematic presentation of the policy framework influencing the ECD environment in Namibia

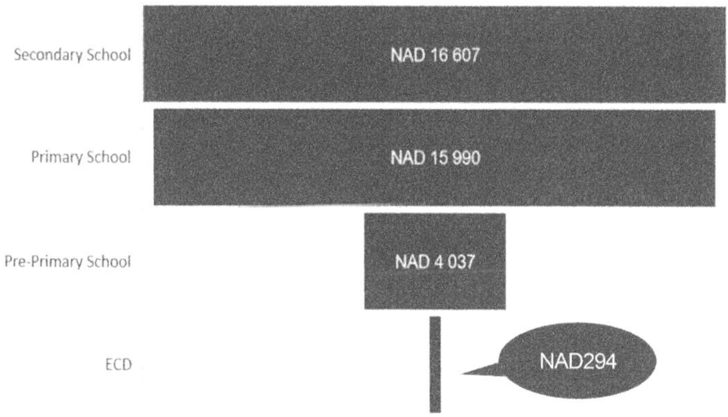

Fig. 2 Expenditure per child per year. Source: Children and the Namibian Budget, Windhoek: UNICEF 2018

coming directly through the MGECW in capacity of the Directorate of Community Affairs and Child Welfare. The amount spend per child per year is not adequate or at least un-relational as the following Fig. 2 compiled by UNICEF shows.

Looking at the role of the different stakeholders in the ECD sector will shed some light on the rather incoherent policy implementation.

As mentioned above the MoHSS is in charge of pre-natal, post-natal and actually the first 1000 days in a child's life through multiple health interventions. These start with pre-natal maternal health and care via safe delivery and post-natal care to a fully immunized child. From then on the MGECW is taking over in support with kindergarten/pre-school at community level. This in particular through infrastructure support and much more pronounced through stipends for trained educarers who are caring and teaching the children. The MoEAC at this stage is indirectly supporting through NAMCOL—a distant learning institution that offers diploma courses for educarers. MGECW's funding is inadequate for the task and the aim to bring children to a level of school preparedness. The lack of adequate infrastructure and well qualified educarers/teachers is pronounced and obvious. The payment for the educarers is covered by a small contribution from the MGECW and by the fees that parents have to pay as a school fee for their children. However, although Namibia is classified as an upper middle income country the disparity of wealth is highly unequal, leading to one of thc highest GINI coefficients in the world. This leads more than often to situations where parents simply cannot afford pre-school or kindergarden-fees for their children.

The strategy of the MoEAC in that space is the rapid implementation Pre-Primary classes at local Primary Schools from the age of 5 years for the children. This is hampered by lack of finance since this requires additional infrastructure (equipped classrooms) and additional qualified teachers. However, the aim to deliver children prepared for Grade 1 for Primary School is met by a targeted syllabus that dovetails with the ensuing curriculum in Junior Primary School. Pre-Primary Education is free of charge, hence much preferred by the parents to send their children there.

Engagement in the ECD sector is lively but highly fragmented. Besides the major government stakeholders there are numerous private initiatives related to ECD. These are found mostly in an urban context where private businesses, churches and parents with good paying employment and other well-wishers support individually the ECD institutions. The key players are not many since the NGO sector in Namibia is not well established and organized. This is due to the fact that the state in Namibia is functioning relatively well in comparison to the regional and continental neighbours. Hence grants and other social funding is state borne and driven. Child Line/Life Line and the Church Alliance for Orphans are major operators in terms of ECD related topics in the country and are funded by the Roger Federer Foundation. Perivoli Foundation from Switzerland is implementing relatively big programmes in various regions in the sector, but completely independent from the aforementioned consortium. Other major service providers in the sector are municipalities and mostly communities. The communities are the ones that benefit from grants given for infrastructure and allowances for the trained educators. The obvious risks for ECD in such an environment are:

- Ownership for ECD in a highly fragmented public service environment (3 Line Ministries plus planning plus finance)
- Investment into ECD is not seen as an investment with a quick ROI for economic advancement of the society
- Lack of experienced implementers outside the public service providers

On the other hand, Namibia shows good conditions to create opportunities for ECD

- Creating a platform pro-ECD for a multi-stakeholder engagement at various levels
- Making investment into ECD understood by the major decision makers in state, business and society at large
- Enhancing the already high public spending in general education through better and targeted investment in ECD
- Demonstrating that RBF can be successful in the social sector in Namibia and hence could become a new instrument for wider investment in that sector

2 Exploring a Result Based Financing Model for Early Childhood Development in Namibia

Namibia shows some good conditions to implement a result based finance strategy for early childhood development (ECD) centers. The government is aware of the need for solid basic education and good care in the ECD centers. In addition, governments and NGOs are collecting data regarding the quality of their education system. Various multinational organizations such as UNICEF and EU are already operating in Namibia and have built up a good local network. Furthermore, cooperation with a foundation can mobilize the necessary capital to implement the project. Namibia has the potential to play a pioneer role in high quality ECD training and become an exemplary transition process from kindergarten to primary school for many countries in sub-Saharan Africa. Furthermore, a result based financing approach can lead to cost-effectively basic educational system and better quality education for the government of Namibia at the same time. However, initial investment and the willingness to act as outcome payer from the government side are necessary. A political will and ability from the different government line ministries is inalienable and has to be present.

For the implementation of a result based financing strategy two conditions must be met:

1. Identification of ECD capacity strengthener as well as an intervention strategy which supports the ECD center to provide scalable high quality service.
2. In order to justify increased government investments, long-term cost savings for the government must be possible.

The feasibility study[2] carried out by Instiglio revealed the following finding:

- Inadequate infrastructure of ECD centers
- Inadequate training of caregivers
- Lack of cost efficiency of ECD centers in Namibia
- Lack of capacity building in the ECD centers
- ECD Centers Namibia are not ready to be included in an RBF structure
- Significant investment is needed to build and expand ECD centers infrastructure/framework to provide high quality ECD services
- The current data availability and quality are still insufficient for a RBF structure
- Although improving the quality of ECD center is part of the government education agenda, there is a lack of adequate financial support for childcare, ECD centers and primary schools.

To successfully implement a result based financing intervention, a two-step plan is recommended[3]: The Plan is further depicted in Fig. 3 and explained below.

The first step is to improve the quality of ECD centers. For this purpose one to three service providers has to be selected, which provide the necessary training to the ECD centers and establishing a quality assessment framework. The goal of the first phase is to make the ECD centers ready for a result based financing intervention. This will result in a pipeline of high quality ECD centers including a measurement framework for high quality education, where the government is

---

[2]Improving early childhood development in Namibia with Results-Based Financing, Instiglio 2018.

[3]Improving early childhood development in Namibia with Results-Based Financing, Instiglio 2018, page 43.

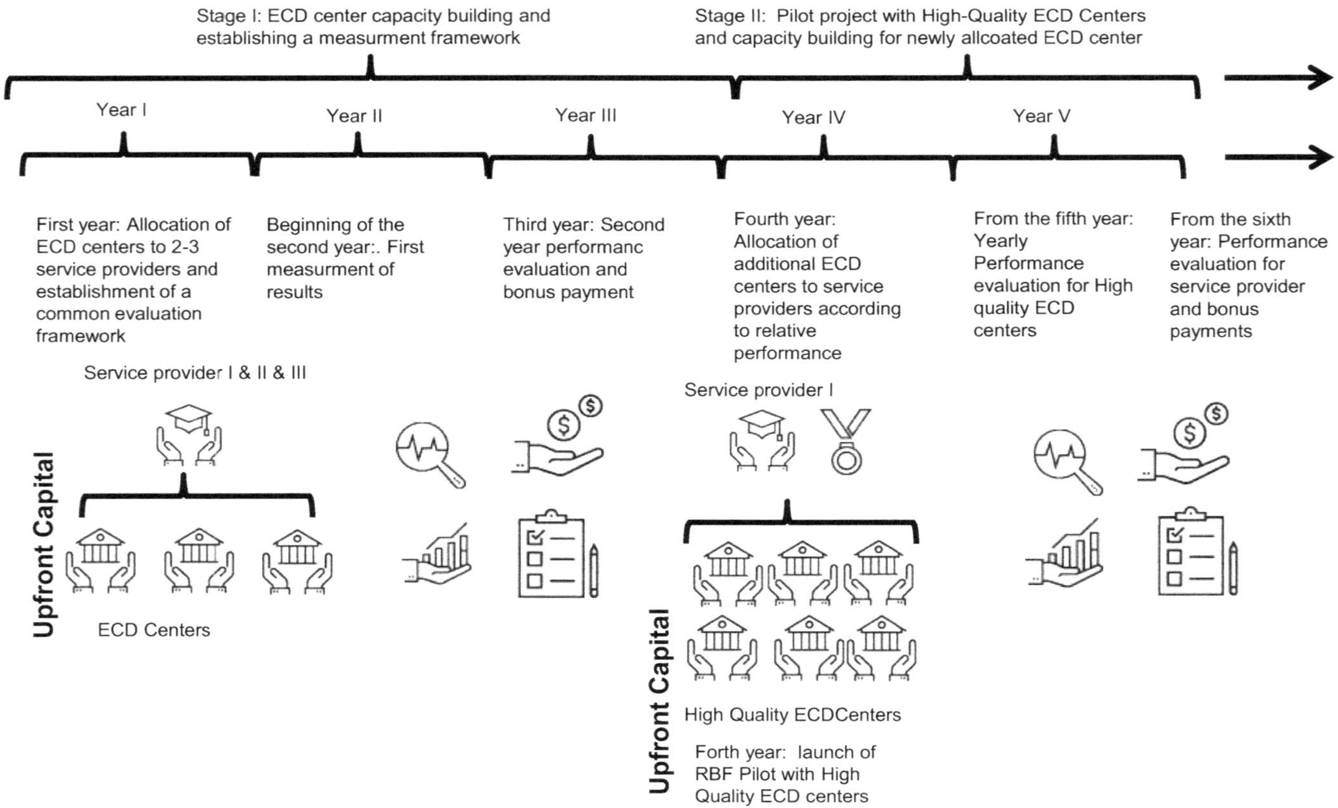

Fig. 3 Result based financing intervention. Source: Own representation based "Improving early childhood development in Namibia with Results-Based Financing", Instiglio 2018, p. 4

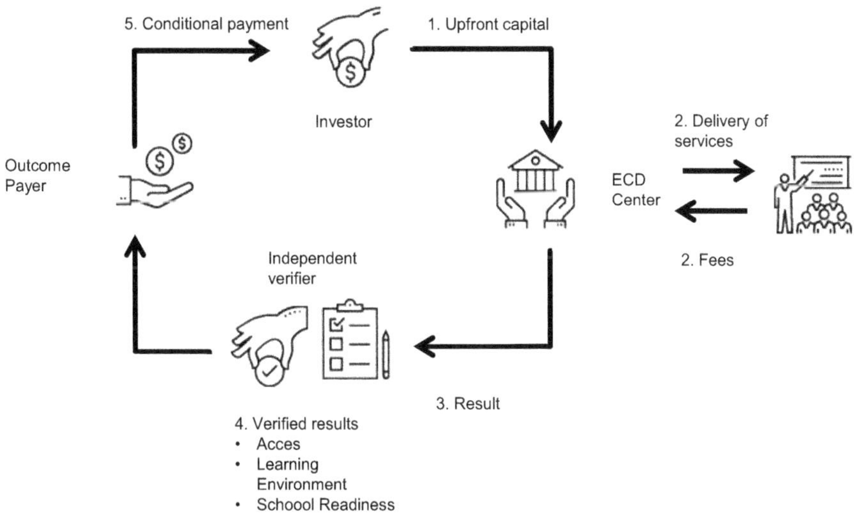

Fig. 4 RBF Approach using a Social Impact Bond (SIB) Scheme Source: Own representation based "Improving early childhood development in Namibia with Results-Based Financing", Instiglio 2018, p. 50

willing and able to invest into it. The first phase will be based on grant funding with corresponding bonus payments for successful service providers.

Figure 3 gives a RBF strategy overview.

In the second phase, the expansion of high quality ECD centers will be continued with the help of one or two service providers financed by foundations or similar institutions using a Social Impact Bond (SIB) Finance Scheme. The main pillars and dependencies of the SIB are depicted in Fig. 4. Furthermore, a pilot project will start with already established high quality ECD centers with the government of Namibia as outcome payer. The school fees will be partly covered by the parents. Funding for the additional operating cost for the ECD centers will come from Ministry of Gender Equality and Child Welfare subsidies. The necessary upfront capital can be secured by an impact bond model. Investors provide the upfront capital and if the corresponding goals in the sense of improved school readiness according to the defined parameters are achieved, the government of Namibia acts as an outcome payer. The school readiness is verified and confirmed by an independent verifier.

Figure 4 RBF approach with upfront capital provided by investors (Impact Bond)

An alternative concept of upfront financing would be via loans from banks for ECD centers. This model could be supported by Opportunity International. They have experience in working with local financial institutions, which lends money to schools to promote the quality of education services. This approach reduces for ECD

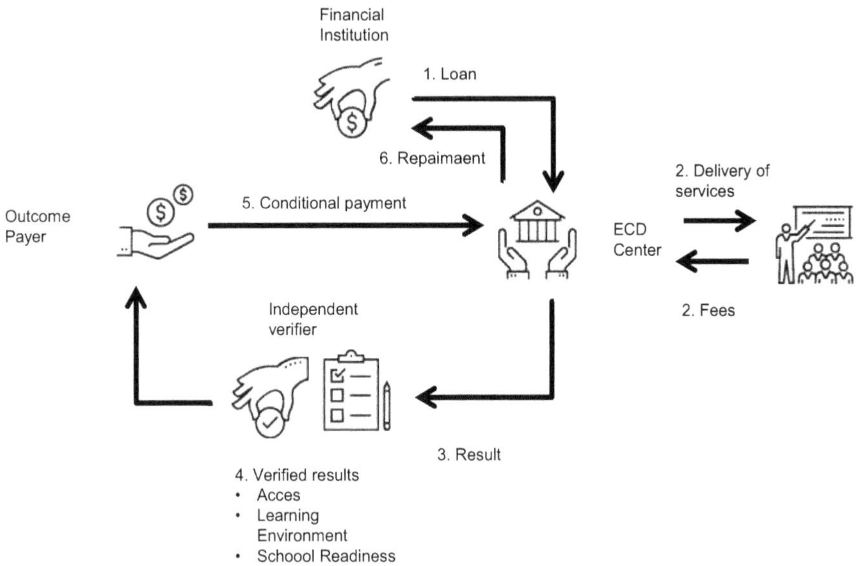

Fig. 5 Impact linked credit for Namibian RBF approach with upfront financing provided by financial institutions. Source: Own representation based "Improving early childhood development in Namibia with Results-Based Financing", Instiglio 2018, p. 51

centers dependence on foreign investors. In this setup, the ECD centers obtain loans from banks in addition to the parents' school fees. The government pays premiums to ECD centers if they are achieving their goal in providing better school readiness, which is assessed by an independent evaluator. The loans are repaid directly by the ECD centers to the financial institutions. This approach has been depicted below in Fig. 5.

In both models, it is recommended to have a lead contractor who takes care of the administrative work as well as the coordination of the individual contracts between the parties (investors, government, and independent evaluator). Another role of the lead contractor could be the takeover of the performance management system.

2.1 Capacity Building for High Quality ECD Centers and for All Involved Stakeholders

With the first study about RBF being launched in May 2018, Interteam facilitated stakeholder meetings with Instiglio, the consulting group for the study. It then became obvious that such a stakeholder meeting became very beneficial for all stakeholders since there was a sentiment that a new platform of information sharing and collaboration had been created—although not by design but rather by default. Interteam took this notion up and transformed this stakeholder group into the steering committee of the second study "Cost of no Action in ECD Investment in Namibia" with a clear task of ownership of the study and owning the results thereof. This steering group became the quasi sub-committee "Finance for ECD" within the NIECD platform in Namibia. Numerous meetings and exchanges had been facilitated with other members then the NIECD but from the same stakeholders which in turn created more and better communication and dialogue between the line ministries and the other major stakeholders. Furthermore, with the continued support and commitment from Fondation Botnar, this working group became enlarged and very instrumental in the co-funded project of creating a better environment for ECD investment in Namibia. This comprises the branding of ECD under a unified nationwide campaign and long-term social media presence for parents, parents of tomorrow and the decision makers in Government, private sector and society. The ultimate aim for the aforementioned is to enhance better ECD service delivery which would have to start with quality ECD centres that would provide adequate care and nurture for children in order to get them prepared for (pre) primary school education. Since most present ECD facilities are privately and community owned and managed, one has to see where and how these major stakeholders could be supported and motivated best. Retaining ownership at community level is most critical in such an undertaking and support. Hence the public sector can support with more and better training offers for Educators in ECD, better support in basic infrastructure (water, sanitation, basic shelter) and public recognition. The private sector and external donors should be offered a platform where investment (grants for infrastructure, soft loans, stipends and special projects) could be bundled and channelled. Obviously, it has to be recognized and put into perspective that ECD is the foundation of education and therefore has to be an integral part of Government Service leading to quality education. This could be either Ministry but would be best placed under the MoEAC with support from MGECW for actual Child Welfare rather than Early Childhood Education which should be led by MoEAC.

3 Conclusion

The uniqueness of this project is the collaboration of the private, public and nonprofit sectors as well government and aid organizations and the involvement of the local communities. The selection and cooperation of the individual project partners is the key to success for this result based financing project. To what extent can UNICEF and the EU support the MGECW ministry in data management and help sustain with the lobbying work for an effective ECD system has to be verified. Furthermore, it is crucial to what extent investors can be found for each financing stage. Another key are Interteam abilities to provide coordination support for this project with theirs years of experience in development work in Namibia and countless contacts in the education sector. In terms of technical advice and advocacy, the know-how of organizations like the Bertha Center, the Brookings Institution and the Center for the Developing Child are crucial. Furthermore, cooperation with a foundation, which has covered the feasibility cost and can mobilize further capital to implement the project. A key for the project is also the willingness and ability of the government of Namibia to act as outcome payer. A political willingness and ability from the different government line ministries is inalienable. On the bottom line, success factors for a RBF project will be:

- Up to now there are already a couple of visible factors that would lead to a success, like having a platform for all major and peripheral stakeholders for ECD
- Enhanced and targeted dialogue about ECD
- Putting ECD as a National topic
- Demonstrating tangible impact to financiers and key decision makers in politics, society and the private sector
- Unity among the engaged ministries
- Confined Pilot Programme with low risk and tangibility will create chance for bigger investment

On the other hand, the following potential risks have to be kept in mind:

- Continued fragmentation due to political or personal reasons
- No political will to venture into new (RBF or blended) financing models in the public social sector
- Lack of motivated and skilled service providers
- Red tape and administrative bottlenecks in the public sector
- Further financial contraction of the Namibian economy
- Financiers are not taking up the risk
- Conditions of RBF are not clear to Government
- Pilot Project for RBF or similar is designed too big

In conclusion, the present interaction and awareness of all major stakeholders in the ECD in Namibia make it a pressing issue to act further within that window of opportunity. Creating an enhanced environment for better investment in ECD starts with better communication and a relevant platform for meaningful dialogue, in particular within Government first but as well with society at large.

Investing with new finance vehicle's like RBF in this sector is realistic in Namibia, looking at the considerable modernity in the sector and the motivated key decision makers in charge of today's policy implementation. The project will succeed if it succeeds to achieve a close cooperation of all involved stakeholders.

Daniel Gächter is an Impact Investing and Sustainable Finance specialist. Daniel is the founder of Swiss Impact Investing Network (SIIN) a peer-to-peer know-how sharing platform. Daniel has a longstanding and professional track record in the area of advisory service for Foundation, Social Entrepreneurs and Impact Funds. Daniel is an advocate of a conscious approach to investing and a regenerative capital market.

Beside this, he has a traditional financial background with over 15 years of experience in the Asset Management area with focus on Fixed Income. Daniel has spent years immersed in the sustainability challenge of our age while still following his Banking career. In the past, Daniel has worked for several major banks in Switzerland.

Daniel holds a Diploma in Business Administration FH specializing in Banking and Finance. He has completed his postgraduate studies at University of Oxford (Said Business School) in Impact Investing and at Center for Philanthropy Studies (University Basel), in Foundation Management. He has just completed his degree in Sustainable Finance at University of Zurich.

Martin Suhr is a Project Management Specialist and currently Country Programme Director of Interteam Namibia, a Swiss based NGO that employs 10 Swiss Development Workers with the Ministry of Education, Arts and Culture. Martins professional background is Civil Engineering but evolved to complex multi-stakeholder project management during his past 34 years experience in development work worldwide, but mainly in southern Africa.

Martin calls himself a champion of networking and collaboration with a "We" approach that works successfully in complex tasks across cultures, hierarchies and different interest groups. For him, Youth Development is the most important task for Africa and therefore his focus is in children and youth related programmes.

Apart from Civil Engineering, Martin is a qualified Business and Leadership Coach (St. Gallen Model) under the Swiss Coaching Academy.

An Analysis on Impact Measurement: How Do We Measure Impact?

Kuno Roth

Abstract There is no question that dedicated campaigners and volunteers are keen to achieve intended effects of a project or campaign. As a rule, they want to know what are the effects and indirect effects of their actions—the intentional, unintentional, short-term and long-term. Yet how does one determine these? What model is employed to measure effect or impact, what approach is used? To find answers to these questions is not easy. Particularly since almost all dedicated people are invariably under time constraints.

Keywords Theory of change · Theories of change · Qualitative data · Small data · Stories as data · Choice of indicators · Impact models · Metaphor of impact measurement · Happiness index · Systemic view · Cynefin model · From theory to practice of change · SDGs · Sustainable development goals · Impact investing · Impact measurement

There is no question that dedicated campaigners and volunteers are keen to achieve intended effects of a project or campaign. As a rule, they want to know what are the effects and indirect effects of their actions—the intentional, unintentional, short-term and long-term. Yet how does one determine these? What model is employed to measure effect or impact, what approach is used? To find answers to these questions is not easy. Particularly since almost all dedicated people are invariably under time constraints.

The following discussion should serve to initiate the reader into the uses and challenges of gathering and monitoring data and effects on collective behaviour of participants in campaign initiatives. Closer observation is on the application of four

---

This article reflects the personal attitude of the author, so it is not an official Greenpeace position. Kuno joined Greenpeace back in 1986 as volunteer, and is working as an employee since 1990, first for Greenpeace Switzerland and since 2016 for Greenpeace International.

K. Roth (✉)
Greenpeace International, Zurich, Switzerland
e-mail: kuno.roth@greenpeace.org

K. Wendt (ed.), *Theories of Change*, Sustainable Finance,
https://doi.org/10.1007/978-3-030-52275-9_10

current impact models, namely, The Kirkpatrick Model, the Logical Framework Approach, The Happiness-Index and the Theory of Change. The latter will be described with case studies in further detail.

Because activist people want to invest as much time as possible in activities, they may risk measuring only what can be measured with minor effort as they tend to "evaluate quickly". For example, when working with online platforms that deliver a massive quantity of data, free of charge and ultra-fast. Hence, one forms a certain impression, undoubtedly often a skewed and biased one. That is like measuring a patient's temperature, blood pressure and pulse; and deriving from that, the intervention for a "healing-the-patient" project. Efficient it is, but not necessarily effective: It can go well, but one can also be wrong with the diagnosis and thus the intervention and not cure the disease as a result. In the case of a serious illness, more indications and expertise are needed for analysis and interpretation. For the evaluation of a campaign project this means deliberating about what data is needed (and how it is collected) in order to get an overall picture in a useful time frame. To understand this, an analogy to photography can be helpful, in which a high-resolution photograph would correspond to the one extreme of a maximum imaging of everything. White paper would be the other extreme. Staying in this metaphor: How many and which pixels would be needed to recognise a face? In the case of a head of a well-recognised figure, such as Albert Einstein's, a few dozen specifically positioned pixels are sufficient. These pixels might then correspond, so to speak, to the indicators for a project profile or outline.

Finding the right balance between the two extremes means searching for indicators relevant the overall picture. It may be necessary to give up on an important one, because the effort involved in conducting surveys, for example, would be too great. However, beware, "too time-consuming" is easy to say. Adjustments can perhaps be made by questioning a small(er) group of respondents in order to obtain at least some "direct data", i.e. from primary sources. And that may even be enough for a start. In any case, the point is not to restrict oneself to "secondary data" and simple indicators. To exclusively evaluate such data would be as if one would only capture Einstein's chin in high resolution and then think one can recognise his entire head (and a video call with Einstein would quickly unveil the truth . . .): Validity and shades of grey can be less questionable if there is an exchange with the various stakeholders in random samples or focus groups. How qualitative "small data" can be collected, is described by C. Otto Scharmer in "The Essentials of Theory U"[1] (p. 91f): *«Another practice is called 'Voices from the Field'. We sit or stand in a circle and speak from the authentic voice of the people that we have met. Someone might say 'I am a social entrepreneur, and I have a very clear vision but cannot communicate it well'. We do this one by one. Then, when all voices have been heard, the individual participants [stakeholders] make entries in their journals about what they have observed and heard, and then take a thirty-minute dialogue walk with a partner, share their observations and reflections with each other, and return to discuss the emerging themes. . .»*, i.e., what is 'burning', what are crucial issues, what brings joy, etc. (see box "Stories as Data" below).

[1]C. Otto Scharmer: "The Essential of the Theory U", Berrett-Koehler Publisher, 2017.

1 Impact Models

An impact model is used to describe the means and activities by which a desired effect is to be achieved, the so-called "impact on the ground". For this purpose most impact models establish a chain of causal relationships: If this measure (intervention) is taken, it is assumed that reality will change in this (or that) way. There are numerous impact models; and outlined here are four models in brief, including two older, established models and two recent ones, one of which is discussed in further detail.

1. **Kirkpatrick-Modell (1955):** This has been used for the evaluation of trainings and courses. The model captures the learning effect on four levels: The first two levels are the familiar standard assessment at the end of a course: Get feedback (Level 1: *Reaction*) and the exam (Level 2: *Immediate Learning*). From this one can deduce and extrapolate information. Yet what happens to learned material back at work or during the stages of a project (Level 3: *Behaviour*); and whether that produces the desired effects in whole or in part (Level 4; *Results*) is rarely recorded. This is because levels 3 and 4 can only be determined after a few months, and are therefore "forgotten". The Kirkpatrick method is very suitable for a relatively less extensive evaluation of learning interventions. Since basically every Greenpeace campaign and every project is a request or invitation to learn, it is in principle also useful in project work.
2. **Logical Framework Approach (1960s):** This method was developed by USAID in the 1960s. It is still very common, namely, in development cooperation (see ZEWO[2] for more information), often in a derived form. Success in this case is measured by the goals that have been developed in a linear logic in advance using the so-called Problem Tree and Target Tree and then transferred to the so-called Logframe. The logframe is a matrix table which summarizes the effects on four levels: over-all impact, outcome, output and activities. At each level it provides how and when something is measured (indicators) how the information is collected, and which assumptions have to be fulfilled in order to achieve the effect. One of the qualities of this method is to explicitly enquire about the assumptions (intermediate objectives or preconditions) that reduce the risk of bias.
3. **Happiness Index Method:** The Happiness Index method, which was developed in the Himalayan state of Bhutan, is impressive but also very complex: the index examines the government's policy, i.e. whether its measures lead (or might lead) to the well-being of the majority of the population. Listening to respondents is the

[2]ZEWO Abstract: The Logical Framework approach is a systematic, analytical planning process for the goal-oriented planning of a project and its monitoring and evaluation system. The basic idea (...), based on a well-founded analysis of the situation and the problems, is to condense the planned impact of the project ultimately into a relatively simple, linear impact model. This serves as a basis for the planning of the monitoring and evaluation system by recording the outputs and impacts of the project using quantitative or qualitative indicators.

underlying principle of statistical surveys. A representative sample of 7000 Bhutanese (1% of the population) is interviewed on average every 3 years. The questions cover the nine Happiness areas of life, i.e. the model is more holistic than the Western model of sustainable development with its three areas (more on this in the FN[3]). It comprises 124 indicators, which are surveyed both "objectively" statistically and "subjectively": In personal conversations "measuring" is, i.e. not meant in the physical sense, but as the best possible approximation. Of course such a comprehensive approach overtaxes every project and every organisation, but it is still inspiring. Therefore, the Eurasia Learning Institute (see FN iv) tries to break down Bhutan's method and insights into organisations and companies. This means that out of 124, a dozen indicators relevant to an organisation are identified. They are used to determine how "Happiness Interventions" affect the well-being of employees. Such an intervention can be, for example, a "Coaching Clinic" (peer consulting group), a new meeting ritual or training in "Active Listening".

4. **Theory of Change (ToC) Method:** The "Theory of Change" method is based on an improvement of the Logical Framework and similar methods. It emerged in the 1990s as a result of impact research in development cooperation and health care. The research showed that the scientific-technical view of development that had prevailed until then did not take sufficient account of the "human component" in social systems and that, therefore, effects could not be measured successfully. To be more precise: the insight that one can only approach the effects of an intervention by taking different perspectives led to the multidisciplinary approach of the Theory of Change (ToC). The central questions are: How does the ToC process develop on the ground, based on a first (speculative) ToC? How to continuously monitor and evaluate with few but significant indicators (see above)? How to adapt ToC to the emerging practice, so that quasi both theory and practice may improve? More about the ToC method can be found below.

2 Cynefin Model: A Practical Aid

To measure or identify effects and ramifications of a project implies finding the balance between "measuring as much as necessary and as little as possible". But how? At first it will be obvious to avoid both extremes: One extreme occurs when the "least possible" is no evaluation at all (or only one for the drawer). This is the case if you think you know what's going on or if you want to stay in your comfort zone. At

[3]The nine areas of the Gross National Happiness Index are: psychological well-being, health, time use, education, cultural diversity and resilience, good governance, community vitality, ecological diversity and resilience, and living standards. The first survey was conducted in 2008, the second in 2010 and the third one in 2015. For an induction see the blog: "Living well and protecting the climate. That would be great". And for information about the Eurasia Learning Institute see: www.eurasia.org.vn

the other extreme, every detail is recorded. One can expend considerable effort, so that either there is nothing left for the project or those involved feel harassed and their enthusiasm for the project is stifled by bureaucracy. So how can a holistic, systematic view have influence on the measuring of impact without overtaxing the project? How can bias be avoided? A simple example to illustrate this: If a part of the population in a village in a poor country receives a solar power installation, and thus access to electricity, the impact is usually determined by questioning the recipients. For example, 6 months after installation, conducting another survey or paying a visit is not standard practice in many projects. Even less common is to interview those villagers who did not buy a solar power system. To interview them as well could, however, provide useful information.

This systematic perspective is missing from the Kirkpatrick and LogFrame methods. Indeed these approaches are very systematic, but in a cause-effect logic. This is not wrong, but not complete: The two methods only capture the rational superficially. However not complexity, which can be described as the "chicken-egg quandary", i.e. where it's not possible to determine what came first, where human interactions take place that influence each other. Complex effects of an intervention can only be determined in retrospect or in the course of the project, but are important for further project development.

The Cynefin-Modell has proven to be simple and helpful for a systematic approach. It depicts reality in four domains: The obvious, the complicated, the complex and the chaotic domains. All four are always represented in human interactions (see chart, taken from Wikipedia[4]).

COMPLEX	**COMPLICATED**
Cause and effect coherent only in retrospect, do not repeat	Cause and effect relationships separated over time, not apparent to everyone (expertise needed)
Emergent practice - System thinking Perspective filters	**Good practice** – not full standard possible Scenario planning
Course of action: Probe – Sense - Respond	**Course of action: Sense – Analyse - Respond**
CHAOTIC	**KNOWN**
High turbulence - no cause and effect relationship perceivable	Cause and effect relations repeatable and predictable
Rapid response (stability focused intervention) Crisis management - enactment measures	**Best practice** (because it's easy) Standard operations procedures
Course of action: Act – Sense - Respond	**Course of action: Sense – Categorise – Respond**

Adapted from David Snowden, The Cynefin Framework

[4] https://en.wikipedia.org/wiki/Cynefin_framework

Illustrated in the image of a sick person: The obvious—fever, blood pressure, pulse—can be self-tested. By yourself, at any rate, is better than nothing. Yet expert knowledge is needed to measure and interpret a blood count. This is the complicated, but also strictly causal domain: If too little of X is present in the blood, then it has a Y effect on health. Medication prescribed by the doctor can also have undesirable side effects. This is the complex domain, the chicken-egg quandary: side effects depend on the constitution as well as the psychological state of the patient and how symptoms affect her. Although it is known from laboratory studies what could happen, what happens in individual cases cannot be predicted. Experience, i.e. many cases where a doctor could "look back", allows him to make assumptions.

If, for example, a side effect is particularly strong, and a person panics—we enter into the chaotic domain, in which nothing more can be predicted. One should anticipate this; and can therefore react as in a crisis-intervention, to which thanks to experience one is prepared. As with the fire brigade: gear is at the ready, but nobody knows when and where a fire will break out.

3 Change in Campaign(ing) Style

Indeed, the Cynefin Model is a supporting framework. For example, the boundaries between the domains are not clear or natural. The model however helps in the awareness of ever present complex constituent parts, which no project manager can control. In other words, with a systematic view, the campaign approach changes from "What have we planned?" to "What is happening, and who has contributed how? Simply put: 'reality is no longer adapted to the plan' or analysed with unconscious filters (e.g. with a bubble filter) but rather an attempt is made to pursue results—positive and negative, expected and unexpected—by listening, observing and working together. Campaign approaches are changing further:" How does what has happened relate to what we thought would happen? And what follows next, how do we integrate what we have learned? In short: collect the significant results and side-effects, describe them in consultation with participants and, if necessary, supplement them with research, i.e. Outcomes Mapping.

The "Probe-Sense-Respond" Process of the Cynefin model [(i) Try out, (ii) perceive empathically and with anticipation; (iii) adjust & do] is a proven instrument for this: putting into practice "swimming with the current", taking note of what happens and trying to control with other participants ("responsiveness"): a refined trial-and-error-principle.

Moreover, a systematic approach means not only taking into consideration the interrelationships and perspectives of the various participants, but also noting the system's limits. Often these are not taken into account. A simple example would be to interview not only the participants of a course, but also non-participants from the target group one would want to reach.

<u>Note</u>: If you are interested in social, i.e. systematic, transformation, you can't miss "Theory U" by C. Otto Scharmer: A systematic view of every process of change that has emerged from the analysis of genuine transformations in notable companies and

organisations. The "Systems Concepts in Action"-Toolkit,[5] is also recommended: In addition to the Cynefin Model, this practice-oriented book also discusses other methods, in particular for describing and analyzing situations, such as the Outcome Mapping for measuring the impact of social change processes with a mix of quantitative and qualitative data collection—see also the box "Stories as Data".

Stories as Data (Excerpts of an Internal Greenpeace Guideline)

How to measure progress, and how to define success indicators? Not with SMART objectives or SMART indicators. Instead, with small stories that arise and are collected. By observations and experiences from the people you'd like to see change: citizen, stakeholders, supporters, activists, product users, employees etc. Indicate what stories you like to see more of, and what stories you like to see less of. This provides a tangible outcome and impact-oriented direction as well as a database for measuring success.

Allow as many people as possible to form part of your "human sensor network". Such networks can amend or replace traditional research tools, polling and focus groups. They also create networks for ordinary purposes that can be activated for extra-ordinary need. (. . .).

Such short first hand-stories provide rich insight in a short form: they capture what people would naturally exchange by the water-cooler or the camp-fire (. . .). It is in these fragmented, anecdotal, not composed stories how we communicate and make sense of the world. They are valuable data. Called small, primary or qualitative data that can be used to identify patterns across your field of research (emergent properties), e.g. your organisational culture, as well as opportunities for change (levers). With traditional questionnaires such patterns can hardly be recognized as they only provide average values. And if the stories come from many different perspectives, this method can also be used to avoid more likely blind spots as thy can occur quite easily in focus groups because of the "bubble problem".

Once you sourced enough of these stories, you can use quantitative techniques to measure success. While you can easily harvest large numbers of stories using survey and questionnaire methods, they can't be interpreted by computers. (. . .). Even experts are at risk to provide misinterpretations because of their own socialization and their limited perception. Therefore, the people who bring in the stories (or their representatives) should decide what meanings the anecdotes have. Roughly speaking, respondents are asked to tell a story in a few sentences, which they rate and classify to reveal their meaning(s), e.g. as follows: "On a scale of 1 to 10, how do you rate your story as an example of good listening?". The main characteristics and benefits of this method are:

(continued)

[5]Bob Williams, Richard Hummelbrunner: "Systems Concepts in Action—a Practitioner's Toolkit", Stanford University Press, 2011.

- People self-index their stories, thereby adding additional meaning to their experiences, not just interpreting the content.
- Fragmented mini-stories are unconstrained by pre-conceived structures (e.g. questionnaires), resulting in significantly less bias, and more meaningful data.
- The removal of intermediaries (e.g. focus group facilitators, expert questionnaires interpreters) allows the original material to be easily accessed in a variety of forms by decision makers.

4 How Does Theory of Change (ToC) Lead to the Practice of Change?[6]

The Theory of Change impact model is firstly a planning method and particularly suitable for complex projects and programs aimed at real societal change. The basic framework of the ToC is similar to project planning. Using a fictitious example of "a new kind of cake with cabbage", the project starts with the goal of baking a cake with the new ingredient cabbage to make it taste good. From that point think backwards. Based on existing cake recipes and one's own baking experience, one determines the preconditions and intermediate goals that have to be met as milestones on the way to the project goal. And the criteria that must to be met in order to achieve the project goal of the "successful cake" are ultimately determined. These milestones indicate the progress of the project: For example, the purchase of ingredients, allocating a budget and the required equipment as provided resources or, for example, "the dough is smooth" as an intermediate goal. Then one considers which indicators are there to point to the success of the project; for example, a taste test of the raw dough or the colour of the cake, which can be seen by looking into the oven. Finally, imagine the cake being served to a hundred guests on the anniversary of the cabbage lobby, where carrot representatives are also present. Then it would be a good idea to start with test cakes and, for instance, let some cabbage lobbyists, as well as potential new cabbage friends and carrot lovers, take part in the tests and thus gather tips and suggestions.

Of course, social baking is infinitely more difficult; and there are no simple recipes. The example nevertheless shows the central elements that matter:

1. The assumptions, from where one proceeds, e.g. that the ingredients are available in good enough quality or that the blender and oven work. In the social context, the question arises as to what assumptions must or can be confirmed and which are agreed upon.

[6]This chapter is an edited version of a written interview with the author published in Zeitschrift OrganisationsEntwicklung (1/2018).

2. The indicators: What is the best indicator of the quality of the process and the approach to the project intention? The oven temperature? Just because it's easy to measure may not be enough.
3. Participation and practical learning during testing, which allows continuous improvement so that ultimately as many people as possible find the cake tasty.

5 The Steps for a Theory of Change

From this (and from the example) resulted the steps for the development of a ToC:

- Those involved agree on the long-term objective and the project objectives derived from it. More precisely, they agree on the intentions, because in dynamic systems flexibility is necessary so that, for example, objectives can be adapted to changing framework conditions. The cake doesn't have to taste good primarily for me, but for as many participants as possible.
- The second step is to determine which assumptions have to be fulfilled in order for these intentions to be achieved. For this purpose, a rough road map is prepared, taking into account a similar procedure, and the expected interim results are described. These are the preconditions that must first be achieved for the project objective. They are described as outcomes as the assumptions on which they are based can be reviewed from time to time. Typically, often unspoken assumptions are how an intermediate objective is linked to the project goal, or why one believes that a particular outcome is the result of an intervention. It is therefore essential to check the assumptions made. The results of this step are an impact model presented, e.g. in a flow chart, and the so-called Outcomes Framework: This is the summary of how those involved imagine the pathway to change. And the tools are planning process, activities, monitoring and evaluation.
- Indicators are sought which continuously highlight the progress and quality of the project or warn of undesirable developments. It is central to choose them carefully and to test them.
- The next step will be the measures with which one hopes to create the preconditions. As this point it is now determined which activities or interventions should take place, when and where on the impact diagram. This completes the flowchart and Outcomes Framework with indicators, assumptions, activities and interventions. **This is the Theory of Change of the project: the expectation of how the desired change could happen in the specific context.**
- Last but not least, a narrative must be developed, i.e. the narrative motif that gives meaning, or a story, respectively, that illustrates the project's intention and becomes the booster of the project.

A productive exercise is to analyse a completed project and map backwards a Theory of Change to learn for a next project. For instance the solar revolution in rural Bangladesh, which is based on a business model: Its success factors serve as base for the ToC of a next practice.

The Marketmakers: Solar for the Hinterland of Bangladesh
Bangladesh is the only developing country that has created a rural market for solar home systems: Four million solar home systems have been installed to illuminate as many households. But could this market approach be feasible in other countries in the Global South, where 70–80% of the rural population still has no access to electricity?

Nancy Wimmer describes vividly how this market came about in her book "The Marketmakers"[7] for which she spent 3 years researching in Bangladesh, India and Washington DC. She is convinced "*this market's success is not entirely determined by a certain country and product. Rather, its success stems from a market-oriented approach carried out by rural entrepreneurs (. . .). Its development approach could be adapted to work elsewhere. But only if its inner mechanics are well understood. Therefore this book.*" Here a summary of the success factors of this approach, which can serve as a basis for a Theory of Change for transfer to another country or to a pilot community.

This solar market did not develop in the megacity Dhaka—but in village markets, in tribal hamlets, on islands in the Brahmaputra River and in the fishing villages of the Bay of Bengal. This is Bangladesh's *hinterland* where 18 million villagers—who for generations had lived in the dark after dusk—now have solar powered light. Here solar power was needed most and here a rural market will continue to provide it. Within a decade, 50 rural enterprises were installing up to 65,000 solar home systems a month, expanding their solar business, creating over 25,000 village jobs and developing the local economy.

Nancy Wimmer reveals in detail how this market developed. Her analysis takes an unusual approach by describing the market's evolution from the very different perspectives of the players who made it happen: The **World Bank** provided credit for start-up and growth. **IDCOL**, Bangladesh's Development Finance Institution, designed the financial model and managed the market's many players. The **local entrepreneurs** promoted a solar technology village people had never heard of and ensured quality service to remote households scattered across a river delta. It is from the diverging views of a donor, the administrator and the practitioners that readers gain deep insights.

(continued)

[7]Nancy Wimmer: "The Marketmakers: Solar for the Hinterland of Bangladesh", MCRE Verlag, 2019.

The Marketmakers thus goes far beyond explaining the obvious ingredients of success: technical quality, monitoring and training, business models, financing schemes and the crucial role of incentives. Its actors also reveal the intangibles crucial to rural market creation:

- the crucial importance of leveraging the expertise of rural entrepreneurs with financial and technical support— and the joint monthly meetings with IDCOL managers for feedback from the market and problem solving
- how to manage the balancing act between gaining political support and keeping political interference at bay
- the challenges of creating cooperation between partners with diverse interests
- the need to take a strong stand against corruption before it takes hold in procurement, a notorious field of fraud

And the all-important role of steadfast leadership to steer an emerging system of rural entrepreneurs, multilateral donors and technical suppliers that make things happen large-scale. This book doesn't provide a theory, but far more than a checklist of what to consider when attempting rural market development and change. Readers will understand why rural business can be a driving force for sustainable progress in developing countries—and why it takes time to develop.

Last but not least, this success story was triggered by an emotional impact. Initially, IDCOL's CEO was not convinced of the suitability of small solar home systems for rural households. But he was ready to give it a try. He purchased two solar systems for his cousin and a nearby mosque on a remote island and was amazed to hear their grateful response months later for reliable light and solar power. This convinced the CEO to bring solar home systems to the hinterland of Bangladesh.

The ongoing checks and reviews of projects in progress, whether the impact assumptions are accurate, are helping them to be more effective. At least if one is prepared to adapt one's actions to the realities. For example, it emerged that the classic Greenpeace campaign instruments tended to have a diminishing effect, i.e. that the previous impact assumptions often turned out to be incorrect. As a result, there are fewer but more varied GP public campaigns, but especially also of other intervention methods, such as participatory campaigns. These so-called "open campaigns" (3–5-year initiatives with a myriad of activities) are also the result of the insight that major real changes can only be achieved in cooperation with others.

6 Lessons from Bihar/India

One example of this is a Greenpeace campaign in northeastern India. The long-term goal is to establish organic farming in the entire state of Bihar (similar in size to Germany). Greenpeace India set "100 model villages" as the campaign goal, which was accepted because of its critical mass and intermediate goal of "creating a model village" as a precondition. This intermediate goal was achieved in 2017. The campaign goal was brought one big step closer in January 2018 when the government of Bihar recognised the model village as a bellwether for its agricultural policy (see[8]). However, the work in this first village proved to be very complex and the original ToC for this implementation project was wrong. In addition to the usual practical problems, there was also the complex problem of castes. The urban campaigners had not foreseen that this could pose a major disruption: Because there was no relationship of trust in the beginning, nobody drew their attention to it during the planning phase. In particular, the ongoing exchange with those involved was introduced as a kind of indicator which helped to identify (and to question) assumptions and biases, to broaden perspectives, to follow-up, and (unconsciously-automatically) to adapt the ToC. As the campaigners noticed the interest matched by rising enthusiasm, they knew that they were together on course.

The Theory of Change method can also be used if global impact is intended. Yet already in large, long-standing campaigns no detailed ToC can be produced; and even less so on a global level, where one of the intentions of Greenpeace is to transform consumer culture into a sustainable, resource-saving one. The ToC is a set of guidelines at this level; the principal one, plainly stated: "Ensure that people can experience the solutions for which we strive, to achieve a kind of implicitness: By experiencing a truly new way of doing things, people will sooner seek out a desired change of culture".

7 Advantages and Disadvantages

Important advantages are that the ToC helps to clarify contents and assumptions for discussion and decision making and sets intermediate goals; agreements are made specifying what progress and successes are and how they are measured. The ToC establishes a link between on-the-ground activities and project goals. It forces us, so to speak, to think together about the preconditions/prerequisites and measurement of the project's progress, i.e. the interventions are justifiable and reasonable. Whilst all depends on communication between constituent elements: committed stakeholders, impact-oriented monitoring and evaluation, the pulse of the project so is felt quasi continuously. This dialectic, the interplay between top-down theory and bottom-up

[8]http://www.greenpeace.org/india/en/Blog/Campaign_blogs/three-years-of-ecological-agriculture-has-cha/blog/61045/

practice, is the main advantage. The ToC lends itself to verify or falsify assumptions in practice: Working with focus groups, stakeholder conferences, prototypes and models are some of the key words. The ToC thus permits a systematic view and ensures with its participative approach that partners involved know where they stand in the project.

The Difficulty of the Theory Is Applying It the Practice Because the ToC is a detailed impact model, it is very time-consuming to implement 1:1. Furthermore, the lack of resources and time pressure can overshadow the advantages (e.g. by applying it like a mechanical model with a linear logic). Of course, time pressure is sometimes a reality, e.g. in disastrous situations. Very often there simply isn't money to plan and monitor comprehensively, or the entire budget would have to be spent on it. Among other things, this presents a danger of using only those indicators in underfunded situations that are cheap.

In my opinion, however, most of the time one puts pressure on oneself. If one thinks something has to be done immediately, it often leads to activism or treating a matter as if it were an eleventh hour-urgency to impel others. In the face of such a threat, this is all too understandable, however one might shoot oneself into one's own leg: Time pressure can render us blind. It would be better to heed the maxim, "If you are in a hurry, go slowly"; bluntly stated: "It's too late anyway, so we have time". However, patience is not the job of environmentalists; and where there is no time, participation often turns into a top-down or misuse of participants.

8 Conclusions

It is an art form not to cut back too early, and yet not to wait too long. Processes can be tedious, and it's important to stay agile. For this reason tests or pilot projects are important: the first practice run happens relatively quickly, one learns from practice and gets to know one another, one builds trust. Risk is reduced: partial failure only on a small scale saves resources and makes it possible to learn from mistakes.

In conclusion: there is no one single effect, there are always several. Some of these effects can be measured directly, others only indirectly. For a complete overall picture, this means not only relying on superficial big data, but also on qualitative "small data" beneath the surface. To ensure that the "right" data is collected, the indicators should be chosen carefully. The sales figure of a product is undoubtedly an indicator, but it may say too little, e.g. nothing about sustainability. Here is an example: In the solar project of Nicaraguan women[9] the number of solar cookers built was initially used as an indicator of the progress of the project—the more, the better. Until 1 day, the project managers noticed that many stoves were left unused in a neighbourhood where they had organised construction courses. As a result, they

[9]https://fuprosomunic.org/

decided to use the "number of stoves in actual use" as the main indicator. This had major consequences, because this indicator requires a qualitative survey. One can no longer simply count the output, but must record the outcome in the kitchens, *in situ*. This meant that some of the resources were now used to visit every solar cooker owner every 2 months for 2 years after the construction course (see also above Kirkpatrick Method). In this way, the project managers were able to see exactly what promotes or hinders the use of the solar cooker in everyday life. Some of the findings led to adjustments in the construction courses, others to an increased concern for the social dimension of the project. This qualitative survey is costly, but led to the fact that now 90% of the cookers built are actually used; and a community of a thousand women has emerged—this is the real success of the multiple award-winning project (e.g. the Nicaraguan prize for innovative promotion of micro-enterprises).

This leads to the recommendation that evaluations should be designed in such a way that the interviewees do not only possess the factor of cost, but primarily an inherent equivalent value. Anecdotes (see box above "Stories as Data") or conversations can therefore be configured in, so that the participants in a group discussion can learn from each other. Or in an individual discussion, where small but concrete things can be learned and accomplished. In the example of the 'solar women', such things have been repairs to a cooker or recipes for improved cooking.

Caution: to always follow up on project participants after a few months with comprehensive questionnaires can border on harassment and result in a somewhat numbing rather than inspiring and manageable amount of data.

Kuno Roth PhD in chemistry, human ecologist, writer, Greenpeace International, Global Learning & Development, Mentoring Coordinator.

The Lessons of Microcredit

Peter W. Heller

"He that has lost his credit is dead to the world."
(German and English Proverb)

Abstract Microcredit is a prominent sector in the field of sustainable development finance. This article addresses the lessons learned in its rise and fall over thirty years. It examines the conceptual barriers as a result of its commercialisation, driven by the underlying neoliberal paradigm: the asymmetric debt relationship, the use of an arbitrary poverty line for the assessment of its performance, the absence of the inequality perspective, the unsubstantial belief in a 'natural' market equilibrium. A systemic failure of market forces lies beyond that paradigm, hence an alternative post Keynesian theory is illustrated by Mader's application of Minsky's financial instability hypothesis to the collapse of the regional microcredit market in India. It follows a brief overview of the feeble response of the microfinance industry to the distortions in the microcredit markets. In the final part, two alternative approaches to sustainable development finance are outlined, the universal basic income and the "Jubilee" type debt cancellation challenging usury and systemic overindebtedness. A thorough understanding of the lessons learned in microcredit opens new windows of opportunities to achieve a meaningful theory of change in sustainable development finance.

Keywords Financial instability (Hypothesis) · Jubilee (Law of) · Microcredit · Microfinance · Minsky moment · Poverty line · Universal basic income · Theory of change · Theories of change · Sustainable development goals · SDGs

---

P. W. Heller (✉)
Canopus Foundation, Freiburg, Germany
e-mail: pwheller@canopusfund.org

K. Wendt (ed.), *Theories of Change*, Sustainable Finance,
https://doi.org/10.1007/978-3-030-52275-9_11

1 Introduction: Sustainable Finance, a Concept in Danger of Dilution

In the wake of the controversial debates triggered by the *Limits to Growth* report of the Club of Rome, the concept of *sustainable development* emerged as a new paradigm for the global environmental, social and economic agenda. Soon it began to affect financial markets, too, where it led to an "increasing awareness of the risks which may have an impact on the sustainability of the financial system itself, and the need for financial and corporate actors to mitigate those risks through appropriate governance." (European Commission 2019) Over the last 10 years, in the aftermath of the financial crisis of 2007/2008, the term *sustainable finance* has gained traction in the private sector and the political arena: recently, on 21st March 2019 the European Commission organised its second high-level conference on sustainable finance. The event was held to encourage a global approach to sustainable finance and to discuss ways to channel private capital towards sustainable projects in a coherent way.

The idea of sustainability was first conceived in the early eighteenth century in the field of forest management: it requires to manage forests in a way that the extraction of wood does not exceed its reproductive abilities. In 1987, when the Brundtland Commission coined the widely used definition of sustainable development,[1] there was already sound evidence that not only environmental externalities and resource markets, but also financial markets were on unsustainable trajectories. Volumes of stocks, bonds and derivatives were rising exponentially against the market volumes of goods and services, spinning off at a yet unimaginable pace and in 2007 ultimately out of control, which created a new awareness of the systemic risks embedded in the disjuncture of the real and the financial economy. Sustainable development was perceived by the international community as a much needed response to the unlimited but unreliable reign of the globally unleashed market forces. However, the more the term was used in a broader sense (in forest management things were clear and easy to capture), the more its meaning multiplied and lost its practical operability, and the core message of sustainable development became diluted, a victim of its own success. In debates on policies for economic development it has been subsequently used as a preferred formula by the advocates of private sector solutions who consider *old style development aid*, dependent on the steady flow of public money for development causes, as outdated, even 'unsustainable', distracting the market forces to do better: "As the twenty-first century began, the idea of delivering poverty reduction through sustainable business principles and practices was powerful … With sustainability used as a hallmark of success for both development intervention and institutions, microfinance embodies one of the most successful international development industries and a sector in its own right" (Maîtrot 2019: 144). After the rise and fall of microfinance, outlined in the next chapter, the adoption of the 2030

[1] "'Sustainable Development' is development that meets the needs of the present without compromising the ability of future generations to meet their own needs." (Report of the World Commission on Environment and Development: Our Common Future 1987: 41).

Agenda for Sustainable Development and its 17 *Sustainable Development Goals (SDG)* by the UN in 2015 brought forth a new attempt to carefully balance the neoliberal[2] and the post Keynesian concepts of sustainable finance. The tension between these two economic schools of thought had a direct impact on the development of the microfinance narrative. This chapter examines the lessons learned after the rise and fall of microfinance. It exposes the conceptual barriers of the current paradigm of development finance and outlines some elements of a new theory of change which takes into account the failures of the past. Those conceptual barriers are strong in the world of microfinance: first, there is the myth of substantial poverty mitigation by the commercialisation of highly asymmetric debt relationships. In practice, microfinance contracts are a far cry from any transaction between equal partners, even if a sufficient number of lenders have entered the markets. Second, an arbitrary poverty line is applied in tracking the performance of microfinance products which defines development down and claims progress where there is none, turning statistics into politics. Third, we see a significant preference on the lenders' side for the poverty narrative over the inequality narrative, turning semantics into politics. Fourth, in the field of economic theory and policy applied to microfinance, the neoliberal belief in a natural trend to economic equilibrium and the stability of financial markets, based on the principles of neoclassical economics, evidently fails to provide a convincing explanation for the real market distortions and the inherent instability of the microfinance markets.

Those barriers are not carved in stone. There are other approaches to sustainable development finance which have the potential to overcome the limits of the neoliberal paradigm. Two of them will be briefly introduced in the final part of this chapter. The first element of a new theory of change is the implementation of a universal basic income (UBI) which replaces the credit based access to money and prevents systemic overindebtedness. The second element is a carefully orchestrated debt cancelling policy.

2 The Microfinance Narrative

Microfinance[3] got global recognition when the UN declared 2005 as the 'UN Year of Microcredit' and Muhammad Yunus, the founder of the *Grameen Bank* in Bangladesh, was awarded with the Noble Peace Prize in 2006. Yunus has been widely credited as the leading pioneer of microcredit[4]; he famously claimed that

---

[2]I use the term 'neoliberal', often lacking precise meaning, in the way Ph. Mirowski defines the 'neoliberal thought collective' as the group of economists who developed the neoliberal core agenda in the Mont Pèlerin Society since 1947 (Mirowsky 2014).

[3]*Microfinance* encompasses diverse microfinancial services to the poor, f.e. microcredit, microsaving, microinsurance, microleasing. Although the term is used synonymously with *microcredit*, the latter in its strict sense refers to the provision of credit only.

[4]A claim repeatedly challenged by Acciòn, a microfinance institution which provided its first microloans in Brazil in 1973.

microcredit would "make a break in the historical continuation of poverty"(Yunus 2006).

In a broader historical perspective, microfinance is nothing entirely new. The idea of bringing small credits to the poor was much earlier conceived in Northern Italy at the time of the *Renaissance*, where municipal lending institutions were built to challenge the rampant usury by the commercial money lenders—a quite similar situation to Bangladesh before the emergence of microfinance institutions (MFI), although there is no direct lineage or linkage between the early European approaches to cooperative banking and contemporary microfinance. In 1462 the city of Perugia established the first *Mons Pietatis* to distribute small credits to poor people in urgent need to escape the firm grip of money lenders. Soon the cities of Orvieto, Siena and other municipalities in Northern Italy followed the example of Perugia's Mons Pietatis. Annual interest rates varied between 4% and 12% (Holzapfel 1903: 32–66), significantly lower than the interest rates of commercial money lenders or *Montes Profani* which regularly exceeded 40%. The Montes Pietatis of the fifteenth century had a management structure and *social banking* mode of operations closely resembling those developed by the Grameen Bank, Acciòn and other pioneer MFIs. However, an essential feature of the Renaissance MFIs is their status as purely non-profit, charitable institutions.

Pursuing at first a non-profit strategy, too, Yunus started as a social banker, acquiring capital first from private donors and increasingly from development finance institutions (DFI). He built a *soft money* capital stock for the Grameen bank to protect its social purpose. After the launch of the Grameen Bank in 1983 its microcredit model was embraced by the international development community as an innovative and *unique* tool for poverty reduction and rural development, 10 years later it caught the attention of the World Bank (Robinson 2001).[5] Financial engineers in the DFI world quickly realised that the young microfinance sector had a huge potential for commercialisation: to phase out the old style development aid model based on continuous subsidies, and gradually replacing capital of public agencies and philanthropic donors with for-profit investments by private providers of capital. In cooperation with the World Bank, IFC, Asian Development Bank and other DFIs the investment companies which entered the microfinance sector applied the familiar business mindset and its tools to the reengineering of the non-profit model of microfinance, they convinced private investors to pump billions of dollars into the microfinance industry. Looking back to 2006, the story was easy to capture in a marketing perspective:

- Microfinance is pursuing a noble social mission, the mitigation of poverty;
- Microcredits are an 'alternative' financial product or asset class, and thus more resilient to disruptions in the mainstream capital markets;
- Risks of default are limited, as the repayment rates of borrowers have been consistently high (>95% for a majority of MFIs).

[5]see also Bateman and Chang (2012: 15).

That commercial shift urged Yunus and his fellow pioneers to completely revise the first business model of the Grameen Bank and other early MFIs. In 2002 he and his senior staff launched the 'Grameen II' project, adapting the bank to the commercialised version of microcredit (Hulme 2009: 168–169). As the world famous leader of the microfinance movement and Noble Prize Laureat he had no other choice if he wanted to stay at the forefront and ride the new wave of excitement in the halls of the World Economic Forum in Davos and the Clinton Global Initiative in New York. It took a few more years before the outcome of the *Faustian pact* that he and his fellows had forged became visible.

After the peak of the popularity of microfinance in 2006 the cracks in the shining façade of magic poverty reduction began to multiply. The first distortions occurred when, coincidentally, the global crisis on the financial markets fully hit the world economy in the wake of the collapse of Bear Stearns and Lehman Brothers in 2007: "The turning point came in April 2007 when Mexico's largest microcredit bank, Banco Compartamos, undertook an Initial Public Offering (IPO). The IPO process inadvertently revealed two crucial things: first, in spite of its self-described role in poverty reduction, it became clear that there was no real evidence whatsoever that Banco Compartamos had been instrumental in resolving poverty among its poor, mainly female, client-base; . . . and even more damaging, the IPO revealed a simply astonishing level of private profiteering engineered by Banco Compartamos's co-CEOs, its senior managers and its investors." (Bateman 2019: 7). In Andhra Pradesh, India, SKS Microfinance, at that time the largest MFI in the country, followed with its IPO in 2010, 5 years after it had shrugged off its non-profit status. Soon after going public, SKS Microfinance dragged Andhra Pradesh in a destructive subprime-style microcredit meltdown with severe collateral damage in other states of India and beyond.[6] The subsequent crises of the microfinance sector in Pakistan, Bangladesh, Nicaragua, South Africa, Morocco, Bosnia and Cambodia after 2008 provided ample evidence that the new concept had major flaws:

- The theory of change pursued by Yunus and his followers has been built on *Say's Law*[7]: the idea that 'supply creates its own demand' (Bateman 2019: 49). In fact, the local demand of rural and urban low income communities is often constrained, and the explosion of microenterprises fueled by the easy access to microcredits is not balanced by an adequate purchasing power on the side of the customers.
- Even when sufficient local demand would exist, the narrow scale and scope of microenterprises and self-employment ventures does not offer them enough opportunities to benefit from economies of scale and the deployment of new technologies and product innovations.

---

[6]The SKS Microfinance case shall be outlined in more detail in the chapter "India's Minsky Moment".

[7]Say's Law assumes, in the classical tradition of economics, that in the absence of state interventions markets clear and the economy is close to full employment. Keynes' *General Theory* has been the most prominent falsification of Say's Law.

- From an empirical perspective, six randomized evaluations of microcredit in 2015 found a "lack of evidence of transformative effects on the average borrower" (Banerjee et al. 2015: 3), and confirm that generally microcredits have not lifted people out of poverty.

The disturbing news coming in from the world of microfinance had a tangible impact on the financial service providers which had developed and were successfully marketing microfinance investment funds. After 2011 they switched step by step to the sufficiently vague term *financial inclusion*, using the new meta-brand for a redesign of the microfinance model. In particular they shifted their attention from household based microenterprises in the informal economy to small and medium enterprises (SME) in the formal sector, as governmental development aid has preferred to do in the past. That move recognised the relevance of local demand and economies of scale for microentrepreneurs. The fund managers and their client MFIs have been increasingly cautious to lend money for business activities below the minimum efficient scale of production of goods and services.

From an investor's perspective, today the microfinance industry is by and large in good health. MIX Market, one of the leading market intelligence agencies in the microfinance sector, estimates a global volume of US $ 112 billion microcredits borrowed by 120 million clients[8] for 2017. An increase in loan portfolios from 2016 to 2017 of 15.6% shows the robust growth of the microfinance industry with a current capital allocation exceeding pre-crisis levels. The 100 largest MFIs account for 76% of both the loan portfolios and the number of clients. An average portfolio yield of 20.9% and an IRR on equity of 12.6% (2016) prove the strong performance of the sector and confirms its prominent position among alternative assets (BNP 2018: 2). The persistent low-to-zero-to negative interest rates offered on the mainstream bond markets make returns of microfinance funds attractive and provide a competitive advantage. However, market intelligence of MIX Market and BNP refer to *increasingly challenging environments* indicated by a higher portfolio at risk (repayment delays of >30 days) from 4.7% in 2015 to 7.2% in 2016. The microfinance industry acted in response by lowering its projections for 2018.

3 Theoretical Implications

After 2007 the managers of MFIs and microfinance funds, most of them economists and bankers by training, were in a serious predicament: neoclassical microeconomics taught them that the subcritical production scale of microenterprises would not let them operate in a sustainable way, an issue which could be tackled by shifting their lending policy to SMEs. But a *systemic* failure of market forces was not what they had expected. Their toolkit for the design of primary and derivative financial

[8]Based on information submitted by >700 MFIs; BNP Paribas estimates a total volume of US $ 114 bill. and 139 mill. clients (BNP 2018: 2).

products is firmly anchored in the *efficient market hypothesis*, conceived by Louis Bachelier in 1900 and integrated into neoclassical mainstream economics by Paul Samuelson in his theory of financial market dynamics after World War II. Samuelson's modern interpretation of the efficient market hypothesis is basically a reinstatement of Say's Law in the language of modern economic theory of rational expectations. The efficient market hypothesis claims that stock prices include all relevant market information available, ergo securing a *fair* valuation of financial assets such as stocks, bonds, and property over time. In 1965 Eugene Fama added to the efficient market hypothesis the *random walk theory* which, based on his empirical research, asserts that stock prices move randomly around their 'true' value and cannot be predicted by market analysis in order to generate superior returns. Mainstream economists were guided by the efficient market hypothesis and the random walk hypothesis in their research on the dynamics of financial markets. They applied that conviction to all financial asset classes, including market driven microfinance products.

The flooding of the Global South with microfinance products followed the conviction that those 'bottom-of-the-pyramid'[9] markets in poor communities would absorb all the fresh capital and lead to rapid and robust steady state growth. The historically unique provision of billions of dollars by microfinance funds and banks would, as efficient markets are always supposed to do over time, build a new economy for the poor and push entire nations out of poverty: Bangladesh, the home of Grameen Bank and the other large MFIs BRAC and ASA with more than 27 million active borrowers as a shining example (MIX Market 2019a).

Alas, the new *equilibrium in theory* did not materialise, instead the microfinance markets in Asia, Africa and South America were pushed in an acute financial instability. The neoclassical belief in the magic wand of the efficient market hypothesis to make market distortions and risks vanish did not work better for the alternative asset class of microfinance as it did for the mainstream stock and bond markets. In retrospective, the bigger and smaller crashes after 2007 gave an edge to post Keynesian economics over their neoclassical counterpart. In particular H. Minsky's *financial instability hypothesis* offered a view of the boom and bust closer to the real dynamics of the microfinance sector. Minsky followed the insights of Keynes in the behaviour of actors in financial markets under uncertainty. He ascertained that in well functioning markets, cautious behaviour and risk aversion tends to decrease over time, as more speculative investment strategies with more leverage are rewarded by significantly higher returns. At a tipping point called the *Minsky Moment*, the high flying expectations and heavily leveraged investments start to falter when external events, not necessarily unique or catastrophic, lead to the downscaling of expectations in the market performance. The ensuing phase of de-leveraging triggers a vicious downward cycle. Minsky concludes that "the tendency to transform doing well into a speculative investment boom is the basic

[9]A frequently used term coined by C.K. Prahalad in *The Fortune at the Bottom of the Pyramid* (Prahalad 2005).

instability in a capitalist economy" (Minsky 1977: 24). A gradual shift towards more risk-taking moves the behaviour of investors forward in three phases:

- hedge financing, a cautious use of capital under the condition that debt obligations can still be fully covered by the investor's income;
- speculative financing with higher leverage. Interest can still be paid by income, but not repayment installments on the principal which have to be covered by new debt;
- *Ponzi*[10] financing, where constantly fresh capital is needed to cover the increasing debt and to postpone default, usually leading into a full-fledged crash situation (Mader 2019: 197).

Counter-intuitively, so Minsky's argument, "[i]t follows that the fundamental instability of a capitalist economy is upward" (Minsky 1977: 24). The financial instability hypothesis is grounded in Keynes' insight that the disequilibrating forces operating in financial markets "directly affect the valuation of capital assets relative to the prices of current output, and this price ratio, along with financial market conditions, determines investment activity" (Minsky 1977: 21). Those forces not only work on markets for stocks, bonds and derivatives in the OECD world, but also guide investment activities on markets in the Global South, including microfinance.

4 India's Minsky Moment

The world's largest domestic microfinance market, India, with over 50 million active borrowers (MIX Market 2019b), is a good example of the validity of Minsky's theory. When India entered the microfinance world after 2000, relatively late, markets in rural areas were hit by the deregulation of the agricultural sector awkwardly managed by the federal government and state governments. States like Andhra Pradesh, where neoliberal reform initiatives pushed parts of the rural population into forced economic migration and failed to create a sufficient number of new jobs, microcredits were most welcome as a substitute for the virtually non-existent social welfare system. The exploding volume of microcredits in Andhra Pradesh from 2005 to 2010 was driven on one side by the low regulation of MFIs (the full exemption from regulative oversight by the Reserve Bank of India), on the other side by federal financial policy which channelled 40% of the credits of Indian banks into *priority sectors* including the rural low income areas. Access to capital was easy for Indian MFIs, and international private investors were keen on seizing the opportunity to provide them with capital. Microfinance has already been acknowledged as a distinguished class of alternative assets, its regional markets largely disconnected from the mainstream money markets. Microfinance clients

[10]The *Ponzi scheme* is named after Charles Ponzi who in Boston 1920 conceived a 'snowball' rollover borrowing system with increasingly ruinous speed and volume.

were considered by the microfinance industry as *hedge units* who borrow money to realise economic opportunities, not to service existent debt. But many already had such debt from other sources and were in need to refinance it. As predicted by the financial instability hypothesis, MFIs started to drift from cautious, donor driven lending practices to more speculative strategies with increasing leverage. The boom ground to a halt in 2010 after the Initial Public Offering (IPO) of SKS Microfinance, at that time the largest MFI in Andhra Pradesh and entire India, raising "US $ 358 million, in spite of serious doubts about the soundness of the company's governance" (Mader 2019: 202). In fall 2010 the microcredit market in Andhra Pradesh reached its *Minsky Moment* and was at the brink of collapse. The State Government saw no other choice than, 6 weeks after the suicides of 30 borrowers, to impose an *emergency ordinance* to immediately stop microfinance operations. Nationwide the SKS Microfinance multi-million deal at the borrowers' expenses and the increasing pressure from MFI agents fueled a growing repayment defiance among microcredit clients. "Competition led MFIs to lower their own lending standards, to the point of refinancing unrepaid loans with further loans and systematically lending to clients of other lenders. The effects of these ... poor lending decisions were even obscured by the rapid loan growth itself, as new (and still 'good') loans numerically outweighed older (already potentially distressed) loans, creating a false semblance of healthy lending. India had, by all accounts, a widely applauded, exemplarily competitive, and commercially successful microfinance sector. These successes were the key to both its spectacular growth and its downfall." (Mader 2019: 208). After microfinance markets in parts of India had reached the Minsky phase 3 of ruinous Ponzi financing, it took them years to recover.

5 The Feeble Response of the Microfinance Industry

Yunus was well aware of the risk that the SKS Microfinance case would tarnish the reputation of the movement he has been spearheading, and released an op-ed comment in the New York Times on what went wrong: "I never imagined that one day microcredit would give rise to its own breed of loan sharks. But it has. As a result, many borrowers in India have been defaulting on their microloans, which could then result in lenders being driven out of business. India's crisis points to a clear need to get microcredit back on track." (Yunus 2011) He referred to the *aggressive marketing and loan collection* as a direct outcome of the commercialisation of the sector, and called for stricter government regulation, in particular the need to set up microfinance regulatory authorities in every country. He proposed a cap for the annual interest rate charged to microcredit clients of 25% which is fairly close to the global average interest rate of microcredits, although some rates are much higher. Yunus' comment is based on his conviction that the crisis of the microfinance industry is caused by bad corporate governance, the greed of shareholders and managers, and dysfunctional government interventions. However, he does not acknowledge a crisis of the microfinance model *itself*, its systemic,

Minskyian instability. Since the crisis has become evident, he has never renounced his Faustian pact with the hard nosed and unsustainable commercialisation of the sector.

Although Yunus' call to order was broadly recognized, it withered away as a lonely voice in the microfinance industry. Other MFIs and their investors preferred to keep low profile in the tough period of 2008–2015 while, having switched their rhetoric from *microfinance and microcredit* to *financial inclusion*, they were gradually getting back to pre-crisis turnovers and profitability. The fast progress of digital payment technologies has opened a new window of opportunities: the ubiquitous outreach of mobile phone applications to even the remotest areas enables lenders to offer their microfinance services at lower cost almost everywhere. Those opportunities bring new challenges to the sector: "... while creating completely new IT-based transactions and markets in the Global South might make good business sense, it can also represent a slow-moving incremental disaster for those vulnerable individuals and communities on the receiving end" (Bateman 2019: 11).

Distress is persisting in many places indeed. According to undisclosed reports of October 2017 to BMZ/KfW,[11] the number of overindebted clients in Cambodia has reached 50% (Steinmetz 2019). In Sri Lanka 2018, the finance minister accused microfinance companies of ruining Sri Lanka's financial sector. The *Economist* comments: "Sri Lanka needs properly enforced rules that prevent overindebtedness and ensure fair treatment of borrowers. Until then, microfinance will be a cause not for hope but for despair" (Economist 2019: 58).

Today the total private capital invested in microfinance funds is estimated—with moderate reliability—at US $ 12–14 bill. Not New York or London are the hotspots of microfinance fund management, but Switzerland. A significant part of private investments are directly managed or controlled via advisory mandates by three Swiss companies, Blue Orchard and responsAbility in Zurich, and Symbiotics in Geneva. Since 2001 Blue Orchard has been the Swiss pioneer whose founder had launched the first European microfinance fund at Banque Dexia in 1998. Recently Schroders aquired a major stake in Blue Orchard, bringing its US $ 3,5 bill. of microfinance assets under the firm regime of Schroder's empire of US $ 537 bill. assets under management and a global workforce of 5000 employees. Blue Orchard's oldest and largest flagship product, the Blue Orchard Microfinance Fund, for professional investors only, still proudly bears its old name and defied any relabelling to financial inclusion. Commercially the fund has done well over the last 20 years, only in 2013 it generated a loss for investors due to the microfinance crisis in India. Other funds of the company cover the thematic areas of energy and climate, health and education. On its homepage Blue Orchard celebrates its contribution to the mitigation of poverty and implementation of SDG #1 by a graphic ticker counting the number of *microentrepreneurs* (their clients) supported by a loan from MFIs financed by Blue Orchard, which in 2019 has exceeded 40 million people. Another graphic ticker

[11]BMZ: German Federal Ministry for Economic Cooperation and Development; KfW: Kreditanstalt für Wiederaufbau, Germany's state-owned Development Bank.

counts the number of people who have escaped poverty, now over 575 mill., the term poverty defined by a *poverty line* of US $ 1.90 a day.[12] However, neither on its website nor in its impact report (Blue Orchard 2019/2020) anything tangible can be found in response to the critical examinations of the systemic instability of microfinance and its role in perpetuating and widening the inequality gap within and between countries - in violation of SDG #10.

responsAbility, Blue Orchards competitor in Zurich and a close second with US $ 3 bill. assets under management, has chosen a similar spread of its products across the thematic fields of microfinance, energy, and agriculture. The relabelling of its microfinance investment fund, the former responsAbility Global Microfinance Fund, to *responsAbility Micro and SME Fund* acknowledges the new preference of the microfinance industry given to small and medium enterprises which at the peak of the microcredit hype had a hard time to get access to growth capital of public and private investors alike. In fact, responsAbility is one of the players in the microfinance industry whose intention is to avoid the impending *crowding out* scenario where informal microenterprises with low productivity and poor households are overloaded with microcredits, while lending to the more productive SMEs is abandoned (Bateman 2019: 280). As a consequence, the volume of individual loans is constantly rising: at responsAbility the average loan size in 2017 was US $ 2.254 (responsAbility 2017: 34). The industry has come a long way indeed from Yunus' first US $ 27 loans to the women in the village of Jobra 40 years ago. But the share of SME finance in the portfolios is still small in relation to the volume of microcredits, typically below 10% of the assets under management.

The response of the microfinance industry to the huge wave of critique about the impact of microfinance in the Global South has been feeble. Its mindset is anchored in the practitioners' micro level world, the larger picture, the *macroeconomic effects* of microfinance and its systemic implications, is largely absent on its horizon. In a joint effort a group of international DFIs, including the IFC and the Asian Development Bank, have established a *smart campaign* for the protection of borrowers, offering a certification process for MFIs which have to meet a number of client protection principles. At a closer look, the standards raised by the smart campaign ring hollow and touch, at best, the surface of the problem. The director of the campaign sets the bar low for the microfinance industry: "We don't see it as our role to set any limits on interest or profits" (Barrès 2015). That stance falls even short of Yunus' intervention in 2001 and is far from any substantial protection of poor people lured into overindebtedness, which would definitely require to curb profitability for investors and prevent usury in charging clients. Among smaller lenders there are notable exceptions, like GLS Bank in Germany, which go beyond the smart campaign criteria and have a closer look at the level of microfinance market penetration in regions where they are vetting MFIs.

---

[12]see next chapter.

6 Essential Elements of a Meaningful Change

As commercialised microfinance has not lived up to its promises, the looming question is: what are the key elements of a meaningful change, how can development finance be updated to pursue a sustainable trajectory? We have explored microfinance as an important narrative of sustainable finance to understand how the neoliberal approach has failed to provide guidance for the implementation of the SDG agenda at a larger scale. At that point we ought to think *a bit more radical* about the ways and means to overcome the limitations of mainstream thinking. For that purpose the term *poverty* has to be reviewed and clarified.

The advocates of microfinance tell us that market driven poverty mitigation, apart from the occasional crises here and there, has been mostly successful over the last 20 years. That statement is usually based on the old poverty line benchmark of US $ 1.90 a day, endorsed by the World Bank until 2017,[13] an income equivalent of what US $ 1.90 could buy in the US in 2011. Blue Orchard shows on its homepage how many poor people have been lifted out of (1.90) poverty in the last 20 years. Only 770 million people are estimated to live below that poverty line today; do we really have a success story at hand? The former World Bank economist and Harvard scholar Lant Pritchett strongly disagrees and sees the (1.90) poverty line as "defining development down... paternalistic and discriminatory ... with no economic rationale at all" (Pritchett 2017). Given the dramatic drop of subsistence economies and the high inflation in major parts of the Global South, Pritchett and other researchers have argued for a much higher poverty line, securing at least basic nutrition and an average human life expectancy, at US $ 7.40 a day. Below that more realistic (7.40) poverty line are living not 770 million, but 4.2 billion poor people; hence the poverty mitigation narrative becomes elusive (Hickel 2019).

Instead of arguing about poverty lines which do or do not confirm the effectiveness of microfinance, a shift from the *poverty focus of SDG #1* to the *inequality focus of SDG #10* might give a more insightful picture of the situation. The poverty narrative has "given rise to watered-down theories of change that are personal, individual, depoliticized, respectful of the status quo and the system, and not in the least bit disruptive" (Giridharadas 2018: 120). Concepts about poverty mitigation are met with less resistance than those about the reduction of inequality. Although the two ideas are closely related, "poverty is a material fact of deprivation that does not point fingers, and inequality is something more worrying: It speaks of what some have and others lack; it flirts with the idea of injustice and wrongdoing; it is relational" (Giridharadas 2018: 122).

The idea of a *universal basic income* (UBI) has gained traction over the last 10 years as a potential solution to tackle inequality and close the gap between the rich and the poor. It represents a fresh and valid alternative to debt based strategies. The UBI is a regular local, regional or national payment delivered by the public authorities to its residents. It is *unconditional* of gender, employment, and living costs and *non-withdrawable*, i.e. it does not constitute any debt relation between the

[13]Since 2017 the World Bank routinely calculates and reports multiple international poverty lines.

state and the individual. The basic idea has a long history: Marquis de Condorcet, Th. Paine and B. Russell have promoted different versions of a UBI, more recently H. Daly has applied the UBI concept to his framework of a *sustainable or steady-state economy* (Daly 2013). Theoretically it is not necessarily at odds with neoliberal economics: M. Friedman planted a UBI concept in the mould of a *negative income tax* firmly in the garden of the Chicago School.

At an amazing speed the debates about the UBI and the diverse options of its design have spread in the OECD world and led to various local tests in the Netherlands, Switzerland (where it was the subject of a federal referendum), Canada, California and Italy. In the Global South UBI pilot projects have been conducted in Namibia, India and Brazil. Where the idea of a basic income with no strings attached, guaranteed by the government as a legal right, emerges, it shifts the underlying message in a subtle but pervasive way from the *poverty narrative* to the *inequality narrative*. High net worth individuals, their foundations and fund managers are not amused about that shift, as the inconvenient truth of a growing gap between the rich and the poor in many countries becomes more visible, more urgent, more controversial. The message of *poverty mitigation by making the poor bankable* loses its credibility in the context of the UBI discourse. The unconditional transfer of regular payments which constitutes no debt obligations follows a completely different path to implement the sustainability agenda than the full commercialisation of poor communities at the *bottom of the pyramid* in the Global South.

Complementary to the UBI, the rampant overindebtedness of poor borrowers we see today in Cambodia, Sri Lanka and other countries provides a strong argument to reinvent a very old tradition of debt release: the *Law of Jubilee* (Graeber 2011: 82). In his seminal study on the history of debt ("the first 5000 years"), Graeber introduces the Law of Jubilee by a reference to a passage in the Old Testament of the Bible giving the following command: "At the end of every seven years you must cancel debts. This is how it is to be done: Every creditor shall cancel any loan they have made to a fellow Israelite. They shall not require payment from anyone among their own people, because the LORD's time for canceling debts has been proclaimed. You may require payment from a foreigner, but you must cancel any debt your fellow Israelite owes you." (The Holy Bible: Deuteronomy 15, 1–3) An extension of that system of solidarity among the Israelites to all world citizen in need would lead us to another approach to sustainable finance, "not just because it would relieve so much genuine human suffering, but also because it would be our way of reminding ourselves that money is not effable, that paying one's debts is not the essence of morality, that all these things are human arrangements and that if democracy is to mean anything, it is the ability to all agree to arrange things in a different way." (Graeber 2011: 390). Obviously the Law of Jubilee violates the rule of reciprocity or equivalent material exchange in transactions between the lender and the borrower which governs the financial markets, including the microfinance sector, and its assessments of credit default risks today.

A first step would be a carefully orchestrated international debt cancellation policy by DFIs addressing emergency cases where repayment rates are close to usury and debt volumes are too high to give borrowers any chance to recover. Such a debt cancellation initiative would depend on a concurrent mechanism, set up by international development banks, to hedge the portfolio risks of non-speculative private investors. The political road to an international agreement for a regular *Jubilee type* debt cancellation would be arduous, as even a limited violation of the reciprocity rule would undermine the basic fabric of the commercialised structure of development finance.

Graeber argues that in proto-capitalist economies, that rule of exchange reciprocity had never been strictly applied. The evolution of property rights, monetary exchange mechanisms and ultimately financial markets in the history of capitalism brought an end to this. It is about time to reconsider the sanctity of the reciprocity rule in the same way as the *Limits to Growth* discourse on sustainable development reconsidered the sanctity of the paradigm of unlimited growth in man's *dominium terrae,* his right to exploit natural resources *ad infinitum* and to undermine the basic preconditions for human survival in the age of the *Anthropocene*.

7 Conclusion

In the previous brief chapters I have examined the microfinance sector as a prominent example of sustainable finance where major barriers obscure the perspective of a meaningful change. Those barriers are

- the exclusive development of microcredit as a for-profit asset class which sacrifices basic human needs to loosely controlled market forces and creates highly asymmetric debt relationships;
- performance assessments of microcredit products and portfolios based on the application of an arbitrary low poverty line in order to define development *down* and, therefore, prove progress;
- the dominance of the poverty narrative and the avoidance of the inequality narrative in the sector;
- the lack of insight into the systemic instability of financial markets as a legacy of neoclassical economics.

If we detach our approach towards a new theory of change from those barriers, other options emerge on the path to a meaningful concept of sustainable finance:

- a universal basic income which replaces the credit based access of poor people to money and prevents systemic overindebtedness;
- a Jubilee type policy which cancels debt in emergency situations.

A more comprehensive theory of change reviewing those options in greater detail is, I have to admit, beyond the reach of this article. But understanding what has not worked over the last 30 years, and what has yet to be tested at a larger scale, might give an idea of the opportunities that lie before us. The proverb's anathema "He that has lost his credit is dead to the world" should be overcome by a meaningful theory of change for sustainable finance.

References

Banerjee, A., Karlan, D., & Zinman, J. (2015). Six randomized evaluations of microcredit: Introduction and further steps. *American Economic Journal: Applied Economics, 7*(1), 1–21.

Barrès, I. (2015). *Defining 'good practices' in microfinance: Smart campaign director Isabelle Barrès addresses the thorny issues of profits and pricing – And discusses its next steps, interview by J. Militzer*. Retrieved August 10, 2019, from https://nextbillion.net/defining-good-practices-in-microfinance/

Bateman, M. (2019). Impacts of the microcredit model: Does theory reflect actual practice? In *The rise and fall of global microcredit: Development, debt and disillusion* (pp. 42–68). London: Routledge.

Bateman, M., & Chang, H.-J. (2012). Microfinance and the illusion of development: From hubris to Nemesis in thirty years. *World Economic Review, 1*, 13–36.

Bateman, M., Blankenburg, S., & Kozul-Wright, R. (Eds.). (2019). *The rise and fall of global microcredit*. London/New York: Routledge.

Blue Orchard Impact Report (2019–2020). Retrieved August 10, 2019, from https://www.blueorchard.com/wp-content/uploads/BlueOrchard-Impact_Report_2019-2020.pdf

BNP Paribas Microfinance Barometer. (2018). Retrieved August 15, 2019, from http://www.convergences.org/wp-content/uploads/2018/09/BMF_2018_EN_VFINALE-1.pdf

Daly, H. (2013). *Top 10 policies for a steady-state economy*. Retrieved August 20, 2019, from https://steadystate.org/top-10-policies-for-a-steady-state-economy/

European Commission. (2019). Retrieved August 26, 2019, from https://ec.europa.eu/info/business-economy-euro/banking-and-finance/sustainable-finance_en

Giridharadas, A. (2018). *Winners take all*. New York: Alfred A. Knopf.

Graeber, D. (2011). *Debt: The first 5000 years*. New York: Melvillehouse.

Hickel, J. (2019, Jan 29) Bill gates says poverty is decreasing. He couldn't be more wrong, *The Guardian*. Retrieved August 20, 2019, from https://www.theguardian.com/commentisfree/2019/jan/29/bill-gates-davos-global-poverty-infographic-neoliberal

Holzapfel, P. H. (1903). *Die Anfänge der Montes Pietatis, 1462–1515*. München: J.J. Lentner.

Hulme, D. (2009). The story of the Grameen Bank: fRom subsidized microcredit to market based microfinance. In D. Hulme & T. Arun (Eds.), *Microfinance: A reader* (pp. 163–170). London/New York: Routledge.

Mader, P. (2019). The instability of commercial microfinance: understanding the Indian crisis with Minsky. In M. Bateman, S. Blankenburg, & R. Kozul-Wright (Eds.), *The rise and fall of global microcredit: Development, debt and disillusion* (pp. 194–215). London: Routledge.

Maîtrot, M. (2019). Sustainability paradigm to paradox: A study of microfinance clients' livelihoods in Bangladesh. In M. Bateman, S. Blankenburg, & R. Kozul-Wright (Eds.), *The rise and fall of global microcredit: Development, debt and disillusion* (pp. 143–165). London: Routledge.

Minsky, H. (1977). The financial instability hypothesis: An interpretation of Keynes and an alternative to 'standard' theory. *Challenge, 20*, 20–27.

Mirowsky, P. (2014, September). *The political movement that dared not speak its own name: The neoliberal thought collective under erasure*, INET Working Paper No. 23, 1–34. Retrieved August 20, 2019, from https://www.ineteconomics.org/uploads/papers/WP23-Mirowski.pdf

MIX Market. (2019a). *Bangladesh market overview*. Retrieved August 13, 2019, from https://www.themix.org/mixmarket/countries-regions/bangladesh

MIX Market. (2019b). *India market overview*. Retrieved August 13, 2019, from https://www.themix.org/mixmarket/countries-regions/india

Prahalad, C. K. (Ed.). (2005). *The fortune at the bottom of the pyramid: Eradicating poverty through profits*. New Delhi: Pearson.

Pritchett, L. (2017). *Getting kinky with chickens*. Retrieved August 11, 2019, from https://www.cgdev.org/blog/getting-kinky-chickens

Report of the World Commission on Environment and Development: Our Common Future. (1987). Retrieved July 25, 2019, from https://sustainabledevelopment.un.org/content/documents/5987our-common-future.pdf

responsAbility. (2017). *Impact report 2017*. Retrieved August 10, 2019, from https://www.responsability.com/sites/default/files/2018-12/rA_IMPACT_publication_2.pdf

Robinson, M. (2001). *The microfinance revolution: Sustainable finance for the poor*. Washington, DC: World Bank Publications.

Steinmetz, V. (2019). Mikrokredite in Kambodscha - Lukratives Geschäft mit der Armut, *SPIEGEL online* 7.8.2019. Retrieved August 20, 2019, from https://www.spiegel.de/politik/ausland/mikrokredite-in-kambodscha-lukratives-geschaeft-mit-der-armut-a-1280064.html

The Economist. (2019, August 17). *Distress Signals, 58*.

The Holy Bible, New International Version. (2011). *Deuteronomy* 15, 1–3. Retrieved August 11, 2019, from https://www.biblegateway.com/passage/?search=Deuteronomy+15%3A1-3&version=NIV.

Yunus, M. (2006). *Nobel lecture*. Retrieved August 10, 2019, from https://www.nobelprize.org/prizes/peace/2006/yunus/26090-muhammad-yunus-nobel-lecture-2006-2/

Yunus, M. (2011, January 14). Sacrificing microcredit for Megaprofits, Op-Ed in the *New York Times*. Retrieved August 13, 2019, from https://www.nytimes.com/2011/01/15/opinion/15yunus.html

Peter W. Heller, born in 1957, studied economics (PhD 1988) and philosophy in St. Gallen (CH), Lausanne (CH) and Freiburg (D). 1990–1997 he served as Deputy Mayor for Environmental Protection, Energy Management and Forestry in the municipal administration of the City of Freiburg. 1993–1997 he was Chairman of the Executive Committee of ICLEI, Cities for Sustainability. Heller is a co-founder of BASE (Basel Agency for Sustainable Energy), Chairman of the Board of HUMBOLDT VIADRINA Governance Platform gGmbH, Berlin, and a member of the Advisory Council of Cusanus University, Bernkastel-Kues (D). Heller is the founder and sole shareholder of forseo GmbH, a holding company investing in early stage enterprises in the field of renewable energies and energy efficiency. The portfolio of forseo comprises wind and solar project development companies in France and Chile, and energy technology providers in the US and Germany. He serves as a member of the Board of Fahrenheit GmbH and as Chairman of the Board of Streb AG.

Impact Investing Practice Report: Impact Analysis and Impact Reporting at BonVenture

Erwin Stahl and Paul Garte

Abstract Impact investing is on the verge of becoming mainstream. Yet, due to an "impactwashing" wave of conventional investment practices it is evermore crucial for impact investors to differentiate themselves through transparent and well-grounded impact measurement and impact reporting practices. As pioneer in financing social ventures, BonVenture successfully demonstrated the integration of social and economic goals for impact investments. This article seeks to provide insights on the impact analysis and impact reporting process conducted at BonVenture to foster transparency but also to promote the conduct of profound impact investing practices.

Keywords Theory of change · Theories of change · Impact investing · Reporting · Impact reporting · Impact analysis · Bonventure · Transparency · Sustainable development goals · SDGs

1 Introduction

Following the claims of major banks and asset managers, it appears that sustainable or impact investing strategies have grown from a niche to a major trend in the investment industry in recent years. While on hand players of this (former) niche seek for it to become mainstream. Some now fear the misappropriation of terms and the erosion of practices that were established in this young industry over the past two decades in the realm of a greenwashing or 'impactwashing' wave.

To make things worse, the impact investing industry itself, even in its niche, is still very heterogeneous with regard to its practices. Probably the most common denominator is the proactive pursuance of social and/or environmental goals in the investment strategy instead of a passive strategies such as negative screening. Further, the investment evaluation in impact investing almost always incorporates an elaborative

E. Stahl (✉) · P. Garte
Munich, Germany
e-mail: erwin.stahl@bonventure.de; paul.garte@bonventure.de

K. Wendt (ed.), *Theories of Change*, Sustainable Finance,
https://doi.org/10.1007/978-3-030-52275-9_12

impact assessment as basis for an additional impact reporting. The integration of social and financial dimensions within a business model as well as investment strategy is commonly described double-bottom-line or lock-step approach.

Impact investing, from our perspective, follows an 'impact first' approach as delineated in the EVPA Spectrum (2018) and operates within the SDGs (Sustainable Development Goals). Thereby, it can be distinguished from ESG and negative screening approaches subsumed under 'finance first'. The initially described transformation, however, challenges this distinction, reframing 'finance first'-practices as impact investing. Consequently, it becomes more and more important for 'impact first'-investors to differentiate themselves. This resulted, for instance, in reframing 'impact investing' to 'high impact investing' or 'deep impact investing' in a first reaction. The following article seeks to shed light on impact analysis and impact reporting practices as key differentiators of 'impact first' investors.

2 Impact Reporting at BonVenture

2.1 Conceptual and Regulatory Basis

Being one of the first social venture funds in Europe in the early 2000s, the conceptual development and practical implementation of impact assessment and reporting practices played a crucial role for BonVenture to establish its then new investing approach. A key milestone in the professionalization of these practices was the contribution in the joint effort of developing the Social Reporting Standard (SRS) together with research institutions and impact investing intermediaries. Besides these efforts and further internal improvements, impact measurement and reporting practices also underwent an ongoing institutionalization. A major step was BonVenture's registration as European Social Venture Fund (EuSEF) which made previously voluntary conducted impact analysis and reporting practices mandatory. This registration also linked the fund manager's performance to the portfolio's impact performance to ensure an alignment of interests with regard to maximization of the social return alongside the financial return. These practices are embedded in the limited partnership agreement (LPA) of the fund as a prerequisite for being eligible to an investment of the European Investment Fund (EIF) through the Social Impact Accelerator (SIA) program.

2.2 Impact Analysis

2.2.1 Goal

The impact analysis stands at the core of any impact investment. The proactive approach of understanding if and how impact is generated by a venture is a key differentiator from so called negative screening practices. As part of the due diligence process, the insights from the impact analysis are crucial to the ultimate investment decision. Further, the analysis identifies social key performance indicators (KPIs) in order to achieve measurability and traceability of the impact created. At BonVenture, no investment will be made without a clear perspective on an additional positive impact by addressing a social or ecological issue as described within the SDGs.

Apart from guiding the investment decision and setting up the impact reporting, the impact analysis is also key in the communication to the fund's investors. While it demonstrates to existent investors how their allocated capital is invested to generate impact (as agreed upon in the LPA). It also helps to attract new investors who look for impact investment approaches that are more proactive than, for instance, negative screening approaches. Hence, it signals credibility in the field of impact investing.

Lastly, conducting an impact analysis can also contribute to sharpen a venture's vision and strategy. Although we see more and more entrepreneurs that are familiar with the concept of social entrepreneurship and underlying logics of impact creation. The insights gained in the impact analysis often lead to a better understanding of the market and target group, and support the communication to external stakeholders.

2.2.2 Process

Till this date there is no standardized approach across the industry to analyze the impact of an organization—a circumstance we will touch upon later (see discussion). As earlier mentioned, BonVenture has been involved in a prominent attempt for standardization—the development of the SRS. In practice, however, we apply the very comprehensive methods and formal steps outlined in the SRS in a very focused and condensed manner.

At the core, our impact analysis stems from two approaches: the Theory of Change and the logic model approach. According to Rauscher et al. (2012, p. 7) who build upon Weiss (1998), "[...] the logic model reflects what is to be achieved [...], the theory of change focuses on the question how and under what preconditions specific effects are to be achieved [...]". Moreover they highlight the importance of empirical evidence upon which the assumptions for a systematic change through certain interventions are built.

In the following, we describe the main elements of the impact analysis as conducted at BonVenture.

The Societal Challenge

In a first step, we seek to get a profound understanding of the societal challenge a venture is addressing. When looking at a societal challenges we usually look a very complex systems. For our purposes, however, it is important to reduce this complexity in a meaningful way and to expose causal links that are key to a challenge and its solution based on empirical evidence. Not surprisingly it can take several iterations to apply a sufficient level of abstraction. If not already explicitly mentioned by the venture, we also interpret its activities in context of the SDGs and the societal challenges it is addressing accordingly.

The Solution/Business Model

In our understanding, as for most in the field of social entrepreneurship, a social venture's business model should be directly linked to the societal challenge it addresses. The impact analysis should, therefore, reveal a clear causal link between the business activities and the previously described societal challenge in the logic of a Theory of Change.

Theory of Change and IOOI-Logic-Model

Having described the societal issue as well as the causal links of a social venture's business activities addressing it, we then summarize these findings and give an outlook of what is ought to be achieved using the IOOI-Logic-Model (IOOI = Input, Output, Outcome, Impact). This model of abstraction helps us, to depict the various immediate and long-term as well as quantitative and qualitative effects that we are anticipating based on our analysis. Further, directly measurable as well as indirectly calculable KPIs are developed reflecting the IOOI abstraction levels based on empirical findings. These venture-specific KPIs are crucial to keep track of a venture's impact. The following case example will illustrate the different levels of abstraction and provide exemplary KPIs.

2.2.3 Portfolio Venture Example

The case example of a "Sustainable Mobility Venture" represents a very condensed version of an impact analysis. The causal links that are described as well as the development of KPIs shown need to be based empirical findings. Despite an elaborate research, there is often a need to include proxies or even collect primary data to support the impact hypotheses.

With regard to the KPIs, only at the output level they are directly measurable. Outcome and impact are usually only indirectly calculable or they are qualitative. Calculating those estimates, one should be aware of spurious accuracies. When developing KPIs, we recommend to limit the ultimate selection to a view key figures in order to reduce complexity and underline the impact hypotheses.

Box 1 Impact Analysis "Sustainable Mobility Venture"

Societal Challenge:

- Individual traffic is key driver for greenhouse gas and pollutant emissions in cities as well as for environmental degradation through resource depletion
- Scientifically shown relation between anthropogenic CO_2-emissions & global warming

(continued)

Box 1 (continued)

- High number of emission-related respiratory diseases

The solution/business model

- Substitution of resource-inefficient and pollutant mobility concepts
- Highly scalable mobility concept for cities with significantly reduced emissions

Theory of Change and IOOI-Logic-Model

1. *Input*
   - External investments to date: €XXm, internally generated revenue: €XXm
   - No. of FTE: XX; No. of locations: XX
   - Development of expertise
2. *Output*
   - No. of registered customers to date: XX
   - Distance travelled to date: XX km
   - No. of vehicles to date: XX

   The planned impact budget values for each KPI are based on the financial planning as they are linked to the core business. They should, therefore, scale at the same rate. Please note that the impact analysis and KPIs shown in the following Box 1 are only exemplary and do not depict an exhaustive impact analysis.
3. *Outcome*
   - Substitution of inefficient vehicles
   - CO_2 savings
   - Resource savings
   - Reduction of pollutant emissions
   - Non-intended negative effects are deducted
4. *Impact:*
   - Reduction of greenhouse gas emissions leads to deceleration of global warming
   - Reduction of fossil and non-fossil resource repletion reduces environmental degradation
   - Reduction of pollutant emissions reduces respiratory diseases and increases life quality

(continued)

Box 1 (continued)

– Change of mobility habits within the society

Key performance indicators

			Year 1 (actual)*	Year 2 (plan)	Year 3 (plan)	Year 4 (plan)	Year 5 (plan)	Year 6 (plan)
Output	Customers	No.	3000	5000	10,000	18,000	28,000	40,000
Output	Distance travelled	km	10,000	40,000	90,000	170,000	330,000	600,000
Outcome	CO_2 savings	t	500	1500	3500	6000	9500	14,000
Outcome	Resource savings (metals)	Fe t	300	600	1100	2000	5000	12,000
Outcome	Resource savings (fossils)	Oil t	3000	10,000	30,000	45,000	70,000	90,000

*Actual values of Year 1 are considered as starting point before investment. They do not contribute to an investment's impact performance

2.3 *Impact Reporting at Portfolio Venture Level*

2.3.1 Goal

Besides analyzing a venture's impact and considering these results within the investment decision, keeping track of the impact performance is a further key element of impact investing. Only by tracking the impact of a venture until the exit, impact investors can demonstrate that impact was generated through their investment.

Technically, keeping track of a venture's impact also enables us to identify a potential mission drift. In practice, however, we seek for investments whose business models would simply not function without impact as their core business activities are irrevocably linked to impact creation. At the same time, there is often space for improvements. Through an active impact management on a strategic level we can contribute to a more effective and comprehensible impact creation.

Lastly, and as earlier mentioned, the impact reporting is required through the investor agreement as well as the EuSEF-regulation. In this context, a continuous impact reporting is needed to evaluate our performance as fund managers which is linked to the impact performance of our investments.

2.3.2 Process

As mentioned in the previous section, only KPIs at the output level are directly measurable and, hence, trackable. The impact reporting follows the logic of the financial reporting. For each given period, a portfolio venture reports its achieved KPIs at the output level.

In addition, the investor's board of a fund decides on (output) target values for each KPI (based on a proposal of the investment team) which usually equals the expected value 3–4 years after the investment. Based on the target achievement of each KPI and by using a weighting we then calculate the overall social impact target achievement of a startup for a given period as shown below.

$$\sum_{X=1}^{n} \frac{AV_{KPIX_Y}}{TV_{KPIX}} * WF_{KPIX} = TA_Y$$

*AV = Actual Value; *Cumulative values in period or year Y; TV = Target Value; WF=Weighting Factor; TA = Target Achievement; Y=Period or Year; X = No. of KPI*

This, rather synthetic, target achievement value translates all the different KPIs with varying units into one comparable figure. This enables us to keep track of the impact performance of our ventures at fund level as we will discuss in one of the next sections.

2.3.3 Portfolio Venture Example

Box 2 Reporting Social Key Performance Indicators at Venture Level

			Year 1 ([a])	Year 2 (actual)	Year 3 (actual)	Weighting/target value
Output	Customers	n	3000	4400	12,000	40%/28,000
Output	Distance travelled	km	10,000	39,000	93,000	60%/ 330,000
Target achievement		%		13%	34%	

[a]Values before investment

Box 2 shows an exemplary reporting sheet 2 years after an investment. The target values in the last column are based on the values for Year 5 of the original impact analysis (see Box 1). If the KPIs develop according to plan, the target achievement will be at 100% in Year 5.

2.4 *Impact Reporting at Fund Level*

2.4.1 Goal

At fund level, we seek to have an overall overview of our impact performance similar to a financial reporting. As the impact performance is linked to our performance as fund managers, we have an intrinsic motivation understand and further optimize the impact creation of our portfolio ventures. Further, a representation of the fund's overall impact performance helps in the communication to our existent as well as potential investors.

2.4.2 Process

As previously described, the individual impact values of the venture-specific KPIs cannot be aggregated directly. Due to this reason, we developed a system of target achievement values through we can aggregate the individual impact performance of all portfolio ventures at fund level. The calculation, as shown below, is very straightforward. Each venture's yearly target achievement value is weighted by its monetary share of the total fund's investment. Then all weighted target achievement values are accumulated at fund level for a specific period.

$$\sum_{X=1}^{n} TA_{VentureX_Y} \times \frac{Investment\ Size_{VentureX_Y}}{Total\ Fund\ Investment\ Size_Y} = Fund's\ Overall\ TA_Y$$

TA = Target Achievement; X = No. of Venture in Fund; Y=Period or Year

Similar to the portfolio venture level, the fund's target achievement will reach (and ideally exceed) 100% towards the end of the fund's lifetime given a development according to plan.

2.4.3 Fund Example

Box 3 Fund Impact Reporting

Reporting of Target Achievement at Fund Level (after 3 years)

	Investment size	Year 1 (actual	Year 2 (actual)	Year 3 (actual)
Venture 1	1,000,000	–	13%	34%
Venture 2	500,000	20%	28%	46%
Venture 3	1,500,000	28%	43%	67%
Venture 4	500,000	–	–	19%
Overall target achievement in %	3,500,000	26%	31%	48%

The following Box 3 shows an exemplary aggregation of portfolio ventures' target achievements at fund level 3 and 6 years after inception (including 'Venture 1' from Boxes 1 and 2).

(continued)

Box 3 (continued)

Illustration of Target Achievement at Fund Level (after 6 years)

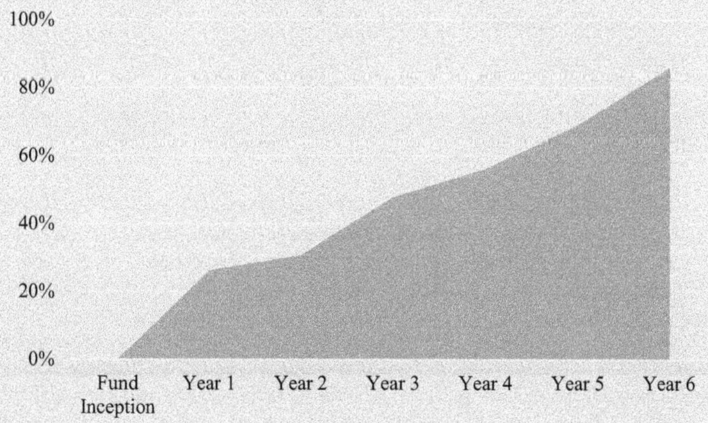

3 Discussion

Impact analysis and reporting practices still remain heterogeneous in the impact investing industry. A recent survey among 8 EIF-backed impact funds within the SIA program showed that all were using Theory of Change as main method (NGII 2019). Other approaches such as SROI or IRIS or IRIS+ were only used by very few intermediaries in Europe as supporting tools.

What is used in practice, can be extended by specific measures like 'lives touched', 'jobs created' or 'CO_2 saved'. Metrics of KPIs can be recalculated to financial values. Together with additional and venture specific information this can lead to a better information on the level of the venture and is requested by some investors, especially if those investors have to report the additional measures to their sources of financing.

Strengths and weaknesses of current practices should be discussed further on (see work of the Global Steering Group for Impact Investing). This should lead to better guidelines and systems for impact communication in the future. There are already several initiatives for general impact measurement and reporting guidelines ongoing in the field. Examples are IRIS+ (established by GIIN), the Impact Management Project (initiated by UNDP), SROI (Social Return on Investment), IMM (impact multiple of money), the Operating Principles for Impact or contributions of the EVPA, just to name a few.

From our experience, aggregating and communicating impact remains challenging. Different from financial KPIs, there is no uniform and established social KPI. At the same time there is a resource constraint with regard to the conduction of impact analysis and reporting practices. Hence, concepts such as the SROI or the SRS become too extensive for the application in practice. Finding a right balance between profound impact practices and competitive investing practices in the venture capital industry is a key challenge.

Besides the discussion on different measuring and reporting systems that will hopefully lead to one common accepted frame or set of guidelines. Introducing an auditing of the applied and reported impact figures (KPIs) would a crucial step for the differentiation of the impact investing industry. The auditing could be done, for instance, by certified accountants.

References

EVPA. (2018). *A practical guide to venture philanthropy and social impact investment.* Retrieved from European Venture Philanthropy Association website https://evpa.eu.com/knowledge-centre/publications/venture-philanthropy-and-social-impact-investment-a-practical-guide

NGII. (2019). *Impact practice survey among conference participants. Next generation impact investors 2019.* Milan, Italy.

Rauscher, O., Schober, C., & Millner, R. (2012). *Social impact measurement and social return on investment (SROI) – Analysis.* Working paper. Retrieved from: http://socialvalueint.org/wp-content/uploads/2012/12/Social-Impact-Measurement-andSROI_English_Version_final_2.pdf

Weiss, C. H. (1998). *Evaluation: Methods for studying programs and policies.* Englewood Cliffs, NJ: Prentice Hall.

Erwin Stahl more than 22 years of successful track-record in investing in seed and early-stage companies; graduated from Regensburg University, Germany, with a degree (Dipl.-Kfm.) in business management; PhD (Dr. rer. pol.) in economics. From January 1996 to March 1999 project manager venture capital with Wellington Partners, Munich (venture capital fund). From April 1999 to December 2002 managing partner of Upside Ventures, Munich (consulting and seed investments for entrepreneurs) and consultant to the EU (5th framework programme SME). From January 2003 (concept/start-up stage) to date Erwin Stahl is Managing Partner of the BonVenture Group, Munich (foundation and impact investing fund with about 50 impact investments up to now; www.bonventure.de).

Paul Garte is an Investment Analyst at BonVenture focusing on early and growth-stage impact companies. Graduating in Management & Technology from Technische Universität München (TUM), he spent semesters abroad at FGV-EAESP (São Paulo) and TU Delft. He finished the certification program for social innovation from the Social Entrepreneurship Akademie and worked as a student in the private equity department of Bain & Company prior to joining the BonVenture Group, Munich (foundation and impact investing fund with about 50 investments and supported projects up to now; www.bonventure.de).

Part IV
Quantitative Analysis in Investing

When Transparency Clouds Rather Than Clarifies: A Closer Look at Transparency Bias Within ESG Scores

Ruben Feldman

Abstract As more attention is paid to ESG and more data vendors enter the ESG ratings market, the importance of data quality cannot be understated. ESG scores and data are increasingly being integrated into investment decisions in order to enhance the sustainability profile as well as improve portfolio performance. However, ESG data is not immune to bias and although data transparency and disclosures seem to be a virtuous aim of and valuable indicator for sustainability, it too can be a source of bias. As discussed here, this bias can lead to over- or underestimating the true sustainability performance of companies, reducing the reliability of ESG scores.

Using regressions and other statistical methods on standard ESG data sets of more than 5000 publicly-listed firms, this paper demonstrates the clear presence of transparency bias within ESG scores, how, if uncontrolled, it leads to erroneous sustainability scores, as well as explains how RobecoSAM's Smart ESG methodology can be used to effectively neutralize systematic transparency bias in order to distill idiosyncratic ESG scores that are more reflective of a company's true sustainability performance. Armed with refined Smart ESG scores, investors can make better informed investment decisions and increase the predictive power of ESG data for a portfolio's sustainability, risk and return performance.

Keywords Theory of change · Theories of change · Transparency · ESG · ESG scores · RobecoSAM

1 Introduction

Investors increasingly incorporate ESG metrics throughout the asset management cycle to aid stock selection and asset allocation, making better informed investment decisions. Whether to reduce risk, increase performance, or to improve a portfolio's sustainability

The original version of this chapter was revised with correct author name "Ruben Feldman". The correction to this chapter can be found at https://doi.org/10.1007/978-3-030-52275-9_30

R. Feldman (✉)
ESG Strategy & Business Development Department, Swisscanto, Zürich, Switzerland
e-mail: ruben.feldman@robecosam.com

K. Wendt (ed.), *Theories of Change*, Sustainable Finance,
https://doi.org/10.1007/978-3-030-52275-9_13

profile, investors should be aware of the pitfalls ESG data may contain. In this paper, we highlight the presence of transparency bias in untreated ESG data and propose a solution to overcome it. An ESG data set that is free of noise induced by transparency bias enables investors to use the true ESG signal that is contained in the data absent the extraneous biases that can mar ESG scores and impair investment decisions.

2 Analysis of Standard ESG Scores

The data collection process begins with companies completing an industry-specific questionnaire that includes a wide variety of topics relating to environmental (E), social (S) and governance (G) criteria. Companies receive a score for each question that is based on both the information supplied (either directly or indirectly via publicly-available sources) as well as on the specific scoring mechanics of the ESG data provider. Moreover, each question score rolls up into a total score that is also dependent on the proprietary weighting methodology of the respective ESG data provider. Our research shows that ESG scores are generally biased towards companies that have a higher level of transparency; so much so, that the strength of the underlying information provided is practically irrelevant, overshadowed by the strength of the transparency bias. As a result, the principal driver of ESG strength, in most ESG datasets, is not based on a company's sustainability but rather a company's transparency.

3 Transparency Bias Present in Standard ESG Scores

Simply defined, transparency is the percentage of questions that have been answered on a given company questionnaire. Were we to create a score for each company by simply taking the scores of all questions and aggregating up to total scores, we would obtain a Standard ESG Score. This simple methodology generally describes the ESG scoring process of the most widely used ESG scores on the market.

Plotting scores against the transparency of each company, as can be seen from Fig. 1, we clearly see a strong positive relationship between the two variables with a correlation of 84%. A regression analysis not only indicates that transparency is a statistically significant predictor of Standard ESG Scores, but with a regression slope of 81%, it also shows the convincing *strength* of transparency's predictive power on scores. The larger the regression slope the more powerful the effect of the independent variable (here, transparency) on the dependent variable (here, Standard ESG scores).

Furthermore, the regression has an R-squared of 70%, demonstrating that most of the variance found in the Standard ESG Scores can be explained by transparency.

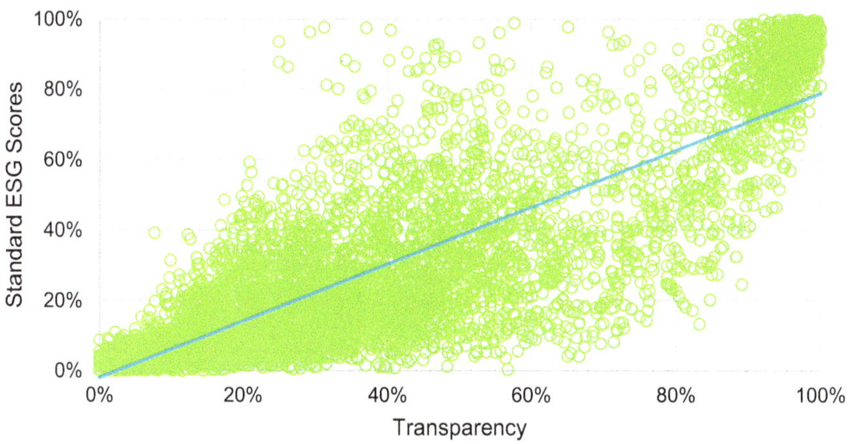

Fig. 1 Standard ESG Scores vs. transparency. Source: RobecoSAM, June 2019 data

3.1 Transparency: Highly Predictive of Standard ESG Scores

Undoubtedly, there is a clear link between sustainability and transparency. This is a rather obvious statement given truly sustainable companies do, in fact, exhibit higher levels of transparency. After all, any serious effort towards sustainability would involve collecting, analyzing and documenting ESG-related information that would be used by a company's itself to measure its own progress as well as submitted externally to justify internal processes and ESG claims. However, it should not be the case that companies *appear* to be more sustainable just because they disclosed more information, or made it more easy to find in processable languages for data collection agencies (i.e. higher transparency).

The causal relationship between sustainability and transparency is one-way only; that is to say, sustainability should encourage and enhance transparency but transparency alone should not enhance sustainability.

4 Transparency Bias Concealed as Regional Bias

Some segments of the market are significantly more transparent than others and this tends to hold true when looking at countries, regions, company size and even sectors.[1] Therefore, a region with significantly higher transparency, which may be driven by regulatory disclosure obligations or social pressure rather than higher levels of company sustainability, will have significantly higher Standard ESG

[1]ESG scores are usually standardized within sectors (or questionnaire groups), neutralizing sectorial transparency biases.

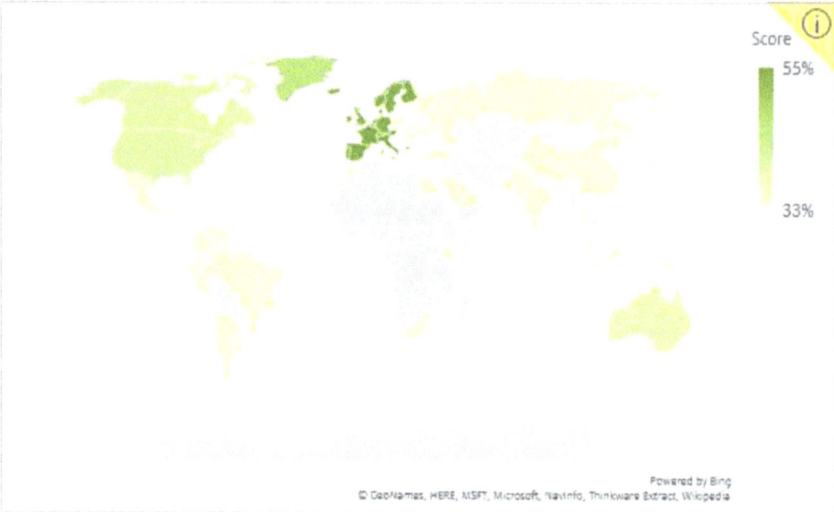

Region	Average Transparency	Average Standard ESG Score
Europe	55%	45%
North America	39%	32%
Asia-Pacific	37%	27%
Emerging Markets	33%	22%

Fig. 2 Standard ESG Scores by region. Source: RobecoSAM, June 2019 data

Scores. The same is true for country and company size. Certain countries and larger companies that have higher transparency also have higher Standard ESG scores. With this in mind, the use of Standard ESG Score-tilted investments will naturally favor parts of the market with higher transparency, regardless of whether these are actually more sustainable.

Breaking down the world into four regions: Developed Asia-Pacific, Developed Americas, Developed Europe and Emerging Markets, we note that there are major discrepancies in average Standard ESG Scores, as can be seen in Fig. 2.

4.1 ESG Scores Vary Significantly by Region: European Firms Perform Best, Emerging Markets Worst

Comparisons between regions show that there are considerable differences in transparency, as well as *perceived* strengths in sustainability. European firms have more pressure to report on ESG issues, stemming from tougher regulatory requirements, investor demands and perhaps even social pressures. The resulting transparency bias artificially boosts their ESG scores and erroneously amplifies differences with other regions.

While we do not argue all regions should have an equal level of sustainability, we do not think it viable to assume that Europe is one and a half times better than the next best region and twice as good as the weakest. One should bear in mind that regardless of region, all evaluated companies included within the analysis are public and mostly international firms that must adhere to the prescribed statutory standards of their respective listed exchanges, governing bodies and regional jurisdictions that regulate company disclosure, stakeholder servicing, rule of law et cetera.

5 Transparency Bias Concealed as Size Bias

From a size perspective, it is also obvious that there is a strong transparency bias in Standard ESG Scores, as can be seen in Fig. 3. It is rather intuitive that large companies have a distinct advantage over their smaller counterparts in terms of the financial and non-financial resources they can apply to collect, organize, formalize and disclose ESG-related information. Moreover, smaller companies with more limited resources may not go the extra lengths necessary to prove and report on criteria they deem to be immaterial and/or non-strategic to their business model and activities.

5.1 Sizing Up Transparency Bias: The Larger the Company, the Bigger the Bias

From the data (Fig. 3), we can clearly see that there are differences in the transparency levels of companies of different sizes. We can also clearly see consistent

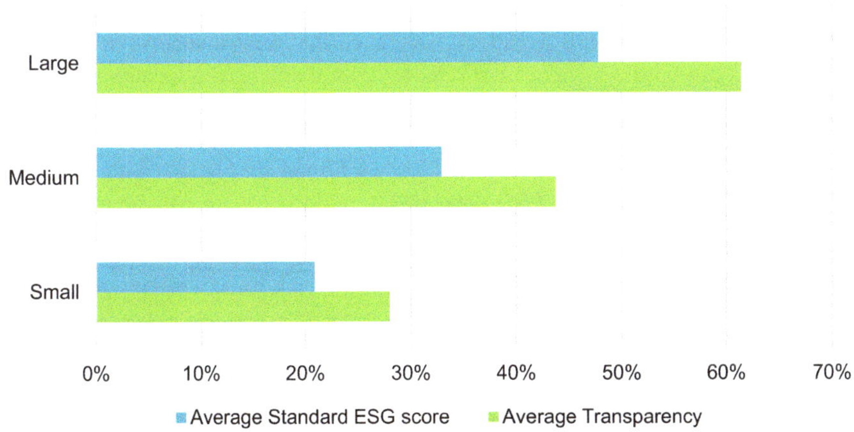

Fig. 3 Standard ESG Scores and transparency by company size, companies have been grouped into 3 size categories—Large: largest 20%, Medium: next 30% and Small: smallest 50%. Source: RobecoSAM, June 2019 data

differences in the Standard ESG scores across companies of different size. What we would like to know is if these results are purely by chance or whether there is some underlying trend captured in the data that substantiates the differences between the groups and renders the differences meaningful to explore. To answer whether the data differences are simply the product of chance, we need to demonstrate a statistical difference between each sample group's mean.

A two-sample t-test is a statistical method of testing whether the mean of two different data sample groups (here mean Standard ESG scores of Large and Small companies) are significantly different from each other. Carrying out a two-sample t-test on Standard ESG Scores for Large and Small companies, we see convincing results showing that there is a statistically significant difference in the average Standard ESG Scores for Large and Small companies.

Again, we do not argue that size cannot have an impact on the real sustainability performance of companies, but we can easily infer that larger companies (with bigger budgets) can afford better transparency thereby artificially boosting their Standard ESG Scores. Moreover, the magnitude of the bias seems difficult to justify.

6 Transparency Bias and Portfolio Performance

If Standard ESG Scores are used in the construction of a portfolio, it would be natural to assume that all biases stemming from this transparency bias will be introduced into the portfolio to some degree. Therefore, it is likely that biased scores will cause an over allocation to European listed securities and large firms (as measured by market capitalization).

Over the last 15 years, Large companies have underperformed Small companies by 2.1%.[2] In the same period, Europe has underperformed the other three regions on aggregate by 31.4%[3]. Clearly, an uncalibrated over-exposure to Large caps and European companies would negatively influence the performance of a portfolio which integrates biased Standard ESG Scores with unintended allocations to these areas.

There is generally no consensus on the impact of adding ESG to the portfolio construction process in terms of returns, as confirmed by Fig. 4. With so many extraneous risks contained in ESG data, investors do not get a consistent sustainability signal and so it is understandable that investors are not united in their opinions. If investors load unintended risks onto their portfolio by using scores which contain transparency bias, it is no wonder that investors cannot reach firm conclusions on the usefulness and value of ESG data.

---

[2]Calculated using the RobecoSAM All Assessed Universe from 28.02.2005 to 28.06.2019 in the Axioma risk model, with equal weighted position weights.

[3]See footnote 1.

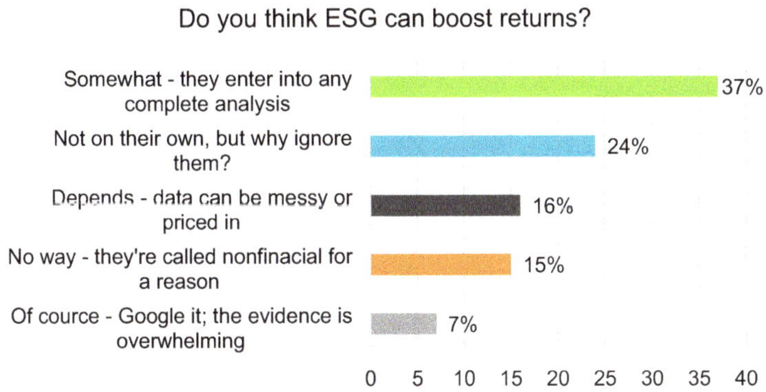

Fig. 4 A 2016 CFA public study on the perception of the value of ESG data in enhancing returns. Nearly two thirds of respondents express a neutral or negative. Source: https://blogs.cfainstitute.org/investor/2016/09/01/does-esg-boost-returns/

6.1 Investor Sentiment on the Value of ESG Ratings for Portfolio Performance

Most investors currently use a score similar to the Standard ESG Score used for this analysis, which makes no allowance for transparency bias. The comparatively weak performance of European equities and large cap stocks illustrates the downside of having extraneous risk introduced into portfolios by integrating biased ESG data in the investment process. In addition to region and size, there are other systematic/structural biases (e.g. investor sentiment, media coverage) that can induce companies to be more transparent. However, we focus our evaluation on regional and size biases as they tend to be the most significant.

Using biased data can introduce unintended risk into investment portfolios and lead to misguided allocation decisions. Moreover, without disentangling ESG scores from transparency bias, investors cannot make clear assessments on sustainability and its benefits—the noise of transparency bias drowns the true ESG signal. As a result, risk-return evaluations are primarily based on the risk-return of the transparency bias (i.e. did Europe outperform), in effect, voiding sustainability as an assessment consideration. Risk-return considerations aside, even a portfolio's sustainability cannot be accurately assessed using untreated Standard ESG score—it would largely indicate the transparency of a portfolio and not its ESG performance.

7 Sustainability Does Not Equal Transparency

In order to generate a score that reflects sustainability and is free of the effects of transparency bias, RobecoSAM developed Smart ESG Scores. Using a systematic transparency regression, which we use to eliminate the systematic bias within Standard ESG Scores to obtain an unbiased Smart ESG Score.

A more simplistic approach to removing the correlation between transparency and sustainability would be to run a regression on sustainability performance using transparency as the predictive variable, as shown in Fig. 1. If we believe that transparency biases scores upward (more transparency, better scores), then we could simply remove the bias in scores by removing the degree to which companies are rewarded for having higher scores. The degree of reward would be the slope of the regression line. However, this would create two major problems.

Firstly, and as previously discussed, while transparency does not cause sustainability, we can state with certainty that sustainable companies do tend to have higher transparency (which partly explains the steepness of the slope in Fig. 1). As a result, we can infer there is some meaningful amount of transparency that is induced by sustainability. However, the simplistic approach described above would not only entirely eliminate the transparency bias, it would also completely eliminate any meaningful correlations between transparency and sustainability variables—even those which may be causal and therefore appropriate to maintain.

Secondly, such a simple regression would remove any advantages of transparency, which, in effect, would punish companies for higher transparency and reward companies for lower transparency. As a result, companies could improve their score by simply providing less ESG information, whereas truly sustainable companies would see no added advantage in providing too much information and may even be systematically punished.

8 Smart ESG: Free of Transparency Bias

The RobecoSAM Smart ESG approach, which only regresses against the systematic part of companies' transparencies aims to maintain the causality of sustainability leading to transparency. Indeed, transparency can be broken down into two parts:

$$Transparency = Systematic\ Transparency + Idiosyncratic\ Transparency$$

The systematic transparency is the amount of transparency that comes from the systematic characteristics of the firm, such as its country and region of incorporation, sector and size. The idiosyncratic part is that which is unique to each company. A company may be more or less transparent than the average company with similar characteristics, which will determine its idiosyncratic transparency.

The first step is to calculate the systematic transparency for each company. To do this, we run a multiple regression using the continuous variable of log(market cap) and three dummy variables for country, region and sector. This gives the betas for each parameter, thereby enabling the estimation of the systematic transparency of all companies. The idiosyncratic transparency is then just the difference between the actual and the systematic transparency.

The second step is to regress the Standard ESG Scores against the systematic transparency in order to neutralize the effect of the latter on the resulting Smart ESG Scores. Figure 5 shows the slope of the regression (which is clearly weaker than in Fig. 1) where we have removed all relationship of ESG to transparency.

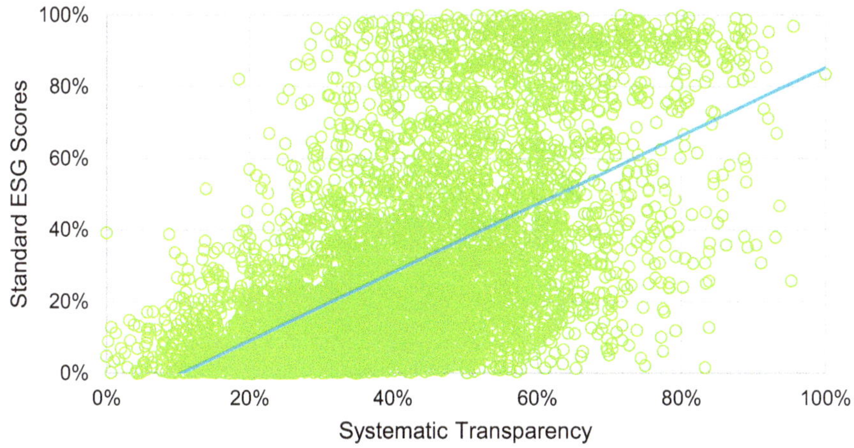

Fig. 5 Regression of Standard ESG Scores vs. systematic transparency. Source: RobecoSAM, June 2019 data

Using the Smart ESG approach, the causality of sustainable companies having more transparency is preserved. The slope is 35% with an R-squared of 33%, which are both less than half the output found in Fig. 1. Therefore, while transparency explains approximately 70% of Standard ESG scores, we can argue that only half of it is due to sustainable companies having better transparency, while half of the effect induces a transparency bias.

8.1 Determining the Degree of Systematic Transparency Bias Within Standard ESG Scores

Indeed, as can be seen on Fig. 6, Smart ESG scores retain a relationship to transparency, with a regression slope of 58% and an R-squared of 32%. This is the justified relationship between the two aspects of companies which arises as a result of sustainable companies having better transparency.

8.2 Smart ESG Corrects the Inflated Effect of Systematic Transparency Bias on ESG Scores

Transparency is but one of many systematic biases that impact ESG scores. So though Smart ESG Scores correct for systematic *transparency* bias, they still contain other systematic biases which have not been explicitly formalized and controlled. These biases are the true biases of sustainability—meaning that if Smart ESG Scores are stronger in some regions, we can infer that those regions contain more sustainable companies on average.

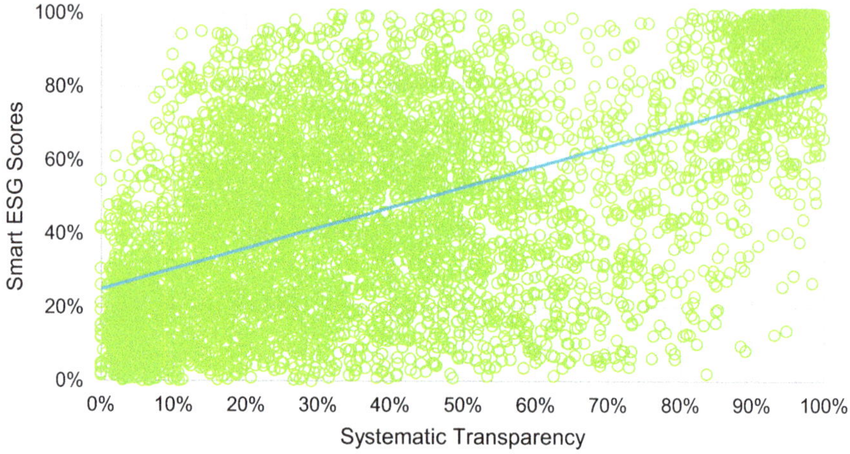

Fig. 6 Regression of Smart ESG Scores vs. systematic transparency. Source: RobecoSAM, June 2019 data

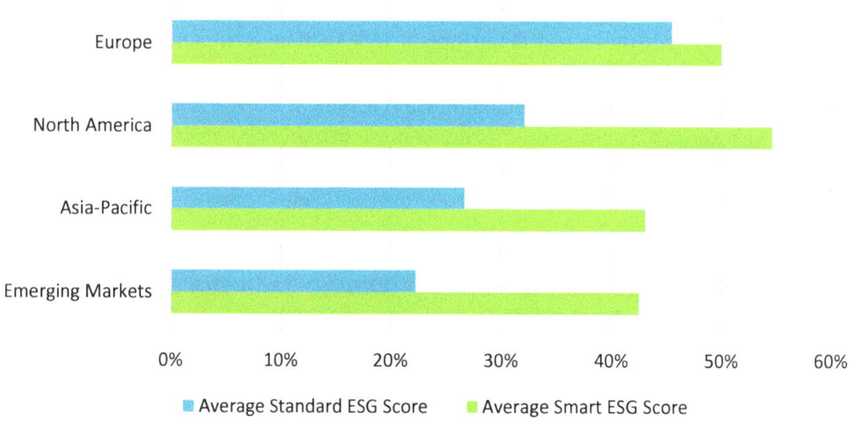

Fig. 7 Regional score averages. Source: RobecoSAM, June 2019 data

Indeed, we see that Smart ESG is not neutral for regions, but the magnitude of differences is much more representative of the truth when compared to Standard ESG Scores. Furthermore, some biases disappear altogether, which indicates that transparency bias was the only reason for those biases to exist in the first place.

8.3 *Standard ESG Scores Versus RobecoSAM Smart ESG Scores: Comparing Scores Highlights Major Regional Discrepancies*

Figure 7 shows the resulting regional score averages when we compare Smart ESG Scores with biased Standard ESG Scores. We note that North America actually outperforms Europe on an aggregated basis even though, historically, Europe has been consistently stronger. We can infer, at present and historically, that Asia-Pacific and Emerging Market companies are on average much weaker when it comes to ESG performance. However, were we not to remove the transparency bias, this weakness would be perceived to be much larger.

We have also conducted a two-sample t-test to check the likeness of Europe to other developed regions and the hypothesis that their means are equal can be rejected with 99% confidence if we use Standard ESG scores. This is no longer the case when we conduct this same test using Smart ESG Scores. According to Fig. 8, we can deduce that the Standard ESG Scores only had a size bias because of the transparency bias. Once this has been accounted for in Smart ESG, we no longer see significant differences between the size groups—especially among large companies.

8.4 Harmonizing ESG Scores: Eliminating Transparency Noise Reduces Size Differences

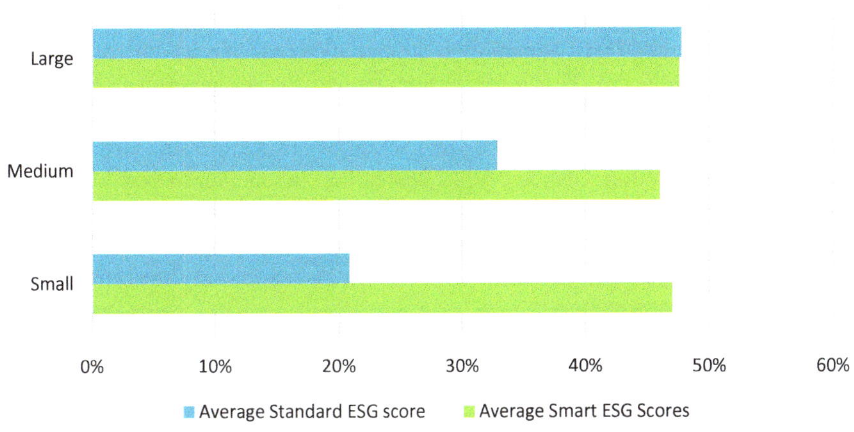

Fig. 8 Score averages by company size. Source: RobecoSAM, June 2019 data

9 Smart ESG Characteristics

There are two main reasons for removing transparency bias from ESG scores. The first is to ensure they are used to paint an accurate picture of company and portfolio sustainability and not simply to highlight company transparency. The second is to disentangle it from potentially extraneous risk factors that bias scores and that are subsequently loaded into investment portfolios.

To add Smart ESG to a portfolio adds only sustainability and the strength of that signal can directly contribute to portfolio management decision. To test the performance of ESG as an investment signal, we break down the RobecoSAM assessed universe of approximately 5000 companies into three quantiles and equal weight their components to represent three portfolios. Comparing Q1, the leaders, vs. Q3, the laggards, give us a good idea of the value that can be extracted using Smart ESG Scores.

9.1 *Smart ESG Scores: Extracting Sustainability from Data, Enhancing Performance for Portfolios*

Figure 9 show that there is relatively stable outperformance of sustainability leaders (Q1) vs. the laggards (Q3), summing to around 12% over the period (or a 0.66% annualized performance). This result is encouraging for any investor interested in improving the sustainability of their portfolio, while getting remunerated for the effort. We also point out that over the same period and using the same methodology, the signal obtained from Standard ESG Scores has an annualized performance of 0.45%. While this is still an interesting number, we argue that focusing on a true

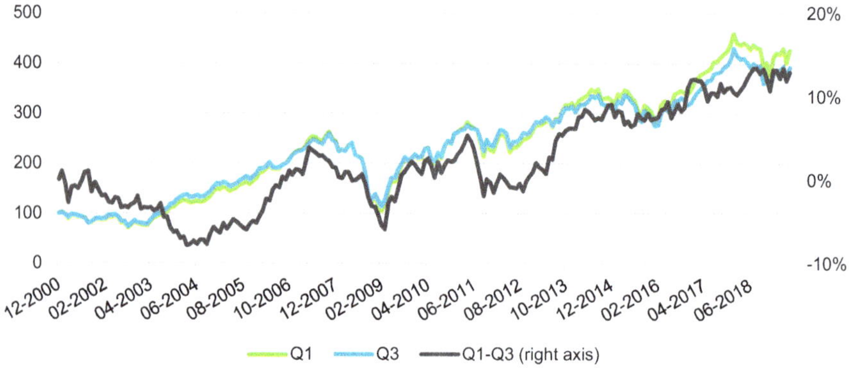

Fig. 9 Equal weighted top and bottom tertials (left axis) and Q1's outperformance over Q3 (right axis). Source: RobecoSAM data from December 2000 to June 2019, universe size varies through time

sustainability signal, such as Smart ESG, can improve sustainability in a much more targeted way and contribute more significantly to returns.

10 Conclusion

Investors should be aware of how differing transparency standards across many structural factors can affect the perceived sustainability of companies and negatively affect both the implementation of sustainable investment strategies and investment returns.

Transparency bias needs to be neutralized in order to extract a purer and stronger sustainability signal. To treat transparency bias, we propose an approach which prevents the unintended penalization of companies which supply more data, reduces the reward for companies which supply less data, and preserves the causality of sustainable companies with higher transparency. Our research suggests that the Smart ESG approach and resulting Smart ESG Scores removes the bias that clouds standard ESG data and helps clarify the true sources of sustainability. As a result, investors are better equipped to reduce risk, spot opportunities and improve portfolio performance.

Ruben Feldman is a Managing Director at Swisscanto, where he is heading the ESG Strategy & Business Development Department. Before joining Swisscanto Invest, he was Head of Quantitative Research and Licensing Business at RobecoSAM. Ruben is an experienced investment professional with a demonstrated track record in creating and raising funds for advanced portfolio management solutions to the benefit of investors.

Comprehensive Simulation Meta Model for Transition Planning and Decision Analysis with Sustainable Impact

Salomon Billeter

Abstract A comprehensive simulation meta model for transition planning and decision analysis is proposed and outlined. This model is designed to provide insight on the effects of a proposed agenda ahead of time, and to support an optimization of means and resources available to decision makers in governments, organizations, businesses, or to private persons to reach their goals across different time horizons and considering different quantities of relevance.

The model supports multiple use cases. The system of interest, the decision makers, the nature of the decisions to be made, and the quantities relevant to the decision makers do not need to be defined *a priori*. The results of the simulation can be aggregated onto diverse observables relevant for business, economy, society, and environment.

The meta model is modular, combining existing domain-specific models into one framework. It will gradually be extended to cover all domains and scales relevant for sustainable business, sustainable finance, and sustainable development.

The article outlines the approach and gives examples of applications. It also shows how the model will gradually be developed during its application, allowing a targeted and fast application while allowing continuous learning and improvement.

Keywords Sustainable finance · Theory of change · SDG · Sustainability · Simulation · Meta model · Integrated assessment model · Forward-looking model · Synthetic model · Economic model · Environmental model · Social model · Network model · Sustainable development goals

1 Introduction

After all progress in science and technology of the past decades in so many areas, shouldn't it be possible to provide enough food and water to all people on earth, and shouldn't the destruction of our own natural basis of life and all economic activities

---

S. Billeter (✉)
scaling4good, Riehen, Switzerland
e-mail: salomon.billeter@scaling4good.com

K. Wendt (ed.), *Theories of Change*, Sustainable Finance,
https://doi.org/10.1007/978-3-030-52275-9_14

be history? While very few would oppose the goals of sustainability, why is global progress in the sustainability area that slow? What can we do to change this? Admittedly, it is less than trivial to orchestrate the collective behavior of billions of people, especially as long as some people or groups may gain an advantage over others by acting unsustainably.

However, several communities have successfully demonstrated that clear norms and actions with understandable impact let them avoid the pitfalls of personal gain at the expense of the sustained business of all, without requiring the rest of the world to follow them. A good example is the traditional alp farming: Since centuries, the interdependencies between farming activities, mechanisms in nature (soil, weather, plants) and economic developments have been well-known. Respecting these interconnections has assured traditional alp farming to provide a basis for living throughout centuries without destroying the fragile alpine pastures.

Why is it so difficult to establish generally accepted norms and actions aimed at sustainability at a larger scale? Are they really as ineffective or prone to side-effects as is often claimed? Or do they possibly just threaten some vested interests of powerful groups as is often claimed, too? Or do they even open new unprecedented opportunities for all? Certainly, it is less clear at this scale how individual behavior affects the common resources. Therefore, wouldn't clarity on all consequences of individual actions help to provide a better and more acceptable basis for change? Was William White right after all suggesting we first and foremost would need better computer models as a response to the financial crisis of 2007/2008 which he has warned of as early as in 2003?

As an answer to the challenge, this paper proposes and outlines the model for Sustainable Impact through Simulation and Action Leverage (SISAL).

This article publishes the approach for the first time. The model is summarized in Sect. 2, and the key concepts are introduced in Sect. 3. Some techniques are outlined in Sect. 4. The means to ensure accuracy and consistency of results are explained in Sect. 5. Sect. 6 outlines the development approach, and Sect. 7 illustrates the concepts with an example.

2 Model Summary

This paper proposes and outlines a comprehensive simulation meta model that serves to reach decisions and transition strategies of societal relevance in transparent collaboration based on facts, stated goals, and declared values. This includes providing insight on the effects of a proposed agenda ahead of time and optimizing means and resources available to decision makers in governments, organizations, businesses, or private persons to reach the stated goals over time.

The model links the actions with their outcomes by dynamically producing information about the system of interest in the future from its current state under the influence of itself, its environment, and the actions of the decision maker. This information is then aggregated onto the quantities of interest using the simulated data about the future just like data from the past.

By nature, the simulation approach to tackle such complex problems must be synthetic, i.e., combine structural, statistical, and other modeling techniques as no single model alone will solve the problem. Also, the intent is to re-use available domain-specific simulation models and data wherever possible instead of developing them from scratch.

The unique strength and emphasis lie on consistency across applications, results, domains, scales, and data sets. First, it provides comparability across actions and key performance indicators across time horizons: All actions to be evaluated are simulated from the same starting conditions using the same methods, and the outcomes therefore can be compared to each other. Second, it provides consistency across use cases, domains, scales, and scopes: For most of the use cases, data quality and availability inherently limit the accuracy of the quantitative forecasts. The primary remedy consists in the employment of the consistency: identical starting conditions (and possibly constraints) and consistent methodology make the results robust against errors in the starting conditions. Third, it supports comprehensive monitoring of accuracy against data and various models: The modeling approach will offer multiple ways to monitor and control the accuracy of results through consistency checks between different models, and through back testing of results of the model in the past against data from the past.

The simulation meta model is not yet implemented in a computer code and data set but exists as a concept with a few proofs of concept. Instead, with the simulation meta model framework, a *per se* unsolvable simulation challenge is broken down into a structure that allows to solve it, providing early validated results while enabling continuous and structured learning. The system of interest, the decision makers, the nature of the decisions to be made, and the quantities relevant to the decision makers are not defined *a priori* but depend on the application (use case). Currently, pilots are set up together with project consortia.

The evolutionary implementation, extension, and improvement in real use cases is an essential part of the model concept: Given the enormous diversity of systems relevant for the different use cases in terms of time scale, domain and spatial coverage, granularity, and quantities important to the model user, it won't be possible to develop such a model beforehand. Nevertheless, a consistent modeling approach across the use cases allows using the partial overlap in terms of these criteria in order to re-use data, lessons learned, validations, and to provide consistency across the use cases. An evolutionary development approach ensures continuous progress by building on previous work consistently.

Synthetic (integrated) modeling approaches have been shown to be able to solve problems that cannot be solved by any of their component models alone.[1] Moreover,

[1]Synthetic approaches are used in different areas. In molecular simulation for example, mixed quantum-classical simulations at various levels allow the simulation of transitions as complex as enzyme reactions, involving 100,000s of electrons and spanning 10 orders of magnitude in time, from femtoseconds to microseconds, see e.g. Billeter et al. (2001). In social sciences, synthetic modeling has recently been established, see e.g. Billeter and Salghetti (2016), Bollinger et al. (2017), and Pauliuk et al. (2017).

the re-use of component models ensures an economic development of the overall model and a high and well-understood quality of the results.

3 Model Concept

3.1 *Overview of the Simulation Meta Model*

The SISAL meta model integration framework combines various pre-existing models for different domains, scales and granularities, and different levels of specificity into one loosely coupled model framework. This allows the integration of data flows and the evaluation of impact across system borders, e.g. the influence of business actions on macroeconomy, public well-being, and climate.

The SISAL dynamic simulation framework propagates the current state of the system of interest (the initial conditions) into the future[2] under the influence of the system itself, its environment, and the actions of the decision maker, allowing them to be analyzed as if there were data from the future.

A structural approach is chosen to loosely couple the different domain-related component models into a comprehensive modular forward-looking model. Back tests will challenge both the meta model and its components, checking if they would have predicted the present and past, and the diversity of the domain-related models allows a consistency check where no data is available.

3.2 *Synthesis of Domains*

Most of the sustainability-related challenges are complex and span diverse parts of the world across the partitions customarily used for modeling. Therefore, several domains usually covered by individual calculation models are relevant to sustainability matters. Instead of developing these parts from scratch, the SISAL model combines pre-existing component models into one meta model in a modular way.

3.2.1 Overview of Modules

An *a priori* overview of the meta model with its modules is given in Fig. 1.

Each component model covers a defined part of a domain, as outlined in Table 1.

[2]The achievable time horizon depends on the nature and scale of the use case as well as the constraints put into the calculation. It generally ranges from a few years to a few decades.

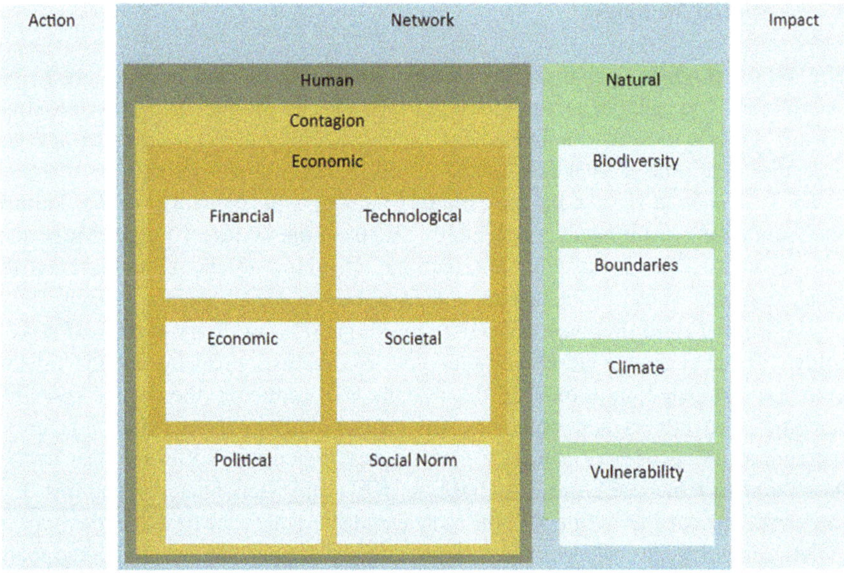

Fig. 1 Overview of modules and components reflecting the domains of the simulation meta model

Table 1 Coverage of domains by different models

Domain	Module	Component	Description
Real economy	Economic	Economic	Economy of heterogeneous societies
Financial economy	Economic	Financial	Financial economy
Society	Economic	Societal	Society beyond economic activities
Real economy	Economic	Technological	Disruptive new technologies
Society	Contagion	Social norm	Collective motives (e.g. ethics, hot topics)
Politics	Contagion	Political	Political, regulatory, and judicial
Climate—Weather	Natural	Climate	Climate, impact on water, ground
Planetary boundaries	Natural	Boundaries	Limited resources of the planet or a system
Biodiversity	Natural	Biodiversity	Living species and their distribution
Assets and supplies	Economic/ natural	Vulnerability	Impact of climate on capital
(All)	Network		Connections between agents/entities
(All)	Action		Policies and scenarios to be probed
(All)	Impact		Answers from simulated world

3.2.2 Special Modules

The **action module** formalizes the agenda whose effects and impacts are to be determined. The agenda[3] is a model input provided by the user and can consist of one-off actions such as an investment capital redeployment or series of actions concerted over time such as continually raised fuel economy standards.

For each agenda variant, the **core model** (denoted with "Network" in Fig. 1) runs one simulation, resulting in a trajectory, i.e., the time series of properties of the relevant entities[4] in the system. The baseline agenda is no change or business as usual. A family of trajectories contains the trajectories for all agenda variants.

The **impact module** gives answers to questions relevant to the users and stakeholders. It calculates the effects and outcomes of each user-provided agenda variant from the simulated trajectory of the system and compares them to a baseline outcome. The effects and outcomes are measured by user-provided indicators, aggregating the trajectory onto key performance indicators (KPIs) relevant to the stated goals of the use case, e.g., business KPIs and SDG-related quantities. By comparing the corresponding KPIs of each agenda variant to the baseline, the impact of the agenda variants is calculated on immediate business goals, sustainability goals and other desired effects as well as undesired side-effects. This allows to challenge, reject or confirm expected effects, to detect unexpected effects, and to quantify and optimize the expected and unexpected effects.

3.3 Synthesis of Scopes, Scales and Granularities

It is not feasible to simulate the whole world in terms of billions of individuals, millions of companies, and all the individual parts of all ecosystems. Most of the effort would be spent on entities that do not matter to the question at hand. In addition to prohibitive costs to obtain the necessary data and to calculate the interactions, the interpretation of the results would be near-impossible.

If the system relevant for the problem is too large to be described in terms of individual entities throughout the system (which is always the case), a partition of the world into subsystems helps solve each part of the problem at an appropriate scale. For example, the system might be split into a city and its environment.

Such a partition into system and environment is not only used to adapt the granularity (i.e., the level of detail) to the requirements of the problem at hand but also to control other levels of resolution, most importantly the level of specificity and the degree of dynamics (see corresponding Sections).

Coarse graining is easiest done with a static partition determined upfront. However, an adaptive partitioning is part of the model concept, too.

[3]For a definition, see the glossary.

[4]For example wealth of actors such as natural or juristic persons, or the water supplies of a habitat.

3.3.1 Scale

The "nano", "micro", "meso" and "macro" scales of economic activities[5] can be generalized from the economic domain to other domains. The simulation meta model differentiates between four scales:

- Nano: In the economic domain, this scale corresponds to individual natural persons
- Micro: In the economic domain, this scale corresponds to companies
- Meso: In the economic domain, this scale corresponds to industries or other habitat of companies
- Macro: In the economic domain, this scale corresponds to countries or even the whole world

For many domains, available taxonomies split the world quite naturally into parts at all four scales. For example, geographic scope can be partitioned into continents, countries, states, municipalities, neighborhoods, and parcels of land. Coordinate systems would be even more fine-grained.

3.3.2 Scope: Dimensions of Spatial Coverage

The size of the system of interest is determined along several dimensions which may depend on the domain. Examples of such dimensions include geographic, political, habitat, companies, species, people, products, type of business, etc.

Geographic scope by political context such as country or municipality often serves as a proxy for other scopes. For example, a country is often used to identify an economic space or a jurisdiction. Moreover, it is not uncommon to infer a company ecosystem from a country. This approach however has several limitations. For example, the alpine ecosystems are not congruent with any country's scope, and some jurisdictions extend over several continents. Also, corporations have a complex system of legal entities and locations which has little to do with the country of the headquarters.

To overcome these limitations, the SISAL model uses dimension-specific identifiers of scope, even where geographic scope by political context is a generally accepted proxy.

3.3.3 Granularity: Controlling the Computational Cost

Most of the sustainability-related challenges are complex and not only span diverse parts of the world but also multiple scales for these parts of the world. Obviously, too coarse resolution into details limits the accuracy and the transparency of the model.

[5]See reporting 3.0 New Business Model Blueprint (Baue and Thurm 2018).

However, unnecessarily high resolution of the system into details not only increases the computational cost, but it also introduces unnecessary parameters and the associated model uncertainty.

With each additional dimension, the configurational space would increase dramatically. The SISAL model provides a few controls which are given in the subsequent Sections.

3.4 Synthesis by Model Specificity

The SISAL model is neither a pure bottom-up nor a pure top-down model. Instead, it resolves the trade-off between high-level and detailed modeling by bridging between three model specificity levels. These levels determine to which extent groups are resolved into their parts:

- Systems level using aggregated quantities of direct relevance to the use case
- Agents level using entities representing people, companies, governments, goods, species or groups thereof
- Individual connections level using explicit connections between individual entities

The systems level can be implemented by system dynamics[6] structural models and best summarizes the dynamics. This is the highest level where quantities of interest are not resolved into the entities they are derived from.

The agents level can be implemented in agent-based and related structural models. It connects the high-level dynamics with the underlying dynamics.

A special case of the agents level is the individual connections level where individual entities are connected to individual entities.

Networks are the common language of the model. Each type of network (see Sect. 4.1) corresponds to one model specificity level.

3.5 Time Scales and Degrees of Dynamic Response

Complex systems do not react linearly to an external influence[7] applied to them, owing to feedback mechanisms within the system. Such feedback mechanisms consist of parts of the system influencing themselves with a time lag indirectly via

[6]System dynamics has a good track record in solving sustainability-related challenges. For Millen nium Institute's iSDG model, see e.g. Arquitt et al. (2018).

[7]Depending on community, such influences may be called "stress" or "perturbation". In the SISAL model, the action module influences the other modules, and the environment acts on the core system. Hence, an agenda consists of external influences.

other parts of the system, leading e.g. to (local) cyclic behavior and equilibria in case of negative feedback and to exponential growth in case of positive feedback. Therefore, a static treatment is not sufficient to predict the future consequences of our actions.

However, the time scales characteristic of the different feedback loops range from hours to years. Moreover, the large and relevant collective transitions such as economic and political paradigm shifts, i.e. transitions involving millions of agents and billions of transactions, are even less frequent.

A brute-force algorithmic solution, i.e., the simulation over a long time span with time steps short enough to capture potential transitions and therefore covering a time scale range of more than a few orders of magnitude is computationally too expensive, leads to the build-up of errors, and its results are difficult to interpret.

Instead, the SISAL model employs three methods to solve this challenge: Multi time stepping, adapted degrees of dynamic response, and system stability measures for the detection of likely large-scale transitions. The partition of the system into subsystems (see Sect. 3.3.1) and the integration of multiple models into one framework simplify the use of these methods. For example, the environment may use a coarser description of the dynamics than the embedded system.

Multi time stepping uses differentiated time steps to solve the equations of motion. This is naturally achieved using the integration of various component models which have their own integrators.

Differentiated degrees of dynamic response limit the flexibility of a system in its reaction to changes within the system or of another system. From totally rigid to fully flexible, the SISAL model includes predetermined static simulations where the whole evolution of the system is predetermined, scenario-based static simulations, with multiple possible pathways into the future, inelastic dynamic simulations with internal feedback but no influence from other systems, and fully dynamic simulations, where all parts of the system move under the influence of each other.

System stability measures help identify time spans where large-scale transitions are likely to occur. Whenever this happens, a more detailed simulation of the large-scale transition[8] is triggered.

3.5.1 Degrees of Dynamic Response

The model offering the most elaborate dynamic response and most comprehensive number of feedback loops is not necessarily the most accurate model. Dynamic freedom decreases the model stability which in turn might limit the time horizon. Moreover, the additional parameters increase the parameterization effort and the

[8]Such methods have successfully been used to accurately simulate enzyme reactions which occur at a rate approximately ten orders of magnitude slower than the atomic motions, see Billeter et al. (2001).

unavoidable parameterization errors. Therefore, it will be useful to restrict the freedom of some systems to dynamically respond to changes within or outside of it.

The SISAL model knows four levels of dynamic response:

- In the fully dynamic simulation, all parts of the system move under the influence of the other parts of the system and under the influence of other systems.
- Inelastic dynamic simulations include dynamic feedback within the system but neglect the influence to other systems. For example, an environment might influence a core system, but the core system is too insignificant for the environment. This allows pre-calculated and pre-aggregated trajectories of the environment. A more flexible variant of inelastic dynamic simulations is the semi-elastic dynamic simulation where heterogeneities in the neighboring systems are neglected, i.e., the impact from them is pre-aggregated.
- Scenario-based static calculations include multiple probable predetermined evolutions of a subsystem which usually is the environment of the core system. Therefore, not only heterogeneities in other systems are neglected but also any dynamic feedback including the internal dynamics of the system.
- In predetermined static (one predetermined evolution of the environment) calculations, the evolution of the system is predetermined. This includes the neglect of less probable evolutions in addition to heterogeneities, dynamic feedback, and any internal dynamics.

3.5.2 Time of Knowledge and Real Time

A forward-looking model not only includes the history but also the present and forecasts of the future. Any forecast will be revised based on new knowledge. Moreover, any knowledge base is partial, and the learning process necessarily implies a lag. Since a model prediction about a time span depends on the knowledge base used (e.g. data), a model prediction about the same time span will be revised multiple times.

For example, the forecasts of interest rates in 2012 were substantially higher before the financial crisis than thereafter. Many financial predictions that depend on the interest rates needed to be revised.

If decisions are based on forecasts, changes in the knowledge base may imply adjustments of these decisions, and for consistent action planning and impact reporting, it is important to keep track by how much the basis of decision changes when and why.

The SISAL model therefore differentiates between two times:

- The real time represents the world we are looking at, identifying e.g. the climate in the 1990s, the GDP of a country in 2008, or
- The time of knowledge represents the knowledge base available at a given point in time, identifying e.g. differentiating between the state of knowledge as of May 2019 and the one as of May 2029 in a prediction about 2030.

Any data used and generated depends on these two times. This bi-temporal model permeates the entire model with a common representation of information. Where data and/or component models do not reflect this principle, the interfaces trigger a reconstruction of the two time spans, ensuring compatibility by encapsulation, i.e., hiding the complexity from the data set and/or component model.

3.6 Synthesis of Modeling Techniques

To tackle the diverse range of challenges, the meta model is built on various existing complementary modeling techniques[9]:

- Structural models[10] both as overall skeleton and as components
- Network models[11] are special structural models, connecting all parts of the model
- Statistical models[12] for parameterization and back test
- Judgmental models[13] complementing the data and calculations by human reasoning

Structural models provide explanatory power, the needed granularity, and allow an integration of all parts.

Networks are the central piece of the meta model, formally connecting all its parts with each other using a graph structure.

Descriptive statistical models are used to determine the initial state of the system, to parameterize observable relationships, and to determine observed targets for model back test.

Human judgement is an essential part of any large-scale modeling effort. The SISAL model formalizes human judgement into an own class of models, the judgmental models. An example of wide-spread judgmental models are political and economic scenarios.

Although the modeling process starts from the systems level and therefore with a macro-founded view, the meta model is micro-founded to ensure transferability of findings between contexts and across fundamental transitions. To avoid misinterpretation and overparameterization, it uses estimated rather than calibrated parameters wherever possible. Preferably, microstates will be aggregated to macro results rather than macro results broken down into micro states to avoid arbitrary and hard-to-explain decisions on break-down.

---

[9]For examples on model integration, see Billeter et al. (2001), Bollinger et al. (2017), and Pauliuk et al. (2017).

[10]See e.g. Dawid et al. (2016), Aznar-Siguan and Bresch (2019), Battiston et al. (2016a), Billeter and Salghetti (2016), Rudolf and Zurlinden (2014).

[11]See e.g. Battiston et al. (2016b).

[12]Examples include simple regression models, generalized linear models, autoregressive models, and a wealth of additional techniques.

[13]Since decades, the RAND Corporation has formalized human judgement. An entry point is e.g. Sackman (1974). Moreover, scenario analysis has been successfully applied since a long time. A review is provided in Kosov and Gassner (2008).

3.6.1 Structural Models

Structural models provide explanatory power, the needed granularity, and allow an integration of all parts.

Since they mirror the structure of the cause-effect chains in the system, they connect numbers with narratives, i.e., quantitative calculations with qualitative explanations and reasonings.

There are different classes of structural models known in the literature.

3.6.2 Statistical Models

The descriptive statistical models exploit data sets from various sources and provide quantitative descriptions of the initial state of the system under consideration and of the influences of quantities on each other along cause-effect chains.

Moreover, a quantitative description of the past is essential for back test, i.e., the check if the simulation was able to predict the past from the more remote past.

The statistical models are well established, and the reader is referred to the rich literature and meta literature on statistical modeling, predictive modeling, regression modeling, etc.

3.6.3 Judgmental Models

Judgmental models formalize human judgement such that even a computer code can understand it. The most prominent judgmental models in the SISAL model are the “issue chains”, postulated networks of issues relevant to the use case impacted by other issues.

Judgmental models are also used to fill inevitable gaps in data by expert judgement, to obtain initial quantifications of impact functions, to critically interpret results, and to orchestrate the calculation in intelligent ways around rare events such as tipping points which in turn may be identified by the model. While fully automatic simulation will be possible, an intelligent human-machine interaction is expected to provide superior results.

4 Techniques for Model Synthesis

4.1 Networks, the Glue of the Model

Networks are the common language of the SISAL model, connecting all components and specificity levels of the model and therefore forming the uniform formal language across the otherwise heterogeneous landscape of model components. By formalizing the influence of one node in the network on another node in the network, they provide an unambiguous connection between qualitative reasoning and quantitative parameterization.

Three types of networks are required:

- Issue chains (roughly correspond to "Channels of Transmission") represent dependencies between issues[14] which are deemed relevant and which have a telling name. Depending on the maturity level of the model part under consideration, the relevance of the individual dependencies might be hypothetical or proven. Each model use case[15] will bring more issues into the model. For illustrative examples, see the example from "Holistic Investment Performance" below. The issue chains belong to the systems level.
- Dependency maps represent the rules reflecting the interactions between entities[16] or their properties. Dependency maps provide the main link between the numbers and the narratives: Each interaction corresponds to a quantitative formula. Examples include the influence of central banks "printing" money on the liquidity available to banks or the impact of malnutrition on a population's life expectancy. The dependency maps belong to the agents level.
- Entity networks represent the relationships between specific entities and make the difference between "a company doing business with a company" and "this company doing this business with that company". Examples include supply chains, value chains, OTC business, and company ownership networks. The entity networks belong to the individual connections level.

4.2 *Levels of Attention: System and Environment*

Even though the details of a remote part of the world might be irrelevant to another part of the world, the combined mid-term evolution of it is not in our interconnected world. For example, a local election result in another continent has little impact on local politics somewhere else, a paradigm change in local elections in the remote part may be decisive, and the price development of a single security mostly does not change the world economy, but price drop of many stocks is likely to cause major financial turmoil everywhere.

The need for focus on processes that matter to a specific set of questions by a user or stakeholder requires a split of the world into systems and their environments. A system is treated in full detail and under the influence of its environment which is larger and treated with less detail.

[14]May involve several entities and relationships.

[15]See Section "Use Cases".

[16]People, companies, governments, goods, etc.

With the treatment of the environment in a much coarser granularity than the system, relevant time scales become accessible without the need to neglect the environment altogether which would make the simulation totally unrealistic, possibly neglecting even the most important aspects[17] of the system.

In addition to the neglect of detailed resolution (coarser levels of granularity), other aspects of the environment might be neglected, resulting in additional computational speed and stability:

- Higher model specificity levels: neglect of heterogeneities (e.g. system dynamics instead of agent-based)
- Smaller system: neglect of entities that are more remote from the center of the system (e.g. a country instead of the whole world)
- Coarser level of granularity: neglect of resolution (e.g. down to states instead of communities)
- Lower degree of dynamic response: Neglect of dynamic feedback loops and system interactions (e.g. inelastic dynamic instead of elastic dynamic)

Neglect of more aspects does not necessarily mean a less realistic calculation as it enforces the focus on the essentials.

The partition into system and environment can be nested, i.e., the environment of the system itself can have an environment that is even more coarse-grained. The split is most easily done by domain and spatial criteria, i.e., by type of entity and by the entity of a given type. For example, the environment of the companies in Switzerland is formed by companies in other countries and the natural and regulatory boundary conditions of Switzerland.

4.3 Model Specificity Levels: Top-Down and Bottom-Up

Networks are also used to connect between the different model specificity levels.

Issue chains at the systems level are the starting point, formally capturing domain experts' hypotheses up for verification and quantification. At the same time, they provide a link to scenario analysis, providing a high-level generic quantitative description exogenous influences on the system of interest. Moreover, aggregation of results onto issue chains allows an explanation of the simulation results. The latter is a non-trivial task and goes beyond the scope of this article.

Explicit dependency maps at the agents level both help construct the model and link its results to detailed data and transferable insights obtained in controlled settings and experiments. They play a special role in the interaction between the component models: all incoming connections in the dependency network represent a specific exogenous influence from another component model.

[17]For example in biochemistry the protein around the reactive core, in finance the macro economy around the company, in society the other societies interacting with it.

The entity networks at the individual connections level are very data intensive but, in some cases, make a decisive difference on the results. An example where issue chains and dependency maps alone are insufficient and entity networks are required is the over-the-counter business of banks which has a decisive impact on the banking system's resilience against exogenous stress. Entity networks can only be used if the two higher specificity levels of network are well understood and reflected in the model.

The three specificity levels of network complement each other: more detailed levels add differentiation and heterogeneity to the more generic levels whereas the more generic levels provide a system overview and help ensure completeness.

5 Model Accuracy and Consistency

5.1 Use and Generation of Data

Simulation does not replace data but rather complements data sets in various ways. Simulation fills gaps in data, provides a bridge between different scales in different data sets, and it generates information on the future as if there were data sets from the future. For simulated action analysis, data sets are used in several ways. Figure 2 provides an overview.

First, the initial state of the simulation is set according to the best knowledge on the current state of the system under consideration and its environment. Wherever data are available, these data sets are used. The inevitable gaps in any data set, e.g. caused by materiality thresholds, are filled using simulation and expert judgement. Record linkage techniques utilize overlapping data sets to reconcile between them, and to enrich the information beyond the scope of the individual data sets.

Second, the boundary conditions might need to be quantified for the time span relevant to the simulation. These boundary conditions include both constraints (prior knowledge the simulation must observe, e.g. from expert judgement) and the quantification of the impact the environment has on the system if the time evolution is not available from another part of the model. The latter is especially relevant in the early stages of model development where, most likely, the model does not yet cover the environment of the system under consideration.

Third, back-testing is an essential part of model quality assurance and the establishment of credibility. In the back-testing process, the past is simulated, and the simulation results are compared to the data from the past. If the simulation does not reproduce the past, it needs to be corrected. In synthetic and structural modeling, a deep analysis of the root causes of the mismatch precedes any corrective action such as extension of the model structure, re-assessment of estimated parameters, or even a recalibration.

Fourth, predictive modeling techniques make use of the lag between a signal (the predictor) and its effect (the dependent variable). The delayed impact of the signal

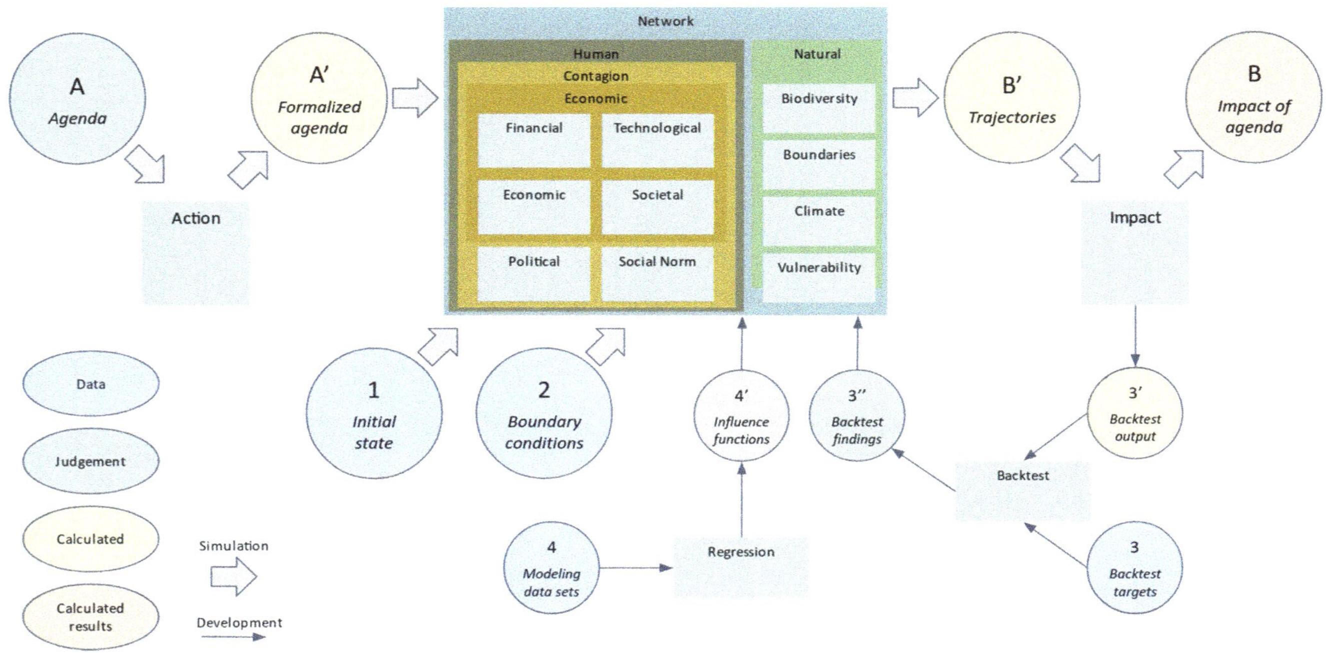

Fig. 2 Use and generation of data in the SISAL model. In the main usage of the model, an agenda (**a**) is fed into the model, resulting in the impact of the agenda (**b**), starting from an initial state of the system (1) subject to the boundary conditions (2). Back testing compares aggregated output on the past (3′) with data from the past (3) to check if and where the model was able to predict the past (3″). Regression analysis derives impact functions (4′) from modeling data sets (4)

gives an opportunity to predict the future evolution of the dependent variable for a limited time window. There is a vast literature on predictive modeling.

Fifth, data are used to parameterize the estimated parameters of the model. The methodology depends on the family of structural models and can range from simple regression models to complex transforms of information.

The data model is an essential part of the SISAL model. Since networks are at the core of the SISAL model, the data model is a graph model. The data model however goes beyond the scope of this document.

5.1.1 Data Availability Requirements

The exact data requirements depend on the use case and the component models employed. Preferably, open data are used. Where possible, data gathered for the SISAL model are also fed back into the organizations providing open data.

5.1.2 Data Processing Requirements

In general, structured data sets are preferred over unstructured data sets, at least initially. Information in tabular form is best accessible for the model. This kind of data can take different forms, for example time series. To minimize the information loss and the effort inherent in any transform, normalized data sets with records categorized by untranslated classifications are best suited. Also, time series are easy to use.

The model can cope with sparse data: No completeness is required, but obviously, it is easier to work with data sets that are complete for practical purposes. However, it is essential that materiality thresholds can be quantified or characterized.

The data must not be pre-filtered. Instead, unreliable, immaterial, or wrong records or rows should be flagged for deletion but not deleted. A good documentation (metadata) is extremely helpful.

In a second step and for the human interpretation of data, unstructured data provides a wealth of information, so it is essential that text is not separated from the more structured parts of data.

5.1.3 Expert Judgement

Where no data are available, the fallbacks are expert judgments[18] and quantified assumptions. In addition to appropriate expert elicitation techniques, it is important to manage expert judgments and assumptions transparently, including a seamless and formalized link back to the sources. The SISAL model maintains a complete

[18] See Sects. 3.6 and 3.6.3 and references therein.

data lineage back to the master source for data, expert judgments, and formalized assumptions alike.

However, even where data are available, gaps and biases in these data sets are unavoidable. For example, materiality thresholds are often implicit and therefore not quantifiable. Where unsure, the SISAL model uses both data and expert judgment for the same quantity along with appropriate consistency checks and a complete data lineage back to both types of sources.

5.1.4 Data Format Requirements

For the pre-analysis and pre-processing, any standardized format goes. A few formats however help minimizing the pre-processing overhead. These formats include for example:

- Relational databases, especially in clean, normalized data models
- CSV, MS Excel (preferably in normalized tables)
- Linked data feeds, graph databases
- Other data APIs

For the model, the data will be processed into a fully normalized bi-temporal graph data model (physical representation: relational database, linked data, or graph data).

5.1.5 Data Output

The impact module translates the trajectories into categorized time series in a tabular form that can be exported into Excel or CSV. Moreover, multiple output tables can relate to each other, for example for visualization of the results.

5.2 Controlling Accuracy

In addition to back testing described under Sect. 5.1, diversity of types of the component models is essential for the reliability of the model. By nature, models neglect parts of reality, and therefore, the level of consistency between different models solving the same problem can be used to assess the level of accuracy achievable. In a meta model, model consistency checks are possible on two levels: on the level of the integrated meta model (package of component models) and at the level of each domain-related component model. Consistency checks at both levels are intended.

If different models arrive at different results beyond the expected accuracy margin, this might be a call for correction (like in the case of back testing mismatches) and/or of manual intervention in the simulation, e.g. by adding specific constraints.

If the instability is inherent, this might be an indication of a likely large-scale transition or uncertain circumstances. In case of a likely large-scale transition, a more detailed simulation is started (see Sect. 3.5). In case of uncertain circumstances, scenario analysis is helpful, i.e., multiple simulations are run using different assumptions on how the uncertain part of the system or its environment will evolve. The probability of each scenario-related trajectory is determined using standard expert elicitation techniques.

5.3 Model Locators

Given the enormous diversity of systems relevant for the sustainability-related challenges in terms of time scale, domain and spatial coverage, granularity, and quantities important to the model user, it is not possible to develop a comprehensive simulation model for all sustainability-related challenges beforehand. On the other hand, a specific ad-hoc model for each challenge would be too expensive to build. Moreover, it would lead to inconsistencies across the applications, and it would be hard to transfer learnings from an application to the following applications.

A consistent modeling approach across the use cases employs the partial overlap in terms of model coverage to re-use data, model parts, learnings, and validations, and to provide consistency across the use cases.

The model locators identify each data point and therefore ensure consistency within and across applications by pointing to the areas of overlap. They therefore serve as a means for continuous learning and improvement.

Technically, the model can be described by a directed graph between model locators, and its information could be kept in a graph database or a triple store.

The details of the model locators are part of the model ontology which goes beyond the scope of this document (see Appendix "Model artefacts").

5.4 Model Selection Criteria

The quality of the model results crucially depends on the quality of the component models embedded into the meta model. Although an *a priori* answer to the selection of component models cannot be given, a few selection criteria can be outlined such as model coverage (domains and scope), specificity level and granularity, degree of dynamic response, quality, diversity, and availability.

5.4.1 Model Coverage: Domain and Scope

An obvious criterion for model choice is the model coverage: the model needs to contain the domains relevant to the application (for example real and financial economy), and the scope needs to span the system of interest (for example the European Union).

The component model's coverage needs to be adequate: As large a system as required, but not larger.

5.4.2 Model Resolution: Granularity and Level of Specificity

The resolution must fit the scale of the application. The simulation of a city's financial and social sustainability requires a different scale than the simulation of the entire world. This applies both to the granularity as well as the level of specificity.

The granularity reflects the resolution into detailed categories such as for example country, state, county, community, and fractions of communities. The level of specificity reflects the resolution of groups into individual parts of the group such as for example the resolution of a proxy investment goods firm in system dynamics modeling into several specific competing investment goods firms in agent-based modeling.

The component model's resolution needs to be adequate: As specific as required, but not more specific.

5.4.3 Degree of Dynamic Response

The model offering the most elaborate dynamic response and most comprehensive number of feedback loops is not necessarily the most accurate model. Dynamic freedom decreases the model stability might which in turn limits the time horizon. Moreover, the additional parameters increase the parameterization effort and the unavoidable parameterization errors.

Therefore, model parsimony rules also apply to the level of dynamic response: The component model needs to offer as much dynamic response and freedom as required to solve the problem in a non-trivial way, but not more.

5.4.4 Required Resources: Data, Computing Power, and Parameterization Effort

Large scope, many domains, fine granularity, high level of specificity, and a high degree of dynamic response all require computational power as well as effort and data for parameterization and back test.

Given all these resources are limited and, a balance across all component models is required since the law of diminishing returns applies to computational models as well.

The best overall model performance is achieved if the resource requirements of all component models in terms of data, computing power, and parameterization effort are comparable to each other and reflect the relative importance of the subsystem they cover approximately.

5.4.5 Model Quality

The considerations on controlling the model's accuracy and consistency hold for the component models as well. Ideally, the developer of the component model has already done and published all the quality checks in a reproducible and repeatable way, and a full data lineage exists. An explicit estimate of the model inaccuracy is preferred over a high but unquantifiable accuracy.

The law of diminishing returns mandates the accuracy to be balanced across all component models rather than maximized.

The consistency of the overall model results not only crucially depends on the consistency of the component models but also on the approach combining them. Therefore, the effort required to adjust them in order to combine them in a consistent way[19] is an essential model selection criterion.

Finally, the transparency requirements of the component models combined into a meta model is even more important than the transparency requirements of their standalone use.

5.4.6 Model Diversity

It is highly desirable to have several models covering the same system. This applies both to the component models and to combinations thereof into a meta model. In case of several models in parallel, they should be as diverse as possible according to all criteria, especially the modelling techniques, the level of specificity, and granularities as well as the data sets used to parameterize them. A good design is often referred to as a combination of "top-down" and "bottom-up" approaches.

However, averaging over different parallel models greatly reduces the benefit of model diversity: Instead, a critical review of model results is required wherever the results of the different models diverge substantially.

5.4.7 Practical Considerations

Finally, a few obvious practical considerations are game-changing: is it legally possible and economical to use, embed, and if necessary, extend the model under consideration? Is it technically feasible to embed the model into an overall framework? Has the model reached a certain level of maturity? Will it be maintained? Is there a way to feed back the findings to the developers of the model?

The appendix gives a few models along with a rough classification.

[19]Both for upfront integration and for updates.

6 Model Development Approach

The development approach is a decisive factor in the creation of the SISAL model: The upfront development of a model that potentially covers all life on earth and their circumstances is impossible. The goal of such a modeling effort can therefore not be to cover everything, but rather to model what needs to be covered for an application, and to consistently re-use what has already been modeled for another application.

Moreover, the results of the model are required in order to understand which part of the model needs to be improved.

6.1 Development around Use Cases

A problem-driven and application-oriented approach will be adopted, i.e., the model will be developed while solving problems in use case applications. Early application is as important as the constant incorporation of learnings into the stock of the model, iteratively improving the model in an agile way. An evolutionary development approach ensures continuous progress by building on previous work consistently.

The structural approach of the model makes it possible to extend and employ it to unforeseen use cases, and to re-use existing simulations to explore unforeseen questions.

6.2 Analytics and Early Deliveries

As in any undertaking that includes research, many relevant qualitative and quantitative questions can only be formulated concretely considering preceding results. Therefore, early result delivery and scrutiny with subsequent gradual improvement and extension are essential for large-scale model development. A decisive success factor is the delivery of the minimum viable product (MVP) as early as possible. The MVP represents the first meaningful results as coarse and simplified as they might be, for example a relationship map showing the most important postulated issue chains for an application, followed by the system dynamics resulting from it.

For the client or user, early results provide useful, non-trivial insight which also clarifies the expectations on subsequent deliveries. For the use case project, they help clarifying and sharpening the case continuously.

However, also the model benefits from these early results, providing early insight into the mechanisms that matter most. The conceptual pilots clarify the areas requiring attention, their link to the existing model, and they point to missing parts in the overall meta model or in component models.

Finally, the public receives early insight and the project early concrete material for sharing.

Early results are not created with the full simulation meta model but with explorative analytics which initially might merely be inspired by the model but might not yet build on the already implemented parts of the model. As the model is continuously extended based on the analytics findings, the analytics increasingly builds on the implemented model rather than on ad-hoc analytics.

6.2.1 From Scenario Analysis to a Fully Dynamic Simulation

Table 2 outlines an *a priori* strategy for early interim results deliveries, iterative results improvements and extensions, and continuous model development for the investment case (see Sect. 7). This strategy will be adapted continuously to the results of each step. The application can be structured into two threads, a vulnerability quantification and an impact quantification. The resilience thread quantifies the effect of environmental and social risks and opportunities on the financial performance of the assets and asset classes, and the impact thread quantifies the environmental and social impact of these assets and asset classes

In addition to starting with a top-down approach, i.e., with the systems level (see Sect. 3.4), it is particularly useful to restrict the flexibility of the system in its reaction to changes within the system or of another system (see Sect. 3.5).

A predetermined static calculation at the beginning helps identify the key mechanisms requiring a dynamic or scenario-based treatment.

For an initial assessment of the impact, a predetermined static calculation will already be sufficient, and for the assessment of the resilience against environmental and social risks, a scenario analysis with scenarios representing the potential development of these risks over time will be sufficient.

Once the key feedback loops driving the future of the system are identified, a simplified system dynamics calculation will provide early insight on the completeness and stability of the system. Moreover, the results of these calculations will serve as a background for the more detailed calculations.

Beyond a simplified system dynamics calculation, any development of models from scratch will no longer make sense, and the simplified calculations are consolidated into a component model of SISAL. At the same time, available suitable component models are adapted, extended, and embedded into the SISAL framework. A comparison between top-down and bottom-up results is important for the validation of model results (see Sect. 5.2). Moreover, the links between top-down and bottom-up approaches help explain the model results.

6.2.2 Examples of Minimum Viable Products

The MVP is agreed-on with the use case project team in an early project stage. The examples given here shall only serve as a collection of ideas to build on and most importantly, to show how simple the MVP can be.

Table 2 Potential interim results deliveries of the investment case (see Sect. 7) from an a priori view, for continuous adjustment considering the results already available

Thread	Step	Description	MVP	Launch
R	Investments parameterization	Classification of assets, investment decisions, financial KPIs, and pre-financial KPIs in a consistent overview, top-down, for gradual refinement and quantification	Outline with examples	Overview and tables
R	Asset stress scenario pre-analysis	Compilation of threat scenarios and *a priori* estimation of threats and vulnerabilities of different asset classes and assets	Summary	Summary and time series
R	System impact scenario analysis of asset vulnerabilities	– Prioritized and characterized channels of transmission overlaid with the values from scenario analysis. – Summary of relevant trade-offs that are neglected, impossible to resolve, or resolved in scenario analysis. – Overview of key mechanisms that need to be better understood and/or quantified.	Visual	Chart, graph data, time series, and key story lines
R	Key dynamics quantification	– Key feedback loops in the system with relevant lags are taken into account – Agreement with the static systems view using scenarios is understood. – Overview of key dynamics that need to be better understood and/or quantified.	Visual	Overview, visualization, time series
I	Investments parameterization	Classification of assets, investment decisions, financial KPIs, and pre-financial KPIs in a consistent overview, top-down, for gradual refinement and quantification	Outline with examples	Overview and tables
I	Impact estimation of investments	Impact of investments in selected assets and asset classes for selected pre-financial KPIs from an *a priori* estimation	Numbers with explanations	Report, table with visualization
I	System impact pre-analysis of investments	System impact of investments in selected assets and asset classes for selected KPIs and reporting scopes, replacing impact estimation by calculation using key channels of transmission	Numbers with explanations	Report, table with visualization

(continued)

Table 2 (continued)

Thread	Step	Description	MVP	Launch
I	Systematic system impact pre-analysis of investments	System impact pre-analysis extended to many asset classes and assets by using a variety of channels of transmission	Insights with explanations	Report, table with visualization
I	System impact analysis of investments	– System impact pre-analysis improved with selectively added and/or resolved channels of transmission based on outcome of the pre-analysis. The emphasis lies on traceability and reproducibility. – Prioritized and characterized channels of transmission. – Summary of relevant trade-offs that are neglected, impossible to resolve, or resolved in scenario analysis. – Overview of key mechanisms that need to be better understood and/or quantified.	Visual	Chart, graph data, time series, and key story lines
I	Systematic system impact analysis of investments	– System impact analysis extended to many asset classes and assets by using a variety of channels of transmission. – Prioritized and characterized channels of transmission.	Visual	Chart, graph data, time series, and key story lines
I	Key dynamics quantification of investment impact	– Key feedback loops in the system with relevant lags are taken into account. – Agreement with the static systems view using scenarios is understood. – Overview of key dynamics that need to be better understood and/or quantified.	Visual	Overview, visualization, time series
I	Initial dynamics quantification of investment impact and vulnerabilities	Initial synthesis of impact of investments and vulnerabilities of assets and asset classes.	Visual	Overview, visualization, time series

Thread "R" represents a quantification of the resilience of assets and asset classes against environmental and social risks, and thread "I" represents an investment impact quantification

- Relationship map: Identification of key issues and relationships
- Driver map: Identification of key drivers (most relevant parts)
- Scenario vulnerability analysis: Static impact calculation of assumedly known outside development on own business (scenarios related to external development)
- Scenario impact analysis: Static impact calculation of own action scenarios on selected target KPIs (scenarios related to own action)
- Core dynamics: Simplified system dynamics simulation of key drivers (most relevant parts)

6.3 Model Application and Development Cycles

A model of this dimension can only be developed using agile approaches: the effort of modeling *a priori* would be prohibitive. Five cycles structure and align the work and allow a continuous progress while delivering results.

1. Pre-analysis

   (a) Set the objective: Together with the clients, users and the project team, the use case giver formulates a challenge and a corresponding project. Start outlining model.
   (b) Context analysis (part 1 of system analysis): Together with the clients, users, direct stakeholder representatives and the project team, the context of the use cases is being mapped. This includes a schematic description of the current situation including problems, challenges and future issues as well as available and needed resources such as data, skills, finance, knowledge, etc.
   (c) Initial dependency modeling: (Issue Chains—part 2 of system analysis). Following the context analysis, the interdependencies are being mapped. The first step here is to include the highest level of networks, the issue chains
   (d) Stakeholder analysis: in order to find out which stakeholders are involved in processes, decisions and actions regarding the overarching use case. Stakeholders to be considered as most critical or influential are being identified.

2. Analysis and prototyping

   (a) Define hypothesis: Formulate a hypothesis on a cause-effect chain relevant to the challenge at hand. This can include new aspects, data, entities, or higher granularity, or also the rejection of something considered wrong or irrelevant that might obfuscate the overall picture.
   (b) Quantitative (pre-)analysis: A quick-and-dirty study assessing the quantitative impact of the hypothesis using the information at hand.
   (c) Collect data: Following a data hunt, the quality, usefulness, and the effort to make use of the data sets are assessed.
   (d) Model data and function: The results of the preceding steps are cast into the structure of the model. Overlaps and potential conflicts are outlined.

(e) Test in model: The results of the analysis are put into the context of the model and therefore into a realistic environment. A critical review of inconsistencies may lead to an improvement or corrections to any of the results of the preceding steps and/or evidence to correct the model.
(f) Evaluate with client: A critical and thorough review of the results and the reasons together with clients, stakeholders, and experts concludes a research and prototyping cycle. Any non-trivial finding and result gets formulated and stored centrally.

3. Model elaboration and implementation

(a) Model analysis: Model findings are mapped onto the existing model, and gaps or mismatches are identified. In case of improvement or correction needs, a root cause analysis is performed.
(b) Domain modeling: The model structure is specified in the two parts of the domain model: the domain entity and the domain functional model. Extensive use is made of model locators and the model architecture artefacts.
(c) Model implementation: The extensions and adaptations to the domain model are implemented in the software code implementing the meta model and/or the component models, the structure of the databases hosting the parameters, and/or the model parameters of the meta model and/or the component models.
(d) Model regression and back test: Two types of results quality assurance are performed. The regression tests ensure that the changes are indeed in line with expectation (impact analysis) and there are no unintended side effects (false positives check) whereas the back test ensures that the model predicts the past wherever data on the past exist.

4. Client results delivery

(a) Client result delivery: A results delivery consists of at least four parts: the conclusion and recommendation, the quantitative reasoning behind the conclusion, a confidence level with the evidence supporting and potentially limiting the conclusions, and a recommendation on next steps.
(b) Client scaling: In a deep collaboration with the client, a holistic assessment on impact maximization is performed across the whole organization.

5. Impact scaling

(a) Result evaluation: Continuous learning and improvement is deeply embedded in the agile model pursued by Simulated Action Analysis. It includes but is not limited to content and model learning, business model and process optimization, and client value improvement.
(b) Application scaling: With each use case it will become clearer which companies or organizations will have a direct benefit of the project results. Depending of the profitability or ability to pay for knowledge sharing and specific implementation, a scaling approach will be used. There will be two modes of scaling: more use cases or more users of the same use case.

6.3.1 Model Application and Development Phases

A successful application of a use case has five phases (see project timing). The organization by phase helps determine if a use case/application is on track:

1. Pre-pilot: This phase ends with the agreement to start the collaboration e.g. in a client relationship. It consists of steps of the pre-analysis cycle.
2. Pilot: This phase ends with the delivery of the MVP. It consists of the steps of the analysis and prototyping (A&P) cycle and results delivery.
3. Prototyping: This phase ends with the start of the model elaboration and implementation cycle for the use case. It consists of the steps of the A&P cycle and results deliveries.
4. Deliver & incorporate: This phase ends with the conclusion of the use case application. It consists of the steps of the A&P cycle, the model elaboration and implementation cycle, and results deliveries.
5. Post-conclusion: This phase starts after the conclusion of the use case application and ensures that the impact is maximized beyond the use case application. It consists of the steps of the impact scaling cycle and the model elaboration and implementation cycle.

7 Example: Financially, Societally, and Environmentally Outperforming Investments

The use case "financially, societally, and environmentally outperforming investments" shall illustrate how the model concept works.

7.1 Use Case

Corporate and individual investment has a large power over our future. Successful investors provide solutions which are more than just compliant with existing regulations. The trillions of dollars of investment funds have a decisive power over which products, business practices, and technologies will be pursued and developed, both for the better or the worse of our societies and our planet.

The application "financially, societally, and environmentally outperforming investments" envisions corporate investment paving the way for a sustainable economy while being financially performing.

The model simulates *ex ante* which investment will have the maximum return in terms of risk-adjusted financial key performance indicators (KPIs) and SDG-related KPIs across different time horizons consistently using the same methodology, data, and assumptions for both the financials and non-financials. As time progresses, the anticipated results will be seamlessly adjusted, in order to detect early corrective action where needed and for consistent reporting and impact measurement.

7.2 *System Overview*

Figure 3 shows an *a priori* overview of the meta model with its modules. Illustrative example issue chains are overlaid at the systems level.

In the example, the user rebalances a portfolio (a), replacing e.g. coal bonds by bonds in a wind farm, and is interested in the risk-adjusted mid-term financial performance of the new bonds compared to the old ones (b) and the net effect his investment decision has on greenhouse gas emissions including indirect emissions (c).

7.2.1 Issue Chains

Very simplified cause-effect chains shall illustrate Fig. 3: The effect on the portfolio's financial performance (b) is directly determined by expected the relative financial performance (d) of the two bonds affected by the decision (a). The financial performance (d) in turn is influenced by the mid-term economic performance of the two companies (e) and therefore by economic opportunities (i) governed by regulatory acts (j). The anticipated effect on greenhouse gas emissions (c), (g) depends on the economic performance (e) of the two companies, boosted or suffocated by liquidity provided by own (a) and following investments (f), changing price levels (k), etc.

The different lags and connection strengths in the different influence functions connecting the issue nodes create the non-linear dynamic system where we can observe the leveraged effects of paradigm changes with tipping points such as market disruptions, climate change, or extinction of species, and collective phenomena such as bank runs or the mass adoption of specific new technologies.

Technically, the issue chains are retained in a graph database, and the graphical rendering shows the nodes and relationships that are material to the use case, based on the simulation results. The selection of relevant relationships is done by prioritization and by aggregation of several parallel relationships onto one combined relationship.

7.2.2 From the Input to the Output

The simulation process outlined in Fig. 2 is illustrated here for the investment use case.

The starting conditions (1) are derived from data e.g. on the financials and activities of companies potentially in the portfolio, on the economies surrounding them, on their value chains, and on the carbon footprints of the companies and people in the value chain.

The boundary conditions (2) contain e.g. macro-economic forecasts as well climate forecasts under various scenarios. Depending on the model results, some of these scenario forecasts will be complemented or replaced by full simulations of macro economies and/or the climate for areas of interest.

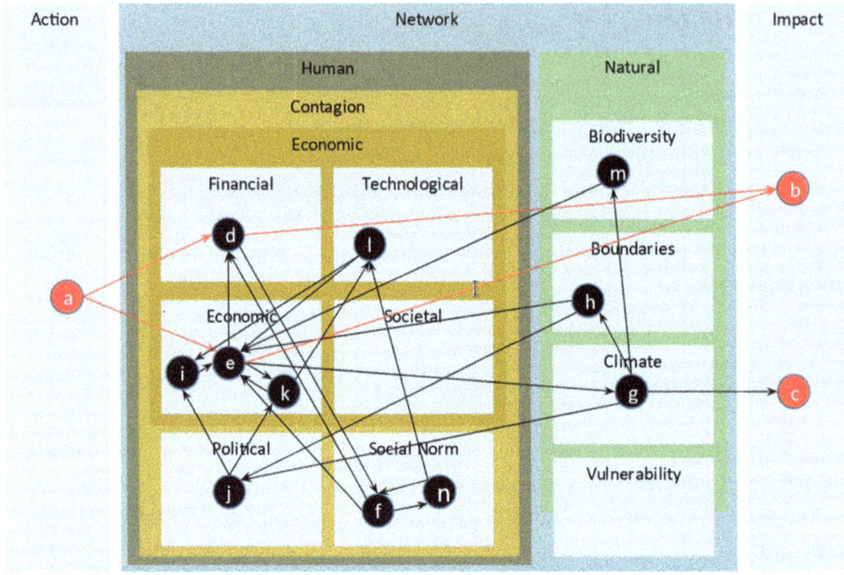

Fig. 3 Illustrative issue chains related to the use case "Financially, societally, and environmentally outperforming investments". The depicted issue nodes represent: (**a**) investment decision, (**b**) investment performance, (**c**) greenhouse gas emissions, (**d**) Valuation, (**e**) economic performance, (**f**) following investors, (**g**) greenhouse gas emissions, (**h**) natural resources, (**i**) economic opportunities, (**j**) regulatory response, (**k**) price levels, (**l**) Energy consumption, (**m**) natural resources, (**n**) acceptance

Using the influence functions (4′), the quantification of the interactions e.g. between the companies, the participants of the value chain including end customers, financial stakeholders, other players such as regulators, and of the direct and indirect greenhouse-gas emissions, the initial state (1) is propagated into the future subject to the boundary conditions (2), resulting in a baseline trajectory (B′), i.e., time series of key properties of all relevant actors in the system.

For each agenda variant (A), the investment decisions influence the system by adding, removing, or changing properties of influence functions (A′) representing investments in specific companies or asset classes. The simulation is repeated, resulting in a trajectory (B′) for each agenda variant (A). Aggregation and comparison of these trajectories (B′) to the baseline trajectory (B′) and the corresponding agenda variants (A′) results in the time series of the key performance indicators of interest (B), described in more detail in Sect. 7.3.

Since each entity in the system (1) or its boundary conditions (2) as well as each influence function (4′ and A) are not only represented by numbers but also have a counterpart in reality and therefore a narrative, carrying a link to the sources, the model results (B) can be explained by a reconstruction of all relevant cause-effect chains.

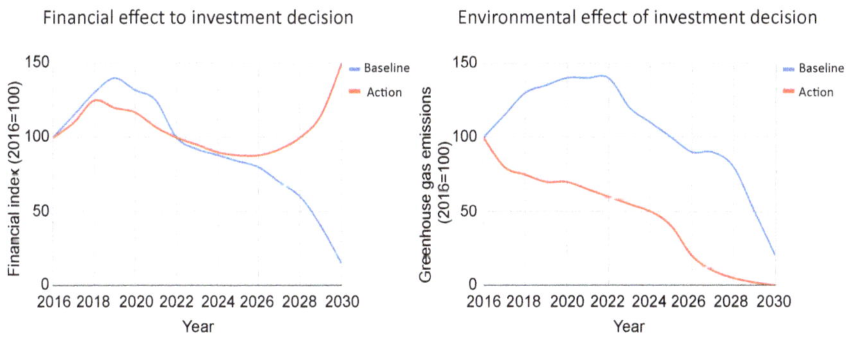

Fig. 4 Illustration of aggregated model results. The future performance of an investment portfolio after capital redeployment (with action) is compared to the future performance of the same portfolio without capital redeployment (baseline). Performance is measured by key performance indicators (KPIs) over time: investment return and greenhouse gas emissions caused by the companies in the portfolio

7.3 Anticipated Results

As Fig. 4 illustrates, the model will aggregate its results onto trajectories of various observables over time, both in the presence of the action (in the example capital redeployment) to be probed and in its absence (baseline). The action can be both a private action (in the example below an investment decision) and a policy action (not shown).

Both the targeted performance measures (in the example investment return) as well as important externalities (in the example greenhouse gas emissions "GHG emissions") can be observed on a consistent basis. The simulation replaces biases and *a priori* assumptions on how the observed quantities will progress by verifiable model results and links the results to data and assumptions used to obtain them. As time progresses, the simulated trajectories will gradually be replaced by observed ones, allowing both a gradual reduction of the uncertainty of the remaining predictions and an improvement of the model.

Moreover, it will be possible to further drill into the model results to investigate the reasons of the observed results such as the depicted widening financial performance gap observable in the later years, and to find potential additional relevant effects such as impact on local unemployment rates (not shown) or potential roadblocks to the desired effect of the action under consideration (in the example capital redeployment).

Simulating several agenda variants such as different capital redeployments allows the user to find the most effective action.

As time progresses, the simulated trajectories will gradually be replaced by observed ones, allowing both a gradual reduction of the uncertainty of the remaining predictions and an improvement of the model. For simplicity, the uncertainty interval has been omitted in the illustrative figure.

8 Conclusions

Computer simulation has become an indispensable tool for the assessment and quantification of outcomes of decisions ahead of time in various fields. However, many sustainability-related challenges are seemingly too complex to be simulated realistically given the enormous range of systems, scales, and quantities of interest.

With the presented simulation meta model framework, this *per se* unsolvable simulation challenge has been broken down into a structure that allows to solve it, providing early validated results while enabling continuous and structured learning.

Since neither individual models nor individual modeling approaches solve the challenge, a synthetic approach has been presented, combining techniques in a mutually complementary way. Specifically, the synthesis of domains, scopes, scales, granularities, time scales and modeling techniques has been outlined. It has been shown how a gradual complement of top-down and bottom-up approaches lead to increasing explanatory power.

The synthetic modeling approach ensures comparability across applications, actors, actions, and quantities of interest. The structural approach not only ensures transferability but also traceability of results to data and assumptions, and it adds explanatory power. Most importantly, this connection invites all actors and stakeholders to participate actively in the entire analysis and modeling journey and therefore opens the pathway to using the results for more sustainable decisions.

Finally, an agile development approach has been introduced, supporting both early delivery of results and continuous improvement. It was shown how the development approach makes a decisive difference, guiding the effort to the areas which matter most and allowing an early detection of oversimplifications or invalid assumptions, and letting subsequent applications build on earlier work.

Acknowledgements I thank Karen Wendt for the invitation to contribute this article to the book "Theories of Change".

This work and its applications would not have been possible in isolation.

Many thanks to Katrin Hauser and Francesca Mancini for their thorough review of this manuscript.

I would like to thank Anaïs Sägesser and Britta Rendlen for putting faith and great collaboration into the endeavor when it was merely a concept from a short sabbatical, and for encouraging me to pursue it further.

I am particularly grateful to Katrin Hauser who has been an invaluable project partner going through the ups and downs of this startup ever since her joining, challenging me and spending countless hours together on getting it going. I am very grateful to the colleagues in the first SISAL team Katrin Hauser, Francesca Mancini, and Brunhilde Mauthe.

This work has benefited greatly from discussions and workshops with countless people who are too numerous to be mentioned individually here and whom I stay gratefully and respectfully connected with.

Last but not least, I am deeply grateful to my wife Renata Vasella Billeter and our daughters Mira and Corina for their continuous support and the decisive encouragement to take the risk and make SISAL the new center of my professional life.

Appendix

Terminology and Key Term Definitions

Term	Description	Examples	Section	Belongs to
Model method	The model method categories classify the model by how it works	System dynamics, statistical static, judgmental scenario-based	(see parts of model method)	
Model coverage	The model coverage categories classify the model by the scope of the system it covers, i.e., by what is contained in the system	Economy of the United States of America	Model coverage: domain and scope	
Model resolution	The model resolution categories classify the model by the level of detail it resolves the system into	Single companies, groups of people, cities	Granularity: controlling the computational cost	
Scale	Order of magnitude of the system and the resolution of detail	Macro, meso, micro, nano	Scale	
Specificity level	Specificity of the model approach can reach. This dimension covers the spectrum between top-down and bottom-up modeling. There are three levels: systems, agents, and individuals	System dynamics, agent-based model	Synthesis by model specificity	Resolution, method
Technique	Technique employed to describe, simplify, and quantify the system to be understood	Structural model, statistical model, judgmental model	Synthesis of modelling techniques	Method
Degree of dynamic response	(define when writing the section)	Inelastic dynamic, elastic dynamic, scenario-based static	Degrees of dynamic response	Method, resolution
Domain	Subject matter area the model covers	Real economy, society, politics, climate	Synthesis of domains	Coverage
Scope	Coverage of the model in terms of size and location (spatial coverage)	City of Zurich, France, World	Scope: dimensions of spatial coverage	Coverage, scale
Granularity	Level of detail in terms of size the model resolves the system into	Cities (meso), companies (micro), employees (nano), square km	Granularity: controlling the computational cost	Resolution, scale

(continued)

Term	Description	Examples	Section	Belongs to
Level of attention	Methodological focus a sub-system receives in case of a partition into system and environment or a nested partition into system and environment: differentiated model specificity levels, granularities, degrees of dynamic response.	Split into Zurich (high specificity, fully dynamic, high granularity), Switzerland (low granularity), rest of world (low specificity, scenario-based static)	Levels of attention: system and environment	
Boundary condition	Boundary conditions include both constraints (prior knowledge the simulation must observe) and the quantification of the impact the environment has on the system if the time evolution is not available from another part of the model.	Expert judgement on reasonable range of national GDP growth, time series of world's output growth as a context for national GDP growth	Use and generation of data	
Agenda	The agenda is a model input provided by the user and can consist of one-off actions or series of actions concerted over time	One-off investment capital redeployment, continually raised fuel economy standards	Special modules	
Agenda variant	Agenda variants are mutually exclusive parameterizations of an agenda, used to find the optimum agenda to achieve the desired impact.	Fast-paced raise of fuel economy standard (as opposed to slow increase of one-off).	Special modules	Agenda
Issue chain	Series of high-level dependencies between issues which are deemed relevant, have a telling name. It has an overarching narrative and represents a selection from the high-level dependency graph at the systems level. Depending on the maturity level of the model part under consideration, the relevance of the individual dependencies might be hypothetical or proven.	The effect of the investment decision on the portfolio's financial performance is directly determined by the expected relative financial performance of the two bonds affected by the decision.	Networks, the glue of the model	Network

(continued)

Term	Description	Examples	Section	Belongs to
Issue node	The issue node formalizes and quantifies an issue which is deemed relevant and has a telling name. It may carry one or many quantities or proxies of quantities. The issue node represents a node in the high-level dependency graph at the systems level.	Investment decision, economic performance, economic opportunities	Networks, the glue of the model	Network, issue chain
Issue link	A connection between two issue nodes. The issue link represents an edge in the high-level dependency graph at the systems level	Impact of liquidity provided by investment on the economic performance of a company	Networks, the glue of the model	Network, issue chain
Influence	The influence reflects a change to one or more properties of an entity in the system caused by an entity within or outside the system. It has a name, a direction, and an influence function. In system dynamics, it is often called flow. In agent-based modeling, it is often called rule. In network modeling, it is often called transaction.	Influence of microclimate on available fresh water, financial disruption caused by economic downturn, a customer purchasing a good, effect of a central bank "printing" money on liquidity available to banks, a supply relationship, company ownership relationship.	Time scales and degrees of dynamic response	Network
Influence function	The quantification of an influence, usually consisting of several parameters relating to the strength, timing (lag), and polarity (sign) of the influence.	Covariance and lag between defined open-market operations and loan cash reserves of business banks, high/medium/low assessment of the influence of a defined change of microclimate on the fresh water supplies as initial guess	Time scales and degrees of dynamic response	Network, influence
External influence	Influence on parts of the system from outside. In other communities also stress or perturbation.	Action (action module), influence of world economy on a country's prosperity	Time scales and degrees of dynamic response	Network

(continued)

Term	Description	Examples	Section	Belongs to
Master source	A master source contains the sources of evidence behind a quantity used in the model. The sources of evidence are the endpoints of a data lineage, i.e., the ultimate sources.	Defined records in a data set, formally captured expert judgments in a database, original statements that can be referred to.	Use and generation of data	Data

Interaction Between Use Case and Model Development

Goals of the different use case delivery phases are:

- Pilot and prototype: speedy delivery of first insight with as little constraint as possible
- Prototype: constraint-free leverage of pre-existing model and
- Deliver and incorporate: continuous progress and innovation, sustainable and reproducible creation of results

Phase	Direction	Matter	Notes
Pilot, prototype	Model—use case	Base model as starting point	Experimentation
Prototype	Use case—model	Data for the public domain	
Prototype	Use case—model	Insight and guidance for model extension	Including prioritization by importance
Prototype	Use case—model	Test cases, insight about back test	
Prototype	Modely—use case	Continually improved and extended model	
Prototype	Model—use case	Controlled framework	Repeatability, reproducibility, consistency

Model Artefacts

Name	Purposes	Priority	Description	Notes
High-level description	Get into the model, published reference	H	Description of the model for a knowledgeable person as a first reading	Publication in the Springer Book chapter in "theories of change"

(continued)

Name	Purposes	Priority	Description	Notes
Formal description	Establish the model in scientific world	M	Description satisfying standards of a peer-reviewed journal	Scientific publications
Model ontology	Guide through the details of the model graph	H	Gives a context for the details and outlines the model locators	Highlights implemented parts of full model and ensures consistency via the model locators
Domain entity model (model graph)	Formal reference language across the component models	H	Condensed formal description and specification of the entities in the model	Meta language and technical form need to be ready before details are worked out (migration is cumbersome)
Domain functional model	Formal reference language across the component models	H	Condensed formal description and specification of the functions in the model	Meta language and technical form need to be ready before details are worked out (migration is cumbersome)
Data catalogue	Find and re-use important information	H	According to established data catalogue standards	Form needs to be established early on
Domain data master sources	Resolve potential conflicts between data sets	M	A reference repository of data processed for model use and a reproducible methodology for refresh and update	Includes data lineage, tracing information back to all sources
Data backbone	Get the results in a reproducible, consistent way, allowing progress	L	Technical infrastructure for data brought into a common form	Follows the domain entity model
API specification	Establish a common reference for model integration	M	How the component models communicate with each other	Concept and proof of concept need to be established as soon as the domain model, follows the domain entity model
Model implementation	Get the results in a reproducible, consistent way, allowing progress	L	Meta model reference implementation, aspiration: can power even a game	Architectural artifacts need to be ready first

References

Arquitt, S., Pedercini, M., Onasanya A., & Herren, H. (2018). *Addressing climate-sustainable development in long-term low-carbon strategies: The role of Millennium Institute's iSDG model.* Retrieved from https://www.wri.org/climate/expert-perspective/addressing-climate-sustainable-development-linkages-long-term-low-carbon

Aznar-Siguan, G., & Bresch, D. N. (2019). CLIMADA v1: A global weather and climate risk assessment platform, Geosci. Model Dev. Discuss, https://doi.org/10.5194/gmd-12-3085-2019

Battiston, S., Mandel, A., Monasterolo, I., Schütze, F., & Visentin, G. (2016a). *A climate stress test of the financial system*, SSRN-id2726076.

Battiston, S., Caldarelli, G., D'Errico, M., & Gurciullo, S. (2016b). Leveraging the network: A stress-test framework based on DebtRank. *Statistics and Risk Modeling, 33*, 117.

Baue, B., & Thurm, R. (2018). *Blueprint 4: New business models, integral business model design for catalyzing regenerative and distributive economies, reporting 3.0.* Retrieved from https://reporting3.org/wp-content/uploads/2018/06/R3-BP4.pdf

Billeter, S., & Salghetti, F. (2016). *Bringing a forward-looking perspective into liability modelling: Liability risk drivers*, Swiss Re.

Billeter, S., Webb, S. P., Iordanov, T., Agarwal, P. K., & Hammes-Schiffer, S. (2001). Hybrid approach for including electronic and nuclear quantum effects in molecular dynamics simulations of hydrogen transfer reactions in enzymes. *Journal of Chemical Physics, 114*, 6925.

Bollinger, L. A., Davis, C. B., Evins, R., Chappin, E. J. I., & Nikolic, I. (2017). Multi-model ecologies for shaping future energy systems: Design patterns and development paths. *Renewable and Sustainable Energy Reviews*. https://doi.org/10.1016/j.rser.2017.10.047.

Dawid, H., Harting, P., Hoog, S., & Neugart, M. (2016). *A heterogeneous agent macroeconomic model for policy evaluation: Improving transparency and reproducibility.* Universität Bielefeld, Working Papers in Economics and Management.

Kosov, H., & Gassner, R. (2008). *Methods of future and scenario analysis: Overview, assessment, and selection criteria.* SSOAR. Retrieved from https://www.ssoar.info/ssoar/bitstream/handle/document/19366/ssoar-2008-kosow_et_al-methods_of_future_and_scenario.pdf

Pauliuk, S., Arvesen, A., Stadler, K., & Hertwich, E. G. (2017). Industrial ecology in integrated assessment models. *Nature Climate Change, 7*, 13.

Rudolf, B., & Zurlinden, M. (2014). *A compact open economy DSGE model for Switzerland.* SNB Economic Studies 8/2014.

Sackman, H. (1974). *Delphi assessment. Expert opinion, forecasting, and group process.* RAND Corporation published research, Reports, Delphi. Retrieved from https://www.rand.org/pubs/reports/R1283.html

Salomon Billeter initiated Simulated Action Analysis for Sustainable Impact, a comprehensive decision support meta model and consultancy, intended to serve business and sustainability goals alike, for and beyond sustainable finance. Started during a sabbatical in 2016, he made it his focus from 2018. At Swiss Re, he led the casualty model development team and activities until 2018, having built up forward-looking modeling from scratch including the patented Liability Risk Drivers™ model for costing, underwriting, risk accumulation control, and other purposes. Until 2006, he has developed computer simulation methods at IBM Research to overcome fundamental scaling limits in solid-state electronics. Prior to joining IBM, his academic research in the US and Europe focused on simulation techniques aimed at understanding bio-reactions to treat metabolism-related diseases. Salomon has graduated in physics and chemistry at ETH Zürich and holds a PhD from ETH Zürich in physical chemistry.

Part V
Ecosystems

Banking 4.0: Digital Ecosystems and Super-Apps

Daniel Fasnacht

It is not our feet that move us along, it is our minds!
[Ancient Chinese proverb]

Abstract Banking 4.0 is characterised by digital innovations, fusing the physical, artificial, and biological worlds, affecting societies, industries, and companies with ever higher speed and intensity. In the process to a new world order with new competitive forces and uncertainty, where goals are continually changing, and resources must be flexibly reorganised, there is no room for traditional ways of strategic thinking. With old management concepts, linear value chains, and rigid and closed organisational structures, established firms will be the losers. This article explains why the banking industry is ripe for disruption. It introduces a conceptual framework based on a case study research of Chinese juggernauts, including value constellations, platform business models and super-apps. Our journey from the industrial economy to the digital era opens up new vistas on how to create and capture value for businesses and clients of the next generation. We describe why modern leaders must embrace change, learn from Asia, and develop strategies through the lens of the ecosystem theory. Digital ecosystems focus on clients and data and consolidate interconnected goods and services. To achieve sustainable financial growth, we suggest an agile management approach that takes the digital transformation as a chance and builds upon partnerships to connect with diverse actors—technologically, socially, and culturally.

Keywords Theory of change · Theories of change · Ecosystems · Financial ecosystems

D. Fasnacht (✉)
Department of Banking and Finance, University of Zurich, Zurich, Switzerland

K. Wendt (ed.), *Theories of Change*, Sustainable Finance,
https://doi.org/10.1007/978-3-030-52275-9_15

1 Panta Rhei

If we want to understand what changes people and businesses, we cannot ignore megatrends. Megatrends are significant social, economic, political, and technological changes that influence us for some time—usually more than 10 years.[1] Futurologist, John Naisbitt defined 1980 ten megatrends, completely redefined them for the Millennial and together with his wife published books that cover a variety of megatrends such as China's megatrends or megatrends for women.[2] As he has been studying and visiting China since 1967 and also worked as a professor at Nanjing University, Nankai University and Tianjin University of Finance and Economics, we acknowledge his expertise and forecasts. However, after a google search, we compiled our own set of six megatrends that are more or less aligned with the big consulting firm's evaluations and grouped sub-trends relevant to the financial sector into market, client, regulation, and technology. The sub-trends, or macrotrends, refer to a time horizon of five to ten years and directly affect the business (see Fig. 1).

As never before in history, several trends hit the financial sector simultaneously. They not only accelerate the transformation, instead they lead to increasing volatility, uncertainty, complexity, and ambiguity. Especially noteworthy is the ability to manage complex and conflicting tasks such as efficiency and innovation, commoditization and customisation, control and entrepreneurship—through the dynamic reconfiguration of resources and capabilities. The concept of organisational ambidexterity was developed upon organisation design and dynamic capability literature.[3] Architectural ambidexterity in the context of technology and in an age of hypercompetition is the collective ability that enables an organisation to integrate know-how and processes and systems to enact forms of connectivity that ensure endurance and accommodation to an unpredictable future.[4] It builds an overarching basis for stability, requisite uniformity, facilitatory flexibility and anticipative connectivity. Here, transformation knowledge comes in. Understanding trends is just the first step on a journey that offers a myriad of opportunities.

Change is the only constant in life as Greek philosopher Heraclitus found 500 BC. In today's business world, we have experienced one more time the constant flow of everything. Even megatrends, as introduced previously, are continuous processes. Because everything flows, everything is subject to eternal creation, and

[1]Naisbitt J (1982) Megatrends: Ten New Directions Transforming Our Lives, Warner Bros, New York.

[2]See, Naisbitt J and Naisbitt D (1991) Megatrends 2000, HarperCollins, New York; Naisbitt J and Naisbitt D (2010) China's Megatrends: The 8 Pillars of a New Society, HarperCollins, New York; Aburdene P and Naisbitt J (1992) Megatrends for Women, Villard Books, New York.

[3]O'Reilly CA and Tushman ML (2004) The ambidextrous organization, Harvard Business Review, April; March JG (1991) Exploration and exploitation in organizational learning. Organization Science, 2, 71–87.

[4]Huang, J., Fasnacht, D., Starkey, K., Tempest, S. (2006) The Development of Architectural Ambidexterity: Information Technology in an Age of Hypercompetition. In: Best Paper Proceedings, Academy of Management, Vol. 2006, No. 1.

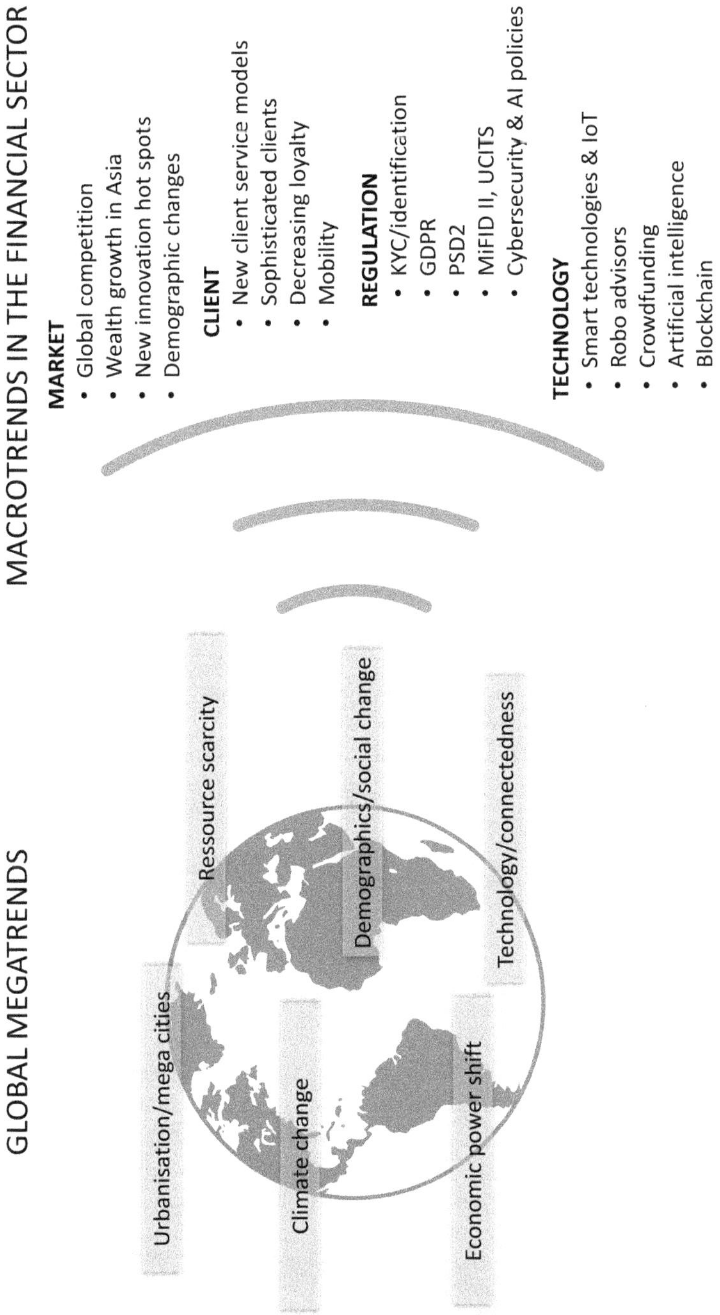

Fig. 1 Trends that hit the financial sector

every economic development is preceded by the process of change known as *creative destruction*.[5] In other words, traditional business models do not last forever. The renewal of business models results in new structures and combinations of production factors that are necessary to trigger further innovative impulses.

Trends cause changes, hence, leaders must embrace change.

During the Industrial Economy, markets and competition were clearly defined, and market power abuses by incumbents normal. Porter's five forces,[6] a framework for analysing the microenvironment, and the concept of value chains have worked for the last 40 years in a relatively stable environment. The world of industry verticals has given way to dynamic client journeys. Today we live in an interconnected and digital world with strategic discontinuities and disruptions. The COVID-19 crisis has put digital interactions to utmost importance and will boost the adoption of digital platform and ecosystem business models. To master new ways of doing business, we need entrepreneurial flexibility, agile leadership, and a framework that explains what could happen in the future. In a world were volatibility and complexity end up in chaos and unpredictability, with no stable forecasting and unclear cause-effect trajectories in a complex web of relationships, we need new transformation knowledge.

Bank managers have a direct responsibility to organise collective resources and reconfigure them to generate capabilities to handle conflicting composite requirements. Ambiguity and non-linearity call for flexibility and chaos could be met by resilience. The pandemic has accelerated a shift in values that amplified the transition to holistic and networked thinking, empathy and responsible corporate governance. Leaders must systematically develop opportunities out of trends and crises and prepare the organisation for change and disruptive business models to achieve sustainable financial growth.

2 Trends Trigger New Business Scenarios

Banking goes back 2000 years with evidence of money lending in China and India. Original banks were merchant banks with the aim to finance long trading journeys along the Silk Route. The Industrial Revolution and growing international trade increased the number of banks. Modern banking came in 1861 to the people with the postal savings system to provide depositors who did not have access to banks. Banking today is the network of institutions and laws that provide a great variety of financial services that involve an institution holding money on behalf of customers that is payable to the customer on demand, either by appearing at the bank for a withdrawal or by writing a check to a third party. It offers customers the payment of

[5]Schumpeter J (1942) Capitalism, Socialism and Democracy, Harper, New York.

[6]Porter M (1980) Competitive Strategy: Techniques for Analyzing Industries and Competitors, The Free Press, New York.

interest on deposits and reception of interest on loans (not applicable for Islamic banking) and is regulated by the laws and central banks of individual countries.[7] Is this all going to change with non-banks and fintechs—companies leveraging technology to digitise and streamline processes? Yes, it is because challenger banks usually offer competitive products and services such as digital current and savings accounts, loans, insurances, crowdfunding, crypto-investments, robo-advice, and payment services through mobile devices and digital platforms. They disrupt traditional business models as they target untapped markets and underserved demographics or radically improve user experience. Their app-based banking services epitomise the digital economy.

Everybody intuitively agrees that there is a correlation between early scouting trends, transformation skills and success. Nevertheless, leaders at established conglomerates often neglect the importance of continuous renewal. They spot the trends, but can hardly translate them into business model innovations. Implementations of transformation programmes fail due to misapplication of impending technologies and the lack of organisational agility. The Fourth Industrial Revolution, referring to the World Economic Forum founder Klaus Schwab,[8] has long since begun and is leading to an economic reorganisation with significant changes. Established Western companies will be driven out of the market if they do not collaborate with innovators outside their core industry. There is no other option than strategic renewal. Start with a new way of thinking, referring to the lessons learned of Apple's and IBM's near-death experience at the end of the 1990s.

Understanding megatrends is essential, but the more you should explore the macrotrends with wide-ranging impact on your industry. Because these critical forces will not only change your industry but impact your businesses in the future. Therefore, they will have a specific impact on your markets, products, services, organisation, staff, and clients. Use scenario planning techniques as they need to be SMART, in other words, specific, (clearly define what needs to be done in the business), measurable (clear metrics), actionable, (clear segmenting the problem), realistic (problem can be solved with the available resources, time, and cost constraints), and time-bound (clear statement of when the solution opportunity expires). Further, four simple questions additionally help firms to manage the very first step of the transformation:

- What macrotrend is relevant to your industry?
- What is the impact of the trend?
- What are the implications of the critical forces for the future?
- What business scenarios do we need to develop?

Investment banks and asset managers use megatrends as a sales approach for their products. For instance, investing in a fund linked to climate change and resource

[7] https://financial-dictionary.thefreedictionary.com/Banking

[8] Schwab, K. and Davis, N. (2018) Shaping the Future of the Fourth Industrial Revolution, Penguin Books, New York.

scarcity makes sense and does something right. Blackrock, the largest asset manager, explains that curbing carbon emissions requires significant spending on green infrastructure and a reduction in fossil fuel subsidies. This can create tremendous investment opportunities in areas that attract capital or industries at risk of disruption.[9] The future of investment banking must include social responsible and positive impact-investing.[10] Banks should not just redirect capital into the companies that deliver and show the best change dynamics; moreover, they must contribute to the economics of the 17 sustainable development goals of the United Nations.[11]

3 The Future Digital Ecosystem

In biology, change is natural law and tells us what we need to know about ecosystems. A business ecosystem models the economic rather than the energy dynamics of the biological ecosystem operations because, in the business context, complex interactions are formed between participants with the functional goal to enable technology development and innovation.

Open innovation is embedded in the notion that the sources of knowledge for innovation are widely distributed in the economy.[12] The entire innovation process from discovery, development, to commercialisation, is open to third-party providers and the public if we consider co-innovation with clients, competitors, communities, robots, machines, and in future with everything that has sensors (Internet of Things). In this context, we see the ecosystem as the next dimension of open collaboration, reflected by the extent to which firms interact internally and externally. They are the result of organisation and industry boundaries dissolving and value chains consolidating into digital ecosystems. Primarily as sharing information and knowledge, artificial intelligence and adopting cognitive technologies determine current socio-economic behaviour.

A business ecosystem consists of interdependent as well as sometimes independent businesses across sectors, linked through a digital infrastructure (platform) that facilitates the sharing of knowledge, ideas, and capabilities. It is characterised by value-creating services that are distributed throughout the actors in which the client's data access and sharing are symbiotic. The performance of the entire ecosystem exceeds the sum of the individual contributions of all the actors involved. Each actor delivers a piece of the client solution; in other words, a part of the value-creating

---

[9]Blackrock Investment Institute [online 21 September 2020]. www.ishares.com/ch/individual/en/themes/megatrends/climate-change-and-resource-scarcity

[10]Wendt K (2015) Responsible Investment Banking, Springer, Groebenzell.

[11]United Nations, Sustainbale Development Goals [online 21 September 2020] www.un.org/sustainabledevelopment/

[12]Chesbrough H and Bogers M (2014) *Explicating open innovation: Clarifying an emerging paradigm for understanding innovation*, In Chesbrough H, Vanhaverbeke W, West J (eds) New Frontiers in Open Innovation: 3–28. Oxford University Press, Oxford, p 17.

process with its resources and capability. Accordingly, the value the ecosystem generates is larger than the combined value each of the actors could contribute individually.

In today's business practice, ecosystems consist of a network of usually few large cross-sector orchestrators and lots of smaller actors. Those actors can be businesses, clients, communities, universities, governments, regulators, but also machines and robots that are either geographically localised or strategically linked to provide the best constellation for developing and distributing solutions for businesses and clients. The *orchestrator* aims to control and offer products and services from diverse businesses through a digital platform with all the actors working together to create value for clients by defining, developing, and executing market-creating solutions. Other roles of ecosystem leadership are the aggregator and the innovator/ supplier.[13] The *aggregator* coordinates supply and demand from diverse players for distribution to customers but can also be a provider of a marketplace. Managing the client journey and delivering superior services and client experiences is at its core. *Suppliers* enable and encourage innovation, also by providing data to be used by other actors in the ecosystem. They also offer infrastructure and core banking among various other financial services. Usually, they have specific product development capabilities and operate in a niche market.

The novelty of the digital ecosystem is that it is a fluid inclusive web that embraces digital technologies to put the client and data in the centre of all activities. Sharing client information across diverse businesses is at the center of big-tech business models to harness their smart data capability. Such cross-business data sharing enables new applications, including distributed ledger technology (DLT), quantum computing, deep learning, and the cloud. An open infrastructure is eminent for instance for the transition from machine learning to the next level of deep learning that has evolved with natural language processing (NLP), voice recognition, and pattern matching in the 2010s. NLP is concerned with the interactions between computers and human (natural) languages. While computers learn the language of their own mind, this will enable new customer services and business interaction with digital personal assistants and chatbots. Bank of America already communicates with their clients using Facebook's Messenger.

The enormous amount of data banks have accumulated from their clients over the years would potentially allow advanced analytics. The real power of data relies on the capacity to ingest, clean, and validate data from different sources at large scale and at high speed. Since the efficient and smart use of data provides real business value, banks must catch up and learn from Internet, social media, and e-commerce firms. If incumbents resist, non-banks will jump in and offer complementary services using their technological advantage in the role of the orchestrator of business ecosystems.

We suggest the prefix *open* because this characterises data sharing and free flow of information that enables new constellations for data analysis and consumption.

[13] Accenture (2017) Your Role in the Ecosystem, Accenture Strategy.

Examples are predictive analytics and insight-driven decision making. The so-called *open ecosystem* is dynamic and describes networking as the socio-economic process that automatically accelerates value with increasing interaction points between all players. Based on that, and with the support of surrounding technology, *hyperconnectivity* drives the *network effect*—both seen as the operational logic for all actors in an ecosystem.[14]

We take a distinctive view on technology; on the one hand, it is a means for achieving greater efficiency through digitalisation and on the other hand, it provides the basis for the digital transformation. Later, in turn, enables the development of disruptive innovations and new business models based upon ecosystems. In sum, our open ecosystem approach aggregates capabilities and resources across sectors, thus, leverages a firm's businesses in terms of innovation, diversification, and growth. This strategic infrastructure connects, integrates, and facilitates all value-generating processes to a unique value constellation.

4 Alibaba: The Ultimate Ecosystem Case

4.1 Cross-Sector Diversification

Amazon disrupted commerce 1995 after its founder Jeff Bezos was stunned by the first growth rate of the Internet. Technological innovation and a strategy and business plan that uses an electronic marketplace considering the network effect of the Internet were part of Amazon's journey to becoming one of the most successful and largest company based on market value. At the same time, Pierre Omidyar, the founder of eBay, had similar ideas for his original auction site and e-commerce firm. Both marketplace-startups bet on the rise of the Internet. Another young entrepreneur, Jack Ma from China, visited the Silicon Valley for business purposes at a time China had no computer and Internet at all. Today, about 95% of households in Beijing and Shanghai have Internet access and many young people (average age of Internet users is 28 years) exclusively use mobiles in their daily lives. Silicon Valley has been the epicentre for venture capital, so though Jack Ma when he visited over 30 venture capitalists in 1999 asking for funding for his Chinese Internet and e-commerce startup called Alibaba. Based on the misjudgement of all venture capitalists that no firm can beat eBay with a market share of over 90% by that time, he did not raise a single dollar.

Alibaba was founded anyhow and reached the highest initial public offering (IPO) in history in 2014. Meanwhile, the group became one of the top-ten companies worldwide. It became the largest e-commerce firm in the world and one of the most relevant firms in terms of venture capital, investments, and artificial intelligence. Its

[14]Fasnacht D (2018) Open Innovation Ecosystems: Creating New Value Constellations in the Financial Services, Springer, Berlin, p. 132.

market capitalisation is half of Amazon, revenues are equal, but profits are 50% more than Amazon and eBay combined.

Alibaba is an exemplary case to show an evolving global ecosystem with uncountable simultaneous activities belonging to different value creation processes. Officially the network of businesses provides the fundamental technology infrastructure and marketing reach to help businesses leverage the power of the Internet to establish an online presence and conduct commerce with hundreds of millions of international consumers and businesses. The main difference between the Silicon Valley firms where all businesses are under one roof is that Alibaba is divided into three core businesses, i.e. Alibaba (B2B), Taobao (B2C), and Tmall (B2C). Based on their webpage, Alibaba Group's major businesses include:

- **Alibaba.com**
  China's largest integrated international online wholesale marketplace for small businesses and global trade.
- **Taobao**
  China's largest online shopping marketplace and mobile commerce with a personalised user experience, optimised by smart data analytics.
- **Tmall.com**
  World's largest third-party online and mobile commerce platform for international brands and retailers.
- **Freshippo**
  Proprietary grocery retail chain that fosters the convergence of online and offline activities with rich and fun experience for customers who shop instore.
- **1688.com**
  Leading domestic wholesale marketplace in China, supplying online transaction services by connecting manufacturers and wholesale sellers and buyers.
- **Lazada**
  Leading e-commerce platform in Southeast Asia for SMEs, regional and global brands.
- **Alimama**
  The Group's monetisation platform using data technology to match marketing demands of merchants, brands, and retailers with the media resources on Alibaba's own platforms and third-party properties, websites and apps.
- **AliExpress**
  Retail marketplace for international consumers to cheaply purchase goods directly from manufacturers and distributors in China.
- **Ele.me**
  On-demand food delivery and local services platform, linked with Alipay, Taobao and Koubei mobile apps.
- **Youku**
  Third largest long-form video platform in China that drives customer loyalty to Alibaba's core commerce business in the form of complementary content offerings.
- **DingTalk**

Digital collaboration workplace for modern enterprises and organisations, including schools and education institutions.

- **Alibaba Cloud**

  Digital technology and intelligence backbone of Alibaba Group with a complete suite of cloud services for various businesses, including data analytics, machine learning, IoT, PaaS, IaaS.
- **Cainiao**

  Smart one-stop-shop logistics network that fulfils consumer orders within 24 h in China and 72 h worldwide.
- **Ant Group**

  Leader in the development of open platforms for technology-driven inclusive financial services with Alipay, China's largest payment app, Ant Fortune, a comprehensive wealth management app, Yu'e Bao, one of the world's biggest money-market fund and MYBank, a complete online bank.

Besides buiding a proprietary ecosystem and acting as an orchestrator, firms can capitalise by expanding their network and product and service portfolio on the digital platform.[15] Tencent, a major competitor of Alibaba, provides two social networking services, WeChat and QQ, respectively, thus the firm captures value from multiple sources. On one hand consumers pay for new products and services, on the other hand, the firm generates a quarter of its total revenues with merchant fees for e-commerce, finance, and social media content.

Alibaba continuously incubates new businesses and acquires firms or launches new strategic partnerships. Its business expansion with investments and equity sharing is touching many sectors, including cloud computing, digital media, entertainment, health, food delivery, and financial services with a distributed core banking platform. Major investments include Sina Weibo, a Chinese micro-blogging website similar to Twitter, Youku Tudou, China's answer to YouTube or US firms like Snapchat and Lyft. At the core of the business model, there is a strong focus on technological capabilities for data aggregation and analyses of client touchpoints and their behaviour. This opens many opportunities, for instance connecting health data with banking. People wish to live long and remain healthy, and the healthier they are, the more they can spend, and the more attractive they become for wealth managers. Health and wealth are the ultimate goals of most people. Cognitive technologies are ready to make such connections and provide the client advisor on one hand and the medical doctor on the other with specific information about the condition and behaviour of clients, respectively, patients.

[15]McKinsey & Company (2019) How the best companies create value from their ecosystems, 21 November.

4.2 The Golden Triangle of Ecosystems

One effect of the digital transformation is increasing collaboration and interaction with more and more services becoming interconnected. Our research found that global and robust ecosystems evolved from a core business, expanding the network and portfolio to other areas to create and capture value. Alibaba has made considerable efforts to unite e-commerce, logistics, and finance. All three dimensions are essential for the success of the ecosystem as a whole and stimulate and support each other. Therefore, we suggest to rely on seamless process integration between these dimensions that connect across what we call the *golden triangle of ecosystems.* With increasing convergence and blurring business lines, the golden triangle may vary from industries, but the dimensions include similar services. While e-commerce is clearly defined, logistics is a broader area where we added social media and messaging services. For our purposes, we analysed the financial dimension, where convenient and mobile payment services are central to ensure the flow of goods (see Fig. 2).

Ant Group, former Ant Financial Services, acts as the financial arm of the Alibaba Group, dedicated to bringing the world more equal opportunities through building a technology-driven open ecosystem and collaborating with hundreds of financial institutions to support the future financial needs of society. The network also includes the big four Chinese banks, among many other financial institutions across the globe. A strategic partnership with Standard Chartered Bank aims to boost financial inclusion in countries targeted by the Chinese government's Belt and Road Initiative (BRI).

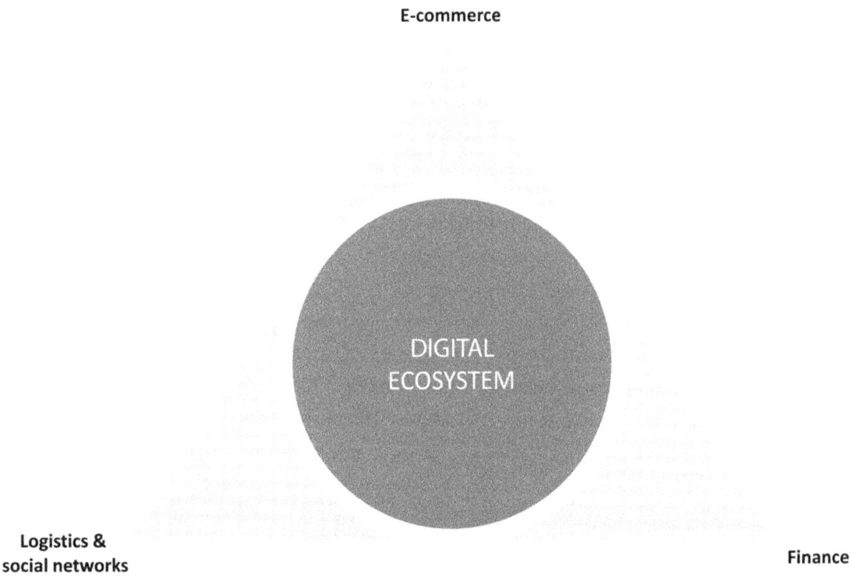

Fig. 2 The golden triangle of ecosystems

Ant runs five primary lines of business: payment, wealth management, insurance, credits, and financing. Noteworthy, the firm raised in 2018 as much venture capital as all US and European fintech firms combined and plans its IPO. Ant is aiming for a valuation of US$ 200 billion which is about the same as the combined market capitalisation of the largest banks in Switzerland and Germany. Ant Group counts about 9000 staff and is about to expand its ecosystem with offices in Japan, Korea, Singapore, Thailand, Germany, France, Italy, the Netherlands, Australia, United Kingdom, and the United States. As of September 2020, Ant would be the fifth largest financial conclomerate in the world with twice the market capitalisation of Citigroup with its over 200,000 employees.

Years ago, Jack Ma coined the term "TechFin" as a countermovement to fintech. We assume he wanted to set an example, demonstrating that all financial services firms such as Ant evolved from emerging technology with the attempt to primarily collect data on clients and secondly analyse and learn from the data collected, and thirdly translate these into business models and solutions that create value to clients. In 2020, the firm changed its name from Ant Financial to Ant Group, to emphasise that it is a digital and innovative, rather than a financial services, firm. Overall, the core strength of the TechFin company is its global digital financial service platform, leading breadth and scale across the financial service spectrum, its unrivalled technological capabilities, and that they are an integral part of the Alibaba ecosystem. Relevant for our study is the ecosystem among Ant's businesses, where we can learn much about disruptive business models, its value creation logic, and how to harness technology for business purposes.

Alipay, the payment solution of the Alibaba Group, was founded in 2004 and spun off from the group in 2010. Ant Financial was officially founded in 2014 and originated from Alipay. In 2007, Alipay had over 50 million users, while China only had 30 million credit card users at that time. During the financial crisis, they kept innovating and launched a voice-controlled payment for mobile users in China. After first payment services for water bills and utilities, the consumer version of Alipay, including payment with barcode, was launched. Today, Alipay is the world's leading third-party payment platform with one billion active mobile users and over 300 partners, offering payment services for around 20 million small and micro-merchants covering 54 countries and regions. Its market share of China's mobile payment market based on transaction value reached 70%.

One reason for the rising mobile payment market in China with innovative solutions such as the QR (quick response) code payment systems is due to the limited credit and debit card infrastructure and the high mobile device penetration. Cashless settlement and processing by scanning QR codes at the point of sales became the norm for many young Chinese. In many cases, they exclusively use online bank accounts. In other words, they do not need cash, credit cards, and no brick-and-mortar bank, which, to a certain extent, support the safe and secure transfer of money. Alipay is continuously striving to make online finance simpler and comfortable. The latest innovation includes gamification technology for payments. Savings strategies become a competition when users' returns can be compared with those of others. As the user base is getting younger, they demand even more intuitive solutions and financial transactions that are perceived as fun. This was realized with the ability to add voice messages, pictures, or emoticons to their peer-to-peer money transfers.

Alipay has evolved from a digital wallet to many other services, spanning from travel arrangements, book movie tickets, make appointments with doctors, pay utility bills, or buy wealth management products directly from the app. For instance tax reimbursement via Alipay is supported in many countries around the world, including a network of overseas financial institutions and payment solution providers to enable cross-border payments for Chinese tourists. Alipay has recently expanded offshore payments in and outside of China with tens of millions of merchants accepting Alipay. Recently they got an e-money licence in Luxembourg and are about to introduce their payment app to European clients without a bank account in China.[16] By using big data technology while penetrating many consumption scenarios and touch points, over time, they can (automatically) generate more comprehensive client profiles. If the firm feeds its algorithms with new data sets from European customers, Alipay may soon be able to offer customised products and services for this new client segment.

The value-generating potential of this kind of digital supermarket for other players is huge because everybody that transact via Alibaba's marketplaces is generating turnover. Alipay earns interest income while proceeds of transactions are temporarily deposited, in addition to commissions to merchants and advertisement fees. Alipay found its way into Alibaba's growing e-commerce and logistic services just 6 years ago. Its transition from a digital provider of financial services to an aggregator of a billion consumers for other firm's services was exemplary. Alibaba's considerable consumer and merchant-funded platform is today fully driven by data technology and while it is generating revenues, it has significantly contributed to the global payment network.

> The golden triangle of the ecosystem includes e-commerce, logistics and social networks, and finance - all required to thrive each dimension.

The all-in-one integration of logistics services with the other two dimensions, namely, e-commerce and financials is pivotal. Domestic as well as international consumers, value rapid and fault-free delivery of goods and services. Alibaba's early strategy to develop a smart logistics network with Cainiao, including express delivery providers such as Best Logistics, Star Express or YTO paid out. Since they are mutually dependent, Alibaba thoughtfully maintains a good relationship. Also, to reduce its dependence, Alibaba is steadily increasing its investments into external delivery companies. Logistics becomes a collective strategic impact if large areas must be equipped with e-commerce capabilities. Since this is part of the Chinese government's socio-economic development plans for rural areas and to fight poverty, Alibaba is also a strong ally in support of these efforts.

[16]Fasnacht D (2019) Chinesische Touristen wollen anders bezahlen, Bankmagazin, Sringer Professional, Nr. 12, 27 September.

Chinese e-commerce giants have adopted a social model where their business is anchored by a social pillar that drives user engagement and growth. To complete the dimensions discussed, messaging services providers can leverage their infrastructure as one-stop shop to combine everything a company has to offer but also to enhance its offering. Accordingly, we consider social networking as a lever to complement the other dimensions of the golden triangle, even though it appears to be shedding younger users only. From banking, we know the importance of data privacy. In Europe, this is, for the time being, slowing down the progress of the monetarisation of client information. However, regulations will come along and soon address the shortcomings. Social media and messenger services will become increasingly crucial for human-machine interactions, and that is why we assign these services to logistics. Conclusively, our analysis confirms that the golden triangle works; hence, it should become a fundamental part for designing ecosystem strategies.

4.3 Platform Business Models

The ties between Alipay and the Alibaba Group are strong, and we saw that being a member of Alibaba's multi-business digital ecosystem enables almost boundless opportunities and enormous scale. Alibaba's all-embracing platform business model has meanwhile combined elements of many of the leading e-commerce, technology, social media, and logistics companies in the U.S. rather than mirroring any one business in particular. Clients can enjoy an end-to-end experience for various products and services, hardware to software, and tangible to intangible services, all accessible through a digital platform without leaving Alibaba. With Alipay, Ant owns the technology pathway that enables functions and innovative initiatives that go way beyond payments. The data and information of their clients are continuously reused to improve the client journey and to offer additional value.

The vision of challenger banks is to specialise in niche products and services or increase the client experience or use data and technology or disrupt underserved markets. Alipay has closed gaps in all these areas at the same time. This strategy goes in the direction of *the winner takes it all* where the top players in China, in that case, Alipay and WeChat Pay, capture a disproportionately large share of the market, while the rest are left with extremely little. Smartphone-apps offer enormous upsides for e-commerce in China. For instance, on Single Day 2017, Alipay processed 256,000 payment transactions per second, about six times more than leading payment systems in the United States. To compare, the theoretical maximum speed for Bitcoin is seven transactions per second. Single Day 2018 even broke all retail records; Alibaba Group was selling US$31 billion in gross merchandise volume, which is triple what U.S. consumers spent online in 2017 for Black Friday and Cyber Monday combined. Thanks to its cloud infrastructure and artificial intelligence, Alibaba had zero downtime when it processed 550,000 orders per second on Singles' Day 2019, equivalent to US$38 billion in total sales. Besides the enormous domestic market power, the world market would be a new and potentially broader market to attack.

China's relatively young population fosters the penetration of mobile financial services. The mobile access penetration in this segment is over 90%. Digital platforms and mobile channels are cutting intermediation and reduce overheads, so platform providers can choose what to offer without giving up profits of one product against another. The modern shopping experience asks for an ecosystem that has for each client an individualised solution and a provider ready. The analysis of the interaction points—even with globally hundreds of millions of users—is vital, though challenging. Besides buiding a proprietary ecosystem and acting as an orchestrator, firms can capitalise by expanding their network and product and service portfolio on the digital platform.[17] Tencent, a major competitor of Alibaba, provides two social networking services, WeChat and QQ, respectively, thus the firm captures value from multiple sources. On one hand consumers pay for new products and services, on the other hand, the firm generates a quarter of its total revenues with merchant fees for e-commerce, finance, and social media content.

The cross-market approach, referring to our golden triangle of the ecosystem, made aware that first and foremost, clients do not seek financial products and advice since they are busy living their lives. However, they may make use of offered financial services easily accessible through digital platforms in the ecosystem once they are happy with other purchase processes, for instance, music and movies. Digital platforms enable consumers to access information and services around the product, while providers profit from the captured transaction data and easy integration of business partners. It seems to be a win-win situation. The provider takes the chance to engage the consumer as long as possible online and is positioning itself early into the client journey, offering an interconnected set of tailored solutions based on the client's historical traces, behaviour and lifestyle.

In future, the majority of consumers will most likely acknowledge that he or she must disclose information in turn for a convenient shopping experience with cheap and individualised solutions. Constant and efficient monitoring and assessing client experiences are dissipating privacy protection. Such platform businesses face the chicken-and-egg challenge. However, with the case of Ant, WeChat respectively, it becomes clear that the ownership of the client relationship and client data is a considerable competitive advantage. These firms are disintermediating traditional banks from their clients, using their wealth of diverse data and analytics capabilities. If non-banks and fintechs increasingly claim parts of the bank's client journey, offering targeted solutions through convenient mobile apps, incumbents can no longer resist to adapt. Otherwise they will lose competitive edge.

> Banking 4.0 means mobile access to all financial and non-financial matters—everywhere and every time and without going to a bank.

---

[17]McKinsey & Company (2019) How the best companies create value from their ecosystems, 21 November.

4.4 Embracing Change and Become Big

The vision of Jack Ma was initially *born in China, grow for the world* with Alibaba Group's ambitions to double its gross merchandise volume to US$1 trillion by 2020. Long-term Alibaba wants to double its active buyers to 2 billion, create 100 million jobs and support ten million businesses on its platforms by 2036.[18] In 2013, Jack Ma continued his moral concept of embracing change and adapted the strategy from organic growth to investment expansion to strengthen the interdependent ecosystem. Building up such a system includes tacit knowledge and social capital—assets that can hardly be acquired and almost not copied.

Embracing change became one of the six company values. Accordingly, in a fast-changing world, flexibility, innovation, and the adaptability to new business conditions in order to maintain sustainability and vitality in business are critical.[19] As an incubator and large investor, Alibaba's organisational culture is about championing small businesses. Without referring to ecosystem theory, all participants in the digital economy must become an opportunity to prosper. The success and rapid growth of Alibaba is built on the spirit of entrepreneurship, innovation, and an unwavering focus on meeting the needs of its customers. The mission to make it easy to do business anywhere and to enable businesses to transform the way they market, sell and operate and improve their efficiencies is a mantra that has paid out.

Though a digital economy of thousands of actors has evolved around Alibaba's platforms and businesses, it seems that the way the ecosystem was formed was not initially planned in 1999. Jack Ma, a visionary genius, did most likely not follow a systematic strategic plan as management theory of the industrial age would propose. Note, the translation of Porter's *Competitive Strategies* in mainland China in 1997. The static strategies from the book with linear value chains and stable organisational borders came into its ages with young entrepreneurs in Silicon Valley and did not fit the challenges of emerging China. Without discussing this in depth, we conclude that traditional management theories and practices are of little help if one wants to disrupt businesses in the digital economy.

For rapid growth, Alibaba's leadership was steadily embracing change to adapt and move strategically. Innovations fostered data and knowledge sharing, which in turn supported resource sharing and synergy effects, which accelerated efficiency and economies of scale. Ex post, we can summarise that as a side effect of embracing change, the ecosystem evolved to what it is today. To compare, China's gross domestic product (GDP) for the twelve months ended 30 June 2020 are estimated US 14.5 trillion, China's consumption US$5.7 trillion and Alibaba's digital economy gross merchandising volume (GMV) US$1 trillion.

Lean innovation, agile leadership and many other approaches have recently been conceptualised. Still, there is no blueprint for designing value-creating ecosystem

---

[18]Investor Day (2020) Hangzhou, China.

[19]Alibaba company homepage [online, 21 September 2020]. www.alibabagroup.com/en/about/culture

strategies. The pendulum of thriving digital ecosystems can easily swing in the other direction due to over-diversification, lack of management focus, cash flow, or the increasing bureaucracy for orchestrating fast-growing, large, global, and self-regulating cross-sector ecosystems. We saw that with established universal banks that seemed too big to fail. What about Amazon, Apple, Google, Microsoft, Facebook, Alibaba, and Tencent? Can all these giants sustain flexibility and agility that they all built on during their rise?

5 The Super-App Is the New Bank

Millennials and generation Z organise almost everything in their daily lives with smartphones and would instead use an app than visiting a bank branch. In the 2010s, the young Chinese populations demonstrated what they expect from their mobile interactions. Beginning with shopping, travelling, entertainment, they adopted as the first individualised, integrated, and mobile financial services. User ergonomics, time savings, and costs are the most significant sales arguments. In contrast, Westerners value security, discretion, and data protection. While the former is relevant for all consumers, the values of traditional banking will dissolve by the millennials. Studies assume that one-third of all digitally affine consumers in Europe is ready to share their data with non-banks if they see an advantage in this.[20] Open banking is a millennials opportunity as they favour convenience over security, integrating everything, accessing everywhere and every time. Challenger banks are increasingly offering financial services on their digital platforms because digital banking traverses organisational, geographical, and cultural borders.

The latest trend from China are super-apps that we believe will boost the smooth integration of services. A super-apps is a stripped-down version of an app that runs within an all-in-one platform, allowing users to bypass an app store like that of Apple. It is a single portal to access a suite of services that one uses in daily life. While Alipay's super app includes services that see high-frequency transactions like retail, and travel booking payments, rival WeChat's messaging service has already integrated functionalities from Amazon, Uber, Skype, Facebook, Instagram, Expedia or Pay-Pal. Super-apps facilitate ordering all kinds of goods and services and use a digital wallet to pay for them. Alongside mobile payment and wealth management services, transferring money to friends or businesses, paying utility bills, rent or mortgages became the new standard in China quickly. Alibaba also focuses' on super-apps, and as it runs with Tianhong Yu'e Bao, the largest money-market mutual fund (after it took over JPMorgan's US government money market

[20]Deloitte (2019) Global Millenial Survey 2019, Deloitte; Finra & CFA Institute (2018) Millennials and Investing [online 21 September 2020], www.cfainstitute.org/-/media/documents/support/advocacy/1801081-insights-millennials-and-investing-booklet.ashx; Gallup (2018) 4 Ways Banks can Win and Keep Millennial Customers [online 21 September 2020], www.gallup.com/analytics/237734/ways-banks-win-keep-millennial-customers.aspx

fund in 2017), a cash transfer from an Alibaba account into their money fund, using the Alipay mobile payment system takes just one-click. Note that two-thirds of all fund subscribers do this via mobile phone apps. This digital fund sales by smartphone lead the world, and with the other advances in wealth management services, this will be shaking traditional private as well as investment banks.

Super-apps will integrate everything you need in everyday life.

This diversification provides Tencent and Alibaba with comprehensive information about customer behaviour. With the help of self-learning algorithms, future customer needs can be optimally identified. There are many ways to analyse the digital preferences of consumers in the new growth markets and take them into account for highly individualised solutions. The art will be to reconcile the new with the traditional values of private banking and, despite all the new possibilities, to keep an overview and focus on what is essential—the satisfaction of customer wishes. The experience that the customer makes during this process can best be managed when wealth managers become data specialists. Therefore, it is pivotal to link the findings from historical investment data and behavioural finance with other consumer activities.

The examined Chinese firms exemplify the super-app in its open ecosystems where they have seamlessly linked e-commerce, logistics, payments along evolving social media, travel, healthcare, and mobility services where people can use super-apps exclusively. Multilateral ecosystems are expanding globally, and as they penetrate more and more businesses, they will become a severe threat to traditional businesses. Remember, WeChat was initially a simple message service. Imagine if U.S. tech giants go the same route? Facebook, is persistently trying to create its golden triangle; from social media to a one-stop shop messaging services, including e-commerce and financial services. Facebook, a copycat of WeChat? Apple is trying the same from a different basis with its iMessage as well as Microsoft with WhatsApp. Facebook's Messenger newly let users order and digitally pay for everything they purchase. Super-apps are a new trend to watch, though a China phenomenon. We see it as a game-changing innovation that interacts with many other service providers transcending industry borders. The shift in consumer preferences and the versatility of super-apps make them a potential disruptor for the next phase of digital banking, in which financial services are just a function of a lifestyle app.

6 The *New* Role of Banks

The days are over when banks were able to operate exclusively in their well-known markets. The client journey has become more complex, and we need to figure out how the creation of value with different actors can be managed. Collaborations with players outside the industry to enter into this relationship makes sense and provides access to resources, diversified knowledge, and new markets. But how to start? Find out who offers your company the relevant access to a digital ecosystem and which players you need to partner with. Because only those who face the challenges early on, think openly and act agilely will find the right cooperation partners and reinvent banking with them. Otherwise, they will face decreasing profits or at least disappear from the private banking map of young, wealthy Asians.

Banks are good at offering financial products and services, transact them and give clients a certain degree of confidentially and trust through intimate relationship management—at least in private and corporate banking. The next generation client is entirely mobile and digital, seeking fully individualised solutions 24 h, 7 days. He or she is combining private leisure with business and wants to have exciting client experiences. So far, so good. The European Payment Services Directive (PSD2) requires banks to allow third parties to access account information and payment services via electronic interfaces, called open APIs (application programming interfaces). This policy paves the way for open banking and forces traditional banks to open up their business models and processes to third parties with wide-ranging consequences. There is no other chance than to adapt their business model and identify the mid- and long-term role of the organisation. The strategic challenge goes beyond repositioning the brand in the global competition. The question is more whether the bank has the technological capacity to take a leadership role in terms of building up and running an ecosystem as in future data monetarizing will become a key asset. Therefore, super-apps are just one more effort to leverage open banking to create value from digital ecosystems by bringing together various industry players.

If one wants to become an *orchestrator* of an ecosystem would mean to coordinate and ensure efficient and effective collaboration within a dynamic web of interdependent businesses. Diversification, as one key feature of future ecosystems, is additionally increasing complexity. Developing and marketing disruptive service offerings—products and services that are not within financial services—calls for flexibility, interdisciplinary human capital, and an open organisational culture. Finally, as we learned from Alibaba, an ecosystem usually evolves, and once it meets the demand of the market, the environment and conditions change. Leadership must be able to master change since an open ecosystem is continuously co-evolving with its business context.

The *aggregator* role determines to not necessarily own the overall customer journey, which may be a shock for traditional banks in a first raw. The role includes to harness their extensive distribution network and to become a trusted partner for suppliers, clients, and other market participants. Their role is that of an intermediary with advisory skills to recommend the best of breed solution to a broadly diversified clientele. Assuring a seamless service integration and customer experience is vital in that role. Having the verticalization of ecosystems in mind the aggregator must develop a new set of capabilities beyond financial services as this will add customer value in future. Also, note that they must be able to build up the capability to accumulate data and convert it into value related to marketing and sales activities.

Eventually, the *supplier* acts as a specialised solution partner instead of remaining a universal brick-and-mortar bank. By rebundling and white labelling financial products and services and distribute them via a digital marketplace, suppliers are generating profits by selling products, services, and infrastructure, including non-bank services. As banks are under regulatory supervision based on their bank licence in their country of operation, they established governance models. They can offer their banking infrastructure and efficient operational processes to third parties. Collaborations with fintechs and regtechs for client identification, compliance, risk management or accounting and reporting services could be possible business scenarios that enrich their service portfolio. Leveraging customer data and insights to develop integrated and flexible solutions that meet the individual needs of clients would increase the scope of business activities. Based on the legacy of a bank, with an agile management team, we assume that the supplier role could be easy access to an ecosystem. The scalability of such a global distribution network can be very interesting for banks struggling with the increasing complexity of their proprietary multi-distribution channels. If the supplier becomes a strategic partner of a dominant ecosystem player, it may even go the route to co-evolution of a specific ecosystem.

Banks must get engaged in ecosystems and invest in mobile platforms as a part of their digital transformation strategy.

One crucial part of the digital transformation is to understand the trends and changing competitive environment before you approach the relevant business scenarios. Next, you should carefully consider your role in the future ecosystem. To take this decision, you need to find the future wealth spots, review your strategy, values and evaluate your golden triangle. Finally, you will find with whom you should partner to achieve sustainable growth. Besides, Western banks have to decide which block they are going to join—the American and European or the Asian block.

7 How to Create Value from Digital Ecosystems

We learned that digitalisation with focus on efficiency gains, and digital innovations alone will not create new markets. Open ecosystem and platform-oriented thinking build the new conceptual framework through that firms can launch innovative business models that will one day disrupt traditional core businesses. Value delivery in financial services will be performed in a radically different way through ecosystems as a set of coherent digital services. Incumbents, startups, and firms from outside the financial sector all have other strategies. They need to determine which parts of their value generation to perform within the firm, which to distribute to their direct partners, and which to take to the open market. However, it is the ecosystem that allows them to create value that no single firm could create alone. Through open interactions of all actors and hyperconnectivity, the system as such becomes a constellation of value. Every market player must focus on delivering a dedicated added value and serve as a trusted node connecting individual participants in the innovation ecosystem.

Not only the boundaries of firms are fading; business models dynamically transcend industries since banking services are increasingly distributed across markets. We assume a shift to a service-dominant logic and multi-actor value creation,[21] in which digital platforms consolidate the linear value chain into ecosystems. In this scenario, the competition will move from legal entities within an industry to interspecific competition across sectors. Global competition will be the interaction between firms in a network, whereby the most innovative and effective ecosystem ends up as the winner. Ecosystems in financial services with associated platforms to consolidate and disseminate knowledge leverage co-innovation and distribution. Therefore, we suggest matching core business models to revised innovation strategies to be viewed through the ecosystem perspective.

We also found that the competitive advantage of firms depends on the strength of the ecosystem in which they operate. Especially banks with global ambitions should proactively seek ecosystems where they can, as an early member, participate in the creation process of the ecosystem. Collaborate with existing ecosystems and embed organisational skills and offerings as a supplier to drive innovation. A role as aggregator to consolidate services is an effective strategy too. Incumbents should not lose much time to find their role because first moving players have been active for years with digital platforms and super-apps, consolidating a myriad of solutions for millions of paying customers. Firms that hesitate will lose competitive edge as stand-alone business models are a leftover of the closed innovation paradigm. Becoming a late partner in an established cross-sector ecosystem is the last opportunity. Value constellations evolve rapidly, and thru constant interactions, network ties between participants are strengthening. Large incumbents can grow by cannibalising their core products while cross-selling new digital products, precisely, services. However, unlocking the full potential of a digital ecosystem requires an assessment and the reconfiguration of the organisation's capabilities. We suggest to strategicaly focus on open innovation, open data, open banking as well as advanced analytics, lean innovation, resilient operations and agile leadership.

8 Conclusion

Besides macrotrends, digitalisation efforts have accelerated during COVID-19. Non-banks started entering financial services as the next adjacency five years ago and juggernauts from China are about to reshape the global economy. Challenger banks offer new business models and superior value to its clients. With the combination of horizontal integration through value constellations and vertical integration through interconnectedness, they provide a diverse set of capabilities required to satisfy sophisticated clients of the next generation. Our observation of the affiliates of the Alibaba Group confirms the value-generation potential of open innovation ecosystems in the context of the golden triangle (see Fig. 2). *Firstly*, it facilitates

[21] Lusch, R.F. and Nambisan, S. (2015) Service Innovation: A Service-dominant Logic Perspective, MIS Quarterly, 39, 155–175.

collaboration to harness digital innovations effectively. *Secondly,* the firm's agility supports its global partner strategy, which in turn creates increasing interactions that lead to economies of scale and increase the scope of products and services. *Lastly,* the cross-sector ecosystem enables constant learning processes that support market entry strategies into non-core businesses.

Diversified digital ecosystems are winner-take-all platform business models.

Global trade and efficiently functioning capital markets have had a positive effect on the rate of innovation over the last hundred years. If capital markets remain secure and sustainable investments will continue to flourish, this will affect innovation and new patents. The question though is from where the majority of future patents will come from—Silicon Valley or Shenzhen. The current environment may be interpreted differently based on the country, region, development stage, political circumstances, or whether you work for an incumbent or a challenger bank. Despite that fact, some always develop opportunities that are unseen by other actors and make our lives better, while others resist changing.

Embracing change is one approach to offer financial inclusion and allow us to build a better world for the increasing population, to recall one megatrend. Pioneers like Ant Group or super-apps like WeChat in China have expanded financial services to millions of people who never could save, manage, and transact money before. Therefore, banking of the future calls for open and digital ecosystems, accessible through super-apps to leverage cross-market network effects!

To build organizations that are adaptable and innovative at their core, we will need to borrow principles from systems that already are resilient—like the Internet, ecosystems, cities, and free markets. [Gary Hammel]

* * *

Daniel Fasnacht is a thoughtful leader with more than 25 years of international experience in the financial sector, where he held senior positions at SAP, Accenture, Credit Suisse, Julius Baer, among other asset managers. As the CEO and founder of EcosystemPartners AG, a consulting firm for strategy, innovation, digital transformation, and ecosystems, he helps incumbents to transform but also supports startups to grow.

He is a fellow of the Department of Banking and Finance of the University of Zurich and lecturer for other educational institutes. His recent book "Open Innovation Ecosystems" was published by Springer in December 2018.

He holds degrees in business informatics, information management, an MBA from the University of St. Gallen, Switzerland in collaboration with the University of Berkeley, Haas School of Business, USA, and a PhD in Strategic Management from the University of Nottingham, UK.

Orchestrating Value Co-Creation in Business Ecosystems

Shifting from an Idiocentric Towards an Allocentric Perspective on the Business Model Concept

Marc Burkhalter, Christian Betz, Stefanie Auge-Dickhut, and Reinhard Jung

Abstract In increasingly digital enabled business environments, value is generated through information sharing and manipulation among interdependent social and commercial actors operating in business ecosystems. With the aim to collaboratively create and capture value in this structural context, a company needs to be effective and efficient in orchestrating resources rather than acquiring and independently owning them. This implies that a company has to move from a purely subjective (idiocentric) perception on value creation and value capturing towards a more intersubjective (allocentric) one. Leveraging business ecosystems from a service-dominant perspective, this chapter illustrates how successful companies achieve this by applying an allocentric perspective on their business models. By building their business models upon a shared value purpose that is materialized through a service resulting from value co-creation among complementary actors including the beneficiary, it is shown how these companies successfully leverage the opportunities resulting from innovative digital technologies. Thus, this article emphasizes the shift from an idiocentric perspective on business models where value creation is perceived as a result of firm self-centered activities. Towards an allocentric perspective, where value occurs when heterogeneous social and business partners work together toward mutual benefits, the key being the orchestration of resources between these parties.

Keywords Ecosystems · Orchestration · Theory of change · Theories of change

M. Burkhalter (✉) · R. Jung
Institute of Information Management, University of St. Gallen, St. Gallen, Switzerland
e-mail: marc.burkhalter@unisg.ch; reinhard.jung@unisg.ch

C. Betz · S. Auge-Dickhut
Business Engineering Institute, St. Gallen, Switzerland
e-mail: christian.betz@bei-sg.ch; stefanie.auge-dickhut@bei-sg.ch

K. Wendt (ed.), *Theories of Change*, Sustainable Finance,
https://doi.org/10.1007/978-3-030-52275-9_16

1 Introduction

Information technology accelerates the speed and quality with which data is processed and exchanged between organizations. By embedding information technology into physical objects, almost any asset of value gains the capability to capture, to process as well as to store data and hence, to communicate with its environment. In the financial industry, regulatory developments such as the Payment Services Directive 2 (PSD2) in the European Union even accelerate this trend by requiring organizations to provide the technical infrastructure for interoperability. With accessible Application Programming Interfaces (API), internal data will be selectively made available for others, therefore increasing the interconnectivity and simplifying the exchange of data. Other technological developments, for example the tokenization of assets allows the digital representation of property rights related to transactions of these assets in incorruptible, distributed digital ledgers, such as the Blockchain. Once digitized and tokenized, programmable transaction protocols (smart contracts) that autonomously display, execute and enforce the terms of contracts associated with the asset, make a digital transfer possible. Being in its early stage of technological convergence, this combination of sophisticated communication solutions together with trustable contract mechanisms liberates social and economic actors from constraints in the way they co-create and co-capture value in today's economy (Beck 2006). According to Normann (2001), value creation is particularly affected in terms of time (when value is created), place (where value is created), actors (who create value) and constellation (how value is created). Consequently, through digitization and tokenization as well as a common communication infrastructure, assets of any value become accessible, sharable and exchangeable with negligible transaction and coordination costs. These steadily decreasing costs driven by ongoing innovations in information and communication technology have led to increased dynamic and interdependent business environments (Picot et al. 1996).

However, in order to transform data into meaningful information that supports value creation, context is essential. The latter defines "*the circumstances that form the setting for an event, statement, or idea, and in terms of which it can be fully understood*" (Oxford Living Dictionary 2019). Inspired by biological ecosystems, Rothschild (1990) and Moore (1993) introduced the notion of business ecosystem[1] as a means to describe the value creation mechanisms in increasingly dynamic and interdependent business environments. Ecosystems can hence be perceived as a structure (Adner 2017), helping to outline a particular context where multiple actors, dynamically organized around a shared value purpose, mutually co-create value.

With the aim to collaboratively create and capture value in this structural context, business actors need to be efficient at mobilizing, managing, and using resources rather than acquiring and independently owning resources—a significant contrast to

[1]In the further course of this article, the terms business ecosystem and ecosystem are used as synonyms.

a classical mindset (Normann, 2001). Osterwalder and Pigneur (2013) suggest that the business model (BM) concept seems particularly apt to provide an overarching framework in which novel value creation architectures in the digital era can be strategically structured, analyzed and designed. However, most researchers typically limit the concept to a single organization's focal plan for its idiocentric (self-contained) value creation and value capturing (e.g. Osterwalder et al. 2005; Kamoun 2008; Teece 2010) thereby ignoring that in today's interdependent business environment, value is rather co-created and co-captured by multiple actors (Vargo and Lusch 2004). Consequently, this idiocentric (self-contained) perspective on the BM, is not suitable for organizations that reside and evolve in ecosystems (Iivari 2016; Iivari et al. 2016). Thus, current idiocentric BM concepts are no longer able to explain how companies can achieve sustainable competitive advantage in emerging ecosystems of which they are a part of. In fact, idiocentric BM concepts are unable to provide practitioners with insights on how they can design their BM in the uprising knowledge economy, where the *orchestration of value co-creation* among different business model participants is critical. Therefore, an allocentric perspective seems promising. In contrast to the idiocentric BM concept, the allocentric (not only depending on the viewer's (being the firm) current position) BM concept can be defined as a companies' overarching framework to orchestrate value co-creation and value co-capturing among participants in the same business ecosystems.

Aiming towards this goal, this article guides the design of the allocentric BM concept through leveraging business ecosystems under a service-dominant logic perspective (Vargo and Lusch 2004, 2008, 2016, 2018). This analytical lens helps to contextualize the structure of increasingly interdependent business environments in which value co-creation upon digitized and eventually tokenized assets is essential. Against this backdrop, the results offered in this chapter represent selected parts of a three- and a half-year research project. Based on a Design Science Research methodology and following a consortium research approach (Österle and Otto 2010), various industry experts—mainly from the financial services sector—from Austria, Germany and Switzerland significantly contributed to the presented results and conclusions.

2 Value Creation in a Digital Enabled Business Environment

To understand the impact of digitalization on value creation two major aspects seem to be of particular interest. First, the unique benefits of *digital technologies as a system of resources* compared to earlier (analog) technologies. Second, the exceptional characteristics of value creation and value capturing upon digitized and eventually tokenized *information as a resource*. Before taking a more detailed look at these two aspects, it is important to specify a working definition of the concept of value. For the moment, the notion of value is defined as the perceived subjective benefit related to the effective use, allocation and exchange of resources for the involved actors. This benefit can be measured in economic as well as in functional, emotional, symbolic or ecological terms.

2.1 Value Creation Based on Digital Technologies

Digital technologies allow to separate the information aspect from the physical world (Normann 2001). Hence, digitization can be defined as the process of converting data into a digital (i.e. computer-readable) format, in which the information is organized into bits (Collins English Dictionary 2019). According to Yoo et al. (2010) digital technologies differ from earlier technologies in terms of their re-programmability, the homogenization of data and their self-referential nature. The fact that a digital enhanced asset (e.g. a device) allows executing any digitally encoded instruction by storing and transmitting both instructions and data in the same format, makes it possible to perform a wide array of functions. Hence, this ability to being re-programmed limits the devices application only by the fantasy (and programming skills) of its users. Additionally, the digital representation of any analog signal into bits and bytes leads to a homogenization of all data involved in the value creation process (Yoo et al. 2010, p. 5). Hence, any digital content can be stored, combined, processed, transmitted and displayed using the same digital devices and networks. Therefore, the homogenization of data separates the content from one specific medium which in turn dissolves product and industry boundaries and builds the foundation of entirely new value creating systems. Against this backdrop, the self-referential and thus continuously self-improving characteristic of digital technologies that act upon each other accelerates this development even more.

2.2 Value Creation Based on Information as a Resource

> When one shares a material good, one divides it. When one shares an immaterial good, one multiplies it.—(Serge Soudoplatoff)

The above-mentioned law, summarizes the foundational basis between value creation based on information (an immaterial asset) compared to value creation limited to purely physical assets. Assuming a given context, where *information extracted from data is synonymous with knowledge* for its actors to perform actions with beneficial outcomes for themselves and/or others, this fundamental law comes along with some important non-trivial consequences.

First, knowledge exchanges are positive sum (Aberkane 2017, p. 5). Hence, when "giving away" knowledge, no one loses it. Evidently, this is not the case by giving away one apple or the ownership of 10 Swiss Francs. This signifies that the usage of a specific "knowledge amount" is non-rival. Meaning that as long as the communication infrastructure is performant enough, everyone at the same time and at any given place can simultaneously use it without negatively impacting other users. Hence, from an economic perspective the accessibility and sharing of an existing bit of knowledge—once it is created[2]—goes in line with nearly zero-marginal costs. In contrast, to accessing and sharing physical goods, the monetary aspect slowly drops out of the equation when it comes to using dematerialized goods.[3]

Second and consequently, through sharing the amount of accessible knowledge grows in a super-linear way (Aberkane 2017, p. 5). Hence, knowledge represents a quasi-infinite resource, while the amount of physical assets grows linearly and is bound by physical constraints. For instance, when adding one apple to a basket of apples, the basket grows exactly by that one apple. Additionally, the total number of apples in the world is finite. Contrarily, the composition of two bits of knowledge systematically generates a third one and the amount of knowledge that can be generated, processed and stored is only negligibly limited by physical constraints (e.g. computation/storage hardware). This super-linear growth of information leads to an abundance of knowledge and in many cases to *an overload* of accessible information. Considering that fact, it becomes obvious that the value creation logic related to purely dematerialized goods has to work exactly opposite to physical goods. While in the physical world, value is generated by creating user access to valuable limited material resources. In the digital world, value is created by liberating users of all the irrelevant, undesired information by communicating only what is valuable to them. In that sense, the Google "search" engine and its related services offer a good illustration example. Too often one thinks that the overall value purpose of Google is to make the worlds information digitally available. However, the actual value for a particular user group (e.g. web content searchers) is not to get access to all the available web content but to the most *relevant* for their requests. The same applies to web content providers (e.g. advertisers) who only want to be displayed to the most promising users of their services.

Third, the value of knowledge increases the more it is used and consequently updated. This phenomenon is called network effect (Shapiro et al. 1999). Again, this is in total opposition of material resources which deplete the more they are used. Hence, in order to create value upon its knowledge, a company has to guarantee that it is used and updated as much as possible. This can be achieved by making sure that the users have the possibility to manipulate it (combine it with their own knowledge) in order to increase the knowledge's value for a particular user context. Consequently, a company does well in considering a *user as a value co-creator* rather than a passive recipient. Though, by allowing users to manipulate a specific bit of its

---

[2]In fact, only the initial creation of the bit of knowledge necessitates a one-time cost (first copy cost). This cost however, can be quite substantial.

[3]In their book Abundance, Peter Diamandis and Steven Kotler refer to this phenomenon as demonetization and provide exhaustive facts and figures from different sectors supporting that phenomenon (Diamandis and Kotler 2014, p. 289).

knowledge through a digital medium, a company does not lose it, rather it increases its value by enhancing its quality as well as its applicable reach. Thereby, to profit from these huge opportunities, a company needs the capability to orchestrate knowledge feedback loops allowing itself and other users to profit from the constantly re-programmed knowledge (i.e. functionalities) based upon a digital medium (i.e. platform). This is exactly what successful value co-creation orchestrators such as Tencent, Amazon or SAP have perfectly understood. However, their success should not disguise the fact that there remain a lot of data-related economic and social issues to be solved (e.g. data sovereignty, data manipulation, filter bubbles, unethical digital nudging).

2.3 The Company as an Orchestrator of Value Co-Creation

Essentially, the value creation logic based on information shared and manipulated through information technology, infers that a company can generate value by perceiving its consumers, suppliers and other partners as value co-creators. In fact, by addressing any stakeholder as a value co-creator, a company is able to leverage its knowledge-based value creation. Consequently, successful companies in the digital enhanced economy naturally shift from dictating value creation to orchestrating value co-creation. Thus, by enhancing its resources with digital technology, a company can be perceived as an *orchestrator of value co-creation* coordinating various complementing participants that collaboratively maximize their individual knowledge-driven value in a specific context. From a normative standpoint, orchestrating value co-creation implies continuously collecting, processing, filtering, sharing and updating the most relevant aspects of (infinite) digitized information with other actors of the ecosystem. This guarantees the most efficient and effective use and allocation of the community's scarce (finite) physical resources in terms of economic, social and ecological value. The business as an orchestrator of value co-creation takes a perspective far beyond its formal boundaries. Hence, rather than limiting its business model to the value generated through its hierarchically controlled, unilaterally produced and marketed product and service offerings, an orchestrator takes an ecosystem-oriented perspective. In this contextualized, dynamic network-like structure, the company's business model is characterized by rather heterarchical controlled, multilateral co-created product and service offerings.

In an extensive empirical study of the S&P 1500, Libert et al. (2016) highlight the success of US companies conceptualizing their BM to orchestrate value co-creation. In their analysis the authors distinguish business archetypes based on four asset types (Libert et al. 2016, p. 7 ff). Asset Builders (focusing on physical things); Service Providers (people); Technology Creators (information/ideas); and Network Orchestrators (connections/relationships). The fact that the connections established by orchestrators may provide access to any of the other asset types, puts them in a strategically strong position and is in line with the above-mentioned value creation characteristics in a digital enabled economy. Unsurprisingly, the authors conclude that orchestrators "*on average grew revenues faster, generated higher profit margins and used assets more efficiently than companies utilizing the other three business models*" (Libert et al. 2016, p. 9). However, despite the rapid advancement of digital technology by leveraging value co-creation based upon digitized assets, only 2% of the companies analyzed by the authors, are able to put the orchestration of value co-creation at the heart of their BM so far (Libert et al. 2016, p. 12). This fact is even more irritating when taking a closer look at two additional numbers. On the one hand, according to Brand Finance 500 most valuable brands 2018 (Brand Finance 2019), four companies (Amazon, Apple, Google, and Facebook) out of the top five have all achieved sustainable competitive advantage by setting up their business models around the orchestration of value co-creation in ecosystems, including devices, books, games, music, media, and search, storage or payment services. On the other hand, a vast majority of startups ranked on the Wall Street Journal and Dow Jones Venture Source tracking list of unicorns (startups valued at $ 1 billion or more), are building BM's based on the orchestration of value co-creation. By December 2018, the list included for instance Uber, its Chinese competitor DIDI, Airbnb, WeWork, as well as payment service provider Stripe and P2P lending/trading platforms such as SoFi or Robinhood. Unique to all of these companies is their ecosystem-oriented BM, characterized by the orchestration of value co-creation among users, service providers and contributing partners.

Although these numbers speak for themselves, it is obvious that especially established companies seem to lack mental and conceptual framing tools allowing them to orchestrate value co-creation in todays' networked economy and thus to position themselves in different roles in the emerging ecosystems. This is especially astonishing, when considering the fact that every organization is always—and has always been—embedded in latent networks, nowadays full of value creating opportunities based upon digitized assets.

3 An Allocentric Perspective on the Business Model Concept

It is only until recently that BM researchers have recognized the importance of contextual issues, by acknowledging that partnerships can have a great impact on value creation and thus BM participants need to be considered as value co-creators in a focal firms' BM (e.g. Iivari 2016; Wirtz et al. 2016; Zott et al. 2011). Some authors started expanding the BM concept towards a network scope, by covering aspects of the firm's interaction with its environment, through the analysis of open BM (e.g. Frankenberger et al. 2014; Chesbrough 2007) or the examination of the role of networks within new BM (e.g. Maglio and Spohrer 2013). However, the focus of value creation and value capturing of these studies remains highly idiocentric (firm self-contained), with limited attention drawn towards the role of business partners and mutual value creation. Considering the emergence of ecosystems and the underlying value creation logic, the misfit between existing BM concepts and empirical evidence is hence obvious. This was made transparent by a survey conducted by Wirtz et al. (2016) among BM researchers. The survey highlights the lack of a deeper conceptual understanding of mutual value creation and value capturing processes among business partners.

Existing BM concepts and related ontologies and representations are either fully idiocentric (e.g. Osterwalder 2004; Osterwalder and Pigneur 2010; Al-Debei and Fitzgerald 2010; Sinfield et al. 2012) or ignore to provide a company an *intersubjective*, yet unifying perspective, on a particular BM allowing it to orchestrate the resulting interactions among actors of the ecosystem it is part of (e.g. Gordijn 2002; Lüftenegger 2014; Zolnowski 2015). Consequently, when neither an idiocentric perspective on the BM concept nor alternative derivatives are able to fully describe and to explain a company's' value co-creation endeavor within a business ecosystem, a change of perspective seems to be at the time.

Rooted in Perceptual Psychology—a subfield of cognitive psychology—the term allocentric defines reference systems that do not only depend on the viewer's (being the firm) current position or orientation (Klatzky 1998). Etymologically, allocentric comes from ancient Greek and literally means "centered in something else (állos = other)" (Wiktionary 2019). From a behavioral point of view, allocentric actors emphasize interdependence by considering and being responsive to the needs of other in-group members (Triandis and Suh 2002). Hence, compared with idiocentrics, allocentrics think in a more holistic way and *define their identity by the context that they share with others*. An allocentric perspective makes it possible to consider a multi-actor context from a more holistic, multilateral standpoint. Obviously, this is particularly relevant when orchestrating value co-creation.

Looking with an allocentric perspective on value creation two major implications have to be considered. First, an allocentric perspective on value creation implies not to limit the resulting value to products and services uniquely offered and fully controlled by one specific corporation or holding. Second, from an allocentric perspective value creation happens through mutually beneficiary interactions among multiple participants (in-group members) sharing their resources in a specific context. Hence, the notion of value co-creation is an inherent part of an allocentric mindset.

As from an allocentric perspective value is always co-created, it can be followed that every co-creator also co-captures a share of that value. Though, an allocentric perspective implies to empathize with the needs and constraints of other value co-creators to specify the nature of value (oftentimes this is a mix between economic, functional, emotional and symbolic value) that each actor expects to capture. Secondly, an allocentric perspective infers that the value captured by a specific firm is never isolated from other value co-creators. It implies that individual profit maximization can only be achieved in interdependence to other actors' perspective on the nature of value to be captured. However, having an allocentric perspective on value capturing should not be confounded with altruism. Rather than altruistically maximizing the gain of others disregarding its own outcome (Hulbert et al. 2001), a company adopting an allocentric perspective simply increases its own profits with regard to- and in dependence on the value captured of other members in the ecosystem it resides.

Combining the above-mentioned characteristics, permits to highlight the main conceptual differences between a purely idiocentric and an allocentric perspective on a company's BM. In idiocentric BM, the final goal of value creation and value capturing is fully self-centered. Hence, idiocentric BM's are defined by a value proposition resulting from the creation and distribution of products and services that are fully controlled by a specific company. Thereby, the profit maximization is perceived to be decoupled from other parties. Hence, customers, suppliers and other contributing partners are rather seen as a means to reach a purely self-referral goal.

In contrast, in allocentric BM the final goal of value creation and value capturing is ecosystem-oriented. Value results from co-created and allocated products and services that are only under partial control of a specific company. Despite the prevailing economic motive to maximize profits, the allocentric business model acknowledges profits as a function of the well-being of other participants involved. An allocentric perspective on the business model therefore allows a company together with other social and business actors to *orchestrate their value co-creation in a unified frame*. A shared value purpose, which manifests itself in a service, functions as an intersubjective reference point for such a frame. Thereby, a service is defined as the *"(...) mutual application of competences (knowledge and skills) for the benefit of another entity or an entity itself"* (Lusch and Vargo 2014, p. 12; see also Vargo and Lusch 2004). Compared to an idiocentric BM approach, allocentric BM put higher emphasis on a service-dominated (Vargo and Lusch 2004) (eco)system-level activity approach (Zott et al. 2011), by defining the roles and the relations of value proposing business partners who are, directly or indirectly, mutually creating value for each party involved.

The proposed allocentric approach however strongly differs from the research stream about open BM concepts that cover aspects of a firm's interaction with its environment. In the context of open BM, collaboration of a firm with its ecosystem is what mainly drives value creation and value capturing specifically for this firm (Frankenberger et al. 2014). Unfortunately, these models bind their focus on value creation and value capturing to one specific firm (idiocentric), while disregarding the other actors' contribution to the same BM. While the open business model concept is shedding light on the importance of synergies (bilateral value flows) between a company and its direct partners, this model however remains idiocentric in itself. In fact, although partners help to enhance the value proposition restricted by particular products and services of a specific firm, it is still strictly dictated by the latter. Consequently, neither a "closed" nor an "open" perspective on the business model concept are fully able to capture the interactions and the interrelated value creation and value capturing between not just the firm and its direct partners, but also between the partners related to the shared value purpose around which an ecosystem emerges. Thus, both of these perspectives can be considered as idiocentric as Fig. 1 highlights.

To conclude, an allocentric perspective on the BM is necessary to offer a more comprehensive understanding of how a company can orchestrate value creation and

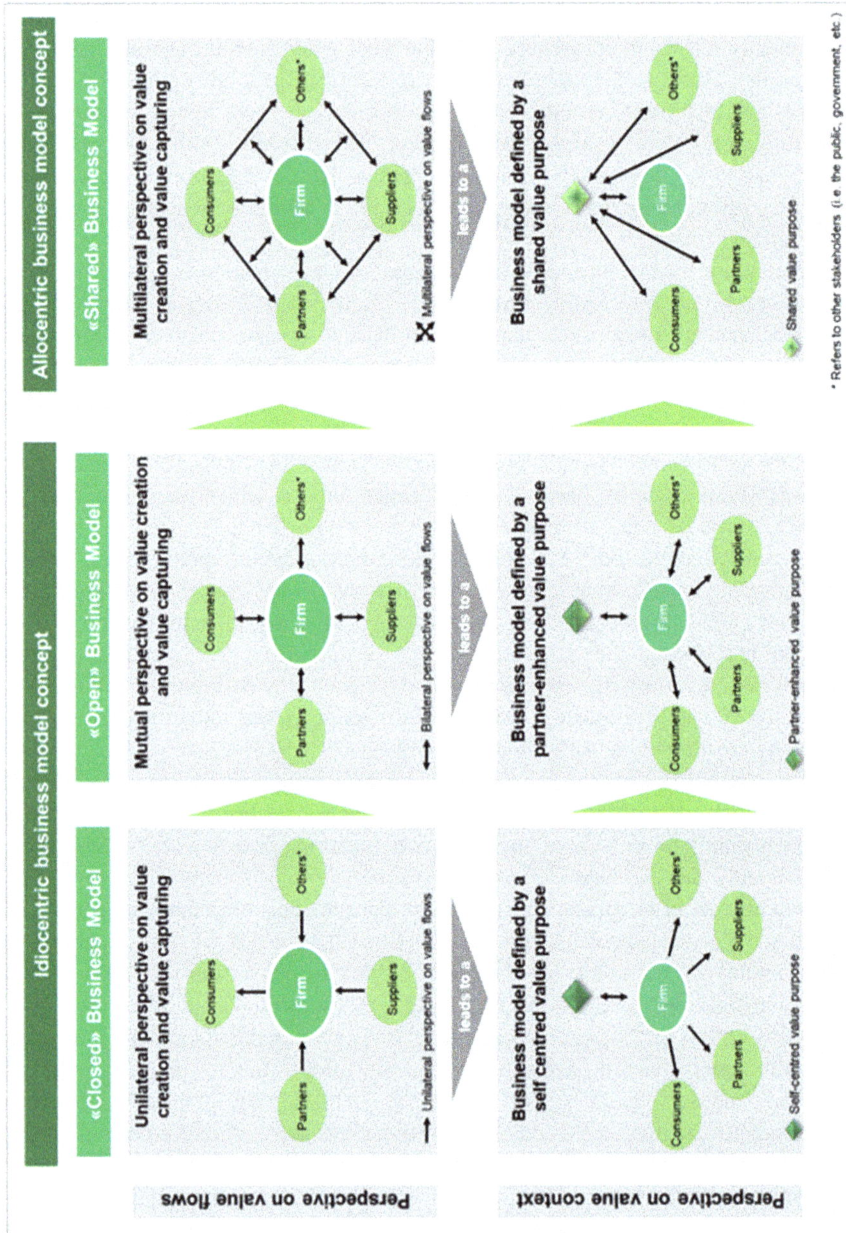

Fig. 1 Towards an allocentric perspective on the business model. Source: Own illustration

value capturing between various actors contributing to the functioning a of a particular ecosystem. Especially in the strategic management literature, arguments in that direction are not completely new (see Nalebuff et al. 1996 or Sull and Ruelas-Gossi 2010). However, so far, these arguments remained largely unnoticed by the research community and practitioners. Hence, in order address this matter, the next section takes a closer look at the conceptualization of the allocentric BM.

4 Conceptualizing the Allocentric Business Model

While this slight but fundamental shift in perspective on BM's is observable through various practical examples (see Chapter "Y.1: The Biological Code for Evolutionary Transformation"), it is important to understand what constitutes this shift. Therefore, two major concepts have to be discussed in this context. First, the shift from a goods-dominant towards a service-dominant business logic, where every actor engages in value co-creation. Second, the fact that these actors align their value co-creation around a shared purpose, leads to the emergence of dynamic, multilateral network structures—so called business ecosystems.

4.1 Service Dominant Logic Theory

Vargo and Lusch (2004, 2008, 2016) postulate a paradigmatic shift from a goods-dominant to a service-dominant logic (SDL), which moves the focus of economic exchange and value creation from a focal firm to an actor-to-actor ecosystem—including service providers, customers, suppliers and contributing partners—all acting as resource integrators (Vargo and Lusch 2004). In this multi-actor context, SDL defines service[4] as the *mutual* process of applying specialized competences (knowledge and skills) for the benefit of other actors and the actor itself (Vargo and Lusch 2004; Lusch and Nambisan 2015). Accordingly, the theory builds on the premise that value occurs when heterogeneous business partners work together toward mutual benefits, the key being the orchestration between these parties (Blaschke et al. 2017). This however, is in contrast with the former Goods-dominant

[4]According to SDL, the notion of *Service* is not to be confounded with *services*. The latter can be defined as the exchange of intangible goods as unit of outputs. As Lusch and Vargo (2014, p. 20ff) point out, under a GDL perspective, an accommodation *service* is "reduced" to producing and selling bed-nights (units of output). However, in SDL, accommodation service includes the mutual application of available resources among different actors including the beneficiary. Hence, an accommodation service includes mutual offerings in the form of products and services among complementary actors contributing and benefiting from the realization of the accommodation service.

logic (GDL), where value creation and capturing are mainly understood when taking place in a specific firm.

However, the GDL is still profoundly rooted in many of today's BM concepts. These concepts still consider business partners only as resource suppliers and customers as an extension of a focal firms' production process (Clauß et al. 2014; Storbacka et al. 2012). Therefore, in order to get a better understanding of value creation in the broader context of the relationships' network between complementary and competing business partners (Vargo and Akaka 2012), SDL Theory takes in a fundamentally different perspective regarding how value creation and value capturing among business partners should be seen and carried out. In this context, four main components can be distinguished and must be explained in detail, the actor, the service, resources, and the concept of value.

Actors can be defined as purpose-driven and decision-making entities. Operating within structures that allow and constrain purposeful actions, all actors can be viewed as "value centric, effectual, enterprising, resource integrating entities" (Vargo and Lusch 2016, p. 56). Put differently, all actors are understood to follow economic targets and leverage the multilateral configuration of resources, knowledge and skills to achieve these collaboratively. Although, the explicitly visible or latent structural context in which they operate can constrain the actors in their decisions, without some degree of agency, there would be no emerging actor-to-actor structure.

The **Service** can be defined as the application of resources for the benefit of another entity or an actor itself. Under an SDL perspective a good is always perceived as an appliance or distribution mechanism for a service. In line with the presented introduction of the allocentric perspective on the BM concept, a service representing a shared value purpose between several actors can be seen as an entry point to design allocentric BM. For this service to materialize (e.g. a financial service, a mobility service or an entertainment service) several actors (in different roles) have to act as mutual resource integrators (value co-creators) by exchanging their resources (e.g. in the form of products/services, money, information or other social currencies, such as attention). Consequently, the beneficiary is always considered as a value co-creator of a particular service.

Resources can be defined as anything that actors draw on to correspond to their particular explicit or latent needs. In this context, SDL differs between *operand* and *operant* resources. Whereby, operand resources (i.e. natural resources or tools) require other resources to act on them to provide benefit, operant resources (i.e. intellectual skills or manpower) are capable on acting upon operand resources to provide value. It is evident that both types are always interlinked.

Value can be perceived as the increase in the well-being of a particular actor respectively of an actor community. Due to the fact, that value is an actor subjective concept, every occurrence of benefit can be defined as unique and *context-dependent*. Against this backdrop, SDL argues that resources from multiple sources (through value co-creation) are integrated to generate value for a particular actor. Thereby, value can only be proposed from one actor to another. Hence, a value proposition is a representation of how an actor proposes to participate in value co-creation with another beneficial actor (Vargo and Lusch 2016, p. 57).

SDL represents a fundamental paradigm shift away from a linear value chain towards an interconnected network of value co-producers, whose actions and decisions are interdependent from each other. In order to distinguish this concept from the traditional GDL, Vargo and Lusch (2004, 2008, 2016) proposed the subsequent set of 11 foundational premises (FP's). Service is defined as the fundamental basis of exchange (FP1) that is oftentimes masked by an indirect exchange (FP2) mediated through money. Consequently, goods can be seen as distribution mechanisms for *service* provision (FP3). Against this backdrop, operant resources (e.g. knowledge) characterized by their ability to act upon operand resources are the fundamental source of strategic benefit (FP4) within economies that all represent *service* economies (FP5). In service economies, value is co-created always including the beneficiary (FP6). In doing so, actors engage in value co-creation by offering value propositions (FP7) that are inherently beneficiary oriented and relational (FP8). Hence, all social and economic actors can be considered as mutual resource integrators (FP9). Consequently, the perceived value by the beneficiaries is always context-specific (FP10) and captured by the orchestration of value co-creation trough actor-generated institutional arrangements (FP11).

While Vargo and Lusch lay the foundation for a fundamental new perspective on collaboration and value creation with the SDL, this meta-theoretical framework can be regarded as basis to understand value creation in complex networks of actors. Therefore, SDL represents an overarching theoretical lens to explain value co-creation in business ecosystems, which gained significant interest during the last years.

4.2 Business Ecosystems

By applying biological ecosystems as a metaphor to describe the value creation mechanism in increasingly dynamic and interdependent business environments, Rothschild (1990) and Moore (1993, 1996) introduced the notion of ecosystems. Since its appearance, the term "business ecosystem" has itself grown to encompass an ecology of meanings both in the research community as well as in the industry. In ecosystems, human actors and corresponding legal entities, try to design these structures through institutions with the aim to decrease risk and increase certainty. Due to their agency, characterized by bounded rationality, human actors in ecosystems align themselves around a shared purpose. It is clear that each individual actor has a slightly different perception of that shared purpose, however if a business ecosystem does not evolve for this greater good over time, it is at risk of being eliminated or becoming obsolete (Mars et al. 2012, p. 278).

Especially in the field of strategy, the concept of "ecosystems" has seen a boom. Jacobides et al. (2018, p. 2256) note that searching the keyword in the title or abstract of the top strategy journals shows a sevenfold increase during the last 5 years. Both managers and academics attest particular value to the metaphor by its ability to explain the complex network of business relationships within and across industries (Harte et al. 2001). Accordingly, definitions mainly stress the interconnectedness and mutual dependency of social and economic agents for their success and survival (Peltoniemi 2004; Anggraeni et al. 2007). Initially the metaphor provides a contextual structure to study the company as an interconnected part of its larger environment by defining different roles and related strategies it has in the ecosystem (Iansiti and Levien 2006). These initial thoughts resulted in a substantial list of considerations both in terms of the perspective researchers apply on the concept as well as on properties that are derived. Hence, ecosystems have been overlappingly analyzed from an innovation- (e.g. Adner 2006), an entrepreneurial—(e.g. Isenberg 2010), a service- (Vargo and Lusch 2011), a customer—(e.g. Manning and Thorne 2002; Voima et al. 2011), a digital—(e.g. Ammon and Brem 2013) as well as most recently from a platform-based perspective (e.g. Tiwana 2013; Parker et al. 2017). Against this backdrop, the contributions to the body of research from these various perspectives are manning fold. For instance, Adner (2017) highlighted the corresponding structure by which value is created and captured. Iansiti and Levien (2006) and Dedehayir et al. (2018) among others analyzed particular roles of actors in this structure. Baldwin and Woodard (2009) and Jacobides (2018) have emphasized the modularity and types of complementarities between actors. Finally, Williamson and De Meyer (2012) as well as Parker et al. (2017) suggested the potential network effects arising from the complementarities between actors operating in an ecosystem structure.

While multiple perspectives on the business ecosystem have been used to analyze the concept, there is also an abundant number of definitions available. Moore (1993) describes Ecosystems as a set of actors that cooperatively co-evolve while at the same time competitively supporting new products which bring value to a customer, while Manning and Thorne (2002) view Ecosystems as a set of companies, partners, suppliers, as well as customers who benefit from their connection. Iansiti and Levien (2006) describe business ecosystems as focus on the lose networks of different actors including suppliers, product or service providers, and others around a focal company. Voima et al. (2011) emphasize the relationship between the actors, including service providers, customers and any other actor with a directly or indirectly related service. Williamson and De Meyer (2012) describe ecosystems as a network of different organizations who evolve their skills and capabilities cooperatively in order to create value, emphasizing the individual role that an actor can hold. Adner and Kapoor (2010) conclude that ecosystems are defined by the alignment structure of various actors around a central value proposition.

While there are other literature streams, that investigate the concept from different angles, three important components of ecosystems can be aggregated. Firstly, it can be observed that ecosystems emerge and evolve around a *shared value purpose* of its participants. This shared purpose can be materialized through a service whose realization necessitates multilateral relationships among different actors. The shared purpose can be defined by one or several actors that orchestrate the other actors towards its materialization. Even if the shared purpose is defined by one specific ecosystem member, the latter is obliged to find other participants that share the purpose in order to materialize it. Although, the subjectively perceived respectively expected value related to the shared purpose might differ between ecosystem participants, it builds the glue helping ecosystem participants to find common ground in the pursuit of their individual goals.

Secondly, actors operating in ecosystems-as-structures take in particular *role archetypes*, which specify how they contribute respectively position themselves in relation to the collaboratively created and captured value. Taking in a strategic behavioral point of view Iansiti and Levien (2006) distinguish between keystone, niche, dominator and landlord. Den Hartigh and Van Asseldonk (2004) on their side view the shaper, the adapter and the opportunist as particular roles in an ecosystem. From an actor-centered perspective, Adner and Kapoor (2010) differ between the focal firm and complementors. However, most of the conceptualizations define the roles either through an actor's particular behavior (i.e. dominator or opportunist), through a particular functional contribution (i.e. sponsor, assembler, regulator) or through a specific actor-related characteristic (i.e. landlord, entrepreneur). Consequently, these roles remain conceptually detached from a shared value purpose that builds the common anchor point around which the ecosystem emerges. Voima et al. (2011) however, offer an interesting entry point by taking in an SDL-perspective and highlighting that roles can be defined in relation to a service (materialized shared purpose). Accordingly, in relation to the shared value purpose materialized through the realization of a specific service, Burkhalter (2019) defines the following role archetypes. *Users* apply their capabilities (resources and activities) to profit from the service output. *Providers* apply their capabilities to generate offerings for the service realization. *Orchestrators* apply their capabilities to coordinate the users and providers' capabilities. Finally, *contributors* apply their capabilities to support either the users, the providers or the orchestrators in their specific function. Each role archetype can be occupied by one or several legally independent but socially and economic interdependent actors. These actors follow a specific set of individual goals that are expressed through explicitly stated or latent needs. In order to fulfill their needs, the actors engage in value co-creation activities. Thereby, transforming their production factors in the form of different complementary resources. This is in line with SDL, where the actors co-create value by applying their heterogeneous capabilities towards mutual benefits.

Thirdly, the *relationships* of these individual actors are of high importance. The relationships among actors residing in a particular ecosystem can be considered as *inherently multilateral*. This implies that the relationships among different actors are not decomposable to an aggregation of bilateral interactions (Adner 2017, p. 42). Additionally, the relationships in an ecosystem are not unilaterally hierarchically controlled by one specific actor no matter the specific role that the latter occupies. According to Jacobides et al. (2018, p. 2266) all ecosystem members retain residual control and claims over their assets in terms of their prices and quantities. Based on that, the following logically related components can be derived when describing the multilateral relationships among ecosystem participants. First, value flows, representing mutual offerings (resources, resource bundles or resource claims) in the form of products and services that actors exchange to mutually materialize a service upon which is based their shared value purpose. Second, the interface, describing the physical, digital (or a mix of both) channels through which the actors engage in their mutual value creation and value capturing endeavor. Finally, the relationship metrics which represent the formalized terms and conditions underlying the multilateral relationships among the ecosystem participants.

To conclude, ecosystems can be considered as *dynamically evolving communities of interdependent social and economic actors which interact through coordinated technologies, norms and rules to co-create and co-capture value in relation to a shared purpose representing the intersection of their individual goals*. This definition sets the shared value purpose into the center of attention functioning as a reference point for all actors within the ecosystem. It also addresses the different, heterogenous and dynamic community of actors in various roles with individual needs and leveraging their specific capabilities. Finally, it emphasizes that the ecosystem is constituted by relationships which can take the form of formal or informal rules and norms leveraging a technological basis that defines the physical or digital means of interaction.

4.3 Business Model Dimension and Components

After having provided an overview on the analytical background helping to conceptualize allocentric BM, this section provides an overview of existing BM components (elements or building blocks). This investigation is based on several meta-analysis (i.e. Wirtz et al. 2016; Csik 2014; Schallmo 2013) and previous research on the topic of one of the authors of this article (see Burkhalter 2019). The review of different BM conceptualizations makes it clear that the definitory delimitations of their components both with regard to their content as well as the number of components vary from author to author. However, in order to clarify the distinct characteristics of these components, the latter can be grouped into business model dimensions (Schallmo 2013; Csik 2014). Accordingly, each of the five below listed BM dimensions describe the underlying logic of a distinctive group of BM components.

The WHY Dimension: Why to Participate in a Business Model?
The WHY dimension contains BM components that are related to the unifying goal of the BM. These components serve as narrative reference points for the BM operator and/ or other involved participants, by providing them a reason to participate. However, among the reviewed BM conceptualizations, this dimension received the least attention. Hence, the sole component that can be attributed to the WHY dimension is the "vision". One explanation could be that components ranging in that dimension further blur the line between the notion of business strategy and the one of BM. Although, the BM concept is not similar to a business strategy and can rather be defined as "strategy-as-a-practice" (Johnson et al. 2008), there exists a long debate on the communalities and distinctiveness of the two

research streams (see for instance: Arend 2013 or George and Bock 2011). Hence, BM researchers naturally put particular attention to not further blur the lines with ambiguous constructs.

The WHO Dimension: Who Participates in a Business Model?
The components in the WHO dimension characterize the BM participants and their roles. In this regard, the perspective on value creation and value capturing deserves special attention. Most BM components in that dimension differentiate between a focal organization (the BM operator) and other BM participants. Hence, most of the time the components are defined from a focal operator's self-centered point of view. In general, components falling into the WHO dimension are "actor", "focal organization", "consumer"/"market segment", "partner" and "governance". The "actor" component represents a consolidation of all involved stakeholder in a BM. However, in many conceptualizations and related ontologies, the "actor" component is limited to the focal organization operating a particular BM (i.e. Osterwalder 2004). Additionally, "market segment" is mostly used to describe a particular customer segment, hence the two components are grouped together. Furthermore, almost every conceptualization contains a "partner" component. In some ontologies (i.e. Gordijn 2002) this element is subsumed in the more generic "actor" element. Finally, the "governance" element is used in rather earlier conceptualizations (i.e. Linder and Cantrell 2000). However, most of the later conceptualizations (i.e. Osterwalder 2004) ignore that element. This can be explained by the fact, that these conceptualizations put their focus on the focal organization by ignoring the various roles and interrelations between other BM partners. Consequently, the authors do not see the relevance for an explicit governance component.

The WHAT Dimension: What Do the Business Model Participants Offer Each Other?
The WHAT dimension contains components that describe the value delivery logic to either the customer and—in rare cases (i.e. Zolnowski 2015)—to other BM participants. Against this backdrop, the participants deliver value by exchanging offerings (products and services) via an interface. However, most BM conceptualizations define the components in the WHAT dimension in a unilateral way, by describing what a particular focal actor is offering to a particular customer (i.e. Magretta 2002; Osterwalder 2004; Johnson et al. 2008). This is particularly true for authors framing the BM concept on a company-level and underlying a purely idiocentric value creation and value capturing logic. Although, the descriptions of components slightly differ from author to author,[5] the following components can be grouped into the WHAT dimension: "value proposition"; "value offering"; "channel/interface"; "relationship".

[5]For a detailed overview see for instance: Gordijn et al. (2005) or Burkhart et al. (2012).

The HOW Dimension: How Do Business Model Participants Create Their Offerings?
Components that fall in this dimension describe how BM participants create their offerings. Oftentimes, this dimension is described as infrastructure (Osterwalder 2004) or value architecture (Al-Debei and Avison 2010). Compared to the other dimensions however, the different conceptualizations are rather consistent in defining its components. Overall, the following three constructs can be attributed to the HOW dimension: "resources", "activity" and "capability". However, when taking a closer look on the component's granularity and interdependences, it can be noted that there exists some confusion. For instance, Osterwalder (2004) defines capabilities as a combination of different resources while the activity element is treated separately as being part of different activity configurations. However, in a later publication (Osterwalder and Pigneur 2010) this rather cumbersome separation disappears and the authors forgo the "capability" component while the "resource" and "activity" component remain. Other authors express either "resource" (i.e. Al-Debei and Fitzgerald 2010) or "activities" (i.e. Razo-Zapata et al. 2012; Lüftenegger 2014) as single elements of the HOW dimension.

The VALUE Dimension: How Do Business Model Participants Benefit from Their Participation?
The VALUE dimension contains components that explain BM participants' benefits (monetary or other) resulting from their participation. Most researchers however, describe VALUE in terms of monetary "revenues" and "costs" for the focal organization. While the benefits for a particular customer group are subsumed in the "value proposition" (i.e. Osterwalder 2004). A notable exception is the ontology proposed by Lüftenegger (2014) who differentiates between financial and non-financial costs and benefits not just for the focal organization, but for all the stakeholders involved in the BM. However, components taking into account the reciprocity in terms of costs and benefits between business models stakeholder remain rather the exception.

This condensed overview on different BM dimension and their components, builds the starting point for the conceptualization of the allocentric BM in the next section.

4.4 Key Components of Allocentric Business Models

In order to conceptualize the allocentric BM and to highlight how it complements existing idiocentric BM concepts, Table 1 puts it in relation to the BM Ontology respectively the Business Model Canvas (Osterwalder 2004; Osterwalder and Pigneur 2010). Especially among the practitioner community, the Business Model Canvas can be considered as the leading firm self-centered (idiocentric) BM conceptualization tool. Thus, it seems a logically choice for that contrasting exercise (see Table 1). However, the purpose of this exercise is not to diminish the value of the latter. Nor is it the purpose to suggest that it becomes redundant. The aim is rather

Table 1 Idiocentric vs. allocentric business model conceptualization

Dimension	Components of the Business Model Canvas	Description (Osterwalder and Pigneur 2010, p. 22ff)	Allocentric business model components	Description
The "WHY" Purpose	n.a.	n.a.	Shared value purpose (1)	This component describes the unifying goal (usually proposed by the orchestrator) that underlies the BM. The shared purpose is expressed through a service outcome composed of mutual offerings between BM participants taking in different roles in relation to that outcome
The "WHO" Actors	Focal organization (BM operator)	The focal organization component refers to the actor (oftentimes an independent legal entity) that operates a BM	User (2a)	Describes one actor or different groups of people or organizations engaging in activities by converting their resources to profit directly from the service cutcome.
			Provider (2b)	Describes one actor or different groups of people or organizations providing their resources to create the service outcome. Hence, providers profit indirectly from the service outcome (i.e. through monetary compensation, social currency such as reputation/status or barter goods)
	Customer segment	Describes different groups of people or organizations a focal organization aims to reach and serve	Orchestrator (BM operator) (2c)	Describes one or different groups of people or organizations that operate the BM by engaging in activities to apply their resources for the orchestration of mutual offerings between users and providers to realize the service outcome
	Key partners	Describes a focal company's network of suppliers and partners that enable the functioning of the BM	Contributor (2d)	Describes one or different groups of people or organizations that engage in activities by converting their resources to support users, providers and orchestrators in the realization of the service outcome

(continued)

Table 1 (continued)

Dimension	Components of the Business Model Canvas	Description (Osterwalder and Pigneur 2010, p. 22ff)	Allocentric business model components	Description
The "WHAT" Value Propositions	Value proposition	The value proposition describes bundles of products and services that create value for a specific customer segment. Thus, it characterizes the offer which complements a need or problem of a specific customer segment	Value proposition (3a)	The value proposition describes the monetary, functional, emotional or symbolic value related to an offering (products and services) from one BM participant to one or several other participants to respond to their needs
			Needs (3b)	Describe basic necessities as well as wants (psychological amenities) a BM participants is striving to fulfill through its value co-creation with other participants
	Channel	Takes into account how a company communicates with and reaches its customer segment to deliver a value proposition	Channel (3c)	The channel (interface) component describes how and where two or several BM participants interact in order to co-create value by exchanging their offerings
	Customer relationship	Describes the types of relationships a company establishes with specific customer segments	Relationship metrics (3d)	Describe the terms and conditions expressed through governance metrics helping the BM participants to decrease risk and increase certainty in their multilateral relationships
The "HOW" Value creation	Activities	Describe the most important tasks a company must undertake to make its BM work	Activities (4a)	Describe the most important tasks a BM participant has to engage when converting resources to fulfill its needs
	Resources	Describe the most important assets required to make a focal company's BM work	Resources (4b)	Correspond to the most important assets a BM participant requires (either through direct use or through the exchange for others) to fulfill its needs

The "VALUE" Value capturing	Revenue stream	Describes the monetary returns a company generates from each customer segment	Benefits (5a)	Represent the monetary and non-monetary (psychological well-being) benefits a BM participant generates through the mutual value creation with other participants
	Cost structure	Represents all the monetary costs incurred to operate the company's BM	Costs (5b)	Correspond to the monetary costs as well as psychological efforts and risks a BM participant faces when engaging in mutual value creation with other participants

Source: Own illustration

to compare the different points of focus that arise from the two perspectives and to close the conceptual gap when it comes to the orchestration of value co-creation among different BM participants being part of the same ecosystem. Hence, the next paragraph outlines the components of the allocentric BM.

Allocentric BM are built around a shared value purpose (1). Usually proposed by the BM operator (the orchestrator), it defines a desired state that is materialized through a service that is co-created. Hence, a service represents the outcome that is reached through the mutual application of resources among different groups of people and/ or organizations. In order to structure their value co-creation, these actors occupy different mutually non-exclusive roles determined by their relation to the service outcome. First, users (2a) that have a direct interest in the service outcome and apply their capabilities for that cause. Second, providers (2b), that apply their capabilities to generate an indirect benefit out of the service outcome (e.g. a monetary compensation). Third, the orchestrator that applies its capabilities to coordinate users and providers and contributing partners (2c). Finally, contributors (2d), leveraging their capabilities to support either users, providers or the orchestrator in the realization of the service outcome through which the shared purpose is materialized. Unified through the shared value purpose, BM participants in their roles (2a–2d) engage in multilateral relationships to co-create value. These relationships consist of mutual value propositions (3a) that the actors propose to each other through their offerings to fulfill their needs (3b). In order to exchange their mutual offerings, the participants interact through channels (3c). To increase certainty and decrease risk in relation to the co-created value, the participants define mutually agreed relationship metrics (4d). Accordingly, the mutual value propositions respectively the offerings by which they are provided, the interaction channels- as well as the relationship metrics depend on each participants' individual activities (4a) and applied resources (4b). Thus, for each actor, the engagement in value co-creation is related to subjectively perceived benefits (5a) and costs (5b). Accordingly, only when the perceived benefits exceed the costs, an actor—regardless of its role—is willing to participate in an allocentric BM. To conclude, an allocentric BM can only work if the value co-creation is orchestrated by the BM operator in a way that each participant can realize a subjectively perceived value (monetary or other) that corresponds to its expectations.

5 Orchestrating Value Co-Creation through Allocentric Business Models

McKinsey & Company estimates, that by 2025 roughly $60 trillion in revenues of global production could be distributed across industry borders in new ecosystems such as housing, health or travel and hospitality among others (McKinsey and Company 2008). On a company-level, this huge market potential is oftentimes controversially discussed by pointing on the enormous success and power, US companies such as Google, Apple, Facebook and Amazon (GAFA) or their Chinese counterparts Baidu, Alibaba and Tencent (BAT) have achieved by establishing allocentric BM and orchestrating value co-creation through digital platforms. It is correct that with their business models, they achieved to secure disproportionate rents from participants with whom they co-evolve in their respective ecosystems. However, it should not be forgotten that they have contributed to the further beneficial emergence of these ecosystems, as thousands of small businesses/e-shops (e.g. Alibaba, Amazon), App developers (e.g. Apple, Google) or social content creators and service providers (e.g. Facebook, Baidu, Tencent) would certainly confirm. However, by highlighting other apparent—but also less obvious—examples of companies that achieved to successfully orchestrate value co-creation in different ecosystems (see Table 2), this article provides evidence that the discussion should not only be reduced to the above-mentioned tech players.

Airbnb successfully leverages an allocentric perspective on its business model. After starting in 2008 with only an air mattress (hence the name: "airbedandbreakfast"), the company managed to leverage a network with more than 6 million listings across 190 countries and more than 2 million stays per day. Airbnb matches the millions of available spare rooms with people in need for a place to sleep. The slogan "Anyone can belong anywhere" functions well as a central reference point or shared value purpose not only for the users and providers but also for several partners or contributors. Delta Air Lines clearly supports the user to get to the preferred location, while Sonos and Nest complement the user experience during the stay, hence functioning as user-oriented contributors. Keysafe, on the other hand, supports the provider with the key transaction, hence, functioning as provider-oriented contributor.

Zillow, on the other hand, established a platform hosting more than 110 million homes for about 195 million registered users. How could Zillow help to foster interactions between the different actors? The answer is simply to integrate partners and to connect them with the users and the providers at the right time. Homesmart, for example, is a brokerage company, which not only uses the platform to list their own offerings, but which supports it by providing market insights and advice with their 11,000 agents. AlphaVision—specialized in home building technology, i.e. interactive floor plans, or 3D home renderings—helps by providing a digital solution for a virtual visit when a potential home owner cannot visit an apartment in person. Professional advertisement is another important aspect, where Rearview Advertising supports providers in displaying their real estate. Zillow also offers several features to request a mortgage while integrating local financial services contributors in this process. All this is subsumed under the shared purpose "Find your way home".

UBER connects providers who have a car and are willing to provide their time with users who wish to travel from one place to another. The ecosystem offers high transparency to both the users and the providers, e.g. by showing a price estimate even before the actual ride has started. Furthermore, the UBER app provides the possibility of ratings: both the users and the providers are able to rate each other after a ride—reducing the uncertainty about unpleasant guests or drivers in the future. To expand the ecosystem for example, UBER partnered with Lime which offers electric scooters for its users, if they look for a convenient and fun way to move around. UBER users are able to book the Lime scooter directly within the UBER app in available cities. Another partnership was established with Volvo to integrate their

Table 2 Examples of allocentric business models

Ecosystem		Accommodation	Housing	Mobility	Health	Collaboration	Entertainment	Education
Shared value purpose		**Anyone can belong anywhere**	**Find your way home**	**Move the way you want**	**A healthy life for everyone**	**Decentralized, trusted collaboration**	**Broadcast yourself**	**Ideas worth spreading**
Roles	User	**Tourists and business travelers**	**Home buyers/ renters** (Individuals/ Businesses)	**Riders** (Individuals/Groups)	**Health trackers** (Individuals)	**Token Holders** (Individuals/ Businesses)	**Viewers** (Individuals/ Groups)	**Audience** (Individuals/ Businesses)
	Provider	**Hosts** (Individuals/Businesses)	**Home sellers/ owners** (Individuals/ Businesses)	**Drivers** (Individuals/ Businesses)	**Health Insurers** (Businesses)	**Application developers** (Individual/ Businesses)	**Broadcasters** (Individual/ Businesses)	**Speakers** (Individuals/ Businesses)
	Orchestrator	**Airbnb**	**Zillow**	**UBER**	**Dacadoo**	**Ethereum Foundation**	**YouTube** (Alphabet)	**TED** (Sapling Foundation)
	Contributors (non-exhaustive)	**Delta Air Lines** is partnering with Airbnb to offer special discounted airfares. **Keycafe** is key exchange simplified. Hosts may store their keys at nearby Keycafe locations **Sonos** can easily enhance the guest experience	**HomeSmart** provides 11,000 agents an easy way to market their listings and users their service skills and knowledge **Alpha Vision** Is a home builder technology provider of interactive floor plans,	**Lime** promotes Lime in its mobile application and slap its logo on the scooters **Volvo**: UBER leverages Volvo and their autonomous driving capabilities to provide driverless cars **Wageworks**: commuter benefits cards to pay	**Apple HealthKit; Nike Fitbit; Garmin; Google Fit; Polar; Runkeeper; TomTom:** health tracking apps (among others) that can be connected to Dacadoo **Loylogic** allows providers using Dacadoo to	**Several thousand Ether Miners** validate through their computation power the transactions in the network **Coinbase; SIX Digital Exchange** are digital currency exchanges that allow (among others) to trade Ethereum and	**Restream** service allows its users to broadcast live content to multiple streaming platforms **Sony PlayStation; Microsoft** allow to live-stream videos from their consoles on YouTube **Tribeca Film**	**Independent private & corporate TedX Event Hosts** organize TED conferences in their regions **YouTube** allows to broadcast TED talks all over the world **Professional Translators** translate

		through more than 80 music services worldwide and access to over 100,000 TuneIn radio stations **Nest** makes homes more comfortable, safe and secure for Airbnb guests	interactive site maps, 3D home renderings **Rearview Advertising** Is a full-service advertising, design and interactive marketing agency for sellers **Local mortgage contributors**: Zillow connects users with local mortgage providers for financing solutions **Buildium** is a residential and association management software connected Zillow to allow post rentals on Zillow platform	for uberPOOL rides when commuting **Regional Transportation District (RTD)**: Users in the Denver area will be able to choose public transportation as an option directly through the Uber app **Starbucks:** UberEats offers delivery service for more than 2000 Starbucks stores in the US in 2019	create customized loyalty points experiences. **Oracle:** supports Dacadoo in the development of their health platform by integrating gamification- and social network elements	Ethereum Classic **Meet-Up** organizes regional crypto meetings. The regional Ethereum groups have several thousand members	**Festival** awarding the best YouTube videos **GoPro** provides action-filming equipment allowing its users to live-stream on YouTube and other social medias. **Hootsuite; Broadband TV:** allow to manage among others YouTube content and provide access to YouTube creator community	conference speeches in multiple languages for the international audience **Speaker nominators:** Identify and suggest interesting speakers for the conferences **Boston Consulting Group; Cartier:** Contribute education material and sponsor special events/ awards

(continued)

Table 2 (continued)

Ecosystem	Accommodation	Housing	Mobility	Health	Collaboration	Entertainment	Education
Key facts	>6M Airbnb listings globally >81K cities with Airbnb listings >191 countries with Airbnb listings >2M average number of people staying every night	>195M users in 2018 >110 million homes in data base >5.6 million mortgage requests 2018	>75 million riders >3 million drivers >15 million rides per day >Available in 600 cities globally	N.a.	>353 million transactions to date >1.2 million smart contract calls per day >2.354 DApps on Ethereum Blockchain >200 k developers	>1.9 billion monthly active users >5 billion videos watched per day >300h of videos uploaded per minute >1 billion hours of YouTube content are watched per day	>3100 TED talks currently available >17 Mio YouTube channel subscribers >3 Bio YouTube views >56 Mio viewers of the most popular TED talk

Source: Companies' official websites

capabilities in the field of autonomous driving. Starbucks partnered with UBEReat to offer food and beverage delivery to their customers, effectively making Starbucks products available whenever and wherever which is all integrated under the shared value purpose: "move the way you want".

A less known example is **Dacadoo**, a Swiss-based online health and wealth platform. With the shared value purpose that consists in allowing "a healthy life to everyone", the company orchestrates value co-creation among individuals that track their health through different health tracking apps, such as the Nike Fitbit, Garmin GPS or the Apple Health Kit and health insurers offering them personalized insurance solutions. The key being, a real-time health score upon which users (individuals), providers (insurance companies) together with contributing partners (e.g. health tracking apps, social media contributors) co-create value for themselves and other participants in Dacadoos' BM.

Another more popular example—at least for Crypto Aficionados—is **Ethereum**, an open-source, blockchain-based distributed computing program and operating system. Allowing participants that do not have to trust each other to organize their collaboration without the need of, at least theoretically, any trusted intermediary. With its cryptocurrency Ether respectively Ether Classic and its decentralized virtual machine that is able to execute smart contracts (pre-defined collaboration scripts including terms and conditions related to transactions among different participants), Ethereum achieved to leverage an entire ecosystem consisting of Crypto Token holders, miners (orchestrator-oriented contributors that validate transactions) and decentralized application developers. All orchestrated through the Ethereum foundation and unified by the shared purpose to leverage the technology to allow "decentralized, trusted collaboration" on a global level.

One of the oldest examples of a highly successful orchestrator of value co-creation is certainly **YouTube** that for several years has been owned by Alphabet. Through the shared value purpose "broadcast yourself", the company achieved to orchestrate value co-creation between mainly video content providers, viewers and a multitude of contributing partners, such as other social media sites/management tools (i.e. Hootsuite), gaming platforms (e.g. Sony PlayStation), filming equipment manufacturers (e.g. GoPro) and even film festival organizers (e.g. Tribeca Film Festival).

Another fascinating example of how value co-creation can be orchestrated through an allocentric BM is offered by the Sapling Foundation, better known by their Technology, Entertainment and Design **(TED) Conferences**. Guided by the shared value purpose to diffuse "ideas worth spreading", the Foundation orchestrates the value co-creation of a multitude of legally independent, yet socially and economically interdependent, complementary partners all sharing the same goal. To conclude this chapter, Fig. 2 provides an illustrative example on how TED orchestrates value co-creation through its allocentric BM.[6]

[6]The illustrative example of TED's business model is based on publicly available data, extracted from the organization's website: https://www.ted.com/about/our-organization (Retrieved March 7, 2019).

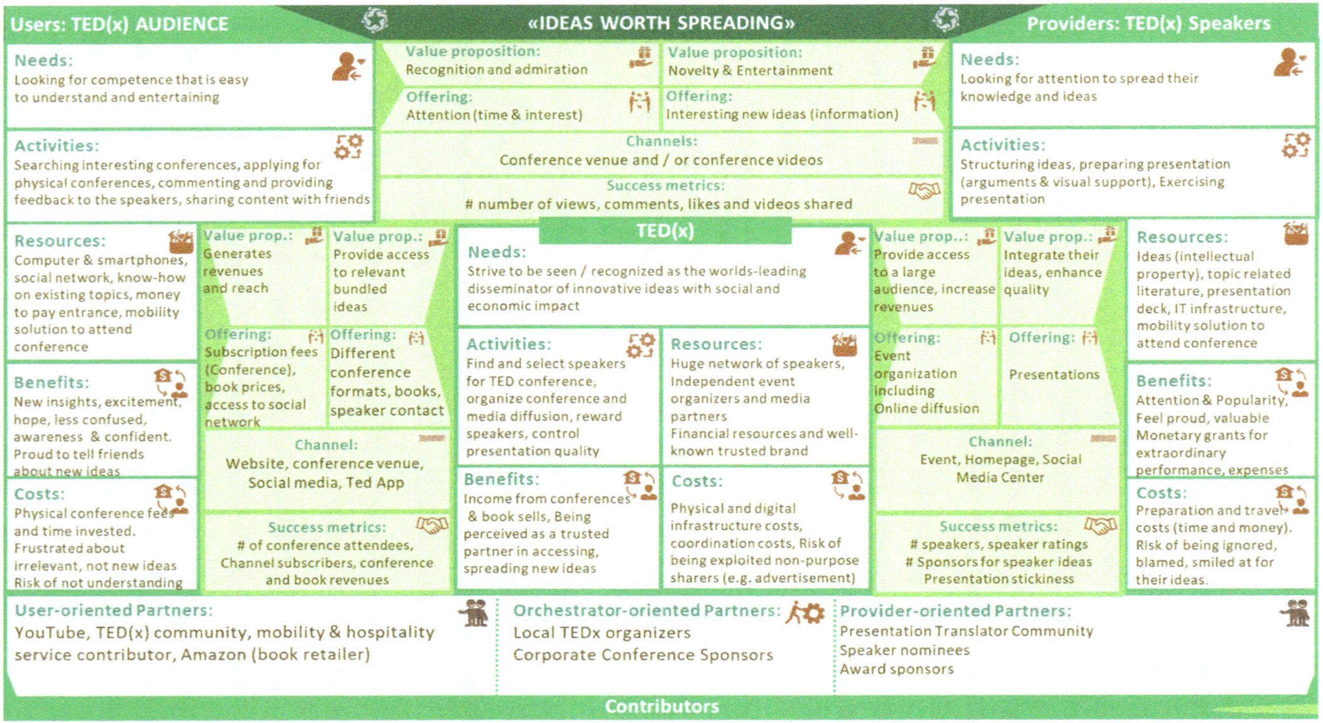

Fig. 2 Illustrative example of TED's business model. Source: Own illustration based on data from TED's official website

6 Conclusion

This article offers a change in perspective on how humans, as enterprising species with bounded rationality, co-create and co-capture value. The proposed shift in perspective from an idiocentric (limited by the perspective of one single company) towards an allocentric (inter-subjective) perspective on the BM concept is explained through a SDL point of view in the context of the emergence of business ecosystems. From a historical perspective, ecosystems are not an entirely new phenomenon. Network structures with the goal to connect various actors for mutually beneficial interactions, such as market places, have always have been used in ancient times already. However, due to the changing nature of our economic activities with knowledge and information as the fundamental basis, as well as with ever more technological possibilities, structures such as ecosystems emerge at an unprecedented speed. With the interconnectedness provided by the internet and technological innovations such as application programming interfaces, cloud computing or distributed ledger technologies, the effort which is necessary to deeply integrate the customers into the process of value creation decreased as well, leading to a paradigm shift in the fundamental economic mindset. These developments, however, challenge the organizational perspective on itself and its environment. A company can no longer look at a simple linear value chain, nor can it ignore all the other parties that are involved in the process of value creation. Hence, it is argued that by contextualizing BM's through a business ecosystem structure, value occurs when heterogeneous social and business partners work together toward mutual benefits, the key being the orchestration between these parties.

In this context, BM's are designed around a shared (an inter-subjective) value purpose that is materialized through a service which is always co-created by complementing actors including the beneficiary (the user of the service output). Accordingly, through an allocentric perspective on its business model, a company perceives itself as an orchestrator of value co-creation that goes far beyond its legal boundaries. Leveraging digital technologies and the opportunities of value co-creation based upon digitized and eventually tokenized assets, organizations such as Tencent, Amazon, Ethereum or TED have successfully implemented an allocentric perspective on their BM's. However, although highly successful many established companies and entrepreneurs with great ideas seem to struggle in understanding how to design innovative business models centered around the orchestration of value co-creation. To address this shortcoming, the conceptualized and illustrated example of allocentric BM's in this article offer a mental framework. With this slight, but yet fundamental, shift in perspective on BM research the authors hope to support companies in the orchestration of value co-creation and value co-capturing between mutually complementary social and business actors based upon innovative digital technologies.

However, we are still at the beginning of understanding how ecosystems work, in particular, how value is co-created, to what extent a specific actor contributes to value co-creation and how they are able to extract value from this organizational structure. Especially how collaboration is orchestrated, and what basic mechanisms of value co-creation are present, is still not fully understood. This chapter, therefore, provides a starting point with the necessary change in perspective to understand and conceptualize value co-creation in new organizational structures such as ecosystems.

References

Aberkane, I. J. (2017). A simple paradigm for nooconomics, the economy of knowledge. In P. Bourgine, P. Collet, & P. Parrend (Eds.), *First complex systems digital campus world E-conference 2015* (pp. 271–283). Cham: Springer. https://doi.org/10.1007/978-3-319-45901-1_30.

Adner, R. (2006). Match your innovation strategy to your innovation ecosystem. *Harvard Business Review, 84*(4), 98.

Adner, R. (2017). Ecosystem as structure. An actionable construct for strategy. *Journal of Management, 43*(1), 39–58. https://doi.org/10.1177/0149206316678451.

Adner, R., & Kapoor, R. (2010). Value creation in innovation ecosystems: How the structure of technological interdependence affects firm performance in new technology generations. *Strategic Management Journal, 31*(3), 306–333. https://doi.org/10.1002/smj.821.

Al-Debei, M. M., & Avison, D. (2010). Developing a unified framework of the business model concept. *European Journal of Information Systems, 19*(3), 359–376. https://doi.org/10.1057/ejis.2010.21.

Al-Debei, M. M., & Fitzgerald, G. (2010). The design and engineering of mobile data services: Developing an ontology based on business model thinking. In J. Pries-Heje, J. Venable, D. Bunker, N. L. Russo, & J. I. DeGross (Eds.), *IFIP working conference on human benefit through the diffusion of information systems design science research* (pp. 28–51). Berlin: Springer. https://doi.org/10.1007/978-3-642-12113-5_3.

Allo- [Def. 1]. (n.d.). In *Wiktionary. The free dictionary*. Retrieved January 14, 2019 from https://en.wiktionary.org/wiki/allo-

Ammon, T., & Brem, A. (2013). Digitale Ökosysteme und deren Geschäftsmodelle: Analyse und Implikationen für klassische Buchverlage. In F. Keuper, K. Hamidian, E. Verwaayen, T. Kalinowski, & C. Kraijo (Eds.), *Digitalisierung und Innovation* (pp. 91–121). Wiesbaden: Springer Gabler. https://doi.org/10.1007/978-3-658-00371-5_6.

Anggraeni, E., Den Hartigh, E., & Zegveld, M. (2007). Business ecosystem as a perspective for studying the relations between firms and their business networks. In F. van Eijnatten & J. Peters (Eds.), *Phase transitions in ortanisations* (pp. 1–28). Veldhoven: TVA.

Arend, R. J. (2013). The business model: Present and future—Beyond a skeumorph. *Strategic Organization, 11*(4), 390–402. https://doi.org/10.1177/1476127013499636.

Baldwin, C. Y., & Woodard, C. J. (2009). The architecture of platforms: A unified view. *Platforms, Markets and Innovation, 32*. https://doi.org/10.2139/ssrn.1265155.

Beck, R. (2006). *The Network(ed) economy - The nature, adoption, and diffusion of communication standards* (pp. 15–40). Wiesbaden: DUV. https://doi.org/10.1007/978-3-8350-9213-6.

Blaschke, M., Haki, K., Riss, U., & Aier, S. (2017). Design principles for business-model-based management methods—A service-dominant logic perspective. In A. Maedche, J. V. Brocke, & A. Hevner (Eds.), *DESRIST 2017: Designing the digital transformation* (pp. 179–198). Cham: Springer. https://doi.org/10.1007/978-3-319-59144-5_11.

Brand Finance – Global 500 Report 2018. (2019). *Brand Finance Global 500 2018*. Retrieved March 02, 2019, from http://brandfinance.com/knowledge-centre/reports/brand-finance-global-500-2018/

Burkhalter, M. (2019). *Allocentric business models - An allocentric business model ontology for the orchestration of value co-creation using the example of financial service ecosystems* (Unpublished doctoral dissertation). University of St. Gallen, St. Gallen.
Burkhart, T., Wolter, S., Schief, M., Krumeich, J., Di Valentin, C., Werth, D., et al. (2012). A comprehensive approach towards the structural description of business models. In *Proceedings of the international conference on Management of Emergent Digital EcoSystems* (pp. 88–102). New York: ACM. https://doi.org/10.1145/2457276.2457294.
Chesbrough, H. (2007). Business model innovation: It's not just about technology anymore'. *Strategy and Leadership, 35*(6), 12–17. https://doi.org/10.1108/10878570710833714.
Clauß, T., Laudien, S. M., & Daxböck, B. (2014). Service-dominant logic and the business model concept: Toward a conceptual integration. *International Journal of Entrepreneurship and Innovation Management, 18*(4), 266–288. https://doi.org/10.1504/IJEIM.2014.064209.
Context [Def. 1]. (n.d.). (2019). In *Oxford living dictionaries*. Retrieved January 14, 2019, from https://en.oxforddictionaries.com/definition/context
Csik, M. (2014). *Muster und das Generieren von Ideen für Geschäftsmodellinnovationen* (Doctoral dissertation). Retrieved from https://www1.unisg.ch/www/edis.nsf/SysLkpByIdentifier/4263/$FILE/dis4263.pdf
Dedehayir, O., Mäkinen, S. J., & Ortt, J. R. (2018). Roles during innovation ecosystem genesis: A literature review. *Technological Forecasting and Social Change, 136*, 18–29. https://doi.org/10.1016/j.techfore.2016.11.028.
Den Hartigh, E., & Van Asseldonk, T. (2004). *Business ecosystems: A research framework for investigating the relation between network structure, firm strategy, and the pattern of innovation diffusion*. ECCON 2004 Annual Meeting: Co-Jumping on a Trampoline, The Netherlands.
Diamandis, P. H., & Kotler, S. (2014). *Abundance. The future is better than you think*. New York, NY: Free Press – Simon & Schuster Inc.
Digitize [Def. 1]. (n.d.). In *Collins dictionary online*. Retrieved March 02, 2019, from https://www.collinsdictionary.com/de/worterbuch/englisch/digitize
Frankenberger, K., Weiblen, T., & Gassmann, O. (2014). The antecedents of open business models: An exploratory study of incumbent firms. *R&D Management, 44*(2), 173–188. https://doi.org/10.1111/radm.12040.
George, G., & Bock, A. J. (2011). The business model in practice and its implications for entrepreneurship research. *Entrepreneurship Theory and Practice, 35*(1), 83–111. https://doi.org/10.2139/ssrn.1490251.
Gordijn, J. (2002). *Value-based requirements engineering - Exploring innovative e-commerce ideas* (Unpublished doctoral dissertation). Vrije Universiteit, Amsterdam.
Gordijn, J., Osterwalder, A., & Pigneur, J. (2005). Comparing two business model ontologies for designing eBusiness models and value constellations. In *8th Bled Electronic Commerce Conference (Bled'2005)*.
Harte, A., Shireman, B., Burke, A., & Scarlett, L. (2001). A roundtable discussion. Business as a living system: The value of industrial ecology. *California Management Review, 43*(3), 16–25.
Hulbert, L. G., Corrêa da Silva, M. L., & Adegboyega, G. (2001). Cooperation in social dilemmas and allocentrism: A social values approach. *European Journal of Social Psychology, 31*(6), 641–657. https://doi.org/10.1002/ejsp.53.
Iansiti, M., & Levien, R. (2006). The keystone advantage: What the new dynamics of business ecosystems mean for strategy, innovation, and sustainability. *Academy of Management Executive, 20*(2), 88–90. https://doi.org/10.5465/AMP.2006.20591015.
Iivari, M. (2016). *Exploring business models in ecosystemic contexts* (Doctoral dissertation). Retrieved from http://jultika.oulu.fi/files/isbn9789526212401.pdf
Iivari, M., Ahokangas, P., Komi, M., Tihinen, M., & Valtanen, K. (2016). Toward ecosystemic business models in the context of industrial internet. *Journal of Business Models, 4*(2), 42–59. https://doi.org/10.5278/ojs.jbm.v4i2.1624.
Isenberg, D. J. (2010). How to start an entrepreneurial revolution. *Harvard Business Review, 88*(6), 40–50.

Jacobides, M. G., Cennamo, C., & Gawer, A. (2018). Towards a theory of ecosystems. *Strategic Management Journal, 39*(8), 2255–2276. https://doi.org/10.1002/smj.2904.
Johnson, M. W., Christensen, C. M., & Kagermann, H. (2008). Reinventing your business model. *Harvard Business Review, 86*(12), 57–68.
Kamoun, F. (2008). Rethinking the business model with RFID. *Communications of the AIS, 22*(1), 635–658. https://doi.org/10.17705/1CAIS.02235.
Klatzky, R. L. (1998). *Allocentric and egocentric spatial representations: Definitions, distinctions, and interconnections*. Berlin: Springer. https://doi.org/10.1007/3-540-69342-4_1.
Libert, B., Beck, M., & Wind, J. (2016). *The network imperative: How to survive and grow in the age of digital business models*. Harvard: Harvard Business Review Press.
Linder, J., & Cantrell, S. (2000). Carved in water: Changing business models fluidly. *Accenture Institute for Strategic Change Research Report, 12*, 1–13.
Lüftenegger, E. (2014). *Service-dominant business design* (Doctoral dissertation). Retrieved from https://research.tue.nl/en/publications/service-dominant-business-design. https://doi.org/10.6100/IR774591
Lusch, R. F., & Nambisan, S. (2015). Service innovation: A service-dominant logic perspective. *MIS Quarterly, 39*, 155–175. https://doi.org/10.25300/MISQ/2015/39.1.07.
Lusch, R. F., & Vargo, S. L. (2014). Service dominant logic. Premises, perspectives, possibilities [Kindle DX version]. Retrieved from Amazon.com
Maglio, P. P., & Spohrer, J. (2013). A service science perspective on business model innovation. *Industrial Marketing Management, 42*(5), 665–670. https://doi.org/10.1016/j.indmarman.2013.05.007.
Magretta, J. (2002). Why business models matter. *Harvard Business Review, 80*(5), 86–92.
Manning, B., & Thorne, C. (2002). *Demand driven: Six steps to creating an ecosystem of demand for your business*. New York: McGraw-Hill.
Mars, M. M., Bronstein, J. L., & Lusch, R. F. (2012). The value of a metaphor: Organizations and ecosystems. *Organizational Dynamics, 41*(4), 271–280. https://doi.org/10.1016/j.orgdyn.2012.08.002.
McKinsey & Company. (2008). *Winning in digital ecosystems*. Digital McKinsey, 3. Retrieved from https://www.mckinsey.com/business-functions/digital-mckinsey/our-insights/digital-mckinsey-insights/digital-mckinsey-insights-number-3
Moore, J. (1993). Predators and prey: A new ecology of competition. *Harvard Business Review, 71*, 75–86.
Moore, J. (1996). *The death of competition*. New York: Harper Business.
Nalebuff, B. J., Brandenburger, A., & Maulana, A. (1996). *Co-opetition*. London: Harper Collins Business.
Normann, R. (2001). *Reframing business: When the map changes the landscape*. Chichester: Wiley. https://doi.org/10.1108/09564230410523367.
Österle, H., & Otto, B. (2010). Consortium research: A method for researcher-practitioner collaboration in design-oriented IS research. *Business & Information Systems Engineering, 2*(5), 283–293. https://doi.org/10.1007/s12599-010-0119-3.
Osterwalder, A. (2004). *The business model ontology: A proposition in a design science approach* (Doctoral dissertation). Retrieved from http://www.hec.unil.ch/aosterwa/PhD/Osterwalder_PhD_BM_Ontology.pdf
Osterwalder, A., & Pigneur, Y. (2010). *Business model generation: A handbook for visionaries, game changers, and challengers*. Hoboken, NJ: Wiley.
Osterwalder, A., & Pigneur, Y. (2013). Designing business models and similar strategic objects: The contribution of IS. *Journal AIS, 14*, 237–244. https://doi.org/10.17705/1jais.00333.
Osterwalder, A., Pigneur, Y., & Tucci, C. L. (2005). Clarifying business models: Origins, present, and future of the concept. *Communications of the Association for Information Systems, 16*(1). https://doi.org/10.12691/jbms-3-2-4.
Parker, G., Alstyne, M. V., & Jiang, X. (2017). Platform ecosystems: How developers invert the firm. *MIS Quarterly, 41*(1), 255–266. https://doi.org/10.25300/MISQ/2017/41.1.13.

Peltoniemi, M. (2004, September). Cluster, value network and business ecosystem: Knowledge and innovation approach. In *Organisations, innovation and complexity: New perspectives on the knowledge economy conference* (pp. 9–10).

Picot, A., Ripperger, T., & Wolff, B. (1996). The fading boundaries of the firm: The role of information and communication technology. *Journal of Institutional and Theoretical Economics, 152*, 65–79.

Razo-Zapata, I. S., De Leenheer, P., Gordijn, J., & Akkermans, H. (2012). Fuzzy verification of service value networks. In J. Ralyte, X. Franch, S. Brinkkemper, & S. Wrycza (Eds.), *International conference on advanced information systems engineering* (pp. 95–110). Berlin: Springer. https://doi.org/10.1007/978-3-642-31095-9_7.

Rothschild, M. (1990). *Bionomics: Economy as business ecosystem.* Washington: Beard Books.

Schallmo, D. (2013). *Geschäftsmodell-Innovation: Grundlagen, bestehende Ansätze, methodisches Vorgehen und B2B-Geschäftsmodelle.* Wiesbaden: Springer. https://doi.org/10.1007/978-3-658-00245-9.

Shapiro, C., Varian, H. R., & Becker, W. E. (1999). Information rules: A strategic guide to the network economy. *Journal of Economic Education, 30*, 189–190. https://doi.org/10.1080/00220489909595956.

Sinfield, J. V., Calder, E., McConnell, B., & Colson, S. (2012). How to identify new business models. *MIT Sloan Management Review, 53*(2), 85.

Storbacka, K., Frow, P., Nenonen, S., & Payne, A. (2012). Designing business models for value co-creation. In *Special issue – Toward a better understanding of the role of value in markets and marketing* (pp. 51–78). Bingley: Emerald Group Publishing. https://doi.org/10.1108/S1548-6435(2012)0000009007.

Sull, D. L., & Ruelas-Gossi, A. (2010). Strategic orchestration. *Business Strategy Review, 21*(4), 58–63. https://doi.org/10.1111/j.1467-8616.2010.00707.x.

Teece, D. J. (2010). Business models, business strategy and innovation. *Long Range Planning, 43* (2), 172–194. https://doi.org/10.1016/j.lrp.2009.07.003.

Tiwana, A. (2013). *Platform ecosystems: Aligning architecture, governance, and strategy.* Boston, MA: Newnes.

Triandis, H. C., & Suh, E. M. (2002). Cultural influences on personality. *Annual Review of Psychology, 53*(1), 133–160. https://doi.org/10.1146/annurev.psych.53.100901.135200.

Vargo, S. L., & Akaka, M. A. (2012). Value cocreation and service systems (re) formation: A service ecosystems view. *Service Science, 4*(3), 207–217. https://doi.org/10.1287/serv.1120.0019.

Vargo, S. L., & Lusch, R. F. (2004). Evolving to a new dominant logic for marketing. *Journal of Marketing, 68*(1), 1–17. https://doi.org/10.1509/jmkg.68.1.1.24036.

Vargo, S. L., & Lusch, R. F. (2008). Service-dominant logic: Continuing the evolution. *Journal of the Academy of Marketing Science, 36*(1), 1–10. https://doi.org/10.1007/s11747-007-0069-6.

Vargo, S. L., & Lusch, R. F. (2011). It's all B2B... and beyond: Toward a systems perspective of the market. *Industrial Marketing Management, 40*(2), 181–187. https://doi.org/10.1016/j.indmarman.2010.06.026.

Vargo, S. L., & Lusch, R. F. (2016). Institutions and axioms: An extension and update of service-dominant logic. *Journal of the Academy of Marketing Science, 44*(1), 5–23. https://doi.org/10.1007/s11747-015-0456-3.

Vargo, S. L., & Lusch, R. F. (2018). *The SAGE handbook of service-dominant logic.* New York: Sage.

Voima, P., Heinonen, K., Strandvik, T., Mickelsson, K.-J., & Arantola-Hattab, J. (2011). A customer ecosystem perspective on service. In *QUIS 12: Advances in service quality, innovation and excellence* (pp. 1015–1024).

Williamson, P. J., & De Meyer, A. (2012). Ecosystem advantage: How to successfully harness the power of partners. *California Management Review, 55*(1), 24–46. https://doi.org/10.1525/cmr.2012.55.1.24.

Wirtz, B. W., Pistoia, A., Ullrich, S., & Göttel, V. (2016). Business models: Origin, development and future research perspectives. *Long Range Planning, 49*, 36–54. https://doi.org/10.1016/j.lrp.2015.04.001.
Yoo, Y., Henfridsson, O., & Lyytinen, K. (2010). Research commentary—The new organizing logic of digital innovation: An agenda for information systems research. *Information Systems Research, 21*(4), 724–735. https://doi.org/10.1287/isre.1100.0322.
Zolnowski, A. (2015). *Analysis and design of service business models* (Doctoral dissertation. Retrieved from https://owl.purdue.edu/owl/research_and_citation/apa_style/apa_formatting_and_style_guide/reference_list_other_print_sources.html
Zott, C., Amit, R., & Massa, L. (2011). The business model: Recent developments and future research. *Journal of Management, 37*(4), 1019–1042. https://doi.org/10.1177/0149206311406265.

Marc Burkhalter is a PhD student at the Institute of Information Systems at the University of St. Gallen and co-author of this paper. As part of his dissertation project, he is working on business modeling in the context of ecosystems. In collaboration with the Business Engineering Institute, the Ecosystem Design Toolkit was developed in this context, which supports companies in business modeling within ecosystems. https://ccecosystems.news/ecosystems-positionierungsmoeglichkeiten-fuer-die-finanzindustrie/

Christian Betz is research associate and PHD candidate at Business Engineering Institute St. Gallen. His focus is on value creation and the underlying value infrastructure within Business Ecosystems. This includes the design of artifacts related to orchestration of value co-creation as well as collaborative process models according to the design science research approach. He has accumulated project experience in the areas of Distributed Ledger Technology/Blockchain, Ecosystem development, and Digital Transformation with financial services providers in Switzerland, Germany and Turkey.

Stefanie Auge-Dickhut, Main Research Themes: Financial Industry & Ecosystems, AI & DLT, Client Centric Banking, Sustainability, Valuation. Prof. Dr. Stefanie Auge-Dickhut is Head of CC Ecosystems at the Business Engineering Institute St. Gallen. Within the scope of application-oriented research, models, solutions and prototypes in the field of ecosystems, digital transformation and innovative technologies in the field of artificial intelligence (AI) and blockchain/distributed ledger technologies (DLT) are developed for partners from the financial industry.

Reinhard Jung is Professor of Business Engineering at the University of St. Gallen (HSG) and Director of the Institute of Information Systems and Director of the Institute for Information Systems (IWI-HSG). Academic Director of the Executive MBA HSG in Business Engineering and Executive Diploma HSG in IT Business Management and Head of the Master Program Business Innovation. Board member of SIRA (Swiss Informatics Research Association). His research interests are business engineering, change management, business intelligence, data and integration management and customer relationship management. He is a speaker at national and international conferences on current business engineering as well as social CRM topics.

Part VI
Blockchain, Chryptoeconomics and Sustainability

Change Through Crypto-Economics

Michal Natora

Abstract Blockchains incentivize the network participants to stick to the rules of the network by creating economic benefits to them. That mechanism drives change on the level of each network participant through a pure voluntary opt in mechanism, and it changes how networks are operated. On the latter, centralized networks are transformed into open markets. In particular, current financial and energy networks can be replaced by networks run by communities resulting in the emergence of sustainable societies.

Keywords Blockchain · Impact SDGs · Sustainable development goals · Theory of change · Theories of change

1 Introduction

This article is about how blockchains can be used to steer behavior towards sustainability. To this end, firstly a blockchain is analyzed not only as a novel protocol technology but as an economic system: Creation of blockchain networks is equivalent to creation of incentive structures in self-sustaining economies. Next, applications of blockchains to sustainable financing and renewable energy are discussed.

2 What Is a Blockchain?

The concept of a blockchain was derived from Bitcoin which was invented by an anonymous person or collective, under the name of Satoshi Nakamoto. More recently, the term "distributed ledger technology" became popularized supposedly as a generalization to blockchain, as it also aims to encompass chains other than

M. Natora (✉)
Emerald Technology Ventures AG, Zürich, Switzerland
e-mail: michal.natora@emerald-ventures.com

K. Wendt (ed.), *Theories of Change*, Sustainable Finance,
https://doi.org/10.1007/978-3-030-52275-9_17

proof-of-work for example methods based on directed acyclic graphs. In this article we will stick to the term blockchain, as in our opinion the term "distributed ledger technology" overly highlights the "ledger" aspect. Distributed ledgers or more generally distributed databases have been around for a long time, and the innovative aspect around blockchain is not that data is stored redundantly in many distributed ledgers. The innovative part is how network participants interact with each other. In particular, a blockchain allows the enforcement of rules between network participants without having to resort to third parties or middlemen.

Let us illustrate how a blockchain works with an example, which will also demonstrate why a blockchain...

1. ...is a trust generator
2. ...is an incentive machine

Say we have three parties trading goods with each other and which want to run some logistics software in order to keep track of who sent which good to whom, when it was shipped and delivered etc.

With pre-blockchain technology it is likely that due to trust and security reasons each party will keep their data in its own database/cloud, and also keep track of the data it got from the other parties in order to reconstruct the data flow and interdependencies. Communication between the various clouds might happen through some APIs (application programming interface) which, might differ for each cloud and which are provisioned on a completely voluntary basis by each party.

On the other hand, with a blockchain based system, standardization is achieved. Every party is storing and exchanging data according to the same protocol, and the data is kept as a record immutably in the distributed ledger; see Fig. 1. Hence, a blockchain is a trust generator; it creates trust in the code and data for all parties in the network.

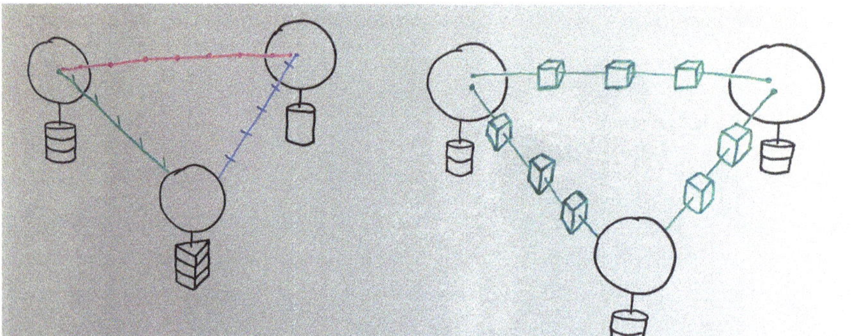

Fig. 1 Left-hand side: Three parties interacting with each other through various APIs and each party storing data in a different format/database. Right-hand side: Three parties interacting with each other through a blockchain. Communication and data storage are standardized through binding protocol rules [Illustration allowed to be modified/re-created by Springer in order to fit design requirements]

At the same time, because there is no central authority, every network participant has to contribute to the working of the blockchain. This is the reason why a network token comes into play and is the currency of the blockchain network. It is rewarded to parties which validate and execute code, store data and so on (in case of the logistics example, this could be storing of shipment data and execution of contracts such as confirmation notices and payments whenever a good arrives at certain locations, such as at an interim storage facility or at the final customer). On the other hand, parties who want to access the network, e.g. ask about the status of a good or want to view a shipment contract, have to pay for that by expending tokens. Hence, blockchains are incentive machines; they incentivize users with token rewards to contribute useful work to the network and ask for tokens from users who want to consume the network's services.

From the last aspect it also directly follows that blockchains lead naturally to a monetization of networks. Useful work to the network has to be rewarded in order to sustain the operations of the network. As a consequence, the network cannot be for free but requires a mechanism for distributing tokens to parties who provide useful work to the network and conversely a mechanism for requesting tokens from parties who claim work from the network (this includes punishment by subtracting tokens from parties who attack the network).

3 How Blockchain Links to Economics

Economic theories are based on concepts such as supply and demand, monetary economics (e.g. unit of account) and game theory (and more broadly agent-based modeling).

On the other hand, the fundamental concepts on which blockchain is based are all coming from pure mathematics and computer science, most notably from cryptography, such as public key encryption, zero-knowledge proofs, hash algorithms, and Merkle trees.

The interesting thing is that a blockchain network turns out to be a self-sustaining system, and as such can be viewed as a closed economy; this is the reason why the design and analysis of blockchain networks is also being called "crypto-economics". Some high-level relationships between blockchains and economics are summarized in Fig. 2.

In particular, a blockchain network has a token which is the native currency of the network and is used to get services from the network. The network participants correspond to the agents from economic theory. Every network participant is forming its own opinion about what value he/she sees in the services of the network. In conjunction with the rules of token supply (issuance rates, limits, token burns, . . .) network participants value the token individually, which on an aggregate level leads to a market value of the token and of the associated network functionality.

Each network participant might have a different motivation, same as agents in an economy can have different profit functions. However, through the concept that a

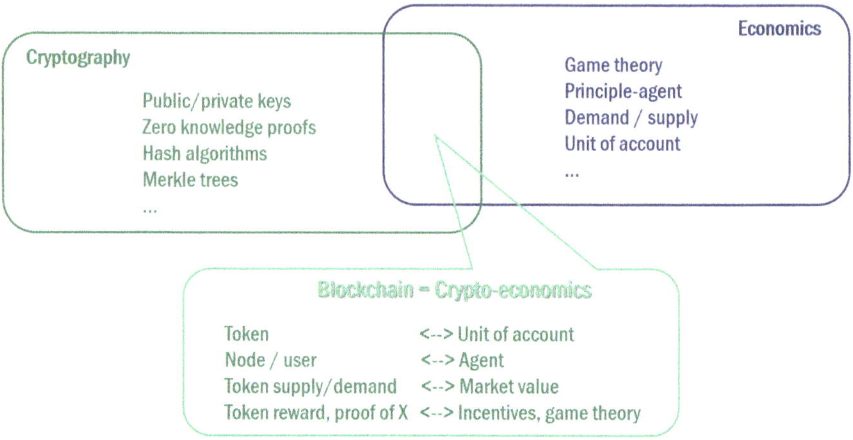

Fig. 2 A blockchain can be viewed as a self-sustaining economy. Designing and analysing blockchain networks is an interdisciplinary task of combining technical knowledge from cryptography with economic knowledge. The latter is needed for understanding incentive structures and resulting behaviour of network participants [Illustration allowed to be modified/re-created by Springer in order to fit design requirements]

blockchain creates incentives and penalties by rewarding or subtracting tokens, a blockchain steers the behavior of the network participants. Since each individual network participant has limited knowledge about the motivation of the other network participants (similarly as in game theory), it is difficult for the participants to collude and attack the network, or generally to work against the rules of the blockchain network.

In other words, the main protection of a blockchain network is the absence of incentives to perform an attack against it. An attacker would need to dedicate substantial resources and accumulate a large portion of the networks' tokens only to try to harm the network. Even if the attack was successful, it would undermine the value of the network at the moment the attack is exposed, leaving the attacker with a large number of worthless tokens; hence, the attacker has limited potential to gain direct financial benefit from an attack.

In summary, it makes much more economic sense for every network participant to contribute to the network and adhere to its protocol rules than to try to work against its rules. Blockchains incentivize the network participants to stick to the rules of the network by creating economic benefits to them.

4 How Blockchains Can Be Used to Drive Change

A blockchain can be used for driving change on two levels. The first one is the level of the individual network participant. Secondly, blockchains also fundamentally change the structure of networks.

4.1 Blockchain as a Driver to Change User Behavior

In the previous section we have seen that there is a link between blockchain and economics. Blockchain networks can be viewed in the same way as closed economies, hence when designing and building a blockchain network, the key question becomes what goal one wants to achieve within the network. The task is then to design crypto-economic primitives, that is the reward and penalty mechanisms relying on the token of the network, such that in the end the network participants will be incentivized to exhibit behavior converging towards the set goal of the network.

Previously, we were talking very generally about "network participants", referring to any entity somehow participating or being part of a blockchain network. One can distinguish three layers in a blockchain network and their associated network participants. For each layer we also mention some of the crypto-economic primitives that were developed so far.

Technology layer: This is the layer of computer nodes that run the network according to the blockchain protocol, execute the code, validate transactions and store data. Token rewards are distributed for providing the basic functionality of the network for it to operate. Some crypto-economic primitives that were developed are proof-of-work, proof-of-stake-time, delegated proof-of-stake, proof-of-space, proof-of-replication, and others.

User layer: This layer entails the interaction between the various users[1] enabled through the blockchain network. Token rewards are distributed to users for contributing to the network and subtracted for utilizing network services. Some of the known blockchain projects rely on crypto-economic primitives such as curated registry, curved bonding, curated proof markets, data transmission and others.

On-chain governance layer: The on-chain governance layer describes how changes regarding the very goal of the blockchain network are made. In particular, crypto-economic primitives such as voting and bounty mechanisms can be used to reward users for proposing ideas for network evolvement, active decision making, and for contributing new functionality or improving existing code.

Crypto-economic primitives can be viewed as the elemental units from which blockchain networks are built. The design of crypto-economic primitives on each layer and their combination across layers allows creating incentive mechanisms and resulting behavior of network participants in a similar way as in economies driven by market forces and regulations.

[1]Users can be humans or machines.

4.2 *Blockchain as a Driver to Change Network Topology*

Many systems surrounding us can be viewed as networks (e.g. by viewing the vertices as representing entities/people/organizations and the edges as representing a relationship between them). Examples include financial networks, logistics networks, social networks, transportation networks, etc.

Currently, most of those networks are centralized in the sense that there is an entity with elevated power which essentially operates and controls the network. Examples of such centralized entities are the central bank (in a financial network), a utility company (in an electricity network), a corporation (in an online social network), etc.

In existing networks, it is the central authority which provides most of the network services, and the network participants have to pay for them either with a fiat currency or with another resource desired by the central authority (such as your attention, your data, etc.).

In the previous section we have seen that a blockchain network cannot be free: a blockchain tokenizes the network and as such a native currency is introduced. This changes the topology of the network. The function of the central authority is replaced by meritocratic contribution of each network participant. Network participants do not have to rely on an external unit of account anymore, but all native services to the network are denominated in the native token which can be earned through network contribution (Fig. 3).

There are of course examples of networks operated by communities. What those community-driven networks have in common with centralized networks is that they are not self-sustaining: Meritocratic participation in the network is rarely possible and the unit of account is an external currency on which the network has no influence, most notably a fiat currency.

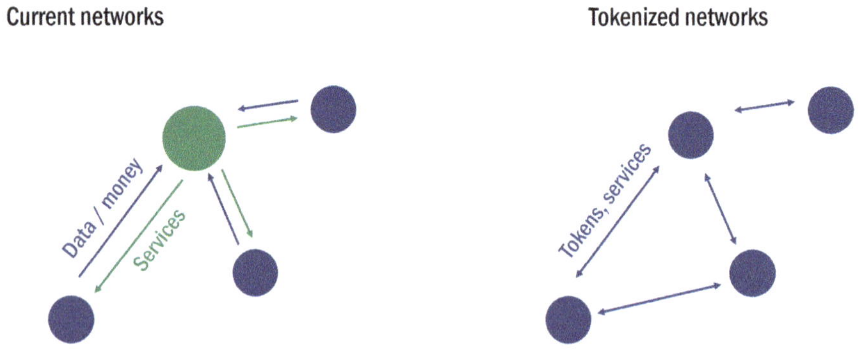

Fig. 3 Left-hand side: Current networks are operated by a central authority, which provides services to the other network participants in exchange for fiat money. Right-hand side: Blockchain networks allow the meritocratic participation of all network participants. The native network token is used to track and compensate for the merit of each network participant [Illustration allowed to be modified/re-created by Springer in order to fit design requirements]

For community-driven networks which have to rely on contributions from volunteers or finance themselves through donations, blockchain gives the opportunity to transition to a self-sustaining model where consumption of network services and contribution to the network are balanced through the market value of the token.

In summary, a blockchain

3. . . . is a mechanism to transform networks into open markets.

Blockchains allow everyone to contribute to the network on a meritocratic basis. The token of the blockchain network is used to track the contribution of every network participant. Since each blockchain will have different crypto-economic primitives and requires different kind of contributions, different blockchains rely on different tokens.

5 Examples of Blockchains for Change Towards Sustainability

5.1 Sustainable Monetary System

Money should be sound, that is money should be hard to produce. This concept has proven to work over centuries and mankind used technology available at that time best suited for sound money, such as wampum, large rocks or precious metals. If money is not sound, this ultimately leads to some party simply creating money, from which, however, only that party and the initial receivers benefit (this is called the Cantillon effect), whereas the value of the savings held by other parties erodes. In essence, money should be the measurement stick that measures the economic activity of a nation or society, not a good which quantity can be manipulated arbitrarily. However, this is exactly what happened since the introduction of fiat currencies which allowed nation states to finance unstainable spending through ever-growing debt. Easy money does not benefit the society, instead, it allows wealth that was earned by individuals through hard work to be exchanged for something that is easy to produce.

Hence, we think that the very first blockchain, namely Bitcoin, is actually one of the most significant disruptions which will have the largest positive impact on sustainable behavior. Bitcoin is currently the technologically most advanced form of money offering a mathematical guarantee of soundness while at the same its large base of network participants makes it censorship resistant.

Using the notions from section "Blockchain as a driver to change user behavior" the crypto-economic primitives of Bitcoin are as following: On the technology layer, computer nodes are rewarded with bitcoins (the native token of the Bitcoin protocol) for ordering valid transactions into blocks. On the user layer, users have to pay for using the Bitcoin network, i.e. whenever they want to send a transaction a transaction fee has to be paid. Bitcoin does not have an on-chain governance layer; all changes to the protocol are adopted on a purely voluntary basis.

The impact of Bitcoin on the level of an individual is that people could have their savings in form of sound money, allowing them to focus on their work and creating value. Instead, the inflationary pressure of current fiat currencies leads individuals to spend time thinking on how to protect their wealth and seeking speculative investments which have to yield returns beating inflation. In short, sound money protects wealth across time and as such lowers the time preference of individuals. Lower time preference is equivalent with long-term thinking and sustainable decision making. It is long-term thinking that allows the building of societies which cooperate with each other and which care about issues which seem to be far in the future such as the impact of global warming. In addition, a return to sound money would stop states from being able to compete unsustainably through conflicts (including artificial currency devaluations and market-distorting subsidies) financed by printing money for prolonged periods.

5.2 Renewable Energy

In contrast to financial networks, energy networks are networks in which the physical network component plays a significant role. There are parties who own the physical assets encompassing the energy generator units, transmission grids, and substations. Hence, we do not think that blockchain can disrupt the energy industry completely, however, there is a trend to decentralized energy especially in renewables, which is in line with the decentralized nature of blockchain. So what is the additional benefit blockchain can bring to a decentralized renewable energy network?

Again, the tokenization of an energy network can be used to incentivize the behavior of network participants towards a set goal without having to rely on an external unit of account. For example, on the user layer token rewards can be distributed to users who generate renewable energy in excess of self-consumption, to users who provide energy storage capacity to the grid and to users who provide other services beneficial to the network (e.g. cleaning of solar panels). The crypto-economic primitives could be designed in such a way, that the goal of the network is to achieve a self-sustaining energy network, i.e. the community does not have to rely on external energy supply or operations services.

Blockchain in energy networks enables some further use cases:

- Energy generating and storing equipment could be sold to new network participants with a discount, i.e. the token wallet of the equipment would contain a negative token balance. Once those network participants start contributing to the network, the initially rewarded tokens (through generated energy or provided energy storage) are offset against the initial discount. Such a pre-financing mechanism allows lowering the entry barriers to join a network, even if the network prerequisites a capital-intensive hardware component.

- Once data from a trusted source (e.g. a smart meter or sensor running a blockchain light client in a trusted environment) enters the blockchain, it gives network participants transparency and trust about its origin. Hence, generated energy could have trusted attributes such as time of generation, source and condition of generation (e.g. wind turbine model, location of turbine, wear condition/efficiency of the turbine, etc.) and also information about the owner and operator of the energy generating unit. This would allow users to value energy based on attributes, e.g. users could pay above average prices for energy which was for example generated in their vicinity or on the premises of a school.

The lastly mentioned use case of blockchain could partially solve the current challenge that a lot of consumers simply do not care about their energy and view it as a brandless commodity. In contrast, people do care about communities and associated value systems. Hence, the possibility to connect in the energy network in a similar way as in other social networks based on attributes would allow the transition from consuming a commodity to supporting and participating in a community with which the user can identify.

6 Implications of Blockchain on Investing and Conclusion

Blockchains are self-sustaining economies and allow the transformation of existing centralized networks into open markets. In contrast to the existing networks, such open markets function on a meritocratic basis by network participation and do not rely on a central authority nor on fiat money. Such a transformation could have profound implications as today's societies and governments are built on many layers of mostly centralized networks.

From an investor point of view, blockchain is a further step towards the democratization of finance:

- As with every other good, users should have a choice in selecting their preferred money. Bitcoin is already competing with fiat currencies. Especially in countries with high inflation or where the financial network is abused by the government or by corporations to censor unwanted opinions, Bitcoin is adopted quickly. Sound and censorship resistant money is essential for personal freedom as well as for the sustainable development of societies.
- The financing of projects and private enterprises were already partially democratized through the rise of crowd-financing, crowd-investing and crowd-lending platforms. Blockchains not only allow the financing through a community, but they also allow a meritocratic contribution to the project. This will allow the realization of more projects, and will also allow people to contribute and earn an income from projects they are truly passionate about.

- Current trading systems of fiat currencies and of securities are expensive (due to intermediaries), slow (due to opening only during business hours on weekdays) and risky (the user does not actually own the security, but it is a company such as Cede & Co. or a custodian bank who keeps ownership). In contrast, blockchain tokens are tradeable in a peer-to-peer way, allowing for trading around the clock and for direct ownership of the asset by the users. Such increased efficiency and security will lead to more investment inflows and consequently more financing for innovative projects.

All of this is also beneficial to financing decentralized renewable energy projects. In addition, depending on how the crypto-economic primitives are designed, blockchains can incentivize users to contribute work useful to the energy network. In the end, currency is language for value sharing. Tokens, hence, are a way of getting users involved into communities they care about and incentivize continuous participation.

Current developments suggest that decentralization enabled by blockchain will change the current value sharing structures towards open meritocratic networks; terms such as "Internet of Value" are being already formed to describe this new reality. Second order and higher order effects of this transition have yet to fully emerge, but they will likely have an even more significant contribution to the development of sustainable societies, similarly as it was observed from previous major technological revolutions.

Disclaimer The views and opinions expressed in this article are those of the author and do not necessarily reflect the official policy or position of Emerald Technology Ventures AG.

References

This article draws on ideas developed in:

https://medium.com/paratii/on-the-immaturity-of-tokenized-value-capture-mechanisms-1fde33f2bc8e
https://blog.coinbase.com/the-emergence-of-cryptoeconomic-primitives-14ef3300cc10
https://blog.oceanprotocol.com/can-blockchains-go-rogue-5134300ce790
https://twitter.com/naval/status/877467629308395521
The Bitcoin Standard: The Decentralized Alternative to Central Banking; Saifedean Ammous; April 2018; ISBN: 978-1-119-47386-2.
https://ruben.verborgh.org/blog/2017/12/20/paradigm-shifts-for-the-decentralized-web/#decentralization-as-the-way-forward-p-3
https://medium.com/@sebnem/parte-finale-the-energy-tokens-5b5f7c4fdacd
https://solarcoin.org/wp-content/uploads/SolarCoin_Policy_Paper_EN-1.pdf
https://hackernoon.com/a-primer-on-ethereum-blockchain-light-clients-20d715255ff0
http://www.iflr.com/Article/3807306/Blockchain-could-transform-securities-transfer-systems.html

Dr. Michal Natora Based in the Zurich office, Michal Natora is the Investment Director in Industrial Information Technology at Emerald Technology Ventures. Within this sector he performs sourcing, evaluation and due diligence. Moreover, Michal is responsible for developing and providing open innovation services for Emerald's corporate investors who are looking for strategic value in addition to financial returns. Prior to joining Emerald in 2014, Michal worked as a consultant for Daimler. He was responsible for managing the quality of software development and data generation processes for electronic control units. Prior to that, Michal was a scientist for three years at the neural information processing group of the TU Berlin where he conducted research in signal processing, stochastic optimization and machine learning. Michal holds a MBE from the Steinbeis Center of Management and Technology which included seminars at the Jönköping International Business School, Kelley School of Business and SKK Graduate School of Business. He received his PhD from the TU Berlin and completed his Diploma in Physics at the ETH Zurich and Ecole Polytechnique in Palaiseau.

Blockchain and Sustainable Development Goals: From Blue Skies Estimates of Impact to Bottom-Up Essentials

Katherine A. Foster, Deanna MacDonald, and Marc Johnson

Abstract This chapter takes a "Theory of Change" approach in examining the opportunities and challenges of blockchain in sustainable development and social impact. It addresses the manner in which both the discourse and the use cases of blockchain and initiatives related to sustainable development and social impact have evolved, from the discourse of the Pillar of the 4th Industrial Revolution and the effects of the silicon valley "style" ventures, the overestimation of "market opportunity", the conflation and confounding of different of types of blockchain initiatives and offerings combined with key assumptions about readiness and capacity not only of the technological elements—as blockchain as a "ready service"—but also within the social impact and sustainable development landscape. It then examines key use cases and loops back to address the key needs and barriers for scaling up (As opposed to the issues surrounding technical transactional scaling issues related to the need for blockchain platforms to process hundreds of thousands of transactions per second as well as the increased need for miners, developers, businesses and other stakeholders) of blockchain solutions and impact in sustainable development.

Keywords Theory of change · Theories of change · SDGs · Sustainable development goals · Blockchain

---

K. A. Foster (✉)
Green Digital Finance Alliance (GDFA), Geneva, Switzerland
e-mail: fosterkat@gmail.com

D. MacDonald
BLOC, Copenhagen, Denmark
e-mail: deanna@un-bloc.com

M. Johnson
Bunker Trace, Westminster, London, UK
e-mail: marc@bunkertrace.co

K. Wendt (ed.), *Theories of Change*, Sustainable Finance,
https://doi.org/10.1007/978-3-030-52275-9_18

1 Blockchain Use in Sustainable Development

The Blockchain for Sustainable development landscape which we define as distributed ledger technology projects, initiatives and discourse across any of the Sustainable Development Goals, has changed dramatically in the 3 years since the emerging technology received global attention for its potential implications on the economy, business, and government at the World Economic Forum in 2017. A 20-year vision of adoption was optimistically delineated across all facets of the real economy wherein businesses and governments would be able to achieve unprecedented efficiency, with global operations and supply chains fundamentally reorganized, enabled by new business and service models and relationships.[1] Blockchain promised to offer approaches and solutions not possible using other technologies or systems, and a unique opportunity to simultaneously create accountability, transparency, and security of systems, especially appealing at a moment when trust in institutions was in question and continues to decline.[2]

While several use cases had been propagated, the WEF 2017 marked a new wave of blockchain for sustainable development scoping, development, dialogue and speculation across economic sectors, and stakeholders. For sustainable development, the vision focused on specific areas where the most activities and impact were likely to occur. These included but were not limited to "utilities or renewable energy developers seeking a more efficient way of pricing and selling clean power; at consumer products companies and retailers seeking a better way of validating supply-chain claims; and among banks and insurance companies interested in verifying the provenance of minerals, commodities or raw materials.[3] In addition, key potentials for impact investment, for emerging markets, and for financial inclusion as viable business strategies[4] were highlighted.

While applications and use cases specifically aligned with the Sustainable Development Goals have been growing and organizations are investing more in emerging technology and potential blockchain applications, scaled solutions remain limited, the concrete benefits have been challenging to demonstrate and the "revolutionary" capacity envisioned remains elusive. As suggested by Deloitte in its 2018 survey, a certain "Blockchain Fatigue" has set in among those who feel its capacity and potential has been over communicated.[5]

---

[1]Maguire, E. (19 January 2017). Global Financial Services Lead, Digital Ledger Services, The quiet hero: Blockchain at the WEF, https://www.weflive.com/#!/story/e9cfa9e0de8b11e6a1c6a7ee941bc7e8

[2]"We Need to Talk about Blockchain—Together." Inside Financial & Risk, 1 June 2018, blogs.thomsonreuters.com/sustainability/2018/06/01/we-need-to-talk-about-blockchain-together/

[3]Clancy, Heather. "The Blockchain's Emerging Role in Sustainability." GreenBiz, GreenBiz Group Inc., 6 Feb. 2017, www.greenbiz.com/article/blockchains-emerging-role-sustainability

[4]"Banks Can Grow Profitably in Emerging Economies by Being More Inclusive." The Future of Work|Accenture, https://www.accenture.com/us-en/insight-banks-grow-profitably-emerging-economies

[5]Deloitte Breaking blockchain open Deloitte's 2018 global blockchain survey, https://www2.deloitte.com/content/dam/Deloitte/us/Documents/financial-services/us-fsi-2018-global-blockchain-survey-report.pdf

1.1 *Blue Sky Estimation of "Market Opportunity" and Social Impact*

Despite the growing number of use cases, to date they have been too nascent to demonstrate tangible impact, and the **estimates of impact** for blockchain and sustainability were largely based on figures pulled from key institutional reports providing general "market opportunity" estimates for achieving the SDGs in the billions and even trillions. For example, a "*US$12 trillion in market opportunities in four economic systems: food and agriculture, cities, energy and materials, and health and well-being*" from the Better Business Better World report by the Business & Sustainable Development Commission, and a $380 Billion market opportunity in Financial Inclusion from Accenture and CARE International UK Study, were often cited in presentations and pitches. Yet, these figures and findings have no direct link to the role of blockchain in achieving them nor the relevancy and applicability of the technology within these areas.

BLOCKCHAIN IN VC

The venture capital community invested nearly 1 billion into Distributed Ledger Technology (Blockchain) related startups between 2014 and 2016 but Blockchain reached a new level of global attention for its implications on the economy, business, government, and the Sustainable Development Goals (SDGs), most notably at the World Economic Forum in 2017 where a 20-year vision of adoption was optimistically delineated

These and similar figures were held up as "estimated market" without addressing assumptions about technical capacity and resources, available data, interoperability between emerging technology and legacy systems, regulation, socio-political and even temporal considerations, among other key factors.[1] Instead, the estimates of inefficiencies, corruption, and the cumbersome centralized processes of legacy system and processes, or the absence thereof, were held up as the "new market opportunity" where theoretical blockchain builds were prominent and necessary processes, data and infrastructure readiness were assumed yet often absent.

The estimates also overlooked core governance elements as multi-stakeholder collaborations are required to combine and leverage the financial resources of actors across sectors to even achieve a fraction of the impact suggested. This is a key element outlined in the same reports being quoted, SDG 17 which calls for partnerships, concerted action, integrated models and collaboration across a range of sectors and stakeholders. The many "interdependencies, synergies and trade-offs across sectors, which affects investment requirements and financing needs" [2] as well as the capacity to deliver, were not factored in to the discourse on blockchain for SDGs and social impact.

The rise of crypto-economics and Initial Coin Offerings (ICOs) as SDG project crowdfunding, combined with the high failure rates of ICOs, the mismatched culture and incentives, the fundamental conceptual gap between investment requirements and the collaboration and integrated models required, all overshadowed if not derailed the opportunity for revolution in building and scaling real world sustainable development blockchain applications.

The role of blockchain in sustainable development has insofar resulted in a fundamental conceptual gap between the investment, governance and technical requirements necessary to achieve the promised impact. Arguably, this is due to the short time frame since initiatives began, combined with somewhat unrealistic expectations and understanding of the technology itself, the rise of short-term financial gain and mismatched incentives brought forward by Initial Coin Offerings as a means of raising SDG crowdfunding, the advent of cryptoeconomics which promised new incentives that have yet to be realized, and the immaturity of the technology at scale combined with its isolated development communities. This, in turn, has overshadowed if not derailed the true opportunity afforded for transformation within sustainable development, through feasible and tested blockchain applications, as but one part of the solution for impact and global change.

2 Why Blockchain?

2.1 Blockchain Basics

In simple terms, blockchain is predominantly described as a digital, distributed ledger that records transactions that take place across a peer-to-peer network. The societal innovation behind this technology is based on the theory that open immutable ledgers would enable transparent decision-making procedures and decentralized incentive systems for collaboration and cooperation. Generally, an open source technology, blockchain is positioned as a common, digital ledger secured with cryptography and shared via public and private keys. It can store verified digital tokens representing anything of value.

A real-time copy of this ledger is stored on thousands of computers worldwide making it decentralised and incorruptible. Protocols are built into this distributed ledger database that specifies the governing rules of the system generally for tracking and trading tokens to ultimately unlock new sources of value in society if connected to the physical world. Additionally, blockchain technology can increase the difficulty to hack the system to the degree of virtual impossibility. With the protocols for these systems being stored on thousands of different servers at the same time, it is not enough to hack just one server. The fault-tolerance of the system depends on the consensus mechanism employed. For instance, the consensus mechanism used for Bitcoin, the most widely known use of blockchain, more than 50% of the servers need to be hacked to enable a change of the information being stored.

There are three salient points that need to be made when demystifying and clarifying the often over-inflated properties and functions of blockchain. These are:

- First, this technology is in fact not a technology but, rather, it is a combination of several technologies and scientific tools that we have possessed for the greater half of this century that have also proven themselves previously on the market. What is unique and definitive about the blockchain movement, however, is how these technologies are combined to create a decentralised system that is designed, in theory, to be sovereign, incorruptible and globally accessible.
- Second, and an important point of departure is the issue of heterogeneity, in that that while many speak of 'THE blockchain', there in fact exist several different blockchains. There is no one agreed upon global standard, framework or best practices approach to the creation of these blockchains.
- Third, and each of these blockchains are currently operating in siloed environments from each other. There is little to no interoperability that exists between these solutions and this will be key going forward to transform the current system and not simply duplicate the current data silos and centralised, privatised data storage solutions available.

2.2 *Blockchain Opportunities*

Blockchain technology, being decentralized by nature, can enable communities of all sizes to reach consensus and "implement innovative forms of self-governance", provided that the rules of the system were developed inclusively with these communities. Essentially blockchain-based systems could be the key to changing market-based mechanisms dramatically, if implemented correctly.

These market mechanisms include potential for delivering productivity gains and connecting digital infrastructure across multiple industries, from supply chains, to energy markets and utilities, to the public sector, intellectual property management and more. In emerging markets, the use of blockchain could be highly attractive, enabling markets and capturing value creation that would otherwise be extracted, confined or otherwise too expensive to account for. Rather than replacing centralized digital infrastructure, a digital system founded upon blockchain could inherently enable physical infrastructure by providing security, access and self-governance. This would in theory allow the creation of lean capacity where no critical infrastructure exists or where it is highly cumbersome and fraught with challenges.

There are a number of regulatory and technical risks that still need to be worked through, which could challenge the success of its application at present. Some of these risk areas include its ability to be scaled, the security that underlies it, the data privacy and issues of governance. Due to the lack of governmental or regulatory oversight, caution needs to be taken when creating a new blockchain for use in any market, particularly within sustainable development initiatives and emerging markets. Especially with the hype since 2017 and its presence in the mainstream media, blockchain and cryptocurrencies have moved from something in which only "techies" participate to an inclusive global financial system where inventing a new form of digital currency has become real.

To be feasible in the long term, development needs to continue with compliance tools, wallets, hardware and payment gateways being further developed and built out. Since the technology is in it is infancy this development also needs to take place at its core infrastructure and governance mechanisms. Besides blockchain, cryptocurrencies can have great potential as in some developing countries (e.g. Venezuela), where bitcoin is more trusted than the local currency due to high inflation rates and government control. As no bank account but only an internet connection is required, this also gives access to the system to everyone.

While the ICO market has stemmed due to the falling prices of cryptocurrencies (extreme market fluctuations are common in this space), ICOs have traditionally been the focus of blockchain development and are simply a rebranding of crowdfunding models. Due to their infancy, they are essentially under regulated and unlicensed securities and do not necessarily mean real technology is being developed. Given the utopian visions set forth by the blockchain community for inclusive financial markets, distributed power structures and an alternative economic system to capitalism, the current ICO markets are at risk of reproducing and perpetuating the very same centralised system it sought to overturn. Beyond the moral and philosophical implications, ICOs and their potential for creating real-world value within society beyond get rich quick schemes, have yet to be proven.

3 Evolving Blockchain Landscape

In terms of blockchain applications and platforms, we have moved beyond digital currencies—from bitcoin to other cryptocurrencies, into the tokenization of other "assets" (diamonds, agricultural commodities, property and even identity) through to smart contracts which facilitate the exchange of digitized assets. This trajectory shows the evolution of underlying blockchain technology within a range of industry applications.

In addition, there are now many different blockchain applications and platforms on the market and in development, from simply being able to hold and transfer wealth throughout different cryptocurrencies, to transferring ownership of large assets such as land. These applications and platforms operate under different rules of access defined as public, private or semi-private terms that outline "permissions":

- Chains like bitcoin are "permissionless", meaning that anybody with a computer can view and access the blockchain.
- Permissioned systems allow certain users to do specific things on the blockchain, but these are not "open" for everyone to use.
- Each offers different advantages and perhaps disadvantages ranging across security, flexibility, scalability and energy efficiency.[6]

While there is a certain fluidity in the evolution of the blockchain landscape and the potential for its capacity continue to evolve – it has become a saturated, confusing and moreover, a highly speculative arena. This includes in relation to the emerging discourse and "offerings" for sustainable development and social IT being made through the blockchain industry.

The core common elements to any of these applications is the provision of a common database of transaction history (a digital ledger globally accessible within each network) which allows for accessibility, the cryptography (public and private keys) which offer security, and the Distributed Network (which allow transparency and accountability). This unique combination of features offers users a shared history of business network transactions, with a high degree of immutability. The real novelty of blockchain technology is that it is more than just a ledger of transaction history but that it can also set rules about a transaction (business logic)

[6]Morrissey, Erin, and Erin Morrissey. "*Breaking Down the Blockchain—Capital One Tech—Medium.*" *Medium.com. September 12, 2018*, https://medium.com/capital-one-tech/breaking-down-the-blockchain-f4b87422481b

that are tied to the transaction itself.[7] This contrasts with conventional databases, in which rules are often set at the entire database level, or in the application, but not in the transaction".[8] The ability to execute smart contracts semi-automatically (according to specific predetermined conditions and algorithms established by parties), along with transactional transparency (the ability to create secure, real-time networks with partners to communicate not only about monetary transactions but any data).

Combined, these capacities offer the potential of increasing efficiencies, reducing friction, lowering risks and costs, reducing leakage, fraud and eliminating double counting that offers an added value proposition to social impact and sustainable development applications. "It is about the algorithmic technologies that enable (Blockchain) and their power to transform ledgers as tools to record, enable and secure an enormous range of transactions."[9] In this way, blockchain holds the potential to help revitalize, if not overcome, cumbersome and disjointed indices, accounting, tracking and reporting capacity which can increase the possibility for more inclusive and effective means to drive fundamental shifts in connected value chains. Theoretical predictions point to more robust and interlinked effects—to a theory of change and systems—with a major role in sustainable development.

3.1 The Rise and Fall of the Whitepaper for Initial Coin Offerings

Initial Coin Offerings (ICOs) use blockchain technology to issue digital assets (usually referred to as tokens or coins) to investors rather than equity stakes. For the investor, the ICO offered an ability to quickly profit from something that is not open to taxation and being able to reinvest those profits to continually speculate to attain more. Organizations have been able to take risks due to the lack of regulatory oversight that would normally be underlying any security issuance.

In some countries, like the USA, a virtual currency is considered a form of a commodity and when they are traded to US dollars, they are subject to taxation. Rather than transfer their virtual currency to cash and be liable for taxation, it is possible to trade them to another form of virtual currency and avoid any capital gains tax. While investors in ICOs come from around the globe, by date of submission,

[7]Chuen, David Lee Kuo, and Robert Deng. *Handbook of Blockchain, Digital Finance, and Inclusion, Volume 2*, 2018, pp. xix-xxvi., doi:https://doi.org/10.1016/b978-0-12-812282-2.00029-2

[8]David LEE, Kuo Chuen (Editor), Robert H. Deng (Editor) (2018) *Handbook of Blockchain, Digital Finance, and Inclusion, Volume 2: ChinaTech, Mobile Security, and Distributed Ledger 1st Edition Academic Press. Pg. 306.*

[9]*Distributed Ledger Technology: beyond block chain A report by the UK Government Chief Scientific Adviser pg. 6 UK Government Report* https://assets.publishing.service.gov.uk/government/uploads/system/uploads/attachment_data/file/492972/gs-16-1-distributed-ledger-technology.pdf

they were overwhelmingly a North American phenomenon.[10] It is also important to note that most recent ICOs lacked revenues, customers and even product prototypes due to their early stages, so creative investors toyed with metrics such as the number of developers in the community and other purported indicators of development such as code commits.[11]

The whitepapers which back these ICOs are fraught with the potential for legal trouble, as they are expounded on theory that is more often than not, unregulated or banned in the consumer/reader's jurisdiction. They are vulnerable to speculation and exploitation and are virtually unregulated globally. As US SEC Chairman Jay Clayton noted in his statement on Cryptocurrencies and Initial Coin Offerings, the manner in which ICOs are currently operating means that "there is substantially less investor protection than in our traditional securities markets, with correspondingly greater opportunities for fraud and manipulation."[12] Indeed, while countries such as the USA, Russia and Singapore allow ICOs for fundraising under heavily regulated terms, most countries have yet to back the concept.[13]

4 Difference Between Crowdfunding and Using an ICO

In standard crowdfunding, participants do not expect a "return on investment" but with ICOs, at least two models are in use in the social impact landscape, one in which the participants receive a "token" in return for their contribution with the expectation that the token has the potential to grow in monetary value through crypto exchange. For the sustainable development and social impact space, the ICO seemingly offered "win-win" designs intended to revolutionize impact investment models by linking the value of the coin to the cost of delivering impact.[14] This brought new potential offers for both fundraisers and for investors. "The ICO illustrated the hope that anyone could be involved in both soliciting and investing in enterprise while

[10]see Galka, Max. "Token Sale Geography." Elementus. January 31, 2018, https://elementus.io/blog/token-sale-geography/. "Stats and Facts." ICObench. https://icobench.com/stats "CoinDesk ICO Tracker." CoinDesk. https://www.coindesk.com/ico-tracker

[11]Maguire E, Maguire E (2017) The big blockchain and ICO boom: have we seen this movie before? In: medium.com. https://medium.com/cryptolinks/the-big-blockchain-and-ico-boom-have-we-seen-this-movie-before-271330515735

[12]Initial Coin Offering (ICO) Mania and Its Implications for Technology-Led Social Enterprise. In: Center For Global Development. https://www.cgdev.org/blog/initial-coin-offering-ico-mania-and-its-implications-technology-led-social-enterprise

[13]ICO Regulations Guide: World's Initial Coin Offering Country By Country. (2018) In: BitcoinExchangeGuide. https://bitcoinexchangeguide.com/ico-regulations-guide-worlds-initial-coin-offering-country-by-country/

[14]The Real Game-Changer: Impact Investment and the Blockchain Iulian Circo In Medium June 5, 2017. https://medium.com/@icirco/the-real-game-changer-impact-investment-and-the-blockchain-c1e21e728b55

bypassing the hugely regulated, bureaucratized, and impenetrable apparatus of traditional financial markets, including rarefied venture capital funding".[15]

The start-ups involved in most of the ICOs conducted to date have been able to side-step the disclosure and investor protection requirements normally associated with securities issuance because regulation has naturally lagged behind technological innovation. This does not mean however, that regulators have been unaware of the need for ICO regulation. In fact, some countries such as Estonia are looking to use ICOs for their own fundraising. Nations across the globe are reviewing their positions on ICOs and the use of blockchain particularly and regulation is expected to be developed and initiated on a country by country basis as the risk relating to ICOs become known.[16] While ICO's come in a variety of type ***the weakness of these models mainly rest in the fact that, more times than not, the tokens do not fluidly interact with their underlying business models.***

The proposed blockchain revolution for sustainable development was detoured into the focus on ICOs and the process of investing and raising money in order to support—projects. But the hope has been tempered by the ongoing wave of ICO failures (with estimates of 59% for ICOs launched 2017 failing or "semi-failing" by February 2018[17] and more recent figures reaching even higher estimate).[18] This risk and failure rates have led to many countries and trading commissions to step up efforts to ensure companies cannot simply circumvent tried and tested regulatory frameworks. Countries such as China have banned ICOs outright[19] whereas others, such as Switzerland, offer help in navigating ICOs to innovators.[20]

5 The Conflation Issue

While ICO based solutions are still a long way from being able to prove the benefits that they purport to offer, there are blockchain based projects and initiatives that are beginning to demonstrate potential for global companies, organizations and perhaps

[15]August 18, 2018, Jeffrey Tucker in FORBES, Despite What You Hear, The ICO Is Not Over. https://www.forbes.com/sites/jeffreytucker/2018/08/18/despite-what-you-hear-the-ico-is-not-rip/#6459c9373192

[16]For a relatively recent overview in this rapidly shifting landscape. https://bitcoinexchangeguide.com/ico-regulations-guide-worlds-initial-coin-offering-country-by-country

[17]The Impact of Blockchain Technology on Finance: A Catalyst for Change, Geneva Reports on the World Economy 21 Michael Casey, Jonah Crane, Gary Gensler, Simon Johnson, Neha Narula *July 2018 VOX CEPR Policy Portal.* https://voxeu.org/article/blockchain-catalyst-change

[18]August 18, 2018, Jeffrey Tucker in FORBES, Despite What You Hear, The ICO Is Not Over. https://www.forbes.com/sites/jeffreytucker/2018/08/18/despite-what-you-hear-the-ico-is-not-rip/#6459c9373192

[19]https://www.cgdev.org/blog/initial-coin-offering-ico-mania-and-its-implications-technology-led-social-enterprise

[20]https://www.finma.ch/en/news/2018/02/20180216-mm-ico-wegleitung/

for impact investors.[21] A key consequence of the ICO rise and fall was that it detracted from the concrete initiatives and practical use cases in development and scaling phases and collaborative projects.

In fact, there was a conflation of blockchain technology applications (ICO, crypto currencies with concrete blockchain builds and use cases) which was only exacerbated by the hype and chatter and gave way to assumptions of knowledge and understanding by individuals, organizations, and companies that were just embarking on the blockchain journey (i.e. that ICO was synonymous with Crypto and practical builds). In the SDG blockchain landscape, social innovation and social-entrepreneurship, merged with what Forbes reporter Jason Bloomberg called a "carnival huckster atmosphere" which infiltrated blockchain for social impact conferences and events, overshadowing the "rare but essential business models" where blockchain was delivering a real impact and business value.[22] Some toyed with the notion of metrics such as the number of developers in the community, code commits and bolstered their credibility with a heavy-weight list of investors or advisors.[23] There was an immediate atmosphere of competition and urgency of pitching and gaining early position for tech startups but also for social impact thought leaders and initiatives, all of which was amplified as international institutions became involved through conferences, hackathons, working groups, internal initiatives, and innovation calls. The result has been a cacophony of mismatched voices all purporting the same sustainable development credentials and offering a venture capital style pitching platform. A sense of blockchain fatigue and even distrust emerged.

6 Repositioning the Discourse

Despite the conflation and general blockchain fatigue, many companies and organizations are looking to take a more strategic approach to deciding which opportunities and initiatives to pursue, research or support. Moreover, international organizations such as the OECD, the World Bank, and the United Nations continue to explore and expand initiatives and pilots, and 40 percent of institutional

[21]*The most common use cases for these "blockchain for good" initiatives are payments and money transfers (25%) and records and verification (26%). Furthermore, the initiatives evaluated, 55% are estimated to deliver positive impact to intended beneficiaries by early 2019—Stanford 2019.*

[22]Jason Bloomberg 2018, Massive Consensus Conference Succumbs To Blockchain 'Echo Chamber'

In Forbes. https://www.forbes.com/sites/jasonbloomberg/2018/05/17/massive-consensus-conference-succumbs-to-blockchain-echo-chamber/#366adf41a3d4

[23]Maguire E, Maguire E (2017) The big blockchain and ICO boom: have we seen this movie before? In: medium.com. https://medium.com/cryptolinks/the-big-blockchain-and-ico-boom-have-we-seen-this-movie-before-271330515735

investors still believe that blockchain could be the most transformative technology since the internet."[24]

The concrete capacities of blockchain include:

- **Decentralized Information Sharing**: allows different parties that do not know nor trust each other to share information without requiring a central administrator.
- **Immutability**: data transactions cannot be changed as every node in the network is creating the same shared system of record simultaneously.
- **Efficiency and trust through smart contracts**: reduce friction and improving efficiency by automatically executing business logic agreed by participants.
- **Privacy**: visibility into transactions that correspond to their own role in the network.
- **Reduced Risks**: through shared reference, lineage and contract in an immutable ledger.
- **Provenance**: transparency and accountability across the supply chain through an immutable shared ledger.
- **New business models**: new participants of different types can join the network providing new value.

Discussions surrounding the delineation of standards, frameworks and protocols across crypto currency, tokens, ICOs and has multiplied as have concrete use-cases across sectors.

For those who can delineate the theoretical from the practical and the ICO from implied economic utility, the outlook for potential application remains optimistic with significant areas of dialogue and use cases related to sustainable development. So rather than a derailment of the blockchain revolution, perhaps we have instead reached what Deloitte calls "an inflection point" with "momentum shifting to the building of practical business applications".[25] Therefore, it is essential to sift through the noise and conflation and outline concrete real-world applications to address the overall issues and barriers, and to increase capacity and the potential for scalability of impact.

While numerous reports and books have been published on the potential of blockchain for sustainable development, most are caught up in the issues outlined above.

There are few use case analyses related to blockchain sustainable development and impact published in academic journals or in peer reviewed articles. A key exception is a 2018 Stanford study[26] which identified nearly 200 active blockchain

[24]Suberg W (2019) 40% of Investors Say Blockchain Could Be 'Most Transformative' Tech Since Internet: Survey. In: Cointelegraph. https://cointelegraph.com/news/40-of-investors-say-blockchain-could-be-most-transformative-tech-since-internet-survey

[25]*Deloitte Breaking blockchain open Deloitte's 2018 global blockchain survey pg. 5.* https://www2.deloitte.com/content/dam/Deloitte/us/Documents/financial-services/us-fsi-2018-global-blockchain-survey-report.pdf

[26]Blockchain for Social Impact. By Doug J. Galen, Nikki Brand, Lyndsey Boucherle, Rose Davis, NatalieDo, Ben El-Baz, Isadora Kimura, Kate Wharton, Jay Lee. *Center for Social Innovation, RippleWorks*. April 11, 2018. https://www.gsb.stanford.edu/faculty-research/publications/blockchain-social-impact

initiatives designed to deliver social impact and sustainability benefits. Both for-profit and non-profit initiatives were examined, ranging from decentralized models for solar energy distribution, peer-to-peer trading of existing and emerging commodities, identity and banking the unbanked, aid distribution, initial carbon market exchanges, and logistics chains and supply chains. The study concluded at that time (April 2018) that 74% of blockchain for social impact initiatives were still in early stages but with 55% estimated to impact beneficiaries by the end of 2018, and that blockchain was providing solutions where none were possible before or material improvements over existing solutions. However, the study found that the leading use cases were generally limited to records, verification, payments and money transfers with the primary benefit of reducing risk, fraud and inefficiency.

7 Use Cases

This brings us back to the question about the initial vision for blockchain and sustainable development, before it was conflated with the ICO landscape: What is the appropriate way to facilitate the transfer of lessons learned for a robust discussion, cross sectoral learnings, capacity building and the scaling of innovation results? Some of the early use cases, which have scaled in terms of capacity, stakeholders, and business models are worth re-examining—to better understand commonalities, and to uncover any unforeseen implications and issues of introducing new and integrated technology. To this end, this section focuses on four different supply chain use cases that illustrate common practical capacities and advantages to consider, and introduces some of the common barriers to increasing capacity and to scaling impact initiatives. It is our belief that this type of examination enables practitioners to learn not only about the issues addressed, but also the scope, processes and engagement models, key elements of success, and unforeseen implications; all of which lend insights to cross-cutting issues.

USE CASE No. 1—EVERLEDGER: Diamond Time Lapse Protocol Case
PROOF OF ORIGIN AND CERTIFICATION

Process and Engagement: Two user interfaces combining public and permissioned protocols are employed allowing everyone across the value chain to have viewing accessibility to the provenance of the diamond. The DTL platform benefits industry stakeholders across the value chain including miners, artisans, distributors, certifiers, retailer, and consumers as well as insurance companies and law enforcement agencies such as Interpol and Europol.[27]

[27]View a sample Diamond Time-Lapse report here.

Issues Addressed: The Diamond Time-Lapse (DTL) Protocol proposed to engage industry participants including miners, polishers, manufacturers, retailers and consumers to provide a historical ledger of the movement of each diamond—its lifetime journey—using standardized industry data and certification.

Scope: Proof-of-origin; traceability of luxury raw material goods; provenance; and certification.

Takeaways: Integration of different technologies, sound science-based processes, digital capacities and metadata, strong partnership ecosystem developed in stages and over time, and a secure supply chain were key elements of success and scaling. Key understanding of the successes and challenges of the Kimberley Certification scheme as well as the broader scope of issues (labour, environmental issues, etc.) were also central to the success of the initial pilot and the capacity to scale it and the approach to other materials and sectors.

USE CASE No. 2—PROVENANCE: Clothing Supply Chain (two pilot projects)[28]

SUSTAINABLE RAW MATERIALS

Process and Engagement: Wash-proof chip which is stored inside the clothing and can be scanned with a phone camera to unlock a link detailing each item of clothing's journey and locking in verified supply chain information from material sourcing, NGO projects and the individual craftspeople and workers.

The Martine Jarlgaard pilot includes the Fashion Innovation Agency (London College of Fashion, University of the Arts London), A Transparent Company Ltd., Fashion for Good, Circle Economy, Plug and Play Fashion Accelerator.

The Martina Spetlova project focuses on a small supply chain ecosystem ensuring chrome-free leather, integrating recycled plastic bottles into materials, and employs a collective of Syrian refugee craftspeople in Turkey (in partnership with NGO Small Project Istanbul).

Issues Addressed: Ethical and environmentally sound material sourcing, Gender (and refugees), Decent Work, Innovation, Responsible Consumption and Production, Partnerships human rights (labour, gender and refugees).

Scope: Provenance; sourcing assurance; embedded data in chips and sensors; traceability; certified data sources and integration of technologies (i.e. ID holding, location mapping, content and timestamps).

Takeaways: Providing consumer window on digital history of a garment requires information across complex supply chains, incorporating verifications and certifications from multiple platforms, organizations and individuals therefore trust and capacity of inputs was key as was integration of technologies across these.

---

[28] Increasing transparency in fashion with blockchain. In: Provenance. https://www.provenance.org/case-studies/martine-jarlgaard

USE CASE No. 3—MARITIME BLOCKCHAIN LABS: Marine Fuels Assurance and Compliance[29]

END-TO-END PRODUCT TRACEABILITY

Process and Engagement: Piloted with an industry-wide consortium representing the shipping bunkering (fuelling) supply chain. Gather quality assurance (QA) data from Certificates of Quality and bunker fuel drip sample, as assurance of the quality of bunker delivered from the terminal to the barge, and to gather data of the quality test currently performed from independent third-party testing labs. The objective is to demonstrate the use of blockchain to provide transparency and accountability around the bunkering supply chain and inform the buyers of bunker fuels as to the quality and compliance levels of the fuels prior to purchase. In the long-term, a system for informed decision making, monitoring, reporting and verification of the fuel accounting system and emissions data will emerge. Industry consortia members Consortium members include Lloyd's Register Fobas (testing facility); GoodFuels (biofuels supplier); Precious Shipping and Bostomar (shipping operators/fuel purchasers); BIMCO (legal bunkering contracts and terms); and International Bunkering Industry Association (standards, ISO and advocacy). The project has now entered technical scaling phase, onboarded additional partners with the intention of commercialization.

Scope: Traceability, transparency and chain of custody for the marine fuels supply chain.

Impact Issues Addressed: Quality and sustainability of marine fuels; compliance and enforcement of environmental regulations; anti-corruption; data standardization and verification. Global compliance for the IMO 2020 Global Sulphur Cap, which sets specific restrictions on Sulphur content in fuel.

Takeaways: The inclusion of science-based processes and the development of a collaborative consortium of stakeholders along a supply chain was an essential element including in providing additional insights such as the need for greater upstream focus on suppliers interested in showing their fuel tests, brokering systems, upstream data points and additional continuous sampling. Understanding the limitations of automation of data and current manual documentation processes which need to be supported by the system was also a key takeaway.

USE CASE No. 4—Bext360: Moyee Coffee

SUPPLY CHAIN FINANCE

Impact Issues Addressed: The coffee supply chain is notoriously complex, with increasing uncertainty, unfairness, and countless middlemen, each taking a piece of the pie along the way including 99.9 percent of roasting done outside country of origin. Coffee farmers and producing economies are always at the short end of the stick with only 2% of the added value of every cup of coffee ending up in their pockets. Origin and Fairtrade certification and traceability is complex.

[29]Maritime Blockchain Labs. https://www.maritimeblockchainlabs.com/#

Process and Engagement: Cultivators load their daily haul into a Bext360 machine which sifts and sorts coffee cherries, uses sensors and optical recognition technology to analyse and image each cherry at point of cultivation (size, colour and soon density), assigns a grade based on quality and therefore the price, automatically generates an agreement to sell, generates the digital payments to the farmer, the cooperative, taxes etc. and provides immediate feedback on harvest. There is also the optional feature to create new tokens that represent the coffee haul, which increase in value as the beans move through the supply chain from source of origin to end-user product. This application enables local growers, co-ops, and communities, producers, retailers and consumers alike to engage directly in an integrated value chain, thereby enabling suppliers to better verify the provenance of goods.

Scope: Closing the loop on efficient supply chain traceability, including cheaper transaction costs, accountability, monitoring, reporting and verification, asset value additionality, labour, accessible finance, land rights and economic development.

Takeaways: In the case of Bext360, the harvesting machines collect the coffee haul, conduct their analysis, and store the beans onsite for extended periods of time. For fresh coffee beans, the time lapsed through the analysis process, from initial harvest to further downstream shipping and production processes, has the potential to impact the quality of the individual beans.

The key common element to these projects is their capacity to focus on an integrated and transparent supply chain that clearly identifies stakeholder inputs, ensures that quality standards are met across processes, and that compensation is fairly rendered. Supply chains are notoriously complex so one of the primary challenges is appropriately scoping the processes and identifying stakeholders.[30] When used judiciously, blockchain can assist in addressing many of the biggest challenges in today's interconnected value chains, and affords businesses and suppliers alike the opportunity to create transparent, equitable, and sustainable supply chains for society, including enhanced:

- Management of human rights risks
- Allocation of financial resources and incentives
- Support for smallholder livelihoods that supports resilience of supply
- Environmental protection that maximizes productivity
- Transparency of logistics that lower costs and waste, while increasing security
- Authenticity of product and company storytelling that drives brand equity and loyalty

While the introduction of technology generally provides efficiency gains in the form of increased transparency and in some cases productivity gains, there are situations in which unintended consequences occur. While the Moyee coffee case offers 1 min example, the key takeaway is that when introducing new technology

[30]Kamath, Reshma. Blockchain for Women Next Generation for Sustainable Development Goal 5. In Journal of Poverty Alleviation & International Development. Jun2018, Vol. 9 Issue 1, p 88–109. 22p.

and/or reconfiguring legacy processes, it pays to be mindful of the potentially adverse impacts from the unknowns and to build capacity to learn from and address these eventualities in any technical and commercial scaling plans.

While the genesis of each of these use cases certainly varied, they, like other viable use-cases, all share similarities with respect to ecosystem and stakeholder engagement and inputs, to track and trade assets or commodities in a transparent, fault-tolerant, and universally accessible manner. For each of these cases, the technology was not offered top down but instead by scoping the initial problem with stakeholders who understand the political, social, economic and environmental context and linking to specific sustainability certification, policy or reporting frameworks is a common factor.

7.1 The Challenges

In considering the overall challenges facing sustainable development initiatives and blockchain applications, three common themes emerge: heterogeneity, incentives, and credibility.

7.2 Heterogeneity

Just as there are multiples of initiatives, actors, frameworks and approaches in sustainable development with little standardization and few systemic inputs for impact investment, there is currently, no standardization of blockchain applications in the sustainable development arena. Blockchain for sustainable development pilots and projects are building into silos and risk exacerbating an already disjointed landscape. Many are often focused on technology and fundraising rather than directly building in reference to SDG reporting, certification, carbon trading and other established frameworks. Furthermore, there is much discussion about blockchain but little focus on interoperability between systems but also with legacy systems and other emerging technology.

7.3 Incentives

Another challenge that runs in parallels across emerging initiatives and sustainability projects is the pressure to promote high-volume, least-cost projects, which is exacerbated with the hype and silver bullet approach being promulgated with the blockchain discourse. This pressure, including the approach to compensation, investment, and procurement, combined with regulatory and governance uncertainty, is driving innovation deeper into competitive silos with the risk of impeding long-term stability and impact. Furthermore, the data silos which are used in blockchain creation act to further discourage open standards and interoperability. Initiatives need to link to existing ecosystems and infrastructure including the physical, digital, and even regulatory (including sectoral standards and data standards) to better address specific needs and constraints.

7.4 Credibility

Credibility is a significant issue, not only in terms of the predicted versus real and scalable blockchain capacities, and regulatory uncertainty, but also in terms of data inputs, and issues within and across projects and practical applications. These issues include, but are not limited to, data readiness, verification, validation and evaluation, access, and participation, all of which risk increasing the digital divide. These issues are mainly related to linking the physical and the digital world, and the ability to prevent their occurrence rests on the blockchain applications capacities to prevent data errors from manual entry, formatting differences, and other issues related to human-to-nonhuman interactions. From a technical perspective, the primary way in which this is facilitated is through oracles and crypto-anchoring mechanisms that interface with data-sources & the blockchain to translate and verify the information being provided.

One of the main issues against the application of ICOs in relation to SDG's is that it lays down principles as being incontrovertibly true without ever examining the input position and systems perspective assumptions which form the foundation of the idea. It is important to remember where the inputs are secured and implemented, and have full data on origin, from local producers or artisans, to all other factors relevant to the project. The digital infrastructure for a verified data flow across any value chain can be constructed (such as smart contractual agreements, automated certification, human rights, capacity building). Taken together, this can create a holistic value chain solution and framework.

8 Conclusions and Recommendations

While it is clear that the formation of successful blockchain initiatives applied to the area of sustainable development can be achieved, the current blockchain landscape is comprised of a dogmatic grouping of initiatives and projects operating independently, under the idea of finding new forms of governance, each of which relying upon internal cooperation. This is also true within the sustainable development and social impact landscape.

There have been misaligned intentions with regard to the use of blockchain in sustainable development. There is a conflation of the Silicon Valley style, venture capital, social entrepreneurship, impact investment and institutional procurement processes and incentives. While social enterprises have historically been in "competition" for limited funds, the sense of common purpose seems to be overshadowed within the blockchain discourse which has in turn, amplified the sense of competition.[31] Rather than creating a culture of collaboration, those most vested in creating social change have been positioned in increased competition with each other to be recognized as thought leaders, to attract investors, contracts, and clients, all largely coupled with the blue sky estimates of capacity and impact.

These initiatives and individuals are set up to be in competition and to set inflated estimates and promises which can only fail to achieve, thereby casting shade on the entire space. Even the ecosystems are in competition with each other which goes against the entire ethos of the industry. Blockchain is inherently a collaborative technology; it will only succeed to the degree that everyone adheres to a collaborative approach. The way forward will continue to require bottom-up private sector innovation, followed by top-down (regulatory reforms for institutional investors) responses. Sustainable finance practices are still far from mainstream, and their adoption is driven by corporate decisions and initiatives and this has implications when it comes to blockchain as well.

8.1 *Shifting Value Chains as Investment Opportunity*

Due to the infancy of the technology and industry, to date, blockchain applications primarily exist as a type of "nascent industry" that is expected to drive future policy formation through its ability to enable suppliers, purchasers, and regulators to make and enforce informed decisions. Where some blockchain applications are focused on financial transactions, document management, content delivery, data storage, gaming, luxury brands, and other areas that resonate with select audiences, practitioners of sustainable development need to have blockchain applications that examines trade finance, aid delivery, renewable energy deployment, regenerative agriculture practices, risk insurance, infrastructure financing, afforestation, carbon markets, and other related projects.

As a very concrete example: If a blockchain solution for traceability in sustainably grown vanilla is not trusted by vanilla farmers and thus not used, the value of that vanilla gets lost before it is even harvested. If fragrance and food companies sourcing this vanilla have not agreed on the kind of data they would like to see or the underlying blockchain framework to use before deploying a solution, they risk a duplication of systems, which would run counter to the promise of distributed, open protocols.

[31] C. Grieco, 2015 Assessing Social Impact of Social Enterprises, SpringerBriefs in Business, DOI https://doi.org/10.1007/978-3-319-15,314-8_2 https://www.springer.com/cda/content/document/cda_downloaddocument/9783319153131-c2.pdf?SGWID=0-0-45-1495679-p177229414

When it comes to building solutions with this technology, it is important that this is done in conjunction with actors that represent the key links in the value or supply chain being addressed, and likewise, the industries and sectors it is meant to serve. We therefore, recommend that solutions be developed inclusively and through an ethos of progress by trial and error together with a consortium of actors sharing in collective challenges and needs. Just as impact does not stem from innovation but from the scaling of innovation results, so does this apply for the potential of blockchain. Only through an ecosystem approach and adhering to SDGs as an underlying principle of collaboration will significant advances be made.

There is great discussion about technical interoperability between blockchain platforms and systems, but the interoperability must also focus on legacy systems, emerging technology, policy frameworks, and collaborations across all types of projects. The current focus is too much about scaling innovation in market and Silicon Valley style approaches, not just in terms of investment, but also in terms of framing the proposed "solutions" and huckster approaches, rather than clear delineation of the problems scope, stakeholders, collaboration, and real capacity. The theory of change ethos should be brought into the development of blockchain "solutions" and initiatives.

In addressing the considerable challenges, shifting infrastructure, incentives, collaboration and the approach to incentivising innovation needs to be part of the strategy:

- Collaboration—a key factor to success is ensuring stakeholders across the value chains or ecosystems are involved at all stages, from problem definition through to design and piloting. This includes taking a deliberate and rigorous approach to the selection of those potential collaborators referencing geo-political, cultural, and ethical considerations.
- Iterative Process—There is a potential for disruption by considering and implementing strategic objectives, addressing key inefficiencies, building for interoperability and scaling through an iterative process. The goal should be to seek evolution not revolution. Once an optimal system is identified it should have the ability to be replicated.
- Innovation—A focus on shifting the approach to and notion of innovation will improve the trajectory. Only a small percent can follow the route through venture capital and on to success within the social innovation space. We need to stop focusing solely on unicorns and need hack the hackathons.
- Using Vertical Strengths—Ensuring that initiatives are building in reference to legacy systems and hard won sustainability frameworks as this creates the least friction and by integrating legacy industries the existing ecosystem can be used.
- Create partnerships for training and talent—The aim of these partnerships will be to ensure that the process can continue to be implanted and replicated ongoing, and most importantly, adhered to in the proper way from the outset. Cross sectoral dissemination on frameworks, best practices, business models, etc.
- Focus on creating systemic solutions for systemic change—stakeholders and actors should gather to confer as well as to create robust ecosystems. Apply the

same level of integrity and value developed within partnership ecosystems to the potential research, adoption and employment of new technologies, and to consider the reputational risks that could be associated within this emerging technical landscape particularly regarding providers and collaborators.

The UN System Task Team on the Post-2015 UN Development Agenda Working Group on "Financing for Sustainable Development" notes that current governance engages in "negative screening" and sorting out the negative impacts and that it does not stem from innovation, but instead from the scaling of innovation results. This requires key elements, collaboration and ecosystem approaches which are not part of the current integration and not quickly available or easily seen. There should be a paradigm shift away from actually looking at what market forces will scale. Market forces will not be enough in themselves and blockchain could help to drive positive change across many actors and sectors.[32] However, we need to recognize that adding the new level of blockchain to the equation brings key assumptions that have no basis in practice. Since technology is not a neutral platform, it needs proper verifications and end points to begin with for success to be achieved.

Despite the capacity and the ever-growing number of use cases, these have been limited and are difficult to draw cross cutting data on impact. Hence, a focus on results-based financing and impact investing is more preferable, since it is not fraught with challenges such as ensuring there is transparency across all channels. We have only scratched the surface but should next examine the way sustainable development is financed and examine the capacity of DLT for terms to be created which all channels would have to follow to create full transparency. At present, UNFCCC and SDGs use results-based financing, there should be stage gates for funding release requirements, with tranches created that must be met before each next step can happen. There should also be a way of holding back all stakeholders until all stakeholders have passed the current round of requirements, to ensure that the projects move forward at a set pace in line with each other. Blockchain clearly has the capacity to attain this result, but it will be imperative to create a sustainable process that involves stakeholders in the real world and the technological world to benefit increasingly with each level of progress that all stakeholders meet.

[32]Vali N (2017) More than philanthropy: SDGs are a $12 trillion opportunity for the private sector. In: UNDP. http://www.undp.org/content/undp/en/home/blog/2017/8/25/More-than-philanthropy-SDGs-present-an-estimated-US-12-trillion-in-market-opportunities-for-private-sector-through-inclusive-business.html

Katherine A. Foster has been spearheading systems innovation at the nexus of technology, policy, climate change and sustainable development for over 25 years. She served as a Canadian Diplomat, specializing in human security, the NAFTA Environmental Agreement and Climate Change, and as Innovation Lead Switzerland and Business Development Lead Europe for the EU's Climate-KIC which accelerated 1000 clean tech startups and 300 partnership across sectors. In her most recent roles as Chief Intelligence Officer of the Green Digital Finance Alliance (UNEP – Ant Financial NGO), and International Strategy Officer of Open Earth Foundation, Katherine focuses on harnessing emerging technology, open innovation and collaborative platforms and tools for the systemic issues of climate change, energy and biodiversity loss. She is also a globally recognized program advisor, facilitator and speaker on new business model, radical collaboration and emerging tech for impact.

Deanna MacDonald is Co-Founder of BunkerTrace, a company using synthetic DNA and blockchain to tag and trace fuels and emissions in the shipping sector, and Founder and CEO of BLOC (Blockchain Labs or Open Collaboration). Trained as a global political economist she brings over a decade of experience in applying and scaling industrial technologies in the agriculture, energy and health sectors. Her work targets fostering transformational change for decarbonisation of global industries. She focuses on business and application development, systems architecture and acts as a bridge between business, technology and society. She is also a global speaker and workshop facilitator on blockchain and new forms of governance and business models needed to support the transition into a new paradigm.

Marc Johnson is a driven sustainability leader who has spent the majority of his career working on technological solutions to problems faced by the energy-water-food nexus. For the past several years, much of his work has focused on how frontier technologies can upend traditional business models to create more economic inclusion for underserved segments of the global population. Marc holds an MSc in Sustainability Management from Columbia University.

The Tokenization of Assets: Using Blockchains for Equity Crowdfunding

Jakob Roth, Fabian Schär, and Aljoscha Schöpfer

Abstract In this chapter, we present tokenization of equity crowdfunding on a Blockchain as a possible approach to ease access to capital for startups. We propose a categorization of token standards into UTXO-based, layer-based and smart contract-based tokens. In a second step, we analyze the advantages that tokenization can bring, such as cryptographically secured ownership, programmability of assets, access to the Blockchain-ecosystem, enhanced divisibility of shares as well as the formation of a well-functioning secondary market. Tokenization allows to decouple the ledger of assets from the crowdfunding platform, thus lowering the cost of secondary market trading and the intermediary's power. We conclude by mentioning several drawbacks including information asymmetries between investors and campaign creators, regulatory issues and high energy intensity of Proof-of-Work-secured Blockchains.

Keywords Tokenization · Blockchain · Token standards · DLT · Crowdfunding · Secondary markets · Sustainable finance · Sustainability

1 Introduction

One of the biggest challenges for small startups and new projects is to find investors, willing to support the company with seed capital (Tomczak and Brem 2013; Schwienbacher 2019). After having accessed all available resources from the FFF group (friends, family and fools), startups tend to turn to banks or angel investors for funding in the earliest stages (Tomczak and Brem 2013). However, due to the lack of collateral of these young firms and the high information asymmetries involved, financial intermediaries are usually reluctant to invest (Deffains-Crapsky and Sudolska 2014). Tomczak and Brem (2013) argue that small startups in particular

J. Roth · F. Schär (✉) · A. Schöpfer
Center for Innovative Finance, Basel, Switzerland
e-mail: jakob.roth@unibas.ch; f.schaer@unibas.ch; aljoscha.schoepfer@unibas.ch

K. Wendt (ed.), *Theories of Change*, Sustainable Finance,
https://doi.org/10.1007/978-3-030-52275-9_19

have a lower probability to obtain funding. In the last decade, this fueled the rise of crowdfunding[1] as a new way to raise seed capital for small startups, through the consolidated investment of investors (Tomczak and Brem 2013).

Crowdfunding[2] models are usually categorized in two broad classes: (1) reward- and donation-based crowdfunding and (2) investment-based crowdfunding (Belleflamme et al. 2015). In reward- and donation-based crowdfunding, investors are not reimbursed financially, but receive some other kind of reward (e.g. the product once the first production round is realized) or have other motivations for supporting the project. The second class is divided into lending-based, equity-based and royalty-based crowdfunding, from which investors expect to receive interest, dividends or other forms of financial gains. In this chapter we will focus on the field of equity-based crowdfunding. Crowdfunding is usually organized by an internet-based intermediation platform which connects investors with campaign creators[3] (Belleflamme et al. 2015). Platforms charge various fees for their services from the creators (if the campaign was successful), accumulating to approximately 7–10% of the total amount raised (Belleflamme et al. 2015).

Investors in equity-based crowdfunding on the other hand are facing the problem that their investment is locked in. Their only exit options (besides liquidation) are trade sales,[4] share buyback schemes or sale on the stock market after an initial public offering (Schwienbacher 2019). In traditional markets, an additional option to exit investments is provided through secondary markets on which investors can sell their assets to other investors (Freedman and Nutting 2015). In the crowdfunding sector, this option is widely missing (Schwienbacher 2019). There are however platforms which have identified the need for a secondary market for crowdfunded equity shares, such as Seedrs[5] and CFX Markets.[6] Nevertheless, CFX Markets is limited to accredited investors (CFX 2018a) which will not be covered in this chapter. Seedrs, on the other hand, allows trading for non-accredited investors, but they are restricted to trading cycles (Seedrs 2019a). Both platforms need 1–2 weeks for settlement. To sum up, creators of crowdfunding campaigns are facing high intermediation costs, while investors cannot exit their investments or are confronted with highly limited marketplaces.

A wide range of scholars (Ante and Fiedler 2019; Schwienbacher 2019; Sahdev 2017) therefore propose to use Blockchain technology to set up secondary markets for crowdfunded equity shares. Through this rather new technology, assets can be represented by digital tokens, which then can be transferred in a peer-to-peer manner

[1]For a definition of the term see Belleflamme et al. (2015).

[2]Messeni Petruzzelli et al. (2019) provide a comprehensive and detailed summary of the current research front and its implications for sustainable crowdfunding projects.

[3]Agrawal et al. (2013) have given a great overview about the incentives and disincentives to engage in crowdfunding for these three actors.

[4]I.e. all outstanding shares are bought by a third party which acquired the startup.

[5]https://seedrs.com/.

[6]https://cfxtrading.com/.

amongst all network participants. In particular, the exchange would not be limited to a particular crowdfunding platform. In recent years, this practice has gained much attention through the highly successful initial coin offerings (ICOs) which have been studied in great detail by Chen (2018), Rohr and Wright (2019), Howell et al. (2018) and Nyffenegger and Schär (2018). Ante and Fiedler (2019) have laid their focus on the new phenomenon that is the very current shift from ICOs to security token offerings (STOs). Zhu and Zhou (2016) have combined the two topics of tokenization and crowdfunding by analyzing the possible application of Blockchain technology for equity crowdfunding in China. In this chapter, we also want to explore the potential of tokenizing assets to counteract the current limitations in the equity crowdfunding market, but have chosen a more technical approach. We will therefore start our analysis by explaining the key strengths of Blockchain technology. Thereafter, we will explain three different ways to tokenize assets, i.e. to represent real world assets digitally on a Blockchain. In the main part of this chapter we will then explore seven advantages tokenization could bring to crowdfunding and present three problems that arise or remain unsolved due to tokenization.

With the growing awareness of social and environmental problems in the public, the world bank (infoDev 2013) identified crowdfunding to have great potential to be a solution to channel additional financial resources into small scale projects for sustainability. By exploring how tokenization can be used to make crowdfunding more attractive, this chapter contributes a small piece towards achieving sustainability goals.

2 Blockchain and Token Standards

In this section we provide a short overview of the technical concepts. We briefly explain the key characteristics of Blockchain, followed by a more detailed analysis and categorization of token standards. For the sake of brevity, we assume that the reader already has some familiarity with the topic. For a more detailed introduction into Blockchain see Antonopoulos (2014), Antonopoulos and Wood (2018) and Berentsen and Schär (2017, 2018).

2.1 Blockchain

A public Blockchain (hereafter just referred to as Blockchain) is an open and distributed ledger where data can be stored immutably. Originally, Blockchains are primarily used to transfer digital assets such as native coins (e.g. Bitcoin or Ether) or tokens in a peer-to-peer manner (see Nakamoto 2008). Hereby, asymmetric cryptography is leveraged to ensure both privacy (pseudonymity) as well as authenticity and integrity of transactions through the use of cryptographic signatures.

Ownership of assets is tracked on the Blockchain and secured by its consensus protocol,[7] which makes it almost impossible for an attacker to manipulate the ledger.

Recent years have brought the advent of Blockchains that allow complex scripts, so-called smart contracts, to be deployed and executed on the Blockchain. This in turn simplified issuance of tokens and enabled the development of decentralized applications (DApps).

2.2 *Token Standards*

Public Blockchains (Nakamoto 2008) have created an infrastructure that allows anyone to own and transfer digital assets without the need for an intermediary. The process is permissionless and, under certain circumstances, more efficient than centralized systems (see Berentsen and Schär 2018, in the place of many). However, the assets that can be represented on a Blockchain natively are limited to assets that are created as part of the protocol, such as Bitcoin in the case of the Bitcoin Blockchain. If we want to track and trade external assets on a Blockchain, these assets must be tokenized, i.e. each asset needs a token that represents its existence and allows the asset to be transferred just like native protocol assets.

Tokens are rivalrous, digital units of value, which entitle the owner to an asset or a utility. They may include promises for the delivery of goods and services, or represent the ownership of an asset. Rosenfeld (2012) describes that tokens may represent virtually any kind of asset or promise and Buterin (2013) mentions a few examples, including currency (stablecoins), commodities, stocks, bonds and property.

Moreover, tokens have significant advantages as shown by Rosenfeld (2012) and Chen (2018) and discussed later in this chapter. In particular, they may lead to more efficient funding processes with more equal access for potential investors and severe cost reduction.

Tokens are based on a special data structure within the Blockchain that tracks the current owner of each token (alternatively, the balance of each address). As we will see in this section, the exact implementation varies. There are numerous token standards on a variety of platforms, all with their own advantages and drawbacks. We propose three categories, namely UTXO-based, layer-based and smart contract-based tokens. The three categories are discussed below and summarized in Table 2 at the end of this section.

Table 1 provides an overview of the main token platforms, the respective token standards, the number of tokens and the aggregate market capitalization per platform.

[7]E.g. Proof-of-Work (PoW) or Proof-of-Stake (PoS).

Table 1 Tokens per platform

		Number		Market capitalization	
Platform	Type	Absolute	Relative	Absolute	Relative
Ethereum	Smart contract-based	1108	89.43%	8,695,655,366	77.91%
Neo	Smart contract-based	27	2.18%	83,100,800	0.75%
Waves	Smart contract-based	24	1.94%	34,593,249	0.31%
Stellar	Smart contract-based	15	1.21%	97,214,953	0.88%
BitShares	Smart contract-based	13	1.05%	21,896,211	0.20%
Qtum	Smart contract-based	10	0.81%	15,434,624	0.14%
Omni	Layer-based	7	0.57%	2,007,734,292	19.11%
Nem	Smart contract-based	6	0.48%	31,442,156	0.29%
Counterparty	Layer-based	6	0.48%	7,629,517	0.07%
EOS	Smart contract-based	5	0.40%	16,772,483	0.15%
Other	Various	18	1.45%	20,488,711	0.19%

Bitcoin has been omitted in this table due to the negligible significance of its token standard. Data sources: Coinmarketcap (2019), Tether (2019). Accessed February 2019

2.2.1 UTXO-Based Tokens

UTXO-based token standards are usually referred to as colored coins (Hakim 2012; Assia et al. 2012). They use a native Blockchain asset, e.g. a fraction of a Bitcoin, and attach an external promise to it. The Bitcoin fraction, or more precisely the unspent transaction output (UTXO), serves as a container to which the additional value can be attached. Its value may rise as the result of an external promise by an issuing party or a Schelling point (Rosenfeld 2012).

Colored coins are created through a genesis transaction which uses an additional output to add metadata to the transaction graph. Compatible wallets will thereafter treat the corresponding outputs separately from any other Bitcoin unit making them non-fungible (Rosenfeld 2012; Shomer and Zach 2015).

The term colored coin highlights the fact that these Bitcoin fractions represent something else in addition to the Bitcoin itself. To use an analogy, one can think of a five-dollar bill on which someone writes a promise to deliver an ounce of gold. The five-dollar bill could freely circulate—including the attached promise. Consequently, any asset could be attached to a Bitcoin fraction, transferred on-chain and thereby be used to leverage potential efficiency gains (Schär 2019).

UTXO-based tokens are relatively straightforward to implement. However, they also have some drawbacks. In particular, they require external coordination and can be lost quite easily. If someone uses a Bitcoin wallet that does not support the colored coin standard (most wallets do not) and is therefore unable to identify colored outputs, the wallet might select a Bitcoin fraction with additional value for an ordinary Bitcoin transaction. In this case, the token would be lost and the additional value discarded. Moreover, colored coin transactions are subject to Bitcoin transaction fees and scalability solutions are more difficult to implement if compatibility with colored coins is to be guaranteed. Accordingly, the standard today has a negligible significance.

2.2.2 Layer-Based Tokens

Layer-based tokens are a similar, yet distinct way to issue tokens through the use of new transaction graphs. Instead of employing existing outputs, as in our UTXO-based example, new ones are created and tracked separately. These new outputs are generated through OP_RETURN transactions. This op_code allows anyone to add arbitrary data to the Blockchain. While Bitcoin-like Blockchains cannot interpret this data natively, it is possible to create a corresponding transaction graph on a second layer. Consequently, the base layer (original Blockchain) can be used for some security guarantees, while the second layer allows for more features, including additional consensus rules, transaction types and requirements. Some layered solutions even include functionalities for decentralized asset exchanges.

To employ another analogy, layer-based tokens could be compared to establishing a transaction system based on public letters in newspapers. An agent intending to transfer an external promise (i.e. token) to someone would publish this transaction in a codified and compressed manner in the newspaper (representing the underlying Blockchain). An external layer (transaction graph) would then interpret the information from the newspaper and include the corresponding transfer in its transaction system. This creates a system for the exchange of value which benefits from the properties of the first layer.

Just like UTXO-based tokens, layer-based tokens also have their drawbacks. They depend on both layers[8] and usually require a full node for transaction validation. Some scripts on the base layer tend not to work with layer-based tokens and consensus may get messy during base layer "reorgs".

The two most prominent examples of layer-based tokens are OMNI, formerly Mastercoin (Willett 2012), and Counterparty (Zuber et al. 2015). Both provide a second layer on top of the Bitcoin Blockchain.

Layer-based tokens lost much of their appeal with the increasing popularity of smart contract platforms. However, despite the complicated implementation and a somewhat confusing fee schedule, there are still relatively large token projects based on this standard. By far the most popular one is the OMNI-variant of the Tether stablecoin, which corresponds to approximately 95% of the total market cap of all layer-based tokens (see Table 1). Other prominent examples include Bitcrystals (Counterparty) and MaidSafeCoin (OMNI).

---

[8]In our analogy: If either the newspaper or the consensus system for the external transaction graph are compromised, the system will fail.

2.2.3 Smart Contract-Based Tokens

Most tokens are based on smart contracts. These contracts create and track states that represent token ownership. In particular, they map tokens to current owner addresses. Whenever someone wants to transfer a token, this person needs to interact with the contract and make a corresponding transfer call. If successful, i.e. if a person can provide cryptographic proof of ownership, the state of the contract gets adjusted accordingly.

While there is a large variety of smart contract-based token standards, the vast majority are built on Ethereum's ERC-20[9] standard. There are almost 200,000 ERC-20 compatible token contracts on the Ethereum mainnet (Etherscan 2019), over 1000 of which are listed on exchanges with a total market capitalization corresponding to approximately 8.5 billion USD as of February 2019 (Coinmarketcap 2019).

The main advantage of ERC-20 is the rich ecosystem and broad developer base. There is a variety of open source implementations and all major hardware (software) wallet manufacturers (developers) do support ERC-20. Tools such as tokenfactory[10] even allow people with no prior experience to easily create new ERC-20 tokens. Additionally, the risk of severe bugs is relatively low, considering the significant bug bounty and the number of people working on implementations of this standard.

However, ERC-20 also has certain drawbacks. In particular, wallets do not get a notification when they receive new ERC-20 tokens. If agent *A* wants to transfer tokens to agent *B*, he calls the transfer function in a hypothetical ERC-20 smart contract. The contract verifies the legitimacy of the transaction and updates its internal state. Agent *B* does not get a notification, but instead has to proactively scan his balance with this contract. Moreover, token interactions with other (smart) contract accounts require two function calls. If a person accidentally calls the wrong function, the funds may end up stuck in the receiver contract. This is a severe problem and many ERC-20 based cryptoassets have been lost that way. Similar standards for other Blockchains include NEP-5[11] (NEO) and QRC-20[12] (QTUM).

ERC-223[13] and ERC-777[14] are new standards based on Ethereum. They mitigate the problem of lost tokens by allowing tokens to always be sent with the same function—independently of whether the person interacts with a smart contract or an externally owned address. Moreover, incoming tokens trigger an event which can be responded to by the recipient's contract. An account may even reject non-supported tokens. Last but not least, the transfer is more efficient, especially when sending

[9]See http://eips.ethereum.org/EIPS/eip-20.

[10]https://tokenfactory.surge.sh.

[11]See https://github.com/neo-project/proposals/blob/master/nep-5.mediawiki.

[12]See https://docs.qtum.site/en/QRC20-Token-Introduce.html.

[13]See https://github.com/ethereum/EIPs/issues/223.

[14]See http://eips.ethereum.org/EIPS/eip-777.

Table 2 Summary of the three categories of token standards

Category	Description	Examples
UTXO-based	Uses a fragment of a native Blockchain asset as a container to which additional assets can be attached.	Colored coins
Layer-based	Uses metadata transactions and a separate transaction graph to create and track tokens.	Omni (Mastercoin), Counterparty
Smart contract-based	A dedicated smart contract creates and tracks states that represent token ownership. It maps tokens to current owner addresses.	ERC-20, ERC-223, ERC-721, ERC-1155, NEP5, NEP11, QRC-20

tokens to contract accounts. Despite these advantages, ERC-20 remains dominant so far.

Smart contract-based tokens can also be used for non-fungible assets, like collectibles. The dominant standard for non-fungible tokens is ERC-721.[15] Several proposals, including ERC-1155[16] try to make non-fungible token contracts more efficient, e.g. by allowing batch transfers and the creation of semi-fungible tokens. NEP11[17] is an example of a non-fungible token standard on a different Blockchain (NEO) (Table 2).

3 Tokenization and Crowdfunding

With the key concepts of Blockchain explained and the three token standards presented, we now turn to the practical advantages and drawbacks of their implementation in the crowdfunding sector. We first explore the advantages, which are divided into two categories. The first consists of general advantages of tokenized equity shares. These advantages are not bound to the availability of a secondary market, but rather present the basic advantages of tokenizing assets on a Blockchain. Thereafter, we discuss the advantages of using tokenization in secondary markets for crowdfunded equity shares. In both categories we identify to which of the actors (investors, creators and platforms) tokenization would be advantageous and with which of the three token standards the respective advantage could be best availed of. At the end we turn to three drawbacks, which are not solved by tokenization or which arise due to its implementation.

[15] See http://eips.ethereum.org/EIPS/eip-721.

[16] See http://eips.ethereum.org/EIPS/eip-1155.

[17] See https://github.com/Splyse/proposals/blob/4947667b57a7d05825bf20fec52b6db15a467726/nep-11.mediawiki.

3.1 General Advantages

3.1.1 Cryptographically Secured Ownership

One of the key characteristics of Blockchain technology is its immutability. Ownership rights are secured by a long cryptographically linked sequence of state changes and transactions are secured by public key cryptography as well as the consensus protocol of the Blockchain. In particular, a valid transaction can only be initiated by a person who controls the corresponding private key and therefore is able to provide a cryptographic signature.[18]

As such, cryptoassets, including tokens, are subject to a large degree of autonomy and self-responsibility. Whoever controls the private key is in control of the corresponding assets. By tokenizing the crowdfunded assets, investors would therefore have full control over them (Zhu and Zhou 2016). Their assets would be safe from arbitrary manipulation and confiscation attempts by malicious platform hosts or third parties. Moreover, it would make the platform more robust and reduce risks regarding a single point of failure.

The cryptographically secured ownership would clearly benefit investors, but might also be in the interest of the platform hosts, as it relaxes their need for security and may make the platform more attractive to new investors. Furthermore, it might have legal implications, since the platform may no longer be considered a custodian in certain jurisdictions.

Since this is a fundamental concept shared by all public Blockchain implementations (at least to some degree), all three token standards are equally capable of introducing this benefit. That being said, neither one of them resolves the counterparty risk involved with the securitization of assets. If the issuer is unable or not willing to fulfill the promise to deliver the underlying asset, the token will be worthless, despite being represented on a Blockchain (Berentsen and Schär 2017, 2019). However, this is not a problem related to the technology but rather a consequence of the securitization of assets.

3.1.2 Programmable Assets

In many cases, the only condition that must be met in order for a cryptoasset to be spendable is a signature with a specific private key. However, Blockchain asset transfers can also be restricted by powerful scripts (see Sect 3.2).

The Ethereum Blockchain (Buterin 2013) has enhanced this concept with a more versatile (Turing complete) scripting language, the concept of contract accounts and state variables. Instead of adding these scripts to a specific UTXO in the form of a spending condition, they can be deployed in the form of a contract account. A

[18] Alternatively, a variety of additional requirements can be added, such as the need for additional signatures or timelocks.

contract account is an address which is not governed by the private key, but rather follows the instruction in the script. The programmability of these smart contracts opens a wide field of "arbitrary rules of ownership, transaction formats and state transition functions" (Buterin 2013).

If we assume that the token is governed by a smart contract, many tasks, such as dividend or interest payments, could be coded in the contract (Wall and Malm 2016). Additionally, the assets could represent voting rights and votes could be conducted through the Blockchain infrastructure.[19] Yet another smart contract could be set up as a fund, hold a basket of tokens as collateral and issue fund tokens that represent partial ownership of the fund.[20] This would allow a broad diversification and at the same time publicly prove that the underlying assets are indeed present, i.e. locked up in the smart contract.

Even the crowdfunding platform itself could be set up as a construct of smart contracts. Early examples include lighthouse (Higgins 2015) and the DAO (Jentzsch 2016). Both of these attempts failed, albeit for very different reasons and with varying degrees of severity. While Lighthouse failed to generate user adoption, the DAO has fallen victim to a programming error and put millions of dollars in user funds at risk. This sheds light on one of the disadvantages of the programmability of assets when combined with the Blockchain's immutability. If there is an error in the script, this could have catastrophic consequences and ultimately lead to the loss of the assets.

Apart from this drawback the set of potential applications is immense and may potentially lead to more efficient crowdfunding markets. We suspect that creators and investors will profit most from these opportunities and that we might experience a shift in power away from the platform hosts.

With regard to the different token standards, smart contract-based tokens seem to be the best choice in this category due to their very flexible application.

3.1.3 Access to the Blockchain Ecosystem

The use of Blockchain technology facilitates the access to a wide range of services provided by other actors of the Blockchain ecosystem. As many projects are active on public Blockchains, there is great potential to use synergies and to combine various projects. One example which could be applicable to crowdfunding are projects providing know-your-customer (KYC) verification. Moyano and Ross (2017) have proposed a system (for banks) in which KYC is only done once by one actor, who then shares the result on a Blockchain with other actors. With this new system cooperating actors can avoid performing the same process redundantly and therefore save costs (Moyano and Ross 2017). The same system is also applicable to crowdfunding platforms, which could rely on a third party to perform KYC

[19] See for example https://solidity.readthedocs.io/en/v0.4.24/solidity-by-example.html.

[20] See https://melonport.com/ and https://tokensets.com.

and to fulfill anti-money-laundering (AML) requirements. However, some issues regarding privacy arise when real world identities are linked to addresses on a public Blockchain.

Other examples (without claiming completeness) could be the more general approach of digital identities, oracles (providers of real-world data on the Blockchain), decentralized exchanges or the use of tokens as collateral for loans.

The ecosystem has the potential to benefit all three crowdfunding actors and may greatly increase social gains. With Ethereum being the most popular platform for Blockchain-based services (see Table 1), smart contract-based tokens are arguably best capable of providing this advantage.

3.1.4 Divisibility

A fundamental characteristic of equity crowdfunding is the relatively low price per share (Mollick 2014). With the minimum amount required to invest in a project being comparatively low, crowdfunding therefore favors financial inclusion, making more diverse investment portfolios available to less wealthy individuals (Jenik et al. 2017; Klein 1973). Furthermore, investors can reach their optimal portfolio more precisely with smaller unit prices of each asset (Klein 1973).

Blockchain could further enhance this advantage with its capabilities to divide assets into very small fractions. The native coins of the two most important Blockchains, Bitcoin and Ethereum, can be divided into 8 and 18 decimals respectively. Tokenized assets can be divided into similar fractions.

Building on the argument about small prices per asset favoring financial inclusion, a lower denomination per asset usually has a positive effect on the number of asset holders and with it the probability to find a trading partner (see Sect. 3.2). Thus, markets allowing higher divisibility and lower prices per unit tend to be more liquid than markets of assets that trade only in large batches (Muscarella and Vetsuypens 1996).

The properties described above mainly provide advantages for investors. However, with more investors being interested in the project, creators benefit as well. In particular, it might increase the likelihood of a successful campaign. The relatively low investment barrier, however, also bears the risk of attracting investors that do not have the capability and knowledge to assess the risks involved. This is why in many jurisdictions access is limited to accredited investors, i.e. investors who have a high income or net worth (infoDev 2013).

Although all three token standards are divisible to a certain extent, it is usually more complex to maintain the divisibility for UTXO-based tokens. Moreover, current UTXO-based implementations lead to relatively high transaction fees, which implicitly limits the divisibility of the asset. Batch transactions of smart contract-based tokens, as proposed by ERC-1155, may be more suitable for the transfer of multiple small token amounts.

3.2 *Secondary Market*

To continue our analysis of tokenization, we take up the prevailing discussion in scientific literature about secondary market trading in equity crowdfunding. Signori and Vismara (2016), Murray (2015) and Schwartz (2013) identify the absence or limited presence of secondary markets as an enduring problem. The main reasons at the time of writing are arguably legal obstacles.[21] However, Turan (2015) argues that from an investor's perspective dividends are the only realizable financial gains given the absence of well-established secondary markets. This is a risk factor that hinders equity crowdfunding to flourish healthily.

Similar to Ante and Fiedler (2019) we propose that tokenization of crowdfunded equity can ease the formation of a liquid secondary market from an economic perspective.[22] We further extend the analysis by assessing the ability of different token standards presented in Sect. 2.2 to tackle barriers that prevent secondary market trading from happening.

3.2.1 Intermediaries

In secondary markets on conventional stock exchanges there are numerous fees and commissions that have to be paid to third parties. Bell et al. (2006) provide a comprehensive overview on costs that occur in secondary market trading on major stock exchanges such as NYSE, NASDAQ, LSE, and others. These costs include admission fees for exchanges, annual exchange fees, broker commissions as well as other fees and are estimated to be between 0.16 and 0.4%. According to Domowitz et al. (2001) these costs tend to be higher in developing countries and emerging markets.

There are some crowdfunding platforms that allow investors to trade their equity (Seedrs 2019b; CFX 2018b). In the case of Seedrs there is only one fee that applies to sellers of shares, which amounts to 7.5% of the profit (Seedrs 2019c). Buyers do not have to pay fees. With this fee, investors pay for all the services of Seedrs including the provision of the platform and settlement of transactions. However, this fee does not include any fees charged by the investor's bank to move funds to and from the platform. These frictions limit the access to capital for startups that want to approach sustainability-related problems.

Some of these third-party services would not be needed anymore when assets are tokenized. Tokenization brings the advantage of decoupling the crowdfunding platform and the ledger. Platforms would no longer be in charge of maintaining the balances of investors (as investors control their assets themselves with their private keys). Instead, balances would be recorded on the Blockchain and this layer is where alterations would occur. Each platform could then obtain data directly from

[21] See for example the U.S. JOBS Act (https://sec.gov/spotlight/jobs-act.shtml).

[22] Legal obstacles might still prevent secondary markets from developing.

the Blockchain and balances are updated automatically when the transaction is confirmed. Therefore, crowdfunding platforms would have to charge significantly lower fees since the settlement of transactions would be outsourced to the Blockchain and the platform itself would not have to deal with any more paperwork. However, some fees would presumably remain as the platform itself is still likely to be powered by a centralized provider. Early attempts to create a decentralized crowdfunding platform have failed to succeed (see Sect. 3.1). Still, the matching of buyers and sellers could be completely detached from a central provider and be conducted by smart contracts. This approach is called decentralized exchange (DEX) and is already being put into practice by some projects.[23] The fees in this setup are arguably lower than in the case of a centralized matching. In both cases, investors would not have to pay transaction fees charged by banks to deposit funds in their account on the platform. This implies that the transacting parties are mainly left with the transaction fees of the Blockchain.[24] With the advent of state channels, fees will arguably decline and might even play a negligible role in the future (Seres et al. 2019).

This advantage clearly benefits investors, who face lower transaction fees and are not limited to a platform anymore to transfer their tokens. Platforms on the other hand would arguably lose power due to the decentralized nature of Blockchain and therefore might not profit from this advantage. This, however, depends on the implementation as well and will differ from case to case.

In order to avail of these advantages, each token standard could be considered because all of them would make the aforementioned third party-services unnecessary to some degree. However, it would be easiest to implement a decentralized exchange with smart contract-based tokens. This way, the most cost savings could be achieved.

3.2.2 Standardization and Interoperability

The secondary market provided by Seedrs is a closed ecosystem. This means that there are no more potential buyers and sellers than the number of users of the platform. Sellers from platform *A* cannot sell their securities to buyers from platform *B* and vice versa. In other words, secondary markets on crowdfunding platforms are not interoperable. This is a rather serious limitation, since a large fraction of potential market participants are excluded from taking part in the trading activity.

As explained above, by isolating the ledger from the platform, crowdfunding platforms would get data on investor's balances from the underlying Blockchain. Since different platforms could rely on the same Blockchain as its transactional layer, transactions between different platforms would be enabled easily. Moreover,

---

[23]See for example https://uniswap.io/.

[24]Note that in order to acquire coins, one must often resort to exchanges where the investor is charged a fee to buy coins or tokens.

tokens could be traded over the counter without the need for any platform at all. Even inter-Blockchain token exchanges are feasible.

Another advantage stands out when we further consider the decoupling of the platform and the ledger. In every traditional stock exchange, there are trading hours where investors can buy and sell securities. Also, in secondary markets on crowdfunding platforms, investors are bound to trading periods. In the case of Seedrs, there is a 1 week trading period every month starting on the first Tuesday of the month and lasting exactly 1 week (Seedrs 2019b). The weeks in between are needed for preparation and paperwork (Seedrs 2019a). Smith (2001) proves formally that this friction is undesirable to the investor who prefers to be able to adapt his/her portfolio at any given time. Since Blockchains are usually decentralized, the ledger is maintained around the clock and can be used for transactions 24/7. Consequently, as soon as equity is represented as a token on a Blockchain, buyers and sellers are no longer bound to trading periods. The removal of this friction can lead to welfare gains (Smith 2001).

In order to create a standardized system, crowdfunding platforms must agree on one cross-platform infrastructure that can be used by each platform to record transactions. By isolating the transactional layer through the introduction of a Blockchain this requirement is fulfilled. Therefore, it is not relevant which token standard is used in order to create a standardized and interoperable system. It can rather be seen as a coordination game with positive network effects for all agents. Smart contract-based tokens and the Ethereum ecosystem are currently in the best position to become the dominant infrastructure.

The possibility to trade assets between multiple platforms without friction would be very advantageous for investors. Creators on the other hand could also benefit from the resulting interoperability, because tokenization could already introduce this advantage at the level of the initial crowdfunding campaign. This allows creators to run their campaign on multiple crowdfunding platforms simultaneously.

3.2.3 Atomic Transactions and Multisig Assets

In traditional secondary markets, clearing houses are responsible for reducing counterparty risk (Bernstein et al. 2019). They do so by stepping in between the two transacting parties (i.e. the buyer and the seller) and performing the obligations of each of the two parties. Therefore, counterparty risk of the transacting parties is transferred to this centralized intermediary (the clearing house). In secondary markets on crowdfunding platforms, the platform provider himself checks whether the seller's shares are eligible to be sold and whether s/he has released his/her signed transfer agreement. The platform provider also verifies whether the buyer has made the payment and only allows the transaction to be executed when both the buyer and the seller have fulfilled their obligation (Seedrs 2019b). This way, both systems of secondary markets require centralized parties to reduce counterparty risk. Consequently, this raises the question how this problem is approached in a decentralized system where the transacting parties interact directly with each other without any third parties involved. Naturally, the seller wants to receive the funds before releasing his tokenized equity share and the buyer, conversely, wants to be in possession of the token before paying for it.

A common approach to counteract the risk of a counterparty not performing his/her obligations are so-called atomic transactions. Berentsen and Schär (2017) explain how atomic transactions work in the case of an asset that is attached to a fragment of a Bitcoin unit (UTXO-based tokens). Both the token and the payment transfers could be combined to one transaction message. Since transactions can only be confirmed if all components are valid, the two transfers would be inseparable. Either both of them are valid or neither one of them is, effectively removing the counterparty risk.

The solution looks different when we turn to smart contract-based tokens (Cuccuru 2017). In this case, the transacting parties have to set up a smart contract to which the buyer can send the funds and the seller, accordingly, the tokenized assets. The smart contract must be set up in such a way that the funds and the tokenized assets are only forwarded to the counterparty if both parties fulfill their respective obligations. If they fail to comply with the agreement within a predefined time frame, there must be a `withdraw` function within the contract that can be called to withdraw the funds and the tokens, respectively.

Layer-based atomic transfers are possible but much more complex. One has to be very careful, since the base layer cannot protect from double spends when there is a separate transaction graph (Killerstorm 2015).

In addition to the advantage of atomic transactions, tokenized assets could be managed by so-called *m*-of-*n* multisig-wallets (Berentsen and Schär 2017; Antonopoulos and Wood 2018). This allows very flexible conditions that can emulate joint accounts (2-of-2), or mitigate the risk of key loss (2-of-3).

Eliminating the counterparty risk during the exchange of assets poses another advantage for trading investors. For platforms, the effect requires further examination. On one hand they would benefit from the elimination of the counterparty risk as well (as it is transferred to them in a centralized approach). On the other hand, they could also lose a business model.

3.3 Drawbacks

3.3.1 Quality of Project

The core problem of early investing, be it by business angels, venture capitalists or crowdfunding, is to correctly assess the quality and potential of the supported startup (Wilson and Testoni 2014). For angel investors and venture capitalists the cost to perform thorough due diligence is low in relation to the total amount for them at stake. In crowdfunding on the other hand, the size of the investment of each individual investor is usually small, as are the incentives to perform proper due diligence (Agrawal et al. 2013). Therefore, many studies show that crowdfunding investment may lead to herding behavior with investors free-riding on the investment decisions of others instead of conducting due diligence (Astebro et al. 2019; Belleflamme et al. 2015).

The implementation of tokenization and Blockchain in crowdfunding does not mitigate the information asymmetries between investors and creators. The numerous fraudulent or unsuccessful ICOs in recent years are great examples of this issue (see EY 2018).

3.3.2 Regulatory Issues

Both the emergence of Blockchain technology as well as the increased popularity of equity crowdfunding are rather young phenomena. This implies that numerous legal questions remain unanswered. Currently, many countries are working on frameworks outlining how to deal with Blockchain-based crowdfunding. Although this chapter focuses on technological and economic aspects of tokenization, we would like to briefly mention the main regulatory issues related to the topic.

Generally, in the U.S., tokenized assets are treated as securities that must comply with federal securities law according to SEC (2019). However, each country follows its own policy and within every jurisdiction local laws apply (for an overview of security regulation see Hornuf and Schwienbacher 2017).

In 2012, the U.S. Jumpstart Our Business Startups Act (JOBS Act) became effective, its goal being to ease equity crowdfunding in principle. With the JOBS Act, startups are allowed to raise capital by selling equity from non-accredited investors under certain circumstances (McGowan 2017). Yet, one main restriction that hinders trading of crowdfunded equity shares remains. The JOBS Act prohibits trading of shares to a large extent during a 1-year period after the initial investment (Freedman and Nutting 2015). Of course, tokenized assets would be no exception. However, such restrictions could easily be implemented in a Blockchain-based solution through timelocks and grace periods (Ostrowski 2018).

3.3.3 Energy Consumption

There has been an ongoing discussion about energy-related problems of Blockchain technology. The reason for Blockchain technology to be energy-intensive is the PoW consensus protocol implemented in many Blockchains (including Bitcoin and Ethereum). Miners have to solve cryptographic tasks by computing numbers on a trial-and-error basis (see Berentsen and Schär 2017, in the place of many). This process requires them to provide computing power, which consumes energy. De Vries (2018) estimated the energy consumption of the Bitcoin network as a whole in 2018 to add up to 2.55 GW. This is close to the electricity consumption of Ireland (3.1 GW).

Some argue that Bitcoin's energy consumption is a severe problem that must be tackled by all available means. Others (e.g. Almasi 2017) justify Bitcoin's energy intensity by arguing that this is a natural consequence of a decentralized payment system and a reasonable cost for the creation of an immutable ledger. Domingo (2017) further highlights that it might not be fair to compare Bitcoin, which provides the whole infrastructure of a payment system, to VISA (or other credit card associations), which are only small links within entire payment systems. He calculates that, once accounted for the electricity consumption of the whole payment system, VISA is not less energy-intensive than Bitcoin. We also want to mention that public Blockchains are more than simple payment systems. They provide an immutable store for arbitrary data that can be leveraged in various applications. In addition to that, comparing VISA transactions to Blockchain transactions does not make much sense since a single transaction has a completely different meaning in a Blockchain system. It may for example transfer assets to several people or trigger a smart contract that can perform a variety of tasks. Moreover, there is no threat of a chargeback nor the requirement for a separate settlement process.

While the high energy consumption in terms of absolute numbers cannot be negated, everyone has to decide for themselves whether the cost of a PoW-Blockchain's energy intensity is adequate for the benefits that a decentralized and immutable ledger provides.

4 Discussion and Conclusion

In this chapter we have presented the tokenization of crowdfunded equity shares as a possible approach to improve access to capital for startups. With more and more sustainable initiatives relying on crowdfunding as a source of funding, this is an important precondition to master the challenges facing the world and to address the global sustainability agenda.

We introduced different Blockchain-based token standards that can be used to tokenize equity shares in crowdfunding markets. These token standards can be categorized into UTXO-based, layer-based and smart contract-based tokens. All three standards differ significantly from each other concerning the technology behind them. However, all of these token standards are similar in the sense that an external promise is attached to the token.

In a second step we analyzed advantages and drawbacks of tokenization in equity crowdfunding. We started with the general advantages of tokenizing assets on a Blockchain, which are not bound to a secondary market. Through the integration of asymmetric cryptography, investors have full control over their assets without having to trust a central custodian. Additionally, the programmability of Blockchains introduces a wide set of potential functionalities. The access to the Blockchain ecosystem leads to new opportunities through synergies with other projects on the same Blockchain. In addition to that, the divisibility of tokenized assets improves the liquidity of the market and favors financial inclusion.

We then focused our analysis on secondary market trading for crowdfunded equity shares, where we identified several key advantages of tokenization. First of all, costs caused by third party services such as banks and clearing houses could be lowered significantly because these services could (partially) be automated on the Blockchain. Second, Blockchain could offer a standardized framework by decoupling the crowdfunding platform and the transactional layer. Therefore, both intra- as well as inter-platform transfers would be feasible without the friction of trading periods. Furthermore, the ability to implement atomic transactions eliminates the counterparty risk during the exchange. Finally, assets could be controlled by several private keys through m-of-n multisig wallets.

In addition, we discussed three problems that remain unsolved or arise due to tokenization. We argued that tokenization cannot solve the problem of information asymmetries about the project quality. Also, legal and regulatory issues remain and must be considered carefully before implementing a token-based solution. Moreover, major Blockchains such as Bitcoin and Ethereum are currently secured by PoW consensus protocols that consume large amounts of electricity.

In contrast to the existing literature, we have taken a close look at the technical side of tokenizing assets. Furthermore, we identified which token standard would be best capable of unlocking the advantages of tokenization. Although further study of the different token standards as well as tests of their suitability are needed, (e.g. with case studies), according to our evaluation, smart contract-based tokens are arguably the most flexible option of the three. In this chapter we also analyzed the effects of tokenization on the three actors in crowdfunding. Arguably, tokenization would benefit investors most, as they profit from secured ownership of tokens, more functions and the access to more efficient secondary markets. Campaign creators benefit indirectly, because the advantages to the investors will consequently stimulate their interest in crowdfunding and lead to a higher success probability for the campaigns. Most of the time, tokenization and Blockchain have a negative impact on the platforms, as they foster decentralized systems with less power for the intermediary.

It is important to note that although we have limited ourselves to equity crowdfunding in this chapter, most of our findings can be applied to all investment-based and reward-based crowdfunding. This results from the fact that virtually any asset or external promise can be tokenized (Rosenfeld 2012). In this chapter we have focused on the advantages that could be enabled by a public Blockchain. In private and permissioned Blockchains, some of the initial advantages of public Blockchains are weakened, mostly because agents have to rely on central actors again.

In addition to further research using case studies of tokenization and trading projects in equity crowdfunding, future studies could investigate the impact of a (Blockchain-based) secondary market on the success of the initial crowdfunding campaign. In particular, it would be interesting to collect data and conduct an empirical analysis on the matter.

Acknowledgements The authors would like to thank Karen Wendt, the editor of this book, as well as the two anonymous reviewers for their valuable inputs. Furthermore, we thank Florian Bitterli, Raphael Knechtli, Emma Littlejohn and Tobias Wagner for their valuable support during the process of writing.

References

Agrawal, A. K., Catalini, C., & Goldfarb, A. (2013). Some simple economics of crowdfunding. Accessed July 15, 2019, http://www.nber.org/papers/w19133

Almasi, P. P. (2017). Bitcoin's energy consumption overblown? Accessed July 15, 2019, https://hackernoon.com/bitcoins-energy-consumption-overblown-31a4eded91f3

Ante, L., & Fiedler, I. (2019). Cheap signals in security and token offerings (STOs). Accessed July 15, 2019, http://dx.doi.org/10.2139/ssrn.3356303

Antonopoulos, A. M. (2014). *Mastering bitcoin: Unlocking digital crypto-currencies* (1st ed.). Sebastopol: O'Reilly Media.

Antonopoulos, A. M., & Wood, G. (2018). *Mastering ethereum: Building smart contracts and DApps*. Sebastopol: O'Reilly Media. Accessed July 15, 2019, https://github.com/ethereumbook/ethereumbook

Assia, Y., Buterin, V., Lior, H., Rosenfeld, M., & Lev, R. (2012). Colored coins whitepaper. Accessed July 15, 2019, http://www.ma.senac.br/wp-content/uploads/2018/05/ColoredCoinswhitepaper-DigitalAssets.pdf

Astebro, T., Fernandez, M., & Lovo, S. (2019). Herding in equity crowdfunding. SSRN, Accessed July 15, 2019, https://dx.doi.org/10.2139/ssrn.3084140

Bell, L., da Silva, L. C., & Preimanis, A. (2006). The cost of capital: An International Comparison. Tech. rep., Oxera Consulting Ltd, Accessed July 15, 2019, https://www.londonstockexchange.com/companies-and-advisors/main-market/documents/cost-of-capital-aninternational-comparison.pdf

Belleflamme, P., Omrani, N., & Peitz, M. (2015). The economics of crowdfunding platforms. Accessed July 15, 2019, http://dx.doi.org/10.2139/ssrn.2585611

Berentsen, A., & Schär, F. (2017). *Bitcoin, Blockchain und Kryptoassets*. Norderstedt: BoD - Books on Demand

Berentsen, A., & Schär, F. (2018). A short introduction to the World of cryptocurrencies. *Federal Reserve Bank of St Louis Review, 100*(1), 1–19. https://doi.org/10.20955/r.2018.1-16

Berentsen, A., & Schär, F. (2019). Stablecoins: The quest for a low volatility cryptocurrency. In A. Fatás (Ed.), *The economics of Fintech and digital currencies* (pp. 65–71). London: CEPR Press.

Bernstein, A., Hughson, E., & Weidenmier, M. (2019). Counterparty risk and the establishment of the New York stock exchange clearinghouse. *Journal of Political Economy, 127*(2), 689–729.

Buterin, V. (2013). Ethereum: A next-generation smart contract and decentralized application platform. Accessed 15 July 2019, https://github.com/ethereum/wiki/wiki/White-Paper

CFX. (2018a). Accessed July 15, 2019, https://cfxtrading.com/pages/about/#faq

CFX. (2018b). Accessed July 15, 2019, https://cfxtrading.com/

Chen, Y. (2018). Blockchain tokens and the potential democratization of entrepreneurship and innovation. *Business Horizons, 61*(4), 567–575.

Coinmarketcap. (2019). Accessed July 15, 2019, https://coinmarketcap.com/tokens/views/all/

Cuccuru, P. (2017). Beyond bitcoin: An early overview on smartcontracts. *International Journal of Law and Information Technology, 25*, 179–195. https://doi.org/10.1093/ijlit/eax003

de Vries, A. (2018). Bitcoin's growing energy problem. *Joule, 2*(5), 801–805.

Deffains-Crapsky, C., & Sudolska, A. (2014). Radical innovation and early stage financing gaps: Equity-based crowdfunding challenges. *Journal of Positive Management, 5*(2), 3. https://doi.org/10.12775/jpm.2014.009

Domingo, C. (2017). The bitcoin vs visa electricity consumption fallacy. Accessed July 15, 2019, https://hackernoon.com/the-bitcoin-vs-visa-electricity-consumption-fallacy-8cf194987a50

Domowitz, I., Glen, J., & Madhavan, A. (2001). Liquidity, volatility and equity trading costs across Countries and over time. *International Finance, 4*(2), 221–255.

Etherscan. (2019). Accessed July 15, 2019, https://etherscan.io/tokens

EY. (2018). Initial coin offerings (ICOs) The Class of 2017 – one year later. Accessed July 15, 2019, https://www.ey.com/Publication/vwLUAssets/ey-study-ico-research/<currencydollar>FILE/ey-study-ico-research.pdf

Freedman, D. M., & Nutting, M. R. (2015). *Equity crowdfunding for investors: A guide to risks, returns, regulations, funding portals, due diligence, and deal terms*. Hoboken: Wiley.

Hakim, L. (2012). Bitcoin 2.x (aka colored bitcoin) – Initial specs. Accessed July 15, 2019, https://yoniassia.com/coloredbitcoin/

Higgins, S. (2015). Bitcoin-powered crowdfunding app lighthouse has launched. Accessed July 15, 2019, https://coindesk.com/bitcoin-powered-crowdfunding-app-lighthouse-launches-open-beta

Hornuf, L., & Schwienbacher, A. (2017). Should securities regulation promote equity crowdfunding? *Small Business Economics, 49*(3), 579–593. https://doi.org/10.1007/s11187-017-9839-9

Howell, S. T., Niessner, M., & Yermack, D. (2018). Initial coin offerings: Financing growth with cryptocurrency token sales. Working Paper 24774, National Bureau of Economic Research. Accessed July 15, 2019, https://doi.org/10.3386/w24774, http://www.nber.org/papers/w24774

infoDev. (2013). Crowdfunding's potential for the developing world. Accessed July 15, 2019, https://www.infodev.org/infodev-files/wb_crowdfundingreport-v12.pdf

Jenik, I., Lyman, T., & Nava, A. (2017). Crowdfunding and financial inclusion. Accessed July 15, 2019, https://www.cgap.org/sites/default/files/Working-Paper-Crowdfunding-and-Financial-Inclusion-Mar-2017.pdf

Jentzsch, C. (2016). Decentralized autonomous organization to automate governance. Accessed July 15, 2019, https://download.slock.it/public/DAO/WhitePaper.pdf

Killerstorm. (2015). Colored coins or mastercoin? Accessed July 15, 2019, https://w3.reddit.com/r/coloredcoin/comments/1o6yke/colored_coins_or_mastercoin/ccpgy0x/

Klein, M. A. (1973). The economics of security divisibility and financial intermediation. *The Journal of Finance, 28*(4), 923–931. https://www.jstor.org/stable/2978344

McGowan, E. (2017). The SEC JOBS act and title III crowdfunding. Retrieved July 10, 2019, Accessed July, 15 2019, https://www.startups.com/library/expert-advice/american-jobs-act-title-iii-crowdfunding

Messeni Petruzzelli, A., Natalicchio, A., Panniello, U., & Roma, P. (2019). Understanding the crowdfunding phenomenon and its implications for sustainability. *Technological Forecasting and Social Change, 141*, 138–148. https://doi.org/10.1016/j.techfore.2018.10.002

Mollick, E. (2014). The dynamics of crowdfunding: An exploratory study. *Journal of Business Venturing, 29*(1), 1–16. https://doi.org/10.1016/j.jbusvent.2013.06.005

Moyano, J. P., & Ross, O. (2017). KYC optimization using distributed ledger technology. *Business & Information Systems Engineering, 59*(6), 411–423. https://doi.org/10.1007/s12599-017-0504-2

Murray, J. (2015). Equity crowdfunding and peer-to-peer lending in New Zealand: The first year. *JASSA The Finsia Journal of Applied Finance*. Accessed July 15, 2019, https://ssrn.com/abstract=2595354

Muscarella, C., & Vetsuypens, M. (1996). Stock splits: Signaling or liquidity? the case of ADR 'solo-splits'. *Journal of Financial Economics, 42*(1), 3–26. https://doi.org/10.1016/0304-405X(95)00872-C

Nakamoto, S. (2008). Bitcoin: A peer-to-peer electronic cash system. Accessed July 15, 2019, https://bitcoin.org/bitcoin.pdf

Nyffenegger, R., & Schär, F. (2018). Token Sales: Eine Analyse des Blockchain-basierten Unternehmensfinanzierungsinstruments. *Corporate Finance, 5*(06), 121–125.

Ostrowski, R. (2018). Time-locked wallets: An introduction to ethereum smart contracts. Accessed July 15, 2019, https://medium.com/bitfwd/time-locked-wallets-an-introduction-to-ethereum-smart-contracts-3dfccac0673c

Rohr, J., & Wright, A. (2019). Blockchain-based token sales, initial coin offerings, and the democratization of public capital markets. *Hastings Law Journal, 70*(2), 463–524. http://www.hastingslawjournal.org/wp-content/uploads/70.2-Rohr-1.pdf

Rosenfeld, M. (2012). Overview of colored coins. Accessed July 15, 2019, https://bitcoil.co.il/BitcoinX.pdf

Sahdev, N. (2017). Crowdfunding meets blockchain. Accessed July 15, 2019, http://dx.doi.org/10.2139/ssrn.3047682

Schär, F. (2019). Blockchains: How they work and what they are used for. In *Crypto Finance*.

Schwartz, A. A. (2013). Crowdfunding securities. *Notre Dame Law Review, 88*(1457). https://scholarship.law.nd.edu/ndlr/vol88/iss3/8

Schwienbacher, A. (2019). Equity crowdfunding: Anything to celebrate? *Venture Capital, 21*(1), 65–74. https://doi.org/10.1080/13691066.2018.1559010

SEC. (2019). Spotlight on initial coin offerings (ICOs). Accessed July 15, 2019, https://www.sec.gov/ICO

Seedrs. (2019a). Accessed July 15, 2019, https://seedrs.com/learn/help/what-is-a-trading-cycle

Seedrs. (2019b). Accessed July 15, 2019, https://seedrs.com/secondary-market

Seedrs. (2019c). Accessed July 15, 2019, https://help.seedrs.com/en/

Seres, I. A., Gulyás, L., Nagy, D. A., & Burcsi, P. (2019). Topological analysis and of bitcoin's and lightning network. Accessed July 15, 2019, https://arxiv.org/abs/1901.04972

Shomer, A., & Zach, E. (2015). Colored coins protocol specification. Accessed July 15, 2019, https://github.com/Colored-Coins/Colored-Coins-Protocol-Specification/wiki/Introduction

Signori, A., & Vismara, S. (2016). Returns on investments in equity crowdfunding. Accessed July 15, 2019, https://dx.doi.org/10.2139/ssrn.2765488

Smith, R. T. (2001). Price volatility, welfare, and trading hours in asset markets. *Journal of Banking & Finance, 25*(3), 479–503. https://doi.org/10.1016/S0378-4266(00)00086-8

Tether. (2019). Accessed February 24, 2019, https://tether.to/

Tomczak, A., & Brem, A. (2013). A conceptualized investment model of crowdfunding. *Venture Capital, 15*(4), 335–359. https://doi.org/10.1080/13691066.2013.847614

Turan, S. S. (2015). Stakeholders in equity-based crowdfunding: Respective risks over the equity crowdfunding lifecycle. *Journal of Financial Innovation, 1*(2), 141–151. https://doi.org/10.15194/jofi_2015.v1.i2.34

Wall, E., & Malm, G. (2016). *Using Blockchain Technology and Smart Contracts to Create a Distributed Securities Depository*. Master's thesis, Lund University. Accessed July 15, 2019, http://lup.lub.lu.se/luur/download?func=downloadFile&recordOId=8885750&fileOId=8885765

Willett, J. R. (2012). Mastercoin specification (version 0.5). Accessed July 15, 2019, https://sites.google.com/site/2ndbtcwpaper/2ndBitcoinWhitepaper.pdf

Wilson, K., & Testoni, M. (2014). Improving the role of equity crowdfunding in Europe's capital markets. Accessed July 15, 2019, http://dx.doi.org/10.2139/ssrn.2502280

Zhu, H., & Zhou, Z. Z. (2016). Analysis and outlook of applications of blockchain technology to equity crowdfunding in China. *Financial Innovation, 2*(1). https://doi.org/10.1186/s40854-016-0044-7

Zuber, I., Krellenstein, A., Unsystemizer, Rippler, Weller, D., Dermody, R., et al. (2015). Counterparty documentation. Accessed July 15, 2019, https://counterparty.io/docs/assets/

Jakob Roth is a research and teaching assistant at the Center for Innovative Finance at the University of Basel. He has a bachelor's degree in business and economics with a major in economics from the University of Basel and is currently in the master's program at the University of Basel. His research focus lies on the implementation of Blockchain technology and Smart Contracts for renewable energies, especially microgrid electricity trading, which has been the subject of his bachelor's thesis and further scientific works.

Prof. Dr. Fabian Schär is Professor for Distributed Ledger Technology/Fintech at the Faculty of Business and Economics. In addition, he is the Managing Director of the Center for Innovative Finance at the University of Basel. His research focus is on interdisciplinary analyses of Smart Contracts, asset tokenization and Blockchain applications. He has a Ph.D. in Cryptoassets and Blockchain Technology and co-authored several publications including the bestselling book "Bitcoin, Blockchain and Cryptoassets" and several scientific articles, some of them published in the prestigious Federal Reserve Bank of St. Louis Review. He is the organizer of the "Blockchain Symposium", the "Blockchain Challenge", member of the organizing committee of a conference with the Swiss National Bank and co-initiator of a project to secure academic credentials on a Blockchain. In addition, he is a board member of Crypto Fund AG, the first FINMA regulated crypto asset manager, teaches at various universities and at Deutsche Börse and is an invited speaker at numerous conferences, including the G20 Global Financial Stability Conference. Prior to that, he worked as a consultant in various positions at banks and bank-related companies.

Aljoscha Schöpfer is a research and teaching assistant at the Center for Innovative Finance at the University of Basel. He holds a bachelor's degree in business and economics from the University of Basel and is currently enrolled at the Norwegian School of Economics (NHH) as a master student. Throughout the last years, he has gained deep know-how both in the economic and technical analysis of Blockchain technology as well as comprehensive hands-on experience within the matter of cryptocurrencies. He works closely with Dr. Fabian Schär, Professor for Distributed Ledger Technology/Fintech, and supports him in his research activity. Furthermore, Aljoscha teaches courses about distributed ledger technology.

Blockchain and the Evolution of Information Society

Mihai Alisie

Abstract Today we are witnessing a multi-layered metamorphosis of our culture and society, accelerated by the technological developments of the last decades. The main drivers of this metamorphosis are information and interconnectivity. Here we will try to analyze this transformation from a holistic perspective.

Keywords Theory of change · Theories of change · Blockchain · Information society

Today we are witnessing a multi-layered metamorphosis of our culture and society, accelerated by the technological developments of the last decades. The main drivers of this metamorphosis are information and interconnectivity. Here we will try to analyze this transformation from a holistic perspective.

It's important to note that this transformation is not just about the most powerful microchip or the fastest Internet connection. It is also about how citizens and our social systems fit into this emergent bigger picture as we become part of an information society.

Instant information creation, sharing and consumption, international collaboration, and real-time global commerce are just a few of the things we take for granted today, but not so long ago they were considered science fiction. Today, this is the "reality" we live in. But what does tomorrow hold for us?

The worldview encapsulated in the following essay sees the technological puzzle pieces that were uncovered over the course of time as not only completing each other, but also as catalyzing the evolution of a new social operating system at a planetary scale.

M. Alisie (✉)
AKASHA Foundation, Zug, Switzerland
e-mail: mihai@akasha.world

K. Wendt (ed.), *Theories of Change*, Sustainable Finance,
https://doi.org/10.1007/978-3-030-52275-9_20

When it comes to blockchain technology, which presents the latest addition to this puzzle, a decade after the concept of "blockchain" was introduced through Bitcoin as a peer-to-peer electronic cash system, we are still scratching the surface of what can be done with this new type of permanent information medium.

For example, since the introduction of "blockchain", it only took 5 years to expand our understanding from a decentralized ledger designed as a peer-to-peer electronic cash system, to a world computer providing a platform for decentralized applications in the form of Ethereum.

Notably, in this piece we will explore "blockchain" through its possible ramifications at societal level, especially in the context of collective intelligence, self-organization, and socio-economic systems. We will think beyond "cryptocurrency" and see how the underlying problem of trust and coordination Bitcoin first solved for the monetary system, is present in many areas of our society, well beyond finance.

For thousands of years we have used a variety of mediums to engrave rules in the form of laws, constitutions, codes of conduct, and contracts. Depending on the age, the "authenticity" would be checked through handwriting, ink signatures, and wax seals, to name a few.

During all this time, we have constantly advanced both the medium of storage and the way in which the information is stored, distributed, and verified—from pieces of clay to sheets of paper and, more recently, "clouds" of data.

As a blockchain, Ethereum introduced "smart contracts" into the picture. These smart contracts can be seen as agreements between two or more parties signed cryptographically, time stamped, and permanently stored on the Ethereum blockchain.

This marks a big leap from handwritten contracts signed with ink, stamped by a recognized authority and stored physically as information written on a paper file or as bits in a PDF file. And this leap allows us to imagine new systems to store, verify and distribute information in a secure way at global scale.

In the context of an information society, this is more valuable than gold and is truly priceless. Even more than that—it's meaningful in so many ways.

For example permissionless blockchains like Ethereum serve as home for thousands of smart contracts offering an auditable, transparent way for anyone from anywhere to enter a cryptographically secure agreement globally—without the possibility of interference from any third party thanks to its decentralized, neutral, open and public nature.

This is how, for the first time in human history, you can have a really high degree of confidence that your agreement will not be altered or destroyed by anyone in the foreseeable future thanks to open source software, mathematics and cryptography.

Before, you had to trust a person, institution or corporation that the agreement will be there when you need it and, preferably, that it will not be changed without your consent or acknowledgement at least.

The decentralized, open, neutral nature of permissionless blockchains mean that you don't have to blindly trust anymore and that today each of us have in our hands a new way to autonomously transact value, create, store, sign and verify agreements at an international scale without an intermediary.

Through permissionless blockchains humanity has gained a new tool in its informational toolkit designed for processing, distributing, and storing permanently information and wealth at the speed of light.

In a way, just as the Internet allows anyone from anywhere to communicate at a global scale through the Web, Bitcoin allows anyone from anywhere to transact through cryptocurrency. Now, Ethereum is enabling cryptographically secure agreements for anyone at global scale through smart contracts using cryptocurrency.

It's worth mentioning that since Ethereum appeared, a number of other blockchain projects have emerged in the smart contracts space. However, at the time of writing this article, Ethereum remains by far the largest smart contract ecosystem, which is why we will refer to it when discussing various ideas involving a smart contract component.

The purpose of this essay is not to focus on explaining the historical or technical details of the individual puzzle pieces, but rather to gaze at the bigger picture in an attempt to understand the possibilities opened by this unique convergence of ideas and technologies present at this particular point in human history.

This is also not meant to be pitched as a blockchain introduction piece, and I will assume that the reader is at least familiar with blockchain as a concept. However, even if the general knowledge level is low when it comes to blockchain technology, my intention is not to talk about "the tech", but about the social structures that can be built around the tech. The main advantage is that blockchain is based on a distributed ledger technology, so there is no central server where information is stored, but many computers that can be imagined like lego blocks that are connected (Fig. 1).

Fig. 1 Blockchain built on distributed ledger technology

That being said, we will look at institutions and nations as mental constructions with the purpose of continuously evolving and adapting to better serve citizens. We will then attempt to paint a near-future, actionable scenario in which our social nature as human beings is nurtured and harnessed for the common good, both at the level of the individual, and the collective.

Perhaps in the future we will look back with amusement on how some of the things seemingly science fiction now, have become our reality, again. But, before jumping too far into the future, let's travel back in time in order to understand the genesis of our information-based society.

1 A Quick Overview of the (Written) Journey So Far

Over 5000 years ago, one of the earliest socio-economic systems powered by information-storage systems was introduced in Mesopotamia, creating in the process the foundations of our modern society. A key achievement of this civilization presented the introduction of the so called cuneiform script, which is depicted in Fig. 2. This marked the beginning of the information revolution within human society, changing its nature for thousands of years to come.

Looking back, this new method for storing and distributing information and wealth, transformed Mesopotamia into one of the largest and most thriving civilizations of its era. The ripples through time caused by this invention have led to our current information age society, a sort of unintended side effect.

Unlike the computer code powering the digital information society of today, the invention of cuneiform script consisted of creating wedge-shaped marks on clay tablets with a blunt reed. As rudimentary as this might sound today, this invention gave birth to concepts and solutions previously unheard of in a variety of areas, from accounting to the creation of legal contracts.

Fig. 2 Cuneiform script from Mesopotamia

Fast forward to more recent days, our civilization has been through three major information revolutions in the last thousand years:

- Printing press
- Telecommunication
- Internet

In a true domino-effect fashion, these information revolutions furthered progress in most fields by creating accessible mediums of information, resulting in more participation and enlightenment by increasing accessibility to information for the individual, which resulted in fewer social limitations.

Today we witness another phase of exponential advancement: digital information technologies fostered by the occurrence of the Web are fundamentally changing our ways of life and human cooperation. With the recent addition of blockchain technology, I like to call this moment in time the "crypto renaissance."

If we would overlay this with the fourteenth to seventeenth century renaissance, powered by the printing press, we would observe the following:

- The introduction of a new method for storing and distributing information in society
- A period marked by important technical achievements allowing a faster propagation of ideas
- The ignition of (social) experimentation and an intellectual revitalization
- The triggering of paradigm shifts deepening our understanding of the world, ourselves and the universe
- All of this resulting in social, political, and economic transformations

This highlights how, taking the technological perspective aside, the Internet is one of the most powerful social experiments in human history: an international mesh-network connecting billions of humans and machines at a planetary level, enabling in the process a free* flow of information, wealth, and services to be exchanged without boundaries—at least theoretically.

The introduction of the Internet as an information technology has accelerated the spread of new ideas and concepts and also led to the materialization of entirely new ones. The Internet reduced drastically the cost of global coordination and the Web as a service built on top of the Internet's infrastructure became a catalyst of co-creation, exponentially increasing our collaborative potential.

Participants with Internet access became universally connected and within reach of each other, readily available to exchange information. This allowed us as humans to transcend time and space limitations—keystroke by keystroke, tap after tap.

The shifts caused by this information revolution can be felt throughout the fabric of our society as storms of bits eroding the pillars of a centralized paradigm—even if during its accelerated expansion and commercialization, the Internet infrastructure recently has become, yet again, centralized.

Again, let's remember, the information economy paradigm created thousands of years ago in Mesopotamia was, unknowingly, the commencement of a successful social experiment that has ultimately led humanity here. Now we have gained a new tool that can be used to make the leap into the next iteration.

With the addition of distributed ledgers another information revolution is underway. The Ethereum blockchain is a new kind of permanent information processing and storage medium accessible by anyone from anywhere—and no one, not even governments or other powerful third parties, will be able to hinder citizens from accessing it to learn and verify its actual contents.

What can we achieve with this?

Or maybe a better question is what do we want to achieve with this?

2 Thirty Years After the Web: New Superpowers Unlocked by Blockchain

Since the early 1990s, the Web brought humans new "superpowers" similar to a digital nervous system interconnecting us on a planetary scale. The Internet was already around for decades, but it was mainly used for transporting data between machines without much thought put into creating a world-wide information medium easily accessible for humans as well. That's where the Web came in and built on top of the data layer informational interfaces. An example of it is given in Fig. 3.

The first iteration of the Web consisted mainly of static "Web sites" presenting information on a white background page with black text. Fast forwarding, tools like

Fig. 3 Typical computer script for blockchain

Wordpress lowered the barrier of entry and made it clear that Websites are the "killer app" of the Web 1.0.

The second iteration of the Web introduced interactive "Web apps" with the most successful examples exploiting our innate desire to connect with one another and come together as groups, regardless of where we are on the planet. Since humans are social beings by nature, it's hardly a surprise that the "killer app" of Web 2.0 are social networks like Facebook et al.

However, the current state of the Web is in peril. As a result of the network's increasing commercialization, and the fact that almost all aspects of our life today are somehow dependent on the Internet, the emergence of major players that act as centralizers has been favored.

Instead of permitting unfettered freedom of expression and access to information for all people on the planet, misinformation is spreading, and companies and nations alike are limiting free access to information for either economic or political reasons.

Ruthless political players across the world abuse this weakness of today's Web for their own agendas, mass-manipulating minds in an unprecedented manner by abusing technology of social network giants, initially designed as advertising engines, to spread their propaganda.

In an open letter marking the 30th anniversary of the Web, the creator of the Web, Tim Berners-Lee wrote that the "fight for the Web is one of the most important causes of our time." He identified three major "sources of dysfunction" affecting the Web: deliberate malicious intent, system design, and the unintended negative consequences of benevolent design. He added: "You can't just blame one government, one social network, or the human spirit. . . . To get this right, we will need to come together as a global Web community."

The good news is that there is still hope.

Whereas the main "superpowers" we unlocked during the Web 2.0 wave revolved mainly around individual self-expression with "user-generated content", "discussion", and "reactions" on various topics, the next wave of innovation will expand our actions and interactions online beyond comments and likes.

Today it is not yet quite clear how the next wave of blockchain-enabled innovation will pan out, but we do have some examples that can help us to make educated guesses. Let's try to paint a picture of what the future might bring.

To start, let's list some of the new "superpowers" blockchains made possible:

- Permanent data and information storage (permissionless blockchains)
- Unfettered freedom of expression (decentralized publishing platforms)
- Unfettered freedom of transaction (permissionless cryptocurrencies)
- New forms of "value" (token standards like the ERC 20, ERC 721, etc.)
- New forms of organizing & collaborating at scale (decentralized autonomous organizations)
- New forms of distributed decision making (decentralized governance systems)
- Many other things that we probably haven't discovered yet?

With the above in mind, let's do some futurescaping while asking:

- How will these new superpowers transform our interactions at societal scale as an information-based society?
- How can these puzzle pieces fit together when taking into consideration both our individual ***and*** collective abilities to organize and express ourselves?

Thanks to these new puzzle pieces, people are able to do more than "discuss", "like", or "react" to various topics as observers of our world reality (while being observed, analyzed, and monetized).

With the new superpowers unlocked by blockchain technology, we gained the ability to organize, crowdfund, and coordinate collective action as co-creators of our world reality. In fact, it is already possible to exchange "value" in so many new forms and shapes on blockchains—from cryptocurrencies to CryptoKitties, a blockchain based game built around unique, digital collectibles shaped as cute kitties living on the Ethereum network.

We cannot know for sure, but this time, I tend to believe that by combining these puzzle pieces, collective (and intelligent) self expression will become the next "killer app" just like individual self expression became the "killer app" of the Web 2.0 wave of social networking. It will be possible to go beyond just "talking about stuff" and in fact begin "actually doing something about it" in completely new ways.

Self-sustaining communities, medical research crowdfunding, citizen science, open-source software & hardware, activism crowdsourcing, and many other purposeful collective actions are within reach—at a global scale.

In a moment of inspiration, someone might ask: What if we can build something better with the new superpowers we unlocked as an information society? What if we build something designed to enhance our natural ability to come together as one—but this time not around a "common enemy", but instead for the "common good?"

Before leaping into the next iteration of the system, let's look first at the foundations of our information society, in order to understand if they're able to withstand the test of time and ensure that the data, information, knowledge and wisdom generated by our society will be accessible to our future generations as well.

3 From Pyramids in the Desert to the Data Pyramids of Tomorrow

To put information technology into context let us start with the pyramids as a building block for effective information transmission. Mankind has moved from information gathering, through information filtering to information integration and wisdom. In each step the building blocks are smoothened and transformed very much like with the building up of the pyramids pictured in Fig. 4.

According to Wikipedia, an information society is a society where the creation, distribution, use, integration, and manipulation of information is a significant economic, political, and cultural activity. Its main drivers are digital information and communication technologies, which have resulted in an information explosion

Fig. 4 Pyramids of Gizeh as a natural blueprint for our information society

profoundly changing all aspects of social organization, including the economy, education, health, warfare, government, and democracy.

The futurist, Alvin Toffler, best known for his book Future Shock, proposed in his 1990 book "Powershift—Knowledge, Wealth and Violence at the edge of the twenty-first Century "three types of power:

- Force (physical power)
- Wealth (economic power)
- Knowledge (the power of information)

If we look at the news, geo-political conflicts are today less often carried out at the level of physical power. The predominant form of power used to carry modern conflicts at state level revolve around wealth, in the form of various economic sanctions and trade agreements.

In this context, major corporations of the information processing business have emerged as global players holding vastly more economic power than most nation states, by focusing on the power of knowledge asymmetry. Further, we observe a competition for knowledge and the best minds, as well as "information wars" targeting citizens and aimed at shaping public opinion.

An interesting insight comes from Charles McGee and his essay titled "The Age of Imagination: Coming Soon to a Civilization Near You" published in the early 90s where he proposes the idea that the best way to assess the evolution of human civilization is through the lens of communication:

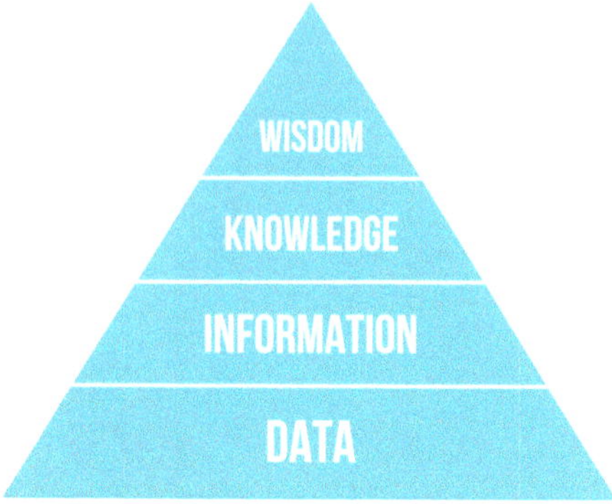

Fig. 5 Rowley, Jennifer E. 2007. "The Wisdom Hierarchy: Representations of the DIKW hierarchy". *Journal of Information Science* 33, no. 2: 163–80

> The most successful groups throughout human history have had one thing in common: when compared to their competition they had the best system of communication.
>
> The fittest communicators—whether tribe, citystate, kingdom, corporation, or nation—had (1) a larger percentage of people with (2) access to (3) higher quality information, (4) a greater ability to transform that information into knowledge and action, (5) and more freedom to communicate that new knowledge to the other members of their group.

In other words, according to this view, future success will not be defined by the biggest weapons, neither necessarily by the largest bank accounts but the ones setting up the best systems of storing, distributing and processing information into knowledge and action. This may occur on a local, or a national scale, but more likely it will evolve in a global arena.

This is also one of the reasons why the current firms built around top-down hierarchies and systems of control providing access to information on a need-to-know basis, may not necessary emerge as the dominant players in their respective fields in the future.

Likely they will be outpaced by new forms of organization leveraging heterarchy, self-organization and open access to information empowering participants with the ability to transform the information into knowledge-in-action, as we will see later.

Seen in the light of an "information society" where "information" is the cornerstone of society, the new paradigm shifts away from military-type control and power towards knowledge with the goal of generating wisdom accessible to as many members of the group or society as possible.

One perspective that can help depict our modern information-based society and the distribution of "mind power" across the various layers is the Data Information Knowledge Wisdom (DIKW) pyramid (Fig. 5).

Like other hierarchy models, the Knowledge Pyramid has rigidly set building blocks—data comes first, information is next, then knowledge follows and finally wisdom is on the top.

Each step up the pyramid answers questions about the initial data and adds value to it. The more questions we answer, the higher we move up the pyramid. In other words, the more we enrich our data with meaning and context, the more knowledge

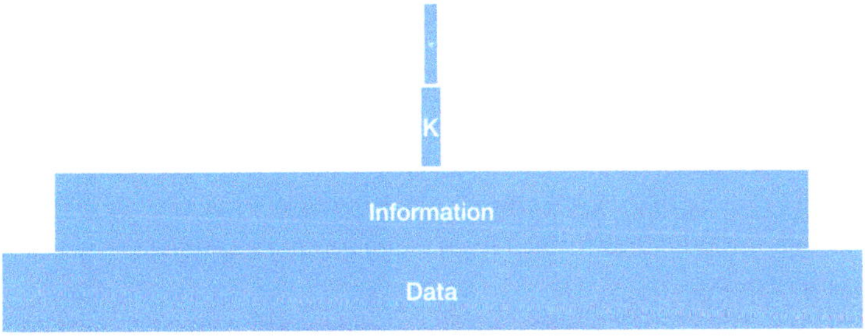

Fig. 6 Own representation: real shape of DIKW without complete market information and information barriers

and insights we get out of it. At the top of the pyramid, we have turned the knowledge and insights into a learning experience that guides our actions.

When looking at today's information society we can observe a number of things such as:

- An enormous amount of data collected by a handful of corporations
- A massive amount of information processed by a handful of corporations
- This data and information being monopolized by for-profit corporations
- Very little, to zero knowledge shared with society from the available data and information
- The knowledge that is derived from the available data and information is proprietary and mainly used to improve advertising algorithms in a pursuit to maximize profitability
- The wisdom layer is almost nonexistent at societal level and currently reserved only for corporations able to exploit the proprietary knowledge generated from all the data and information collected from billions of users around the world

With this in mind, a more accurate representation of the DIKW pyramid has more the shape depicted in Fig. 6. Data and to an extent information it for everyone but the monetization of data is only for large corporations.

This is far from ideal and points to a future where, if the current paradigm of an increasingly commercialized Internet continues unaltered, the vast data and information we generate as citizens of this information society will be collected, analyzed, and potentially "weaponized" by powerful AIs, generating profit more and more efficiently for a handful of powerful corporations.

From the original dream of the Internet and the Web as tools for mass information and empowerment, we find ourselves heading straight into a world continuously shaped through persuasion machines exploiting human vulnerability at a planetary scale.

This didn't happen overnight and started relatively benignly with advertising as a "business model". Gradually the advertisers wanted more information about the "targeted users" seeing the ads so the platforms started collecting more information.

One thing led to another and this marked the beginning of surveillance capitalism as the default business model on the Web.

As if this was not bad enough, we then witnessed how the same mechanisms designed to surveil humanity at a global scale for "better ads" can be used to influence presidential elections and major political decisions with vast geo-political implications such as Brexit. That is when it became clear that, without even realizing, the Web transformed from a tool for mass information to a weapon of mass disinformation.

This is how today we find ourselves living in a world where we have outsourced at planetary scale our collective memory and freedom of expression to a handful of powerful corporations amassing incredible amounts of data—both personal and interpersonal.

This is a very risky proposition when considering the implications of any entity, be it a corporation or a government, dictating what you are allowed to say, what information you are allowed to see, and who you are allowed to talk to.

Coming back to the "force, wealth, and knowledge" analogy of the three types of power, we can appreciate how nations from around the world are basically outsourcing their "mind" on a global scale to a handful of US-centric companies or surrender to total state-controlled enterprises as happening in China that do not always have the interests of citizens at heart.

In a way, this is the dark side of the cloud, seeking to centralize as much control and power as possible under the operator of the Web app in an attempt to maximize profits. A different perspective comes from Vitalik Buterin, the creator of Ethereum, in an article titled "Control as Liability" where he states:

> Before, every bit of control you have was good: it gives you more flexibility to earn revenue, if not now then in the future. Now, every bit of control you have is a liability: you might be regulated because of it.

This is especially relevant when considering blockchain-based applications where control of the data is not an option in many cases, and entrepreneurs try to come up with innovative business models that do not rely on advertising and other privacy-eroding models, tracking users for a quick return on investment.

Today, without a doubt, surveillance capitalism is the default business model of the Internet with advertising being the main driving force behind this trend. But will it continue to be the default business model of the Internet of the future or will we see fresh new takes on this problem?

We currently live in a "collected information society"; what would a "collective information" society look like? If the status quo is maintained and humanity's collective memory and freedom of expression continues to be outsourced at a global scale like now, the future does not look very good.

Can we reimagine the data, information, knowledge, and wisdom distribution at societal level for a brighter future as an information society making a last minute u-turn from becoming a monopolized-knowledge society?

To answer these questions we have to first distinguish better between data, information, knowledge, and wisdom and the process of learning through which shared understanding and wisdom are generated.

4 A Digital Crossroad Marking the Rise of the Learning Society

If we visualize the DIKW model from a different perspective, with the time dimension added to the picture depicted in Fig. 7, we can start to see how the learning process comes into play at various stages, each consuming a particular layer of the DIKW pyramid to ultimately generate shared understanding and wisdom.

In 1973, Donald Schön developed the idea that change is constant in a modern nation and thus, to adapt to this change, there must be a constant state of learning within the society of that nation. Robert Maynard Hutchins also argued that given the ever-changing nature of nation states, particularly in business organisations, it wasn't possible for educational institutions to keep up; in fact, they weren't even expected to.

This theoretical framework has developed since then and it is even more relevant in our days thanks to the interconnectedness facilitated by today's technology and the global nature of the challenges faced by our generation(s).

Fast forwarding to the present, we find ourselves operating in obsolete systems designed for a world that's no longer around. At the same time new paradigms of how we organize our societies have yet to emerge. We are at a point where we have to realize and learn about our information-based world, formulate new systems that can help our civilization to rise to the challenges of today, and emancipate ourselves from the corporate centralizers controlling vast amounts of information.

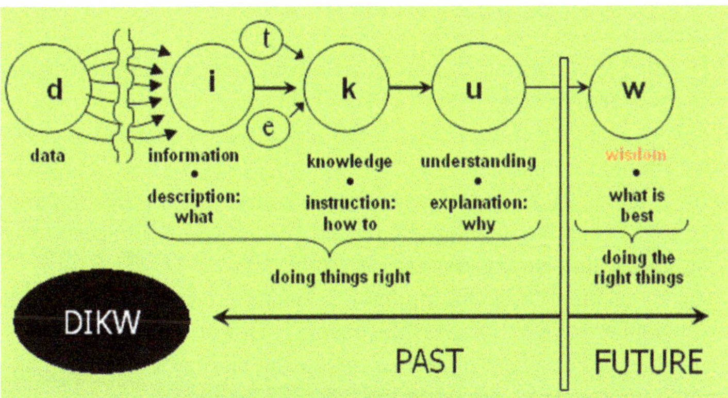

Fig. 7 Flow diagram of the DIKW hierarchy available under creative common license accessed April 172,020 "Educational strategies to reduce risk: A choice of social responsibility" (https://www.researchgate.net/figure/Flow-diagram-of-the-DIKW-hierarchy_fig1_277998122/download)

We are called to be the architects of a better mental construct that can maximize our chances of success for instance when tackling global challenges like global warming. Real-time response and decision making powered by open knowledge and shared understanding empowering efficient, localized, action should be the hallmarks of this new mental construct.

In contrast, the ideal state for many governments around the world appears to be imagined as the "status-quo" with opaque, month-long bureaucratic processes, passing decisions through governance systems designed for a world without Internet, smartphones, strong cryptographic signatures, and blockchains.

On the same note, while speaking of "learning", the educational system is usually associated with the learning concept in the minds of many. However, the modern educational system of today has its roots in the industrial revolution when a big part of humanity was "onboarded" into the industrial society.

In this not-so-distant past, the main mission of the educational system was to teach people how to fit in an industrial society, usually through understanding of how to operate the industrial machines which powered the industrial revolution. We still carry much of this industrial way of thinking in the way we label the children in generations, for example the 2019 batch of graduates, as a sort of "product" of the "educational industry" to be consumed by society.

Today the Web, which has impacted the process of diffusing knowledge in society can lead to the emergence of MOOCs (massive open online courses), TED talks, and global activists and bloggers that help individuals to self-organize and take action, much in the way Buckimster Fuller had envisaged in his work "Education Automation: comprehensive Learning for Emergent Humanity".

As we speak online communities helping each other by answering questions and working together on projects of all kinds. Now people from around the world are using the Web to self-educate and learn about how to participate in an information society. Indeed slowly educational institutions are feeling this change and try to adapt in interesting ways.

The DIKW pyramid has been adjusted by a number of market participants like Fig. 8 illustrates.

Notably another interesting insight comes from contemplating the hierarchical nature of many of our current forms of governmental and corporate organisation. For instance, why do so many of the "Chief X Officer" job titles contain the word "chief" and "officer" in the first place?

We have a rather tribal word "chief" and a military reference of the "officer" which implies a strong hierarchy and a chain of command built around executing-and-not-thinking if the command comes from the "chief".

But even more interesting, the military association brings with it the thinking patterns of planning strategy around "the enemy". This adversarial way of thinking inevitably results in becoming more like the enemy since you are calculating your moves around the enemy moves. And the other way around.

The hierarchy of the firm is an example of a social structure working through invisible social protocols to create a collective taking actions for a specific end-goal.

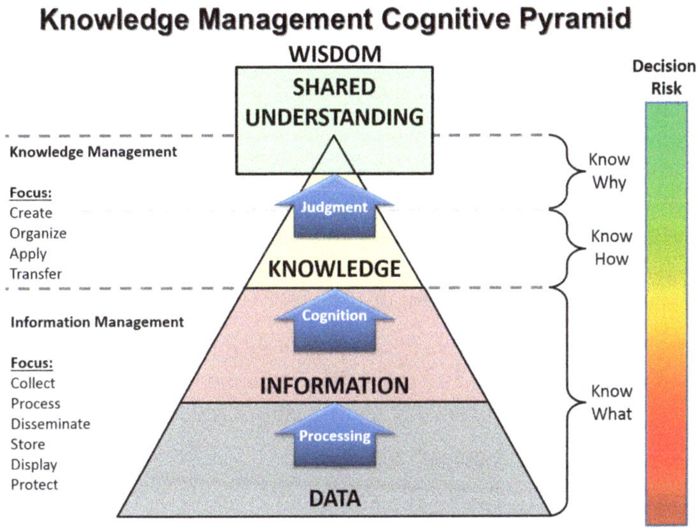

Fig. 8 DIKW pyramid available under creative common licence adjusted (https://www.pngfind.com/mpng/TRwJix_km-pyramid-adaptation-knowledge-management-cognitive-pyramid-hd/)

To exemplify this, here is an adaptation of the DIKW pyramid by US Army Knowledge Managers:

The focus of this entire process of deriving knowledge and wisdom is to decrease the decision risk faced by operatives during missions and improve the chances of success while minimizing casualties. Arguably, the shared understanding and wisdom is not in the service of society at large but to a specific set of interests with a clear objective to take efficient action against another party labeled as "the enemy".

When going even deeper, this way of looking at the world in terms of "us" versus "them" is by large highly problematic: many times this division stands in the way of progress at a global scale, quite ironically since, in an overly-simplified fashion, we could say that in an interconnected world everyone is "we".

Indeed, the short-term gain of outpacing a competitor or withholding innovation by blockchain patents ultimately takes a long-term toll on innovation or leads to unnecessary expenditure of resources or leads to damaging effects for individuals and society.

The reality points to "both-and" thinking instead of "either-or". The borders delimiting humans in terms of "us" and "them" are slowly but surely fading away in a world where language is becoming one of the last frontiers standing in the way of global human collaboration.

Now, if we would try to break away from the industrial military-inspired, old way of thinking putting "the enemy" at the center of our plans (something external) to an approach focused on "the wellbeing of the citizens" (something internal), we have to change the way we both learn and act.

First on the list—hitting both at the trial "chief" and "officer" so deeply ingrained in our social algorithms—the top-down hierarchical way of doing things is not ideal, especially at a global scale.

The bottom-up, self-organizing way of doing things is better suited to localized, real-time action. In this picture we break away from the "globalization" term and move towards "glocalization"—a paradigm prioritizing efficient, real-time, localized knowledge-in-action and citizen satisfaction above top-down control.

The benefits of this approach are vastly underexplored since the default operating system of our society rests on a top-down pyramid of control, however we can imagine some advantages in the form of:

- Smarter citizens making informed decisions in their communities
- Smarter nations that systematize innovation for communities of all scales
- Smarter organizations automatizing many business processes

More specifically these could be translated in:

- Increased citizen engagement and satisfaction
- Efficient governance systems
- More transparent governance processes
- Business-process automatization at city, national, and international scales
- Improved resilience of communication systems against natural disasters
- Accelerated speed of reaction in times of need
- Shared knowledge harnessed for local challenges but generating a global, shared understanding
- Many more things we will uncover?

So how could we nurture this? How could we increase the amount of open data, information, knowledge, and wisdom within societies? But maybe more important, what will be the next phase of our information-based society?

Arguably, some of the best-case scenarios involve leveraging technology with a holistic view in mind to create social structures that serve humanity—not the other way around.

5 Innovation Systems, Collective Intelligence and Decentralized Organizing

According to Wikipedia, a country's innovative performance largely depends on how the various actors involved relate to each other as elements of a collective system of knowledge creation and use, as well as the technologies they use.

Furthermore, in order to promote innovation, the different innovative actors must have strong linkages with each other based on a strong level of trust and governments should promote and facilitate trust among the different innovation actors.

A term used to define this complex set of interactions is "national innovation system". Following a similar line of thought, "The Rainforest: The Secret to Building the Next Silicon Valley", Hwang and Horowitt define such a system as:

> a human social network that behaves like a sociobiological system, wherein people have developed patterns of behavior that minimize transaction costs caused by social barriers resulting from geography, lack of trust, differences in language and culture, and inefficient social networks.

Today large cooperations operate globally with budgets often exceeding that of nation states. Platform economies have emerged that combine the benefits of Internet supported networks with the efficiency of hierarchical organisational structure of the firm, which for a long term has been coined to be the most effective means of human organisation.

The emergence of a firm is favoured when hiring staff internally leads to lower cost than contracting tasks, for instance for producing a specific good. For instance, keeping processes "in house" lowers bargaining cost and the risk of loss of intellectual property.

The hierarchical structure of a firm in principle favours rapid decision making—up to a point. However, firms suffer from an inherent size limitation: when the internal cost of coordination exceeds the value of goods produced firms fail.

This is particularly true for firms that are working in a R&D intensive sector. For instance pharmaceutical industries with a heavy burden on regulation, competition and secrecy with regards to intellectual property suffer from an inverse Moore's Law (Erom) and may soon become unprofitable.

How could we create sustainable innovation systems harnessing the potential of blockchain technology?

In the book "The Wealth of Networks", Yochai Benkler argues that the Internet has lead to a paradigm shift of knowledge production in an interconnected society. He coined the term commons based peer production (CBPP) for this phenomenon that had been for a long time predominantly related to the creation of goods of the free and open-source movements. CBPP however has a major shortcoming: it often does not compensate the creators of a piece of software or their efforts of curating a public domain Wiki page.

While the Web has enabled free exchange of information and expression of individual creativity, the "plumbing" that traditional business structures have enabled to create revenue streams and compensate their workers, is vastly missing so far.

Benkler further argues however that CBPP would be a much more successful approach to wealth creation in a networked society than traditional competitive models of innovation, including firms, if current copyright and patent law legislations would be altered as they have become a limitation of growth and wealth creation in our networked reality.

Along these lines are also the statements of cyberneticists Paul Pangaro who argued in 2014 that "Wealth creation had shifted from prior knowledge to the ability to gain new knowledge in action". He further suggests that "it is more effective to invest in processes to gain insight than material possessions or present-day intellectual property."

With this in mind, it seems that what we need to do is to create favourable environments that bring the right talents and financial support together to tackle major challenges in a collaborative environment.

Blockchain technology will likely play a major role here as means of supporting coordination and lowering transaction cost. Other examples of key technologies in this regard are for instance 3D printing and artificial intelligence, which we will not further address here.

The appearance of blockchain backed smart contracts now makes it possible to lower cost for transactions and coordination even further than the Internet was able to so far. Here a new field of economic study is evolving that is creating so called crypto-economic mechanism and incentive designs.

Crypto-economic systems point to a transition towards an unprecedented new era of collaborative businesses, nurturing diversity and cooperation amongst different, and often intrinsically motivated contributors that organise themselves through the Internet for a defined period of time to contribute and solve a specific task and subsequently may resolve and seek new opportunities elsewhere.

Following a similar thought line, Peter A. Gloor has defined such dynamic networks as "collaborative innovation networks" shortened as COIN in his book "Swarm Creativity: Competitive Advantage through Collaborative Innovation Networks". COINs that operate within the context of blockchain and smart contract backed organisations will enable us to harness effectively the benefits of collective Intelligence.

In a way, Collective Intelligence (CI) can be seen as the organic counterpart to the silicon-based Artificial Intelligence (AI). Whereas the AI represents the "machine thinking" usually shining at analyzing, extracting and creating insights from large amounts of data, the CI represents the "human thinking" usually shining at creative problem solving sometimes operating with incomplete or a very limited amount of data.

Collective Intelligence can be understood as an emergent property from the synergies among: (1) data-information-knowledge; (2) software-hardware; and (3) experts (those with new insights as well as recognized authorities) that continually learns from feedback to produce just-in-time knowledge for better decisions than these three elements acting alone (Fig. 9).

In this context, blockchain technology for the first time unites all required components that leads to the emergence of collective intelligence namely: coordination, cooperation and cognition.

Don Tapscott and Anthony D. Williams also view collective intelligence as mass collaboration. And, in order for mass collaboration to happen, four principles need to exist:

- Openness: Sharing ideas and intellectual property: though these resources provide the edge over competitors more benefits accrue from allowing others to share ideas and gain significant improvement and scrutiny through collaboration.

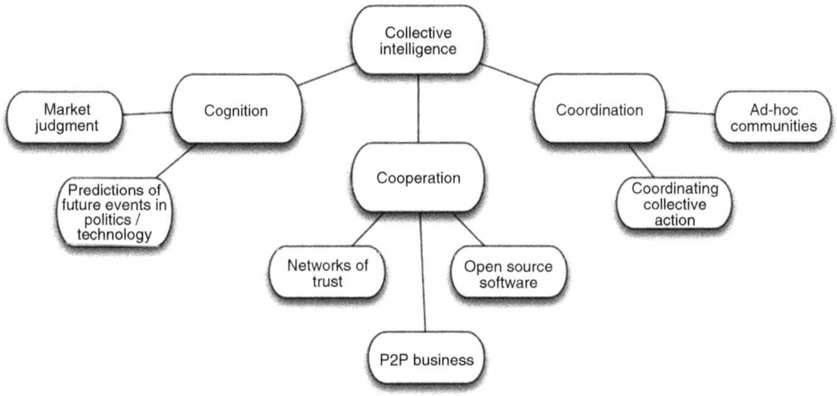

Fig. 9 Collective Intelligence from James Surowiecki "The wisdom of crowds and smart mobs"

- Peering: Horizontal organization as with the 'opening up' of the Linux program where users are free to modify and develop it provided that they make it available for others. Peering succeeds because it encourages self-organization—a style of production that works more effectively than hierarchical management for certain tasks.
- Sharing: Companies have started to share some ideas while maintaining some degree of control over others, like potential and critical patent rights. Limiting all intellectual property shuts out opportunities, while sharing some expands markets and brings out products faster.
- Acting Globally: The advancement in communication technology has prompted the rise of global companies at low overhead costs. The internet is widespread, therefore a globally integrated company has no geographical boundaries and may access new markets, ideas and technology.

While a firm needs to take the risk of hiring the right people, collaborative innovation networks that are governed by blockchain backed protocols can source from a truly global pool of talents. We may ultimately overcome the innovation gridlock within the closed competitive silos of today's corporations.

Cryptocurrencies and incentive design is poised to revolutionize many industries, including engineering and even biomedical and pharmacological research, both fields where talent is scarce and development is resource intensive.

With these new abilities at our fingertips, a new race has started for the creation of new forms of organizing based on social protocols powered by blockchain technology and Internet networks. One of the first manifestations of this new form of organizing is exemplified by Decentralized Autonomous Organizations (DAOs).

DAOs function without any central point of control, are resistant to interference and censorship from external parties and operate based on the collective input of their stakeholders. DAOs will permit the formation of new organizations with the rules of engagement by its participants transparently engraved in their blockchain smart contracts.

Due to their transparent-by-design and permissionless features DAOs will facilitate a far more effective information processing and resource allocation in a self-organizing and market driven process than would be possible in a traditional firm today.

Smart contracts can reflect the agreed-upon social contract and empower communities of people with new capabilities of moving not only information at the speed of light, but also value through a new economic layer secured by cryptography.

With this new perspective in the realm of possibilities, what if we take a more expansive view of our human nature and ponder our humanness as something including both individual *and* collective self-expression, digital *and* physical reality, mind *and* action?

6 Advanced Knowledge Architecture for Social Human Action (AKASHA): From Collected Intelligence to Collective Intelligence

When contemplating the implications of the medium of storage and process of distribution of information at civilization level, we can appreciate its significance better. After all, in an "information society", information is more precious than gold, even if we often don't treat it as such.

In our modern days, social media platforms have become our "public squares" where people voice their concerns. What does this say about our information society when the corporations owning the social media platforms are capable of deplatforming anyone at any point, without any warning in advance?

The current stack of technologies used to build the mainstream information systems, the "social networks" of our information society, are based on paradigm of closed data silos that use unknown means of software tools to strip users from their personal information and abuse the insights gained for their own financial benefit.

Thus Web transformed from a tool originally designed to empower humans, into a dystopian persuasion machine capable of **manipulating** the behavior of billions of people at a global scale. Now we have another window of opportunity, and are invited to (re-)imagine our information society, but this time not as passive observers.

This time we have at our fingertips a technological stack that is founded in transparency and open-source code culture, enabling us to create social protocols and agreements enshrined in an uncensorable global database and executed by a transparent world computer.

Ethereum is a core part of this new tech stack, providing the first layer required to build complex concepts dependent on a secure, public, neutral infrastructure running the agreements as agreed upon without interference from any third party.

One of the unique selling points of Ethereum comes from the synergy effect emerging when thousands of smart contracts powering next-generation decentralized applications share a common blockchain layer. Cross-communication and interoperability represent in this case more of an intended side-effect when building on the same network.

This makes possible all sorts of interesting concepts possible, one example being the "cDAI" building on top of "DAI", an Ethereum-based "stablecoin" with its value pegged 1-to-1 with USD. In this context, cDAI enables Ethereum users to pool together cryptocurrency and choose where the interest accrued goes to—their own pockets, supporting their favorite service or donating to the charity of choice.

This is just one example of how various projects can build on top of each other's work and expand functionality in creative ways without any top-down control at the data-information layer.

As one of the co-founders of Ethereum, I have spent quite a bit of time pondering the potential implications of this new technology and how it could affect (or even better improve) our lives. This is why, after the successful genesis of the Ethereum blockchain, I wanted to explore meaningful use cases of this magnificent, new socio-technological experiment.

This is how the AKASHA foundation was created as a non-profit at the intersection of blockchain and collective intelligence to tackle challenges previously considered "unsolvable". The main mission of the foundation is to nurture projects helping individuals unlock their potential through open systems that expand our collective minds at local, regional, and global scales.

The first project nurtured by the foundation was a decentralized social network that does not rely on a central entity to function (not even the AKASHA foundation) because peers connect directly to each other in a decentralized fashion. Among other things, this approach solves by design many problems associated with freedom of expression, personal data and data privacy.

However, it did not come without its own drawbacks in the form of sometimes slow loading times, unavailable peers and cumbersome blockchain synchronization processes. But we had to start from somewhere. At the time of writing this article we are celebrating over 3 years of playful experimentation with the AKASHA foundation delivering three working applications showcasing that "it is possible" to tackle big problems in new ways.

We are now focusing our efforts on the next phase: compressing all the knowledge gained while trying to create a decentralized social network into an open-source protocol enabling people from around the world to power their own decentralized social structures.

The next phase will encompass the AKASHA World Framework, an open-source framework geared towards developers, maintained and openly distributed by the AKASHA foundation.

The AKASHA World Framework (AWF) will empower people to launch their own customized social networks, backed by an immutable data structure and storage layer, tailored to fit their specific needs. We envision it to spread in a similar manner to how Wordpress once made it easy for people to launch their own Website and customize it to their needs (blog, e-commerce, creative portfolio, etc.).

From communities breeding and trading Crypto Kitties to organizations working on the "next big thing" this toolkit enables anyone from anywhere to create user interfaces that catalyze global collaboration powered by a new information architecture built on open data.

Moreover, because these digital worlds are built on top of an open data layer favoring interoperability by default, there is also an emergent "meta social network" born from the interactions between various social networks.

An interesting image comes to mind when the Ethereum ecosystem is imagined as a synergistic organism. From this perspective we can envision AKASHA as its natural nervous tissue connecting people, ideas and projects through an open, interoperable-by-default, informational architecture built using an advanced open source tech stack.

This potent mix of open technologies can be used to imagine new solutions to old problems. From smart cities designed around increasing the resilience and decreasing the time of coordinated response in times of need to decentralized organizations scaling horizontally to levels previously thought impossible a world of possibilities lies ahead of us.

In a way you could say that the AWF is predestined to be a key component for the creation of a CBPP platform that closely resembles the DAO vision. While DAOs opens the possibility for new, sustainable, financial models and legal structures we also need a communication layer that enables efficient and trusted information processing among the DAO's members around the question of how to most effectively allocate its resources to the challenges at hand.

AWF does so by providing a currently missing means of trusted, censorship-resistant communication that is safeguarding attribution of created work for the contributors, a process that requires identity and notarization of knowledge transactions. This essentially is a prerequisite for its sustainable and fair financial exploitation. Only if we reach this people all over the world will be willing to contribute.

Finally, the next era of networked human development will not succeed, if we do not alter our behaviour towards a more sustainable and inclusive means, both with respect to society as well as to the interconnected network of life we are part of on this planet.

I'd therefore like to finish with an idea from Frederic Laloux who coined the term "teal organisation" in his book "Reinventing Organizations". He defines a new kind of organization that relies on the recent breakthroughs in human collaboration and is driven by the individual's desire for:

- Self management: that is the absence of hierarchy and a central command and control, emergence of consensus
- Wholeness: that is the ability of the individual to "be who they are"
- Evolutionary purpose: that is an organisation comparable to a living organism in which members are invited to listen and take note of the purpose it wants to serve

As we are at a point where we not only understand, but also witness how our species dramatically shaped this planet for the worse we need to adopt a new mindset and formulate new systems that will help our civilization to rise to the challenges.

But this cannot be achieved with a nineteenth century mindset built on the assumption of infinite resources and economic growth with complete disregard of the long-term effects caused, but it requires a mindset that appreciates that we are all part of the "Spaceship Earth" with its life supporting machinery and ecosystems we all depend on.

Increasing resilience and collective intelligence while decreasing the chances of extinction when it comes to life in general, from plants to animals to humans, should be part of a smart civilization living on a pale blue dot in the vastness of space. As Carl Sagan once wisely said, for many of us Earth will be the only home we will ever know. It will likely take decades, if not centuries, until we will inhabit another planet and be able to call it "home".

This time however, we can do more than just "hope" that things will be better. We can actively co-create today a better tomorrow through playful experimentation with a system built around open data, information, knowledge and wisdom. I believe that these things are the critical pieces of infrastructure for a sustainable learning society capable of rising to the challenges not only of today, but also of tomorrow.

The liberation of data from the hands of corporations seeking to maximize profit is going to be one of the biggest fights for freedom in the history of humanity, directly shaping our future as a civilization since we are now looking at billions of souls impacted globally.

And this time the battle is not fought with swords or tanks but with screens and keyboards linking millions of minds into groups rendering geographical boundaries obsolete. It will remain to be seen, where we will go from here and if we will find our way to informational freedom through the digital noise surrounding us in our daily lives or become mere pawns on the chessboard of corporations more powerful than the biggest super-nations.

In any case, I encourage you, the reader, to feed your curious mind and explore the fractal of possibilities opened by these tools because, in the end, it's not information that wants to be free at planetary scale.

It's us.

And now, we can be.

* * *

Mihai Alisie has been actively involved in the blockchain space, since 2011 when he created with Vitalik Buterin the world's first Bitcoin Magazine. He served as Editor-in-Chief for the magazine, until late 2013, when he joined Vitalik in founding the Ethereum project.

In the early days of Ethereum, Mihai led the Swiss efforts to establish the business infrastructure and legal framework crucial for the Ethereum crowdfunding campaign. Following the successful Swiss setup, he served as Vice President of the Ethereum

Foundation and Chief Innovation Officer of Ethereum Switzerland until late 2015.

After the successful Ethereum blockchain genesis in 2015, Mihai focused his attention on building on top of Ethereum. This is what led to the creation of the AKASHA.org project with a declared purpose to explore the applications and implications of blockchain in the context of social networks and collective intelligence, for a better home of Mind.

Cryptography Leads the Next Wave of Societal Change

Efi Pylarinou

Abstract Blockchain technology has already shifted our thinking towards a different way of organizing and collaborating. Cryptography in peer-to-peer immutable networks, has already led to experimentation in alternative Trust mechanisms in several areas of our societal structure. Change is given, even though the most dominant technology of such networks has not yet been decided. The direction of change is towards self-sovereign identity and being your own bank.

Keywords Blockchain · Technical revolution · Trust · Societal change

1 Introduction

We live in very exciting and unstable times. As Ian Goldin[1] frequently says during his talks "Welcome to the slowest day of the rest of your life." The current era is characterized by complexity and accelerated speed of developments with unforeseen consequences. More importantly, we are not clear who is responsible to manage these risks. We seem to agree that the current centralized, hierarchical structure of countries, governments, authorized institutions, are failing to stand up to the circumstances. We realize that several private corporations have grown into powerful and influential entities that are shaping up the societal web in uncontrollable ways.

[1]Ian Goldin is an Oxford University Professor of Globalisation and Development and runs the Oxford Martin program on technological and economic change. He is the author of several books.

E. Pylarinou (✉)
Efi Pylarinou Advisory, Fribourg, Switzerland
e-mail: connect@efipylarinou.com

K. Wendt (ed.), *Theories of Change*, Sustainable Finance,
https://doi.org/10.1007/978-3-030-52275-9_21

GAFAs,[2] FANGs,[3] BATs,[4] are some of the powerful drivers of the convenient digital life in which we are all held captive.

In the West, regulators and governments have been forced to take a position, for or against, the LIBRA association now re-branded to DIEM association. The threat of a private stablecoin used by several large scale corporations, has led to several Central Banks considering the issuance of a Central Bank Digital Currency.

In China, digitalization has enabled a government led initiative, the Chinese social credit system that gathers data from a variety of sources like finances, tax and online purchases, social media activity and more. Over 1.4 billion Chinese citizens are expected to have a publicly available social score that will be used in all realms of life—health, work, education. This score will be adjusted up or down based on behavioral rules set by the government. This controversial state-sponspored Social Credit System that integrates "financial metrics" and "behavioral metrics" is still not implemented. China has already started piloting in specific regions and for specific purposes (e.g. transportation) their retail Central Bank Digital Currency (DCEP).

These facts are masking several moral, ethical and value issues that are the unplanned consequences of the third technological revolution—the Internet tech revolution which was the first large scale open source protocol (TCP/IP) that powers the Web. I identify, three such mega issues:

1. Our collective diminished trust towards established institutional structures (central banks, governments agencies, capital markets, banks, etc.) and information channels.
2. Our painfully slow realization that the economy can no longer operate separately and independently of the ecology.
3. Our realization that societal imbalances and unfairness, are growing despite the permissionless, borderless internet access with its stunning convenience and 'democratization' of information.

Edelman reports that there are four waves characterizing the ***Loss of Trust***, in authorities and institutions. Starting with the fear of job loss to automation and globalization; the undermining of the middle class from authorities and institutions during the financial crisis; the social and economic effects of global migration; and most recently the loss of confidence in all media channels. Media institutions continue to decline in trust with fake news and lack of objectivity of information. There are also great imbalances in these forces at play across different countries. The Edelman Trust Barometer,[5] which analyzes and quantifies the ecosystem of Trust reported in 2017 and 2018 that the US as a country experienced a huge drop on the Trust Index, while China's trust was soaring. Trust inequality between the informed public and the mass population has risen to all time highs, which is more evidence of

[2]GAFA is an acronym for these high growth technology companies: Google, Apple, Facebook, Amazon.

[3]FANG is an acronym for these high growth technology companies: Facebook, Amazon, Netflix and Google.

[4]BAT is an acronym for these high growth technology companies: Baidu, Alibaba, Tencent.

[5]https://www.edelman.com/trust-barometer

an unbalanced world. Media nowadays includes more than journalism, with technology platforms (like the GAFAs) and social media influencers being included in social institutions.

As the Chinese philosopher Confucius said centuries ago: 'A state cannot survive without the confidence of its people'.

The Internet of information has largely contributed to these unintended consequences. It was not built to increase fairness and transparency. The main (albeit simplified) reason is that it needed an application layer to organize and extract value from the innovative and disruptive open source protocol infrastructure. The concertation and abuse of power of the private entities or institutions that undertook the task of building the application layer, has led us to the aforementioned mega issues.

All this has led to a change in the ecosystem of trust. Peer-to-peer networks are gaining traction and facilitate establishing trust within communities with common interests. Confidence is established in rather direct ways instead of trusting a qualified or authorized entity. This change is bottom-up rather than top-down. It is a new tendency that is looking to scale and eventually replace the existing societal structures of institutions and information providers. Change is pulling us towards developing a framework that allows for establishing trust in a peer-to-peer network setup, with an alternative way of validating exchanges of any kind (from information to assets).

We are also confronted with the need to develop an economic theory that combines ecology with business, finance and capital markets. Currently, we treat the economy with a narrow perspective. It encompasses mainly financial values and the infrastructure built for the economies to function, is similarly focused on achieving mainly financial objectives. Economic Value is much broader than Financial Value. It is much more than what is reflected in balance sheets, income statements, and stock market performance. It includes use, abuse, and leveraging of non-market resources, like air, water, sea habitats, forests, biodiversity, and the wellbeing of human beings.

We are heading towards a planet with 9 billion people sharing resources and with an open source protocol (the TCP/IP infrastructure of the Web) for our digital lives that is incapable of dealing with the current complexities of our society. Money as we know it today is issued by governments, managed by Central Banks, stopped at borders, and the defacto measure of power and value in all economies. Money cannot capture economic value but only the narrower financial value. As it is the only incentive built-in to our economic structure, it is partly responsible of the three mega issues identified above and surely, it cannot help us in solving any of them.

2 A New Vision of Money

If only we could design trustworthy peer-to-peer networks, then we could deal with the loss of trust towards the institutions and information channels. Cryptography is presenting us with this possibility. It allows us to exchange cryptographically coded value ('hashed' in the computer science language) directly with one another and without the need for a trusted intermediary to validate the transaction and reconcile. More importantly, without leaving multiple digital copies of this transaction lying around on the web. Without the risk of replicating the same transaction more than once with multiple entities ('the double spending' problem).

Cryptography and the solution to 'the double spending' problem, allows us to transact securely on a peer-to-peer network. The Bitcoin network[6] is one living example that has proved this over a decade now.

If only we could exchange values that are broader than just conventional money, then we could put more emphasis on our ecology and combine it with financial value. We could actually design new incentives beyond money, stock options, and the other financial instruments that we already use. Smart contracts are presenting us with this potential. They are cryptographic code—publicly available—that execute a 'contractual' relationship. One can think of Smart contracts, as autonomous agents in the cryptographically transparent realm, that enforce an agreement. Again, without intermediaries, no need for expensive overhead and full transparency. If we want to bundle together clauses that include tangible and intangible triggers; smart contracts allows to do that. Smart Contracts allow us to "Program Money" that are much broader than just dollars, euros, or yen. Any of the intangible assets that are worth a lot to each one of us and to our communities, that can be measured, can be tokenized via Smart contracts and exchanged in a peer to peer fashion.

We can imagine programmed hybrid money that are a combination of purchasing power in a retail store combined with a fractional ownership in a piece of land for reforestation. Let's call this EATREE coin. My employer gives me the option to be paid in EATREE coin (1:1 to our local currency). The additional value is unlocked when I spend my coins at the retailer and I get automatic cash rebates in EATREE coins real time and directly in my wallet. I also get dividends from the fractional ownership of the land that sells timber as the trees grow in the forest and a certain percentage needs to be cut down. My employer has actually funded the reforestation and is passing the dividends directly to me, as a reward. Operational efficiencies are gained from the transparency, auditability, and lack of intermediaries. The sharing and redistributing of value can occur in an economic fashion and is a new incentive structure that was not possible before.

Marius Schuler talks about the potential of a 'European social capital system' in his book 'Die Zukunft der Blockchain: Ein Systemtheoretisches Leitbild zur Herausbildung der nachsten Internet Technologie'[7] (Schuler 2019) that could be implemented with a Token that rewards Europeans for civic and or voluntary work.

---

[6]The debate as to whether Bitcoin, is Digital money (with the conventional three properties of money) or Digital Gold or something else, is beyond this argument. The fact is that it is a peer-to-peer network operating securely for over 10 years.

[7]Schriftenreihe des The Open Government Institute. https://www.amazon.de/Schriftenreihe-Government-Institute-Universit%C3%A4t-Friedrichshafen/dp/3748547080/ref=sr_1_1?__mk_de_DE=%C3%85M%C3%85%C5%BD%C3%95%C3%91&keywords=schuler+blockchain&qid=1563287120&s=gateway&sr=8-1

This Token would be tradeable and exchanged for social services or for services from other people in the European social capital system. I could earn such Tokens in my 30s and 40s through volunteer and community work and spend them in my 80s when I need to be taken care of. Imagine all sorts of non-monetary Monies that we could program to incentivize behaviors around civic engagement, volunteer engagement, and to reduce the Tragedy of the Commons.

Imagine a Token that incentivizes environmentally sustainable behavior instead of overfishing, wildlife destruction, and water pollution (just to pick a few such mega issues). Ostrom smart contracts are already a possibility. They are smart contracts operating with a token and coupled with intelligent monitoring of environmental data (artificial intelligence). The smart contracts are inspired by the principles proposed by Nobel prize winner Elinor Ostrom[8] for governing the commons sustainably and equitably in a group (Ostrom 2015).

David Dao,[9] is leveraging decentralized technology to prevent deforestation and is leading one of the first use pilots of token based Ostrom smart contracts as the founder of GainForest.[10]

If only we could all agree on a self-sovereign identity global standard that would alleviate the current unsurmountable social imbalances. A self-sovereign identity is a term that has not yet entered the mainstream vocabulary. It remains imprisoned within the tech-informed crowd. It is more of a vision for a dignified digital life rather than a specific piece of identification. It is at its core about handing over the control to each person of their Digital Identity in order to guarantee Freedom and Safety under any circumstances. The Digital Identity can include, information like one's name, birth date, social security number, citizenship, residency, diplomas, licenses, awards, memberships, health data and more. In the physical world, these are recorded on paper, plastic cards, or central databases managed by authorized entities. Refugees are one case that shows clearly how a person can become nobody and lose all dignity simply by not having access or proof of any of these items. The rising large-scale data breaches of organizations like Google, Equifax, Facebook, are also reminders of how our rights are being compromised on the Web. The dematerialization of our lives puts at risk our privacy, data protection, rights to intellectual property and we are coming to realize that it allows hidden but Orwellian style discrimination through algorithms with built-in selection biases.

Michael Casey and Paul Vigna talk about 'The Rise of the Citizen' in their book 'The Truth Machine'[11] and point out the profoundly empowering potential about letting self-sovereign individuals record data to a publicly verifiable record, without

[8]In 2009 Elinor Ostrom and Oliver Williamson shared the Nobel Memorial Prize in Economic Sciences. They were recognized for their work on economic governance, especially the commons. To date, Elinor Ostrom remains the only woman to win the Nobel Prize in Economics.

[9]David Dao is a PhD student at ETH and is also leading research at DS3Lab on machine learning against climate change, mapping the ethical use of AI and directing the Kara research project towards building a market for privacy preserving data for medical research. https://daviddao.org/

[10]GainForest is an award winning not for profit. https://www.gainforest.app/#/

[11]https://www.amazon.com/Truth-Machine-Blockchain-Future-Everything/dp/1250114578

requiring anyone's permission to do so (Casey and Vigna 2018). This potential is enabled by cryptography and the internally consistent language of Mathematics, that we can Trust more than our human irrational nature. This technology presents us with the opportunity to adopt a fundamentally different governance system.

Blockchain is a decentralized mechanism leveraging cryptography, in which trust is built-in with mathematical formulas. As Plato preached, mathematics is the only internally consistent language. As Nick Szabo[12] preached, in his God protocols, mathematics is the language of God. God in this context is the entity that always acts in the interest of everybody. Blockchain protocols are presenting us with an opportunity to build on protocols with built-in consensus mechanisms governed by math. Mathematics governance guarantees fairness and trust.

Cryptography and built-in governance with mathematical formulas that govern consensus mechanisms, is more or less the proposed ideal protocol. These are the core elements that we can choose to adopt and change our societal interactions.

Imagine a design of cryptographically coding Intellectual Property (IP)—that allows to tokenize and therefore, exchange IP securely on a peer-to-peer network. Such protocols are already being launched. They have the potential to distribute revenues, fairly amongst creators of any IP—music, science, or art—and to create an auditable trail of transactions.

Imagine a digital wallet that holds assets with all items that compose a person's self-sovereign identity. Such a digital wallet is unlike our Google Pay or Apple pay Wallets, which are simple accounting logs of our actual holdings in currencies. A Digital Wallet in the cryptographically powered world of distributed ledgers, can actually hold an asset—not a copy of it. A digital wallet with my own self-sovereign identity items, allows me to control who can have access to these items for validation purposes and most importantly, without removing my asset from my wallet or leaving a duplicate copy of it floating around on the web. The cryptographic method that allows this happen is the Zero-Knowledge Proof (ZKP) which permits data to be verified without revealing the data.

There are several such protocols already launched and being adopted slowly and at small scale. The Kiva protocol[13] is one example and a result of a collaborative effort with the UN. Its purpose is to roll out a digital identification system in Sierra Leone first that empowers the country's seven million citizens with a self-sovereign identify. The vision is to empower people with a censorship resistant record of who they are, what they own and what their reputation is. The later asset, reputation, is actually one that falls in the category of our intangible assets that are easily verifiable or tracked. And yet, in almost all business transactions, reputation is valued and remains elusive and difficult to monetize. Cryptography combined with intelligent

[12]Nick Szabo is a recognized computer scientist and legal scholar known for his research in digital contracts and digital currencies. The Gods protocol was originally published in 1997 and is the description of an ideal, fair and transparent protocol. https://nakamotoinstitute.org/the-god-protocols/

[13]Kiva is a non-profit launched in 2005 and focused on financial inclusion. The Kiva protocol was first launched in 2019. https://pages.kiva.org/kiva-protocol-faq

recording of reputational data that is crowdsourced, can unlock value that is currently can only be captured within a limited circle of each person's network.

3 Challenges and Levers

The three mega issues—Loss of Trust, the Silo between Economy and Ecology, the Societal imbalances and unfairness—cannot be overcome by adding layers to the existing societal structure. We continue to add regulations, laws, and fines, which are proving ineffective. A new paradigm with completely different incentives is clearly needed, and the only uncertainty is which design do we intend to choose. Our intention matters more than anything else. Ironically, we could even adopt cryptography and blockchain and some version of peer-to-peer networks and still maintain the same value system. The same one that today has money as the value, second to none; ecology treated in bylaws because borrowing from the future is no sin in our value system; and unfairness as somebody else's problem.

Cryptography and peer to peer networks with built-in decentralized and transparent governance, offer us the option to restructure into a society that empowers citizens starting with a self-sovereign identity. This can grow and include not only our driver's license, our university diplomas and work history, but also our mentoring and humanitarian work, our reputational assets above and beyond our on-time debt payments.

It offers the possibility to use an enriched self-sovereign data locker—with all our tangible and intangible assets—and to act like our own bank. Each citizen will be the custodian of their own valuable assets—much like banks custody our financial assets—and each individual can use these assets to trade in a peer to peer fashion and even borrow against them.

Cryptography and peer to peer networks with built-in decentralized and transparent governance, can allow us through tokenization, to create 'bankable' assets of all sorts. From the real estate that we own and whose value can be unlocked by registering it on a distributed ledger, all the way to our reputation that can be documented and verified in an immutable way.

We currently depend on language and law to organize, collaborate and reach consensus on various issues. We are now stepping into a more advanced era in which mathematics can be trusted in order to reach consensus. Clearly from all the sciences—social, political, physics—mathematics is the branch of knowledge with the highest level of consensus and in which we trust.

4 Conclusions

The current experimentation era around peer-to-peer networks and cryptography, is leveraging several theoretical mathematics that have already been developed with no real-world application in mind. From hash functions to more ‘abstract first’ mathematical concepts like the Zero Proof Knowledge.

We are naturally moving away from trusting forced consensus mechanisms like regulations. We aim to design consensus mechanisms that will allow us to swarm like bird flocks or murmurations of starlings.

References

Casey, M. J., & Vigna, P. (2018). *The truth machine: The blockchain and the future of everything*. New York: St. Martin’s Press.

Ostrom, E. (2015). *Governing the commons: The evolution of institutions for collective action (canto classics)*. Cambridge: Cambridge University Press.

Schuler, M. C. (2019). European social capital system. In *Die Zukunft der Blockchain: Ein Systemtheoretisches Leitbild zur Herausbildung der nachsten Internet Technologie*. Zeppelin University. Retrieved from https://www.epubli.de/shop/buch/Die-Zukunft-der-Blockchain%2D%2D-Ein-systemtheoretisches-Leitbild-zur-Herausbildung-der-n%C3%A4chsten-Internet-Technologie-Marius-C-Schuler-978374854

Efi Pylarinou is a global influencer and a recognized thought leader in Finance and the 4IR technologies. A seasoned Wall Street professional with a Ph.D. in Finance and the founder of Efi Pylarinou Advisory. She has over 200,000 followers on social media, she is the No.1 Finance Global Woman Influencer by Refinitiv 2019 & 2020 and also included in several other rankings. She is a prolific writer & international speaker (Twitter & Medium @efipm & Youtube Efi Pylarinou). She is also the author of Wiley Fixed income books with Frank Fabozzi and a contributing author of the 2018 WealthTech book by Wiley and 2019 4IR, Reinventing a Nation book. www.efipylarinou.com

Machine Learning and Finance

Bernhard Villhauer

Abstract The article provides a short overview of recent developments driven by the application of Artificial Intelligence (AI) or, more specifically, Machine Learning (ML) in the financial sector. The focus is on the practical consequences of ML use, especially at Pretrade analytics, Portfolio Management or in the field of service.

Keywords Theory of change · Theories of change · Blockchain · Machine learning

1 Perspectives

Which areas are currently of importance in the field of Machine Learning (ML) and finance? A literature review for the past years shows that most of the research work focuses on these topics:

- Pre trade analytics
- Risk management
- Portfolio optimization
- Service, man-machine-interfaces

But before we get into the details of these areas, let me first outline something about the terms. It seems important to me to explain what we mean exactly with ML when speaking of "Artifical Intelligence (AI)". The starting point is a classic definition attributed to Arthur Samuel:

> "Machine Learning is the subfield of computer science that gives computers the ability to learn without being explicitly programmed" (although a famous quote, it is presumably a paraphrasing of Samuel 1959).

In ML, algorithms are used, that are self-teaching as the data changes, and they build pattern recognition models working with subsequent sets of data. For each new

B. Villhauer (✉)
Weltethos-Institut (World Ethos Institute), University of Tübingen, Tübingen, Germany
e-mail: villhauer@weltethos-institut.org

K. Wendt (ed.), *Theories of Change*, Sustainable Finance,
https://doi.org/10.1007/978-3-030-52275-9_22

incremental piece of data added, the algorithms change and improve. It is important to emphasize the processual nature and role of pattern recognition in ML. Unlike earlier AI concepts, it deals with processes, developmental paths, vectors and dynamics, not static models. ML is a process happening. ML in Finance is a process happening that interferes with the ongoing processes of financial development. And not without reason: The financial sector is increasingly influenced by ML developments, because the financial industry itself is basically an information-processing industry. ML in finance means the utilization of a variety of techniques to intelligently handle large and complex volumes of information. That is why the financial industry has always played a leading role in previous waves of technological development.

Above all, I want to give an overview of the practical implications of the combination of ML and finance, less the theoretical and mathematical or technical basics for this—there are good overviews of Gyorfi and Ottucsak (2011), Walk, Klaas, Klemelä, Cuchiero, Klein, Teichmann or Hastie, Tibshirani, Friedman et al.

2 Fields of Application

The areas mentioned here are connected by the fact that more and more complex data is being processed in the financial sector. The ML self-improving algorithms handle this storm of information better than humans. Therefore, they can provide faster a good basis for decision-making.

Of course, most of these topics are not exclusive to ML, but are a mix of digitization and ML innovations. For example, ML is being used more and more extensively in algorithmic trading, but ML is not the main driver of development here. In this field, AI and ML have especially strengthened the acceleration factor, as they can make buy and sell decisions millions of times faster. This connects the development with the long-known High Frequency Trading, especially when the perspectives of Big Data use are considered. In a contribution to this (Kearns and Nevmyvaka 2013) we read: "Machine learning provides no easy paths to profitability or improved execution, but does provide a powerful and principled framework for trading optimization via historical data."

3 From Pretrade Analytics to Portfolio Optimization

In order to process the datasets for pretrade analytics, many tools and programs have been developed in recent years, which are based on different programming languages, e.g. Python. Python is commonly used in AI projects with the help of libraries like TensorFlow, Keras, Pytorch and Scikit-learn. TensorFlow for example, is a product of GoogleBrain and primarily allows the creation of models, which are the basis of data analysis. It is highly used in the finance sector, helping people to build, develop or evaluate different model für predicting and pricing Klaas (2019).

The advantages of an ML strategy in stock price prediction and chart analysis are particularly clear. The company valuation is facilitated, including the prediction of future "winning stocks". When analyzing documents about companies and market conditions, ML applications can more easily identify critical passages and find contradictory statements in large documents. In addition, the company comparisons become easier, similar business models are identified faster—an ideal use of pattern recognition. In short: the job description of the analyst changes fundamentally. We see that important changes in the narrower area of quantitative finance have an impact on the entire industry or its strategic development. Deep Learning is currently intervening in the areas of "middle creativity" typical of the analyst profession (not unlike the ML use in journalism, media and design). This development emerged earlier when it was not yet attributed to ML in the strict sense. The potential of so-called "genetic" or "evolutionary" algorithms has been clear for some time now—and the application possibilities in the financial sector have been investigated for about 20 years.

This goes back in Streichert's work (2001), which examines practical problems for such algorithms such as constrained portfolio selections (including cardinality constraints), parameter optimization for regression models, time series forecasting with symbolic regression and the development of trading strategies on exchange rates.

Deep Learning models from the ML act like experienced analysts. Such an expert learns in his career a lot about many companies and formes impressions of them. Over time, he or she develops a sense of pattern in the numbers and balance sheets of companies. By organizing his work in learning processes, the analyst will recognize decisive characteristics. His or her experience allows to quickly and better classify new facts. Deep learning models work similarly. They learn to independently recognize balance sheet patterns, which they can then apply to new data. The more data the system has, the better it can learn and gain experience. The data quality, but also the amount of data are crucial.

However, the data volume also increases the demands on computer performance.

Tools of Deep Learning are useful in portfolio selection problems, because Deep Learning techniques are the best available way to compute any function mapping data (which may be other returns, economic data, accounting data, demographic data, data on the legal regime, etc.) into the value of the return. This is an advanced approach compared with the rather simplistic linear factor models of traditional financial economics and the relatively crude ad hoc methods of statistical arbitrage and other quantitative asset management techniques (Hutchinson et al. 1994).

Two big advantages of Deep Learning models over an analyst are their much greater capacity and their lack of emotion. The system can also find patterns that humans would not recognize. In addition, the algorithm strictly decides based on self-generated rules, which leaves out everything emotional. The classic sources of error and miscalculation, self-deception and overconfidence are bypassed. This has direct economic effects. Therefore, portfolios can be cost-effectively reviewed and reorganized. The portfolio optimization can be carried out at shorter intervals and thus a better result for the asset management can be achieved. Li and Hoi (2014) and Li et al. (2016) discuss that for different tools and different types of portfolio, especially for real world transactions.

It is obvious, why many efforts are invested in optimization, not only for idealized balanced portfolios but for sparse everyday portfolios (Lai et al. 2018).

In this context, the term "Robo Advisory" comes to mind.

We sometimes find "Robo Advisory" as connected with new form of business-consumer-relations. But Robo Advisor companies such as Betterment, Schwab Intelligent Portfolios, WiseBanyan, Wealthfront, or quirion and Scalable in Germany, use algorithms also built to calibrate portofolio to the goals and risks of the user. Portfolio optimization becomes portfolio construction. The Wealthfront software can even implement a variety of strategies, including tax-loss harvesting.

Wealth and Asset Management in the whole is changing quickly—Nutmeg, an online investment management company, has become one of the largest digital wealth manager in Europe, managing over 18 billions Pound of assets in 2017. On their website, this is described as "a mission to democratise wealth management". This socially responsible rhetorics are used by many news firms that cut costs via ML.

One of the other forerunners in this area with a promising name is Rebellion Research, where investment management and robo advisory is integrated, using Bayesian networks. The core strategy here is called "A.I. Global Equity Strategy"; it has been established in 2007 and it holds a diverse portfolio consisting of 90–120 global equities. The firm describes itself as an online financial advisor and claims: "Our AI has outperformed the markets for 13 years." Human revolutionary touch combined with high performance. This works well in the area of wealth management because cost-cutting is one of defining aspects of ML—and this makes it very attractive for a the wealth management business.

4 From Risk Management to B-C

It goes without saying that with increased computing power classical models of probability calculus can be used better and faster. Assessing risks becomes easier, the preparation of decisions as well.

Especially at large firms (big banks and publicly traded insurance companies), ML algorithms can be trained of million of examples of consumer data (job, place of residence, age, marital status) and financial lending or insurance results, such as whether or not a person defaulted or paid back their loans on time. The producing of credit scores is and will be a main field of use for ML.

This can be used in lending- and crowdfunding platforms as well. SoFi for example is an online lending platform that offers home improvement loans, credit card consolidation, student loan refinancing and mortgage refinancing as well as well as investment management.

But the most visible changes com with new communication- and service tools. Speaking of service or of man-machine-interfaces, we find a lot more cheap productivity in the use of chatbots. The company FUJITSU for example has developed FUJITSU Financial Services Solution Finplex Robot Agent Platform (FRAP), an ML-based enterprise chatbot service. FRAP achieves automatic robot support of financial product sales and customer support by having users converse in a chat format with a robot having knowledge accumulated by ML.

What is particularly clear in the field of customer relationships is that every technological innovation has to be embedded in a social and psychological environment. It is not just the new programs and models that are important, but the man-machine interfaces by which it is decided whether the programs and models can be used. This utilization can not be judged without some comments on organizational development. Organizational development means: development *in* organizations, but also development *of* organizations If we look at current trends, we can treat different phases at the level of companies: (1) Start-ups—e.g. Fintechs, that use innovations for new business models. (2) Optimization of existing structures, e.g. Customization, personalization. We see many traditional banks going that way and supporting entrepreneurship within their own firms. (3) Realignment of a fundamental kind—mixture of start-up and optimization: maybe the most important and most creative sector. These transformations are driven by high expectations: A Research and Markets survey indicates that the market for AI financial services software is expected to grow at approximately 40.4% per annum, from $1.3 billion in 2017 to $7.4 billion in the year 2022.

5 Outlooks

So there is a long road in front of us. It is true, that ML excels the large and complex volumes of data, something the finance sector certainly has in excess of. And it is not only the quantity but also the quality of data in finance that is unique. The treasure of historic data provides good reasons to be confident about the standardization, which is necessary for the even better use of ML in Finance.

But it would be fatal to acknowledge the effects of artificial intelligence or machine learning only on the economic level or in organizational development. We should not forget the social and environmental impact Scott (2013). So here we did not discuss the theoretical basics, but the current areas of application in which significant social and environmental added value can be expected. The UN Report "Digital Technologies for Mobilizing Sustainable Finance. Applications of Digital Technologies for Sustainable Finance" (Bayat-Renoux et al. 2018) summarizes various digitization projects from different countries, takes a closer look at some strategic problems, but sheds little light on the specific opportunities of ML related to sustainability.

In the whole discussion, we fail to recognize that the two major waves of transformation in the financial industry, sustainability and digitization, will have a significantly higher impact together, supporting each other. This is partly due to a cultural divide between the AI-/ML-Community and the sustainability scene (Smolinski et al. 2017). But interconnectivity rules: they can complement and reinforce each other. If this necessary connection is recognized in future thinking about finance, then a goal of this article has been reached.

References

Bayat-Renoux, F., Svensson, U., & Chebly, J. (2018). *Digital technologies for mobilizing sustainable finance. Applications of digital technologies to sustainable finance, sustainable digital finance alliance 2018.*

Gyorfi, L., & Ottucsak, G. (2011). *Machine learning for financial engineering*. London: Imperial College Press.

Hutchinson, J. M., Lo, A. W., & Poggio, T. (1994). A nonparametric approach to pricing and hedging derivative securities via learning networks. *Journal of Finance, 49*(3), 851–889.

Kearns, M., & Nevmyvaka, Y. (2013). Machine learning for market microstructure and high frequency trading. In D. Easley, M. Lopez de Prado, & M. O'Hara (Eds.), *High frequency trading—New realities for traders, markets and regulators*. London: Risk Books.

Klaas, J. (2019). *Machine learning for finance. Principles and practice for financial insiders.* Birmingham: Packt.

Lai, Z.-R., Yang, P.-Y., Fang, L., & Wu, X. (2018). Short-term sparse portfolio optimization based on alternating direction method of multipliers. *Journal of Machine Learning Research, 1*, 2547–2574.

Li, B., & Hoi, S. C. H. (2014). Online portfolio selection: A survey. *ACM Computing Surveys (CSUR), 46*(3), 1–33.

Li, B., Sahoo, D., & Hoi, S. C. H. (2016). OLPS: A toolbox for online portfolio selection. *Journal of Machine Learning Research, 17*(1), 1242–1246.

Lopez de Prado, M. (2018). *Advances in financial machine learning*. Hoboken: Wiley.

Samuel, A. L. (1959). Some studies in machine learning using the game of checkers. *IBM Journal of Research and Development, 3*(3), 210–229.

Scott, B. (2013). *The heretics guide to global finance: Hacking the future of money*. London: Pluto Press.

Smolinski, R., Gerdes, M., Siejka, M., & Bodek, M. C. (Eds.). (2017). *Innovationen und Innovationsmanagement in der Finanzbranche*. Wiesbaden: Springer Gabler.

Streichert, F., & Algorithmen, E. (2001). *Implementation und Anwendungen im Asset Management-Bereich, Diplomarbeit Universität Stuttgart 2001.*

Bernhard Villhauer is the Managing Director of the Global Ethic Institute (WEIT) at the University of Tübingen since January 2015. After completing an apprenticeship as an industrial clerk, he studied philosophy, classical studies and history of art at the Universities of Freiburg i.Brsg., Jena and Hull (UK). After his PhD thesis on a cultural-philosophical topic (Aby Warburg and Ernst Cassirer) he worked for various companies in the publishing and media sector, most recently as editorial director of the publishing group Narr Francke Attempto. Before that he held positions in the middle management at the publishing houses Mohr Siebeck and Wissenschaftliche Buchgesellschaft (WBG). At the same time, he taught as a lecturer at the universities of Karlsruhe,

Jena, Darmstadt and Tübingen. His lectures focused on cultural and media science issues as well as theoretical and practical philosophy and economics. He is co-founder of the Institute for Philosophy of Practice e.V. in Darmstadt. Since the summer 2013 he offers a seminar "Money and Ethics" at the Global Ethic Institute. He is also the initiator of the series "Klüger wirtschaften". His current work focuses on monetary theory, financial ethics and investment, topics he bloggs about in his "Finanz und Eleganz" Blog. Bernd Villhauer is Director of the Good Governance Lab at the European School of Governance (EUSG) and head of the research group "Finanzen und Wirtschaft" at the Weltethos-Institut. He is currently writing a book "Finanzmarkt und Ethik. Eine Einführung" and hopes to finish this in autumn 2019.

Part VII
SDG Topic

The Gender Investment Gap

Ulrike Glatz and Siddhartha Sharma

Abstract We are in the twenty-first century, and live in a technologically very advanced, culturally sophisticated and globalized world. In the world of business and investment however, half of humanity still doesn't receive their fair share of trust and financial backing when pitching their business proposals. Still, men are preferred when it comes to VC and other funding. Research shows that there is an immense gender investment gap, still and again placing women at a backseat. This chapter takes a close look at that gap, exploring the historic dimension behind it, and diving into gender roles, the role of perception and of our economic system rewarding and incentivizing "male" qualities. It outlines good reasons to invest in women and offers recommendations for best practices to close the gender investment gap. Not only as an act of justice by giving women a fair chance and a greater share of market and power—it's a change in mindset that could well determine our future quality of life or even survival on this planet.

Keywords Theory of change · Theories of change · Diversity · Mixed teams · Social entrepreneurship · VC · VC capital · Gender gap · Investment gap

1 The Gender Investment Gap

The gender pay gap is well documented: women make about 54% for every dollar that a man earns. Less well known however is the gender investment gap (Tyson and Parker 2019).

U. Glatz (✉)
Global Impact Alliance, Berlin, Germany
e-mail: ulrike.glatz@global-impact-alliance.com

S. Sharma
CredFIC Inc, Jaipur, Rajasthan, India

K. Wendt (ed.), *Theories of Change*, Sustainable Finance,
https://doi.org/10.1007/978-3-030-52275-9_23

Image 1 Women in business and investment

According to research conducted by BCG in partnership with MassChallenge[1] covering 5 years of investment and revenue data, the gender-focused analysis showed a clear funding gap: Women pitching for early-stage capital receive significantly less investment than men (Abouzahr et al. 2018).

In 2017, female-founded businesses received just 2.2% of the total venture capital (VC) funding in the United States and this trend continued during the following year (TechCrunch 2018). Further data compiled by Pitchbook shows that the vast majority of UK VC investments are into all-male teams. In fact, during 2017, all-female teams constituted just 4% of deals, and mixed-gender teams made up only 12%. Also, the average deal size for a woman-led company in 2017 was a bit over $5 million. For a man-led company, that number is around $12 million (Zarya 2018).

Numbers that should surprise considering that we are looking at data from Western countries in the twenty-first century. After decades of equal rights movement and with even men being outspoken feminists, we pride ourselves to be truly egalitarian societies. Still, those are the findings. In the world of business and investment, women don't receive their fair share of trust and financial backing for their business ideas like their male counterparts. A startling situation that requires a closer look—even more so in an era of AI, blockchain and biotechnology where

[1]MassChallenge is a US-based global network of accelerators that offers startup businesses access to mentors, industry experts, and other resources (https://masschallenge.org).

startups have the power to not only disrupt industries, but to profoundly shape society and human evolution.

2 Exploring the 'Why' Behind the Gap

2.1 *One of the Underlying Reasons for Today's Gender Investment Gap Can Be Found in History*

Seen from a historian's perspective, it's a rather recent phenomena that women are allowed to fully participate in the world of finance.

No doubt, there have been progressive societies throughout history, such as e.g. ancient Egypt (3100 BCE and after) where women held equal financial rights with men: Egyptian women were able to acquire, to own, and to dispose of property (both real and personal) in their own name. They could enter into contracts in their own name, could initiate civil court cases and could be sued; they could serve as witnesses in court cases; serve on juries; and could witness legal documents (Johnson 2019). Far more restrictive versions of this existed also in Ancient Hinduism (1500 BC and after), during biblical times (1800 BC and after) under Jewish Law, in the Islamic Middle East (AD600) or during the Byzantine Empire (AD565) thanks to Empress Theodora (McGee and Moore 2019).

However, throughout history and across most cultures, women were only very rarely treated and seen as equals when it came to owning property, receiving a fair share of heritage, having and investing their own money and getting into business. Instead, women had to depend on their fathers, husbands or brothers. Partially, this is still the case in many countries and cultures today. And even in Europe and the US, up to 40 years ago, middle-class women were not allowed to handle money and having a job was seen as a sign of financial desperation (McGee and Moore 2019).

To summarize: For most of human's history, women have been in a position depending on men and this consistent imbalance over the course of centuries had great influence and impact, up until today. In material terms it shows in women holding only 30% of private wealth in the world (Beardsley 2016) while being 49.6% of the population.

Deeply ingrained psychological traces of dependency throughout centuries can of course not that easily be stated in numbers. However, "women need men" and "women and finances don't go together" has been a reality for such a long time for an overwhelming majority of women (and men!) on this planet—and in many countries it still is—that the new concept of women being independent and fully playing their equal role in the world of business and investments is still struggling to become the norm.

To be seen also in the latest attempts to even out the situation in the investment world by introducing "gender lens investing" (Cortes 2019)—certainly a great step forward, but looking at it more closely we see that narrowing the VC gender gap does not seem to enjoy much of importance as the funds meant for plugging the gender gap are less than 1% of the annual total VC spent globally. Probably as still men being the majority in the VC industry (Guynn 2016) and women, still and again, are dependent on men allocating more resources to even out a situation that should not exist in the first place.

2.2 An Economic System Built by and for Men: With a Focus on "Male" Qualities

The core of our globally operating economic system is competition. Its focus is one-dimensional on "winning the business game". By outplaying competitors, fast and if possible, global expansion and making maximum profit in a short time. It's about being better, aggressive and "hunting for' clients, market shares and investors. Women can play that game too—totally. Most of the still rather few female billionaires (for every female billionaire, there are 8.4 male billionaires (Zarya 2019)) made their money, being brilliant entrepreneurs and investors, successfully navigating this economic system.

However, be it now by genes, hormones and/or the education system and society girls are brought up in and women live in—women tend to be more inclined towards cooperation, multi-tasking and focusing on more than one dimension. They prefer stable, long-term growth over fast expansion and winning together versus alone. Hence qualities that are valued, but mostly not helpful to get all the way to the top, and stay there. Hence, being an "alpha-female", a true leader built on feminine strengths and power, is hence not enough. A woman also has to learn to portray and play the "male game" to fully succeed in the business and investment world. However, she also needs to braze herself: If a woman naturally fits or adapts to the rules of the operating system, she needs to live with being deemed 'too aggressive", "too ambitious", "too manly"—all qualities that men would get praised for (Rao Gluckman 2018).

2.3 Gender Roles Influence Us, from Childhood to Pitching

Which leads us to gender roles that encompass a range of behaviors and attitudes that are generally considered acceptable, appropriate, or desirable for people based on their actual or perceived sex (En.wikipedia.org n.d.). The prevalent demeanor women are expected to display is accommodating, nice, nurturing and polite. Furthermore, girls and women are generally expected to dress in typically feminine ways. Men in contrast are expected to be strong, aggressive and bold, and wear pants, suits, ties and shirts—hence the male gender role and expectations corelate with the classical business outfit and the desired characteristics of a successful entrepreneur. Which means that while men can stay in their comfort zone and act the way they are trained since childhood,[2] women need to either adopt "male qualities" and attire or work double as hard to convince investors despite not fitting the commonly expected traits and looks of (male) role-model entrepreneurs.

Furthermore, women's role in society isn't made to go out and hunt for clients and investment deals.

This is true for Western countries, but even more so for least developed and developing nations. Even though 40–50% of all small businesses are owned by women in developing countries (TEDx 2011), it doesn't mean that this is an easy path.[3] As still, the primary and traditional role and responsibility in society for women, especially outside of big cities, is more likely to be mother, housewife and caretaker—rather than businesswoman or owner of an investment portfolio. Choosing an entrepreneurial path or exploring the route of becoming an investor as a woman, hence means not only defying the norms of society, but also constantly dividing one's time and attention between business and tasks at home, between fulfilling professional requirements and family expectations, between personal aspirations and the needs of children, husbands and elderly parents and parents-in-law. Those competing demands on time have been observed in a number of studies across different countries, from Bangladesh to Sweden. The results suggest that lack of time due to societies role expectations towards women, is a barrier for most women, in most economies, independent of the level of development (Oecd.org 2004).

2.4 How Gender Impacts Perception, Language and Funding for Women

Women and men are different, yes. However, when it comes to applying for VC funding, the decision should be about the idea, the timing, the competence and the model of the business presented—not about the stereotypes Venture Capitalists consciously and unconsciously hold in their minds. But it is, as a yearlong study (Malmstrom et al. 2017) in Sweden revealed.

The researchers were allowed to silently observe governmental VC decision-making meetings and their conversations about entrepreneurs that had applied for funding. Their findings were that the attributes used to describe male and female entrepreneurs were radically different (see Fig. 1: "Description of male and female attributes"). Also, qualities were judged differently depending on gender, e.g. being

[2]During puberty, children seem heavily influenced by the traditional gender norms amplified in pop culture. Education research has found that the stereotypes of assertive male and passive female are often reinforced in our schools and in our very classrooms.

[3]Remark by the author: A fact that may be attributed to women from low-income countries without childcare, elderly care and other social security support often seeking an additional means of income to support themselves and their families—and running a small business is possible from home, at flexible hours and an option independent from having a formal degree or not.

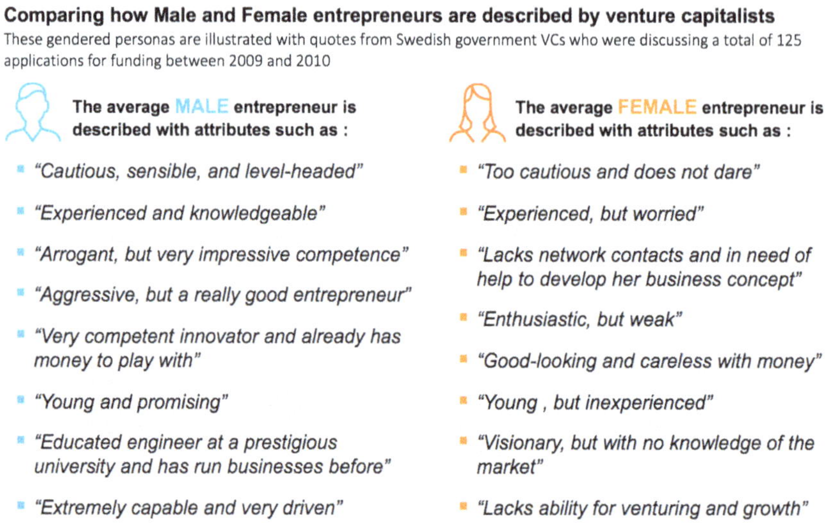

Fig. 1 Description of male and female attributes

young as an entrepreneur was seen as "inexperienced" in the case of a woman, but for men this quality was "promising". Being "aggressive" or "arrogant" was positive for men, whereas women letting their experience known and showing their excitement lead to discussions about their "emotional shortcomings" (Malmstrom et al. 2017). And those differences had very real consequences: Women entrepreneurs were only awarded, on average, 25% of the applied-for amount, whereas men received, on average, 52% of what they asked for. Furthermore, only 38% of men were denied funding in contrast to 53% of the women whose applications were dismissed (Malmstrom et al. 2017).

Another research conducted during TechCrunch Disrupt New York City, and published in the Harvard Business Review (Kanze et al. 2017), showed how questions to entrepreneurs change depending on gender: When pitching their startups, men get asked how they will make money. While women get inquiries about how they will prevent losing the investor's money. According to the psychological theory of "regulatory focus", investors adopt a "promotion orientation" when asking questions to male entrepreneurs while exhibiting a "prevention orientation" in their questions to female entrepreneurs (Kanze et al. 2017). This means that 67% of questions to male entrepreneurs were about hopes, achievements, advancement, and ideals whereas female candidates had to answer 66% of the investor's inquiries concerning the topics of safety, responsibility, security, and vigilance (Kanze et al. 2017).

As seen in Fig. 2, framing questions in those two different ways, gives a chance to the male entrepreneur for inspiring answers. Whereas female entrepreneurs faced with such questions are forced to focus their answer on the risky aspects of their business—which in turn leads to less investment in women entrepreneurs (Kanze et al. 2018).

VCs frame questions in two different ways

Promotion questions focus on potential gains, whereas prevention questions focus on potential losses. VCs tend to ask the former of men and the latter of women

TOPIC	PROMOTION	PREVENTION
Customers	**Acquisition** *Example Question:* "How do you want to acquire customers?"	**Retention** *Example Question:* "How many daily and monthly active users do you have?"?
Income statement	**Sales** "How do you plan to monetize this?"	**Margins** "How long will it take you to break even?"
Market	**Size** "Do you think that your target market is a growing one?"	**Share** "Is it a defensible business wherein other people can't come into the space to take share?"
Projections	**Growth** "What major milestones are you targeting for this year?"	**Stability** "How predictable are your future cash flows?"
Strategy	**Vision** "What's the brand vision?"	**Execution** "Are you planning to Turing test this?"
Management	**Entrepreneur** "Can you tell us a bit about yourself?"	**Team** "How much of this are you actually doing in-house?"

Fig. 2 Promotion versus prevention questions

2.5 *Feminine Behavior in a Male Oriented Investment World*

Interestingly, research (Balachandra et al. 2017) indicates that women are not discriminated against simply because of being a woman, but because of exhibiting stereotypical feminine traits (Balachandra 2018). Interestingly, also men are at a disadvantage when showcasing "feminine" behavior while pitching. Ergo, to be successful in raising money, one definitely is on the winning side when exhibiting stereotypical "male" behavior—no matter if as a man or a woman (Balachandra 2018).

2.6 *Good Old Sexism Still at Play*

Raising investment for a startup in general is a challenge. Even more so as a female founder. As the investment industry still is "an old boy's club" with an unhealthy dose of old-fashioned sexism still at play (Murphy 2019). In other words, by an anonymous female founder who published her experience on Forbes, the VC world is "the wild west of fundraising and I needed to learn how to navigate the alpha male-dominated VC community as a female founder" (Bercovici 2014).

It is mostly hidden, but creeps up into the light when being mistaken as the secretary or receptionist instead of getting a polite welcome as a promising women entrepreneur ready to pitch her business (Murphy 2019).

Misogyny also shows when being invited home for a business discussion by a VC and then being touched inappropriately (Bercovici 2014). It gets evident when getting an invite for a yacht trip with angel investors and VCs to get to know them better in a relaxed setting while the same boat trip gets praised to male entrepreneurs as "epic" as "there are always multiple blondes to every guy" (Bercovici 2014).

2.7 The Profile of the Successful Entrepreneurship Is Male

As women have entered the stage of business and investment only recently compared to men, minds are filled with male examples of successful entrepreneurs and investors: Mark Zuckerberg, Steve Jobs, Bill Gates, Warren Buffet, George Soros. Of course, there are very successful female investors—but how many people have really ever heard of Abigail Johnson or Deborah A. Farrington (Fontinelle 2019)? The same is true for female entrepreneurs—names such as Sofia Vergara, Arianna Huffington, Indra Nooyi might somehow ring a bell (Western n.d.), but they for sure don't come up first in mind when asked for famous entrepreneurs. Hence, says Candida Brush, a professor of entrepreneurship at Babson College, when investors are approached by women entrepreneurs, there is an unconscious bias that they will not be as reliable an investment as their male counterparts, and therefore not as fundable (Hecht 2016).

This lack of female figures coming to mind when thinking of successful investors and entrepreneurs does not only have an impact on investment decisions. It also does influence career decisions—as we all, and especially young people, need and follow role-models we can identify with (Parikh 2017). Men clearly have more and highly prominent figures as role-models to thrive for becoming successful business men or investors. Whereas women need to dig deeper to identify a female role-model for their entrepreneurship or investor career.

2.8 Adding Another Layer to the Gender Bias: Race

Even though this is not the focus of this essay, it's still important to mention that it is even more of a challenge for women of color to raise funding. As additionally to the gender bias, they also need to face racial bias which leads to very little funding for founders of color (Friess 2018). Which can be seen looking at e.g. the report of the analytics firm CB Insight revealing that of the $58 billion invested by venture capitalists in U.S. startups in 2015, only 1% went to black-owned enterprises and 8% to women (Sherry 2015). In East Africa, a study (Strachan Matranga et al. 2017) of 2015–16 by Village Capital found that 90% of the capital invested in the region didn't go to local entrepreneurs, but went to a very small group of businesses, founded by expats (Chiu 2019).

2.9 Investors Invest in What They Fully Understand

Any investor prefers investing in domains he/she fully comprehends, or ideally even has prior experience with (Murphy 2019). A wise move in order to minimize risk—for oneself, the portfolio and the other investors one possibly represents when taking an investment decision. The downside of this for business women is that not too few of them come up with products and services that serve specific needs of women, mothers, babies. A market that is growing, partially untapped and that women understand (Solovic 2016)—from their own experience—very well. Hence, a great case for investing. However, most investors are men. Who, more often than not, simply based on their gender, their role in society and their hence limited, personal exposure to certain topics and situations are no experts of those products and services. Which, being responsible investors trying to minimize risk, may lead to them not investing in women led ventures—leaving female entrepreneurs with no funding, despite their possibly high-potential ideas for a growing niche market.

2.10 Gender Gap on the Investors Side

Women, of course, can turn to female investors for funding. However, despite a growing trend in recent years (The Economist 2019), there is still a considerable gender gap also on the investor side, as can be seen in Fig. 3 below (Garaizar 2016):

In 2015, a group of senior women investors interested in solving this gender gap set out to investigate the reasons why not more women acted as investors—specifically focusing on angel investing (Garaizar 2016). They identified 6 roadblocks stopping women from getting active as investors:

- They don't know about angel investing and its opportunities
- They are not solicited to invest
- They feel ill-prepared for angel investing

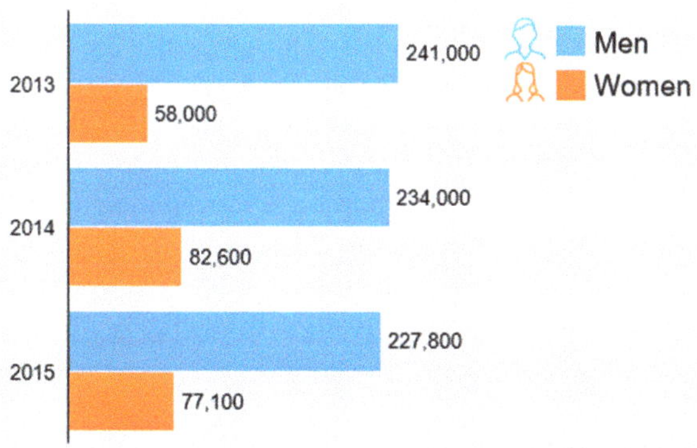

Fig. 3 Number of female investors compared to number of male investors

- They are risk-averse and avoid this risky asset class
- They do not have the right network of angel investors
- They are not exposed to vetted deal flow (Garaizar 2016)

A similar situation can be seen in the VC industry. Under 10% of decision-makers at VC firms were women, and nearly three-quarters of US VC firms did not have a single woman investor. In Canada, 15% of VC partners were women in 2018 (BetaKit 2018), and in the UK only 13% of the senior management in all UK VC investment teams are women, while 48% of investment teams had no women at all. Cumulatively, these figures highlight an imbalance in the composition of investment teams and are one of the many reasons for skewed investments into female-led businesses.

Women are significantly underrepresented as leaders in PE/VC firms, and their lack of representation means that the decision-making teams, responsible for capital allocation in emerging markets, are acutely imbalanced. A recent research (International Finance Corporation et al. 2019) conducted by the International Finance Corporation (IFC) suggests that this imbalance may not only be reducing the returns of PE/VC firms but could also be reducing female entrepreneurs' equal access to capital.

3 Many Good Reasons to Invest (More) in Women

3.1 The Business Case for Funding Female Founders Is Simple: Female Founders Outperform Their Male Counterparts

Data collected for example by First Round Capital indicated that investments in companies with at least one female founder were meaningfully outperforming their investments in all-male teams (First Round 10 Year Project 2015). Indeed, companies with a female founder performed 63% better than investments with all-male founding teams (First Round 10 Year Project 2015).

Further research conducted by the Ewin Marion Kauffman Foundation (Garaizar 2016) found that women-led teams generate a 35% higher return on investment than all-male teams (Fatemi 2019). Privately held tech companies lead by women are more capital-efficient, achieve 35% higher return on investment, and, when venture-backed, bring in 12% higher revenue than male-owned tech companies (Klein 2013).

Boston Consulting Group made it even more evident by evaluating 350 companies that had been part of the "MassChallenge" program.[4] The study showed that for every dollar of investment raised, startups lead by women generated 78% in revenue, whereas their male counterparts generated only 31% (see Fig. 4). And those women

[4]https://masschallenge.org

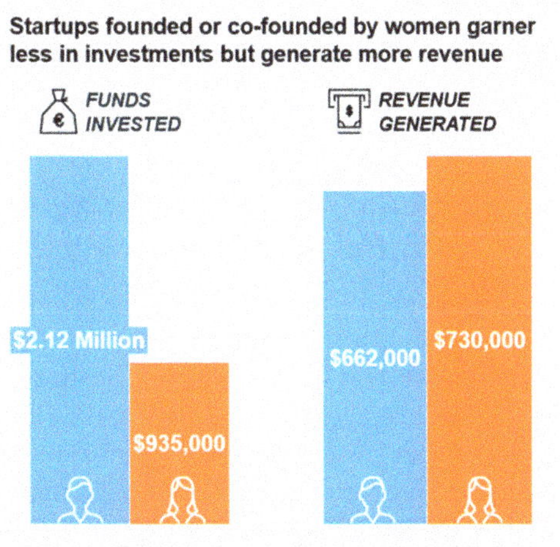

Fig. 4 Less investment, more revenue

entrepreneurs achieved these much better results despite raising less money ($935 K vs. $2.12 M) (Abouzahr et al. 2018). By that measure, if investors had put the same amount of capital into women-run businesses as they did into the ones run by male-leadership, they would have helped generate an additional $85 million in revenue.

3.2 *Furthermore, Women Possess What Is of Interest for Investors: Intrinsic Motivation, Long-Term Thinking and a Sense for Innovation*

Female founders are less motivated by money. Specifically, males are nearly eight times more likely to be motivated by financial gain. 15% of male entrepreneurs are motivated to start companies for financial gain compared to only 2% of female entrepreneurs who are more intrinsically motivated (Fatemi 2019). And this is a good thing. Research has shown that people are more likely to perform well on difficult, cognitive tasks compared to an easier cognitive task when they are intrinsically motivated (Donovan 2015). And this is what most women are—they have a strong desire to create something meaningful and to have a positive impact on the world (Fatemi 2019). Also, intrinsic motivation helps to go the extra mile and to persevere in difficult situations (Fatemi 2019).

Another point to consider is that investing in for profit-driven entrepreneurs can be riskier as they are inclined to make decisions for short-term gains that are unsustainable for the company in the long run (Fatemi 2019).

Women entrepreneurs furthermore have a 5% greater likelihood of innovativeness than men, according to the Women Entrepreneurship Report that covered 74 economies worldwide (Kelley et al. 2017). This means, women were more likely than men to introduce products and services that are new to customers and not generally offered by competitors (Price 2017)—a talent worthwhile an investment.

3.3 *Last But Not Least: Closing the Gender Gap Is Not Only Fair, But Also Means Overall Economic Growth*

The following was proven by Stefan Klasen in his study (1999) that was used to support the World Bank's gender mainstreaming strategy: Societies that discriminate by gender tend to experience less rapid economic growth and poverty reduction than societies that treat males and females more equally. Furthermore, social gender disparities produce economically inefficient outcomes.

The consulting company McKinsey states that gender inequality is not only a pressing moral and social issue but also a critical economic challenge. If women—who account for half the world's working-age population—do not achieve their full economic potential, the global economy will suffer (Woetzel et al. 2015). The management consulting firm's report finds that $12 trillion could be added to global GDP by 2025 by advancing women's equality (Woetzel et al. 2015).

Hence closing the gender gap in the world of business and investment makes total business sense—also for the overall economy of a country.

4 Best Practices for Female Entrepreneurs

Of course, centuries of women not being an equal part of the business and investment equation and mostly unconscious bias and stereotypes can't be eradicated from 1 day to the other—it's a process. Women hence still need to live with the status quo of a rather male oriented economic system and investment world. However, there are a few things, female entrepreneurs can do:

4.1 *Build Your Female Support Network*

Find other female founders and role-models, and build a trusted support network to exchange with. Identify a female mentor with experience in entrepreneurship, leadership and fundraising (Fernandes 2018). Reach out to female investors, and VCs with women on their investment boards (Huston 2015).

4.2 Be Strategic and Clear When Networking

Meet with people relevant to your business and fundraising. Don't hesitate to ask for introductions, advice, recommendations and support. Be clear and outspoken about your value and your company's USP and current requirements (funding, staff, advice etc.) (Marcus 2018).

4.3 Focus on the Figures

This is even more important when pitching a female-focused product to male investors. Give them the bottom line—potential market share, opportunity and margins (Malik 2019).

4.4 Confidentially Ask for What You Need

In equity raising, men tend to ask for more money and provide more optimistic forecasts. Whereas women tend to ask for less than they actually need, but this will cause problems in the long term. It's important to ask for the right amount of money. Believe in yourself, show confidence and don't be shy to ask for what you need (Malik 2019).

4.5 Focus Your Answers on Potential

If you are getting a "prevention oriented" question from investors, shift the focus in your answer to the potential of your venture (Kanze et al. 2018). Not answering every question the way it was meant to be shows confidence and helps your potential investors see the treasure they'd be possibly missing otherwise.

4.6 Team up with Men

Mixed teams are successful, in business and when pitching. It's hence wise to team up with men, and strategically work with their strengths to your company's advantage. In the end, it's about delivering great value to the market, to clients, investors, to one's own life and society—and about doing that successfully as a female leader, not despite men but with them.

5 Best Practice for the World

Closing the gender investment gap is important—no doubt.

What we urgently need however is not only more female entrepreneurs and women investors, but also a transformation of our economic system from one only focusing on and rewarding rather "male qualities and aspects" (fierce competition, fast growth, winning the "faster, better, bigger" race, single focus on profits etc.) to one integrating more "feminine qualities and aspects" as equally—or even more—important:

5.1 Cooperation

We need massive cooperation among nations, corporates, organizations and citizens in global issues, first of all in the very urgent matter of climate change—mitigating the worse and adapting to its effects cannot be done as "lone wolves", but only in a cooperative effort of all players, globally (Powell 2013). The same is true for rapidly advancing fields such as biotechnology and AI—where only globally agreed and implemented guidelines and regulations could prevent potential misuse and downsides of those technologies.

5.2 Contribution

Business could emerge as a real player and solution-provider in the quest to put our world on a better course—and it actually should and must go through a major shift, given the fact that it largely contributed to the environmental degradation, imbalanced accumulation of capital among very few and its resulting tensions in the world. Business needs to redefine itself as a true "force for good" by redefining its definition of success from profits as the main and ultimate objective to positively contributing to the society and the environment being its purpose and core feature of its business model.

5.3 Sharing

The sharing economy with its digital platforms is already no longer a millennial preference, but a part of modern society (Knowledge at Wharton 2019). The model has come to be mainly about convenience, price and transactional efficiency (Knowledge at Wharton 2019). With its credo "access over ownership", it could however have the potential to responsibly mitigate hyper-consumption, enabling more people having access to otherwise unaffordable services, and could build genuine community connections—if it was implemented with those objectives in mind and based on the principle of "truly sharing". It's furthermore recommendable to create and implement more models of shared ownership (like e.g. the cooperative model) in communities and businesses in order to re-install a sense of responsibility, belonging and joint interest within our currently rather alienated members of communities and mostly disengaged employees.

5.4 *Inclusion*

The inclusion of "the unheard", of marginalized groups and minorities into the economic process and discussion is not only fair to those who are members of such groups, but it also is essential for coming up with innovative solutions to our current issues—as there is an inherent degree of innovation in diverse groups (Hewlett et al. 2013) and those affected by certain situations know best what is needed to solve them on the ground.

5.5 *Partnership*

We need to re-establish our partnership with nature—as an integral part of it, not its master. It's in our interest as human species to protect our habitat and to learn from nature's amazingly efficient system of co-creation, co-habitation and cooperation. Nothing gets wasted in nature—a principle that the system of circular economy has taken up as one of its core pillars. Instead of our current linear system of economy (take, make, use, dispose, pollute), it takes up the natural cycle of "make, use, re-use, re-make, re-cycle"—leading to highly responsible consumption of resources and zero waste (Ellenmacarthurfoundation.org. 2019).

To summarize: Closing the gender investment gap is far more than an act of justice giving women a fair chance and a greater share of market and power—it's a change in mindset that could well determine our future lifestyle or even survival on this planet.

References

Abouzahr, K., Brooks Taplett, F., Krentz, M., & Harthorne, J. (2018). *Why women-owned startups are a better bet*. https://www.bcg.com [Online]. Retrieved August 2, 2019, from https://www.bcg.com/en-us/publications/2018/why-women-owned-startups-are-better-bet.aspx

Balachandra, L. (2018). Research: Investors punish entrepreneurs for stereotypically feminine behaviors. *Harvard Business Review* [Online]. Retrieved August 1, 2019, from https://hbr.org/2018/10/research-investors-punish-entrepreneurs-for-stereotypically-feminine-behaviors

Balachandra, L., Briggs, T., Eddlestone, K., & Brush, C. (2017). *Don't pitch like a girl! How gender stereotypes influence investor decisions—Lakshmi Balachandra, Tony Briggs, Kim Eddleston, Candida Brush, 2019*. Journals Sagepub [Online]. Retrieved August 1, 2019, from https://journals.sagepub.com/doi/abs/10.1177/1042258717728028?journalCode=etpb

Beardsley, B. (2016). *Global wealth 2016: Navigating the new client landscape*. https://www.bcg.com [Online]. Retrieved July 29, 2019, from https://www.bcg.com/publications/2016/financial-institutions-consumer-insight-global-wealth-2016.aspx

Bercovici, J. (2014). *What it's like raising money as a woman in silicon valley*. Forbes.com [Online]. Retrieved July 30, 2019, from https://www.forbes.com/sites/jeffbercovici/2014/08/07/what-its-like-raising-money-as-a-woman-in-tech/#70173fe1707d

BetaKit. (2018). *Despite more Canadian women VC partners, LP dollars still go to all-male funds*. BetaKit [Online]. Retrieved August 1, 2019, from https://betakit.com/despite-more-canadian-women-vc-partners-lp-dollars-still-go-to-all-male-funds/

Chiu, B. (2019). *Impact investing needs to rise to the urgent challenge of reducing racial inequalities*. Forbes.com [Online]. Retrieved August 3, 2019, from https://www.forbes.com/sites/bonniechiu/2019/07/22/impact-investing-needs-to-rise-to-the-urgent-challenge-of-reducing-racial-inequalities/#558911264b23

Cortes, E. (2019). *Gender-lens investing strategies for 2019 (SSIR)*. Ssir.org [Online]. Retrieved August 5, 2019, from https://ssir.org/articles/entry/gender_lens_investing_strategies_for_2019

Donovan, N. (2015). *The effects of intrinsic and extrinsic motivation on cognitive performance in humans*. Scholarship@Western [Online]. Retrieved August 2, 2019, from https://ir.lib.uwo.ca/hucjlm/vol53/iss1/5/

Ellenmacarthurfoundation.org. (2019). *What is the circular economy?* [Online]. Retrieved August 6, 2019, from https://www.ellenmacarthurfoundation.org/circular-economy/what-is-the-circular-economy

En.wikipedia.org. (n.d.). *Gender role*. [Online]. Retrieved August 2, 2019, from https://en.wikipedia.org/wiki/Gender_role

Fatemi, F. (2019). *The value of investing in female founders*. Forbes.com [Online]. Retrieved August 2, 2019, from https://www.forbes.com/sites/falonfatemi/2019/03/29/the-value-of-investing-in-female-founders/#30e8a4565ee4

Fernandes, P. (2018). *7 Challenges faced by female entrepreneurs*. *Business News Daily* [Online]. Retrieved August 5, 2019, from https://www.businessnewsdaily.com/5268-women-entrepreneur-challenges.html

First Round 10 Year Project. (2015). *First round 10 year project*. [Online]. Retrieved August 2, 2019, from http://10years.firstround.com

Fontinelle, A. (2019). *7 Outstanding female investors*. Investopedia [Online]. Retrieved August 1, 2019, from https://www.investopedia.com/articles/basics/12/top-female-investors.asp

Friess, S. (2018). In Chicago, black entrepreneurs seeking venture capital face excessive scrutiny and discrimination. *Belt Magazine* [Online]. Retrieved August 3, 2019, from https://beltmag.com/black-entrepreneurs-discrimination/

Garaizar, J. (2016). *Kauffman fellows report, volume 7*. Kauffmanfellows.org [Online]. Retrieved August 1, 2019, from https://www.kauffmanfellows.org/wp-content/uploads/KFR_Vol7/Juliana_Garaizar_vol7.pdf

Guynn, J. (2016). *Venture capital is overwhelmingly white and male*. Eu.usatoday.com [Online]. Retrieved August 6, 2019, from https://eu.usatoday.com/story/tech/news/2016/12/15/national-venture-capital-association-deloitte-diversity-survey/95453926/

Hecht, J. (2016). *Why women entrepreneurs have a harder time finding funding*. Entrepreneur.com [Online]. Retrieved August 1, 2019, from https://www.entrepreneur.com/article/281733

Hewlett, S., Marshall, M., & Sherbin, L. (2013). How diversity can drive innovation. *Harvard Business Review* [Online]. Retrieved August 6, 2019, from https://hbr.org/2013/12/how-diversity-can-drive-innovation

Huston, C. (2015). *Why entrepreneurs reach out to female investors*. MarketWatch [Online]. Retrieved August 5, 2019, from https://www.marketwatch.com/story/why-entrepreneurs-reach-out-to-female-investors-2015-01-30

International Finance Corporation, et al. (2019). *Moving toward in private equity and venture capital gender balance* (1st ed.). Washington: International Finance Corporation.

Johnson, J. (2019). *Women's legal rights in ancient Egypt*. Fathom.lib.uchicago.edu [Online]. Retrieved July 29, 2019, from http://fathom.lib.uchicago.edu/1/777777190170/

Kanze, D., Huang, L., Conley, M., & Higgins, E. (2017). Male and female entrepreneurs get asked different questions by VCs—And it affects how much funding they get. *Harvard Business Review* [Online]. Retrieved July 30, 2019, from https://hbr.org/2017/06/male-and-female-entrepreneurs-get-asked-different-questions-by-vcs-and-it-affects-how-much-funding-they-get

Kanze, D., Huang, L., Conley, M., & Higgins, E. (2018). *We ask men to win and women not to lose: Closing the gender gap in startup funding*. Academy of Management Journal [Online]. Retrieved July 30, 2019, from https://journals.aom.org/doi/full/10.5465/amj.2016.1215

Kelley et al. (2017). *Global entrepreneurship monitor*. Women's Entrepreneurship 2016/2017 Report [Online]. Retrieved August 2, 2019, from https://www.gemconsortium.org/report

Klasen, S. (1999). *Does gender inequality reduce growth and development? Evidence from Cross-Country Regressions*. Siteresources.worldbank.org [Online]. Retrieved August 2, 2019, from http://siteresources.worldbank.org/INTGENDER/Resources/wp7.pdf

Klein, K. (2013). *Women who run tech startups are catching up*. Bloomberg.com [Online]. Retrieved August 2, 2019, from https://www.bloomberg.com/news/articles/2013-02-20/women-who-run-tech-startups-are-catching-up

Knowledge at Wharton. (2019). *How green is the sharing economy?* [Online]. Retrieved August 6, 2019, from https://knowledge.wharton.upenn.edu/article/how-green-is-the-sharing-economy/

Malik, Z. (2019). *Female founders and the equity gap*. Thefintechtimes.com [Online]. Retrieved August 5, 2019, from https://thefintechtimes.com/female-founders-investment/

Malmstrom, M., Johansson, J., & Wincent, J. (2017). We recorded VCs' conversations and analyzed how differently they talk about female entrepreneurs. *Harvard Business Review* [Online]. Retrieved July 30, 2019, from https://hbr.org/2017/05/we-recorded-vcs-conversations-and-analyzed-how-differently-they-talk-about-female-entrepreneurs

Marcus, B. (2018). *How successful women network for their career and business*. Forbes.com [Online]. Retrieved August 5, 2019, from https://www.forbes.com/sites/bonniemarcus/2018/04/10/how-successful-women-network-for-their-career-and-business/#377de62c4782

McGee, S., & Moore, H. (2019). Women's rights and their money: A timeline from Cleopatra to Lilly Ledbetter. *The Guardian* [Online]. Retrieved July 29, 2019, from https://www.theguardian.com/money/us-money-blog/2014/aug/11/women-rights-money-timeline-history

Murphy, H. (2019). Gender bias contributes to blocking female founders out of investment & venture capital. We need to fix this. *Crowdfund Insider* [Online]. Retrieved July 30, 2019, from https://www.crowdfundinsider.com/2019/02/144703-gender-bias-contributes-to-blocking-female-founders-out-of-investment-venture-capital-we-need-to-fix-this/

Oecd.org. (2004). *Women's entrepreneurship: Issues and policies*. [Online]. Retrieved August 1, 2019, from http://www.oecd.org/cfe/smes/31919215.pdf

Parikh, S. (2017). Women entrepreneurs hardly have role models and mentors. *Entrepreneur* [Online]. Retrieved August 1, 2019, from https://www.entrepreneur.com/article/290264

Powell, N. (2013). For global cooperation on climate change. *The Hindu* [Online]. Retrieved August 6, 2019, from https://www.thehindu.com/opinion/op-ed/for-global-cooperation-on-climate-change/article5386955.ec

Price, S. (2017). *As entrepreneurship thrives, women are starting more innovative businesses than men*. Forbes.com [Online]. Retrieved August 2, 2019, from https://www.forbes.com/sites/susanprice/2017/11/15/as-entrepreneurship-thrives-women-are-starting-more-innovative-businesses-than-men/#13a6246a3da5

Rao Gluckman, P. (2018). *When women are called 'aggressive' at work.* Forbes.com [Online]. Retrieved July 30, 2019, from https://www.forbes.com/sites/nextavenue/2018/08/28/when-women-are-called-aggressive-at-work/#762913937bc8

Sherry, J. (2015). *A data-driven look at diversity in venture capital and startups.* CB Insights Research [Online]. Retrieved August 3, 2019, from https://www.cbinsights.com/research/team-blog/venture-capital-diversity-data/

Solovic, S. (2016). *Untapped women's markets hold huge potential for startups, small biz and VC. Women, are you ready to compete?* Linkedin.com [Online].Retrieved August 6, 2019, from https://www.linkedin.com/pulse/untapped-womens-markets-hold-huge-potential-startups-small-solovic/

Strachan Matranga, H., Bhattacharyya, B., & Baird, R. (2017). *BREAKING THE PATTERN: Getting digital financial services entrepreneurs to scale in India and East Africa.* Vilcap.com [Online]. Retrieved August 3, 2019, from http://vilcap.com/wp-content/uploads/2017/06/VC_Breaking_the_Pattern.pdf

TechCrunch. (2018). *Female founders have brought in just 2.2% of US VC this year (yes, again).* TechCrunch [Online]. Retrieved August 1, 2019, from https://techcrunch.com/2018/11/04/female-founders-have-brought-in-just-2-2-of-us-vc-this-year-yes-again/

TEDx. (2011). *Women entrepreneurs, example not exception.* [Video]. Retrieved August 1, 2019, from https://www.ted.com/talks/gayle_tzemach_lemmon_women_entrepreneurs_example_not_exception?language=en

The Economist. (2019). The power of money. Investment by women, and in them, is growing. [Online]. Retrieved August 1, 2019, from https://www.economist.com/finance-and-economics/2018/03/08/investment-by-women-and-in-them-is-growing

Tyson, L., & Parker, C. (2019). *An economist explains why women are paid less.* World Economic Forum [Online]. Retrieved July 29, 2019, from https://www.weforum.org/agenda/2019/03/an-economist-explains-why-women-get-paid-less/

Western, D. (n.d.). *The Top 15 Most Famous Female Entrepreneurs.* Wealthy Gorilla [Online]. Retrieved August 1, 2019, from https://wealthygorilla.com/15-most-famous-female-entrepreneurs/

Woetzel, J., et al (2015). *How advancing women's equality can add $12 trillion to global growth.* McKinsey & Company [Online]. Retrieved August 3, 2019, from https://www.mckinsey.com/featured-insights/employment-and-growth/how-advancing-womens-equality-can-add-12-trillion-to-global-growth

Zarya, V. (2018). *Female founders got 2% of venture capital dollars in 2017. Fortune* [Online]. Retrieved August 4, 2019, from https://fortune.com/2018/01/31/female-founders-venture-capital-2017/

Zarya, V. (2019). The percentage of women billionaires compared to men is shrinking. *Fortune* [Online]. Retrieved July 30, 2019, from https://fortune.com/2016/08/08/female-billionaires-entrepreneurs/

Ulrike Glatz is the Director of Glatz Impact Ventures since 2017, and focuses on supporting impact investment projects and programs, impact entrepreneurs and impact investors to invest their time and capital effectively, and aligned with their purpose.

Ulrike is also the Founder of Global Impact Alliance (GIA)—an Alliance of conscious citizens and purpose driven organizations that utilize their minds, science, capital and technology in a focused manner to serve people and planet. GIA advocates the redesign of our approach and systems to fit twenty-first century's challenges, with the vision for humanity to shift from our current Age of Information & Consumerism into an Age of Wisdom.

With her background in management consulting and entrepreneurship, she regularly speaks at international conferences and teaches business ethics & CSR at the ESCP Business School in Berlin.

Siddhartha Sharma founded CredFIC, an investment technology company, in 2017 and is the Chief Financial & Risk Officer (CFRO) since 2019. He is a Global Shaper (World Economic Forum) and has previously worked with Techstars, Headstart Network Foundation and MiSK Foundation's Entrepreneurship World Cup. He is also an investment consultant for Phi Capital in India, leading new initiatives and its sustainability portfolio in the region.

The Era of New Leadership

Katharina Miller

Abstract This chapter pretends to inspire the reader to consciously balance and honour the feminine and masculine energies as described by Mariana Bozesan (*The making of a consciousness leader in business: An integral approach.* SageEra, 2010) and to reach number 5 of the Sustainable Development Goals which aims the achievement of gender equality and empowerment of all women and girls, also in business. Because values traditionally associated with women create more effective leaders and organizational strategies in today's society. Traits associated with women—flexibility, empathy, and honesty—underpin career mobility and personal fulfilment. Finally, feminine traits help human beings adapt seamlessly and effectively to today's changes. A few stories will support these assumptions. According to the CEO of SUPRACAFÉ: "From our experience, it is clear that resources managed by women have a greater and more positive impact on families, education, child nutrition and health. Also, the empowerment of women makes them less vulnerable to gender-based violence."

Keywords Social enterprise · Sustainable development · Theory of change · Theories of change

1 Introduction

A fish rots from the head down. The meaning of this English proverb is: When an organization or state fails, it is the leadership that is the root cause. The same happens in the corporate world and in business in general. That's why good leadership in business is very important. "Good" is used as the opposite to bad leadership which leads to bad decisions in business. This chapter pretends to inspire the reader to consciously balance and honour the feminine and masculine energies as described

K. Miller (✉)
3C Compliance, Madrid, Spain
e-mail: miller@3ccompliance.com

K. Wendt (ed.), *Theories of Change*, Sustainable Finance,
https://doi.org/10.1007/978-3-030-52275-9_24

by Mariana Bozesan (2010, p. 25) and to reach number 5 of the Sustainable Development Goals which aims the achievement of gender equality and empowerment of all women and girls, also in business.

"If Lehman Brothers had been a bit more Lehman Sisters … we would not have had the degree of tragedy that we had as a result of what happened" (Youtube 2012). Many people use Christine Lagarde's (Managing Director of the International Monetary Fund since 5 July 2011) hypothesis when defending gender equality in leadership in business.

2 The Evidence Is In: So Why Is So Little Being Done?

No Gender-Balance in Leadership There is still no gender-balance in economic decision-making and this is an international phenomenon. The European Union Institute for Gender Equality (EIGE) measures (EIGE 2017) the proportion of women and men on corporate boards of the largest nationally registered companies listed on stock exchanges within the 287 Member States of the European Union. For 2015 they published that only 21.7% women are members of boards in largest quoted companies, supervisory board or board of directors compared with 78.3% men.

Under-Exploited Source of Economic Growth According to the European Commission (2018), "women constitute 52% of the total European population but only 34.4% of the EU self-employed and 30% of start-up entrepreneurs". This European institution is insisting that "female creativity and entrepreneurial potential are an under-exploited source of economic growth and jobs that should be further developed." Sally Krawcheck (2017, p. 23) summed it up perfectly: Women make 80% of consumer purchases, control $5 trillion of investable assets (at least in US) and, given their longer lives, women stand to inherit some $29 trillion in the coming decades. McKinsey (2015) estimates that fully engaging women worldwide in the economy can add $12 trillion in economic growth.

TECH and STEM Without Women In times of fast future (Talwar et al. 2017) and the dark side of Big Data (Cathy O'Neil 2016), good leadership in business is very important, because the needs of many people could easily be forgotten. For example, black people cannot use facial recognition because most applications don't recognise black faces (Buolamwini and Gebru 2018, p. 1). Or let's think of women that own a car which opens by voice recognition. Then these women might have a problem because carmakers "acknowledge that women have a tougher time using speech-recognition technology than men" because the systems have a hard time deciphering what was actually said (McMillan 2011). Finally, according to research released in January 2018, women living in US are more at risk of losing their jobs thanks to tech (WEF 2018; Browne 2018). Women whose jobs are at risk of being lost have fewer opportunities to transition to more high-skilled occupations, the report highlighted. Even with reskilling—which WEF defines as "giving workers the skills and capabilities needed for the future workplace"—women still have fewer options than men to find alternative careers. According to the OECD (2017a), there is still a huge gender parity across disciplines, because only 50% of women entering tertiary-level studies in the OECD countries study natural sciences, maths and stats, only 23% study engineering and only 19% study ICT. This is a problem which could produce even more inequalities worldwide.

Unconscious Bias As mentioned at the beginning of this chapter, number 5 of the Sustainable Development Goals aims to achieve gender equality and empower all women and girls, also in business. Already in 2011, Peninah Thomson and Lloyd (2011, pp. 156–161) asked in her book "Women & The New Business Leadership": "The evidence is in—So why is so little being done?". It seems that people's stereotyped thinking and their own biases are hindering humanity from fulfilling to achieve gender equality and empower all women and girls. A confirmation of this assumption could be that a "good manager" is still described and perceived being androgynous or masculine (Powell and Butterfield 1979). Or saying it with Iris Bohnet (2016) "unconscious bias holds us back, and de-biasing people's minds has proven to be difficult and expensive".

3 The Athena Doctrine

Maybe people's minds don't have to be de-biased. It could be that the feminine traits in business are already socially more accepted than during the last decades. Gerzema and D'Antonio (2013) tried to defend this idea with "The Athena Doctrine". In the following, the basic ideas of the "The Athena Doctrine" shall be described. Finally, two business stories from around the world shall support the not scientifically proved hypothesis which is based on "rigorous data" (Gerzema and D'Antonio): feminine traits are ascending—even in business.

Survey with 64,000 People Since 1993, Gerzema and D'Antonio have been surveying 13 nations representing 65% of global GDP. In total they surveyed 64,000 people. Interestingly, 66% of the interviewed persons agreed with the assumption that the world in general would be a better place if men thought more like women.

Silenced Women During thousands of years, humanity has been influenced by male thinking which even managed to silence women. One famous example, highlighted by Mary Beard (2017, p. 4), can be found in Homer's Odyssey when young Telemachus tells his mother Penelope: "Mother, go back up into your quarters, and take up your own work, the loom and the distaff ... speech will be the business of men, all men, and of me most of all; for mine is the power in this household". It's time to give women back their voices and to listen to them.

Gerzema and D'Antonio (2013, p. 22) called their book "The Athena Doctrine" because according to the authors, the qualities most favoured in their study resembled that character of this Greek goddess, which was honoured for her intelligence, skills, civilizing influence and fairness, responding with clever strategy and wise tactics.

Beard (2017, p. 70) explains, that Athena is one of those difficult hybrids, that, in the Greek sense, is not a woman at all. She dresses like a warrior, when fighting was exclusively male work, she is a virgin, when motherhood was the highlight of a woman's life and Athena was born from the head of her father Zeus. Therefore, Athena offered a glimpse of an ideal male world in which women could not only be kept in their place but dispensed with entirely. As a conclusion it might not have been a good choice for a book that praises the feminine traits to be called "The Athena Doctrine".

Dissatisfaction with the Conduct of Men Another very general question asked by Gerzema and D'Antonio was whether there was dissatisfaction with the conduct of men ("I am dissatisfied with the conduct of men in my country"). Indeed, a majority of the persons surveyed by Gerzema and D'Antonio agreed when asked if they are dissatisfied with the conduct of men in their country. On global average 57% of surveyed adults, 54% of men and 59% of millennials are very critical of male behaviour. Interestingly, there is a double-digit generation gap between millennials and men in Germany, South Korea and India, and in these three countries millennials are much more critical with male conduct than the men themselves.

Male Traits In the survey undertaken by Gerzema and D'Antonio, the following attributes were strongly related to masculine leadership: aggressive, proud, analytical, independent, decisive, resilient. Apparently, they took these items from previous empirical studies on behavioural psychology and gender-related research, however they don't give any more information about their source. It shall be mentioned here, that it seems to be quite popular to measure gender differences and one widely used classification measurement is the Bem sex role inventory (BSRII), which at the same time is also a widely criticized method (Hoffman and Borders 2001). As stated by Hoffmann and Borders, the main criticism of the BSRI is focused on its usage without sufficient attention to its theoretical framework and without clear and deliberate thought to the research questions being studied. On the other hand, even with strong evidence little has been done. And "The Athena Doctrine" doesn't pretend to be a scientific book.

Female Traits Gerzema and D'Antonio used the following characteristics related to feminine leadership and these are plans for future, reasonable, collaborative loyal, expressive, flexible, patient, intuitive, passionate, empathetic, selfless.

In conformity with Gerzema and D'Antonio, values traditionally associated with women create more effective leaders and organizational strategies in today's society. Traits associated with women—flexibility, empathy, and honesty—underpin career mobility and personal fulfilment. They also think that these feminine traits help human beings adapt seamlessly and effectively to today's changes. This last assumption could be debated by the fact that not many women are represented in TECH or in STEM and that apparently, they seem to be the losers of the age of algorithm, as already discussed above.

Humble Leaders Only recently the early retirement of ProSiebenSat.1's CEO, one of Germany's mass media, has been announced. In this context German media Manager Magazin (2018) predicted a change from the "narcissistic go-getter" to the adaptable and flexible leader and the German zeitgeist seems to have chosen Kasper Rørsted, current CEO of Adidas-Group, as role model. Until 2016, Rørsted seemed to be the perfect leader for the German chemical and consumer goods company Henkel, and now he switched to the industry of apparel and accessories. According to the Business Insider (Turula 2017) Rørsted had to learn from his career's worst setback: Getting fired from Hewlett-Packard back in 2004. "I was 42 years old and I was responsible for 40,000 employees. I had a [very successful] career up until that point. It was a giant failure." It was his "bad attitude" that got him fired. "All my numbers were great, and therefore I thought I could act however I wanted to. But I couldn't." From that failure, he eventually gained his career's most important lesson: To have a humbler approach. "It undoubtedly made me a better leader". According to "The Athena Doctrine", "being humble" is a feminine trait.

There are many business stories worldwide that seem to affirm "The Athena Doctrine" and in the following two of them shall be described.

3.1 SUPRACAFÉ: Coffee for Peace and Development

SUPRACAFÉ is a Spanish company dedicated to the coffee production industry and it was founded in 1990 by Ricardo Oteros, Vicente Arregui y Raúl Gil.

In 1999, during a visit to the Coffee Growers Cooperative of the Department of Cauca, Colombia, the CEO of SUPRACAFÉ, Ricardo Oteros, met with a group of women. They told him that they needed support in order to get their families forward; their husbands had died or were displaced because of the war and the women had to maintain their families. They wanted to grow coffee to earn the necessary income for their families.

Oteros explained during the OECD Forum 2017, Bridging Divides (OECD 2017b):

> This is how we began our joint work with them. The first thing they needed was to get financing to buy plants and fertilisers. Coffee needs 3 years to grow before the first crop is harvested. The first major problem they faced at that time, and one they are still facing today, was the lack of funding to establish their small production unit. Credit is either almost impossible to obtain or, if it is given, has interest rates so high that they practically negate any returns. Therefore, the first thing we did was to get the plants and fertilisers to establish their crops and give them technical support through the co-operative.

When they started producing coffee months later, the problem they faced was that they did not have adequate infrastructure to process it, such as coffee pulping machines, fermenters or drying yards. This affected the quality of their coffee. We therefore focused on getting aid to improve profits by financing parabolic dryers and helping improve processes, through technical assistance as well as raising awareness of the importance of quality and its impact on income. We also organised a small competition among the farmers to help them discern the defects of their products and what caused them, with SUPRACAFÉ always guaranteeing the purchase of their coffee at a fair price.

One of our main objectives was to strengthen this group, consolidating it and empowering these women. As the group became stronger, progress was achieved. First, they registered as both a Certified Fairtrade and Certified Organic Coffee producer. While the group initially needed a lot of external support for its administration and representation, it gradually consolidated and became more autonomous. Since then, they have managed to include two of their members on the Board of Directors of the Cauca Coffee Growers Cooperative. They have been able to manage their own administration, set up their small extension and technical assistance service and a small revolving fund.

The group is concerned with ensuring the quality of its coffee and the fulfilment of its commercial commitments. It has managed to sell 100% of its produce to differentiated markets. Today, most of the Fair-Trade coffee that is marketed by our company is produced by the Association of Women Coffee Farmers of Cauca (AMUCC), a high-quality coffee that we are very proud of.

These 18 years of experience with AMUCC have been both highly rewarding and a steep learning curve. First of all, we must bear in mind that these processes are medium- and long-term and, to ensure success, they need constant support. To get where we are today, we need to take a holistic approach, from an initial situation with high levels of poverty and violence, and with little training and access to basic services such as health. I sincerely believe that one of the main achievements of SUPRACAFÉ has been to accompany and support the group continuously since 1999.

From our experience, it is clear that resources managed by women have a greater and more positive impact on families, education, child nutrition and health. Also, the empowerment of women makes them less vulnerable to gender-based violence.

The challenges they face are immense and include: lack of funding, lack of technical assistance, the need to work on the farm and to take care of the family at the same time and lack of participation in institutions and trade organisations where decisions that affect them are made.

Looking at the results obtained during all these years, including improvements in productivity and quality, I feel that this wave of change and progress is unstoppable.

One of the latest achievements of this group has been integrating into the first technological park of TECNICAFE coffee, a laboratory for peace and innovation. I am sure that their contribution will be decisive in placing the woman at the centre of local development. Without innovation there is no progress and no future for new generations. We will continue to strongly support their empowerment. At SUPRACAFÉ we firmly believe that our alliance with the AMUCC group strengthens us and brings many advantages, both in terms of commercial expansion and contribution to sustainability in the broadest sense.

In private interview, Oteros admitted that it was not easy to convince his company's management and other stakeholders of the engagement with AMUCC, however, his own success story proves him right. He proved that perching on women and to empower them economically leads to better results for all stakeholders.

3.2 *Foundation Ana Bella*

Ana Bella was a victim of domestic violence to which her husband subjected her for 11 years. She is the mother of four children born of her marriage. Now, she is a social entrepreneur who helps other women get out of the violent relationships (Compromiso Empresarial 2017).

The story of Bella begins when she runs away secretly with her four small children, after 11 years of suffering.

When she married her now ex-husband she signed the first of many agreements, among which were, for example, not being able to walk more than three meters away from him; commit to deliver all receipts for purchases, no matter how small the spent amount was; not going to the university, in spite of having exams, or, the last one, to stay by his side although he didn't stop beating her. 'Agreements' that Bella ended up signing forced by the threats and beatings, the last one, until almost losing consciousness—and life—suffocated at the hands of her husband while listening: "No, little one, no, you will never separate yourself from me because ours is love or death."

She asked for help and lived in a shelter, however after many months, when she left the shelter she found herself in the street, without work, with four children and a paper that would give her access to financial support for being a victim of gender-based violence: the amount she would receive were 320 Euros a month. She looked for housing and employment and she started to appear in the Spanish media. It was the first time in Spain that a woman was in the news for surviving and recovering from gender-based violence and not as a new dead victim to add to the statistics. Bella changed this perspective.

Soon she began to receive support and also requests for help from other women. The request that most marked her was by the cousin of her ex-husband's new girlfriend. That was the moment when she realized that she had survived, and that there were many other women who continued to be mistreated.

One out of every three women have experienced either physical and/or sexual intimate partner violence or sexual violence by a non-partner at some point in their lives. However, some national studies show that up to 70% of women have experienced physical and/or sexual violence from an intimate partner in their lifetime (UN Women 2017). In Spain, they are one in ten women victims of domestic violence (Instituto de la Mujer 2006).

Ana Bella has been trying since 2002 to reduce this percentage. In 2006, she created the foundation that bears her name, and her main goal was to change the perspective of abuse with positive testimonies. She also wanted to send the following message to the world: we can get out of gender-based violence. In her opinion, posters of dead women or women with bruises are not an invitation for denouncing the perpetrators.

The Ana Bella Foundation has created a network of surviving women where they help each other by providing a home, a job, training, and empowerment. According to Bella, it is a natural network of trust. In its beginnings, the Foundation created the company Servicios Integrales Solidarios, which offered cleaning, catering or sale of craft products. In 2011, Bella was chosen by Momentum Project (now Momentum BBVA) among the ten most promising social enterprises of the year and by the International Ashoka Foundation as social entrepreneur in Spain.

Servicios Integrales Solidarios gave Bella a lot of visibility and the one that provided the most psychological benefits to the employees, because their work was valued and the clients praised them. They felt valued.

That is why, years later, she created the Ana Bella School for the Empowerment of Women. The school offers training, coaching and a job opportunity as brand ambassadors. The first company to lend their support was Danone, placing women survivors of gender-based violence in front of their yogurt shops to promote their products. The results were very positive: employee turnover decreased from 63 to 2% in 2013, absenteeism decreased from 40 to 2% and they obtained 97% positive feedback from the sales force. As Bella says, they know what it is like to have the "worst boss in the world", referring to their violent ex-partners.

Since then and until 2016 about a thousand women have achieved a job opportunity thanks to the different companies that have joined Danone: Bonduelle, Fontvella, Amichi, Clece, Panaria, Disney, Alvalle or Campofrío. Each year the Foundation helps more than 1400 survivors of abuse (more than 20,000 women during these 15 years) to break their silence and start over again.

4 Conclusion

It might be a question of time until more women and girls will achieve gender equality and economic empowerment. Until then, feminine traits will—little by little—be more accepted within business and bring out the best in female and male leaders.

References

Beard, M. (2017). *Women & power: A manifesto* (1st ed.). London: Profile Books.

Bohnet, I. (2016). *What works: Gender equality by design* (1st ed.). Cambridge, MA: The Belknap Press of Harvard University Press.

Bozesan, M. (2010). *The making of a consciousness leader in business: An integral approach* (1st ed.). Redwood City: SageEra.

Browne, R. (2018). *Women are more at risk of losing their jobs thanks to tech, WEF says*. Retrieved February 25, 2018, from https://www.cnbc.com/2018/01/22/women-more-at-risk-of-losing-jobs-thanks-to-tech-automation-wef.html
Buolamwini, J., & Gebru, T. (2018). Gender shades: Intersectional accuracy disparities in commercial gender classification. *Proceedings of Machine Learning Research, 81*, 1–15.
Compromiso Empresarial. (2017). *Ana Bella, superviviente de violencia de género, personaje social del año 2017*. Retrieved February 25, 2018, from https://www.compromisoempresarial.com/tercersector/fundaciones/2017/12/ana-bella-superviviente-de-violencia-de-genero-personaje-social-del-ano-2017/
EIGE. (2017). *Gender equality index*. Retrieved February 25, 2018, from http://eige.europa.eu/gender-equality-index/2015/domain/power
European Commission. (2018). *Female entrepreneurs*. Retrieved February 25, 2018, from https://ec.europa.eu/growth/smes/promoting-entrepreneurship/we-work-for/women_en
Gerzema, J., & D'Antonio, M. (2013). *The Athena doctrine: How women (and the men who think like them) will rule the future* (1st ed.). San Francisco: Jossey-Bass.
Hoffman, R. M., & Borders, L. D. (2001). Twenty-five years after the Bem sex-role inventory: A reassessment and new issues regarding classification variability. *Measurement and Evaluation in Counseling and Development, 34*, 39–55.
Instituto de la Mujer. (2006). *Mujeres en Cifras – Violencia – Macroencuestas "Violencia contra las Mujeres"*. Retrieved February 25, 2018, from http://www.inmujer.gob.es/MujerCifras/Violencia/Macroencuestas.htm
Krawcheck, S. (2017). *Own it* (1st ed.). New York: Penguin Random House.
Manager Magazin. (2018). *NEUES DEUTSCHLAND ELITE: Dreht sich in der Wirtschaft tatsächlich alles um Geld, Macht und Eitelkeit? Nein, der narzisstische Ellbogentyp stirbt aus. Wer in disruptiven Zeiten nach oben will, sollte selbst anpacken können – und zuhören*. Retrieved February 25, 2018, from https://heft.manager-magazin.de/MM/2018/3/155801164/index.html
McKinsey. (2015). *How advancing women's equality can add $12 trillion to global growth*. Retrieved February 25, 2018, from https://www.mckinsey.com/global-themes/employment-and-growth/how-advancing-womens-equality-can-add-12-trillion-to-global-growth
McMillan, G. (2011). *It's not you, it's it: Voice recognition doesn't recognize women*. Retrieved February 25, 2018, from http://techland.time.com/2011/06/01/its-not-you-its-it-voice-recognition-doesnt-recognize-women/
O'Neil, C. (2016). *Weapons of math destruction: How big data increases equality and threatens democracy* (1st ed.). New York: Crown Publishers.
OECD. (2017a). *Education at a glance 2017: OECD indicators, tab. C3.1*. Retrieved February 25, 2018, from http://www.oecd.org/education/education-at-a-glance-19991487.htm
OECD. (2017b). *Empowering women in indigenous communities: SUPRACAFÉ and AMUCC*. Retrieved February 25, 2018, from https://www.oecd-forum.org/users/71432-ricardo-oteros-sanchez-pozuelo/posts/22458-empowering-women-in-indigenous-communities-supracafe-and-amucc
Powell, G., & Butterfield, D. (1979). The "good manager": Masculine or androgynous? *Academy of Management Journal, 22*, 395–403.
Talwar, R., Wells, S., Whittington, A., Koury, A., & Romero, M. (2017). *Beyond genuine stupidity: Ensuring AI serves humanity* (1st ed.). Fast Future Publishing.
Thomson, P., & Lloyd, T. (2011). *Women & the new business leadership* (1st ed.). Great Britain: Palgrave Macmillan.
Turula, T. (2017). *Adidas CEO says his worst career setback was getting fired from HP for having a bad attitude*. Retrieved February 25, 2018, from http://www.businessinsider.com/adidas-ceo-kasper-rorsted-on-his-worst-career-setback-2017-10
UN Women. (2017). *Facts and figures: Ending violence against women*. Retrieved February 25, 2018, from http://www.unwomen.org/en/what-we-do/ending-violence-against-women/facts-and-figures#notes

WEF. (2018). *A survival guide for the Fourth Industrial Revolution*. Retrieved from https://www.weforum.org/agenda/2018/01/the-fourth-industrial-revolution-a-survival-guide/
Youtube. (2012). *Christine Lagarde on women and crisis in women in the world 2012 forum*. Retrieved February 25, 2018, from https://www.youtube.com/watch?v=XtI_BpqoZ30

Katharina Miller I am a committed Non-Executive member of various corporate boards with extensive legal, operational and risk management experience. Qualified lawyer in Germany and Spain with over 15 years of international practice across Western Europe, business owner, Adjunct Professor at the IE Law School, first ambassador of the Global Leadership Academy GIZ for Europe & MENA, President of European Women Lawyers Association (EWLA) and EU delegate for G20 Women20 Engagement Group. German (native), Spanish (fluent), English (fluent), French.

Social Enterprises: Investment in a Sustainable Social Development with Added Value

Markus Zeilinger

Abstract When setting up the first Social Entrepreneurship Venture Capital Funds in Austria, the institutional investor fair-finance had to find a suitable vehicle for this new form of investment in social enterprises. A valid exit strategy via a social bond ensures the fund is suitable for long-term investors. The declared aim of this initiative, launched jointly with the SME & industry stakeholder group "Senat der Wirtschaft", is to increase the number of social entrepreneurs and thus also the number of social business cases in Austria and Germany. Investors placing social impact above profit maximisation are to be given the opportunity to invest meaningfully in companies offering a solution for overcoming social challenges—and in return receive a socially sustainable yield.

Keywords Theory of change · Theories of change

1 Introduction

Sustainable investment also means supporting companies and projects helping to create a society prepared for future challenges. With the Social Entrepreneurship Venture Capital Funds fair-finance wants to play a part in the rethinking process away from a pure return focus towards measurable social and environmental impact. Therefore it is important for us to identify companies generating real added value. We are mainly focusing on business ideas offering solutions for social challenges such as ageing demographics, inequality of income, scarcity of resources, rising sea levels, loss of biodiversity or changes to work environments. For all of these companies we use the term "social business". We use the term 'social' to refer to any aspects affecting society whether they are social or environmental in nature.

M. Zeilinger (✉)
fair-finance, Vienna, Austria
e-mail: markus.zeilinger@fair-finance.at

K. Wendt (ed.), *Theories of Change*, Sustainable Finance,
https://doi.org/10.1007/978-3-030-52275-9_25

Apart from all those meaningful and responsible criteria a Vorsorgekasse managing assets for its members as a fiduciary cannot disregard the aspect of capital market returns. But the impact of our investments on society is not a coincidental or simply a welcome result of our decisions. It is much more a goal in its own rights, i.e. the fourth dimension turning the "magic triangle" of investing into a pyramid made out of four interdependent factors. Our investments in the "social business" sector are in no way donations. They are an investment both in the future of our society but also in the preservation and increase of the value of our members' assets. Therefore we carefully structured the first Social Entrepreneurship Fund in Austria to create an investment case that is a win-win-win situation, as will be shown later.

The first chapter of this article will provide definitions to terms like social business, social impact, Vorsorgekasse etc. In line with the aim of the European Commission's action plan for sustainable finance, it is important for us to be transparent about our investment strategy, its evaluation and the terminology used.

In Chapter two the legal framework for social businesses (also known as social enterprises) will be charted. At the time of writing Austria does not have a special legal structure for these businesses. However, we will outline the debates on the subject. Further, we will give a brief overview on some legal structures for social businesses in other countries.

The third chapter is dedicated to the structure of our investment solution. It will try to answer the following questions: Which form of investment did we choose? What are our return expectations? Were we able to create a sustainable and socially compatible exit strategy? Which criteria do possible investment cases have to meet and what proof do they have to present on their business results?

Afterwards three examples for possible investments will be presented in chapter four. What do companies we are supporting actually look like?

The final chapter is both a conclusion as well as an outlook. It is - particularly in Austria—still very early days for investments in social businesses. With our fund solution we hope to inspire other institutional investors to copy the idea or become co-investors in the fair-finance fund.

2 Terminology

First, it is important to note that for fair-finance *social impact* is the impact an investment has on society. Particularly in the field of sustainable investments and ESG concepts environmental issues are very often prioritised over social impact. Similarly, the current EU action plan for sustainable finance seems to focus almost solely on environmental aspects. As fair-finance we want to differentiate ourselves from other sustainable investors in this field and explicitly help to generate social added value. Until very recently, we mainly did this via a micro finance fund and various other criteria such as considering the tenant structure in evaluating sustainable properties. Of course we also see climate change as a social issue as the impact on food production, availability of water and eventually on migration are clearly visible and will intensify over the next years.

When it comes to social impact many investors are struggling with its measurability. But for our social business investments it made sense to postpone these evaluations onto a later point in time. A lot of good initiatives looking for investors cannot report any meaningful figures in their early stages or the collected data would paint a distorted picture. Additionally, the focus of social entrepreneurs should not be on academic exercises but in taking action. In assessing the social impact of a business model we therefore do not rely on key figures but on an expert panel. A more detailed explanation of this solution to investment hurdles will be provided in the chapter on our investment case and fund concept.

This solution also allows us to skip having to define *social business* for our fund. The often-applied definition via the use of a company's profits did not make much sense for us. In this article the terms social enterprise and social entrepreneurship will be more or less used as synonyms for social business.

Especially in Austria the idea and concept of social businesses still has to take root. Not only legally (as pointed out in the next chapter) but also in the heads of politicians as well as within society. So far social initiatives were mostly non-profit organisations applying for subsidies or relying on patrons. Caring for people's social needs was so far almost exclusively either part of the state's obligation towards its citizens, of a company towards its employees or the region in which a company is headquartered.

For the sake of transparency the business model of an Austrian *Vorsorgekasse* has to be explained in this chapter as well. Since 2003, every company has to accrue a severance pay for each employee via regular contributions (1.53% of remuneration) to one of the eight existing providers of a Vorsorgekasse. Self-employed individuals make similar contributions. These fiduciary capital management companies are run by providers from the financial industry, very often the same companies that are also offering pension funds ("Pensionskassen"). In contrast to pension funds, Vorsorgekassen are paying out the accrued capital plus returns as a lump-sum upon retirement at the latest.

The investment regulations for Vorsorgekassen are mainly characterised by the capital guarantee providers have to give on the contributions made over time. This applies not only to the retirement date but to any point in time as the money can be withdrawn at the latest 3 years after an employment ended. Additionally, fair-finance is the only provider to guarantee a minimum interest on the accrued assets. These guarantees as well as the unpredictable and sometimes very short investment horizon are massively restricting the scope for long-term return targets.

Fair-finance was founded specifically to build and expand fair, socially responsible and sustainable financial services in Austria. Advantages for customers are linked to a public welfare ("Gemeinwohl") service. In 2010, we started with the fair-finance Vorsorgekasse, then added a real estate company, an asset management company solely issuing sustainable investment funds and most recently we set up a sustainable insurance broker. Fair-finance is supported by two strategic shareholders each holding 10% in the listed company: the GLS Bank awarded the German sustainability award and the Concordia Group specialising in ecological life insurances. Additionally, fair-finance has 16 investors sharing the rest of the free float.

Within the Vorsorgekassen industry, where some providers have committed to sustainable investments from the go, fair-finance continues to set new trends. The most recent impetus was the issuance of the first sustainable real estate fund to be certified with the Austrian "Umweltzeichen", a government-approved sustainability label.

3 Legal Framework

Investments in social businesses need the right legal framework. In Austria, a non-profit foundation cannot invest in a social enterprise without endangering its "non-profit" status. For many small businesses setting up a limited liability company ("GmbH") is a major challenge. Compared to other countries, setting up a company in Austria involves quite a lot of bureaucracy and also requires quite a lot of capital.

Additionally, it is currently difficult for investors like fair-finance to identify a socially active company as such. For our future Social Entrepreneurship Venture Capital Funds we therefore created a council of experts together with the SME- & industry stakeholder group "Senat der Wirtschaft". This industry stakeholder group is, among other things, focussing on the promotion of sustainability in the domestic economy. The expert council will screen investments for us and help to make investment decisions.

Taking a longer-term view fair-finance is also supporting a proposal by multi-stakeholder group "GEMSE" which stands for "together more social enterprise". Already in 2017, this group had demanded the creation of an "sGmbH". Similar to what has been established in other countries, the idea was to create a special legal structure or at least an uncomplicated suffix to an existing legal structure for social enterprises. Via small voluntary limitations a limited liability company could opt to identify itself as a social enterprise. In return bureaucratic as well as financial hurdles could be lowered for these and other innovative business cases in future.

"The self-identification of a social enterprise and its social impact have to be measured and processed for investors," stressed Keyvan Rastegar, founder of the law firm RPCK.[1] He is the legal expert for fair-finance in creating the Social Entrepreneurship Fund. The internationally operating attorney describes the legal framework for setting up innovative companies in Austria as "overregulated, cost-intensive and characterised by useless formalities as well as their inconsistent application". At the time of writing this article, there were several campaigns from the business sector as well as the capital market to change the situation. But neither the sGmbH nor other simplifications were on the political agenda.

[1]These and the following quotes by Mr. Rastegar are derived from an interview with fair-finance on 31 January 2019 in Vienna.

Nevertheless, we want to provide a short overview on possible advantages a simple suffix to the legal structure of a GmbH could have and on international models.

First it has to be stressed that both in the USA as well as in Italy attempts by private providers failed to get a fee-based "quality label" for social businesses hardwired into the legal framework.

From a legal point of view Rastegar supports the idea that entrepreneurs who want to get a social business label have to accept certain restrictions. This could, for example, be the limitation to only distribute up to 50% of the profits and commit to this in the company's statutes. "This would offer a simple legitimation and it would make it easier for impact investors questioning the true impact component of a company," Rastegar pointed out. These or similar elements for self-identification are available for social businesses in most countries—apart from Austria and German.

Introducing self-definition also avoids the problem a categorisation into "green", "social" and "environmentally-friendly" companies poses as these goals are constantly changing with shifting social challenges. This is also where Rastegar sees one of the major problems with the fund vehicle for social investments created by the EU, the EuSEF (European Social Entrepreneurship Fund, VO (EU) 346/2013). Compared to the venture capital vehicle EuVECA it "hardly offers any advantages", according to Rastegar. The difference rather lies in additional conditions. One of them is the obligation to invest 70% of the assets in social businesses fitting certain categories and definitions. Currently, there are only four funds in the entire EU that have chosen this vehicle as an investment model. Rastegar and fair-finance finally decided EuVECA to be the type of fund to use for the first Austrian Social Entrepreneurship Venture Capital Funds.

Coming back to the debate of altering the general legal framework it has to be said there is also criticism for the idea of creating a separate legal structure for social enterprises. The fear is that these companies might be put into a corner or even lose competitive advantages because of the self-restrictions. But for Rastegar these concerns are missing the point: "The best-case scenario would be to have a lot of different legal structures for social businesses to choose from. But de facto currently only the GmbH is available for entrepreneurs who want to generate profit (even if it is limited) by avoiding personal liability." And as Rastegar adds the GmbH "is in many ways out-dated". The lawyer describes the Austrian company law as "operating system on which modern software does not run", including social businesses.

Using a legal structure from another country in the EU is also "not practical", noted Rastegar. "Although the freedom of establishment also applies to companies in principle, practically language barriers, cultural differences and administrative hurdles mean that 'shopping' for legal structures across borders has not yet become commonplace within the EU."

4 Investment Case and Fund Structure

Together with the aforementioned "Senat der Wirtschaft" the fair-finance came up with the idea to create Austria's first Social Entrepreneurship Venture Capital Funds in autumn 2018. While fair-finance brings the investment expertise to the table, the industry lobby group has a network of experts and contacts with ideas for investments and skills to evaluate them. For the fund, the Senat will take on the initial screening of companies' investment proposals introduced via an online tool on the website dedicated to the fund www.se-fonds.at (The tool was scheduled to go live before summer 2019). Entries are open to companies from Austria as well as Germany.

The Senate will verify that the entries are complete and that they meet the minimum criteria such as the business requiring early-stage financing but also that it is beyond the start-up phase.

Afterwards, the actual selection of the companies is delegated to an external, voluntary committee panel. It consists of 17 experts from the industry sector, churches and ethical investments. They screen the entries in detail and decide whether or not there is a case for social impact investing. Of course the companies also have to meet fair-finance's general ethical, social and environmental criteria applied to all investments. Companies can also be recommended by the expert panel.

Within 14 days after the entry was uploaded, the panel decides based on a two-third majority if enough members have voted. In case of a sufficiently significant added value as well as a sustainable business model, the panel makes a recommendation to the asset manager of the fund, who will make the final investment decision after an economic and legal due diligence with the participation of Impact Hub Vienna and other experts.

Fair-finance wants to keep the range of companies considered for investments as wide as possible. There is no limitation to the definition of social impact. As noted in the introduction we define social impact as significant contribution to solving challenges and problems (social and environmental) a society is facing. To be considered for the fund, however, a business already has to be beyond the start-up phase.

4.1 *The Investment Model*

With the Social Entrepreneurship Venture Capital Funds fair-finance is aiming to provide comparatively cheap capital to companies with social commitment without necessary profit maximisation. This is, however, by no means a donation. It is a long-term allocation offering a socially sustainable return for sustainable investors.

The company has to present a proven concept as well as a stress-tested business plan with a value appreciation potential of at least 15% per year. No collateral is required. However, on demand, companies the fund is invested in have to provide information on the business performance and allow access to their books.

Per company between € 200,000 and € 500.000 in equity capital can be provided. On this there is a limited (pre-emptive) right for the entrepreneur or its employees to repurchase the equity shares.

For due diligence there is a fee payable at the first instalment which amounts to 1% of the provided equity capital, with a minimum fee set at €5000. Continuous fees of 1,5% per year will be charged for business coaching, fund management and other expenses. Compared to traditional costs of funds this model is considerably cheaper.

Getting access to the Senate's and fair-finance's network as well as that of supporting organisations is an added bonus for the social businesses.

4.2 The Participation Model

The investment is structured as a *private equity* participation. Investors can purchase limited partner shares ("Kommanditanteile") or share certificates ("Zertifikatsanteilsscheine").

As noted no collateral is required from the company and the fund also has *no direct say in the management* of the business. However, the companies the fund invests in commit to continued coaching by business experts chosen by fair-finance. If the business outlook deteriorates considerably, management competences can be limited. Companies also have to provide certified annual accounts and a social impact report for each year.

4.3 The Fund Structure

In Austria, there is as yet no private equity fund focussing on social business. For the joint venture with the Senat der Wirtschaft to create the first Social Entrepreneurship Venture Capital Funds (SEF I) fair-finance is providing €5m in seed capital. The fund is set up under the regulatory framework for Alternative Investment Funds (AIF) as GmbH & Co.KG. Once the Austrian financial market authority FMA has approved the AIF, further investors will be taken on board. It will be a closed-end fund for professional investors with a minimum investment threshold of €500,000.

First investments are scheduled for the last quarter 2020. The targeted fund volume for the SEF I (after licensing and inclusion of further investors) will be €10m. The timeframe for the initial closing can only be determined after the FMA has given its approval.

The target return for fair-finance and potential co-investors follows the socially sustainable return ("gemeinnützige Rendite") of 3.5% p.a. To start with this return is only an estimate derived from the classic three-part formula: One third of the investments has to be strong enough to carry the other two thirds should they not grow or at least not grow profitably.

The fund duration is 8 years with an option to extend by up to 2 years. Capital withdrawals (aliquot) are possible until the end of the investment period of 12 month.

The fees for co-investors are—just like the ones for companies the fund is invested in—lower that the market average. For fair-finance creating more transparency in the capital market including fee structures as well as fair calculation of these fees is an important part of the sustainable investment strategy. In the SEF I investors pay a one-off fee of 2% of the drawn assets. The continuous fund management fee amounts to 0.5% p.a. of the NAV.

For investors such as e.g. philanthropist foundations, sustainable investors, impact fund-of-funds, development banks and funds or ethical investors the fund aims to provide the possibility for risk-diversified social impact investment without using too much of their own time and know-how resources.

4.4 The Exit Strategy

One of the major challenges in structuring the fund model was the exit-strategy. On the one hand, the aim is to guarantee sustainable financing with a long-term investment horizon. On the other hand, institutional investors also need an exit point from investments. Further, a scheduled sale or "giving up" assets is always difficult as investments could again have value years later or they could even still grow in value over time.

As a sustainable solution also fitting a fair capital market thinking, fair-finance opted for a social bond as the exit strategy from SEF I at the end of the fund term of up to 10 years. First off the assets are evaluated via a bidding process and an independent value appraisal.

It is, however, important to ensure that for the social entrepreneurs this exit does not mean a change in ownership or strategy. For them, the risks associated with these changes have to be avoided. Therefor the refinancing of the payout amount by the SEF I GmbH & Co.KG is to be done via a social bond. The idea is to allow existing private equity investors to keep their investment in the company via bonds rather than private equity. Instead of getting their share value paid out they can buy social bonds for up to that amount. This way they can still profit from any future growth in the company. Fair-finance takes on the placement risk of this social bond with variable interest set to mature after up to another 10 years. This ensures a long-term and stable financing option for social entrepreneurs.

4.5 *The Donation Element*

It has to be stressed again that the investments by the SEF I are no donations. But the expected return is considerably lower than that typically aimed for by private equity funds. SEF I is set up to help fill a financing gap for aspiring social businesses. Additionally, investors not solely focused on profit maximisation and increasing returns are to be presented with investment possibilities that make sense and which are yielding socially sustainable returns.

Nevertheless, SEF I is to contain a donation element to increase its social added value. If the fund return is higher than a certain threshold, investors are free to choose which charitable organisation is to receive parts of the excess return. From 3.5% return p.a. 25% of the excess return are donated and above a 5% annual return 50%.

5 Investment Examples

The companies the SEF I is investing in are either selected from the online applications or from recommendations by the expert panel.

As detailed in the investment case chapter, companies already have to have successfully started their business model and they have to present a stress-tested business plan. Profit maximisation is not necessary and more likely a reason for exclusion. The fields in which the social added value is generated are not limited. The social impact has to be convincingly presented.

For fair-finance a strong multiplying effect is important: We are particularly looking for companies whose solutions for overcoming social challenges can be copied or expanded.

Although the fund has not made any investments at the time of writing, we can present a few examples of companies which judging by their business case could be suitable candidates for investments.

5.1 *R.U.S.Z Reparatur- und Service-Zentrum (Austria)*

Use longer instead of buying more often! Under this motto, the R.U.S.Z. repairs household appliances, consumer electronics and computers. The R.U.S.Z. is also a specialist for nostalgic devices and repairs old radios, record players and tube amplifiers. Almost all devices through which electricity flows can be repaired in the workshop. Large household appliances are only repaired on site.

Managing Director Sepp Eisenriegler: "It is our declared aim to fight against the pre-programmed expiration date of products, the so-called planned obsolescence, and to counter the industry's trend towards disposable products with serious customer service". Therefore the R.U.S.Z. now offers a repair café every Thursday afternoon. Here customers can repair appliances such as toasters, mixers and hairdryers themselves in a relaxed atmosphere.

5.2 *Capito (Austria)*

Capito turns technical jargon into easily understandable language. Company information, texts, news and advertising materials are translated into easily understandable language. And the content is so prepared that it can be used digitally at any time. "capito is Italian and means: I have understood. We want everyone to be able to say in the future: "I have understood". But we want a society in which no one is excluded. We want accessibility for all", says Walburga Fröhlich, the managing director of atempo (capito is part of the atempo group). In Austria, Germany and Switzerland, around 24 million people cannot read well. Most information from companies and authorities is difficult for these people to understand. Those who communicate in a way that is easy to understand will be understood better and faster. capito is about giving everyone access to knowledge, breaking down language barriers by adapting the language and complexity of the information to the respective existing language skills and previous knowledge of the target groups.

5.3 *Helioz (Austria)*

According to figures from WHO and UNICEF, over 660 million people have no access to safe drinking water, and every 90 s a child under the age of five dies as a result of diarrhoea, cholera or typhoid. Wadi, an invention of the Austrian start-up company Helioz, has now been confirmed by the World Health Organization WHO as a reliable technology for the treatment of drinking water. When the smiley laughs from the small display, you can drink the water in the bottle without hesitation: From the user's point of view, this is the simple concept of Wadi, the palm-sized UV meter, which is already used thousands of times in countries. It is a safe method to ensure that no harmful bacteria and protozoa (micro-organisms) remain in the water. The actual work of the Wadi method is done by the sun: Water filled in transparent plastic bottles is placed in the blazing sun until the UV radiation has disinfected the contaminated water. The UV-measuring instrument indicates when drinkability has been reached.

5.4 *Nut & Feder (Austria)*

Nut & Feder sees work as a central element of social inclusion. Escaped people face particular barriers in the labor market for legal, social and cultural reasons. As a social enterprise, Nut & Feder aims to involve people with a refugee background in a work and training process related to the woodworking trade from the very beginning. The work of Nut & Feder carries the biographies of its producers within itself and conveys the message that everyone is capable of great things. Christian Penz, Managing Director of Nut & Feder: "We are concerned with sustainable integration for refugees in the workplace. Our goal is to become an independent social business in the labor market".

6 Visions for the Future

As co-initiators of the first Social Entrepreneurship Venture Capital Funds to be issued in Austria for institutional investors, fair-finance is of course convinced of its feasibility and its chances for success. But we can also justify this conviction as the project presents a win-win-win model for various different stakeholders. Additionally, it can help on a small scale to tackle problems our society is facing. Once the ideas get copied and spread into other funds this small-scale approach becomes a network of innovative investment opportunities supporting social aid projects.

On the one hand, the idea behind the Social Entrepreneurship Ventutre Capital Funds is helping those running or building a social business: They get the opportunity to implement social impact in promising business models and do not have to focus on profit maximisation to receive equity capital from investors. This will eventually lead to there being *more social entrepreneurs*—and they are what both the economy as well as society desperately needs.

With the fund the social entrepreneurs are also given the chance to increase the impact of their business cases via expansion. This can lead to *more social business* being created.

The social impact is directly as well as indirectly relieving the national budgets and with it the tax and duties quota. This in turn *helps society* in general.

The money from investors is generating a financial as well as a social return. This way *money can generate purpose*.

Overcoming social challenges is the prerequisite for *peaceful and safe living for this as well as future generations*.

Acknowledgment A case study from fair-finance Vorsorgekasse and its Social Entrepreneurship Fund.

Markus Zeilinger, CEO and founder of the fair-finance Group, Member of the Board of Directors of the Forum Nachhaltige Geldanlagen (FNG).

Fair-finance: Based on the vision of investing the funds of the obligatory pension fund system in Austria exclusively in a "responsible and effect-oriented" way, fairfinance was founded in 2010 together with a group of private individuals, GLS Bank and Concordia Insurance. The search for sustainable and profitable investment opportunities has led to the establishment of an asset management company and a real estate company as well as several participations in the real estate and impact sector (KlimaGut Immobilien, Berlin; faire Windkraft, Vienna). In 2019, "Die Versicherei fair-insurances" was founded, a brokerage company in which fair-finance holds a majority stake. With the Social Entrepreneurship Fund, the first Austrian equity fund for social enterprises (financed and managed by fair-finance) is currently in the start-up phase. The fair-finance group employs almost 40 people and manages assets of around EUR 645 million.

Professional background: After studying commercial sciences and political science, professional experience in marketing consulting. Subsequently management of a direct marketing company. 1996 Change to the financial sector and establishment of Winterthur Pensionskasse, Vienna. Various positions at Winterthur CEE as well as Board Member for Life & Pensions at Winterthur Austria until the merger with Zurich Insurance. Management of the joint subsidiaries of Zurich and Generali in the area of company pension schemes (pension fund and consulting company) from 2002–2007. From 2008, foundation and development of fairfinance.

Part VIII
Climate Change

Domestic Heating and China's Sustainable Energy Goals

Xin Xu, Lei Xu, and Laubie Li

Abstract With proprietary datasets we examine China's domestic heating energy consumptions between 2010 and 2015. We find that, together with the upward trend in the country's total domestic heating energy consumption, electricity and natural gas fast replace coal as major sources of energy. Total domestic heating energy consumption, coal and electricity consumptions are negatively related to the households' disposable income. Steam heating capacity, an energy efficiency indicator, is negatively related to total domestic heating energy consumption. In addition, weather conditions are also key factors towards domestic heating energy consumption in China.

Keywords Domestic heating · Energy consumption · Sustainability · China

1 Introduction

Climate change has now become an outstanding issue faced by human society. Greenhouse gas emissions at dangerous levels have triggered series of environment problems. For example, Pretlove and Oreszczyn (1998) report that significant changes in temperature and solar radiation invalidates historical climate data of London. Noticeable climate changes around the world would have adverse impacts on weathers and consequently domestic energy consumptions (Watson 2001; Wang et al. 2010). The salient environmental impacts on all aspects of economy, human

X. Xu · L. Li
SKEMA Business School, Suzhou, China
e-mail: xin.xu02@xjtlu.edu.cn; Laubiechisumli@gmail.com

L. Xu (✉)
UniSA Business, University of South Australia, Adelaide, SA, Australia
e-mail: lei.xu@unisa.edu.au

K. Wendt (ed.), *Theories of Change*, Sustainable Finance,
https://doi.org/10.1007/978-3-030-52275-9_26

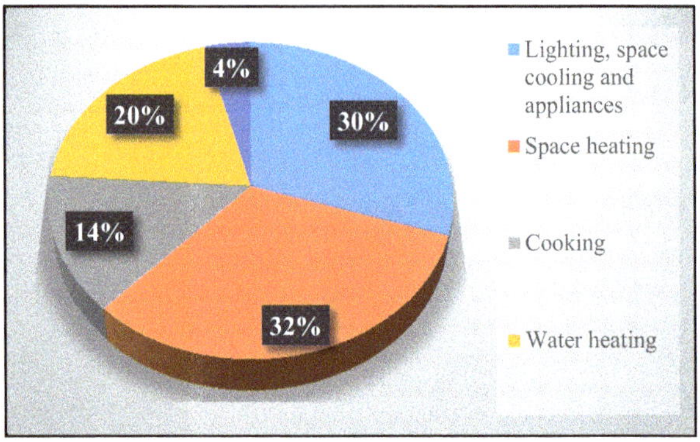

Fig. 1 Domestic energy consumption in China. Source: IEA (2015)

society, and ecosystems alerts that every country aim sustainability in the long run (UN 1992, 2002, 2015).[1]

China, the largest emerging economy, has developed unprecedented sustainability targets in the promotion of clean energy and energy efficiency as part of its environmental efforts. Following the Rio Earth Summit (UN 1992), China introduced China A21[2] and accordingly dedicates significant efforts in achieving its sustainability targets (Tung 2009). The State Council's 2007 Action Plan for Sustainable Development further clarifies China's energy policies before 2020. For example, the National Development and Reform Commission (NDRC) developed Medium and Long-term Development Plan for Renewable Energy in China.[3] The top-down design to achieve sustainability is systematically carried out in the country. Domestic heating contributes to more than a quarter of global energy consumption (Grubb et al. 2014). Given China's population size and energy consumption structure, domestic heating becomes an important research topic (Zhang et al. 2011). Figure 1 describes the components of domestic energy consumption in the most populated country where domestic heating is the lion's share.

This study examines the key factors affecting domestic heating energy consumption through the analysis of proprietary datasets. To our best knowledge, such studies are scarce. Existing survey-based literature mostly focuses on energy saving technology and construction discussions. In addition, through regional and provincial analysis, we could identify patterns in the changes of domestic heating energy

[1]The Paris Climate Change Conference is the 21st session of the Conference of the Parties (COP) and the 11th session of the Conference of the Parties serving as the meeting of the Parties to the Kyoto Protocol (CMP). (UNFCCC website http://unfccc.int/meetings/paris_nov_2015/meeting/8926.php accessed on 10 December 2017).

[2]State Council announced that China A21 was integrated into the Ninth Five-Year Plan and the Long-Term Objectives for the year 2010.

[3]The NDRC 2007 Plan formulated China's target that the share of renewable energy consumptions would increase to 10 percent by 2010 and 15 percent by 2015. Respectively 30 and 70 percent of rural households would use clean renewable energy by 2010 and 2020, (NDRC website http://www.martinot.info/China_RE_Plan_to_2020_Sep-2007.pdf accessed on 13 January 2018).

consumption. Such patterns would provide evidence of the long-term sustainability efforts in the country and be interesting to both practitioners and policymakers.

Through the analysis of proprietary datasets between 2010 and 2015, we find that, together with the upward trend in the country's total domestic heating energy consumption, electricity fast replaces coal as a major source of energy. Total domestic heating energy consumption, coal and electricity consumptions are negatively related to the households' disposable income. Steam heating capacity, an energy efficiency indicator, is negatively related to total domestic heating energy consumption. In addition, weather conditions are also key factors towards domestic heating energy consumption in China.

The rest of the chapter is structured as follows. Section 2 presents a brief literature review. Section 3 describes our data and methodology. Section 4 analyses the measurement results and Section 5 concludes the chapter with policy implications.

2 Literature Review

Domestic heating studies over developed countries have evolved through two strains. One strain focuses the discussion on discrete and continuous energy demands. Assuming perfect elasticity of fuel price and capital cost of heating devices, Dubin and McFadden (1984) adopt a sample of 3249 households from Washington Center and unified models of demand for household durables and fuels. Baker et al. (1989) apply a two-stage budgeting model on household consumption patterns with durables data income. Baker and Blundell (1991) introduce a sequential approach on time series data of household gas and electricity consumption with socio-economic control variables. They find that there is a significant temperature impact on household energy consumption and that energy price and income are also significant to the energy choice and usage. However, both the studies above all concentrated on the overall domestic energy expenditure, rather than specifying the home heating energy consumption. Nesbakken (2001) derives a discrete continuous choice model focusing on the relationship between heating equipment and energy consumption to simultaneously analyse the discrete choice of the heating technology and the continuous choice of utilization of such technology. His finding suggests that capital cost and operating cost of the heating system have significant impact on the choice of domestic heating means. Meier and Rehdanz (2010) argue that discrete continuous models distinguish the choice of durables and the demand for energy due to the use of appliances. Another strain of studies focuses on conditional demand of domestic heating. The discrete continuous models can be defected since the choice of heating energy and devices may be de facto and subject to depreciation factors (Munley et al. 1990; Leth-Petersen and Togeby 2001; Meier and Rehdanz 2010). Rehdanz (2007) find that socio-economics features of households can additionally play significant roles besides building features in heating energy consumption.

Most domestic heating studies on China are survey-based due to data constraints. Since the Open Door policy in 1978, China has introduced aggressive plans to curb the growth in household energy consumption through construction and industrial standards (Zhou et al. 2010). The Ministry of Construction imposes energy saving standards for residential properties in Northern China and consistently updates these standards (Wu 2006). However, only around 60 percent of residential properties meet these standards in last decade. In the meantime, China regulates the household appliances through mandatory/voluntary energy efficiency standards and labelling regimes. Wang and Feng (2001) examine China's rural household energy consumption through effective heat per capita, electricity expenditure per capita and commodity energy ratio. Extending Baker and Blundell (1991)'s study, Zhang (2004) explores China's annual energy consumption per household and heating degree-days between 1990 and 2000 and propose that weather condition has impact on the household energy consumption. Bin and Dowlatabadi (2005) and Wei et al. (2007) suggest that consumer lifestyle also has impact on household energy consumption. Zhang et al. (2011) decompose energy consumption into direct and indirect items to identify its trend in China's urban and rural areas.

3 Data and Research Method

3.1 Data

Our proprietary data are manually collected from China Statistical Yearbook and China Energy Statistical Yearbook. Our sample covers 31 provinces/municipalities in the country between 2010 and 2015. Table 1 presents the province/municipalities covered in this study.

Table 1 Sample provinces/municipalities in China

Northern China (16)	Southern China (15)
Beijing	Anhui
Gansu	Chongqing
Hebei	Fujian
Heilongjiang	Guangdong
Henan	Guangxi
Jilin	Guizhou
Liaoning	Hainan
Inner Mongolia	Hubei
Ningxia	Hunan
Qinghai	Jiangsu
Shaanxi	Jiangxi
Shandong	Shanghai
Shanxi	Sichuan
Tianjin	Yunnan
Xinjiang	Zhejiang
Tibet	

3.2 Research Method

Current studies suggest top-down or bottom-up approaches on household energy consumption studies (Sorrell 2007; Vartanian 2010; Wang et al. 2016). We apply the top-down approach[4] in this study and derivate the following regression model to measure the domestic heating energy consumption $C_{i,\ t}$.

$$C_{i,t} = \beta_0 + \alpha_1 Y_{i,t} + \alpha_2 SHC_{i,t} + \alpha_3 HWHC_{i,t} + \alpha_4 E_{i,t} + \beta_1 ASH_{i,t} + \beta_2 AT_{i,t} + e$$

In this regression model, β_0 is a constant. *Y* represents the disposal income of household per capita as measured in RMB yuan. *SHC* and *HWHC* are respectively steam heating capacity and hot water heating capacity, measured in ton/h and million watt (MW).[5] *E* is energy expenditure in RMB yuan.[6] *ASH* and *AT* are annual sunshine hours and average temperature. *ASH* and *AT are* used as weather condition indicators. The yearly average temperature is the summation of each daily temperature of the whole year divided by actual days of the year. *AT* is measured as the actual hours of sun irradiating the ground.

3.3 Statistical Summary

Table 2 presents the statistical summary of the variables in this study. Households in Northern China has more total energy consumption than that in Southern China. Households in Northern China also have much higher coal, fuel oil, steam heating capacity, hot water heating capacity, and annual sunshine hours than households in the South. But households in Southern China have much higher disposable income and more natural gas and electricity consumptions than the households in Northern China.

We further run the VIF test to examine the multi-collinearity of the variables in our regression model before the formal test. The VIF test results suggest that the variables are suitable for our regression tests (Table 3).

---

[4]Due to the lack of heating device type, age and ownership data, we have to treat the heating device owned by the households as statistically exogenous.

[5]Since energy efficiency is proven a strong indicator of domestic energy consumption, we have to select appropriate efficiency indicator. Most households in China adopt steam, water and electricity for domestic heating purpose. Steam heating capacity and hot water heating capacity can be used directly indicate the energy efficiency. However, due to multi-collinearity reasons, electricity heating is not suitable as energy efficiency indicator.

[6]In China, district heating is always provided by single suppliers without market competition. Energy prices are various in each region in unit price and valuation method. In this study we use energy expenditure to replace unit energy price.

Table 2 Statistical summary

Variables	Mean			Std. Dev.		
	National	North	South	National	North	South
C1: Total energy consumption	480787.30	510492.60	449101.60	328736.00	401049.30	225795.50
C2: Residential consumption (coal)	351.96	472.64	223.24	380.46	448.27	232.23
C3: Residential consumption (fuel oil)	0.21	0.35	0.07	1.84	2.54	0.27
C4: Residential consumption (natural gas)	7.54	6.58	8.58	8.24	5.10	10.55
C5: Residential consumption (electricity)	202.29	147.65	260.58	156.52	126.96	164.51
Y: Disposable income per capita	20364.25	19247.75	21555.18	7156.75	6638.78	7526.17
SHC: Steam heating capacity	2830.34	4665.77	872.57	5211.13	6506.64	1935.85
HWHC: Hot water heating capacity	12328.39	23852.08	36.44	17393.00	17657.03	89.09
E: Water, electricity and fuels	394.99	397.18	392.66	343.34	354.99	332.44
ASH: Annual sunshine hours	1997.49	2390.49	1578.29	590.00	430.92	425.54
AT: Average temperature	14.18	10.30	18.33	5.09	3.50	2.64

Table 3 VIF test results of independent variables

Variables	VIF		
	National	North	South
HWHC (MW)	2.59	2.41	1.43
AT (°C)	2.45	2.40	1.13
ASH (h)	1.69	1.26	1.07
SHC (ton/h)	1.53	2.09	1.42
Y (RMB)	1.21	1.91	1.13
E(RMB)	1.05	1.13	1.05
Mean VIF	1.76	1.87	1.21

4 Results and Analysis

4.1 Domestic Heating Energy Consumption Trend

The trend in China's household heating energy consumption can be illustrated by Fig. 2. Total energy consumption, including coal, electricity, oil and natural gas, demonstrates fast growth and upward trend in our sample period. It is noticeable that total energy consumption outpaced the trend in 2012. This may be caused by the extreme weather in that year.

Traditionally coal is the major source of energy for domestic heating in the country. The noticeable decline in coal consumption from 365 $\times$ 10^4 tons in 2010 to 321 $\times$ 10^4 tons in 2015. This change may be from the expansion of district heating network in the northern part of the country. However, district heating is primarily provided by coal-based thermal projects. Coal consumption in Northern China significantly exceeds that in Southern China (see Fig. 3). China has capped coal consumption since 2012.

Electricity is fast replacing coal as a major source of energy for domestic heating (see Fig. 4). Figure 5 suggests that electricity as a major source of domestic heating energy rose from 31 percent to 40 percent of total energy consumption between 2010 and 2015. By comparison, coal declines from 59 percent to 45 percent. This noticeable change suggests that China's energy policy is effective towards the environment. But at current stage coal still plays decisive roles for domestic heating.

In addition, natural gas rose from 10 percent to 15 percent of consumed energy. This growth may be constrained by the lack of gas reserves in the country. China's huge investment in pipelines connecting neighboring countries may play more positive roles in the near future.

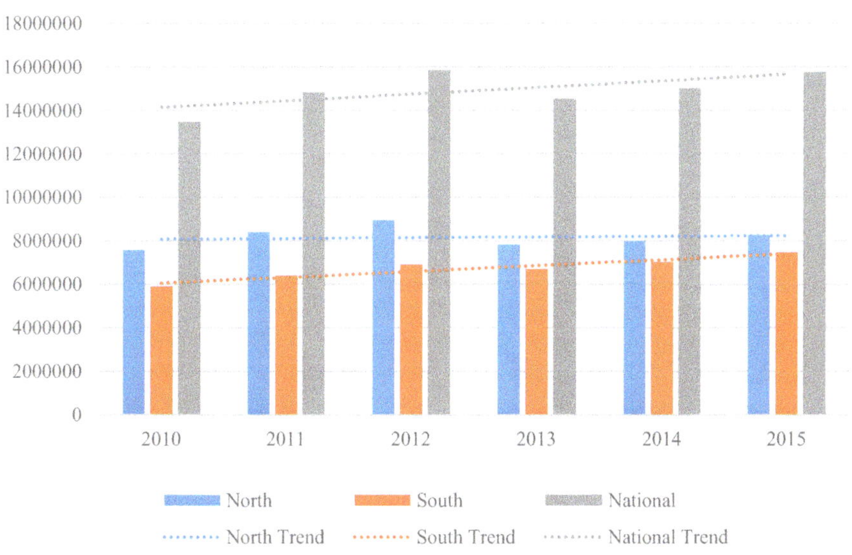

Fig. 2 Total residential energy consumption (unit: 10^8 kcal)

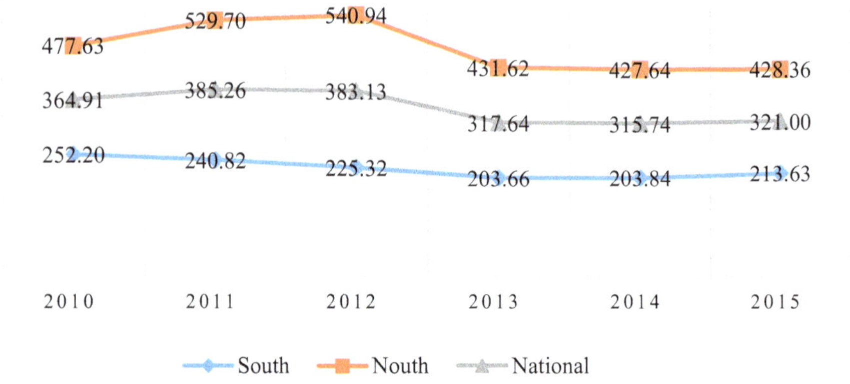

Fig. 3 Average domestic heating coal consumption (10^4 tons)

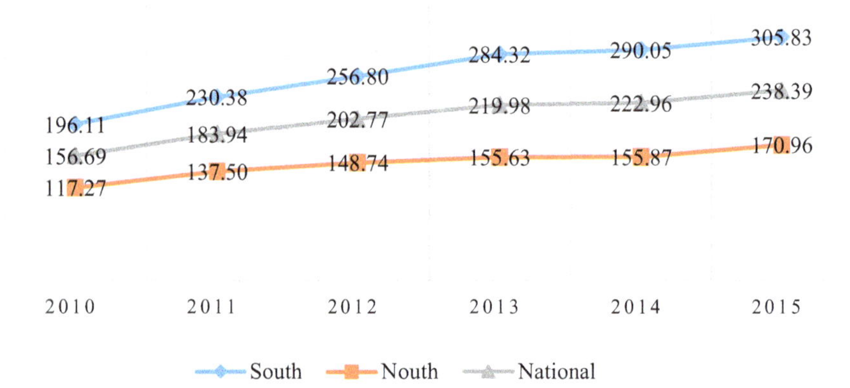

Fig. 4 Average domestic heating electricity consumption (10^8 kWh)

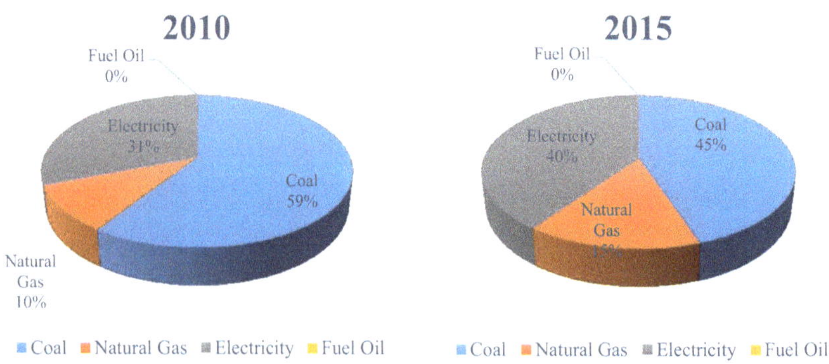

Fig. 5 Domestic heating energy sources in 2010 and 2015

4.2 Regression Results

Tables 4 and 5 respectively report our primary test results of domestic heating energy consumptions in Northern and Southern China. These two tables suggest that disposable income *Y* has impacts on domestic heating energy consumption in the country. Tables 4 and 5 shows a negative relation between *Y* and energy consumption. Households in China have lower *Y* but consume more energy. This suggests that households with lower disposable incomes may not be able to afford districting heating or better technology and therefore consume more with lower energy

Table 4 Measurement results in Northern China

Estimations	Est. 1	Est. 2	Est. 3	Est. 4
Y	2.1490	−2.1716	−2.3777	−26.7418***
	(3.9525)	3.68611	(3.6157)	(5.5767)
SHC		24.0010***	23.8017***	−5.6955
		(5.3032)	(5.4412)	(4.5403)
HWHC		2.1444	2.2200	13.1509***
		(2.1067)	(2.1430)	(2.3772)
E			22.1482	186.0897*
			(110.8755)	(96.6884)
ASH				−110.7408
				(107.8253)
AT				79928.6300***
				(13564.4800)
R Square	0.0013	0.1881	0.1885	0.4713

***, **, and * indicate significance at the 1%, 5%, and 10% levels, respectively

Table 5 Measurement results in Southern China

Estimations	Est. 1	Est. 2	Est. 3	Est. 4
Y	−2.5463	−1.5261	−0.9868	−0.5223
	(2.3186)	(2.5327)	(2.7120)	(3.0017)
SHC		−7.2813	−7.5293	−14.4350**
		(7.5148)	(6.9860)	(7.3636)
HWHC		540.2612***	544.3243***	423.2977***
		(130.2677)	(126.7239)	(108.0846)
E			−66.4856	−83.4641
			(72.6016)	(71.0736)
ASH				−159.3336***
				(41.0502)
AT				−38350.08***
				(8484.8410)
R Square	0.0072	0.0426	0.0519	0.3733

***, **, and * indicate significance at the 1%, 5%, and 10% levels, respectively

efficiency. Wealthier households would pay more attention to social responsibilities and eco-friendly lifestyle. In addition, there may be statistical bias on migrating population in the sample province/municipalities. It is well known that China has huge migration between the under-developed and the well-developed areas even within the same province/municipality.

Energy efficiency indicators, *HWHC* and *SHC*, have mixed impacts on energy consumption. *SHC* is negatively related to heating energy consumption in Southern China. *HWHC* is positive to energy consumption in Northern China. District heating is not commonly used in Southern China. The steam heating has advantages in pressure transmission and high heat transfer coefficient of its radiator compared to the hot water heating. The estimations of *SHC* and *HWHC* would normally indicate the higher energy efficiency the lower energy consumption. However, with the fast growth of real estate sector and expansion of household floor areas, these indicators are not obvious at the country level. Figure 6 suggests that *HWHC* has an upward trend throughout the country. Figure 7 suggests that *SHC* can be significantly improved.

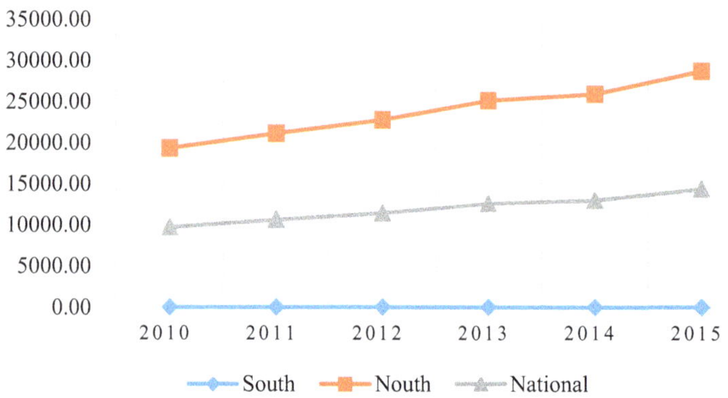

Fig. 6 Hot Water Heating Capacity (MW)

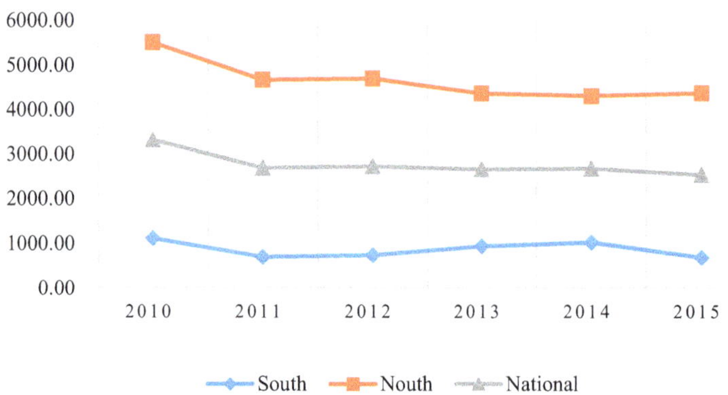

Fig. 7 Steam Heating Capacity (ton/h)

Our measurement suggests that energy expenditure E has positive relation to domestic heating energy consumption in Northern China. This finding suggests that consumption increases when energy price goes up. However, E has insignificantly negative relation to consumption in Southern China. The weather indicator, average temperature AT, has mixed impacts on energy consumptions in Northern and Southern China.

Tables 6 and 7 provide insightful results on electricity and coal consumptions. There is noticeable difference in household energy consumption patterns between Northern and Southern China. There is noticeable difference in household energy

Table 6 Measurement results on electricity consumption

Estimations	North	South
Disposable income of households per capita	−0.0033***	−0.0079**
	(0.0011)	(0.0034)
Steam heating capacity	0.0078***	0.0079
	(0.0011)	(0.0070)
Hot water heating capacity	0.0025***	−0.0327
	(0.0005)	(0.0800)
Water, electricity and fuels	−0.0111	−0.0754
	(0.0178)	(0.0648)
Annual sunshine hours	−0.0470	−0.0106
	(0.0316)	(0.0281)
Average temperature	18.6899***	3.5714
	(3.2967)	(8.6328)
R square	0.8061	0.1521

***, **, and * indicate significance at the 1%, 5%, and 10% levels, respectively

Table 7 Measurement results on coal consumption

Estimations	North	South
Disposable income per capita	−0.0346***	−0.0129***
	(0.0068)	(0.0015)
Steam heating capacity	−0.01941***	−0.0286***
	(0.0058)	(0.0074)
Hot water heating capacity	0.01513***	0.6780***
	(0.0027)	(0.1227)
Water, electricity and fuels	−0.3016**	−0.0186
	(0.1225)	(0.0411)
Annual sunshine hours	−0.0880	−0.0862***
	(0.1068)	(0.03879)
Average temperature	82.2982***	−51.1024***
	(16.3620)	(5.4830)
R square	0.3052	0.6930

***, **, and * indicate significance at the 1%, 5%, and 10% levels, respectively

consumption patterns between Northern and Southern China. The measurement of electricity consumption is significant in Northern China with most variables except annual sunshine hours *ASH* and energy expenditure *E*. Urbanization may have enhanced the incomes of rural residents, relieving energy supply constraints and enriching accessible energy sources in Northern China. More income promotes the switch from coal to electricity consumption. By comparison, in Southern China the weather indicator *AT* is negatively related to coal consumptions. The different weather conditions between Northern and Southern China may the key factor. For example, the rainy season normally lasts 6 months per year and 4 months longer than that in Northern China. The Southern winter is much warmer than the Northern one. Consequently, most households in Southern China prefer to use air-conditioning for heating purpose. However, households in Northern China rely heavily on centralized heating networks during winter times.

5 Conclusion with Policy Implications

This study provides evidence that China has adopted effective means to pursue a sustainable energy policy. We find that disposable income and energy efficiency have negative relations with domestic energy consumptions. Electricity and natural gas are fast replacing coal as major sources of energy. Increased disposal income leads households to a more energy efficient lifestyle. Such improvement in energy efficiency could effectively control the growth in domestic energy consumption. In addition, geographic location and weather conditions are other factors contributing to domestic energy consumption.

Our findings may have the following policy implications. First, if the momentum of increasing disposable income is maintained, China may successfully achieve its energy targets in the future. Second, the top-down energy plans need to be better carried out. The noticeable disparity of energy efficiency allows such improvements. Third, electricity and coal facilities need to improve or downsize. Fourth, natural gas and other clean energies have become strategically more important for improvement. Only with successful energy policies, could China sustainably emerge in the coming Asian era.

References

Baker, P., & Blundell, R. (1991). The micro econometric approach to modelling energy demand: some results for UK households. *Oxford Review of Economic Policy, 7*(2), 54–76.

Baker, P., Blundell, R., & Micklewright, J. (1989). Modelling household energy expenditures using micro data. *Economic Journal, 99*(397), 720–738.

Bin, S., & Dowlatabadi, H. (2005). Consumer lifestyle approach to US energy use and the related CO_2 emissions. *Energy Policy, 33*(2), 197–208.

Dubin, J. A., & McFadden, D. (1984). An econometric analysis of residential electric appliance holdings and consumption. *Econometrica, 52*(2), 345–362.

Grubb, M., Hourcade, J. C., & Neuhoff, K. (2014). *Planetary economics: energy, climate change and the three domains of sustainable development*. Oxon: Routledge.

IEA. (2015). *Energy Technology Perspectives 2015*. Paris: OECD/IEA. Retrieved December 23, 2017, from www.iea.org/etp/etp2015

Leth-Petersen, S., & Togeby, M. (2001). Demand for space heating in apartment blocks: Measuring effects of policy measures aiming at reducing energy consumption. *Energy Economics, 23*(4), 387–403.

Meier, H., & Rehdanz, K. (2010). Determinants of residential space heating expenditures in Great Britain. *Energy Economics, 32*(5), 949–959.

Munley, V. G., Taylor, L. W., & Formby, J. P. (1990). Electricity demand in multi-family, renter-occupied residences. *Southern Economic Journal, 57*(1), 178–194.

National Development and Reform Commission. (2007). *Medium and long-term energy conservation plan*. Retrieved November 30, 2017, from www.ndrc.gov.cn

Nesbakken, R. (2001). Energy consumption for space heating: A discrete-continuous approach. *The Scandinavian Journal of Economics, 103*(1), 165–184.

Pretlove, S., & Oreszczyn, T. (1998). Climate change: impact on the envoironmental design of buildings. *Building Services Engineering Research and Technology, 19*(1), 55–58.

Rehdanz, K. (2007). Determinants of residential space heating expenditures in Germany. *Energy Economics, 29*(2), 167–182.

Sorrell, S. (2007). Improving the evidence base for energy policy: The role of systematic reviews. *Energy Policy, 35*(3), 1858–1871.

Tung, C. (2009). Carbon law and practice in China. In D. Freestone & C. Streck (Eds.), *Legal aspects of carbon trading: Kyoto, Copenhagen, and beyond* (pp. 488–515). Oxford: Oxford Scholarship Online.

United Nations. (1992). *Report of the United Nations conference on environment and development*, Rio declaration on environment and development, Rio de Janeiro. Retrieved January 21, 2018, from http://www.un.org/documents/ga/conf151/aconf15126-1annex1.htm/

United Nations. (2002). *Report of the world summit on sustainable development*, Johannesburg, South Africa. Retrieved January 16, 2018, from http://www.fao.org/fileadmin/user_upload/mountain_partnership/docs/131302_wssd_report_reissued.pdf

United Nations. (2015). *Transforming our world: The 2030 Agenda for Sustainable Development*. Retrieved January 20, 2018, from http://www.un.org/ga/search/view_doc.asp?symbol=A/RES/70/1&Lang=E

Vartanian, T. P. (2010). *Secondary data analysis*. Oxford: Oxford University Press.

Wang, X., & Feng, Z. (2001). Study on rural household energy consumption in China: consumption level and affecting factors. *Transactions of the Chinese Society of Agricultural Engineering, 17* (5), 88–91.

Wang, X., Chen, D., & Ren, Z. (2010). Assessment of climate change impact on residential building heating and cooling energy requirement in Australia. *Building and Environment, 45*(7), 1663–1682.

Wang, Y., Wang, F., & Wang, H. (2016). Heating energy consumption questionnaire and statistical analysis of rural buildings in China. *Procedia Engineering, 146*, 380–385.

Watson, R. T. (2001). Climate change 2001: Synthesis report. Third assessment report of the intergovernmental panel on climate change. *Environmental Policy Collection, 27*(2), 408.

Wei, Y. M., Liu, L. C., Fan, Y., & Wu, G. (2007). The impact of lifestyle on energy use and CO_2 emission: An empirical analysis of China's residents. *Energy Policy, 35*(1), 247–257.

Wu, Y. (2006). *Strengthening the building energy efficiency regulatory system in China. Energy Foundation Forum on Implementing China's 2010 20-Percent Energy Efficiency Target.* Retrieved January 21, 2018, from http://www.efchina.org/Attachments/Foundation-News/news-efchina-20061120/2006%20PAC%20Meeting%20and%20Forum%20Briefing%20Book.pdf

Zhang, Q. (2004). Residential energy consumption in china and its comparison with Japan, Canada, and USA. *Energy & Buildings, 36*(12), 1217–1225.

Zhang, X., Niu, S. W., Shu, W., Zhang, C. H., & Hu, L. L. (2011). The study on household energy consumption and carbon emissions in China's urbanization. *China Soft Science, 9*, 65–75.
Zhou, N., Levine, M. D., & Price, L. (2010). Overview of current energy-efficiency policies in China. *Energy Policy, 38*(11), 6439–6452.

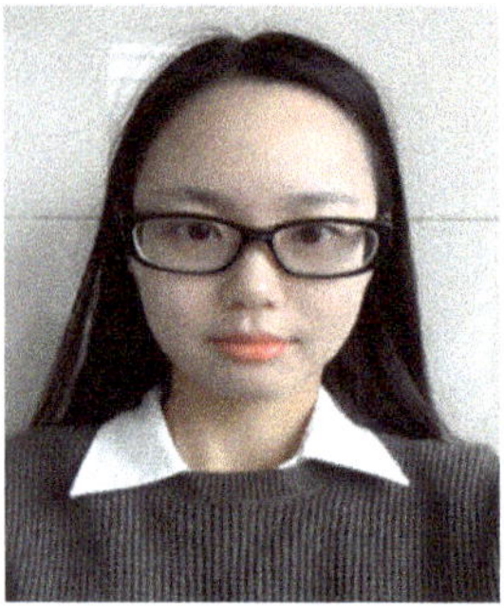

Xin Xu is a PhD student in the Department of China Studies in the Liverpool University based in Suzhou, Jiangsu, China. She gained her BSc in Economics at Xi'an Jiaotong Liverpool University and MSc in Economics and Policy of Energy and the Environment at the University College London. She worked as a research assistant in SKEMA Business School. Her research focuses on issues of environmental policy, the international political economy of environment, and the nexus between environment and development as related to China. She is also interested in the areas related to the environmental governance and institutional theory.

Lei Xu is a Senior Lecturer in Finance at the Business School University of South Australia, a member of the Research Integrity Committee at the University, a member of Academic Unit Board of UniSA Business, a member of UniSA Business Safety and Wellness, Executive of the Association of Overseas Chinese Professionals in South Australia, and a Justice of Peace for South Australia.

His research interests cover banking, financial markets, financial systems, and emerging financial issues. He is currently working with a team of active researchers in the areas of environmental finance and Fin-tech. His continuous research efforts have led to fruitful publications in prestigious international and national journals and conferences.

Before joining University of South Australia, he worked as a Lecturer in Finance at the University of Adelaide and for years at the banking sector in China. Such experience allows him to integrate teaching and research activities with practitioner knowledge in the discipline.

Laubie Li served as Academic Dean of SKEMA Business School's China Campus in Suzhou from July 2014. Laubie reluctantly stepped down from full-time appointment in early 2017 for health reasons.

Laubie holds a PhD degree from the University of New South Wales, Australia. He has had many years of business and industry experience before embarking on an academic career. Most recently (2011–2014), Laubie was Dean of Business and Dean of Research and External Engagement at the University of Wollongong in Dubai (UOWD). From 2003 to 2010, he served as Associate Head of School and Executive Director, MBA Programs as well as Associate Professor of Business at the International Graduate School of Business (IGSB), University of South Australia. He was Associate Dean (Academic) at the Adelaide Graduate School of Business, University of Adelaide, during 1996–2002.

Laubie has been active in international activities, developing and managing business programs and collaboration projects in Asia and Europe. He is also heavily involved in international accreditation of business programs and academic quality audit in both Australia and the Asian region. Laubie regularly chairs academic accreditation panels for the Hong Kong Council for Accreditation of Academic and Vocational Qualifications.

Sustainable Energy Investment in Australia

Will Mackay, Lei Xu, and Greg Meredith

Abstract Securing a stable and reliable energy supply future is a major challenge in Australia in 2018. Ageing energy assets and regulatory uncertainty fuelled by concerns over global climate change and environmental sustainability create significant hurdles to future investment. Resource providers are becoming increasingly concerned with investment sustainability and demand performance metrics beyond profit extending to governance, environmental and social measures. This study develops a Sustainable Development Goals (SDG) Index most relevant to the energy sector and measures the SDG performance of the Australian retail energy market. SDG index scores provide a signal to resource providers including investors, creditors, regulators and the community about the sustainability of energy sector firms.

Keywords Sustainability · Energy futures · SDG

1 Introduction

Securing a stable and reliable energy supply future is a major challenge in Australia in 2018. There are a multitude of factors spanning a lengthy period that have led to this bleak prognosis for retail energy market. Concerns over climate change and regulatory uncertainty combined with the disruptive influence of rising cost fossil fuel costs and improved efficiency of alternative e

nergy production against a backdrop of aging energy assets have combined to create a real threat of an energy shortage in Australia within the next decade. Attracting

W. Mackay · L. Xu (✉)
UniSA Business, University of South Australia, Adelaide, SA, Australia
e-mail: lei.xu@unisa.edu.au

G. Meredith
APA Group, Sydney, NSW, Australia

K. Wendt (ed.), *Theories of Change*, Sustainable Finance,
https://doi.org/10.1007/978-3-030-52275-9_27

financiers to fund the much-needed investment in energy infrastructure and simultaneously ticking all the sustainability boxes is a complex problem.

Awareness of the effects of pollutants on climate change and the significance of greenhouse gases such as fossil fuel generated carbon emissions have focused attention upon the activity of the energy sector. Global climate agreements such as the Kyoto and more recently the Paris Agreement place significant pressure on government to make significant reductions to emissions in the near to medium term. Such constraints influence the viability of all future energy production projects in Australia owing to the duration of the pay-back period associated with large scale efficient clean energy production projects and the stringent hurdles imposed by financiers.

The Australia government has a record of regulatory uncertainty as evidenced by the introduction of a carbon tax through the Clean Energy Act 2011 with an effective date of July 2012 which was subsequently repealed in July 2014. Electricity production is the single biggest contributor to CO_2 emissions in Australia, representing 35% of all CO_2 emissions in 2015. The six highest emitting companies in Australia are from the energy sector, while the top 10 emitters represent over 50% of scope 1 emissions in Australia (CER 2016). The closure of Hazelwood Coal Power Station located in the Latrobe Valley March 2017, a notoriously dirty power station, reduced greenhouse emissions from the energy sector but also reduced the national energy market capacity by more than 5 gigawatts (Potter 2016). Regulatory uncertainty increases the complexity in evaluating the viability of future investment in energy infrastructure and energy generation which in turn increases the risks for investors in this sector.

In addition, the Australian Government passed a Renewable Energy Target (RET) in June 2015 requiring more than 23.5% of electricity generation must be sourced from renewable energy by 2020 (Cwlth 2015). The RET restricts future investment choices for firms in the energy sector although it is aligned with the boarder market push to a shift away from dirty to clean electricity generation.

In this study, we develop a SDG index of the energy sector and measure the SDG performance of Australian energy market. The rest of the chapter is structured as follows. Section 2 presents the institutional background of Australian energy sector. Section 3 describes our research methodology. Section 4 analyses our results and Section 5 concludes the study.

2 Institutional Background

The positive associated with renewable energy generation from solar and wind is a reduction to CO_2 emissions and therefore it is aligned with global climate change policies. The negatives of renewable power include reliability factors: solar electricity generation is impeded by cloud cover and produces no power during the night while wind farms only produce electricity when the wind is blowing. Although there are technologies that can minimise the variability of solar and wind electricity generation, such as large-scale batteries and hydro pumped storage, the delivery of reliable base load power remains a stumbling block with the shift to renewable energy.

The Australian Government committed $29 million in 2017 to fund a feasibility study into Snowy 2.0, the expansion of the existing Snowy Hydro scheme to expand the pumped hydro capacity to tackle the issue of replacing base load coal power generation.

Australian Renewable Energy Agency (ARENA) CEO Ivor Frischknecht said the expansion of the Snow Hydro scheme pumped hydro capability will enable the transition to a wind and solar power in the future.

> As Australia transitions to more renewables and as coal-fired power stations reach their end of life, large scale energy storage coupled with wind and solar can provide dispatchable electricity to replace baseload coal. . . . This study confirms that Snowy 2.0 is an exciting renewable energy project which could play an important role in delivering security and reliability in the National Energy Market.—(ARENA 2017)

The cost of Snowy 2.0 is estimated to be between $6 and $7 billion and is seen as a potential solution to replace base load capacity lost due to the replacement of "dirty generation" from coal and other fossil fuel power generation (Potter 2017).

Securing sustainable finance for future investment presents a major hurdle for players in the energy sector within Australia and across the globe. Disruption to business as usual has come from a combination of the formation of carbon markets, attention on climate change, aging energy assets and improved renewable power generation technologies.

Now more than ever financial markets and governments alike are concerned with a broader suite of performance metrics beyond profitability with increasing attention focused on environmental, social and governance (ESG) metrics. Good ESG performance can unlock access to: equity finance, debt finance, natural resources, energy markets and other government financial support.

Financial markets have evolved to meet the requirements of equity financiers and now include a range of ESG and "green" financial instruments to meet the needs of investors. For example, the UK securities exchange publishes the FTSE4Good Index Series providing a range of "ESG-aware" ratings to assist investors wanting to invest in companies with strong credentials in ESG, supported by strong governance and transparency. The rating allows investors to opportunity to more accurately price in the risk associated with ESG performance including climate risk and the risk of poor green performance.

Most of public companies, in Australia and across the world, are constantly monitored and evaluated on their respective ESG performance by analysts, ratings agencies and other interested third parties. Providers of finance including institutional investors, superannuation funds, portfolio managers, financial institutions, government and other stakeholders are becoming increasing reliant on the extending reporting and performance metrics embedded in the ESG disclosures and the associated ESG ratings to quantify ESG performance across time and among peers within an industry.

3 Research Methodology

3.1 S&P Approach

There are numerous providers of ESG ratings and reports including: S&P Global Ratings Green Evaluation, FTSE Russell's ESG Ratings, Bloomberg ESG Data Service, Dow Jones Sustainability Index, MSCI ESG Research, Sustainalytics Company ESG Reports and Thomson Reuters ESG Research Data. Standard & Poors Green Evaluation Approach is presented in the Fig. 1.

Unfortunately, because the scope, coverage and methodology vary greatly among the various agencies it makes comparison near impossible and produces conflicting score cards for many companies (Huber and Comstock 2017).

Promoters of sustainable financing highlight the opportunities for companies to access considerable long-term finance if they can demonstrate ESG credentials, in particular their environmental (often referred to as "green") credentials, as demonstrated by the quote below:

> Green finance is a major opportunity. By ensuring that capital flows finance long term projects in countries where growth is most carbon intensive, financial stability can be promoted. By allocating capital to green technologies, the prospects for an environmentally sustainable recovery in global growth will increase.

Mark Carney *Governor of the Bank of England and Chair of the Group of Twenty's*

Sustainable development projects that deliver enhanced climate outcomes or societal objectives, national or international, qualify for various private and public sector concessional schemes including market-based climate finance resources. Examples of financial resources available include underwriting, guarantees, concessional loans, grants, risk sharing contracts, permits, credits and other support initiatives. There are three mainstream ways green finance can assist companies to invest in ESG positive ventures: increasing revenues, providing access to equity and providing access to debt. Providing a revenue floor is one mechanism that provides financiers of eligible projects with the confidence their investment will be returned. Mechanisms increasing revenues provide an added impetus for companies to select positive ESG projects above alternate projects in the same sector with lesser ESG credentials. Increasingly institutional investors are selecting investments with high ESG ratings to meet the preferences of their clients and thereby making more equity finance available to qualifying companies. Creditors also face pressure from customers and other stakeholders to divert debt finance away from "poor" ESG firms and encourage issuance of debt to companies that deliver on other positive ESG measures. For example, in Australia the National Australia Bank teamed with The Clean Energy Finance Corporation to facilitate $120 million in concessional loans to farmers to invest in renewable energy projects such as wind, solar and biogas power generation (Marshall 2015).

Green finance offers significant opportunities to deliver environmental benefits by supporting investment for positive Climate Change. It is estimated green bonds

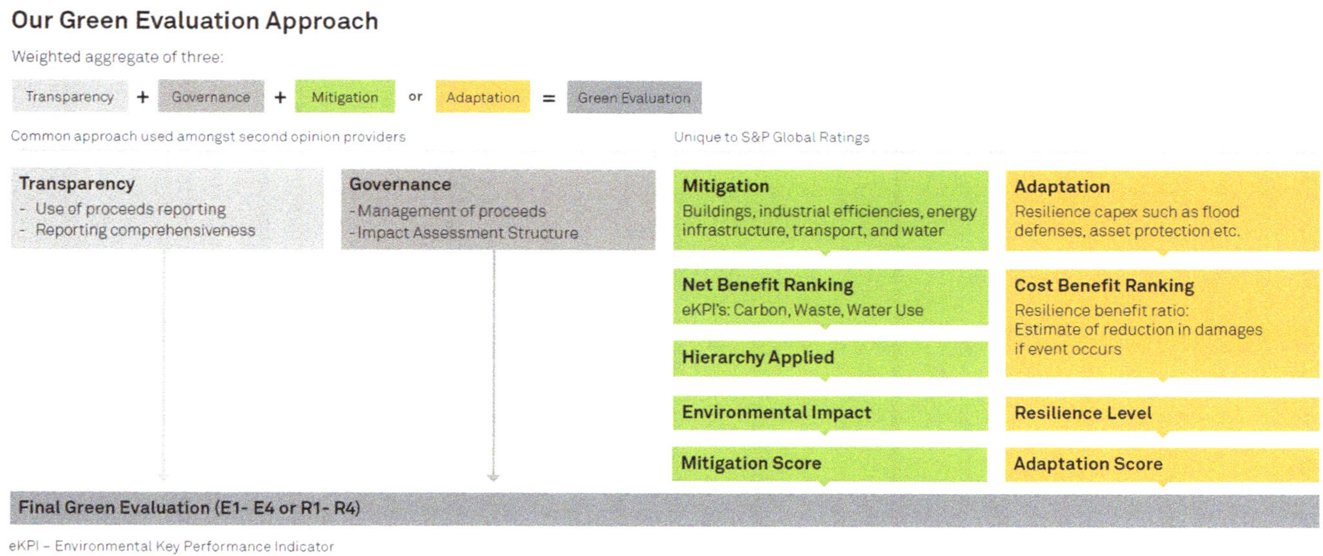

Fig. 1 S&P Green Evaluation Approach. Source: S&P Global Rating Evaluation: Time to Turn Over a New Leaf? Published by Standard & Poor's Financial Services LLC, 2017

mobilised between $200 billion to $250 billion in 2017 alone. Yet the green finance market is struggling to agree on definitional issues concerning relevant ESG metrics and assurance issues around measurement and certification (Rossetto 2017).

3.2 SDG Measurement

The Sustainable Development Goals (SDGs) were established in 2015 to address global poverty and hunger, and the worst effects of climate change. The agreement amongst the 193 countries set 17 SDGs with considerable overlap with the core values embedded within ESG reporting. The SDGs provide a single, consistent framework to measure all companies against and provide a strong signal to financiers on a wide range of factors embedded within tradition ESG reporting and rating metrics.

Below is the full list of 17 SDGs extracted from Transforming our world: the 2030 Agenda for Sustainable Development (United Nations 2015).

Goal 1: No Poverty
End poverty in all its forms everywhere

1.1 By 2030, eradicate extreme poverty for all people everywhere, currently measured as people living on less than $1.25 a day
1.2 By 2030, reduce at least by half the proportion of men, women and children of all ages living in poverty in all its dimensions according to national definitions
1.3 Implement nationally appropriate social protection systems and measures for all, including floors, and by 2030 achieve substantial coverage of the poor and the vulnerable
1.4 By 2030, ensure that all men and women, in particular the poor and the vulnerable, have equal rights to economic resources, as well as access to basic services, ownership and control over land and other forms of property, inheritance, natural resources, appropriate new technology and financial services, including microfinance
1.5 By 2030, build the resilience of the poor and those in vulnerable situations and reduce their exposure and vulnerability to climate-related extreme events and other economic, social and environmental shocks and disasters

Goal 2: Zero Hunger
End hunger, achieve food security and improved nutrition and promote sustainable agriculture

2.1 By 2030, end hunger and ensure access by all people, in particular the poor and people in vulnerable situations, including infants, to safe, nutritious and sufficient food all year round
2.2 By 2030, end all forms of malnutrition, including achieving, by 2025, the internationally agreed targets on stunting and wasting in children under

5 years of age, and address the nutritional needs of adolescent girls, pregnant and lactating women and older persons

2.3 By 2030, double the agricultural productivity and incomes of small-scale food producers, in particular women, indigenous peoples, family farmers, pastoralists and fishers, including through secure and equal access to land, other productive resources and inputs, knowledge, financial services, markets and opportunities for value addition and non-farm employment

2.4 By 2030, ensure sustainable food production systems and implement resilient agricultural practices that increase productivity and production, that help maintain ecosystems, that strengthen capacity for adaptation to climate change, extreme weather, drought, flooding and other disasters and that progressively improve land and soil quality

2.5 By 2020, maintain the genetic diversity of seeds, cultivated plants and farmed and domesticated animals and their related wild species, including through soundly managed and diversified seed and plant banks at the national, regional and international levels, and promote access to and fair and equitable sharing of benefits arising from the utilization of genetic resources and associated traditional knowledge, as internationally agreed

Goal 3: Good Health and Well-Being
Ensure healthy lives and promote well-being for all at all ages

3.1 By 2030, reduce the global maternal mortality ratio to less than 70 per 100,000 live births

3.2 By 2030, end preventable deaths of newborns and children under 5 years of age, with all countries aiming to reduce neonatal mortality to at least as low as 12 per 1000 live births and under-5 mortality to at least as low as 25 per 1000 live births

3.3 By 2030, end the epidemics of AIDS, tuberculosis, malaria and neglected tropical diseases and combat hepatitis, water-borne diseases and other communicable diseases

3.4 By 2030, reduce by one third premature mortality from non-communicable diseases through prevention and treatment and promote mental health and well-being

3.5 Strengthen the prevention and treatment of substance abuse, including narcotic drug abuse and harmful use of alcohol

3.6 By 2020, halve the number of global deaths and injuries from road traffic accidents

3.7 By 2030, ensure universal access to sexual and reproductive health-care services, including for family planning, information and education, and the integration of reproductive health into national strategies and programmes

3.8 Achieve universal health coverage, including financial risk protection, access to quality essential health-care services and access to safe, effective, quality and affordable essential medicines and vaccines for all

3.9 By 2030, substantially reduce the number of deaths and illnesses from hazardous chemicals and air, water and soil pollution and contamination

Goal 4: Quality Education

Ensure inclusive and equitable quality education and promote lifelong learning opportunities for all

4.1 By 2030, ensure that all girls and boys complete free, equitable and quality primary and secondary education leading to relevant and effective learning outcomes

4.2 By 2030, ensure that all girls and boys have access to quality early childhood development, care and pre-primary education so that they are ready for primary education

4.3 By 2030, ensure equal access for all women and men to affordable and quality technical, vocational and tertiary education, including university

4.4 By 2030, substantially increase the number of youth and adults who have relevant skills, including technical and vocational skills, for employment, decent jobs and entrepreneurship

4.5 By 2030, eliminate gender disparities in education and ensure equal access to all levels of education and vocational training for the vulnerable, including persons with disabilities, indigenous peoples and children in vulnerable situations

4.6 By 2030, ensure that all youth and a substantial proportion of adults, both men and women, achieve literacy and numeracy

4.7 By 2030, ensure that all learners acquire the knowledge and skills needed to promote sustainable development, including, among others, through education for sustainable development and sustainable lifestyles, human rights, gender equality, promotion of a culture of peace and non-violence, global citizenship and appreciation of cultural diversity and of culture's contribution to sustainable development

Goal 5: Gender Equality

Achieve gender equality and empower all women and girls

5.1 End all forms of discrimination against all women and girls everywhere

5.2 Eliminate all forms of violence against all women and girls in the public and private spheres, including trafficking and sexual and other types of exploitation

5.3 Eliminate all harmful practices, such as child, early and forced marriage and female genital mutilation

5.4 Recognize and value unpaid care and domestic work through the provision of public services, infrastructure and social protection policies and the promotion of shared responsibility within the household and the family as nationally appropriate

5.5 Ensure women's full and effective participation and equal opportunities for leadership at all levels of decision making in political, economic and public life

5.6 Ensure universal access to sexual and reproductive health and reproductive rights as agreed in accordance with the Programme of Action of the International Conference on Population and Development and the Beijing Platform for Action and the outcome documents of their review conferences

Goal 6: Clean Water and Sanitation

Ensure availability and sustainable management of water and sanitation for all

6.1 By 2030, achieve universal and equitable access to safe and affordable drinking water for all
6.2 By 2030, achieve access to adequate and equitable sanitation and hygiene for all and end open defecation, paying special attention to the needs of women and girls and those in vulnerable situations
6.3 By 2030, improve water quality by reducing pollution, eliminating dumping and minimizing release of hazardous chemicals and materials, halving the proportion of untreated wastewater and substantially increasing recycling and safe reuse globally
6.4 By 2030, substantially increase water use efficiency across all sectors and ensure sustainable withdrawals and supply of freshwater to address water scarcity and substantially reduce the number of people suffering from water scarcity
6.5 By 2030, implement integrated water resources management at all levels, including through transboundary cooperation as appropriate
6.6 By 2020, protect and restore water related ecosystems, including mountains, forests, wetlands, rivers, aquifers and lakes

Goal 7: Affordable and Clean Energy

Ensure access to affordable, reliable, sustainable and modern energy for all

7.1 By 2030, ensure universal access to affordable, reliable and modern energy services
7.2 By 2030, increase substantially the share of renewable energy in the global energy mix
7.3 By 2030, double the global rate of improvement in energy efficiency

Goal 8: Decent Work and Economic Growth

Promote sustained, inclusive and sustainable economic growth, full and productive employment and decent work for all

8.1 Sustain per capita economic growth in accordance with national circumstances and, in particular, at least 7 per cent gross domestic product growth per annum in the least developed countries
8.2 Achieve higher levels of economic productivity through diversification, technological upgrading and innovation, including through a focus on high value added and labour-intensive sectors
8.3 Promote development-oriented policies that support productive activities, decent job creation, entrepreneurship, creativity and innovation, and encourage the formalization and growth of micro, small and medium sized enterprises, including through access to financial services
8.4 Improve progressively, through 2030, global resource efficiency in consumption and production and endeavour to decouple economic growth from environmental degradation, in accordance with the 10 Year Framework of

Programmes on Sustainable Consumption and Production, with developed countries taking the lead

8.5 By 2030, achieve full and productive employment and decent work for all women and men, including for young people and persons with disabilities, and equal pay for work of equal value

8.6 By 2020, substantially reduce the proportion of youth not in employment, education or training

8.7 Take immediate and effective measures to eradicate forced labour, end modern slavery and human trafficking and secure the prohibition and elimination of the worst forms of child labour, including recruitment and use of child soldiers, and by 2025 end child labour in all its forms

8.8 Protect labour rights and promote safe and secure working environments for all workers, including migrant workers, in particular women migrants, and those in precarious employment

8.9 By 2030, devise and implement policies to promote sustainable tourism that creates jobs and promotes local culture and products

8.10 Strengthen the capacity of domestic financial institutions to encourage and expand access to banking, insurance and financial services for all

Goal 9: Industry, Innovation and Infrastructure
Build resilient infrastructure, promote inclusive and sustainable industrialization and foster innovation

9.1 Develop quality, reliable, sustainable and resilient infrastructure, including regional and trans-border infrastructure, to support economic development and human wellbeing, with a focus on affordable and equitable access for all

9.2 Promote inclusive and sustainable industrialization and, by 2030, significantly raise industry's share of employment and gross domestic product, in line with national circumstances, and double its share in least developed countries

9.3 Increase the access of small scale industrial and other enterprises, in particular in developing countries, to financial services, including affordable credit, and their integration into value chains and markets

9.4 By 2030, upgrade infrastructure and retrofit industries to make them sustainable, with increased resource use efficiency and greater adoption of clean and environmentally sound technologies and industrial processes, with all countries taking action in accordance with their respective capabilities

9.5 Enhance scientific research, upgrade the technological capabilities of industrial sectors in all countries, in particular developing countries, including, by 2030, encouraging innovation and substantially increasing the number of research and development workers per 1 million people and public and private research and development spending

Goal 10: Reduced Inequality
Reduce inequality within and among countries

10.1 By 2030, progressively achieve and sustain income growth of the bottom 40 per cent of the population at a rate higher than the national average

10.2 By 2030, empower and promote the social, economic and political inclusion of all, irrespective of age, sex, disability, race, ethnicity, origin, religion or economic or other status
10.3 Ensure equal opportunity and reduce inequalities of outcome, including by eliminating discriminatory laws, policies and practices and promoting appropriate legislation, policies and action in this regard
10.4 Adopt policies, especially fiscal, wage and social protection policies, and progressively achieve greater equality
10.5 Improve the regulation and monitoring of global financial markets and institutions and strengthen the implementation of such regulations
10.6 Ensure enhanced representation and voice for developing countries in decision making in global international economic and financial institutions in order to deliver more effective, credible, accountable and legitimate institutions
10.7 Facilitate orderly, safe, regular and responsible migration and mobility of people, including through the implementation of planned and well managed migration policies

Goal 11: Sustainable Cities and Communities
Make cities and human settlements inclusive, safe, resilient and sustainable

11.1 By 2030, ensure access for all to adequate, safe and affordable housing and basic services and upgrade slums
11.2 By 2030, provide access to safe, affordable, accessible and sustainable transport systems for all, improving road safety, notably by expanding public transport, with special attention to the needs of those in vulnerable situations, women, children, persons with disabilities and older persons
11.3 By 2030, enhance inclusive and sustainable urbanization and capacity for participatory, integrated and sustainable human settlement planning and management in all countries
11.4 Strengthen efforts to protect and safeguard the world's cultural and natural heritage
11.5 By 2030, significantly reduce the number of deaths and the number of people affected and substantially decrease the direct economic losses relative to global gross domestic product caused by disasters, including water related disasters, with a focus on protecting the poor and people in vulnerable situations
11.6 By 2030, reduce the adverse per capita environmental impact of cities, including by paying special attention to air quality and municipal and other waste management
11.7 By 2030, provide universal access to safe, inclusive and accessible, green and public spaces, in particular for women and children, older persons and persons with disabilities

Goal 12: Responsible Consumption and Production
Ensure sustainable consumption and production patterns

12.1 Implement the 10 Year Framework of Programmes on Sustainable Consumption and Production Patterns, all countries taking action, with developed countries taking the lead, taking into account the development and capabilities of developing countries

12.2 By 2030, achieve the sustainable management and efficient use of natural resources

12.3 By 2030, halve per capita global food waste at the retail and consumer levels and reduce food losses along production and supply chains, including post-harvest losses

12.4 By 2020, achieve the environmentally sound management of chemicals and all wastes throughout their life cycle, in accordance with agreed international frameworks, and significantly reduce their release to air, water and soil in order to minimize their adverse impacts on human health and the environment

12.5 By 2030, substantially reduce waste generation through prevention, reduction, recycling and reuse

12.6 Encourage companies, especially large and transnational companies, to adopt sustainable practices and to integrate sustainability information into their reporting cycle

12.7 Promote public procurement practices that are sustainable, in accordance with national policies and priorities

12.8 By 2030, ensure that people everywhere have the relevant information and awareness for sustainable development and lifestyles in harmony with nature

Goal 13: Climate Action

Take urgent action to combat climate change and its impacts

13.1 Strengthen resilience and adaptive capacity to climate related hazards and natural disasters in all countries

13.2 Integrate climate change measures into national policies, strategies and planning

13.3 Improve education, awareness raising and human and institutional capacity on climate change mitigation, adaptation, impact reduction and early warning

Goal 14: Life Below Water

Conserve and sustainably use the oceans, seas and marine resources for sustainable development

14.1 By 2025, prevent and significantly reduce marine pollution of all kinds, in particular from land-based activities, including marine debris and nutrient pollution

14.2 By 2020, sustainably manage and protect marine and coastal ecosystems to avoid significant adverse impacts, including by strengthening their resilience, and take action for their restoration in order to achieve healthy and productive oceans

14.3 Minimize and address the impacts of ocean acidification, including through enhanced scientific cooperation at all levels

14.4 By 2020, effectively regulate harvesting and end overfishing, illegal, unreported and unregulated fishing and destructive fishing practices and implement science-based management plans, in order to restore fish stocks in the shortest time feasible, at least to levels that can produce maximum sustainable yield as determined by their biological characteristics

14.5 By 2020, conserve at least 10 per cent of coastal and marine areas, consistent with national and international law and based on the best available scientific information

14.6 By 2020, prohibit certain forms of fisheries subsidies which contribute to overcapacity and overfishing, eliminate subsidies that contribute to illegal, unreported and unregulated fishing and refrain from introducing new such subsidies, recognizing that appropriate and effective special and differential treatment for developing and least developed countries should be an integral part of the World Trade Organization fisheries subsidies negotiation

14.7 By 2030, increase the economic benefits to small island developing States and least developed countries from the sustainable use of marine resources, including through sustainable management of fisheries, aquaculture and tourism

Goal 15: Life on Land

Protect, restore and promote sustainable use of terrestrial ecosystems, sustainably manage forests, combat desertification, and halt and reverse land degradation and halt biodiversity loss

15.1 By 2020, ensure the conservation, restoration and sustainable use of terrestrial and inland freshwater ecosystems and their services, in particular forests, wetlands, mountains and drylands, in line with obligations under international agreements

15.2 By 2020, promote the implementation of sustainable management of all types of forests, halt deforestation, restore degraded forests and substantially increase afforestation and reforestation globally

15.3 By 2030, combat desertification, restore degraded land and soil, including land affected by desertification, drought and floods, and strive to achieve a land degradation neutral world

15.4 By 2030, ensure the conservation of mountain ecosystems, including their biodiversity, in order to enhance their capacity to provide benefits that are essential for sustainable development

15.5 Take urgent and significant action to reduce the degradation of natural habitats, halt the loss of biodiversity and, by 2020, protect and prevent the extinction of threatened species

15.6 Promote fair and equitable sharing of the benefits arising from the utilization of genetic resources and promote appropriate access to such resources, as internationally agreed

15.7 Take urgent action to end poaching and trafficking of protected species of flora and fauna and address both demand and supply of illegal wildlife products

15.8 By 2020, introduce measures to prevent the introduction and significantly reduce the impact of invasive alien species on land and water ecosystems and control or eradicate the priority species

15.9 By 2020, integrate ecosystem and biodiversity values into national and local planning, development processes, poverty reduction strategies and accounts

Goal 16: Peace and Justice Strong Institutions

Promote peaceful and inclusive societies for sustainable development, provide access to justice for all and build effective, accountable and inclusive institutions at all levels

16.1 Significantly reduce all forms of violence and related death rates everywhere
16.2 End abuse, exploitation, trafficking and all forms of violence against and torture of children
16.3 Promote the rule of law at the national and international levels and ensure equal access to justice for all
16.4 By 2030, significantly reduce illicit financial and arms flows, strengthen the recovery and return of stolen assets and combat all forms of organized crime
16.5 Substantially reduce corruption and bribery in all their forms
16.6 Develop effective, accountable and transparent institutions at all levels
16.7 Ensure responsive, inclusive, participatory and representative decision making at all levels
16.8 Broaden and strengthen the participation of developing countries in the institutions of global governance
16.9 By 2030, provide legal identity for all, including birth registration
16.10 Ensure public access to information and protect fundamental freedoms, in accordance with national legislation and international agreements

Goal 17: Partnerships to Achieve the Goal

Strengthen the means of implementation and revitalize the Global Partnership for Sustainable Development

Finance

17.1 Strengthen domestic resource mobilization, including through international support to developing countries, to improve domestic capacity for tax and other revenue collection
17.2 Developed countries to implement fully their official development assistance commitments, including the commitment by many developed countries to achieve the target of 0.7 per cent of gross national income for official development assistance (ODA/GNI) to developing countries and 0.15 to 0.20 per cent of ODA/GNI to least developed countries; ODA providers are encouraged to consider setting a target to provide at least 0.20 per cent of ODA/GNI to least developed countries
17.3 Mobilize additional financial resources for developing countries from multiple sources
17.4 Assist developing countries in attaining long term debt sustainability through coordinated policies aimed at fostering debt financing, debt relief and debt restructuring, as appropriate, and address the external debt of highly indebted poor countries to reduce debt distress
17.5 Adopt and implement investment promotion regimes for least developed countries

Technology

17.6 Enhance North South, South South and triangular regional and international cooperation on and access to science, technology and innovation and enhance knowledge sharing on mutually agreed terms, including through improved coordination among existing mechanisms, in particular at the United Nations level, and through a global technology facilitation mechanism

17.7 Promote the development, transfer, dissemination and diffusion of environmentally sound technologies to developing countries on favourable terms, including on concessional and preferential terms, as mutually agreed

17.8 Fully operationalize the technology bank and science, technology and innovation capacity building mechanism for least developed countries by 2017 and enhance the use of enabling technology, in particular information and communications technology

Capacity Building

17.9 Enhance international support for implementing effective and targeted capacity building in developing countries to support national plans to implement all the Sustainable Development Goals, including through North-South, South-South and triangular cooperation

Trade

17.10 Promote a universal, rules based, open, non-discriminatory and equitable multilateral trading system under the World Trade Organization, including through the conclusion of negotiations under its Doha Development Agenda

17.11 Significantly increase the exports of developing countries, in particular with a view to doubling the least developed countries' share of global exports by 2020

17.12 Realize timely implementation of duty free and quota free market access on a lasting basis for all least developed countries, consistent with World Trade Organization decisions, including by ensuring that preferential rules of origin applicable to imports from least developed countries are transparent and simple, and contribute to facilitating market access

Systemic Issues

17.13 Enhance global macroeconomic stability, including through policy coordination and policy coherence

17.14 Enhance policy coherence for sustainable development

17.15 Respect each country's policy space and leadership to establish and implement policies for poverty eradication and sustainable development

17.16 Enhance the Global Partnership for Sustainable Development, complemented by multi stakeholder partnerships that mobilize and share knowledge, expertise, technology and financial resources, to support the achievement of the Sustainable Development Goals in all countries, in particular developing countries

17.17 Encourage and promote effective public, public private and civil society partnerships, building on the experience and resourcing strategies of partnerships

17.18 By 2020, enhance capacity building support to developing countries, including for least developed countries and small island developing States, to increase significantly the availability of high quality, timely and reliable data disaggregated by income, gender, age, race, ethnicity, migratory status, disability, geographic location and other characteristics relevant in national contexts
17.19 By 2030, build on existing initiatives to develop measurements of progress on sustainable development that complement gross domestic product, and support statistical capacity building in developing countries

Three out of the four highest greenhouse gas emitters in Australia in 2015–2016 are the three largest energy retailers in the country (see Fig. 2).

Based on the 17 Sustainable Development Goals, an index was devised to measure the performance of each of the energy retailers against the individual SDGs. Scores for each of the SDGs were determined based a review of the content disclosed in the annual published sustainability report for 2016 for each company. Marks awarded ranged from zero for no reference to the Goals in the report, one for a reference to the SDG without a corresponding measure of performance and two for referencing the SDG and disclosing the performance measurement. The possible score range is from 0 to 34.

4 Results Analysis

Table 1 presents our major results of the study.

The results demonstrate a marked difference in reporting of ESG performance against the SDGs by the three energy retailers in Australia.

Energy Australia has achieved the highest rating of 28 out of a possible 34. It is part of the CLP Group which owns and operates energy generation assets in the Asia-Pacific region and has published Sustainability Principles document inspired and informed by the United Nations SDGs. The comprehensive disclosure of SDG information including extensive measurement of company performance indicates Energy Australia is committed to long term alignment with the SDGs.

Energy Australia disaggregates the Sustainability Principles into four focus areas: Economic Sustainability, Our People, Our Environment and Our Community.

CLP Group is in a strong position to capitalise on financial incentives offered under the Clean Development Mechanism (CDM) of the United Nations Framework Convention on Climate Change (UNFCCC). This would provide CLP Group with a lower cost of capital.

SDGs 1 to 4 do not align particularly well with traditional firm level objectives and hence it is not surprising Energy Australia has not published performance metric for these SDGs. However, SDGs 6 (Clean Water and Sanitation) and 14 (Life Below Water) are both concerned with water and performance metrics were not provided. Energy Australia does apply a materiality approach in determining whether to

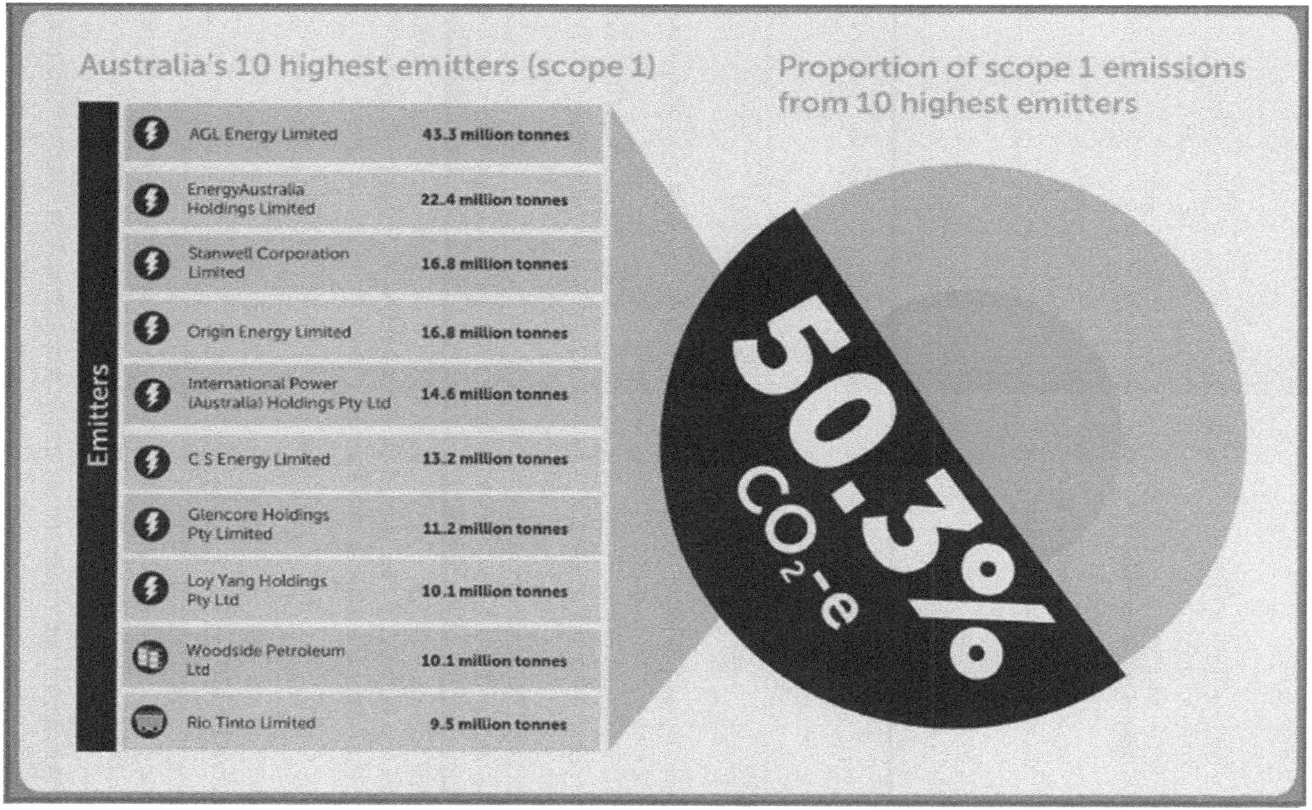

Fig. 2 Major greenhouse gas emitters in Australia. Source: CER (2016) Factsheet, Australia's highest greenhouse gas emitters 2015–2016

Table 1 SDG Index performance of Energy retailers in the Australian Energy Market

Sustainable development goals	Energy Australia	AGL	Origin energy
Goal 1: No poverty	1	0	0
Goal 2: Zero hunger	1	0	0
Goal 3: Good health and well-being	1	0	0
Goal 4: Quality education	1	0	1
Goal 5: Gender equality	2	2	2
Goal 6: Clean water and sanitation	1	1	1
Goal 7: Affordable and clean energy	2	2	2
Goal 8: Decent work and economic growth	2	2	2
Goal 9: Industry, innovation and infrastructure	2	2	2
Goal 10: Reduced inequality	2	2	2
Goal 11: Sustainable cities and communities	2	2	2
Goal 12: Responsible consumption and production	2	2	2
Goal 13: Climate action	2	2	2
Goal 14: Life below water	1	0	0
Goal 15: Life on land	2	2	2
Goal 16: Peace and justice strong institutions	2	2	0
Goal 17: Partnerships to achieve the goal	2	0	0
Total	28	21	20

provide increased levels of disclosure on various ESG factors. It is of no surprise water has a low ranking on their materiality scale.

AGL and Origin Energy perform at a similar level on the SDG index. AGL scored 21 compared to Origin Energy at 20. The only two differences were Origin Energy's omission on SDG 16 concerned with institutional alliances and the inclusion of a reference to SDG 1 relating to quality education.

Although both AGL and Origin publish extensive ESG reporting including references to many of the reporting and rating agencies neither specifically align their respective sustainability reports to the SDGs. This is most likely due to greater emphasis on domestic issues and a lack of recognition by either company for the potential to maximise access to the alternative forms of finance on offer.

5 Conclusion

The major challenge that Australia must face is to secure a stable and reliable energy supply. SDG index scores provide a signal to resource providers including investors, creditors, regulators and the community about the sustainability of energy sector firms. We suggest that Australian regulators, financial markets, energy firms in the market, and the communities do more in the coming years to improve the sustainability of the energy sector.

References

Australian Renewable Energy Agency. (2017). *Snowy 2.0 feasibility study released*. Australian Government, Australian Renewable Energy Agency Media Release, 21 December 2017. Accessed January 31, 2018, from https://arena.gov.au/assets/2017/12/20171221_SNOWY-2.0-ARENA-MEDIA-RELEASE-FINAL.pdf

Clean Energy Regulator Australian Government. (2016). *Australia's highest greenhouse gas emitters*. Clean Energy Regulator Factsheet. Accessed February 10, 2018, from http://www.cleanenergyregulator.gov.au/NGER/Pages/Published%20information/Data%20highlights/2015-16%20factsheets/Australia%27s-highest-10-greenhouse-gas-emitters-2015-2016.aspx

Commonwealth Government of Australia. Accessed March 1, 2018, from http://environment.gov.au/minister/hunt/2015/mr20150623.html

Huber, B. M., & Comstock, M. (2017, July 27). *ESG reports and ratings: What they are, why they matter*. Harvard Law School Forum.

Marshall, A. (2015, June 11). *Cheap loans for farm energy, Fairfax Agricultural Media*. Accessed March 6, 2018, from http://adf.farmonline.com.au/news/nationalrural/agribusiness/general-news/cheap-loans-for-farm-energy/2734634.aspx

Potter, B. (2016, November 3). *Hazelwood power station to close in March 2017. Australian Financial Review*. Accessed March 13, 2018, from http://www.afr.com/news/hazelwood-power-station-to-close-in-march-2017-20161102-gsguse

Potter, B. (2017, December 14). Malcolm Turnbull's Snowy 2.0 project could cost $7b. *Australian Financial Review*. Accessed March 5, 2018, from http://www.afr.com/news/malcolm-turnbulls-snowy-20-project-could-cost-7b-20171213-h04646#ixzz59gt9w6CT

Rossetto, D. (2017, November 28). *Defining green finance for climate change, daily environment report*.

United Nations. (2015, October 21). *Transforming our world: The 2030 Agenda for Sustainable Development, A/RES/70/1*, UN General Assembly. Accessed March 7, 2018, from http://www.refworld.org/docid/57b6e3e44.html

Will Mackay is a Lecturer in Accounting at UniSA Business, University of South Australia, a member of the Centre for Sustainability Governance, Chartered Accountants Australia and New Zealand, the European Accounting Association and Australian Water Association. He is a Visiting Professor at University of Côte d'Azur (Nice, France) and Chairman of the Australian Collaborative Education Network (NT & SA chapter).

Will's research has focused on sustainable governance in listed companies. He has examined the impact of various forms of equity-based compensation and corporate governance regulations in shaping management behaviour. His teaching interests include corporate governance, financial reporting, strategic financial analysis, risk management and work integrated learning.

His current research projects analyse the role of water markets in Australia forestry, energy sector regulation, sustainable corporate governance, shareholder activism, a review of Australia's defence industry capability, and an international study of work integrated learning. His research has received grant funding from the South Australia Government, National Australia Bank, Accounting Finance Association of Australia and New Zealand (AFAANZ), University of South Australia and Adelaide University.

Previously he worked as an auditor for EY and provided professional services in management consultancy within the regulated energy sector, manufacturing sector and to various not for profit organisations.

Lei Xu is a Senior Lecturer in Finance at UniSA Business, University of South Australia, a member of the Research Integrity Committee at the University, a member of Academic Unit Board of UniSA Business, a member of UniSA Business Safety and Wellness, Executive of the Association of Overseas Chinese Professionals in South Australia, and a Justice of Peace for South Australia.

His research interests cover banking, financial markets, financial systems, and emerging financial issues. He is currently working with a team of active researchers in the areas of environmental finance and Fin-tech. His continuous research efforts have led to fruitful publications in prestigious international and national journals and conferences.

Before joining University of South Australia, he worked as a Lecturer in Finance at the University of Adelaide and for years at the banking sector in China. Such experience allows him to integrate teaching and research activities with practitioner knowledge in the discipline.

Greg Meredith is a senior executive with more than 25 years' experience in the energy industry across economic regulation, commercial and treasury management. He has a Honours degree in Economics, a Master's degree in Business Administration and is a Certified Practising Accountant (CPA). Greg has also lectured and tutored in Risk management, Valuation and Economics for Kaplan Professional.

Greg currently works for an ASX top-50 company focused on natural gas transportation, with interests in power generation and other energy infrastructure across mainland Australia and is accountable for funding, treasury policy, liquidity management and hedging the company's interest rates and foreign exchange exposures.

The Money Pipeline: The Role of Finance in the Climate Emergency

Katya Wisniewski

Abstract Climate change is real. It's happening, now. But if the constant flood of record-setting catastrophes in your newsfeed isn't enough to get your attention, it should also be made clear that every foundation stone of the global economy is also at imminent risk of being washed away. The science is clear: to avoid disastrous, runaway climate change, we must prevent the Earth's temperature from rising more than 1.5 °C above pre-industrial levels. Achieving that means emissions must be reduced sharply within the next eleven years, and must reach net zero no later than 2050. We urgently need to bring the fossil fuel era to an end. And with many governments around the world being lobbied, coerced, convinced, or corrupted into continuing with business as usual or outright climate change denial, it is more important than ever that the finance industry step into a position of global leadership.

Keywords Paris agreement · Climate change · Climate urgency · SDGs · Theory of change · Theories of change · Sustainable development goals

Climate change is real. It's happening, now. But if the constant flood of record-setting catastrophes in your newsfeed isn't enough to get your attention, it should also be made clear that every foundation stone of the global economy is also at imminent risk of being washed away. The science is clear: to avoid disastrous, runaway climate change, we must prevent the Earth's temperature from rising more than 1.5 °C above pre-industrial levels. Achieving that means emissions must be reduced sharply within the next 11 years, and must reach net zero no later than 2050. We urgently need to bring the fossil fuel era to an end. And with many governments around the world being lobbied, coerced, convinced, or corrupted into continuing with business as usual or outright climate change denial, it is more important than ever that the finance industry step into a position of global leadership.

Many reasonable-sounding pundits in the financial world have advised us to wait for our political leaders to clarify the policies and regulations that would create a

K. Wisniewski (✉)
Greenpeace, Zürich, Switzerland

K. Wendt (ed.), *Theories of Change*, Sustainable Finance,
https://doi.org/10.1007/978-3-030-52275-9_28

favorable environment for the transition to a low-carbon economy, and the achievement of the Sustainable Development Goals (SDGs). But the pace of change coming from the political arena is simply not fast enough. According to PWC's Low Carbon Economy Index (LCEI) 2018, the global rate of decarbonisation over the last 4 years remained half of what is required to meet the Paris Agreement, with the gap widening more, not less (IISD, 2018). Whilst some G20 and smaller countries are making strides to reduce the carbon intensity of their economies, the absolute number of emissions are still on the rise, hitting an all time global high in 2018 (The Guardian, 2018a). Coal energy, the biggest climate offender, is still assumed by many to figure as an important part of the energy mix for years to come, regardless of the Paris Agreement, let alone the Intergovernmental Panel on Climate Change (IPCC) warnings. According to research by Coalswarm and Urgewald, 1380 new coal-fired power plants or units are either planned or under development in 59 countries. If built, these plants would add 672,124 MW to the global coal plant fleet—an increase of 33 percent (Lewis, 2018). These plans seem simply insane when put in the context of the IPCC's 1.5 °C pathway, which requires a *reduction* in coal use for electricity generation of approximately two-thirds by 2030 (Greenpeace International, 2018).

So if not in the political class, where can powerful financial actors find the direction they so far seem unable to provide for themselves? They can start by looking out their office windows, to the hundreds of thousands of young people around the world who have taken to the streets to march and go on strike from school to demand action to protect their future. Corporations and financiers who fail to treat climate change as a matter of emergency stand to face a profound social backlash for years—and generations—to come. During one of the global student strikes for climate action in December 2018, young people in Zurich nailed a climate change report to the door of Credit Suisse. They demanded, among other things, "system change, not climate change".

The financial industry has a fundamental role to play in the mission of rescuing the planet, and even if somewhat broad, there is a specific mandate for it. One of the three primary objectives set by the international community in the 2015 Paris Agreement is ensuring that financial flows and services are consistent with a pathway towards low greenhouse gas emissions and climate-resilient development (Sustainable Development Goals, n.d.). Unfortunately, no regulator, international body, or central bank has yet provided the *motivation* for action that our young people have demanded and that our scientists have said is necessary. Simply put, averting climate catastrophe will require the financial industry to stop seeing itself in the passenger seat and to start playing an proactive role in saving the planet. It isn't enough anymore to hide behind regulatory uncertainty or to shout about the next quarter's returns. The massive public and investor pressure that has been building in recent years is the key to making financial actors end their support for climate-wrecking industries before it is too late. After all, the trillions in circulation belong to the people—the communities whose homes are destroyed by floods and fires, the workers whose jobs are threatened by industry's willful ignorance, and the investors whose money is subject to reckless schemes. Without sufficient climate action, there will be neither a safe planet nor a working financial system and savings for us all to enjoy.

In Part I we will take stock of progress done in changing the financial industry over the last few years, including the contribution of civil society via finance campaigning. In Part II, we will look at the gaps and show how these efforts, while critical, are still not enough (and outline a few key recommendations for what needs to happen next). Part III will present a case study of a recent and effective campaign that is aligned with some of the recommendations presented.

1 Part I

A lot has changed over the last few years. After most of the world has signed the Paris Agreement and the climate disclosure guidelines were released by the Task Force for Climate Disclosure (TCFD), the pace of climate awareness and action in the world of finance has undoubtedly picked up pace. The ongoing and highly promising work of the European Commission with the implementation of the EU Action Plan on Financing Sustainable Growth, the growing number of companies committing to science based targets (Leggett, 2018), the nascent but growing regulatory changes addressing climate risks in finance—all these are testaments to the fact that climate change has arrived on the agenda of many financial regulators and actors. Banks, insurers, and investors are now paying closer attention to potential climate impacts to their portfolios, lending books, and underwriting business, and are slowly starting to act on climate.

Add to these developments the fact that according to a Bloomberg New Energy Finance (BNEF) report on the levelised cost of energy, wind and solar power prices are expected to beat coal in most places by 2023 (Hodges, 2018). BNEF data indicates that the world has already attained the landmark figure of 1 TW of wind and solar generation capacity installed and that the next TW will be built by 2023 (Bloomberg NEF, 2018). Sustainable mobility is also picking up speed, with global sales of electric vehicles (EVs) as a percentage of all car sales almost doubling year on year in the fourth quarter of 2018, reaching 5.1% or 730,000 units sold globally (Bloomberg New Energy Finance, 2019). All of this has served as the needed incentive for the financial industry to invest more in a wider energy transition. These are important and promising signals.

However, in order to really address the SDGs and impending climate emergency, the financial industry not only has to "impact invest" in the green (low-carbon) but first and foremost reduce the trillions flowing into brown investments (high-carbon and climate negative investments).

Whether by targeted campaigns or widespread movements, civil society has been campaigning to achieve just that. Two core strategies tell the story.

The first, and most visible, is the global fossil fuel divestment movement. According to Goldman Sachs (Goldman Sachs Equity Research, 2018), the coal divestment movement has been a critical driver of the coal sector 60% de-rating over the past 5 years. In their report from November 2018, they referred to a recent study by Arabella Advisors, which showed that almost 1000 institutions overseeing approximately $6.2 trillion in assets had made fossil fuel divestment commitment to date (Goldman Sachs Equity Research, 2018). This shows that divestment works, and thanks to the persistence of many NGOs and climate activists demanding that their pension funds, sovereign wealth funds and insurance companies divest from fossil fuels, it is already having an impact on coal industry.

The second illustration of the movement's success is the spate of (increasingly common) policies by banks, insurance, and reinsurance companies (referred to in combination as "re/insurers" henceforth in this paper) that explicitly exclude funding and insurance to coal and other fossil fuels. According to research by the Institute for Energy Economics and Financial Analysis (IEEFA) (Woodroof, 2019) over 100 major global financial institutions have introduced policies restricting coal funding since 2013. The coal exit announcements have occurred at a rate of over one per month from globally important banks and insurers holding more than US$10 billion worth of assets under management (Woodroof, 2019).

Although most of the higher-profile commitments have been largely coal-related to date (many global banks have some type of "coal exclusion" policies, and several insurers including Zurich Insurance Group Ltd, Allianz SE, Assicurazioni Generali Group S.p.A., Uniqa Insurance Group AG, Vienna Insurance Group AG, Munich Re Group have restricted insurance contracts for the coal industry), civil society is beginning to see signs of more comprehensive, cross-fossil fuels divestment and exclusions by banks, pension funds, sovereign wealth funds and insurers. For example, Axa S.A. no longer invests and insures tar sands, BNP Paribas S.A. and ING Group have started to expand their fossil fuel exclusion policies in terms of lending beyond coal (Rainforest Action Network and Banktrack, 2019). In July 2018 the Irish parliament passed legislation which requires the €8bn Ireland Strategic Investment Fund to dispose of all its coal, oil, gas and peat investments "as soon as is practicable", making it the first country in the world to fully divest public money from fossil fuels (Lorraine, 2018). In March 2019, the Norwegian Oil Fund announced their intention to expand their divestment list to include oil and gas companies—part of key objective that Greenpeace Norway and other NGOs have been campaigning on for years. The Norwegian Ministry of Finance proposed to exclude companies defined by FTSE as upstream oil and gas companies. This round of divestment would only cover about 20% of the oil and gas sector and would not exclude any of the oil majors. Greenpeace commented on this decision as a welcome step, *"but not enough to mitigate Norway's exposure to both global oil and gas prices and the wider financial ramifications of climate change. However, it does send a clear signal that companies betting on the expansion of their oil and gas businesses present an unacceptable risk, not only to the climate but also to investors."* (The Financial Times, 2019)

Moreover, while the divestment from fossil fuels is gaining in speed and normality, the plans to have standardised taxonomy for sustainable investments is also getting closer to reality. In March 2019, the European Parliament has agreed its position on the European Commission's proposal for a sustainability "taxonomy," which will set the framework for establishing which economic activities substantially contribute to environmental objectives such as climate change mitigation (Rust, 2019). Along with the other two important legislative proposals—on low carbon benchmarks and reporting obligations—the sustainable finance should be better equipped to shift the needed trillions to sustainable projects and fight the growing "greenwashing" that has been unfortunately getting more widespread.

Many investors (including insurers) have started actively engaging with companies that they invest in, demanding them to report on their carbon footprint and plans to reduce these footprints. The work of investor group Climate Action 100+ has led to Shell agreeing to set short term carbon emissions targets and reduce its carbon footprint by half by 2050. Glencore also gave in to investor pressure and promised to limit coal production and develop long term targets to reduce its emissions (Bloomberg, 2019).

However, no investor group has so far been engaging with banks (Thamotheram, 2019) and insurers, who are also arguably as exposed to climate financial risks, and as key to drive the transition to low carbon economy as big utility and fossil fuel companies are. Only Norwegian Oil Fund has gone so far as asking the banks that they invest in, like Credit Suisse Group AG, Deutsche Bank AG, HSBC Holdings plc, Citigroup Inc, Wells Fargo & Company, Barclays plc and Nordea Bank abp to disclose how their lending contributes to greenhouse gas emissions (Reuters, 2017). It is therefore essential for investors to remember, asking for plans to reduce indirect carbon footprint and further engagement with global banks and insurers is as important as engaging with utilities and carbon majors.

It is clear that fossil fuel exclusion and divestment is becoming more of a norm than before and it is having the impacts on fossil fuel industry already. More and more projects are being halted and canceled, and it is becoming rarer to see European banks providing lending to the most destructive coal projects or companies in developing South. In some countries, access to funding for coal has almost dried up—for example, private finance in India for new power plants is no longer available (Buckley, 2019). On the other hand, the market share left by the European and US global banks has been taken up by Japanese and Chinese banks, and this has got to change.

Greenpeace report *Uncertain and Harmful: Japanese coal investment in Indonesia (2018)* showed how ongoing Japanese investment in coal-fired power in Indonesia carries increasing financial and political risk to banks and investors and is not in line with global efforts to limit the worst impacts of climate change (Greenpeace, 2018). NGOs like Greenpeace, Rainforest Action Network and 350.com will continue engaging Japanese banks and their investors until they bring their banking policies in line with the Paris Agreement and stop funding coal power expansion in the Global South.

Increasingly, reporting on carbon emissions and reduction plans are also increasingly expected from financial players. As a result of voluntary recommendations issued by Task Force for Climate Disclosure (TCFD), steps being taken to incorporate these recommendations on EU level via EU Non-Financial Reporting Directive 2018/2019. It is expected that this would result in mandatory TCFD reporting from

2021, allowing businesses to prepare and experiment for a few years. Furthermore, some countries' Central Banks are already making different mandatory requirements to their financial players, like requirement to establish a designated board member responsible for climate action/reporting in the UK, or for all investors to report on how their portfolios are aligned with low carbon transition and ESG in France (Article 173) (IPE, 2016). Even UN Principles of Responsible Investments (UNPRI) has just announced (IPE, 2019) that all financial actors who are members of UNPRI are expected to report on TCFD from 2020. So progress on that front is happening, albeit overdue and rather slowly.

2 Part II

While disclosure is important for investors and regulators to assess the situation before taking necessary steps, it is however has proven to be rather time consuming. At the same time, it is seen by some financial actors as the only "climate action" they need to deliver on over the next few years. However, the urgency of climate change does not justify such pace of action, and the financial actors should not congratulate themselves too much just yet. Benchmarking their recent progress to "business as usual" is the perfect recipe to drive the planet closer to its brink. Instead, they need to set their mindset in terms of absolute measures, absolute carbon intensity reductions and absolute sustainability.

Having visibility of carbon risks and scenarios is thought to guide investors, banks and insurers away from carbon-intensive and potentially risky investments and deals. It seems so far, however, that the banking industry has been nevertheless somewhat oblivious to the emerging climate red flags. As the yearly Fossil Fuels Card Report: Banking on Climate Change, 2018 (Rainforest Action Network, 2019) showed—33 global banks have financed USD 1.9 trillion to fossil fuels since the Paris Agreement until end of 2018, with financing increasing year after year. USD 600 billion of this went to 100 companies aggressively expanding fossil fuels (Rainforest Action Network, 2019). This amount dwarfs the annual total investment amounts of roughly USD 350 billion per year that flows into clean energy (Liebreich Associates, 2019).

Why is this unacceptable? According to International Energy Agency (IEA)—the existing infrastructure would "lock in" 550 gigatonnes of carbon dioxide over the next 22 years, which means that there is no more room to build anything new that emits CO_2 (The Guardian, 2018b). Therefore the ongoing funding and insurance of companies involved in expansion should be outlawed as a matter of international climate emergency. No financial institution should continue directly or indirectly fund or insure new oil, gas or coal projects.

The sector continues to provide trillions of dollars to fossil fuel companies, in direct conflict with the Paris goals. Sometimes the indirect emissions of financial actors can outweigh relatively small emissions of the countries they are headquartered in. Greenpeace Switzerland found (Greenpeace, 2019) that in 2017 alone, Credit Suisse Group AG and UBS Group AG financed 93.9 million tonnes of CO_2 equivalent emissions via loans and bond issuance for just 50 of their corporate clients active in extreme fossil fuels. Just this portion of the investment banks' activity resulted in double the level of Switzerland's annual emissions. It is disappointing and unacceptable to see a laissez-faire approach by financial regulators in such situations.

Unfortunately neither being members of the Principles for Responsible Banking, nor the fact that most global banks claim to adhere to UN Guiding Principles for Business and Human Rights, nor the recent set of policies introduced at many global banks—none of that has been holding the global investment banks back from providing these trillions to fossil fuels companies or enabling indigenous rights violations. And whilst many banks have introduced restrictions to designated finance (and project finance) for coal, billions are still flowing via general corporate lending (loans to companies building and operating the projects). Policies for other fossil fuels are still sparse and offer mainly undefined "enhanced due diligence" measures as a safeguard. Without proper processes and systems in place which could screen and flag "prohibited" or "high risk" operations and investments, many banks still struggle to avoid scandalous projects and companies and to operationalise their sustainable policy frameworks. In our experience of working and monitoring banks over the last 5 years, unless a bank has a clear sector exclusion or "prohibited activity" policy in place, many scandalous "high risk" deals slip through the system that is supposed to identify and filter it out.

Therefore this is a massive and urgent gap that needs to be closed. Civil society, central banks, regulators and investors, creditors—all need to urgently step up their game and put more pressure on banks to start decarbonising now.

The timing to expose the ongoing dirty deals is especially important, since many banks and some insurers marketing departments are quickly learning how to professionally greenwash themselves to attract and retain a growing mass of sceptical, environmentally aware customers. Whether it is due to the "great wealth transfer" of close to USD 30 trillion from baby boomers to millenials over the next 30 years (Ernst and Young, 2017), or because this is something that their peers are doing, many financial actors are trying to put on sustainable appearance for the sake of their climate and social impact conscious clientele. What is important is to hold them accountable to their words and slogans and expose when it is just hot air.

Finance campaigning has worked over the last few years, and this is what needs to come next in order for us to achieve 1.5 °C goal.

- **Managed decarbonisation of the financial industry:** As a first and urgent step—no re/insurance for, investment in or finance of new fossil fuel projects. No re/insurance for, investment in or finance of carbon intensive companies without 1.5 °C aligned transition plans.
- **Investor engagement with financial actors:** Investor engagement (either independent or via initiatives) needs to also focus on investee companies from financial sector (insurers, pension funds, fund managers, banks) not only to

achieve disclosure of climate financial risks and financial emissions of financial actors' operations, but also to show their clear decarbonisation plans.
- **Infrastructure investments**: New infrastructure projects need to be sustainable and climate resilient. There is no need to shift trillions of world's savings into something that is based on outdated economic models driven by unsustainable resource extraction, production and consumption.
- **Sustainable and carbon-optimised client advice and investments**: Sustainable finance should be the core offering—not only should climate financial risk be part of all risk-return calculations, but sustainable investments, research and climate optimisation of portfolios should be the core offering for all clients (retail and UHNW).
- **Regulators and central banks** need to introduce brown penalising factors for banks and re/insurers and provide free climate risk tools for the financial industry.
- Investors worldwide should demand that **the board of directors** need to have designated persons who could be held accountable for not enforcing decarbonisation and sustainability agenda in companies they oversee.

Shifting mindsets around what is possible and needed from financial industry to make it happen is an epic challenge. Financial industry practitioners need to feel inspired and compelled to engage, know who is responsible, know the impacts of inaction, and know what the solutions are. The correct mindset and political will of the C-level executives has to be present in order for the financial industry to stop being in the passenger seat and engrain climate action into its DNA.

3 Case Study: Insurance Campaign

It has been more than 45 years since a prominent global reinsurance company first warned about the risks of climate change. However, the industry has largely been maintaining their business as usual model—enabling new fossil fuel projects and companies, whilst knowing better than anyone else, the effects it is having on our climate. If the whole insurance industry as a whole brought its business practices in line with its rhetoric, the result would be fatal for a huge number of fossil fuel projects and companies, and would send an unmistakable signal to the rest of the financial industry that the end of the fossil fuel age has finally arrived.

Greenpeace has been engaging with insurance industry since 2012 in relation to certain projects, like Arctic drilling or mega-dams in the Amazon (Zenger, 2016). In 2017 we have co-launched a systemic campaign called Unfriend Coal with a number of other NGOs aimed at decarbonising the re/insurance industry (Calello, 2018). Since then we and our partners have been calling on the insurance industry to stop underwriting and divest from the coal sector as a first step, and to demonstrate their commitment to protecting their customers from dangerous climate change by bringing their businesses in line with the goals of the Paris Agreement more generally. In other words, the re/insurance industry has been called upon to accept their responsibility as one of the worlds biggest investors and enablers of fossil fuel industry, and take needed action, which goes beyond climate adaptation and green finance commitments.

The reasons behind this campaign are simple. To stop carbon flowing out of pipelines and smokestacks, we have to stop the money flowing into the companies that build them. The global divestment movement and bank campaigns have made some strides on this in recent years, as explained above. Yet re/insurance companies—among the largest sources of financial and operational backing for the fossil fuel industry—have so far had until this campaign largely escaped the attention of the global climate movement.

The re/insurance industry plays a double-enabling role in driving the climate crisis:

1. Fossil fuel projects almost always need insurance coverage before they can get financing from banks, and often before they can get needed permits. Insurance companies routinely provide coverage to projects that they know are dangerous to the climate.
2. Insurers are among the world's largest investors in the fossil fuel industry. According to research by Ceres (2016) and Profundo (Simons & de Wilde, 2017), 55 leading insurers in the U.S. and in Europe have invested at least $590 billion in oil, gas and coal companies.

There are also pragmatic reasons for why re/insurers would benefit from limiting their support to fossil fuels. First of all, a "plus 4°C world is simply uninsurable" (Buberl, n.d.), and "impacts on society beyond 2°C" (Wilson, n.d.) would be nothing short of devastating, which puts the whole insurance business model at risk. This fact, as communicated by the CEO of Axa S.A. and Aviva plc, on its own should be a major concern for all CEOs, the boards, shareholders and creditors with mid to long-term horizon. Munich Re Group recently warned that climate change could make insurance cover unaffordable for most people (The Guardian, 2019). So whilst re/insurance industry is hoping to close the insurance protection gap—they are shooting themselves in the foot at the same time as long as they don't address the root cause of climate change and start limiting their support to fossil fuel industry.

Secondly, whilst the frequency of windstorms, floods, and weather-related catastrophes had increased sixfold since the 1950s (Voysey, 2016), in the absence of a magic ball, even the best re/insurers are already struggling to correctly predict the likelihood and magnitude of such events. Re/insurers' losses from natural catastrophes reached $140 billion and $80 billion in 2017 and 2018 respectively, significantly more than the (inflation-adjusted) 30-year average of $41 billion (Munich Re, 2019).

It is therefore stunning how unfortunately so many insurance CEOs are still not treating this as the core risk and main consideration for business strategy. However, the pace of change is somewhat hopeful. Just two years ago at the start of the insurance campaign, introducing policies limiting insurance to new coal power plants and mines and the most coal intensive clients was unthinkable for most global insurers. Effective engagement and campaigning by the NGOs with the sector has however created the needed dynamic in the industry. In the past two years we have seen encouraging progress with ten major insurance companies—including the world's largest primary insurers and reinsurers—like Zurich Insurance Group Ltd, Swiss Reinsurance Company Ltd, Axa S.A., Allianz S.E., Uniqa Insurance Group AG, Vienna Insurance Group AG, Assicurazioni Generali Group S.p.A. adopting policies to end or limit their insurance services for the coal industry. In addition, more than 20 major insurance companies have divested close to USD 30 billion from coal.

While some of these policies fall short of best practice and many industry laggards, especially those in the US and Asia, remain missing in action, the policies adopted by leading insurance companies have already had a welcome impact in accelerating the transition from coal to clean energy sectors. In its Power and Renewable Energy Market Review 2019 (Willis Towers Watson, n.d.) the broker Willis Towers Watson found that

> insurers' retreat from underwriting coal business has left coal-fired generators with a significant reduction in available capacity. (...) This reduction in available capacity will invariably see upward pressure on rates and coverages as the competition for market share in this specific sector will be much more limited.

The report goes further to say that it is expected that in the short to medium term the independent and smaller coal operators will be already affected by unavailability of insurance.

While this progress is welcome, the urgency of scaling up climate action is becoming ever more manifest. So far not a single US or Asian re/insurer has introduced public policy limiting insurance to coal or fossil fuels projects and companies, thus still leaving more than half of the industry doing "business as usual".

It is clear, that more needs to be done—on coal and also on other fossil fuels and carbon intensive businesses, deforestation companies and mobility. And hopefully some insurers are continuing to innovate on the back of that progress. AXA S.A., the French insurance company, has promised to divest another €3.1 billion from coal, tar sands and pipeline companies and will phase out insurance for new tar sands projects (AXA, 2017). Swiss Re has launched a carbon risk steering mechanism designed to measure the carbon intensity and associated risks embedded in their re/insurance business, with coal exclusion policy being just the first outcome of it.

And whilst marketing departments globally are busy creating sustainable branding for most financial companies, including insurers, around the world, it is important to call out greenwash when we see it and hold financial actors accountable to their promises. One of the campaign's main strategic assumptions is that the global re/insurance industry is prone to competitive pressure, and the companies place significant worth into their brand. The campaign has a global and industry wide approach, leveraging on the race to the top strategy to create competition and move the laggards. When we find an insurer continuing to enable coal projects, we hold them to account and expose their involvement in dirty energy for their customers.

The shift of insurers away from coal has been welcomed by voices such as the Financial Times and the UN Secretary General and is quickly becoming the benchmark for needed climate action (The Financial Times, 2018).

References

AXA. (2017, December 12). *AXA accelerates its commitment to fight climate change*. https://www.axa.com/en/newsroom/press-releases/axa-accelerates-its-commitment-to-fight-climate-change

Bloomberg. (2019, February 20). *Glencore plans to cap coal output in climate shift, sources say*. https://www.bloomberg.com/news/articles/2019-02-20/glencore-is-said-to-plan-to-cap-coal-output-in-climate-shift

Bloomberg NEF. (2018, August 2). *World reaches 1,000GW of wind and solar, keeps going*. https://about.bnef.com/blog/world-reaches-1000gw-wind-solar-keeps-going/

Bloomberg New Energy Finance. (2019, March 5). *Global electrified transport market outlook, 1Q 2019*

Buberl, T. (n.d.). *AXA's CEO indicated that a "plus 4°C world is not insurable"*. https://www.axa.com/en/newsroom/press-releases/axa-accelerates-its-commitment-to-fight-climate-change

Buckley, T. (2019). IEEFA quoted in *"No fad": Global capital flees thermal coal projects*, by Mark Ludlow, 26 February, 2019. https://www.afr.com/news/politics/no-fad-global-capital-flees-thermal-coal-projects-20190226-h1bpw7

Calello, C. (2018, May 25). *Climate chaos, who's in?* Greenpeace International. https://www.greenpeace.org/international/story/16696/climate-chaos-change-coal-insurance-fossil-fuels-investment/

Ceres. (2016, May 24). *Assets or liabilities? Fossil fuel investments of leading U.S. insurers*. https://www.ceres.org/resources/reports/assets-or-liabilities-fossil-fuel-investments-leading-us-insurers

Ernst and Young. (2017). *Sustainable investing: The millennial investor*. https://www.ey.com/Publication/vwLUAssets/ey-sustainable-investing-the-millennial-investor-gl/$FILE/ey-sustainable-investing-the-millennial-investor.pdf

Goldman Sachs Equity Research. (2018, October 25). *GS SUSTAIN: Chart of the week: Is the divestment movement nearing a tipping point?*

Greenpeace. (2018). *Uncertain and harmful: Japanese coal investment in Indonesia*. https://act.gp/2PnlXH5

Greenpeace. (2019, January). *Swiss banks and their financed emissions*. https://issuu.com/greenpeace-switzerland/docs/greenpeace_factsheet_en_v7

Greenpeace International. (2018, October 8). *A coal phase-out pathway for 1.5°C*. https://www.greenpeace.org/international/publication/18866/a_coal_phase_out_pathway/

Hodges, J. (2018, March 28) *Fossil fuels squeezed by plunge in cost of renewables, BNEF says*. https://www.bloomberg.com/news/articles/2018-03-28/fossil-fuels-squeezed-by-plunge-in-cost-of-renewables-bnef-says

IISD. (2018, October 9). *PwC Index finds decarbonization rates are "less than half" needed to meet Paris Agreement*. http://sdg.iisd.org/news/pwc-index-finds-decarbonization-rates-are-less-than-half-needed-to-meet-paris-agreement/

IPE. (2016, February 1). *France aims high with first-ever investor climate-reporting law*. https://www.ipe.com/countries/france/france-aims-high-with-first-ever-investor-climate-reporting-law/10011722.fullarticle

IPE. (2019, February 20). *PRI signatories must report climate change risks from 2020*. https://www.ipe.com/news/esg/pri-signatories-must-report-climate-change-risks-from-2020/www.ipe.com/news/esg/pri-signatories-must-report-climate-change-risks-from-2020/10029579.fullarticle

Leggett, J. (2018, September 13). *480 companies from 38 countries now base climate plans on SBTs*. https://jeremyleggett.net/2018/09/13/480-companies-from-38-countries-now-base-climate-plans-on-sbts-around-one-eighth-of-global-market-capitalisation/

Lewis, M., Jr. (2018). *Coal plant developers still building, investing despite Paris Agreement. Blog*. Washington, DC: Competitive Enterprise Institute. https://cei.org/blog/coal-plant-developers-still-building-investing-despite-paris-agreement.

Liebreich Associates. (2019, May 21). *Global clean energy invested and capacity installations 2004-2018*. https://aee-kongress.ch/files/user/pages/fr/congres/2018/Praesentationen/AEESUISSE-Congres-2018_Michael_Liebreich.pdf

Lorraine, C. (2018, November 23). *Ireland becomes world's first country to divest from fossil fuels*. https://www.theguardian.com/environment/2018/jul/12/ireland-becomes-worlds-first-country-to-divest-from-fossil-fuels

Munich Re. (2019, January 8). *Extreme storms, wildfires and droughts cause heavy nat cat losses in 2018*. https://www.munichre.com/site/corporate/get/params_E-105173115_Dattachment/1708125/natcat-2018-global-20190107_en.pdf

Rainforest Action Network. (2019). *Banking on climate change*. https://www.ran.org/wp-content/uploads/2019/03/Banking_on_Climate_Change_2019_vFINAL.pdf

Rainforest Action Network and Banktrack. (2019). *Banking on climate change: Fossil fuel finance report card*. https://www.ran.org/bankingonclimatechange2019/

Reuters. (2017, June 2). *Exclusive: Norway's $960 billion fund wants banks to disclose carbon footprint of loans*. https://www.reuters.com/article/us-norway-swf-ceo/exclusive-norways-960-billion-fund-wants-banks-to-disclose-carbon-footprint-of-loans-idUSKBN18T26V

Rust, S. (2019, March 28). *European Parliament agrees stance on sustainability taxonomy*. https://www.ipe.com/news/esg/european-parliament-agrees-stance-on-sustainability-taxonomy/www.ipe.com/news/esg/european-parliament-agrees-stance-on-sustainability-taxonomy/10030344.fullarticle

Simons, M., & de Wilde, J. (2017 , May 3). *The involvement of European insurance groups in the fossil fuels sector*. Profundo. http://unfriendcoal.com/wp-content/uploads/2017/06/Profundo-report-final-0417.pdf

Sustainable Development Goals. (n.d.). *Article 2c of the Paris Agreement*. https://sustainabledevelopment.un.org/frameworks/parisagreement

Thamotheram, R. (2019, April). *Long-term matters: Lessons for climate action 100+*. https://www.ipe.com/analysis/long-term-matters/long-term-matters-lessons-for-climate-action-100/www.ipe.com/analysis/long-term-matters/long-term-matters-lessons-for-climate-action-100/10030333.fullarticle

The Financial Times. (2018, January 9). *Insurers join in on the slow squeeze on coal*. https://app.ft.com/cms/s/bdda17ee-f46f-11e7-88f7-5465a6ce1a00.html and UN Secretary-General's remarks on Climate Change, September 10, 2018

The Financial Times. (2019, March 8). *Norway's $1tn wealth fund set to cut oil and gas stocks*. https://www.ft.com/content/d32142a8-418f-11e9-b896-fe36ec32aece

The Guardian. (2018a, December 5). *'Brutal news': Global carbon emissions jump to all-time high in 2018*. https://www.theguardian.com/environment/2018/dec/05/brutal-news-global-carbon-emissions-jump-to-all-time-high-in-2018 and Coal Swarm's "Global Coal Plant Tracker"

The Guardian. (2018b, November 13). *World has no capacity to absorb new fossil fuel plants, warns IEA*. https://www.theguardian.com/business/2018/nov/13/world-has-no-capacity-to-absorb-new-fossil-fuel-plants-warns-iea

The Guardian. (2019, March 21). *Climate change could make insurance too expensive for most people – report*. https://www.theguardian.com/environment/2019/mar/21/climate-change-could-make-insurance-too-expensive-for-ordinary-people-report

Voysey, A. (2016, December 7). *ClimateWise launches two reports that warn of growing protection gap due to rising impact of climate risks*. https://www.cisl.cam.ac.uk/business-action/sustainable-finance/climatewise/news/insurance-leaders-warn-protection-gap-due-to-impact-climate-risks

Willis Towers Watson. (n.d.). *Ready and waiting? Power and renewable energy market review 2019*. https://willistowerswatson.turtl.co/story/power-and-renewable-energy-market-review-2019-online

Wilson, M. (n.d.). *CEO of Aviva said "if we do not take urgent action to limit global temperature increases to within 2°C, the impacts upon the economy, society and our business will be nothing short of devastating"*. https://www.aviva.com/social-purpose/environment/

Woodroof, N. (2019, February 28). *IEEFA report: Every fortnight a bank, insurer or lender announces new restrictions on coal*. World Coal. https://www.worldcoal.com/special-reports/28022019/ieefa-report-every-fortnight-a-bank-insurer-or-lender-announces-new-restrictions-on-coal/

Zenger, Y. (2016, August 5). Freudentanz am Amazonas. https://www.greenpeace.ch/2016/08/05/freudentanz-am-amazonas-erfolg-fuer-munduruku/

Katya Wisniewski is a sustainable finance expert with over a decade of experience in portfolio management, equity derivatives sales, and a lead civil society campaigner on topics such as carbon footprint and sustainable finance. She created and led the sustainable finance campaign at Greenpeace Switzerland, where her focus was on Swiss investment banks and re/insurers as well as Multilateral Development Banks. She monitored and researched bank's financing operations and engaged with global investors, banks, re/insurers, regulators, and credit agencies on issues like corporate responsibility and sustainability, banks' internal policies violations and financial climate-related risks. On the international scene, she coordinated insurance campaign at Greenpeace, which has led to exits from coal and tar sands by some of the biggest re/insurers in Europe.

Prior to 2015, Katya has worked at a number of global banks in different roles including equity trading, equity derivatives sales, and portfolio management and has passed all three levels of the CFA Program. She is a co-founder of Women's March Zurich and is a strong advocate for equality.

Moving the Topic of Climate Change from Politics to Economics

Shruthi Rao and Sandeep Chandur

Abstract Rather than constantly reacting to extreme weather conditions brought on, in the most part by the effects of climate change, is it not now time for the insurance industry to seize the opportunity and take a proactive stance for the greater good? Modern availability of data, innovative analytics products and frankly more importantly a moral obligation, can drive real change into society. With the development of new underwriting coupled with a better understanding of the connected risks, the industry can drive real change. Insuring and managing the risk of those specific industries in vulnerable regions that have far reaching effects on global supply chains and the refusal of some insurers and reinsurers like Allianz not to cover new coal based projects are merely the tip of the metaphorical melting iceberg.

Keywords Theory of change · Theories of change · Sustainable development goals · SDGS · Paris agreemnet · Climate science · Climate change · Global reporting initiative · Carbon disclosrue project · CDP · GRI · Impact investing · Climate disclosure standard board · Integrated reporting foundation · CDSB · IRF · IPCC · Ocean · Cryoshere · World Meteorological Organization · Psychology of change · Capital markets

1 Introduction

The *12th Annual Survey of Emerging Risks* (Rudolph 2019) revealed a perhaps not surprising trend: actuaries ranked climate change as the top risk for 2019, beating cyberattacks, financial stability, and terrorism. No doubt, it is an existential threat on the minds of most of the scientific community. But the politics of climate change have kept it from being a top priority for governments around the world.

S. Rao (✉)
Adapt Ready, New York, NY, USA
e-mail: srao@adaptready.com

S. Chandur
Adapt Ready, New York, NY, USA

K. Wendt (ed.), *Theories of Change*, Sustainable Finance,
https://doi.org/10.1007/978-3-030-52275-9_29

This chapter presents a theory that change can be brought about by linking risks and making them more apparent, relevant, and specific to the affected party—in other words, going further than just putting a price on risk but driving action to mitigate the risks of climate change. While there are a few players that could drive such action, this chapter focuses on the insurance industry and how it can play a pivotal role in reducing the most harmful effects of climate change by putting a dollar cost on climate risk and making the bad actors (e.g. heavy polluters who don't take the necessary action) pay.

2 A Brief History of Climate Science

The science of climate change has developed over the past two centuries. In the 1820s the French physicist and mathematician Joseph Fourier proposed that the atmosphere was trapping heat by examining heat balance equations from incoming solar radiation and outgoing infrared radiation. In the late nineteenth century, the Swedish chemist Svante Arrhenius calculated the possible magnitude of the effects—showing that if CO_2 levels were halved, global temperatures could decrease by about 5 °C (9 °F).

In 1963, the Conservation Foundation convened a meeting of scientific experts called the *Implications of Rising Carbon Dioxide Content of the Atmosphere*, and it was here that concerns about global warming were raised, along with the possibility of a rise in sea levels. This gradually led to the first Earth Day on April 22, 1970, to demonstrate support for environmental protection. After years of effort from the scientific community, non-governmental organizations, and environmental groups such as the Environmental Defense Fund (EDF), parties to the UN Framework Convention on Climate Change (UNFCCC) reached a landmark agreement in Paris, on 12 December 2015.

The Paris Agreement sought to bring together all nations into a common cause to undertake efforts to combat climate change and adapt to its effects, with the central aim of keeping a global temperature rise below 2 °C this century and above pre-industrial levels. As of 2019, most Western countries are not even close to meeting their targets, with one of the worst offenders being the USA. How did we get here? As long as there is a competitive advantage that can be reached by emitting CO_2 without being charged for the damage, there is a clear lack of sense of urgency.

In recent years, a few corporate reporting initiatives around economic, environmental and social impacts came into existence with the aim of increasing transparency and helping companies improve their reporting practices. These include the Global Reporting Initiative (GRI), the Carbon Disclosure Project (CDP) and the Climate Disclosure Standards Board (CDSB) (Integrated Reporting Foundation 2019). While such disclosures are useful to regulators, stock exchanges and investors, this is still a small step in enforcing action against rising temperatures.

The Climate Action Tracker (https://climateactiontracker.org/) tracks government climate action and measures it against the globally agreed Paris Agreement, and Fig. 1 shows the current status of the major emitter countries as of September 2019.

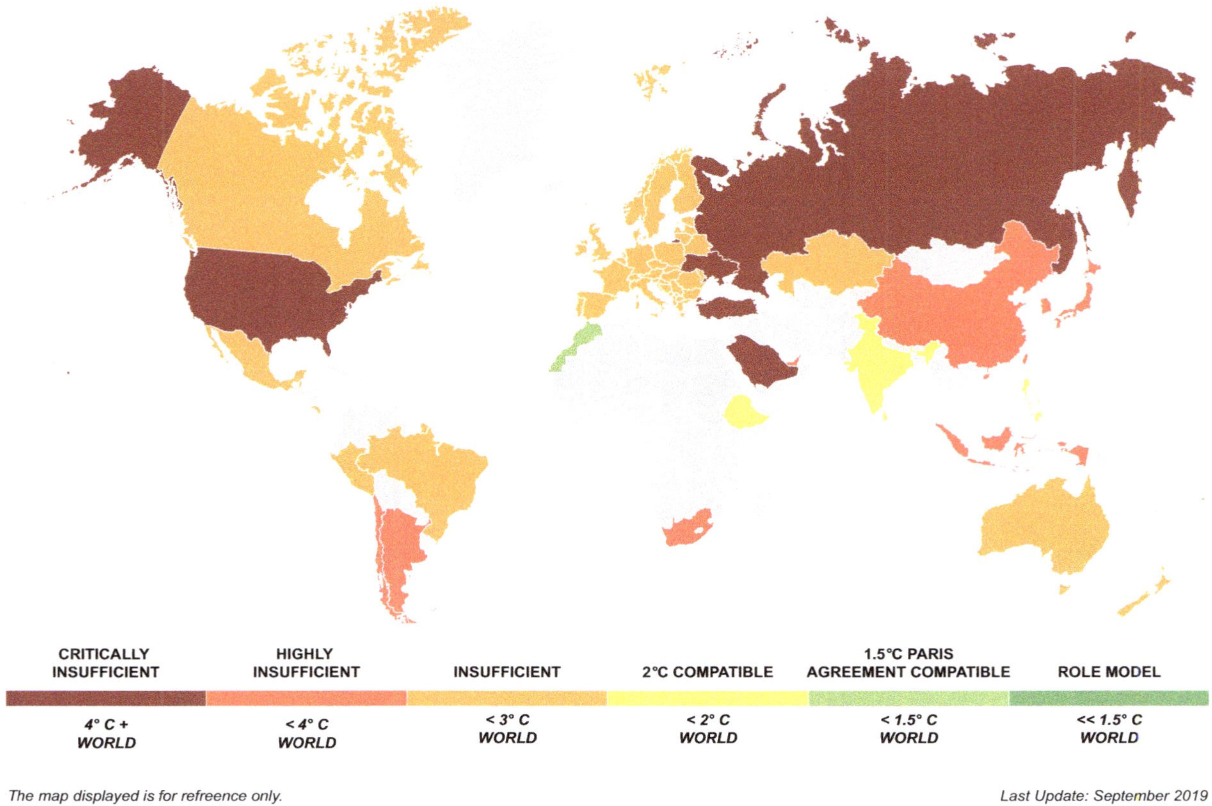

Fig. 1 The Climate Action Tracker covers 80% of global emissions and approximately 70% of the global population, tracking national actions across current policies on emissions, impact of pledges and comparability of effort, rating them from "critically insufficient" to "role model."

3 Current State: IPCC and Recap of Special Report on Ocean/Cryosphere

The Intergovernmental Panel on Climate Change (IPCC), created in 1988 by the World Meteorological Organization, is an intergovernmental body of the United Nations tasked with providing regular assessments of the scientific basis of climate change. It provides governments with the information necessary for policy development, and it currently has 195 member countries.

In September 2019, the IPCC issued a stark assessment of the climate crisis in its special report (IPCC 2019). A summary of some of the key statements from the report are listed below:

- Global mean sea level is rising, with acceleration in recent decades due to increasing rates of ice loss from the Greenland and Antarctic ice sheets.
- Increases in tropical cyclone winds and rainfall, and increases in extreme waves, combined with relative sea level rise, exacerbate extreme sea level events and coastal hazards.
- Coastal ecosystems are affected by ocean warming (see Fig. 2), including acidification, loss of oxygen, and adverse effects from human activities on ocean and land.
- Future shifts in fish distribution and decreases in their abundance and fisheries catch potential due to climate change are projected to affect livelihoods and food security of communities dependent on marine ecosystems.

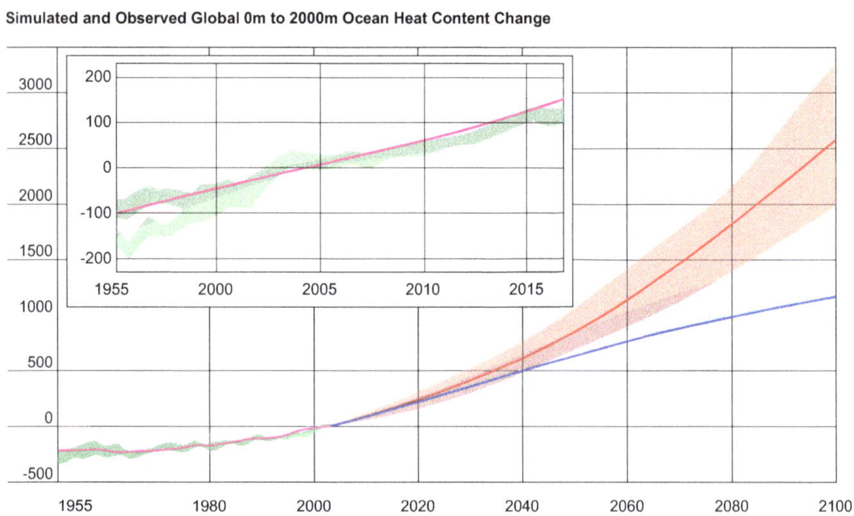

Fig. 2 Time series of globally integrated upper 2000 m ocean heat content changes in zettajoules (ZJ), relative to the 2000–2010 period average. Source: IPCC Special Report on the Ocean and Cryosphere in a Changing Climate (https://www.ipcc.ch/srocc/)

4 Link to Increase in Extreme Events

Extreme sea level events that occur once per century in the recent past are projected to occur at least once per year at many locations by 2050 in all scenarios. Warming seas are causing more intense storms characterized by stronger winds and greater amounts of rain. El Niño and La Niña are the periodic changes in Pacific Ocean sea surface temperatures that have impacts on weather around the world. According to the report, extreme El Niño and La Niña events are likely to increase in the twenty-first century, intensifying existing hazards.

A 2015 study found that some coastal regions, notably the Persian Gulf (including Dubai and the UAE, where tropical storms have never been recorded), may face a risk of unprecedented storm surge in the next century (Lin and Emanuel 2015). These so-called "grey swan" cyclones may be anticipated by combining physical knowledge and global simulations along with historical data.

Currently about 680 million people live in low-lying coastal zones, and this is projected to reach 1 billion by 2050. Around the same time, the number of people living in cities is expected to reach 6.5 billion. That's a staggering level of—mostly economic—migration, which would ultimately be at a higher risk in the years to come. Cities are also highly vulnerable to loss of critical supplies from food distribution to energy provision to water and with 90% of urban areas located in coastal areas, cities face tremendous risk.

In his book "*Why Are We Waiting?*" (Stern 2015) examines approaches to the moral and political philosophy in the context of climate change, starting with moral behavior and conduct. Stern equates virtuous action in relation to the environment and climate change, acting in a way so as not to violate the rights of future generations similar to the way one might avoid buying goods made with child labor, in pursuit of liberty, rights, and justice, to consequentialism. Consequentialism evaluates right and wrong purely by its consequences. The better the consequences, the better the act.

He then introduces a "narrow standard cost-benefit analysis" framework, focusing on ethical issues that arise in analyzing the externality associated with GHG emissions, and concludes that essentially all approaches point toward strong action on climate change.

Despite an abundance of scientific material available to law and policymakers, only a handful of countries are somewhat close to being compatible with the Paris Agreement. So, what needs to happen in order to drive change?

We need to move the discussion from *politics* to *economics*.

5 Psychology of Change

Effecting change in people requires an understanding of behavioral psychology. The Harvard Business Review lists ten ways to get people to change—including the trusty old "carrots and sticks"—incentives and punishments used to change behavior—approach.

When it comes to individuals, there is an emerging school of thought that "nudges"—carefully designed prompts and activities that encourage better outcomes by leveraging how people naturally think and feel—can be a more effective approach (O'Leary and Murphy 2017). But when it comes to organizational change, there is a lot more at play—not least in the people at the top. Moreover, people have a low willingness to accept the perceived short-term costs of policy for the larger medium-to-long-term climate benefits. Many tend to focus on individual gain over public loss, exacerbating the problem. The principle of going the extra mail to catch the carrot is explained in Fig. 3.

In order to effect true change—one where organizations take the risk of climate change more seriously and decide to do something about it—we need to link the corresponding risks and make it apparent, relevant, and *specific* to the organization and the individual.

In other words, it is necessary to put a price on risk to drive change. *This is the crux of this theory of change.*

Fig. 3 The proverbial carrot and stick approach

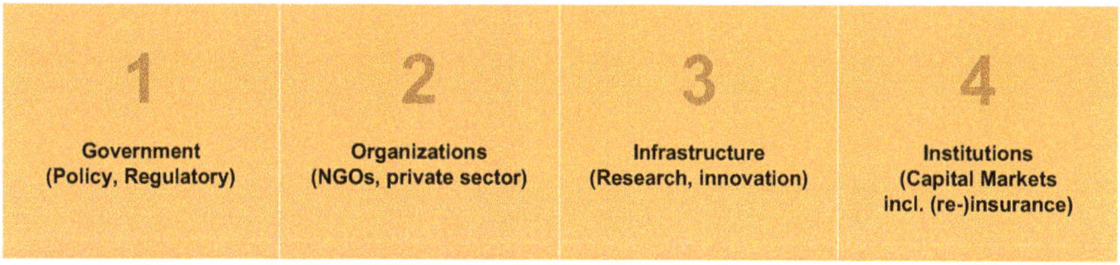

Fig. 4 Framework of active drivers of change (own illustration)

6 The Players

So, who are the major players that can drive change in such an ecosystem? We categorized them into four categoreis, which are depicted in Fig. 4.

Hard scientific evidence of the monetary cost is necessary to create sound policy, which could be in the form of carbon tax, cap-and-trade systems, and regulation. The science is already there with a broad consensus in the scientific community. Organizations, including NGOs and the private sector, have an important role in not only adhering to policy, but also creating methods to monitor and audit the inner workings, and ensuring compliance. Support is needed from an infrastructure viewpoint—whether it is in energy systems or transport or other new and innovative approaches to reduce GHG emissions. Finally, capital markets—particularly insurance and re-insurance—need to take on a more pivotal role in risk reduction.

7 Government/Politics

Despite the advancement made with the signing of the Paris Agreement 4 years ago, little progress has been made. The United States announced its withdrawal from it, in accordance with the current administration's "America First" policy, saying it would help American businesses and workers. This is an indication of how political incentives are biased toward short-term electoral cycles, which is why the topic of climate change within the context of politics has clearly failed.

8 Organizations

Organizations small and large have embraced sustainability in recent years. Though some corporations are accused of "greenwashing", it has embedded itself into the conscious of investors and the general public. In the late 90s, John Elkington coined the term "triple bottom line" (Elkington 1999), referring to the financial, environmental, and social factors included in determining a company or equity's value. This led to creation of ESG (Environmental, Social and Corporate Governance) metrics, a good step, but deeply rooted in instrumentalism. But organizations still see ESG and other such strategies as a separate function outside of the core business—and this gives them the freedom to circumvent them: financial disclosures could say one thing while a firm's sustainability reports would have a whole different spin. With no oversight or accountability to anyone but themselves, the notion that leaving it to organizations is sufficient is a fallacy. In the face of climate change, we need champions in the workplace who act against their short-term incentives (these could be the corporate risk managers, for example) to bring focus onto the potential impacts on the bottom line from extreme events.

9 Infrastructure/R&D

Investments in clean energy ventures totaled $332.1 billion in 2018, and in that, global venture capital and private equity investment jumped 127 per cent over the previous year to $9.2 billion (Bloomberg 2019). This is a good sign, and hopefully a trend that will continue to support low carbon economies worldwide. However, incentive-based programs tend to run out of steam when incentives run out.

10 Capital Markets/(Re-)Insurance

Over a dozen national and sub-national governments have created public green investment banks—banks that are specifically designed to channel private investment (including from institutional investors) into domestic low-carbon, climate-resilient infrastructure. Insurance enables risk sharing, and as we will see in the next section, can drive change through not only its expertise in the quantification of risk but also a measured a carrot-and-stick approach.

11 Zeroing in on Insurance

Insurers are on the front lines of climate change, acting as society's risk managers and economic investors, driving innovation and staying ahead of change. The insurance industry manages $30tn in assets globally, making it one of the most important parts of the financial system. Insurers experienced $155bn total economic losses from natural and man-made catastrophes in 2018 alone, making them key in facing and fighting the effects of climate change by putting a value on today's risk in the interest of a more sustainable tomorrow (Insurance Journal 2018). Insurers' influence goes beyond insureds (policy holders) to capital markets and the world, governing and shaping the behavior of individuals, companies and governments, with mitigation of emissions, energy conservation and creation of initiatives that encourage positive action and economic growth.

Historically, the industry has changed after big disasters. Natural-catastrophe modelling took the forefront after Hurricane Andrew struck Florida in 1992, which caused $15.5 billion in insured losses. It resulted in the liquidation of 13 insurance companies (Hope and Friedman 2018). Property insurance premiums rose rapidly in the aftermath of the 9/11 attack triggering a wave of progress in the modeling of these risks and the acceptance of the need to model them properly and with greater clarity.

Fifty percent of the economic losses from natural catastrophes were uninsured in 2018—and this gap has widened in the last few years. "Insurance protection gap" is the difference between insured losses and economic losses, or uninsured losses. The combined global natural catastrophe (including atmospheric perils and earthquakes) protection gap for 2017–2018 stood at USD 280 billion. On average, economic and insured losses have grown by 5% annually since 1999 (Swiss Re Institute 2019). Many insurers and re-insurers now have in-house climatologists and scientists to help them better understand the risk exposures in a changing climate.

While over 70% of global losses are uninsured, catastrophe insurance is widely available in western countries, but despite this, insurance penetration rates are still low (Munich Re). In Italy's 2016 earthquakes only 1–2% were insured, resulting in heavy economic and societal impacts (Howard 2018). By 2050 7 out of 10 people in the world will live in cities with more than 80% GDP. Cities consume 2/3 of the world's energy with over 70% of global greenhouse gases. Insurance penetration can make an impact on climate change in these communities (The World Bank 2019).

This brings a very interesting challenge to insurance companies. On one side there is an increase in losses. On the other side there is a widening protection gap. There are risks as well as opportunities. The Royal Bank of Canada predicts that, "insurance penetration of catastrophe losses will increase as the protection gap [of uninsured losses] narrows." Jefferies, an investment bank and financial services firm, further expands upon this expecting a "result in higher prices and demand, prompting industry-wide growth... with higher growth and margin." (Jenkins 2019). Closing the insurance gap (Fig. 5) could yield $60–80 billion profit for the industry per year (Shelly 2019).

Zurich Insurance Group's former chief risk officer (now CEO EMEA Region) Alison Martin stated that "our analysis suggests that the current level of efforts to keep global temperatures from rising over 2 °C above pre-industrial levels will likely fail, so businesses should prepare for the physical consequences of a warming planet. Companies must know the magnitude of their climate risk, so that they can prioritize actions based on their particular circumstances." (Ritchie 2018).

Insurers have been putting a price on risk for hundreds of years, and climate risk is naturally the next—albeit inherently more complex—iteration of that endeavor. Traditionally, insurance "punishes" the more vulnerable insureds (policy holders), not the culprits unless the law stipulates it (e.g. liability). Going by the carrot-and-

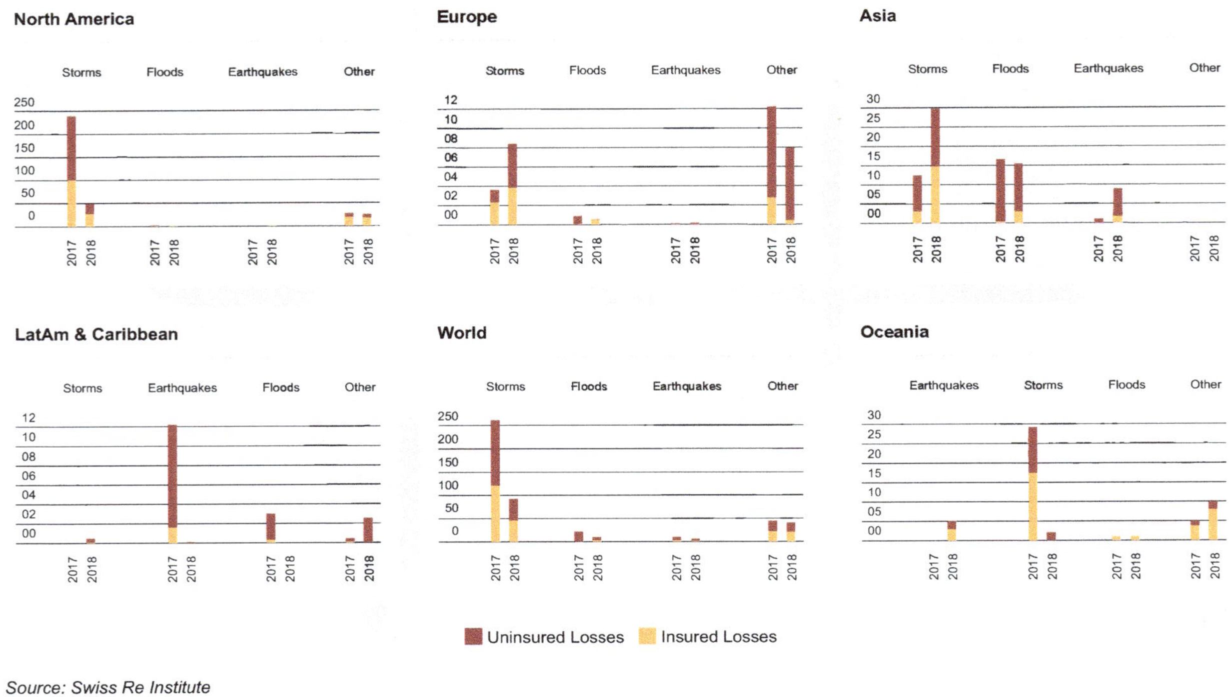

Fig. 5 Insured vs uninsured losses by peril and region in 2017 and 2018 (USD billion, in 2018 prices). Source: Swiss Re sigma No. 2/2019

stick approach then, insurers could effect a behavioral change among organizations by linking premiums to carbon emissions. An example would be raising the premium rates for a company with dismal environmental performance, whereas a company that shows improvement in its carbon footprint could be offered additional discounts in premiums—or a higher claim limits.

The carrot-and-stick approach can be seen on an individual level in auto insurance coverage. In the US and many other countries for example, if a person gets a ticket or gets into an accident, it impacts their ability to get insurance in the future. An individual can then work to lower premiums through defensive driving classes or driving safely after a certain number of months, rewarding them for good behavior. Insurers are beginning to take this kind of action on a global level with climate change. In 2019 commercial insurer Chubb, the largest in the US, became the nation's first insurance firm to take the stance that it "will not underwrite new risks for companies that generate more than 30% of revenues from thermal coal mining … [and] will phase out coverage of existing risks that exceed this threshold by 2022," incentivizing insureds to change their business practices or find a new insurance company, and as insurers continue to take action to punish the bad actors, companies may struggle to find one (Sulakshana 2019).

However, this approach is not without its concerns. Following the California wildfires, Ernst Rauch, Munich Re's chief climatologist, said that the costs could soon be widely felt, with premium rises under discussion with clients holding asset concentrations in vulnerable parts of the state (Neslen 2019). This brings up a concern that climate change could make insurance unaffordable for most people.

Further, insurers pay attention to future risks and act as a watchdog spotting red flags and taking preventative action, while also managing the issues of today. Since insurers benefit financially from capital markets, through individuals' pension funds and other such sources, insurers have a moral obligation to serve the public, which puts them in a good position to govern society in the face of climate change. Insurers were one of the first major industries to warn about climate change, with companies like Munich Re coming out publicly in 1973 (Bosshard 2017). Since then they have been vocal in their concerns and adopted policies to protect and meet the needs of a collective global society in the interest of the greater good.

12 Impact on Regulation

Regulations are tightening in an already heavily regulated industry to protect the public in a changing climate. Within this framework there are two broad, but very different, groups of insureds: the vulnerable and the carbon emitting. The vulnerable are hit the hardest from a catastrophe and struggle with recovery and future insurance as prices rise in the wake of tragedy. This is seen in the 2019 California wildfires where insurers started dropping policies in fire-prone areas. California stepped in to put a one-year moratorium on the practice regulating insurers (Flavelle and Plumer 2019).

Traditionally, insurance puts a price to risk based upon vulnerability, not general causation such as the (bad actor) carbon emitters. This means the acting insurance company would need to be ready to lose these insureds to a competitor as long as the action is voluntary and not all key competitors participate voluntarily and as stated above, with increasing changes in climate, the vulnerable insureds could be priced out. There are several ways to combat this issue: regulation that inhibits this kind of competition, laws that make carbon emitters liable for the damage, a broad insurance industry alliance, or a public opinion about the issue that is strong enough such that insureds start to put pressure onto their insurers.

Current liability against carbon emitters can be demonstrated in a recent 2019 Netherlands Supreme Court ruling to cut greenhouse emissions by 25% by the end of 2020, which could force the government to shut down coal-fired power plants (Schwartz 2019). This is considered to be one of the strongest cases of its kind and represents government regulation that will force the insurance industry to adjust the way that insurance is priced and sold. On the other side, alliance in the industry can be seen in the UN-backed "Net Zero Asset Owner Alliance" from the world's largest investors—pension funds and insurers responsible for nearly $4tn—to commit to carbon-neutral investments by 2050 (UN Government Program 2019). With backers from industry giants like Allianz and Swiss Re, while gaining traction and support throughout the industry, this has the potential to push the needle further on climate regulation and reform.

Further, the court of public opinion is out on climate change and most countries acknowledge that it is a threat to their nation. Residences of California's Butte County and Paradise, who lost much of their community in a 2019 fire, filed suit against Pacific Gas & Co. whose power line started the fire and won $1 billion settlement (Beam 2019). With similar lawsuits against insureds on the rise in the face of catastrophic events insurers will need to adopt new policies.

13 Conclusion

Insurance is the nexus of capital markets and society. As shown in some of the examples from this chapter, insurers should now lead the way forward in combating the worst impacts of climate change. Directing policy that rewards the good and punishes the bad, taking it as their moral obligation, and one that makes sound financial sense as well—not only for the insurers' bottom line but the society at large. This is the insurance industry's time to shine and it will be a shame if it doesn't take it.

References

Beam, A. (2019). California utility company to pay $1 billion to governments for wildfire damage. *USA Today*.

Bloomberg. (2019). *Clean energy investment exceeded $300 billion once again in 2018*. [Online]. Retrieved from https://about.bnef.com/blog/clean-energy-investment-exceeded-300-billion-2018/

Bosshard, P. (2017). *Ten things you didn't know about insurance companies and climate change*, HuffPost.

Elkington, J. (1999). *Cannibals with forks: triple bottom line of 21st century business*. Hoboken, NJ: Wiley.

Flavelle, C., & Plumer, L. A. (2019). *California bans insurers from dropping policies made riskier by climate change*. New York: Times.

Hope, B., & Friedman, N. (2018). Climate change is forcing the insurance industry to recalculate. *Wall Street Journal*. https://www.wsj.com/graphics/climate-change-forcing-insurance-industry-recalculate/

Howard, L. S. (2018). Insurance protection gap is growing global problem; Swiss Re, RenRe & WTW comment. *Insurance Journal*.

Integrated Reporting Foundation. (2019). *Driving alignment in climate-related reporting: Year one of the better alignment project*, s.l. Corporate Reporting Dialogue.

IPCC. (2019). *Special report on the ocean and cryosphere in a changing climate*.

Jenkins, P. (2019). Why climate change is the new 9/11 for insurance companies. *Financial Times*.

Lin, N., & Emanuel, K. (2015). Grey swan tropical cyclones. *Nature Climate Change*.

Munich Re. *Risks posed by natural disasters*. [Online] Retrieved from https://www.munichre.com/en/risks/natural-disasters-losses-are-trending-upwards.html

Neslen, A. (2019). *Climate change could make insurance too expensive for most people*. [Online]. Retrieved from https://www.theguardian.com/environment/2019/mar/21/climate-change-could-make-insurance-too-expensive-for-ordinary-people-report

Net-Zero Asset Owner Alliance surges to nearly $4 trillion at COP25; other investors urged to get on board, UN Environment Programme.

O'Leary, J., & Murphy, T. (2017). *Beyond carrots and sticks*. Toronto, ON: Deloitte University Press.

Ritchie, D. (2018). *Businesses urged to consider climate change-related risks*. [Online]. Retrieved September 23, 2019, from https://www.cirmagazine.com/cir/Businesses-urged-to-consider-climate-change%2D%2Drelated-risks.php

Rudolph, M. J. (2019). *12th Annual Survey of Emerging Risks*, s.l.: Canadian Institute of Actuaries, Casualty Actuarial Society, and Society of Actuaries.

Schwartz, J. (2019). In 'strongest' climate ruling yet, Dutch Court orders leaders to take action. *New York Times*.

Shelly, J. (2019). *The global protection gap has reached $1.2 trillion - But there might be good news still*.

Stern, N. (2015). *Why are we waiting?* Cambridge, MA: The MIT Press.

Sulakshana, E. E. (2019). *Major U.S. insurer says it will no longer underwrite and invest in coal*, Salon.

Swiss Re Institute. (2018). Global insured losses from disasters at $79 billion in 2018: Swiss Re Sigma Estimate. *Insurance Journal*.

Swiss Re Institute. (2019). *sigma 2/2019*. Zurich: Swiss Re.

The World Bank. (2019). *Urban development*.

Shruthi Rao is co-founder and CEO of technology startup Adapt Ready. She leads a dynamic team using her combined background in technology, sustainability and business management and is listed as one of the Financial Times Top 50 Female Future Leaders. Previously Shruthi served as a management consultant, working closely with risk managers and corporates on the insurance buyer's side and helping reshape their sustainability strategy—even winning accolades such as at the Green Enterprise IT Symposium for initiatives on data center sustainability.

Shruthi's company provides a risk intelligence software platform focused on complex lines of business for commercial (re) insurers and brokers. Under her leadership, it has won major awards against incumbents such as RMS and AIR Worldwide, including "Risk Modelling Technology of the Year", "Excellence in Technology" and "Best Customer Service Product for Business".

Sandeep Chandur, co-founder and CTO of Adapt Ready, leads a global technology team in innovating new products and approaches to manage portfolio risk in insurance and investments. With over two decades of experience building software, Sandeep applies his expertise to software architecture and managing product development teams, aligning all technology resources to the founders' vision. Prior to Adapt Ready, he developed software for telecom, finance and other industries from startups to Fortune 100 corporations and won a UN hackathon award for a micro-insurance prototype.

Correction to: When Transparency Clouds Rather Than Clarifies: A Closer Look at Transparency Bias Within ESG Scores

Ruben Feldman

Correction to:
Chapter 13 in: K. Wendt (ed.), *Theories of Change*, Sustainable Finance, https://doi.org/10.1007/978-3-030-52275-9_13

The original version of the chapter was inadvertently published with an error. The author name has now been corrected to "Ruben Feldman".

The updated online version of this chapter can be found at
https://doi.org/10.1007/978-3-030-52275-9_13

K. Wendt (ed.), *Theories of Change*, Sustainable Finance,
https://doi.org/10.1007/978-3-030-52275-9_30

Index

K. Wendt (ed.), *Theories of Change*, Sustainable Finance,
https://doi.org/10.1007/978-3-030-52275-9

GPSR Compliance
The European Union's (EU) General Product Safety Regulation (GPSR) is a set of rules that requires consumer products to be safe and our obligations to ensure this.

If you have any concerns about our products, you can contact us on

ProductSafety@springernature.com

In case Publisher is established outside the EU, the EU authorized representative is:

Springer Nature Customer Service Center GmbH
Europaplatz 3
69115 Heidelberg, Germany

www.ingramcontent.com/pod-product-compliance
Ingram Content Group UK Ltd.
Pitfield, Milton Keynes, MK11 3LW, UK
UKHW022217051026
15624UKWH00001B/203
9783030522742